THE WRITER'S STANCE

THE WRITER'S STANCE

READING AND WRITING IN THE DISCIPLINES

Dorothy U. Seyler

Northern Virginia Community College

Random House • New York

First Edition
987654321
 Published in the United States by Random House, Inc., and simultaneously in Canada by Random House of Canada Limited, Toronto.

Library of Congress Cataloging-in-Publication Data

Seyler, Dorothy U.
The writer's stance.

Includes index.
1. College readers. 2. English language—Rhetoric.
3. Interdisciplinary approach in education. I. Title.
PE1417.S378 1987 808'.0427 87-26327
ISBN 0-394-35548-2

Manufactured in the United States of America

Typographic design: Susan Phillips

Cover design: Lorraine Hohman

Cover: Pierre Auguste Renoir, Monet Painting in His Garden at Argenteuil, 1873. Oil on canvas, 18⅜" × 23½". Wadsworth Atheneum, Hartford. Bequest of Anne Parrish Titzell.

ACKNOWLEDGMENTS

"I Think (and Write in a Journal), Therefore I Am," by Joseph Reynolds. From *The Christian Science Monitor,* February 23, 1981. Reprinted by permission of the author.

"Why I Write," by Joan Didion. From *The New York Times Book Review,* December 6, 1976. Copyright © 1976 by Joan Didion. Reprinted by permission of Wallace & Sheil Agency, Inc.

"The Watcher at the Gates," by Gail Godwin. From *The New York Times Book Review,* January 9, 1977. Copyright © 1977 by The New York Times Company. Reprinted by permission.

"Life in a Bundle of Letters," by Ellen Goodman. From *The Washington Post,* August 10, 1985. Copyright © 1985, The Boston Globe Newspaper Company/Washington Post Writers Group. Reprinted with permission.

"Autobiographical Notes," from *Notes of a Native Son* by James Baldwin. Copyright © 1955, renewed 1983, by James Baldwin. Reprinted by permission of Beacon Press.

"On the Exact Location of the Soul," from *Mortal Lessons* by Richard Selzer. Copyright © 1974, 1975, 1976 by Richard Selzer. Reprinted by permission of Simon & Schuster, Inc.

"With All Deliberate Speed: What's So Bad About Writing Fast?" by William F. Buckley, Jr. From *The New York Times Book Review,* February 9, 1986. Copyright © 1986 by William F. Buckley, Jr. Reprinted by permission of Wallace & Sheil Agency, Inc. and The New York Times Company.

"Foreword" (pp. vii–viii) in *Essays of E. B. White.* Copyright © 1977 by E. B. White. Reprinted by permission of Harper & Row, Publishers, Inc.

"Seeing" (pp. 25–34) in *Pilgrim At Tinker Creek* by Annie Dillard. Copyright © 1974 by Annie Dillard. Reprinted by permission of Harper & Row, Publishers, Inc.

"My Father" from *A Small Personal Voice* by Doris Lessing. Copyright © 1963 by Doris Lessing. "My Father" first appeared in *The Sunday Telegraph,* London, on 1st September 1963. Reprinted by permission of Jonathan Clowes, Ltd., London, on behalf of Doris Lessing.

"Beauty: When the Other Dancer Is the Self," from *In Search of Our Mothers' Gardens* by Alice Walker. Copyright © 1983 by Alice Walker. Reprinted by permission of Harcourt Brace Jovanovich, Inc.

"Education" (pp. 52–54) from *One Man's Meat* by E. B. White. Copyright © 1939, 1977 by E. B. White. Reprinted by permission of Harper & Row, Publishers, Inc.

"Content to Be in My Place," by Ellen Goodman. From *The Washington Post,* August 13, 1983. Copyright © 1983, The Boston Globe Newspaper Company/Washington Post Writers Group. Reprinted with permission.

"Bobcats," by Jeffrey Cooper, 1985. Reprinted by permission of the author.

"Cyclical Time: Reinventing the Wheel," by Floyd C. Stuart. Copyright © 1981 by *Harper's Magazine.* Reprinted from the May issue by special permission.

"Comments on 'Cyclical Time,' " by Floyd C. Stuart, May 1986. Reprinted by permission of the author.

"The Fiction Writer's Materials," from *Living By Fiction* by Annie Dillard. Copyright © 1982 by Annie Dillard. Reprinted by permission of Harper & Row, Publishers, Inc.

"A Worn Path," from *A Curtain of Green and Other Stories* by Eudora Welty. Copyright © 1941, 1969 by Eudora Welty. Reprinted by permission of Harcourt Brace Jovanovich, Inc.

"Is Phoenix Jackson's Grandson Really Dead?" from *The Eye of the Story: Selected Essays and Reviews* by Eudora Welty. Copyright © 1974 by Eudora Welty. Reprinted by permission of Random House, Inc.

"The Secret Life of Walter Mitty," from *My World—and Welcome To It* by James Thurber. Copyright © 1942 by James Thurber. Copyright © 1970 by Helen W. Thurber and Rosemary A. Thurber from *My World—and Welcome To It,* published by Harcourt Brace Jovanovich. Reprinted by permission.

"The Guest," from *Exile and the Kingdom* by Albert Camus, translated by Justin O'Brien. Copyright © 1957, 1958 by Alfred A. Knopf, Inc. Reprinted by permission of the publisher.

"The Magic Barrel," from *The Magic Barrel* by Bernard Malamud. Copyright © 1954, 1958 by Bernard Malamud. Reprinted by permission of Farrar, Straus & Giroux, Inc.

"Report," by Donald Barthelme. Copyright © 1967 by Donald Barthelme. First published in *The New Yorker.* Reprinted by permission of I.C.M.

"Desert Places," from *The Poetry of Robert Frost* edited by Edward Connery Lathem. Copyright © 1936 by Robert Frost. Copyright © 1964 by Lesley Frost Ballantine. Copyright © 1969 by Holt, Rinehart and Winston. Reprinted by permission of Henry Holt and Company.

"Dulce et Decorum Est," from *Collected Poems* by Wilfred Owen. Copyright © 1963 by Chatto & Windus. Reprinted by permission of New Directions Publishing Corporation.

"Dream Deferred," from *The Panther and the Lash: Poems of Our Times* by Langston Hughes. Copyright © 1951 by Langston Hughes. Reprinted by permission of Alfred A. Knopf, Inc.

"The Children of the Poor," sonnet #2, pg. 100 from *The Womanhood* in *The World of Gwendolyn Brooks* by Gwendolyn Brooks. Reprinted by permission of the author.

"Tool," from *Writings to an Unfinished Accompaniment* by W. S. Merwin. Copyright © 1973 by W. S. Merwin. Reprinted with the permission of Atheneum Publishers.

"Mirror," from *The Collected Poems of Sylvia Plath* edited by Ted Hughes (originally appeared in *The New Yorker*). Copyright © 1963 by Ted Hughes. Reprinted by permission of Harper & Row, Publishers, Inc.

"The Third of May, 1808," painting by Francisco Goya, 1814. Reprint permission granted by El Museo Nacional del Prado, Madrid.

"In Search of History," from *Practicing History* by Barbara Tuchman. Copyright © 1963 by Barbara Tuchman. Reprinted by permission of Alfred A. Knopf, Inc.

"An Inquiry into the Persistence of Unwisdom in Government," by Barbara Tuchman. From *Esquire*, May 1980. Copyright © 1980 by Barbara Tuchman. Reprinted by permission of Russell & Volkening, Inc. as agents for the author.

"Foreign Policy and the American Character," by Arthur Schlesinger, Jr. From *Foreign Affairs*, Fall 1983. Reprinted by permission of the author.

"The Indispensable Opposition," by Walter Lippmann. From *The Atlantic Monthly*, 1939. Used with permission of the President and Fellows of Harvard College.

"On Moral Equivalence," by Charles Krauthammer. From *Time* magazine, July 9, 1984. Copyright © 1984 by Time Inc. All rights reserved. Reprinted by permission from *Time*.

"Comments on 'On Moral Equivalence,' " by Charles Krauthammer. Reprinted by permission of the author.

"Duty: The Forgotten Virtue," by Amitai Etzioni. From *The Washington Post*, March 9, 1986. Reprinted by permission.

"The Myth of Sisyphus," from *The Myth of Sisyphus and Other Essays* by Albert Camus, translated by Justin O'Brien. Copyright © 1955 by Alfred A. Knopf, Inc. Reprinted by permission of the publisher.

"A Free Man's Worship," from *Mysticism and Logic* by Bertrand Russell. Reprinted by permission of George Allen & Unwin Publishers.

"Selecting the News: Story Suitability," from *Deciding What's News: A Study of CBS Evening News, NBC Nightly News, Newsweek and Time* by Herbert J. Gans. Copyright © 1979 by Herbert J. Gans. Reprinted by permission of Pantheon Books, a division of Random House, Inc.

"Journalism and the Larger Truth," by Roger Rosenblatt. From *Time* magazine, July 2, 1984. Copyright © 1984 by Time Inc. All rights reserved. Reprinted by permission from *Time.*

"The Sports Craze," by Joseph Kraft. From *The Washington Post,* September 15, 1985. Copyright © by *The Washington Post.* Reprinted by permission of *The Washington Post.*

"Made in Heaven," by Leigh Montville. From *The Boston Globe,* May 15, 1983. Reprinted courtesy of *The Boston Globe.*

"How Not to Aid African Nomads," by Blaine Harden. From *The Washington Post,* April 5, 1986. Reprinted by permission of *The Washington Post.*

"Comments on 'How Not to Aid African Nomads,' " by Blaine Harden. Reprinted by permission of the author.

"Africa: Portrait of a Continent," from *The Africans* by David Lamb. Copyright © 1983 by David Lamb. Reprinted by permission of Random House, Inc.

"Comments on 'Africa: Portrait of a Continent,' " by David Lamb. Reprinted by permission of the author.

"Salvador," from *Salvador* by Joan Didion. Copyright © 1983 by Joan Didion. Reprinted by permission of Simon & Schuster, Inc.

"Playing Dumb: A Form of Impression Management with Undesirable Side Effects," by Walter R. Gove, Michael Hughes, and Michael R. Geerken. From *Social Psychology Quarterly* 43: 89–102 (1980). Reprint permission granted by The American Sociological Association and the authors.

"Playing Dumb," by Michael Hughes and Walter R. Gove. From *Psychology Today,* October 1981. Copyright © 1981 by the American Psychological Association. Reprinted with permission from *Psychology Today* magazine.

"Recasting a Piece of Sociological Research for a Popular Audience: The Case of 'Playing Dumb,' " by Michael Hughes. Reprinted by permission of the author.

"Television and the Young Viewer," by Eli A. Rubinstein. From *American Scientist,* journal of Sigma Xi, 66: 685–693 (1978). Reprinted by permission.

"Television and the Disappearance of Childhood," excerpted from the book *The Disappearance of Childhood* by Neil Postman. Copyright © 1982 by Neil Postman. Reprinted by permission of Delacorte Press.

"How to Get the Poor Off Our Conscience," by John K. Galbraith. From *Harper's Magazine,* November, 1985. Copyright © by *Harper's Magazine.* Reprinted from the November issue by special permission.

"Education: Incentives to Fail and Proposals for Change," excerpted from *Losing Ground: American Social Policy, 1950–1980* by Charles Murray. Copyright © 1984 by Charles Murray. Reprinted by permission of Basic Books, Inc., Publishers.

"Of Grasshoppers and Ants (A Review of Charles Murray's *Losing Ground*)," by Lester Thurow. From the *Harvard Business Review*, July/August 1985. Copyright © 1985 by the President and Fellows of Harvard College; all rights reserved. Reprinted by permission of the *Harvard Business Review*.

"Rebuilding the Foundations of Economics," excerpted from *Dangerous Currents* by Lester C. Thurow. Copyright © 1983 by Lester C. Thurow, Inc. Reprinted by permission of Random House, Inc.

"Scientific Creativity: A Study of Darwin," from *Darwin on Man: A Psychological Study of Scientific Creativity* by Howard E. Gruber and Paul H. Barrett. Copyright © 1974 by Howard E. Gruber and Paul H. Barrett. Reprinted by permission of Georges Borchardt, Inc.

"Were Dinosaurs Dumb?" from *The Panda's Thumb, More Reflections in Natural History* by Stephen Jay Gould. Copyright © 1980 by Stephen Jay Gould. Reprinted with the permission of W. W. Norton & Company, Inc.

"Hot Times over Warm Blood," from *The Riddle of the Dinosaur* by John Noble Wilford. Copyright © 1985 by John Noble Wilford. Reprinted by permission of Alfred A. Knopf, Inc.

"Comments on 'Hot Times over Warm Blood,' " by John Noble Wilford. Reprinted by permission of the author.

"The Mass Extinctions of the Late Mesozoic," by Dale A. Russell. From *Scientific American*, January 1982. Reprinted with permission.

"An Interview with Dale A. Russell," by Dale A. Russell. Reprinted by permission of the author.

"The Origin of Earth," excerpted from the book *Genesis: The Origins of Man and the Universe* by John Gribbin. Copyright © 1981 by John Gribbin. Reprinted by permission of Delacorte Press.

"Black Holes," from *The Roving Mind* by Isaac Asimov. Copyright © 1983 by Isaac Asimov. Reprinted with permission of the publisher, Prometheus Books, Buffalo, New York.

"Competing Models of Mental Illness: Psychodynamic, Behavioral, and Biological," chapter 3 (pp. 20–23) from *The Broken Brain: The Biological Revolution in Psychiatry* by Nancy C. Andreasen. Copyright © 1984 by Nancy C. Andreasen. Reprinted by permission of Harper & Row, Publishers, Inc.

PREFACE

Although I have nurtured each of my books with care, *The Writer's Stance,* like the difficult child in the family, has cost me more energy and anguish than the others. And so now that its turn has come to get to work in the classroom, I send it off with a touch of sadness as well as joy.

I wanted to prepare a special kind of reader, one that might not, therefore, fit easily into a category: rhetorical, thematic, across the curriculum. Insofar as *The Writer's Stance* is a writing-by-discipline text, I wanted the disciplines to be honestly represented by genuine examples of scholarship, not popular writing only. But I wanted this reader to do more, because writing is not primarily characterized by its content—or by the label we put on it; it is characterized by the relationship of content to audience and purpose: by the writer's stance. Finally, I wanted this text to explore with students the kind of reading they actually do, both in classes and in their lives, and to connect that reading to their writing: to show students how understanding the writer's stance will make them both better readers and better writers. These three major concerns have shaped this text.

The Writer's Stance begins with an introductory chapter that establishes principles of good reading and the tasks of the *studentwriter*—the student as writer in an academic discipline. Chapter 2 reinforces the ideas in Chapter 1 by exploring—through essays by writers—key writing issues: the writing process, the reasons for writing, the challenges of writing well. Chapters 3 through 8 present readings in an order from the most personal, imaginative, and inward-looking to the most fact-oriented and outward-looking; from the personal essay, to fiction and poetry, to the disciplines of history and philosophy, journalism, the social sciences and economics, and the sciences. This ordering allows students to see more clearly the part that the nature of the subject matter (facts, fiction, facts from a distance or generated by controlled experiments, facts imaginatively ordered through the stance of a "fictional" persona, and so on) plays in a writer's shaping of a work, or in a discipline's conventions for presenting written work.

Each chapter begins with a detailed introduction that explains the terms and concepts needed to understand a writer's work in that chapter's discipline. These introductions will help students read more accurately, analyze the readings with appropriate vocabulary, and understand how to establish an appropriate stance as a *studentwriter* in that discipline. Each chapter concludes with a student essay illustrating one type of student writing appropriate for college work; exercises on writing or in preparation for writing, such as library exploration; and writing assignments.

One of the greatest pleasures for me in preparing *The Writer's Stance* has been the engaging of authors in each chapter to write about their writing. I hope that both students and instructors using the text will come to cherish the insightful, and frequently moving, "Comments" by Floyd C. Stuart, Charles Krauthammer, Blaine Harden, David Lamb, Michael Hughes, John Noble Wilford, and Dale A. Russell. These postscripts, prepared especially for *The Writer's Stance,* complement the published essays on writing found throughout the text. I want to say a special thank you to the writers of "Comments" and to the many other authors who graciously answered letters and phone calls, offering me both needed biographical details and a special sentence or two about themselves.

No book of any value is written alone. Friends and colleagues have helped me with *The Writer's Stance,* and I am happy to thank them publicly. I am indebted to Richard Wilan for advice on selections and chapter structure, to Jane Friedmann for her endless supply of favorite articles for my consideration, and to Jonathan Yoder for advice and encouragement, especially with Chapter 8. My warm thanks are due, again, to the library staff at the Annandale Campus of Northern Virginia Community College, especially to Jan Jefries, Ruth Stanton, and Marion Denton, who cheerfully aid my research and make it fun. I appreciate, as well, the advice and specific suggestions of the following reviewers: Gary Schmidt, Calvin College; Kathleen Cain, Merrimack College; Helen Isaacson, University of Michigan; Walter Minot, Gannon University; and Richard Larson, Lehman College, City University of New York. My editor, C. Steven Pensinger, deserves a special thank you for his guidance and support. Finally, I want to acknowledge the student writers who allowed me to print their essays and all my students who helped in the selection of student papers and who encouraged me during the Fall 1986 quarter.

Dorothy U. Seyler

CONTENTS

PREFACE xi

CHAPTER 1 **WRITERS AND THE READING PROCESS: ESTABLISHING CONNECTIONS** 3

The Writer in a Writing Course 3
The Student Writer's Roles 6
The Reader in a Writing Course 8
Steps to Accurate Reading 10
The Engaged Reader 12
Reinforcing the Reading Process 14
A Writer's List of First Questions: Aids to Both Reading and Writing 20

EXERCISES 21
WRITING ASSIGNMENTS 23

CHAPTER 2 **WRITING: THE CHALLENGE** 25

INTRODUCTION 25

JOSEPH REYNOLDS *I Think (and Write in a Journal), Therefore I Am* 29
JOAN DIDION *Why I Write* 32
GAIL GODWIN *The Watcher at the Gates* 38
ELLEN GOODMAN *Life in a Bundle of Letters* 42
JAMES BALDWIN *Autobiographical Notes* 44
RICHARD SELZER *On the Exact Location of the Soul* 50
WILLIAM F. BUCKLEY, JR. *With All Deliberate Speed: What's So Bad About Writing Fast?* 56
STUDENT ESSAY *The Business of Writing*, by *J. Penn Jones* 61

EXERCISES 63
WRITING ASSIGNMENTS 64

CHAPTER 3 THE ESSAYISTS SEEING: PEOPLE, PLACES, OURSELVES 67

INTRODUCTION 67

E. B. WHITE *Foreword to* The Essays of E. B. White 70
ANNIE DILLARD *Seeing* 73
DORIS LESSING *My Father* 81
ALICE WALKER *Beauty: When the Other Dancer Is the Self* 90
E. B. WHITE *Education* 98
ELLEN GOODMAN *Content to Be in My Place* 101
JEFFREY COOPER *Bobcats* 104
FLOYD C. STUART *Cyclical Time: Reinventing the Wheel* 109
FLOYD C. STUART *Comments on* Cyclical Time: Reinventing the Wheel 114
STUDENT ESSAY *Alcohol Awareness,* by *Penny M. Potter* 116

EXERCISES 118
WRITING ASSIGNMENTS 119

CHAPTER 4 SEEING II: FICTION, POETRY, THE VISUAL ARTS 121

INTRODUCTION 121

ANNIE DILLARD *The Fiction Writer's Materials* 129
EUDORA WELTY *A Worn Path* 135
EUDORA WELTY *Is Phoenix Jackson's Grandson Really Dead?* 144
KATE CHOPIN *The Story of an Hour* 148
JAMES THURBER *The Secret Life of Walter Mitty* 151
ALBERT CAMUS *The Guest* 157
BERNARD MALAMUD *The Magic Barrel* 170
DONALD BARTHELME *Report* 186
A Collection of Poems 190
WILLIAM SHAKESPEARE *Sonnet 73* 193
JOHN DONNE *The Flea* 194
ROBERT BROWNING *My Last Duchess* 195
WALT WHITMAN *When I Heard the Learn'd Astronomer* 197
ROBERT FROST *Desert Places* 198
WILFRED OWEN *Dulce et Decorum Est* 199
LANGSTON HUGHES *Dream Deferred* 200

GWENDOLYN BROOKS from *The Womanhood* 201
W. S. MERWIN *Tool* 201
SYLVIA PLATH *Mirror* 202
STUDENT ESSAY *A View of War's Horrors*, by *Clark Martin* 203
EXERCISES 205
WRITING ASSIGNMENTS 208

CHAPTER 5 **WRITINGS FROM HISTORY, GOVERNMENT, AND PHILOSOPHY** 211

INTRODUCTION *211*

BARBARA W. TUCHMAN *In Search of History* 215
BARBARA W. TUCHMAN *An Inquiry into the Persistence of Unwisdom in Government* 228
ARTHUR SCHLESINGER, JR. *Foreign Policy and the American Government* 243
WALTER LIPPMANN *The Indispensable Opposition* 260
CHARLES KRAUTHAMMER *On Moral Equivalence* 268
CHARLES KRAUTHAMMER *Comments on* On Moral Equivalence 274
AMITAI ETZIONI *Duty: The Forgotten Virtue* 275
ALBERT CAMUS *The Myth of Sisyphus* 280
BERTRAND RUSSELL *A Free Man's Worship* 284
STUDENT ESSAY *The Quest for Wisdom*, by *Kevin Hite* 293
EXERCISES 295
WRITING ASSIGNMENTS 296

CHAPTER 6 **JOURNALISM: INVESTIGATIVE, EDITORIAL, SATIRIC, LITERARY** 299

INTRODUCTION *299*

HERBERT J. GANS *Selecting the News: Story Suitability* 304
ROGER ROSENBLATT *Journalism and the Larger Truth* 316
JOSEPH KRAFT *The Sports Craze* 320
PAT OLIPHANT *Prayer in School* (cartoon) 323
LEIGH MONTVILLE *Made in Heaven* 324
BLAINE HARDEN *How Not to Aid African Nomads* 328

BLAINE HARDEN *Comments on* How Not to Aid African Nomads 333
DAVID LAMB *Africa: Portrait of a Continent* 335
DAVID LAMB *Comments on* Africa: Portrait of a Continent 343
JOAN DIDION *Salvador* 344
STUDENT ESSAY *Photo Crops–Showing Sexism in Photography,* by *Brian Kreudel* 354
EXERCISES 357
WRITING ASSIGNMENTS 359

CHAPTER 7 **WRITINGS FROM THE SOCIAL SCIENCES AND ECONOMICS** 363

INTRODUCTION *363*

WALTER R. GOVE, MICHAEL HUGHES, AND MICHAEL R. GEERKEN *Playing Dumb: A Form of Impression Management with Undesirable Side Effects* 366
MICHAEL HUGHES AND WALTER R. GOVE *Playing Dumb* 388
MICHAEL HUGHES *Recasting a Piece of Sociological Research for a Popular Audience: The Case of "Playing Dumb . . ."* 394
ELI A. RUBINSTEIN *Television and the Young Viewer* 397
NEIL POSTMAN *Television and the Disappearance of Childhood* 413
JOHN KENNETH GALBRAITH *How to Get the Poor off Our Conscience* 424
CHARLES MURRAY *Education: Incentives to Fail and Proposals for Change* 431
LESTER C. THUROW *Of Grasshoppers and Ants (A Review of Charles Murray's* Losing Ground*)* 440
LESTER C. THUROW *Rebuilding the Foundations of Economics* 448
STUDENT ESSAY *Sailing Against the Tide (A Review of Lester C. Thurow's* Dangerous Currents*)*, by *Gary Isom* 455
EXERCISES 457
WRITING ASSIGNMENTS 458

CHAPTER 8 **WRITINGS FROM THE SCIENCES** 461

INTRODUCTION *461*

HOWARD E. GRUBER *Scientific Creativity: A Study of Darwin* 465
STEPHEN JAY GOULD *Were Dinosaurs Dumb?* 474

JOHN NOBLE WILFORD *Hot Times over Warm Blood* 481

JOHN NOBLE WILFORD *Comments on* Hot Times over Warm Blood 495

DALE A. RUSSELL *Mass Extinctions of the Late Mesozoic* 497

DALE A. RUSSELL *An Interview with Dale A. Russell* 510

JOHN GRIBBEN *The Origin of Earth* 512

ISAAC ASIMOV *Black Holes* 521

NANCY C. ANDREASEN *Competing Models of Mental Illness: Psychodynamic, Behavioral, and Biological* 524

STUDENT ESSAY *Can You Feel the Earth Move?* by *Kristina B. Murmann* 537

EXERCISES 538

WRITING ASSIGNMENTS 540

INDEX 543

THE WRITER'S STANCE

Hans Holbein the Younger, The French Ambassadors, 1533. *Oil and tempera on wood, approx. 6′ 8″ × 6′ 9½″. Reproduced by courtesy of the Trustees of the* National Gallery, London.

CHAPTER 1

WRITERS AND THE READING PROCESS

ESTABLISHING CONNECTIONS

What does it mean to be a student taking instruction in writing? Does this make you a writer—primarily? Or a student—primarily? Or some new species we'll call the *studentwriter*? And how will a *studentwriter* be served by a textbook of readings? Giving these questions some thoughtful analysis is a good place to start the journey through this text and course. When you enroll in a biology class, you have a good idea of how the course will be structured, what will be expected of you, and what you will know when you finish. Your experiences with a variety of English courses, however, may result in your being less certain about the plan and purpose of a college writing course, and the role of a collection of readings in that plan. This chapter will get you started by answering questions, addressing possible anxieties, and offering some guidelines for your reading and writing in this course.

THE WRITER IN A WRITING COURSE

Many of you who are exploring this text for the first time are experiencing a variety of feelings: curiosity about the book itself; a sense of excitement about a new term, a new course, perhaps a new instructor; and most likely, a sense of anxiety or foreboding. Some of you may be looking forward to your new course; more of you are ambivalent; many are, unfortunately, experiencing that dull ache in the pit of the stomach and those sweaty palms—physical indicators of stress—brought on not just because you are beginning a new term—you've done that before—but because you are beginning a composition course. Why do so many of you experience so much anxiety as you start a writing course? One answer is that college composition courses are usually required; students must pass them to take upper-division courses, to transfer, to graduate. The school's requirements place pressure on you. But you've faced—and coped successfully with—required courses before, or you would not be in a college course now. The chief cause of your anxiety, let's face it, is the fact that this is a composition course; you will have to write.

Recognizing fears and their sources often helps to decrease their force. Recognizing that others share our anxieties helps us feel less foolish and alone. Recognizing that our anxieties are valid, appropriate for the situation, may be the most comforting of all. When your casual stroll through a pasture brings you face-to-face with an angry bull, you should be afraid. In the face of a term of writing compositions, a degree of nervousness is appropriate, because writing well is not easy. Searching eagerly for an end to their misery, students often ask when writing will become less difficult. The honest answer is that, with practice, writing should become *easier,* but it will probably never be *easy.*

Let's consider some realities of the writing process. First, writing is a skill, like dancing or driving or playing tennis. To be a competent writer you must develop your skills in the same way tennis players develop a spin serve: through good instruction, a strong desire to succeed, and practice, practice, practice. Reading Shakespeare's *Hamlet* and admiring the grace and force of his language and his keen insights into human character, many conclude that writing is some kind of magic that only a few souls have been blessed with the power to use. This concept of the writing process needs qualification. A second fact of writing to accept is that some are more talented writers than others, just as Ivan Lendl is a more talented tennis player than most. But Lendl's tennis ability did not come from a genie in a bottle, and neither did Shakespeare's skill with language. The exceptional in any field make their abilities look "like magic." Still, we must acknowledge that they also devote years of study, self-discipline, and practice to achieve their excellence. Although we may never match Shakespeare's "magic," we can, with practice, become competent writers.

Even for those willing to practice, learning to write well is not easy because no clear instructions or rules exist. Composition texts—and instructors—can offer strategies for effective writing; but they cannot present, complete with pictures, "Ten Easy Steps to a Good Essay." Literally thousands of writing texts are in print. Teachers continually search for better guidelines and new exercises to help students improve their writing. But students need to see that learning to write is not the same as learning to type or tune an engine. There are a fixed number of keys on a typewriter, and car engines are more alike than different. But topics to write about, audiences to write for, and reasons for writing could never be completely catalogued, and the options for choosing and combining words into sentences are infinite in their variety.

Two further realities create difficulties for students of writing. First, good writing results from repeated revising. Even if we are willing to devote the time to revising drafts, many of us lack skill in judging our own writing. Consequently, beyond trying to catch any errors in spelling or punctuation, we don't know what to revise. One important skill to be gained from this course is the ability to edit drafts: to know what to look for and how to achieve sufficient distance to read with a critic's eye. The difficulty of judging our writing often leads to a second problem: a difficulty in accepting editing advice from others. What we have written "sounds good," so we feel hurt or angry when classmates or instructors comment that a paragraph lacks coherence or a passage is awkward. But group reports, whether in the classroom or in the office, require cooperation both in their drafting and in their editing. Even though bruised egos may result from criticism—because writing is so personal—we need to go beyond hurt, learn from others' suggestions, and strive to imitate the critic.

If learning to write well is so difficult, why work on writing skills? For a good answer to this question, ask any student over twenty-five why he or she is now in college. Many "older" college students are training for a second career; but many more want to learn basic skills so that they can advance in their current careers. They will attest that one skill essential for advancement is writing ability. More immediate and personal goals for writing well can also be noted. The more you develop your awareness of the writing process, the better a reader you will become of the numerous books you will read before completing school.

You will be a better reader because you will understand how writers, guided by their awareness of audience and purpose, select and organize material. Your knowledge of writing will enable you to become an active reader, involved with the text. The more confident a writer you become, the more efficiently you will handle written assignments in all your college courses. Understanding the expectations and conventions of writing in various academic disciplines, you can get started on each assignment without undue anxiety or confusion. And since writing is an act of discovery, the more you write, the more you will learn about who you are and what matters to you.

A composition course creates an artificial writing environment, unlike other classes calling for papers to be written on the subject of the course. In a composition course the subject is writing itself, the purpose is to demonstrate writing skills, and the audience for graded compositions is a "supercritic"–an instructor in writing. No wonder you feel anxious. You will cope better by altering that environment–at least in your mind's eye–as much as possible. Develop a more reasonable, less threatening sense of audience by picturing your readers as members of the class, not just the instructor. (Indeed, in many classes–and offices–your audience will be your peers.) Understand the purpose of each assignment; just as the tennis player spends hours drilling on overheads or sliced backhands to put together a successful game, so your instructor gives assignments for you to practice particular skills to improve your overall writing talent. Finally, consider each topic choice as an opportunity for increased self-awareness. After all, how accurately do you see your parents, your friends, your campus? How well do you understand the advertisements incessantly demanding your attention? Writing will improve your vision of the world around you and your understanding of the world inside you.

THE STUDENT WRITER'S ROLES

Writers frequently wear many hats. Isaac Asimov does not write science fiction only; he also writes about science, usually explaining the complexities of science to nonscientists. Leigh Montville writes a sports column for the Boston *Globe*–except on Sundays. At some point in the week he discards his baseball cap and takes on the penetrating, satiric vision of the essayist. There are probably many Bostonians who regularly read Montville's Sunday magazine column but never read Montville the sports journalist. Both Asimov and Montville write about different subjects for different audiences for different purposes. And each time, they write differently: in a different format, with a different style.

Both in this writing course and throughout the many courses you will take in college, you will need to shift writing roles, to wear many hats. At times you will be asked to write essay exams or prepare summaries of articles on library reserve. Your audience will be the teacher, your purpose to demonstrate knowledge gained through reading and instruction. Although you must write, your primary role is the student one. When your writing instructor asks you to read Doris Lessing's "My Father" and then to compose an essay on your father, she wants you to demonstrate skill in description, in evoking a sense of place and its effect on personality. A demanding task. She will be evaluating you in the role of writer. But when your history instructor requests a critical review of one book from a reading list, he may be expecting you to write that review as if you were preparing it for a magazine or journal. In other words, he will expect you to write for a larger audience, ignoring the fact that you are actually completing an assignment, and to use the format and style of the professional reviewer. Similarly, when you prepare the results of a survey—say, a survey of student attitudes toward record labeling—for your sociology course, your instructor may be as interested in your demonstrating the format, style, and tone appropriate to reports in the social sciences as she is in what you actually have to report from your survey. She wants you to learn the *conventions* of a particular type of writing. These instructors want you to wear your studentwriter hat, to combine roles.

This text is all about the demands of wearing many hats, of writing for different audiences for different reasons. Thus not only will you find articles on a range of subjects, astronomy and psychology, sports and economics; you will also find scientists writing to scientists, to educated nonexperts, and to the general public. These differing audiences provide subtle but important distinctions, affecting a writer's choice of subject matter, vocabulary, and format. You should study assigned readings, then, not only to prepare to discuss content but also to analyze the effect of audience and purpose on content and style and to recognize the different conventions the readings illustrate. In addition, you will want to pay close attention to instructions for each writing assignment so that you will know what role you are being asked to fill: a student demonstrating knowledge, a writer revealing descriptive skills and control of varied sentence patterns, a *studentwriter* practicing the conventions of book reviews or literary analysis or explanation of a process.

THE READER IN A WRITING COURSE

"If this is a writing course, why have I purchased a reader?" What, your question asks, is the connection between reading and writing? Actually there are several connections, each providing a different service—and leading to a different type of writing. You can better understand both reading assignments and subsequent writing assignments if you have a clear view of each reading assignment's primary goal.

READING FOR MODELS

One reason we use readings in a composition course is to illustrate a type of writing: the personal essay, the book review, the scholarly report; or more generally, qualities of good writing: effective use of details, control of contrast structure, effective use of metaphors. When you are asked to read Doris Lessing's "My Father" and then to write an essay about your father, you are being asked to use Lessing's essay as your model or example. Obviously your father's life and work aren't the same as hers, so the precise content is not the point of your reading. Rather, you will want to see how a good writer uses details to reveal personality and analyzes the experiences of her subject to reveal the shaping influences on that personality. If Lessing's essay is your model, then you need to go beyond a listing of events to think about your subject's personality traits and the forces that shaped those traits. Although Lessing's approach to character isn't the only one, it is a valid one and, important for you as a *studentwriter,* an approach you have been asked to practice in a given assignment.

More generally, you may examine assigned readings to observe structure, or the use of details, or varied sentence patterns. You may study the poems in Chapter 4, for example, to sharpen your understanding of metaphors and as the basis for a class discussion of attitudes toward loneliness or failed dreams. Then your instructor might ask for an essay (not a poem) on one of these topics in which you develop your views through the use of several metaphors. The poems' structures are not models, but a study and discussion of them have served as a basis for your practice in writing.

READING FOR INFORMATION

We also read for information, for facts and details, for new ideas and startling analyses. As you study assigned readings as models for writing, you will also be gaining information about many subjects: the moves of a bobcat, the origin of the earth, the influence of American character on foreign policy. Chapter 2, for instance, in addition to providing models of essay writing, provides insight into the writing process and the motivations for writing by several successful authors. In subsequent chapters, at least one article in the chapter offers an analysis of the nature of writing—the sources, the conventions, the concerns—for the field represented in that chapter. You can find much useful information about writing in these articles, information that will be especially helpful whenever you must function in the combined role of the studentwriter, that is, whenever you will be evaluated on both content and the conventions of a particular discipline.

READING FOR WRITING

One of the most important effects of reading for students, scholars, business people, citizens—for most of us—is that it produces writing, more works to read, in a never-ending chain reaction. There are many ways that we respond, in writing, to what we read. One response is *to evaluate.* A novelist writes a new book and generates book reviews—essays combining summary, analysis, and judgment of the book's qualities.

Another frequent response to writing is *to analyze.* Scholars in many fields analyze written works, so you can count on being required to practice analyzing some of the works in this text. You are probably thinking of papers for English classes, papers that analyze a character in a story or the metaphors in a poem. But remember that social scientists seeking, for example, to explain the effects of television on children are engaged in *causal analysis.* The student essays on Goya's painting (Chapter 4) and on photographic bias (Chapter 6) are both analyses.

Papers delivered at conferences and published in journals can be viewed as an ongoing debate among specialists over controversial issues. We write to add to a body of knowledge in our field of interest and, frequently, to disagree with what someone else has written. One current scientific debate is over the causes of the dinosaur's extinction. Some scientists present the results of their studies, results that may point to a galactic catastrophe, such as an asteroid crashing into the earth. Others respond to refute this view, arguing that the dinosaurs died off gradually, perhaps because of much slower changes in the food chain. The debate goes on, in writing. And those debates that seem of general interest eventually generate additional writing: journalists report on the issue to the general public. Journalists, like students, must develop sound reading skills so that they can write with clarity about complex ideas.

As a studentwriter you will frequently be asked to write about your reading, to present summaries, analyses, contrasts, and evaluations of assigned material. Remember that to be successful you must demonstrate *both* a knowledge of the assigned reading and an understanding of the required type of writing. It is not enough to know how to organize a contrast structure if you do not understand, for example, how the psychoanalytic and behavioral theories of human personality differ. It is also not sufficient to understand those theories if you are unable to organize a paper that reveals the key differences between them. One reason that writing well is such a challenge is that reading accurately and thinking clearly are also challenging.

STEPS TO ACCURATE READING

Our responses to written works will of course vary, depending on our purposes for reading. Most of us skim more of the daily paper than we read. When we reach for a favorite magazine, we first flip through to see what's there. When purchasing texts for courses or using library materials, you are wise to begin with a "flip and skim" approach to see what the work contains, how it is organized, what sections will be most useful for your study. But once you become engaged in a particular article or chapter or novel, a work that you must know thoroughly for a test or written project, then accuracy, not speed, is your goal.

To develop accurate reading skills you need first to prepare yourself to be a good reader. A good reader is like the eager theatergoer who is prepared to let the director present, through the actors, the dramatist's story and characters. You watch the players perform, hoping to be caught up in their action; you do not come to take a nap or to be called to center stage. When you read, prepare yourself to receive the writer's message, not to rewrite the work to suit yourself. Remember that not all who write will share your views or express themselves as you do. Read what is on the page, opening yourself to a player's particular interests and talents, participating, if indirectly, in the action, withholding judgment, staying alert until the curtain drops. Remember that intelligent, interesting people soak up new knowledge, are challenged by new ideas, and see each reading experience as a door opening onto an expanding world outside themselves.

Although it is easier to say "Read what is on the page" than to perform that task successfully, you can improve your reading skills by starting with the goal of accurate reading and practicing the following steps:

1. *Prepare to become part of the writer's audience.* This may sound strange, but we all need to understand that writers do not have every one of us in mind when they write. Dale Russell, writing on the dinosaur's extinction for *Scientific American,* anticipates a reading audience with knowledge of geologic periods in the earth's history. Stephen Jay Gould, writing about dinosaurs in *Natural History* magazine, seeks to engage the educated nonspecialist in biology's fascinating history, procedures, and topics. Thomas Paine, addressing American colonists still "on the fence" over separation from England, did not write for any of us in the twentieth century who study his pamphlet *Common Sense* in a history or literature course. You need to prepare yourself to join a writer's audience by learning what you can about the writer, about the time in which the piece was written, about the writer's anticipated audience. For writings in this text, you will be aided by introductory notes.

2. *Consider the title.* Titles are the first words writers give us about their work. Take time to look for clues in each title that may reveal both the work's subject and perhaps each writer's approach or attitude as well.

3. *Read slowly enough for understanding.* Remember that the goal is understanding the writer's message, not completing an assignment as quickly as possible. Only when you slow down will you be able to observe the key words that connect a writer's ideas and establish the relationships among the parts of a written work. Sometimes we focus on subjects and verbs, actors and action, and forget that often it is the little connecting words, the *but*'s, *therefore*'s, and *although*'s, that show key relationships.

4. *Use the dictionary and other appropriate reference works.* Reading a work containing unfamiliar words that you do not look up is like trying to play tennis with some of the strings missing from your racket. Also, if you don't recognize the particular examples writers are using to illustrate their points, you are reading a text with holes in it just as if you did not look up a key term or unfamiliar adjective. As long as you are understanding most of what you are reading, circle unfamiliar words or examples and look them up after you have finished the article or chapter. But if you find a paragraph or section containing a number of key terms you do not know, there is little point in pushing on, pretending that you have understood the passage. Subsequent paragraphs may build on the points established in the paragraph you did not understand.

5. *Make notes.* Use more than just your eyes when you read. The more senses you engage, the more active your involvement. As you read, underline key sentences—such as each paragraph's topic sentence, if there is one, and the writer's thesis (main idea), if stated. Remember, though, that the purpose of underlining is to highlight by contrast; if you underline just about every sentence, you have missed the purpose. When you look up a word's definition, write the definition in the margin so that you can reread that section with understanding. Make other marginal notes that will help you become more fully engaged in the reading process. Don't just underline a writer's main idea; note in the margin that it is the main idea. When you recognize that a writer is providing a series of examples, label them examples and then number each one in the margin. Draw pictures to illustrate concepts; draw arrows to connect example to idea.

THE ENGAGED READER

Experts who study how we read have learned that our success as readers depends on how much information about a topic we bring to our reading of that topic and on how we use that information to interact with the text, to understand what we have just read and anticipate what will come next. Good readers, even when faced with a new subject or with complex writing, still find clues that help them shape a *context of expectations,* clues that aid the reading process.

To help you become more aware of reading clues, more alert to the extent to which you interact with what you read, an informal exercise follows. (It is not a test!) The first few paragraphs of Joseph Kraft's column "The Sports Craze" have been interrupted at key points by questions for you to consider. To benefit most from this exercise, cover the lines you have not yet read and write the best answers you can to each question before reading past the question. Then, after reading the next section, go back to your answer and see how well you anticipated the selection's structure and direction. Finally, you can read the entire article in Chapter 6 to see how accurately you predicted the remaining parts of Kraft's column.

READING EXERCISE

1. What, if anything, do you know about Joseph Kraft? Put down whatever you know.
2. From the title ("The Sports Craze") and whatever you may know about Kraft and the kind of writing he does, what do you expect to read about?

> Pete Rose, Joe Montana, John McEnroe and Larry Bird surpass Ruth, Tilden, Dempsey and Bobby Jones in technique, speed, power, crowd appeal and cash flow. The '80s have replaced the '20s as the Golden Age of American sport.

3. From reading the first paragraph, what do you expect the article to be about? How do you think it will be organized?

> But the sports craze common to the two eras denotes a deeper harmony. The '80s resemble the '20s in many other ways, and a comparison helps to define the spirit of our times.

4. After reading paragraph 2, how have your expectations about the article changed?

> A waning of common purpose set the stage in each case. Just before the turn of the century the sense of national destiny quickened. The war with Spain was one sign, and the building of the

> Panama Canal another. Theodore Roosevelt's Progressivism and Woodrow Wilson's New Freedom both featured what Herbert Croly called the "promise of American life." World War I, and Wilson's call to make the world "safe for democracy," enhanced the sense of mission.
>
> With victory came disillusionment. A provincial backlash fastened Prohibition on the nation and fostered a vogue for religious quackery. Sophisticates in the great cities turned away from larger national goals to the comforts of individual success and good living.
>
> Financial speculation was one, highly approved, form of self-assertion. Making whoopee at speak-easies and country clubs was another. Gangsters enjoyed a vogue as stars who gave thrills. The great figures of sport combined personal achievement with a certain insouciance. They joked and jested. They were innocent heroes who had fun. It figured that they would be wiped out by the Great Depression.

5. What broad topic is common to these three paragraphs?
6. What broad topic will be discussed in the rest of the article?
7. What kinds of details do you expect in the rest of the article? How will they be organized?

REINFORCING THE READING PROCESS

After reading complex material, even when following guidelines for accurate reading and for becoming engaged with the text, you may still feel uncertain about the thoroughness of your understanding. Sometimes we remember a line here, an example there, but we are unsure of the central purpose and direction of the work as a whole. Understanding what is central to a writer's subject and purpose can be aided by a preliminary analysis of the work's thesis, evidence, and structure.

WHAT IS THE THESIS?

Often the first question an instructor asks to initiate class discussion of an assigned essay is: "What is the thesis?" The *thesis* is the main idea or chief point a writer wants to establish and have readers accept. A thesis is not the same as the writer's subject. Rather, a thesis includes the writer's assertion about or attitude toward the subject as well as a statement of the subject. The thesis is what the writer wants to point out, assert, or claim about his or her subject.

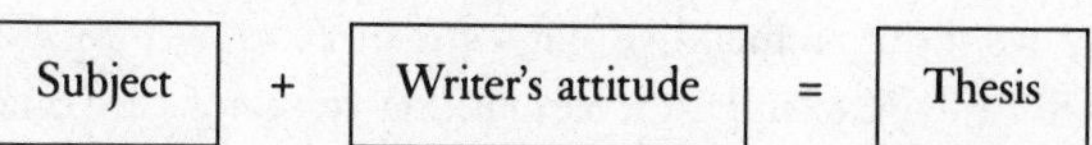

We can illustrate the concept of thesis by applying the above diagram to an essay in Chapter 2, Gail Godwin's "The Watcher at the Gates":

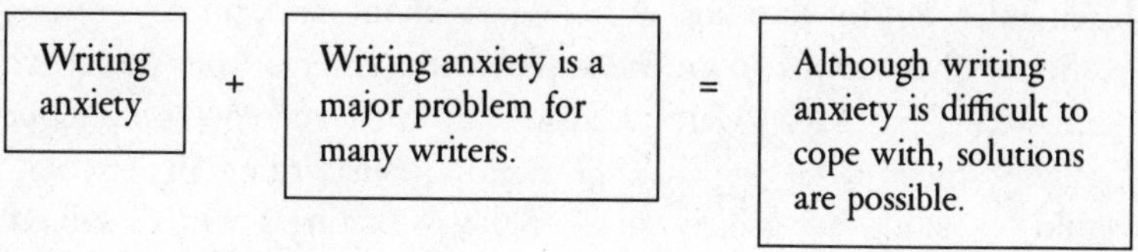

When you are reading the results of scientific research, you will find it more helpful to state the author's attitude as a question, a hypothesis to be tested by experiment or study. The results of the research project become the article's thesis, thus:

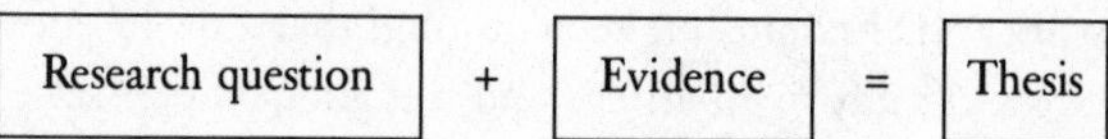

In "The Mass Extinctions of the Late Mesozoic," Dale A. Russell examines the issue of the dinosaur's extinction. Using the above pattern, we can analyze his article thus:

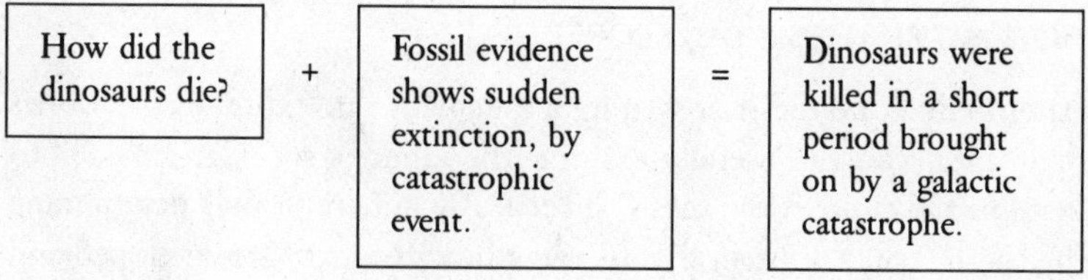

When analyzing novels, short stories, or plays, we generally do not speak of the writer's thesis but rather of the work's *theme* or themes, and we are cautious about reducing a complex literary work into a one-sentence statement of theme. Still, the basic process remains the same: what is the work about (its subject) and what is the writer's assertion about or attitude toward that subject?

Finally, we should remember that some pieces of writing are designed primarily to explain, to impart information. Textbooks are one example. Although as readers we recognize that the selecting and organizing of information may reveal an attitude or theoretical bias, still our primary task is to understand the work's content. For example, in Chapter 8 Isaac Asimov defines black holes. We read his explanation to understand black holes, not to learn how Asimov feels about black holes.

Some observations about thesis statements emerge from the above discussion. First, if you were to answer an instructor's question about Godwin's thesis by saying that she writes about writing anxiety, you would be stating her subject, not her thesis. Stating a writer's subject with precision is a good beginning, but in order to recognize thesis you need to answer the question "What is the writer's assertion about that subject?" or "What is the question to be answered by the research project?" or "What is the novelist's attitude toward—for example—seeking wealth by any means?"

When reading, then, look for one or two sentences that seem to state the work's chief point; but keep in mind that a thesis does not have to be stated specifically in an article, and it is almost never stated directly in fiction. Just because a thesis is unstated, though, does not mean that the work lacks a main idea. Expert writers, writing with force and clarity, can feel confident that thoughtful readers will reach an accurate understanding of their main idea.

HOW IS THE THESIS DEVELOPED?

After finding the thesis or writing a statement that expresses the work's main idea, you can usefully examine the kinds of specifics provided to develop and support the thesis. Indeed, if you have trouble determining the thesis, you can begin by observing how the article is developed and then work toward an appropriate generalization. Does the writer provide a list of examples? If so, what are they examples of? Is the article developed by one lengthy illustration, an amusing anecdote, or descriptive details? If so, what is their point? What generalization emerges from the details or illustrations? Being a good reader involves more than having a good memory for specifics; being a good reader requires understanding what the specifics mean.

WHAT IS THE WORK'S STRUCTURE OR ORGANIZATION?

Analysis of a book's or an article's *structure* (pattern or shape) can also aid the reading process. Becoming aware of shape will help you to distinguish between main ideas and evidence, to follow the steps in an argument, or to see that the writer's purpose is to establish differences (contrast) or to report events. The more clearly you can see what an author is doing and how he or she is accomplishing the task, the better you will understand the author's message. Although there are as many ways to organize a written work as there are writers, some patterns are frequently repeated. Readers can be on the alert for a writer's use of one standard pattern or some combination of several patterns.

1. *Chronological.* The most common structure is a chronological order or time sequence. Stories, of course, use narrative (though sometimes strict chronology is altered for effect), but nonfiction writers can also organize their examples in historical sequence or examine a controversial issue by following the sequence of a particular case through the legal system. Explanation of a process also relies on time sequence.

2. *Spatial.* Descriptive writing frequently employs a spatial order. A writer describing the pleasures of visiting Manhattan can organize details in a logical movement through space from Wall Street in lower Manhattan to the Empire State Building in midtown to Columbia University on the upper West Side.

3. *General-to-particular.* A frequent pattern in essay writing is to state a thesis after a brief introduction and then present evidence—particulars—in support of the thesis. The particulars are then organized by some principle, perhaps time sequence or from the least to the most important. In Chapter 2, for example, Joseph Reynolds provides a list of reasons for keeping a journal.

4. *Particular-to-general.* Reversing the pattern—beginning with examples, or perhaps one longer anecdote, and then concluding with a thesis—is also common, especially if an author is writing about a controversial issue. The advantage of this approach lies in enticing readers by presenting lively examples first and stating controversial opinions last. An essay with an implied thesis, or a story, uses this structure. Both stop short of supplying the generalization.

5. *Question-answer.* A variation of the particular-to-general shape is often found in scientific report writing. The researcher introduces the

subject by stating a hypothesis or question to be answered by experiment or case study, explains the experimental process or methodology, presents the evidence obtained, analyzes the evidence, and draws a conclusion, an answer (or partial answer) to the question.

Keep these patterns in mind as you read, using them as another aid to good reading.

WHAT IS THE WRITER'S STANCE?

We have seen that examining a writer's thesis, evidence, and organization is one useful approach to understanding a piece of writing; but this approach works best with writing that presents and develops a single, clear assertion. Another way to analyze what we read is to consider the relationships among the writer, the writing, and the audience for that piece of writing. We said earlier that writers wear many hats, just as you will as a studentwriter. Writers must consider not only what they want to say but also how best to say it to a particular audience. In this context, "best" means appropriately as well as effectively. For a chemist writing in a scholarly journal, it is inappropriate to present the results of an experiment in the form of a fable. He will be ineffective if he breaks from the expected format and conventions of scientific report writing. For Leigh Montville, writing social commentary in a Sunday newspaper column, a fable may be the best way to present his ideas. The decisions writers make about the form of their works in the light of audience and purpose we can call the *writer's stance.*

We can visualize the concept of stance by use of a funnel image, as in Figure 1.1. In general, the less individuality expressed by a writer, the larger the potential audience and the more central the content of the work. Consider again the scientific report. One of the conventions of report writing is that the writer's personality be suppressed in favor of impersonal language and a standard format. The content is central and can be understood by all who know the language of science, all who can meet the writer in the large universe of scientific endeavor, not the probably more narrow vision of a writer's private world. In journalism and history writing, more individuality of style will be found, but these works must still connect to a world of facts, of shared knowledge of

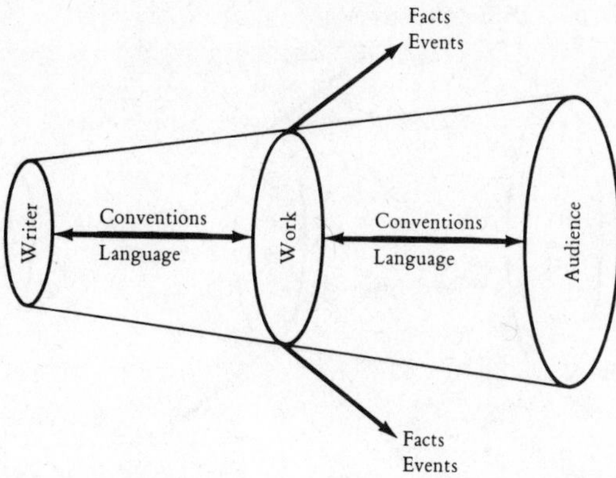

FIGURE 1.1 The Writer's Stance

events. On the one hand, the historian must conform to the "facts out there" to have any audience. A history text with the dates all wrong will have few readers. On the other hand, the amount of background information provided will determine the size and nature of the audience. Junior history books are accessible to every reader, but specialists would not use them. In this stance, the writer is primarily concerned with the best selection and arrangement of material to reflect, accurately and meaningfully, the world the work is about so that the targeted audience can understand that world.

Going in the other direction—or turning the funnel around (see Figure 1.2)—we can see that some works are more highly personal, reflecting the writer and the writer's world of experiences, feelings, dreams. The more private the writing, the more limited the audience, for only those able to enter the writer's world can become readers. The language and form of the work may appear simpler than, for example, the language of science; but in fact the reading is more difficult because the language refers to private experiences, not public events, or it refers to a private understanding of public events. The most private writing would include letters and diaries because we write to friends or ourselves in a private "code" that depends, for understanding, on shared knowledge. Standing somewhere between diaries and technical reports are essays and poems, works of fiction, and philosophy. Some conventions of format and structure aid us as readers, but both the knowledge

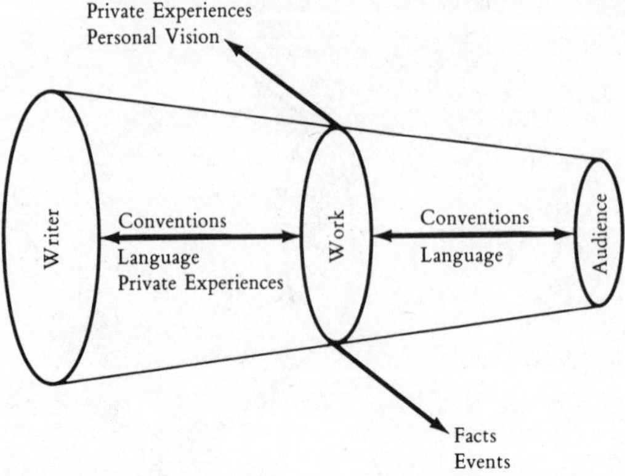

FIGURE 1.2 The Writer's Stance

required and the ability to relate to the writer's personal vision and particular interests will determine the audience. Essayists, poets, novelists, philosophers—all may take us to new worlds, but we as readers may have to work hard to get there. Your ability to read many different kinds of writing will be aided by your being able to recognize each writer's stance.

A WRITER'S LIST OF FIRST QUESTIONS: AIDS TO BOTH READING AND WRITING

We are familiar with the reporter's litany of questions: who, what, where, when, and why. But all writers need to answer some key questions to plan their writing. They need, in short, to determine their stance. Having specific answers to the following questions before you launch into any writing assignment is guaranteed to improve your work. Knowing that professional writers have also answered these questions will help you analyze the works you read. So in addition to answering the study questions following the articles in this text, answer these general questions as well, as if you were the writer, remembering to use all relevant clues from the headnotes, the chapter introductions, and the study questions. And when you are the writer, use these questions to plan your writing.

PREWRITING QUESTIONS

I. Type

What kind or type of writing do I want (or have I been assigned) to produce?

What is the appropriate format for this kind of writing?

What is the appropriate (or assigned) length?

II. Purpose

Beyond completing an assignment, what is my purpose in writing? To inform? To analyze? To evaluate? To persuade?

What do I want my readers to know, to feel, or to do after reading my work?

III. Subject

What is my specific topic?

What main point or thesis do I want to establish about that topic?

Does my choice of topic meet the guidelines of purpose and format that have been established for this piece of writing?

IV. Audience

Who is my audience?

What do members of my audience already know about my topic?

What are their interests and values? What attitudes toward my subject are they likely to hold?

How should answers to these questions guide my choice of approach and tone?

EXERCISES

1. Joan Didion ("Why I Write," p. 32) says college taught her that she was not an intellectual. Years later she realized that she was a writer with a particular approach to writing. How well do you know yourself as a writer? For ten to fifteen minutes, brainstorm about yourself, using the following questions as guidelines:

   a. On what occasions and for what reasons do you most frequently write?
   b. What is most important to you when you write? To persuade others to your way of thinking? To express feelings? To capture an image? To learn about yourself? Does your purpose vary sometimes? If so, why?

c. Does the process of writing give you pleasure, or do you get more pleasure from finishing, from having written?
d. Do you get pleasure from shaping a piece of writing even if no one sees it, or is your pleasure dependent on a reader's favorable response?
e. Do you prefer writing description? Developing an idea logically? Pleading forcefully for a cause?

2. To practice responding to clues and developing expectations when reading, read the following excerpts and answer the questions in turn. Remember to cover what you have not yet read, or you will not benefit from the exercise. When you have completed the exercise, review all your answers, noting the good guesses and those that turned out not to be accurate. Finally, read the complete essay and evaluate your answers again.

1. The author of the following excerpt is Ellen Goodman. Write whatever you may know about Goodman and what you might expect when considering that knowledge.

"Life in a Bundle of Letters"

2. From the title, what do you expect the essay to be about?

Somewhere, in the boxes that I have moved from one address to another, are small packages of summers past. Letters from my parents. Letters from school friends. Love letters. Private history wrapped neatly in rubber bands.

3. On the basis of the first paragraph, what do you expect the essay to be about? Do you have any clues about the essay's organization?

Most of them are, by now, more than 20 summers old. The datelines remind me of camp, college, trips. They also remind me of my father's humor, the rhythms of my mother's daily life, the code words of adolescent friendships–S.W.A.K., sealed with a kiss–the intimacy of the young.

4. What does the second paragraph add to the first? Does it give you further clues about the rest of the essay?

My friends, my family and I rarely mail our thoughts anymore. The mailman brings more catalogues than correspondence to our homes. The letters that come through our mail slot are mostly addressed in robotype. The stamps we buy are to go on bills.

5. After reading the third paragraph, what do you now expect the essay to be about? How do you think it will be organized?

We direct-dial now. Spoiled by the instant gratification and the ease of the phone, we talk. The telephone call has replaced the letter in our lives nearly as completely as the car has replaced the cart.

6. Now what do you think the essay will be about? Does this paragraph confirm your expectations stated above, or does it give you a new sense of where the writer is going? What organizational pattern will Goodman use? What attitude toward letters will emerge in the rest of the essay?

WRITING ASSIGNMENTS

1. What kind of reading do you enjoy the most? Do you like science fiction, romance, a newspaper or newsmagazine, or magazines devoted to a special interest or hobby? In an essay, explain *why* you enjoy reading the kind of material you usually select. Give specific examples of the material you read but organize by the reasons for your preference. Your purpose is not to argue for one type of reading but to share your reading pleasures in a personal essay.
2. Have you had difficulty with writing in the past, or do you feel anxious about this writing course? If so, explain, in an essay, why you have anxiety about writing. Is it hard to get started? Do you worry about grammar or spelling? Do you feel that you express yourself better when you talk than when you write? Be as specific as you can, using your past writing experiences as examples. Think of yourself as a columnist for the college newspaper.
3. What did you expect this writing course to be like? Were your expectations similar to or different from what you have experienced thus far in the course? In an essay compare or contrast your preconceived ideas of the course with the actual course as it has been revealed in class, syllabus, and texts. You are writing this essay for next year's orientation packet for freshmen. Before writing, sort through your ideas and make a list of two to four specific points of similarity to or differences from your expectations. (Remember that your expectations about this course were probably based on other courses you have taken.) Then answer the prewriting questions provided in this chapter so that you will be planning with an audience and purpose in mind. Submit answers to prewriting questions with your completed essay.

Pablo Picasso, The Studio, 1927–1928. *Oil on canvas, 59″ by 7′ 7″. Collection, The Museum of Modern Art, New York. Gift of Walter P. Chrysler, Jr.*

CHAPTER 2

WRITING
THE CHALLENGE

This first collection of readings provides insights into the task of writing. Seven professional writers and a student writer explore several issues: what motivates writers to write, how experiences are forged into a literary work, what rewards a writer receives from writing, what keeps us from being able to write. Your primary concern in Chapter 2, then, will be with content; you will be reading for information about the subject of this course: writing.

As you read, be open to what you can learn from these dedicated writers, from people who have committed themselves to achieving excellence in one of our most demanding tasks. Why do Joseph Reynolds and Ellen Goodman value so highly even the most informal and personal of writing: journals and letters? What are both James Baldwin and Richard Selzer—one a professional writer, the other a professional surgeon—seeking, through writing, whatever the struggle? What important points about writing well underlie William F. Buckley's insistence on writing "with all deliberate speed"? Why do we stare miserably at a half-completed sentence, unable to go on? There is a rich treasure of insights in the essays that follow. As these writers reflect on themselves as writers, they can expand your understanding of yourself as both writer and reader.

Since you have just read about the reading process in Chapter 1 and have now turned to your first chapter of essays, you can probably anticipate that your instructor will use these essays on writing to reinforce techniques for close reading and to check for reading accuracy. So practice good reading skills and prepare solid answers to questions about each writer's subject, thesis, organization, and use of evidence.

Although Chapter 3 is about the essay and this chapter is primarily about writing itself, still the pieces in this chapter are also personal essays, so we should make some preliminary observations about this form. Actually the term *form* is misleading, since the first point to be made is that the personal essay is a vague, amorphous category. We know that a poem must be in verse, that a story will have characters and narrative structure, that a scientific report has a standard format for presenting results, but what can we say about the essay? It is shorter than a book; it is not in verse; it is not a narrative, but it may use time sequence to organize points; there is no specific format, but unity is achieved by its being about one subject, however broad. Although some may use the terms *article* and *essay* as synonyms, we generally use *article* to refer to a factual piece of writing and reserve *essay* for a piece of writing that is more speculative or reflective. This does not mean that essays are without facts but rather that the writer's thoughts about the facts are more important than the facts themselves. If we add *personal* to *essay,* then we have in mind short prose works that draw primarily on personal experience for the facts on which the writer is reflecting. All the essayists in this chapter, for example, draw on their own experiences as writers first to understand then to illustrate their ideas about writing.

Some of the marks of the personal essay include use of the first person pronoun (*I*) and a choice and arrangement of material that is highly individualistic. Often we as readers have the sense that we are engaged in a casual conversation with the essayist who is just now, with us, thinking through his or her ideas. But do not be deceived. To create the sense of casual intimacy may take much planning and revising, for the good writer knows that few people want to read random and carelessly organized thoughts. Remember, from Chapter 1, that the more personal or writer-centered the work is, the greater the writer's task to reach and hold readers. Of course well-known writers can expect to transfer their audiences from one work to the next, but they will keep their readers only if interest is sustained through each new work. James Baldwin, for example, can expect at least some readers of his novels to be interested in his essay about his life as a writer.

You should also note that three of this chapter's essays were published in the prestigious *New York Times Book Review.* This section of the *Times* Sunday edition, subscribed to by readers across the country, always runs an essay about writing or writers. Godwin, Didion, and Buckley can anticipate a large audience eagerly awaiting their reflections.

The first essay in this chapter, by Joseph Reynolds, is about the advantages of keeping a journal—an appropriate topic to start with, for many professional writers find their journals essential to developing the craft of writing. You may also find the journal a helpful tool; indeed your instructor may require journal writing in this course—good reasons for understanding what a journal is. A *journal,* like a diary, records the writer's experiences; but in a journal one is less concerned with listing all the major events of the day and more concerned with capturing reactions to and reflections on one's experiences. From a full day, the journal writer may select one experience to think about—as it were—aloud. In the process of writing thoughts and observations, the journal writer gets practice writing—and finds other advantages, as Reynolds observes.

While making you more aware of writing, the essays in this chapter can also teach you much about style. First, though, you need to think about what it means to analyze a writer's style. Look at word choice: is it formal or informal, colloquial or technical, abstract or concrete, or some combination of possibilities? Consider sentence structure: is it generally long or short, simple or complex, balanced or loose? A writer's style is shaped primarily by combined choices about diction (words) and sentence patterns. A formal style signals a serious purpose and can create distance between writer and reader, the distance of authority or wisdom. Lincoln's "Gettysburg Address" provides an example of a formal style. Instead of choosing the words "eighty years," Lincoln selected "fourscore." And Lincoln crafted long sentences with complex patterns of parallel structure and antithesis (contrast). Compare the following sentences—the first by Lincoln, the second an informal version.

Lincoln: Formal

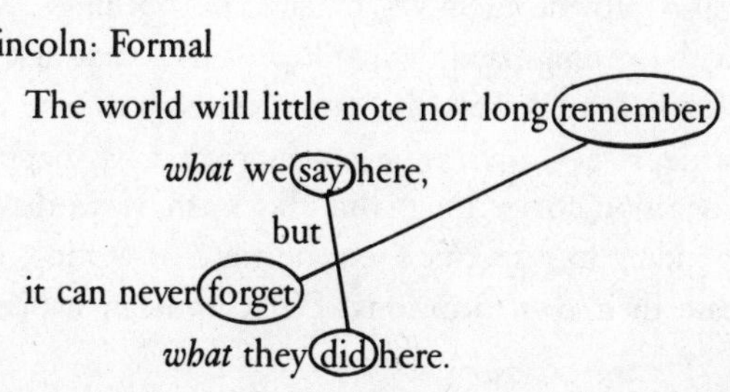

Rewrite: Informal

> The world will always remember what the soldiers did, even though it is likely to forget our speeches.

A writer's selection of words offers a wider range of possibilities than the formal or informal suggested by "fourscore" and "eighty." Richard Selzer's use of medical language ("unguent," "cellular," "albuminoid") reveals his technical training, and makes his essay more formal in tone than, say, Gail Godwin's. Godwin writes about "looker-uppers" and "scaredy-cats," words that would sound inappropriate in Selzer's essay. To achieve an informal style, a writer might select the verb "carry" instead of its more formal synonym "convey." If seeking a particularly informal, chatty style, the writer could discard "carry" and choose "lug" instead. (The following chapters will give you additional guidelines for analyzing style—and opportunities for practice.)

One good way to recognize style is through contrast. Take Reynolds and Goodman on the one hand and Selzer and Buckley on the other, examine several paragraphs of each, and see how they differ in word choice and sentence structure.

We see several qualities of good essay writing at work in this chapter; one is the use of details. As noted earlier, good writing is concrete writing; these writers prove it. When Gail Godwin considers solutions to writer's block, she does not say, "If you just sit at the desk long enough and try really hard, you will think of something to write, so hang in there." The last thing people with writing anxiety want to hear is a pep talk; they need help—specific techniques for getting something worthwhile down on paper. Godwin gives specifics. Similarly, Joan Didion does not assert that her stories come from images in her mind—and then stop. She illustrates the process by discussing the evolution of several novels. As we read the examples, we understand the general point.

These writers also provide examples of effective openings. Many students struggle with openings, and their stilted or irrelevant first lines bear witness to a battle lost. Perhaps the easiest opening to use, when appropriate, is Buckley's: he begins by explaining what has happened that provides his occasion for writing. But this opening works only when you are responding to a specific event or piece of writing; more often essayists create their own occasions. Did Goodman happen to look through some boxes of letters and then decide to write her column? Or did she think about them as a way to get her column started? Notice how many of the writers begin by referring to other writers; Reynolds, Godwin, and Didion begin with a borrowed line or reference to reading. What could be more appropriate for essays about writing? Observe that each opening is relevant to the essay and is simply stated, not "announced." "Here is a quote that fits journal writing" is decidedly *not* the way Reynolds gets started!

I Think (and Write in a Journal), Therefore I Am

JOSEPH REYNOLDS

Joseph Reynolds (b. 1942) teaches English and Latin at Wachusett Regional High School in Massachusetts. He has spent a year in Rome on a Fulbright grant and a summer studying Greek and Greek civilization on an NEA grant. Reynolds is also a free-lance writer who has published over a hundred articles and reviews in newspapers and journals. And he keeps a journal, having averaged four entries a week for over a dozen years! Such dedication to journal writing—launched as a way to improve his prose style—certainly qualifies Reynolds as a spokesperson for the values of keeping a journal.

His article on journal writing was first published in the Christian Science Monitor *on February 23, 1981. In a letter about his journal keeping, Reynolds spoke again of the good reasons for writing in a journal: "If the hundred or so essays and reviews I've published since beginning journal writing is any measure of the success of journal keeping, then I have to admit I've made some progress [on my prose style]. The tangential benefits of keeping a journal are more obvious to me. I have sharpened my powers of observation. I see events more clearly by simply recording them. Also, I make connections more readily with the subtle signs that speak to everyone in life if only we are aware of them."*

> *For a long time I was a reporter to a journal, of no very wide circulation, whose editor has never yet seen fit to*

print the bulk of my contributions, and, as is too common with writers, I got only my labor for my pains. However, in this case my pains were their own reward.

–Henry David Thoreau
Walden

1 "I write, therefore I am," wrote Samuel Johnson, altering Descartes' famous dictum: "I think, therefore I am."

2 When writing in my journal, I feel keenly alive and somehow get a glimpse of what Johnson meant.

3 My journal is a storehouse, a treasury for everything in my daily life: the stories I hear, the people I meet, the quotations I like, and even the subtle signs and symbols I encounter that speak to me indirectly. Unless I capture these things in writing, I lose them.

4 All writers are such collectors, whether they keep a journal or not; they see life clearly, a vision we only recognize when reading their books. Thoreau exemplifies the best in journal writing–his celebrated *Walden* grew out of his journal entries.

5 By writing in my own journal, I often make discoveries. I see connections and conclusions that otherwise would not appear obvious to me. I become a craftsman, like a potter or a carpenter who makes a vase or a wooden stoop out of parts. Writing is a source of pleasure when it involves such invention and creation.

6 I want to work on my writing, too, hone it into clear, readable prose, and where better to practice my writing than in my journal. Writing, I'm told, is a skill, and improves with practice. I secretly harbor this hope. So my journal becomes the arena where I do battle with the written word.

7 Sometimes when I have nothing to write, I sit idly and thumb back through old entries. I rediscover incidents long forgotten.

8 During a recent cold midwinter night, for example, I reread an entry dated a summer ago. My wife and I had just returned after a day at the beach. We were both tired and uncomfortable after the long ride home, but our spirits were lifted when we saw our cat come down the driveway to greet us, her tail held high shouting her presence. By reading this entry, I relived the incident, warming with affection for my cat and a sunny day at the beach.

9 I always try to write something, however, even if it is free writing, writing anything that comes to mind. Often this process is a source of a

"core idea" that can later be developed into a more finely polished piece of writing. The articles I've published had their inception in my journal.

10 Journal writing, in addition, is a time when I need not worry about the rules of spelling and grammar; it provides a relaxed atmosphere in which my ideas and feelings can flow freely onto the page. If I discover an idea worth developing, then my rewriting is done.

11 My journal becomes a place where I can try different kinds of writing, as well, from prose and poetry to letters to the editor. Attempting different kinds is useful; once I find the inspiring medium, my writing improves.

12 When I write in my journal, I seek the solitude of my study. With pen in hand, I become omniscient; I am aware of the quiet, damp, night air, or the early-morning sounds of life. My journal is the place where I discover life.

13 "Usually when a man quits writing in his journal, . . . he has lost interest in life," attests E. B. White, an inveterate journal writer himself.

14 So for these few moments, at least, I hold myself in hand, I am.

QUESTIONS FOR ANALYSIS AND DISCUSSION

1. What is Reynolds's thesis or main point about journal writing?
2. Reynolds provides nine reasons for keeping a journal. List them in order, stating each reason as a phrase (e.g., a place to discover life).
3. Nine reasons make a rather compelling list. Select the one or two reasons you find most convincing and say why.
4. Has Reynolds convinced you of the rewards of journal writing? If not, how would you respond to him?
5. Reynolds assumes a reader who knows Thoreau, Samuel Johnson, and Descartes. Look up each name you don't know in an encyclopedia, and then explain how each writer's quotation contributes to Reynolds's essay about journal writing.
6. Although his organization appears simple, Reynolds's style is complex. He uses a number of effective metaphors or comparisons. Find at least three metaphors, state the two items being compared, and explain why the metaphor provides an effective comparison.
7. Reynolds gives us an example of the personal essay: he uses the pronoun *I* throughout and writes of his experience. What techniques help him avoid sounding self-centered or pompous? What does he do to make his personal experience significant for many readers?

Why I Write

JOAN DIDION

Joan Didion (b. 1934) began her career at Vogue *after graduating from the University of California at Berkeley. She now lives in California, where she writes short stories, novels, reviews, and political analyses, and co-writes screenplays with her husband. (An example of her political writing appears in Chapter 6.) Her novels include* Run River *(1963),* Play It as It Lays *(1970), and* Democracy *(1983). She is also well known for her essays, many of which have been collected in* The White Album *(1979) and* Slouching Towards Bethlehem *(1968). The following essay, adapted from a lecture delivered at Berkeley, was first published in the December 6, 1976, issue of the* New York Times Book Review.

Through a forceful expression of her reasons for being a writer, Didion gives us insight into a writer's creative techniques. She is a good example of the "seeing" writer, one who begins not with ideas but with the telling detail, and finds a story therein.

1 Of course I stole the title for this talk, from George Orwell. One reason I stole it was that I like the sound of the words: Why I Write. There you have three short unambiguous words that share a sound, and the sound they share is this:

I
I
I

2 In many ways writing is the act of saying *I*, of imposing oneself upon other people, of saying *listen to me, see it my way, change your mind.* It's an aggressive, even a hostile act. You can disguise its aggressiveness all you want with veils of subordinate clauses and qualifiers and tentative subjunctives, with ellipses and evasions—with the whole manner of intimating rather than claiming, of alluding rather than stating—but there's no getting around the fact that setting words on paper is the tactic of a secret bully, an invasion, an imposition of the writer's sensibility on the reader's most private space.

3 I stole the title not only because the words sounded right but because they seemed to sum up, in a no-nonsense way, all I have to tell you. Like many writers I have only this one "subject," this one "area":

the act of writing. I can bring you no reports from any other front. I may have other interests: I am "interested," for example, in marine biology, but I don't flatter myself that you would come out to hear me talk about it. I am not a scholar. I am not in the least an intellectual, which is not to say that when I hear the word "intellectual" I reach for my gun, but only to say that I do not think in abstracts. During the years when I was an undergraduate at Berkeley I tried, with a kind of hopeless late-adolescent energy, to buy some temporary visa into the world of ideas, to forge for myself a mind that could deal with the abstract.

4 In short I tried to think. I failed. My attention veered inexorably back to the specific, to the tangible, to what was generally considered, by everyone I knew then and for that matter have known since, the peripheral. I would try to contemplate the Hegelian dialectic[1] and would find myself concentrating instead on a flowering pear tree outside my window and the particular way the petals fell on my floor. I would try to read linguistic theory and would find myself wondering instead if the lights were on in the bevatron up the hill. When I say that I was wondering if the lights were on in the bevatron you might immediately suspect, if you deal in ideas at all, that I was registering the bevatron as a political symbol, thinking in shorthand about the military-industrial complex and its role in the university community, but you would be wrong. I was only wondering if the lights were on in the bevatron, and how they looked. A physical fact.

5 I had trouble graduating from Berkeley, not because of this inability to deal with ideas—I was majoring in English, and I could locate the house-and-garden imagery in *The Portrait of a Lady*[2] as well as the next person, "imagery" being by definition the kind of specific that got my attention—but simply because I had neglected to take a course in Milton.[3] For reasons which now sound baroque I needed a degree by the end of that summer, and the English department finally agreed, if I would come down from Sacramento every Friday and talk about the cosmology of *Paradise Lost,* to certify me proficient in Milton. I did this. Some Fridays I took the Greyhound bus, other Fridays I caught the Southern Pacific's City of San Francisco on the last leg of its transcontinental trip. I can no longer tell you whether Milton put the sun or the

---

[1]A process whereby a higher form of truth is obtained by the synthesis of an idea with its opposite, according to the German philosopher Hegel (1770–1831).—Ed.

[2]A novel by Henry James.—Ed.

[3]A seventeenth-century English poet.—Ed.

earth at the center of his universe in *Paradise Lost,* the central question of at least one century and a topic about which I wrote 10,000 words that summer, but I can still recall the exact rancidity of the butter in the City of San Francisco's dining car, and the way the tinted windows on the Greyhound bus cast the oil refineries around Carquinez Straits into a grayed and obscurely sinister light. In short my attention was always on the periphery, on what I could see and taste and touch, on the butter, and the Greyhound bus. During those years I was traveling on what I knew to be a very shaky passport, forged papers: I knew that I was no legitimate resident in any world of ideas. I knew I couldn't think. All I knew then was what I couldn't do. All I knew then was what I wasn't, and it took me some years to discover what I was.

6 Which was a writer.

7 By which I mean not a "good" writer or a "bad" writer but simply a writer, a person whose most absorbed and passionate hours are spent arranging words on pieces of paper. Had my credentials been in order I would never have become a writer. Had I been blessed with even limited access to my own mind there would have been no reason to write. I write entirely to find out what I'm thinking, what I'm looking at, what I see and what it means. What I want and what I fear. Why did the oil refineries around Carquinez Straits seem sinister to me in the summer of 1956? Why have the night lights in the bevatron burned in my mind for twenty years? *What is going on in these pictures in my mind?*

8 When I talk about pictures in my mind I am talking, quite specifically, about images that shimmer around the edges. There used to be an illustration in every elementary psychology book showing a cat drawn by a patient in varying stages of schizophrenia. This cat had a shimmer around it. You could see the molecular structure breaking down at the very edges of the cat: the cat became the background and the background the cat, everything interacting, exchanging ions. People on hallucinogens describe the same perception of objects. I'm not a schizophrenic, nor do I take hallucinogens, but certain images do shimmer for me. Look hard enough, and you can't miss the shimmer. It's there. You can't think too much about these pictures that shimmer. You just lie low and let them develop. You stay quiet. You don't talk to many people and you keep your nervous system from shorting out and you try to locate the cat in the shimmer, the grammar in the picture.

9 Just as I meant "shimmer" literally I mean "grammar" literally. Grammar is a piano I play by ear, since I seem to have been out of school the year the rules were mentioned. All I know about grammar is

its infinite power. To shift the structure of a sentence alters the meaning of that sentence, as definitely and inflexibly as the position of a camera alters the meaning of the object photographed. Many people know about camera angles now, but not so many know about sentences. The arrangement of the words matters, and the arrangement you want can be found in the picture in your mind. The picture dictates the arrangement. The picture dictates whether this will be a sentence with or without clauses, a sentence that ends hard or a dying-fall sentence, long or short, active or passive. The picture tells you how to arrange the words and the arrangement of the words tells you, or tells me, what's going on in the picture. *Nota bene:*[4]

10 It tells you.

11 You don't tell it.

12 Let me show you what I mean by pictures in the mind. I began *Play It as It Lays* just as I have begun each of my novels, with no notion of "character" or "plot" or even "incident." I had only two pictures in my mind, more about which later, and a technical intention, which was to write a novel so elliptical and fast that it would be over before you noticed it, a novel so fast that it would scarcely exist on the page at all. About the pictures: the first was of white space. Empty space. This was clearly the picture that dictated the narrative intention of the book—a book in which anything that happened would happen off the page, a "white" book to which the reader would have to bring his or her own bad dreams—and yet this picture told me no "story," suggested no situation. The second picture did. This second picture was of something actually witnessed. A young woman with long hair and a short white halter dress walks through the casino at the Riviera in Las Vegas at one in the morning. She crosses the casino alone and picks up a house telephone. I watch her because I have heard her paged, and recognize her name: she is a minor actress I see around Los Angeles from time to time, in places like Jax and once in a gynecologist's office in the Beverly Hills Clinic, but have never met. I know nothing about her. Who is paging her? Why is she here to be paged? How exactly did she come to this? It was precisely this moment in Las Vegas that made *Play It as It Lays* begin to tell itself to me, but the moment appears in the novel only obliquely, in a chapter which begins:

13 "Maria made a list of things she would never do. She would never: walk through the Sands or Caesar's alone after midnight. She would

---

[4]Latin phrase meaning "note well."—Ed.

never: ball at a party, do S-M unless she wanted to, borrow furs from Abe Lipsey, deal. She would never: carry a Yorkshire in Beverly Hills."

14 That is the beginning of the chapter and that is also the end of the chapter, which may suggest what I meant by "white space."

15 I recall having a number of pictures in my mind when I began the novel I just finished, *A Book of Common Prayer.* As a matter of fact one of these pictures was of that bevatron I mentioned, although I would be hard put to tell you a story in which nuclear energy figures. Another was a newspaper photograph of a hijacked 707 burning on the desert in the Middle East. Another was the night view from a room in which I once spent a week with paratyphoid, a hotel room on the Colombian coast. My husband and I seemed to be on the Colombian coast representing the United States of America at a film festival (I recall invoking the name "Jack Valenti"[5] a lot, as if its reiteration could make me well), and it was a bad place to have fever, not only because my indisposition offended our hosts but because every night in this hotel the generator failed. The lights went out. The elevator stopped. My husband would go to the event of the evening and make excuses for me and I would stay alone in this hotel room, in the dark. I remember standing at the window trying to call Bogotá (the telephone seemed to work on the same principle as the generator) and watching the night wind come up and wondering what I was doing eleven degrees off the equator with a fever of 103. The view from that window definitely figures in *A Book of Common Prayer,* as does the burning 707, and yet none of these pictures told me the story I needed.

16 The picture that did, the picture that shimmered and made these other images coalesce, was the Panama airport at 6 A.M. I was in this airport only once, on a plane to Bogotá that stopped for an hour to refuel, but the way it looked that morning remained superimposed on everything I saw until the day I finished *A Book of Common Prayer.* I lived in that airport for several years. I can still feel the hot air when I step off the plane, can see the heat already rising off the tarmac at 6 A.M. I can feel my skirt damp and wrinkled on my legs. I can feel the asphalt stick to my sandals. I remember the big tail of a Pan American plane floating motionless down at the end of the tarmac. I remember the sound of a slot machine in the waiting room. I could tell you that I remember a particular woman in the airport, an American woman, a *norteamericana,* a thin *norteamericana* about forty who wore a big square emerald in lieu of a wedding ring, but there was no such woman there.

---

[5]President, since 1966, of the Motion Picture Association of America.—Ed.

17 I put this woman in the airport later. I made this woman up, just as I later made up a country to put the airport in, and a family to run the country. This woman in the airport is neither catching a plane nor meeting one. She is ordering tea in the airport coffee shop. In fact she is not simply "ordering" tea but insisting that the water be boiled, in front of her, for twenty minutes. Why is this woman in this airport? Why is she going nowhere, where has she been? Where did she get that big emerald? What derangement, or disassociation, makes her believe that her will to see the water boiled can possibly prevail?

18 "She had been going to one airport or another for four months, one could see it, looking at the visas on her passport. All those airports where Charlotte Douglas's passport had been stamped would have looked alike. Sometimes the sign on the tower would say "Bienvenidos" and sometimes the sign on the tower would say "Bienvenue," some places were wet and hot and others dry and hot, but at each of these airports the pastel concrete walls would rust and stain and the swamp off the runway would be littered with the fuselages of cannibalized Fairchild F-227's and the water would need boiling.

19 "I knew why Charlotte went to the airport even if Victor did not.

20 "I knew about airports."

21 These lines appear about halfway through *A Book of Common Prayer,* but I wrote them during the second week I worked on the book, long before I had any idea where Charlotte Douglas had been or why she went to airports. Until I wrote these lines I had no character called "Victor" in mind: the necessity for mentioning a name, and the name "Victor," occurred to me as I wrote the sentence. *I knew why Charlotte went to the airport* sounded incomplete. *I knew why Charlotte went to the airport even if Victor did not* carried a little more narrative drive. Most important of all, until I wrote these lines I did not know who "I" was, who was telling the story. I had intended until that that the "I" be no more than the voice of the author, a nineteenth-century omniscient narrator. But there it was:

22 "I knew why Charlotte went to the airport even if Victor did not.

23 "I knew about airports."

24 This "I" was the voice of no author in my house. This "I" was someone who not only knew why Charlotte went to the airport but also knew someone called "Victor." Who was Victor? Who was this narrator? Why was this narrator telling me this story? Let me tell you one thing about why writers write: had I known the answer to any of these questions I would never have needed to write a novel.

QUESTIONS FOR ANALYSIS AND DISCUSSION

1. What kind of act, according to Didion, is the act of writing?
2. Why is Didion not an intellectual? What gets her attention?
3. What is Didion's definition of a writer? Are you surprised by her definition? How would you have defined a writer?
4. Didion's reference to a bevatron is important in developing her point. What is a bevatron? How does this detail help make her point?
5. By discussing parts of her novels, Didion reveals her writing process. What does she start with? Why does she want to arrange words into sentences? What questions does she want to answer?
6. Although Didion apparently begins her novels with a cluster of images, we know from writers' notebooks or journals available to us that some novelists do begin with character or plot. How might what a writer starts with affect the kind of novel (or poem or essay) that is written? What differences in emphasis or focus might result from beginning a novel with character instead of plot? From beginning with plot instead of images?
7. When discussing getting her pictures into words, Didion draws an effective comparison. Differing arrangements of words in a sentence are compared to what? How does this comparison help us understand the importance of sentence structure?
8. Didion says that the picture in the writer's mind should determine the wording of the sentence designed to describe it, but is writing that uncomplicated a process? What else determines the words we choose and the ways we arrange them in sentences?

The Watcher at the Gates

GAIL GODWIN

Raised by a mother who wrote in her spare time and encouraged her daughter to write, Gail Godwin (b. 1937) took degrees at the universities of North Carolina and Iowa and worked as journalist and English instructor before devoting most of her time to writing. She is best known for her collection of short stories (Dream Children, *1976), her most recent novel* (The Finishing School, *1985), and the highly acclaimed 1982 best seller* A Woman and Two Daughters. *Interviewed by Jean Ross for a* Contemporary Authors *entry,*

Godwin observed that she works every morning when writing a book, may also make notes in the afternoon, and revises extensively as she writes.

Revising and polishing as she goes, rather than working through several complete drafts, may explain Godwin's acquaintance with writer's block, her subject in the following article, first published in the New York Times Book Review *on January 9, 1977. Godwin explained in her interview with Ross that while finding the discipline to revise can be an obstacle to young writers, developing some confidence in their work is also a major problem. In "The Watcher at the Gates" Godwin offers some solutions to the problem of writing anxiety, methods that may help many insecure writers become more productive.*

1 I first realized I was not the only writer who had a restraining critic who lived inside me and sapped the juice from green inspirations when I was leafing through Freud's "Interpretation of Dreams" a few years ago. Ironically, it was my "inner critic" who had sent me to Freud. I was writing a novel, and my heroine was in the middle of a dream, and then I lost faith in my own invention and rushed to "an authority" to check whether she could have such a dream. In the chapter on dream interpretation, I came upon the following passage that has helped me free myself, in some measure, from my critic and has led to many pleasant and interesting exchanges with other writers.

2 Freud quotes Schiller,[1] who is writing a letter to a friend. The friend complains of his lack of creative power. Schiller replies with an allegory. He says it is not good if the intellect examines too closely the ideas pouring in at the gates. "In isolation, an idea may be quite insignificant, and venturesome in the extreme, but it may acquire importance from an idea which follows it. . . . In the case of a creative mind, it seems to me, the intellect has withdrawn its watchers from the gates, and the ideas rush in pell-mell, and only then does it review and inspect the multitude. You are ashamed or afraid of the momentary and passing madness which is found in all real creators, the longer or shorter duration of which distinguishes the thinking artist from the dreamer . . . you reject too soon and discriminate too severely."

3 So that's what I had: a Watcher at the Gates. I decided to get to know him better. I discussed him with other writers, who told me some of the quirks and habits of their Watchers, each of whom was as individual as his host, and all of whom seemed passionately dedicated to one goal: rejecting too soon and discriminating too severely.

---

[1]A German poet and dramatist (1759–1805).—Ed.

4 It is amazing the lengths a Watcher will go to keep you from pursuing the flow of your imagination. Watchers are notorious pencil sharpeners, ribbon changers, plant waterers, home repairers and abhorrers of messy rooms or messy pages. They are compulsive looker-uppers. They are superstitious scaredy-cats. They cultivate self-important eccentricities they think are suitable for "writers." And they'd rather die (and kill your inspiration with them) than risk making a fool of themselves.

5 My Watcher has a wasteful penchant for 20-pound bond paper above and below the carbon of the first draft. "What's the good of writing out a whole page," he whispers begrudgingly, "if you just have to write it over again later? Get it perfect the first time!" My Watcher adores stopping in the middle of a morning's work to drive down to the library to check on the name of a flower or a World War II battle or a line of metaphysical poetry. "You can't possibly go on till you've got this right!" he admonishes. I go and get the car keys.

6 Other Watchers have informed their writers that:

7 "Whenever you get a really good sentence you should stop in the middle of it and go on tomorrow. Otherwise you might run dry."

8 "Don't try and continue with your book till your dental appointment is over. When you're worried about your teeth, you can't think about art."

9 Another Watcher makes his owner pin his finished pages to a clothesline and read them through binoculars "to see how they look from a distance." Countless other Watchers demand "bribes" for taking the day off: lethal doses of caffeine, alcoholic doses of Scotch or vodka or wine.

10 There are various ways to outsmart, pacify or coexist with your Watcher. Here are some I have tried, or my writer friends have tried, with success:

11 Look for situations when he's likely to be off-guard. Write too fast for him in an unexpected place, at an unexpected time. (Virginia Woolf[2] captured the "diamonds in the dustheap" by writing at a "rapid haphazard gallop" in her diary.) Write when very tired. Write in purple ink on the back of a Master Charge statement. Write whatever comes into your mind while the kettle is boiling and make the steam whistle your deadline. (Deadlines are a great way to outdistance the Watcher.)

12 Disguise what you are writing. If your Watcher refuses to let you get on with your story or novel, write a "letter" instead, telling your

---

[2]A British novelist and essayist (1882–1941).—Ed.

"correspondent" what you are going to write in your story or next chapter. Dash off a "review" of your own unfinished opus. It will stand up like a bully to your Watcher the next time he throws more obstacles in your path. If you write yourself a good one.

13 Get to know your Watcher. He's yours. Do a drawing of him (or her). Pin it to the wall of your study and turn it gently to the wall when necessary. Let your Watcher feel needed. Watchers are excellent critics after inspiration has been captured; they are dependable, sharp-eyed readers of things already set down. Keep your Watcher in shape and he'll have less time to keep you from shaping. If he's really ruining your whole working day sit down, as Jung[3] did with his personal demons, and write him a letter. On a very bad day I once wrote my Watcher a letter. "Dear Watcher," I wrote, "What is it you're so afraid I'll do?" Then I held his pen for him, and he replied instantly with a candor that has kept me from truly despising him.

14 "Fail," he wrote back.

QUESTIONS FOR ANALYSIS AND DISCUSSION

1. Godwin's piece is, like Reynolds's, a good example of the personal essay. List specific characteristics that mark this as a personal essay.
2. Where did Godwin find the idea of a Watcher at the Gates? What are the two problem traits found in most Watchers?
3. What are some of the gimmicks Watchers use to keep us from writing? Can you add to Godwin's list from your own experience?
4. What are some of the ways writers can outsmart their Watchers? Again, can you add to Godwin's list the techniques that have worked for you?
5. What, ultimately, do all Watchers, not just Godwin's, seem to fear? Why, in other words, do we have writer's block?
6. Does it help to know that most people share, to some degree or at some times, the experience of writing anxiety? Why or why not? Why do you think that so many people have writing anxiety?

---

[3]A Swiss psychiatrist (1875–1961).—Ed.

Life in a Bundle of Letters

ELLEN GOODMAN

Ellen Goodman (b. 1941) began her journalism career as a researcher at Newsweek; *she became a feature writer at the Boston* Globe *in 1967 and a syndicated columnist in 1976. Her twice-weekly columns appear in over 250 newspapers, and many have been collected in three books:* Close to Home *(1979),* At Large *(1981), and* Keeping Touch *(1985). In 1983 she published* Turning Points, *a study, developed from personal interviews, of the changes in people's lives generated by the women's movement. She has won many awards, including a Pulitzer Prize for distinguished commentary.*

Goodman analyzes social problems and changing life styles as frequently as political issues, as the following column, published in August 10, 1985, illustrates. If witty understatement and clever phrasing are elements of her style, so too is a tough-minded seriousness. Read her essay with care, concentrating both on her writing style and on her comments about the value of letter writing.

1 Somewhere, in the boxes that I have moved from one address to another, are small packages of summers past. Letters from my parents. Letters from school friends. Love letters. Private history wrapped neatly in rubber bands.

2 Most of them are, by now, more than 20 summers old. The datelines remind me of camp, college, trips. They also remind me of my father's humor, the rhythms of my mother's daily life, the code words of adolescent friendships—S.W.A.K., sealed with a kiss—the intimacy of the young.

3 My friends, my family and I rarely mail our thoughts anymore. The mailman brings more catalogues than correspondence to our homes. The letters that come through our mail slot are mostly addressed in robotype. The stamps we buy are to go on bills.

4 We direct-dial now. Spoiled by the instant gratification and the ease of the phone, we talk. The telephone call has replaced the letter in our lives nearly as completely as the car has replaced the cart.

5 When we were kids, I remember, long distance was reserved for announcements. The operator was almost an evil omen. If we had called from camp or campus our parents would have answered the phone with

"What's wrong?" Today, our own children, the products of Sesame Street numbers and telephone-company technology, have grown up knowing area codes before they knew addition. They bounce intercontinental calls off satellites . . . just to say "Hello."

6 I am not railing against this progress. A Frequent Dialer with the bills to prove it, I often choose the give and take, the immediacy of the phone. I accept charges from children with an uneconomical glee. A friend and I, separated by hundreds of miles, have declared our phone bills "cheaper than therapy." It's good to hear a voice. But it isn't the same.

7 Sometimes I think that the telephone call is as earthbound as daily dialogue, while a letter is an exchange of gifts. On the telephone you talk; in a letter you tell. There is a pace to letter writing and reading that doesn't come from the telephone company but from our own inner rhythm.

8 We live mostly in the high-tech, reach-out-and-touch-someone modern world. Communication is an industry. It makes demands of us. We are expected to respond as quickly as computers. A voice asks a question across the ocean in a split second and we are supposed to formulate an answer at this high-speed rate of exchange.

9 But we cannot, blessedly, "interface" by mail. There is leisure and emotional luxury in letter writing. There are no obvious silences to anxiously fill. There are no interruptions to brook. There are no nuances and tones of voice to distract.

10 A letter doesn't take us by surprise in the middle of dinner, or intrude when we are with other people, or ambush us in the midst of other thoughts. It waits. There is a private space between the give and the take for thinking.

11 I have known lovers, parents and children, husbands and wives, who send each other letters from one room to another simply for the chance to complete a story of events, thought, feelings. I have known people who could not "hear" what they could read.

12 There is this advantage to slowing down the pace of communications. The phone demands a kind of simultaneous satisfaction that is as elusive in words as in sex. It's letters that let us take turns, let us sit and mull and say exactly what we mean.

13 Today we are supposed to travel light, to live in the moment. The past is, we are told, excess baggage. There is no question that the phone is the tool of these times. As fine and as ephemeral as a good meal.

14 But you cannot hold a call in your hands. You cannot put it in a

bundle. You cannot show it to your family. Indeed there is nothing to show for it. It doesn't leave a trace. Tell me, how can you wrap a lifetime of phone calls in a rubber band for a summer's night when you want to remember?

QUESTIONS FOR ANALYSIS AND DISCUSSION

1. Goodman actually establishes two contrasts: between the past and present, and between letter writing and phoning as a means of communication. How are the two contrasts connected?
2. In what way does letter writing serve as an image of the past and phoning as an image of the present?
3. Why does Goodman include paragraph 6 in her essay? What point does she feel compelled to make?
4. What does that tell us about her sense of her audience? How might you have reacted if Goodman had not included paragraph 6?
5. What are the characteristics of telephone communication?
6. What are the characteristics of letter writing? What can we do in and with letters that we cannot do with a phone call?
7. Analyze Goodman's style in this column. Describe her sentence structure (Long or short? Simple or complex?), and note her use of repetition with variation and her use of contrasting terms.
8. How would you describe the tone of her essay? How is the tone appropriate for her subject and purpose? How does she create tone?
9. What can we learn about writing, in general, from Goodman?

Autobiographical Notes

JAMES BALDWIN

Born and raised in Harlem, James Baldwin (b. 1924) is the dean of contemporary black writers. A minister's son and a preacher himself at fourteen, Baldwin became an expatriate—first in France, then in Switzerland—to find the distance he needed from the pain of being black in white America so that he could write. He has produced several collections of essays, including Notes of *a Native Son (1955), from which the following piece is taken; numerous short stories and novels, including* Go Tell It on the Mountain *(1953) and* Another Country *(1962); plays; and other works such as his* Rap on Race *with Margaret Mead (1971). While some critics feel that his involvement in civil rights issues, his celebrity status, and the pressure always to speak on black issues have led him away from his best writing, the works mentioned above and another essay collection,* Nobody Knows My Name, *have assured him a place in American literature. In addition, he has done much to shape our understanding of race relations in America.*

In "Autobiographical Notes" Baldwin tells us of the influences on his life and shares his understanding of the difficulties facing black Americans who would be writers.

1 I was born in Harlem thirty-one years ago. I began plotting novels at about the time I learned to read. The story of my childhood is the usual bleak fantasy, and we can dismiss it with the restrained observation that I certainly would not consider living it again. In those days my mother was given to the exasperating and mysterious habit of having babies. As they were born, I took them over with one hand and held a book with the other. The children probably suffered, though they have since been kind enough to deny it, and in this way I read *Uncle Tom's Cabin* and *A Tale of Two Cities* over and over and over again; in this way, in fact, I read just about everything I could get my hands on—except the Bible, probably because it was the only book I was encouraged to read. I must also confess that I wrote—a great deal—and my first professional triumph, in any case, the first effort of mine to be seen in print, occurred at the age of twelve or thereabouts, when a short story I had written about the Spanish revolution won some sort of prize in an extremely short-lived church newspaper. I remember the story was censored by the lady editor, though I don't remember why, and I was outraged.

2 Also wrote plays, and songs, for one of which I received a letter of congratulations from Mayor La Guardia, and poetry, about which the less said, the better. My mother was delighted by all these goings-on, but my father wasn't; he wanted me to be a preacher. When I was fourteen I became a preacher, and when I was seventeen I stopped. Very shortly thereafter I left home. For God knows how long I struggled with the world of commerce and industry—I guess they would say they struggled with *me*—and when I was about twenty-one I had enough done of a novel to get a Saxton Fellowship. When I was twenty-two the fellowship was over, the novel turned out to be unsalable, and I started

waiting on tables in a Village restaurant and writing book reviews—mostly, as it turned out, about the Negro problem, concerning which the color of my skin made me automatically an expert. Did another book, in company with photographer Theodore Pelatowski, about the store-front churches in Harlem. This book met exactly the same fate as my first—fellowship, but no sale. (It was a Rosenwald Fellowship.) By the time I was twenty-four I had decided to stop reviewing books about the Negro problem—which, by this time, was only slightly less horrible in print than it was in life—and I packed my bags and went to France, where I finished, God knows how, *Go Tell It on the Mountain*.

3 Any writer, I suppose, feels that the world into which he was born is nothing less than a conspiracy against the cultivation of his talent—which attitude certainly has a great deal to support it. On the other hand, it is only because the world looks on his talent with such a frightening indifference that the artist is compelled to make his talent important. So that any writer, looking back over even so short a span of time as I am here forced to assess, finds that the things which hurt him and the things which helped him cannot be divorced from each other; he could be helped in a certain way only because he was hurt in a certain way; and his help is simply to be enabled to move from one conundrum to the next—one is tempted to say that he moves from one disaster to the next. When one begins looking for influences one finds them by the score. I haven't thought much about my own, not enough anyway; I hazard that the King James Bible, the rhetoric of the store-front church, something ironic and violent and perpetually understated in Negro speech—and something of Dickens' love for bravura—have something to do with me today; but I wouldn't stake my life on it. Likewise, innumerable people have helped me in many ways; but finally, I suppose, the most difficult (and most rewarding) thing in my life has been the fact that I was born a Negro and was forced, therefore, to effect some kind of truce with this reality. (Truce, by the way, is the best one can hope for.)

4 One of the difficulties about being a Negro writer (and this is not special pleading, since I don't mean to suggest that he has it worse than anybody else) is that the Negro problem is written about so widely. The bookshelves groan under the weight of information, and everyone therefore considers himself informed. And this information, furthermore, operates usually (generally, popularly) to reinforce traditional attitudes. Of traditional attitudes there are only two—For or Against—and I, personally, find it difficult to say which attitude has caused me the most pain. I am speaking as a writer; from a social point of view I am perfectly

aware that the change from ill-will to good-will, however motivated, however imperfect, however expressed, is better than no change at all.

5 But it is part of the business of the writer—as I see it—to examine attitudes, to go beneath the surface, to tap the source. From this point of view the Negro problem is nearly inaccessible. It is not only written about so widely; it is written about so badly. It is quite possible to say that the price a Negro pays for becoming articulate is to find himself, at length, with nothing to be articulate about. ("You taught me language," says Caliban to Prospero, "and my profit on't is I know how to curse."[1]) Consider: the tremendous social activity that this problem generates imposes on whites and Negroes alike the necessity of looking forward, of working to bring about a better day. This is fine, it keeps the waters troubled; it is all, indeed, that has made possible the Negro's progress. Nevertheless, social affairs are not generally speaking the writer's prime concern, whether they ought to be or not; it is absolutely necessary that he establish between himself and these affairs a distance which will allow, at least, for clarity, so that before he can look forward in any meaningful sense, he must first be allowed to take a long look back. In the context of the Negro problem neither whites nor blacks, for excellent reasons of their own, have the faintest desire to look back; but I think that the past is all that makes the present coherent, and further, that the past will remain horrible for exactly as long as we refuse to assess it honestly.

6 I know, in any case, that the most crucial time in my own development came when I was forced to recognize that I was a kind of bastard of the West; when I followed the line of my past I did not find myself in Europe but in Africa. And this meant that in some subtle way, in a really profound way, I brought to Shakespeare, Bach, Rembrandt, to the stones of Paris, to the cathedral at Chartres, and to the Empire State Building, a special attitude. These were not really my creations, they did not contain my history; I might search in them in vain forever for any reflection of myself. I was an interloper; this was not my heritage. At the same time I had no other heritage which I could possibly hope to use—I had certainly been unfitted for the jungle or the tribe. I would have to appropriate these white centuries, I would have to make them mine—I would have to accept my special attitude, my special place in this scheme—otherwise I would have no place in *any* scheme. What was the most difficult was the fact that I was forced to admit something I

---

[1]The quotation is from Shakespeare's *The Tempest*. —Ed.

had always hidden from myself, which the American Negro has had to hide from himself as the price of his public progress; that I hated and feared white people. This did not mean that I loved black people; on the contrary, I despised them, possibly because they failed to produce Rembrandt. In effect, I hated and feared the world. And this meant, not only that I thus gave the world an altogether murderous power over me, but also that in such a self-destroying limbo I could never hope to write.

7 One writes out of one thing only—one's own experience. Everything depends on how relentlessly one forces from this experience the last drop, sweet or bitter, it can possibly give. This is the only real concern of the artist, to recreate out of the disorder of life that order which is art. The difficulty then, for me, of being a Negro writer was the fact that I was, in effect, prohibited from examining my own experience too closely by the tremendous demands and the very real dangers of my social situation.

8 I don't think the dilemma outlined above is uncommon. I do think, since writers work in the disastrously explicit medium of language, that it goes a little way towards explaining why, out of the enormous resources of Negro speech and life, and despite the example of Negro music, prose written by Negroes has been generally speaking so pallid and so harsh. I have not written about being a Negro at such length because I expect that to be my only subject, but only because it was the gate I had to unlock before I could hope to write about anything else. I don't think that the Negro problem in America can be even discussed coherently without bearing in mind its context; its context being the history, traditions, customs, the moral assumptions and preoccupations of the country; in short, the general social fabric. Appearances to the contrary, no one in America escapes its effects and everyone in America bears some responsibility for it. I believe this the more firmly because it is the overwhelming tendency to speak of this problem as though it were a thing apart. But in the work of Faulkner, in the general attitude and certain specific passages in Robert Penn Warren, and, most significantly, in the advent of Ralph Ellison, one sees the beginnings—at least—of a more genuinely penetrating search. Mr. Ellison, by the way, is the first Negro novelist I have ever read to utilize in language, and brilliantly, some of the ambiguity and irony of Negro life.

9 About my interests: I don't know if I have any, unless the morbid desire to own a sixteen-millimeter camera and make experimental movies can be so classified. Otherwise, I love to eat and drink—it's my melancholy conviction that I've scarcely ever had enough to eat (this is because

it's *impossible* to eat enough if you're worried about the next meal)—and I love to argue with people who do not disagree with me too profoundly, and I love to laugh. I do *not* like bohemia, or bohemians, I do not like people whose principal aim is pleasure, and I do not like people who are *earnest* about anything. I don't like people who like me because I'm a Negro; neither do I like people who find in the same accident grounds for contempt. I love America more than any other country in the world, and, exactly for this reason, I insist on the right to criticize her perpetually. I think all theories are suspect, that the finest principles may have to be modified, or may even be pulverized by the demands of life, and that one must find, therefore, one's own moral center and move through the world hoping that this center will guide one aright. I consider that I have many responsibilities, but none greater than this: to last, as Hemingway says, and get my work done.

10 I want to be an honest man and a good writer.

QUESTIONS FOR ANALYSIS AND DISCUSSION

1. What does Baldwin's title lead you to expect about his essay? How does the title accurately announce both the subject and the structure of the essay?
2. One can list Baldwin's subjects as the details of his early life, the influences that shaped him as a writer, his interests, and his goals. What paragraphs are devoted to each subject? Briefly summarize Baldwin's chief points about each subject.
3. What has been the dominant influence on Baldwin the writer? How has this influence created problems for him as a writer?
4. In his discussion of being a black writer, Baldwin makes two key assertions about artistic creation or the making of literature. What are these assertions? How does the second assertion qualify, importantly, the first?
5. Baldwin describes black speech as ironic, violent, and understated. What evidence can you find of these traits in Baldwin's writing?
6. After reading his final two paragraphs, what sense do you have of Baldwin? What is his view of life? Of himself? Of his work?

On the Exact Location of the Soul

RICHARD SELZER

Educated in the Albany, N.Y., area, in general practice in surgery since 1960, and associate professor of surgery at Yale Medical School, Richard Selzer (b. 1928) has also received recognition for his writing. He has published a collection of short stories – Rituals of Surgery *(1974); a blend of fiction and nonfiction –* Letters to a Young Doctor *(1982); and two collections of essays –* Mortal Lessons *(1976), from which the following essay is taken, and* Taking the World in for Repairs *(1986). While continuing to write stories and essays, Selzer is also at work on a mythological treatment of the Civil War.*

As you read Selzer's explanation of why a surgeon should be a writer, you will understand why his essays have been called prose poems. His vivid details, forcing us to accept our human frailties, also continually celebrate the strength of the human spirit. In his praise of the poet, Selzer acknowledges the role of language in the search for life's meanings.

1 Someone asked me why a surgeon would write. Why, when the shelves are already too full? They sag under the deadweight of books. To add a single adverb is to risk exceeding the strength of the boards. A surgeon should abstain. A surgeon, whose fingers are more at home in the steamy gullies of the body than they are tapping the dry keys of a typewriter. A surgeon, who feels the slow slide of intestines against the back of his hand and is no more alarmed than were a family of snakes taking their comfort from such an indolent rubbing. A surgeon, who palms the human heart as though it were some captured bird.

2 Why should he write? Is it vanity that urges him? There is glory enough in the knife. Is it for money? One can make too much money. No. It is to search for some meaning in the ritual of surgery, which is at once murderous, painful, healing, and full of love. It is a devilish hard thing to transmit – to find, even. Perhaps if one were to cut out a heart, a lobe of the liver, a single convolution of the brain, and paste it to a page, it would speak with more eloquence than all the words of Balzac.[1] Such a piece would need no literary style, no mass of erudition or history, but in its very shape and feel would tell all the frailty and strength,

[1]A French novelist (1799–1850). – Ed.

the despair and nobility of man. What? Publish a heart? A little piece of bone? Preposterous. Still I fear that is what it may require to reveal the truth that lies hidden in the body. Not all the undressings of Rabelais,[2] Chekhov,[3] or even William Carlos Williams[4] have wrested it free, although God knows each one of those doctors made a heroic assault upon it.

3 I have come to believe that it is the flesh alone that counts. The rest is that with which we distract ourselves when we are not hungry or cold, in pain or ecstasy. In the recesses of the body I search for the philosophers' stone. I know it is there, hidden in the deepest, dampest cul-de-sac. It awaits discovery. To find it would be like the harnessing of fire. It would illuminate the world. Such a quest is not without pain. Who can gaze on so much misery and feel no hurt? Emerson[5] has written that the poet is the only true doctor. I believe him, for the poet, lacking the impediment of speech with which the rest of us are afflicted, gazes, records, diagnoses, and prophesies.

4 I invited a young diabetic woman to the operating room to amputate her leg. She could not see the great shaggy black ulcer upon her foot and ankle that threatened to encroach upon the rest of her body, for she was blind as well. There upon her foot was a Mississippi Delta brimming with corruption, sending its raw tributaries down between her toes. Gone were all the little web spaces that when fresh and whole are such a delight to loving men. She could not see her wound, but she could feel it. There is no pain like that of the bloodless limb turned rotten and festering. There is neither unguent[6] nor anodyne[7] to kill such a pain yet leave intact the body.

5 For over a year I trimmed away the putrid flesh, cleansed, anointed, and dressed the foot, staving off, delaying. Three times each week, in her darkness, she sat upon my table, rocking back and forth, holding her extended leg by the thigh, gripping it as though it were a rocket that must be steadied lest it explode and scatter her toes about the room. And I would cut away a bit here, a bit there, of the swollen blue leather that was her tissue.

---

[2] A satirical French writer and physician (1494?–1553).—Ed.

[3] A Russian dramatist and short-story writer who was also a physician (1860–1904).—Ed.

[4] An American poet and physician (1883–1963).—Ed.

[5] A nineteenth-century American poet and essayist; chief spokesman for American transcendentalism.—Ed.

[6] Ointment.—Ed.

[7] Pain reliever.—Ed.

6 At last we gave up, she and I. We could no longer run ahead of the gangrene. We had not the legs for it. There must be an amputation in order that she might live—and I as well. It was to heal us both that I must take up knife and saw, and cut the leg off. And when I could feel it drop from her body to the table, see the blessed *space* appear between her and that leg, I too would be well.

7 Now it is the day of the operation. I stand by while the anesthetist administers the drugs, watch as the tense familiar body relaxes into narcosis.[8] I turn then to uncover the leg. There, upon her kneecap, she has drawn, blindly, upside down for me to see, a face; just a circle with two ears, two eyes, a nose, and a smiling upturned mouth. Under it she has printed SMILE, DOCTOR. Minutes later I listen to the sound of the saw, until a little crack at the end tells me it is done.

8 So, I have learned that man is not ugly, but that he is Beauty itself. There is no other his equal. Are we not all dying, none faster or more slowly than any other? I have become receptive to the possibilities of love (for it is love, this thing that happens in the operating room), and each day I wait, trembling in the busy air. Perhaps today it will come. Perhaps today I will find it, take part in it, this love that blooms in the stoniest desert.

9 All through literature the doctor is portrayed as a figure of fun. Shaw[9] was splenetic about him; Molière[10] delighted in pricking his pompous medicine men, and well they deserved it. The doctor is ripe for caricature. But I believe that the truly great writing about doctors has not yet been done. I think it must be done *by* a doctor, one who is through with the love affair with his technique, who recognizes that he has played Narcissus, raining kisses on a mirror, and who now, out of the impacted masses of his guilt, has expanded into self-doubt, and finally into the high state of wonderment. Perhaps he will be a nonbeliever who, after a lifetime of grand gestures and mighty deeds, comes upon the knowledge that he has done no more than meddle in the lives of his fellows, and that he has done at least as much harm as good. Yet he may continue to pretend, at least, that there is nothing to fear, that death will not come, so long as people depend on his authority. Later,

---

[8]Drug-produced unconsciousness.—Ed.

[9]An Irish-born English dramatist (1856–1950) who satirizes the medical profession in *The Doctor's Dilemma*.—Ed.

[10]The pen name of Jean-Baptiste Poquelin (1622–1673), a French dramatist who satirizes doctors in *The Physician in Spite of Himself*.—Ed.

after his patients have left, he may closet himself in his darkened office, sweating and afraid.

10 There is a story by Unamuno[11] in which a priest, living in a small Spanish village, is adored by all the people for his piety, kindness, and the majesty with which he celebrates the Mass each Sunday. To them he is already a saint. It is a foregone conclusion, and they speak of him as Saint Immanuel. He helps them with their plowing and planting, tends them when they are sick, confesses them, comforts them in death, and every Sunday, in his rich, thrilling voice, transports them to paradise with his chanting. The fact is that Don Immanuel is not so much a saint as a martyr. Long ago his own faith left him. He is an atheist, a good man doomed to suffer the life of a hypocrite, pretending to a faith he does not have. As he raises the chalice of wine, his hands tremble, and a cold sweat pours from him. He cannot stop for he knows that the people need this of him, that their need is greater than his sacrifice. Still . . . still . . . could it be that Don Immanuel's whole life is a kind of prayer, a paean to God?

11 A writing doctor would treat men and women with equal reverence, for what is the "liberation" of either sex to him who knows the diagrams, the inner geographies of each? I love the solid heft of men as much as I adore the heated capaciousness of women—women in whose penetralia is found the repository of existence. I would have them glory in that. Women are physics and chemistry. They are matter. It is their bodies that tell of the frailty of men. Men have not their cellular, enzymatic wisdom. Man is albuminoid, proteinaceous, laked pearl; woman is yolky, ovoid, rich. Both are exuberant bloody growths. I would use the defects and deformities of each for my sacred purpose of writing, for I know that it is the marred and scarred and faulty that are subject to grace. I would seek the soul in the facts of animal economy and profligacy. Yes, it is the exact location of the soul that I am after. The smell of it is in my nostrils. I have caught glimpses of it in the body diseased. If only I could tell it. Is there no mathematical equation that can guide me? So much pain and pus equals so much truth? It is elusive as the whippoorwill that one hears calling incessantly from out the night window, but which, nesting as it does low in the brush, no one sees. No one but the poet, for he sees what no one else can. He was born with the eye for it.

12 Once I thought I had it: Ten o'clock one night, the end room off a

[11]Spanish philosopher, poet, and essayist (1864–1936).—Ed.

long corridor in a college infirmary, my last patient of the day, degree of exhaustion suitable for the appearance of a vision, some manifestation. The patient is a young man recently returned from Guatemala, from the excavation of Mayan ruins. His left upper arm wears a gauze dressing which, when removed, reveals a clean punched-out hole the size of a dime. The tissues about the opening are swollen and tense. A thin brownish fluid lips the edge, and now and then a lazy drop of the overflow spills down the arm. An abscess, inadequately drained. I will enlarge the opening to allow better egress of the pus. Nurse, will you get me a scalpel and some . . . ?

13 What happens next is enough to lay Francis Drake[12] avomit in his cabin. No explorer ever stared in wilder surmise than I into that crater from which there now emerges a narrow gray head whose sole distinguishing feature is a pair of black pincers. The head sits atop a longish flexible neck arching now this way, now that, testing the air. Alternately it folds back upon itself, then advances in new boldness. And all the while, with dreadful rhythmicity, the unspeakable pincers open and close. Abscess? Pus? Never. Here is the lair of a beast at whose malignant purpose I could but guess. A Mayan devil, I think, that would soon burst free to fly about the room, with horrid blanket-wings and iridescent scales, raking, pinching, injecting God knows what acid juice. And even now the irony does not escape me, the irony of my patient as excavator excavated.

14 With all the ritual deliberation of a high priest I advance a surgical clamp toward the hole. The surgeon's heart is become a bat hanging upside down from his rib cage. The rim achieved—now thrust—and the ratchets of the clamp close upon the empty air. The devil has retracted. Evil mocking laughter bangs back and forth in the brain. More stealth. Lying in wait. One must skulk. Minutes pass, perhaps an hour. . . . A faint disturbance in the lake, and once again the thing upraises, farther and farther, hovering. Acrouch, strung, the surgeon is one with his instrument; there is no longer any boundary between its metal and his flesh. They are joined in a single perfect tool of extirpation. It is just for this that he was born. Now—thrust—and clamp—and *yes.* Got him!

15 Transmitted to the fingers comes the wild thrashing of the creature. Pinned and wriggling, he is mine. I hear the dry brittle scream of the dragon, and a hatred seizes me, but such a detestation as would make of Iago[13] a drooling sucktit. It is the demented hatred of the victor

[12]English navigator (1540?–1596) who sailed around the world. —Ed.

[13]A cruelly evil character in Shakespeare's *Othello.* —Ed.

for the vanquished, the warden for his prisoner. It is the hatred of fear. Within the jaws of my hemostat is the whole of the evil of the world, the dark concentrate itself, and I shall kill it. For mankind. And, in so doing, will open the way into a thousand years of perfect peace. Here is Surgeon as Savior indeed.

16 Tight grip now . . . steady, relentless pull. How it scrabbles to keep its tentacle-hold. With an abrupt moist plop the extraction is complete. There, writhing in the teeth of the clamp, is a dirty gray body, the size and shape of an English walnut. He is hung everywhere with tiny black hooklets. Quickly . . . into the specimen jar of saline . . . the lid screwed tight. Crazily he swims round and round, wiping his slimy head against the glass, then slowly sinks to the bottom, the mass of hooks in frantic agonal wave.

17 "You are going to be all right," I say to my patient. "We are *all* going to be all right from now on."

18 The next day I take the jar to the medical school. "That's the larva of the botfly," says a pathologist. "The fly usually bites a cow and deposits its eggs beneath the skin. There, the egg develops into the larval form which, when ready, burrows its way to the outside through the hide and falls to the ground. In time it matures into a full-grown botfly. This one happened to bite a man. It was about to come out on its own, and, of course, it would have died."

19 The words *imposter, sorehead, servant of Satan* spring to my lips. But now he has been joined by other scientists. They nod in agreement. I gaze from one gray eminence to another, and know the mallet-blow of glory pulverized. I tried to save the world, but it didn't work out.

20 No, it is not the surgeon who is God's darling. He is the victim of vanity. It is the poet who heals with his words, stanches the flow of blood, stills the rattling breath, applies poultice to the scalded flesh.

21 Did you ask me why a surgeon writes? I think it is because I wish to be a doctor.

QUESTIONS FOR ANALYSIS AND DISCUSSION

1. What is Selzer's reason for writing? (See paragraph 2.) What, exactly, is he looking for? (See paragraph 11.)
2. What reasons for writing does he reject?
3. Who, for Selzer, best understands the meaning of life? What, then, in Selzer's view is necessary for understanding life?

4. Selzer describes the amputation of a woman's leg. Why does he feel that the amputation will make him well, too?
5. Selzer is right in saying that writers have satirized doctors in literature. Why do you suppose doctors have so often been ridiculed? What is the point of Selzer's allusion to Narcissus?
6. What seems to be our attitude toward doctors today? Can you account for this attitude?
7. Selzer contrasts male and female, using a number of scientific terms. Learn the meanings of any terms you do not know and then, in your own words, explain Selzer's contrast.
8. Selzer sees irony in the young man who has been excavating Mayan ruins having a "Mayan devil" or botfly in his arm. Explain the irony of the "excavator excavated."
9. Why does Selzer experience the "mallet-blow of glory pulverized"?
10. Explain Selzer's concluding statement.

With All Deliberate Speed: What's So Bad About Writing Fast?

WILLIAM F. BUCKLEY, JR.

A Yale graduate who worked for the CIA in Mexico before launching a successful writing career, William F. Buckley, Jr. (b. 1925) is viewed by many as the most articulate spokesman for political conservatives. The fury spawned by God and Man at Yale *(1951), an attack on Yale's repression (in Buckley's view) of conservative political thought, brought him national recognition. Since founding the* National Review *in 1955, Buckley has served as its editor-in-chief; his political column* On the Right *has been widely syndicated in newspapers since 1962; and he has hosted a talk show* (Firing Line) *on PBS since 1966. Buckley has given further expression to his political views in several books, including* Up From Liberalism *and* Right Reason, *and has shown his writing versatility in several spy novels about Blackford Oakes, his main character, who is a CIA operative in Europe. Buckley's sophisticated style, consciously clever and learned, is admired by both friends and adversaries.*

Faithful viewers of Firing Line *can recall Buckley's many outrageous assertions tossed to political opponents. The following article, published in the*

New York Times Book Review *on February 9, 1986, may appear to challenge the writing instructor's warnings to review and polish; but careful reading will reveal useful advice to writers and an impressive knowledge of the writing process.*

1 If, during spring term at Yale University in 1949 you wandered diagonally across the campus noticing here and there an undergraduate with impacted sleeplessness under his eyes and coarse yellow touches of fear on his cheeks, you were looking at members of a masochistic set who had enrolled in a course called Daily Themes. No Carthusian novitiate[1] embarked on a bout of mortification of the flesh suffered more than the students of Daily Themes, whose single assignment, in addition to attending two lectures per week, was to write a 500-to-600-word piece of descriptive prose every day, and to submit it before midnight (into a large box outside a classroom). Sundays were the only exception (this was before the Warren Court[2] outlawed Sunday).

2 For anyone graduated from Daily Themes who went on to write, in journalism or in fiction or wherever, the notion that a burden of 500 words per day is the stuff of nightmares is laughable. But caution: 500 words a day is what Graham Greene[3] writes, and Nabokov[4] wrote 180 words per day, devoting to their composition (he told me) four or five hours. But at that rate, Graham Greene and Nabokov couldn't qualify for a job as reporters on The New York Times. Theirs is high-quality stuff, to speak lightly of great writing. But Georges Simenon[5] is also considered a great writer, at least by those who elected him to the French Academy, and he writes books in a week or so. Dr. Johnson[6] wrote "Rasselas," his philosophical romance, in nine days. And Trollope[7] . . . we'll save Trollope.

3 I am fired up on the subject because, to use a familiar formulation, they have been kicking me around a lot; it has got out that I write fast,

[1]Novice of an austere monastic order founded in France in the eleventh century.—Ed.

[2]The Supreme Court, under Chief Justice Earl Warren (1953–1969), rejected "blue laws" prohibiting commercial activity on Sunday.—Ed.

[3]A contemporary British novelist.—Ed.

[4]A Russian-born American fiction writer and poet (1899–1977).—Ed.

[5]A prolific writer (b. 1903), under several pseudonyms, of mysteries, psychological novels, and nonfiction; Belgian-born, now residing in Switzerland.—Ed.

[6]An English lexicographer, critic, poet (1709–1784).—Ed.

[7]An English novelist (1815–1882).Ed.

which is qualifiedly true. In this august journal, on Jan. 5, Morton Kondracke of Newsweek took it all the way: "He [me—W.F.B.] reportedly knocks out his column in 20 minutes flat—three times a week for 260 newspapers. That is too little time for serious contemplation of difficult subjects."

4 Now that is a declaration of war, and I respond massively.

5 To begin with: it is axiomatic, in cognitive science, that there is no necessary correlation between profundity of thought and length of time spent on thought. J.F.K. is reported to have spent 15 hours per day for six days before deciding exactly how to respond to the missile crisis, but it can still be argued that his initial impulse on being informed that the Soviet Union had deployed nuclear missiles in Cuba (bomb the hell out of them?) might have been the strategically sounder course. This is not an argument against deliberation, merely against the suggestion that to think longer (endlessly?) about a subject is necessarily to probe it more fruitfully.

6 Mr. Kondracke, for reasons that would require more than 20 minutes to fathom, refers to composing columns in 20 minutes "flat." Does he mean to suggest that I have a stopwatch which rings on the 20th minute? Or did he perhaps mean to say that I have been known to write a column in 20 minutes? Very different. He then goes on, in quite another connection, to cite "one of the best columns" in my new book—without thinking to ask: How long did it take him to write that particular column?

7 The chronological criterion, you see, is without validity. Every few years, I bring out a collection of previously published work, and this of course requires me to reread everything I have done in order to make that season's selections. It transpires that it is impossible to distinguish a column written very quickly from a column written very slowly. Perhaps that is because none is written very slowly. A column that requires two hours to write is one which was interrupted by phone calls or the need to check a fact. I write fast—but not, I'd maintain, remarkably fast. If Mr. Kondracke thinks it intellectually risky to write 750 words in 20 minutes, what must he think about people who speak 750 words in five minutes, as he often does on television?

8 The subject comes up now so regularly in reviews of my work that I did a little methodical research on my upcoming novel. I began my writing (in Switzerland, removed from routine interruption) at about 5 P.M., and wrote usually for two hours. I did that for 45 working days (the stretch was interrupted by a week in the United States, catching

up on editorial and television obligations). I then devoted the first 10 days in July to revising the manuscript. On these days I worked on the manuscript an average of six hours per day, including retyping. We have now a grand total: 90 plus 60, or 150 hours. My novels are about 70,000 words, so that averaged out to roughly 500 words per hour.

9 Anthony Trollope rose at 5 every morning, drank his tea, performed his toilette and looked at the work done the preceding day. He would then begin to write at 6. He set himself the task of writing 250 words every 15 minutes for three and one-half hours. Indeed it is somewhere recorded that if he had not, at the end of 15 minutes, written the required 250 words he would simply "speed up" the next quarter-hour, because he was most emphatic in his insistence on his personally imposed daily quota: 3,500 words.

10 Now the advantages Trollope enjoys over me are enumerable and nonenumerable. I write only about the former, and oddly enough they are negative advantages. He needed to write by hand, having no alternative. I use a word processor. Before beginning this article, I tested my speed on this instrument and discovered that I type more slowly than I had imagined. Still, it comes out at 80 words per minute. So that if Trollope had had a Kaypro or an I.B.M., he'd have written, in three and one-half hours at my typing speed, not 3,500 words but 16,800 words per day.

11 Ah, you say, but could anyone think that fast? The answer is, sure people can think that fast. How did you suppose extemporaneous speeches get made? Erle Stanley Gardner[8] dictated his detective novels nonstop to a series of secretaries, having previously pasted about in his studio 3-by-5 cards reminding him at exactly what hour the dog barked, the telephone rang, the murderer coughed. He knew where he was going, the plot was framed in his mind, and it became now only an act of extrusion. Margaret Coit wrote in her biography of John C. Calhoun[9] that his memorable speeches were composed not in his study but while he was outdoors, plowing the fields on his plantation. He would return then to his study and write out what he had framed in his mind. His writing was an act of transcription. I own the holograph of Albert Jay Nock's marvelous book on Jefferson, and there are fewer corrections on an average page than I write into a typical column. Clearly Nock knew

[8] An American detective-story writer (1889–1970).—Ed.

[9] U.S. senator from South Carolina; vice president from 1825 to 1832.—Ed.

exactly what he wished to say and how to say it; prodigious rewriting was, accordingly, unnecessary.

12 Having said this, I acknowledge that I do not know exactly what I am going to say, or exactly how I am going to say it. And in my novels, I can say flatly, as Mr. Kondracke would have me say it, that I really do not have any idea where they are going—which ought not to surprise anyone familiar with the nonstop exigencies of soap opera writing or of comic strip writing or, for that matter, of regular Sunday sermons. It is not necessary to know how your protagonist will get out of a jam into which you put him. It requires only that you have confidence that you will be able to get him out of that jam. When you begin to write a column on, let us say, the reaction of Western Europe to President Reagan's call for a boycott of Libya it is not necessary that you should know *exactly* how you will say what you will end up saying. You are, while writing, drawing on huge reserves: of opinion, prejudice, priorities, presumptions, data, ironies, drama, histrionics. And these reserves you enhance during practically the entire course of the day, and it doesn't matter all that much if a particular hour is not devoted to considering problems of foreign policy. You can spend an hour playing the piano and develop your capacity to think, even to create; and certainly you can grasp more keenly, while doing so, your feel for priorities.

13 The matter of music flushes out an interesting point: Why is it that critics who find it arresting that a column can be written in 20 minutes, a book in 150 hours, do not appear to find it remarkable that a typical graduate of Juilliard[10] can memorize a prelude and fugue from "The Well-Tempered Clavier" in an hour or two? It would take me six months to memorize one of those *numeros.* And mind, we're not talking here about the "Guinness Book of World Records" types. Isaac Asimov belongs in "Guinness," and perhaps Erle Stanley Gardner, but surely not an author who averages a mere 500 words per hour, or who occasionally writes a column at one-third his typing speed.

14 There are phenomenal memories in the world. Claudio Arrau is said to hold in his memory music for 40 recitals, two and a half hours each. *That* is phenomenal. Ralph Kirkpatrick, the late harpsichordist, actually told me that he had not played the "Goldberg" Variations for 20 years before playing it to a full house in New Haven in the spring of 1950. *That* is phenomenal. Winston Churchill is said to have memorized all of "Paradise Lost" in a week, and throughout his life he is

---

[10] A highly respected music school.—Ed.

reported to have been able to memorize his speeches after a couple of readings. (I have a speech I have delivered 50 times, and could not recite one paragraph of it by heart.)

15 So cut it out, Kondracke. I am, I fully grant, a phenomenon, but not because of any speed in composition. I asked myself the other day, Who else, on so many issues, has been so right so much of the time? I couldn't think of anyone. And I devoted to the exercise 20 minutes. Flat.

QUESTIONS FOR ANALYSIS AND DISCUSSION

1. What was the occasion for Buckley's writing this article?
2. After reading the first two paragraphs, what can you conclude about Buckley's audience?
3. What, according to Buckley, is the relationship between the time spent and the quality of the writing?
4. When Kondracke asserts that twenty minutes "is too little time for serious contemplation of difficult subjects," what has he failed to consider? What makes it possible for Buckley—and the other speedy writers he mentions—to "write" quickly?
5. When he introduces memorizing music and speeches near the end, Buckley is suggesting, indirectly, another reason (or perhaps two) for his "deliberate speed" in writing. What are these reasons?
6. From reading this article, what image of Buckley emerges? What sense do you get of the man? His knowledge? Interests? Values? Personality? Connect your image to details in the essay.
7. If you were to ask Buckley for ways to avoid writing anxiety, what do you think his response would be?

STUDENT ESSAY

"THE BUSINESS OF WRITING"

J. PENN JONES

"We'd be dangerous if we ever got organized!" I wonder how often I've thought this about my office. Part of the reason for the jumbled method of doing business where I work is that the written word is not precise. I'm convinced that if correspondence, instructions, and documents were first thought through and then put to paper

Introduction

Thesis: Good writing is clear, complete, and concise.

in a logical sequence, much of the confusion would be avoided.

Anticipate the reader's needs when giving instructions

A memo I recently received seemed clear; the memo stated that one of our subsidiaries had had a change of address and then listed the new address. The writer of the memo requested that we insert the new address in our office telephone directory. So far, so good—until I opened the directory. Because our many subsidiaries are arranged within several different "sectors" of business, there is no simple alphabetic listing. Where was I supposed to find the subsidiary that needed its address updated? Had the writer of the memo thought about the process of putting the new address into the directory, she would have provided in her memo the page number we needed. In this case, the omission of one little piece of information from a memo necessitated the preparation of a second, more precise memo. This was an expensive omission; our company has 14,000 employees, and they each had to receive two memos instead of one.

Write down all necessary details of a message

On a smaller scale, confusion may also be avoided even when writing something as simple as a telephone message. By taking the time to write all the details of a message—who, what, where, when, and why—you will avoid the embarrassment of later being asked for clarifying information that you may by then have forgotten. So get the facts, get them straight, and get them down on paper while they are fresh in your mind. Learn to rely on what you've written, not your memory.

Don't assume; give full instructions

In a similar vein, when writing instructions for others, don't assume that the recipient knows what you "really" want. For example, when writing a request for a copying job in the print shop, you should think about how your instructions will be received and acted upon. If you have written, "Two copies, as soon as possible," but what you specifically want is, "Two copies, duplexed, collated, two left-hand side staples, needed by 10:30 A.M.," you will be disappointed to get back papers that are clipped together (not stapled), twice as thick as needed (because they weren't duplexed), and after lunch (because that is when the print shop got around to it). You will soon realize that you need to write enough instructions to get back the desired results.

On the other hand, you do not want to mire down the readers of your documents in excess verbiage. I have found that if you provide enough background information to bring your readers "on-line" and then set forth your subject concisely and logically, you will bring your readers to the same marvelous conclusion you have reached. People in business do not have time to waste plowing through pounds of paperwork to unearth the point of your writing. Have you ever received "junk mail" that you have thrown disgustedly into the trash because after reading the first two pages you still do not know the point of it? If what you have to say is worthwhile, don't lose your reader's attention by taking the long way around to the heart of your document.

Say it concisely

So, if you find yourself working in an office, keep in mind that confusion can begin or end with the tip of your pen. No matter how inconsequential you perceive your written tasks to be, keep in mind the recipient of your writing. What you have written may lead your reader into a maze of confusion or straight to the point of understanding.

Conclusion: Restates thesis, encouraging reader to aim for clarity in writing

EXERCISES

1. Keep a journal for three weeks, making at least five entries a week, on any subjects you choose, of any length from 100 words up. At the end of three weeks, reread your journal and then analyze it to gain insight into yourself and your writing. To analyze, answer the following questions:
   a. What topics do you most frequently write about? Does this focus reflect your interest, or do you believe you were selecting topics with a teacher/reader in mind?
   b. Are your entries usually about 100 words, or much longer? From a consideration of length only, would you conclude that writing is relatively easy or relatively difficult for you?
   c. Did keeping a journal provide you with some of the advantages listed by Joseph Reynolds (pp. 30–31)? If so, which ones? If not, did other reasons for keeping a journal emerge from your work?

d. Examine the writing style in your entries. Is there much variation in your writing, or are sentence length, word choice, and tone about the same throughout? Did you enjoy reading your writing? Do you think some work on writing style would improve your writing? If so, what kind of work?

2. In "The Watcher at the Gates," Gail Godwin recommends getting to know the restraining critic that interferes with our writing process. If you are adept at drawing, begin by drawing a picture of your watcher. Then write a brief description of the person or "thing." If writing comes more easily than drawing, write first and then sketch, as best you can, the person or creature you have described.

3. Listed below are several excuses we've heard—and probably used—for avoiding getting down to writing tasks. Practice coping with these roadblocks by listing two or three ways of getting around each one. For example, one response to the first excuse could be to settle for a simpler goal than finishing—for example, by deciding to write just three paragraphs today.

   a. I don't have time to finish today, so I won't start.
   b. I promised I would go out with a friend, whom I can't let down.
   c. I'm out of typing paper, so there is no point in starting on the draft.
   d. I can only write in the library, but I don't feel like going there now.
   e. I can't start until I can think of a clever opening paragraph.

WRITING ASSIGNMENTS

1. How have you learned to fool your "Watcher at the Gates" (see Godwin, p. 38) so that you can write? In a 500-word essay, give your advice to anxious writers for avoiding writer's block, based on techniques that have worked for you.

2. Both Richard Selzer and William F. Buckley mention a number of writers in their essays, writers they assume readers will know. Select one of the writers mentioned by either Selzer or Buckley and find at least two sources of information about that writer. (Some suggestions: biographies, articles in journals, reviews of their works, and entries in the various biographical dictionaries such as *Who's Who, Contemporary Authors,* the *Dictionary of American Biography,* or the *Dictionary of National Biography.*) Study your sources, take notes, and then from your notes prepare a biographical essay, an essay that could serve as an introduction to a work by that writer. Do not copy from your sources or quote from them. Rather, learn about the writer and then prepare your essay.

3. Selzer writes because he believes that only in writing, not in dealing with life and death as a surgeon, can he begin to understand life's meaning. Why do you think you, given your career plans, should write? In a 500-word essay explain why an engineer, or banker, or teacher—or whatever you plan to become—should write. You can focus either on the practical considerations of the job or on the more philosophical concerns such as those Selzer discusses. Prepare your essay as a feature for your college paper.
4. As you have discovered in this chapter, not all writers write for the same reasons or use the same approaches to achieve their results. Reread Joan Didion's "Why I Write" and Richard Selzer's "On the Exact Location of the Soul," taking notes so that you can explain each author's reasons for writing and show how they differ. As you prepare your contrast of Didion and Selzer, consider as well which writer's reasons are closer to your own. In an essay, contrast the views of Didion and Selzer and explain why you identify more closely with one writer than with the other.

Paul *Cézanne,* La Montagne Sainte-Victoire, c. 1886–1888. 26″ × 35½″. *Courtauld Institute Galleries, London.*

CHAPTER 3

THE ESSAYISTS SEEING
PEOPLE, PLACES, OURSELVES

Chapter 2 is about writing. Chapter 3 is about many things—bobcats, accepting oneself, the geology of central Vermont—but mostly it is "about" a type of writing, the personal essay. Your primary concern in this chapter, then, will be to study assigned readings as models of the essay and for specific strategies of effective writing.

We noted in Chapter 2 that the essays presented there are also personal essays, for although the broad topic is the same—writing—each writer's approach is based on personal experience. The writers in Chapter 2 examine different writing issues and draw from their own writing experiences for examples. Those writers have an advantage over the writers in Chapter 3, however. Because they are established writers writing about their specialty, they are more likely to have a ready-made audience for their essays. Remember that three of the essays in Chapter 2 were published in the prestigious *New York Times Book Review.* A well-known author—Joan Didion or William Buckley—writing in the *Book Review* has an eager audience in hand.

Most personal essayists, however—all but the most famous—must engage readers for each new piece. Even an established columnist such as Ellen Goodman needs to think about holding on to a reader to the end of each column. As E. B. White observes in his discussion of the essayist, essayists have the pleasure of exploring new subjects each time they write, but they are constrained from entertaining "random thoughts" and calling them an essay. For, where is the audience for someone's self-indulgent wanderings?

How, then, do we create an audience for a personal essay? How does

Jeffrey Cooper hold the attention of a reader who may not be especially interested in Arizona's high desert? The essayists in this chapter give us several answers to the question of audience. First, the essayist can engage the reader's attention by providing new information. For most adults who have left the classroom, reading is the chief source of new knowledge. As we follow, with Cooper, the trail of the bobcat, we learn about the Sonoran desert. The facts of the desert fuse with Cooper's experience; each enriches and strengthens the other, blending teaching and sharing. Thus Floyd Stuart gives good advice in his postscript to "Cyclical Time" when he tells us to keep our eyes on the real world out there and to get our facts straight.

A second means of enticing an audience is to report on or re-create unusual experiences. Few of us have the opportunity to trail bobcats in the desert, or to live on a farm in Southern Rhodesia. Thanks to the essayists (and the fiction writers), we can live more lives than one. Readers are not only fascinated by worlds they have not seen or experiences they have not had, however; they are also drawn to moving accounts of the common, the ordinary human experiences. E. B. White and Floyd C. Stuart give voice to a father's love; Alice Walker shares with readers the pain of growing up with a deformity or difference, real or perceived.

Finally, and perhaps most centrally, essayists help us see the larger significances in human events. Whether writing of the unusual or the commonplace, essayists press each drop of meaning from their experiences. Doris Lessing wants us to understand that war can kill the spirit of those not physically killed by bombs or bullets. And Ellen Goodman wants to remind us of the contentment to be found in being one with the natural world. Some essayists offer reflections on their experiences; others retell experiences in a way that implies a larger meaning. Either way, we are being shown that writers who want readers give them good cause to read on.

Although we are drawn to the best essays for the insights we gain, we are also drawn by the pleasure of watching a wordsmith busy at a difficult craft. William Gass, a fine essayist as well as fiction writer, has said of the essay that "it is a great meadow of style and personal manner, freed from the need for defense except that provided by any individual intelligence and sparkle." In the best essays we find that rich union of thought and style: the language selected seems the perfect vehicle for the thought expressed. We delight in listening to a mind at work—or at play—ranging through and drawing together an array of details, charged with nuance, about bobcats or bees or bike riding.

Since we examined, in Chapter 2, the role of vivid details in writing, the rest of this introduction will concentrate on the good writer's attention to sentence structure and the use of metaphors. Reading the essays in this chapter, you may feel at times as if you are reading poetry rather than prose. And you will be on target. The lyric (or musical) quality of many passages in personal essays resembles poetry more closely than does any other kind of prose writing. Part of the reason is the essayist's fusing of particular and general, of rich details and larger meanings, the same fusing we find in lyric poems. (Think, for example, of the Whitman or Frost poems you know.) Part of the reason, as well, is the essayist's attention to varying sentence patterns, to controlling the rhythm of the lines, to shaping the tone of the writing. You can improve your essay writing significantly if you will study, and learn to imitate, the best of the sentence molding illustrated in this chapter. Exercises at the chapter's end will provide good opportunities to practice, to develop an ear for the various melodies you can play by trying different words in different places.

Another reason for the poetic quality of essay writing lies in the essayist's frequent use of metaphors. Because of the time spent finding the metaphors in Milton's sonnets or Shakespeare's plays, students sometimes come away from English classes with the mistaken notion that metaphors are a device found only in poems. In fact, we find more metaphors in casual speech than anywhere else. All the overworked phrases (clichés) that we string together (The rat race is getting me down; my circuits are overloaded) are, of course, metaphors. Avoiding the clichés and trite expressions of colloquial speech, good writers give us fresh, vivid comparisons to help us see their world.

Let's think for a moment about what a metaphor is or does. A *metaphor* is a comparison between two essentially unlike things that, according to the metaphor user, have some traits in common. As Roger Sale explains in *On Writing* (Random House, 1970), a metaphor says that $x = y$, that this is like that. It doesn't matter if the comparison is expressed as a metaphor (Richard the Lion-hearted) or as a *simile* (He fought *like* a lion) because we know that Richard is not a lion, that *x* is not *y*, but that the writer wants us to consider the traits that *x* has in common with *y*. Sale observes that our task as readers is to "unpack" the metaphor, to recognize the two items being compared and to think about the points of comparison. To say that Richard is lion-hearted is to say that he has the strength of spirit, the courage, we associate with the king of the beasts. To say that one's circuits are overloaded is to compare oneself to an electrical device, a machine, that is about to break down because of excessive demand placed on it.

Metaphors, then, have two advantages for writers: they offer a vivid and a brief way to make several points. A writer's choice of metaphors reveals attitudes as well as ideas. There is a big difference in the view of humankind conveyed by a comparison of humans to the gods (godlike Odysseus) and a comparison of humans to machines (My circuits are overloaded). The process of comprehending a metaphor, then, has three steps: recognizing that the writer's language is metaphoric, unpacking the metaphor to understand the points of the comparison, and responding emotionally to the attitudes carried by the comparison. Incorporate these steps into your reading, and you will eliminate much that may have been confusing about "poetic" language, whether in verse or prose.

Foreword to The Essays of E. B. White

E. B. WHITE

For Elwyn Brooks White, the French writer Montaigne set the standard for essay writing; in our time, E. B. White has set the standard against which personal essay writers must be judged. His writing for the New Yorker, *particularly in the "Notes and Comments" section, did much to establish an ironic, understated humor as the* New Yorker's *style and tone. Many of his readers' favorite essays were published from 1938 to 1943 in a regular monthly column for* Harper's *magazine and collected as* One Man's Meat *in 1943. And yet, White the humorist and essayist is probably best loved by readers as the author of three, now classic, children's stories:* Stuart Little *(1945),* Charlotte's Web *(1952), and* The Trumpet of the Swan *(1970).*

White (1899–1985) was born in New York, graduated from Cornell University, lived in Greenwich Village, and made his career as a writer when he began with the New Yorker *in 1926. Later he alternated between New York City and his farm in Maine, a place he wrote about frequently and described as more a private zoo than a real farm. Finally, in 1953 he moved to the farm permanently and continued not only to write essays and his third children's book, but also to prepare a second edition of* The Elements of Style *—a guide originally written by Cornell professor William Strunk but considerably revised and enlarged by White.*

White wrote very little about writing beyond the specific guidelines in The Elements of Style *and the following brief introduction to his collected essays, published in 1977. He wrote an enormous amount, yet he preferred the image of a man busy with many interests who takes time out to tell us what is on his mind. Although he believed that writing is intuitive, he asserts in the following introduction that even this loosest of literary forms has its disciplines. White has taught us, by example, that one of those disciplines is the carefully crafted sentence.*

1 The essayist is a self-liberated man, sustained by the childish belief that everything he thinks about, everything that happens to him, is of general interest. He is a fellow who thoroughly enjoys his work, just as people who take bird walks enjoy theirs. Each new excursion of the essayist, each new "attempt," differs from the last and takes him into new country. This delights him. Only a person who is congenitally self-centered has the effrontery and the stamina to write essays.

2 There are as many kinds of essays as there are human attitudes or poses, as many essay flavors as there are Howard Johnson ice creams. The essayist arises in the morning and, if he has work to do, selects his garb from an unusually extensive wardrobe: he can pull on any sort of shirt, be any sort of person, according to his mood or his subject matter—philosopher, scold, jester, raconteur, confidant, pundit, devil's advocate, enthusiast. I like the essay, have always liked it, and even as a child was at work, attempting to inflict my young thoughts and experiences on others by putting them on paper. I early broke into print in the pages of *St. Nicholas.*[1] I tend still to fall back on the essay form (or lack of

[1]A magazine for young readers that awarded prizes for submitted material and printed the prize-winning works. The magazine printed two of White's pieces, one when he was eleven, another when he was fourteen.—Ed.

form) when an idea strikes me, but I am not fooled about the place of the essay in twentieth-century American letters—it stands a short distance down the line. The essayist, unlike the novelist, the poet, and the playwright, must be content in his self-imposed role of second-class citizen. A writer who has his sights trained on the Nobel Prize or other earthly triumphs had best write a novel, a poem, or a play, and leave the essayist to ramble about, content with living a free life and enjoying the satisfactions of a somewhat undisciplined existence. (Dr. Johnson[2] called the essay "an irregular, undigested piece"; this happy practitioner has no wish to quarrel with the good doctor's characterization.)

3 There is one thing the essayist cannot do, though—he cannot indulge himself in deceit or in concealment, for he will be found out in no time. Desmond MacCarthy, in his introductory remarks to the 1928 E. P. Dutton & Company edition of Montaigne,[3] observes that Montaigne "had the gift of natural candour. . . ." It is the basic ingredient. And even the essayist's escape from discipline is only a partial escape: the essay, although a relaxed form, imposes its own disciplines, raises its own problems, and these disciplines and problems soon become apparent and (we all hope) act as a deterrent to anyone wielding a pen merely because he entertains random thoughts or is in a happy or wandering mood.

4 I think some people find the essay the last resort of the egoist, a much too self-conscious and self-serving form for their taste; they feel that it is presumptuous of a writer to assume that his little excursions or his small observations will interest the reader. There is some justice in their complaint. I have always been aware that I am by nature self-absorbed and egoistical; to write of myself to the extent I have done indicates a too great attention to my own life, not enough to the lives of others. I have worn many shirts, and not all of them have been a good fit. But when I am discouraged or downcast I need only fling open the door of my closet, and there, hidden behind everything else, hangs the mantle of Michel de Montaigne, smelling slightly of camphor.

QUESTIONS FOR ANALYSIS AND DISCUSSION

1. What is the pleasure, according to White, to be gained from essay writing? On the other hand, what is the chief drawback to working in this literary form?

---

[2]An eighteenth-century British poet, critic, lexicographer, and social commentator.—Ed.

[3]A sixteenth-century French essayist.—Ed.

2. White says some unkind things about essayists: they are childish, self-centered, self-serving egoists. Why does the essayist deserve, to a degree, these labels?
3. What limits or constraints does the essay form impose on writers that provide a deterrent to the ego trip of essay writing? What are insufficient reasons for deciding to write an essay?
4. What problem, finally, must the personal essayist solve, if he or she is to write successfully?
5. White introduces a metaphor in paragraph 2 that he returns to in paragraph 4. What is the metaphor, and how does it contribute to our understanding of White's portrait of an essayist?
6. White lists, in paragraph 2, the many poses an essayist can adopt. Which term (or terms) best describes White's pose in these paragraphs defining an essayist? If you don't think any of White's terms apply, what term would you use to label the author's pose?

Seeing

ANNIE DILLARD

A native of Pittsburgh and graduate of Hollins College (B.A. and M.A.), Annie Dillard (b. 1945) has taught poetry and creative writing, served as a contributing editor to Harper's, *and produced several volumes of poetry and nonfiction. Her personal narrative,* Pilgrim at Tinker Creek, *from which the following excerpt is taken, won the 1974 Pulitzer Prize for nonfiction. In addition she has published a volume of poetry (*Tickets for a Prayer Wheel, *1974), a prose narrative (*Holy the Firm, *1978), an essay collection (*Teaching a Stone to Talk, *1982), a work of literary analysis (*Living by Fiction, *1982—see Chapter 5), and most recently, a collection of sketches based on her experiences in China and with Chinese writers in the United States (*Encounters with Chinese Writers, *1985).*

Reviews of Pilgrim *were mixed, with some writers considering Dillard's observations immature and self-centered, while others praised the book's blend of detail and meditation. Notice that the critical comments are exactly the ones E. B. White calls attention to as problems for the essayist. Still, we can learn much from Dillard about the role of sight—and insight—in the work of the writer.*

1 I chanced on a wonderful book by Marius von Senden, called *Space and Sight*. When Western surgeons discovered how to perform safe cataract operations, they ranged across Europe and America operating on dozens of men and women of all ages who had been blinded by cataracts since birth. Von Senden collected accounts of such cases; the histories are fascinating. Many doctors had tested their patients' sense perceptions and ideas of space both before and after the operations. The vast majority of patients, of both sexes and all ages, had, in von Senden's opinion, no idea of space whatsoever. Form, distance, and size were so many meaningless syllables. A patient "had no idea of depth, confusing it with roundness." Before the operation a doctor would give a blind patient a cube and a sphere; the patient would tongue it or feel it with his hands, and name it correctly. After the operation the doctor would show the same objects to the patient without letting him touch them; now he had no clue whatsoever what he was seeing. One patient called lemonade "square" because it pricked on his tongue as a square shape pricked on the touch of his hands. Of another postoperative patient, the doctor writes, "I have found in her no notion of size, for example, not even within the narrow limits which she might have encompassed with the aid of touch. Thus when I asked her to show me how big her mother was, she did not stretch out her hands, but set her two index-fingers a few inches apart." Other doctors reported their patients' own statements to similar effect. "The room he was in . . . he knew to be but part of the house, yet he could not conceive that the whole house could look bigger"; "Those who are blind from birth . . . have no real conception of height or distance. A house that is a mile away is thought of as nearby, but requiring the taking of a lot of steps. . . . The elevator that whizzes him up and down gives no more sense of vertical distance than does the train of horizontal."

2 For the newly sighted, vision is pure sensation unencumbered by meaning: "The girl went through the experience that we all go through and forget, the moment we are born. She saw, but it did not mean anything but a lot of different kinds of brightness." Again, "I asked the patient what he could see; he answered that he saw an extensive field of light, in which everything appeared dull, confused, and in motion. He could not distinguish objects." Another patient saw "nothing but a confusion of forms and colours." When a newly sighted girl saw photographs and paintings, she asked, " 'Why do they put those dark marks all over them?' 'Those aren't dark marks,' her mother explained, 'those are shadows. That is one of the ways the eye knows that things have

shape. If it were not for shadows many things would look flat.' 'Well, that's how things do look,' Joan answered. 'Everything looks flat with dark patches.' "

3 But it is the patients' concepts of space that are most revealing. One patient, according to his doctor, "practiced his vision in a strange fashion; thus he takes off one of his boots, throws it some way off in front of him, and then attempts to gauge the distance at which it lies; he takes a few steps towards the boot and tries to grasp it; on failing to reach it, he moves on a step or two and gropes for the boot until he finally gets hold of it." "But even at this stage, after three weeks' experience of seeing," von Senden goes on, " 'space,' as he conceives it, ends with visual space, i.e. with colour-patches that happen to bound his view. He does not yet have the notion that a larger object (a chair) can mask a smaller one (a dog), or that the latter can still be present even though it is not directly seen."

4 In general the newly sighted see the world as a dazzle of color-patches. They are pleased by the sensation of color, and learn quickly to name the colors, but the rest of seeing is tormentingly difficult. Soon after his operation a patient "generally bumps into one of these colour-patches and observes them to be substantial, since they resist him as tactual objects do. In walking about it also strikes him—or can if he pays attention—that he is continually passing in between the colours he sees, that he can go past a visual object, that a part of it then steadily disappears from view; and that in spite of this, however he twists and turns—whether entering the room from the door, for example, or returning back to it—he always has a visual space in front of him. Thus he gradually comes to realize that there is also a space behind him, which he does not see."

5 The mental effort involved in these reasonings proves overwhelming for many patients. It oppresses them to realize, if they ever do at all, the tremendous size of the world, which they had previously conceived of as something touchingly manageable. It oppresses them to realize that they have been visible to people all along, perhaps unattractively so, without their knowledge or consent. A disheartening number of them refuse to use their new vision, continuing to go over objects with their tongues, and lapsing into apathy and despair. "The child can see, but will not make use of his sight. Only when pressed can he with difficulty be brought to look at objects in his neighbourhood; but more than a foot away it is impossible to bestir him to the necessary effort." Of a twenty-one-year-old girl, the doctor relates, "Her unfortunate father,

who had hoped for so much from this operation, wrote that his daughter carefully shuts her eyes whenever she wishes to go about the house, especially when she comes to a staircase, and that she is never happier or more at ease than when, by closing her eyelids, she relapses into her former state of total blindness." A fifteen-year-old boy, who was also in love with a girl at the asylum for the blind, finally blurted out, "No, really, I can't stand it any more; I want to be sent back to the asylum again. If things aren't altered, I'll tear my eyes out."

6 Some do learn to see, especially the young ones. But it changes their lives. One doctor comments on "the rapid and complete loss of that striking and wonderful serenity which is characteristic only of those who have never yet seen." A blind man who learns to see is ashamed of his old habits. He dresses up, grooms himself, and tries to make a good impression. While he was blind he was indifferent to objects unless they were edible; now, "a sifting of values sets in . . . his thoughts and wishes are mightily stirred and some few of the patients are thereby led into dissimulation, envy, theft and fraud."

7 On the other hand, many newly sighted people speak well of the world, and teach us how dull is our own vision. To one patient, a human hand, unrecognized, is "something bright and then holes." Shown a bunch of grapes, a boy calls out, "It is dark, blue and shiny. . . . It isn't smooth, it has bumps and hollows." A little girl visits a garden. "She is greatly astonished, and can scarcely be persuaded to answer, stands speechless in front of the tree, which she only names on taking hold of it, and then as 'the tree with the lights in it.' " Some delight in their sight and give themselves over to the visual world. Of a patient just after her bandages were removed, her doctor writes, "The first things to attract her attention were her own hands; she looked at them very closely, moved them repeatedly to and fro, bent and stretched the fingers, and seemed greatly astonished at the sight." One girl was eager to tell her blind friend that "men do not really look like trees at all," and astounded to discover that her every visitor had an utterly different face. Finally, a twenty-two-year-old girl was dazzled by the world's brightness and kept her eyes shut for two weeks. When at the end of that time she opened her eyes again, she did not recognize any objects, but "the more she now directed her gaze upon everything about her, the more it could be seen how an expression of gratification and astonishment overspread her features; she repeatedly exclaimed: 'Oh God! How beautiful!' "

8 I saw color-patches for weeks after I read this wonderful book. It was summer; the peaches were ripe in the valley orchards. When I woke

in the morning, color-patches wrapped round my eyes, intricately, leaving not one unfilled spot. All day long I walked among shifting color-patches that parted before me like the Red Sea and closed again in silence, transfigured, wherever I looked back. Some patches swelled and loomed, while others vanished utterly, and dark marks flitted at random over the whole dazzling sweep. But I couldn't sustain the illusion of flatness. I've been around for too long. Form is condemned to an eternal danse macabre[1] with meaning: I couldn't unpeach the peaches. Nor can I remember ever having seen without understanding; the color-patches of infancy are lost. My brain then must have been smooth as any balloon. I'm told I reached for the moon; many babies do. But the color-patches of infancy swelled as meaning filled them; they arrayed themselves in solemn ranks down distance which unrolled and stretched before me like a plain. The moon rocketed away. I live now in a world of shadows that shape and distance color, a world where space makes a kind of terrible sense. What gnosticism[2] is this, and what physics? The fluttering patch I saw in my nursery window—silver and green and shape-shifting blue—is gone; a row of Lombardy poplars takes its place, mute, across the distant lawn. That humming oblong creature pale as light that stole along the walls of my room at night, stretching exhilaratingly around the corners, is gone, too, gone the night I ate of the bittersweet fruit, put two and two together and puckered forever my brain. Martin Buber[3] tells this tale: "Rabbi Mendel once boasted to his teacher Rabbi Elimelekh that evenings he saw the angel who rolls away the light before the darkness, and mornings the angel who rolls away the darkness before the light. 'Yes,' said Rabbi Elimelekh, 'in my youth I saw that too. Later on you don't see these things any more.' "

9 Why didn't someone hand those newly sighted people paints and brushes from the start, when they still didn't know what anything was? Then maybe we all could see color-patches too, the world unraveled from reason, Eden before Adam gave names. The scales would drop from my eyes; I'd see trees like men wallking; I'd run down the road against all orders, hallooing and leaping.

•

10 Seeing is of course very much a matter of verbalization. Unless I call my attention to what passes before my eyes, I simply won't see it. It

---

[1]Dance of death; in medieval art, an allegorical dance showing a figure of death leading people to the grave.—Ed.

[2]Gnostics believed matter was evil and denied Christ's physical existence.—Ed.

[3]An Austrian-born Jewish philosopher and writer (1878–1965).—Ed.

is, as Ruskin[4] says, "not merely unnoticed, but in the full, clear sense of the word, unseen." My eyes alone can't solve analogy tests using figures, the ones which show, with increasing elaborations, a big square, then a small square in a big square, then a big triangle, and expect me to find a small triangle in a big triangle. I have to say the words, describe what I'm seeing. If Tinker Mountain erupted, I'd be likely to notice. But if I want to notice the lesser cataclysms of valley life, I have to maintain in my head a running description of the present. It's not that I'm observant; it's just that I talk too much. Otherwise, especially in a strange place, I'll never know what's happening. Like a blind man at the ball game, I need a radio.

11 When I see this way I analyze and pry. I hurl over logs and roll away stones; I study the bank a square foot at a time, probing and tilting my head. Some days when a mist covers the mountains, when the muskrats won't show and the microscope's mirror shatters, I want to climb up the blank blue dome as a man would storm inside of a circus tent, wildly, dangling, and with a steel knife claw a rent in the top, peep, and, if I must, fall.

12 But there is another kind of seeing that involves a letting go. When I see this way I sway transfixed and emptied. The difference between the two ways of seeing is the difference between walking with and without a camera. When I walk with a camera I walk from shot to shot, reading the light on a calibrated meter. When I walk without a camera, my own shutter opens, and the moment's light prints on my own silver gut. When I see this second way I am above all an unscrupulous observer.

13 It was sunny one evening last summer at Tinker Creek; the sun was low in the sky, upstream. I was sitting on the sycamore log bridge with the sunset at my back, watching the shiners the size of minnows who were feeding over the muddy sand in skittery schools. Again and again, one fish, then another, turned for a split second across the current and flash! the sun shot out from its silver side. I couldn't watch for it. It was always just happening somewhere else, and it drew my vision just as it disappeared: flash, like a sudden dazzle of the thinnest blade, a sparking over a dun and olive ground at chance intervals from every direction. Then I noticed white specks, some sort of pale petals, small, floating from under my feet on the creek's surface, very slow and steady. So I

---

[4]An English author and art critic (1819–1900).—Ed.

blurred my eyes and gazed towards the brim of my hat and saw a new world. I saw the pale white circles roll up, roll up, like the world's turning, mute and perfect, and I saw the linear flashes, gleaming silver, like stars being born at random down a rolling scroll of time. Something broke and something opened. I filled up like a new wineskin. I breathed an air like light; I saw a light like water. I was the lip of a fountain the creek filled forever; I was ether, the leaf in the zephyr[5]; I was flesh-flake, feather, bone.

14 When I see this way I see truly. As Thoreau says, I return to my senses. I am the man who watches the baseball game in silence in an empty stadium. I see the game purely; I'm abstracted and dazed. When it's all over and the white-suited players lope off the green field to their shadowed dugouts, I leap to my feet; I cheer and cheer.

15 But I can't go out and try to see this way. I'll fail, I'll go mad. All I can do is try to gag the commentator, to hush the noise of useless interior babble that keeps me from seeing just as surely as a newspaper dangled before my eyes. The effort is really a discipline requiring a lifetime of dedicated struggle; it marks the literature of saints and monks of every order East and West, under every rule and no rule, discalced[6] and shod. The world's spiritual geniuses seem to discover universally that the mind's muddy river, this ceaseless flow of trivia and trash, cannot be dammed, and that trying to dam it is a waste of effort that might lead to madness. Instead you must allow the muddy river to flow unheeded in the dim channels of consciousness; you raise your sights; you look along it, mildly, acknowledging its presence without interest and gazing beyond it into the realm of the real where subjects and objects act and rest purely, without utterance. "Launch into the deep," says Jacques Ellul,"[7] and you shall see."

16 The secret of seeing is, then, the pearl of great price. If I thought he could teach me to find it and keep it forever I would stagger barefoot across a hundred deserts after any lunatic at all. But although the pearl may be found, it may not be sought. The literature of illumination reveals this above all: although it comes to those who wait for it, it is always, even to the most practiced and adept, a gift and a total surprise.

---

[5]Mild breeze.—Ed.

[6]Barefoot.—Ed.

[7]A French writer and professor of social history (b. 1912) whose primary interest is the role of Christian faith in contemporary society.—Ed.

I return from one walk knowing where the killdeer nests in the field by the creek and the hour the laurel blooms. I return from the same walk a day later scarcely knowing my own name. Litanies hum in my ears; my tongue flaps in my mouth Ailinon,[8] alleluia! I cannot cause light; the most I can do is try to put myself in the path of its beam. It is possible, in deep space, to sail on solar wind. Light, be it particle or wave, has force: you rig a giant sail and go. The secret of seeing is to sail on solar wind. Hone and spread your spirit till you yourself are a sail, whetted, translucent, broadside to the merest puff.

17 When her doctor took her bandages off and led her into the garden, the girl who was no longer blind saw "the tree with the lights in it." It was for this tree I searched through the peach orchards of summer, in the forests of fall and down winter and spring for years. Then one day I was walking along Tinker Creek thinking of nothing at all and I saw the tree with the lights in it. I saw the backyard cedar where the mourning doves roost charged and transfigured, each cell buzzing with flame. I stood on the grass with the lights in it, grass that was wholly fire, utterly focused and utterly dreamed. It was less like seeing than like being for the first time seen, knocked breathless by a powerful glance. The flood of fire abated, but I'm still spending the power. Gradually the lights went out in the cedar, the colors died, the cells unflamed and disappeared. I was still ringing. I had been my whole life a bell, and never knew it until at that moment I was lifted and struck. I have since only very rarely seen the tree with the lights in it. The vision comes and goes, mostly goes, but I live for it, for the moment when the mountains open and a new light roars in spate through the crack, and the mountains slam.

QUESTIONS FOR ANALYSIS AND DISCUSSION

1. Dillard's first seven paragraphs summarize the book *Space and Sight.* Write a brief summary—one paragraph—of Dillard's seven. Leave out quotations and details, stating the general points about the development of sight.
2. From these studies, what can we assume to be the initial experience of seeing by infants?

[8]Greek cry of anguish, usually translated as "sorrow," but frequently used to refer to the moment of the soul's passing from the body at death, thus a cry of release as well as of anguish. In this context, release from the limitations of verbalized seeing to a purer vision.—Ed.

3. Why is it that we—sighted adults—cannot usually see color-patches?
4. How do we normally support the visual process so that we see what is around us?
5. Dillard asserts that there is another way of seeing. What kind of "seeing" is she describing from paragraph 12 on? What do we have to do to "see" this way?
6. How does the material in paragraphs 1–8 relate to the second half of Dillard's essay?
7. In paragraph 12, Dillard explains the two ways of seeing with a comparison to "walking with and without a camera." Explain, in your own words, the point of her comparison.
8. When Dillard describes the second way of seeing, she seems to be describing what kind of experience? (Look up the philosophical term *transcendentalism* in a reference book and see if knowledge of this term helps you understand Dillard.)
9. Richard Selzer's (see Chapter 2) essays have been called prose poems; would this description also fit Dillard's writing? Find several passages that seem poetic to you and analyze them. What elements in her sentences make them read as poetry?

My Father

DORIS LESSING

Born in Persia (now Iran) but reared in Southern Rhodesia (now Zimbabwe), Doris Lessing (b. 1919) left school at fourteen, took various odd jobs, lived, and began to write, in Africa until 1949. She then moved to London, where she lives today. She has steadily published short stories, plays, and novels since 1950 and is considered by critics to be one of the most significant contemporary writers. She has three important short story collections: A Man and Two Women *(1963),* African Stories *(1964), and* The Temptation of Jack Orkney and Other Stories *(1972); several short novels including* The Grass Is Singing *(1950); five interrelated novels forming a unified work called* Children of Violence*; and her most-celebrated novel* The Golden Notebook *(1962). In addition she has written a number of essays and reviews, many, including the essay on her father, collected in* A Small Personal Voice *(1975). "My Father" was first published in 1963 in the London* Sunday Telegraph.

Lessing has expressed the view that the high point of literature can be found in the nineteenth-century novel. Lessing's admirers place her in that great realist tradition that includes Tolstoy and Chekhov, Stendhal and Balzac, Dickens and Conrad. These writers shared, Lessing observes in A Small Personal Voice, *humanistic values, a sense of responsibility, and commitment to moral and artistic honesty. In "My Father" we see Lessing's commitment to portraying her father honestly, and to accepting the person in the portrait.*

1 We use our parents like recurring dreams, to be entered into when needed; they are always there for love or for hate; but it occurs to me that I was not always there for my father. I've written about him before, but novels, stories, don't have to be "true." Writing this article is difficult because it has to be "true." I knew him when his best years were over.

2 There are photographs of him. The largest is of an officer in the 1914–18 war. A new uniform–buttoned, badged, strapped, tabbed–confines a handsome, dark young man who holds himself stiffly to confront what he certainly thought of as his duty. His eyes are steady, serious, and responsible, and show no signs of what he became later. A photograph at sixteen is of a dark, introspective youth with the same intent eyes. But it is his mouth you notice–a heavily-jutting upper lip contradicts the rest of a regular face. His moustache was to hide it: "Had to do something–a damned fleshy mouth. Always made me uncomfortable, that mouth of mine."

3 Earlier a baby (eyes already alert) appears in a lace waterfall that cascades from the pillowy bosom of a fat, plain woman to her feet. It is the face of a head cook. "Lord, but my mother was a practical female–almost as bad as you!" as he used to say, or throw at my mother in moments of exasperation. Beside her stands, or droops, arms dangling, his father, the source of the dark, arresting eyes, but otherwise masked by a long beard.

4 The birth certificate says: Born 3rd August, 1886, Walton Villa, Creffield Road, S. Mary at the Wall, R.S.D. Name, Alfred Cook. Name and surname of Father: Alfred Cook Tayler. Name and maiden name of Mother: Caroline May Batley. Rank or Profession: Bank Clerk. Colchester, Essex.

5 They were very poor. Clothes and boots were a problem. They "made their own amusements." Books were mostly the Bible and *The Pilgrim's Progress.* Every Saturday night they bathed in a hip-bath in front of the kitchen fire. No servants. Church three times on Sundays.

"Lord, when I think of those Sundays! I dreaded them all week, like a nightmare coming at you full tilt and no escape." But he rabbited with ferrets along the lanes and fields, bird-nested, stole fruit, picked nuts and mushrooms, paid visits to the blacksmith and the mill and rode a farmer's carthorse.

6 They ate economically, but when he got diabetes in his forties and subsisted on lean meat and lettuce leaves, he remembered suet puddings, treacle puddings, raisin and currant puddings, steak and kidney puddings, bread and butter pudding, "batter cooked in the gravy with the meat," potato cake, plum cake, butter cake, porridge with treacle, fruit tarts and pies, brawn, pig's trotters and pig's cheek and home-smoked ham and sausages. And "lashings of fresh butter and cream and eggs." He wondered if this diet had produced the diabetes, but said it was worth it.

7 There was an elder brother described by my father as: "Too damned clever by half. One of those quick, clever brains. Now I've always had a slow brain, but I get there in the end, damn it!"

8 The brothers went to a local school and the elder did well, but my father was beaten for being slow. They both became bank clerks in, I think, the Westminster Bank, and one must have found it congenial, for he became a manager, the "rich brother," who had cars and even a yacht. But my father did not like it, though he was conscientious. For instance, he changed his writing, letter by letter, because a senior criticised it. I never saw his unregenerate hand, but the one he created was elegant, spiky, careful. Did this mean he created a new personality for himself, hiding one he did not like, as he hid his "damned fleshy mouth"? I don't know.

9 Nor do I know when he left home to live in Luton or why. He found family life too narrow? A safe guess—he found everything too narrow. His mother was too down-to-earth? He had to get away from his clever elder brother?

10 Being a young man in Luton was the best part of his life. It ended in 1914, so he had a decade of happiness. His reminiscences of it were all of pleasure, the delight of physical movement, of dancing in particular. All his girls were "a beautiful dancer, light as a feather." He played billiards and ping-pong (both for his county); he swam, boated, played cricket and football, went to picnics and horse races, sang at musical evenings. One family of a mother and two daughters treated him "like a son only better. I didn't know whether I was in love with the mother or the daughters, but oh I did love going there; we had such good times." He

was engaged to one daughter, then, for a time, to the other. An engagement was broken off because she was rude to a waiter. "I could not marry a woman who allowed herself to insult someone who was defenceless." He used to say to my wryly smiling mother: "Just as well I didn't marry either of *them*; they would never have stuck it out the way you have, old girl."

11 Just before he died he told me he had dreamed he was standing in a kitchen on a very high mountain holding X in his arms. "Ah, yes, that's what I've missed in my life. Now don't you let yourself be cheated out of life by the old dears. They take all the colour out of everything if you let them."

12 But in that decade—"I'd walk 10, 15 miles to a dance two or three times a week and think nothing of it. Then I'd dance every dance and walk home again over the fields. Sometimes it was moonlight, but I liked the snow best, all crisp and fresh. I loved walking back and getting into my digs just as the sun was rising. My little dog was so happy to see me, and I'd feed her, and make myself porridge and tea, then I'd wash and shave and go off to work."

13 The boy who was beaten at school, who went too much to church, who carried the fear of poverty all his life, but who nevertheless was filled with the memories of country pleasures; the young bank clerk who worked such long hours for so little money, but who danced, sang, played, flirted—this naturally vigorous, sensuous being was killed in 1914, 1915, 1916. I think the best of my father died in that war, that his spirit was crippled by it. The people I've met, particularly the women, who knew him young, speak of his high spirits, his energy, his enjoyment of life. Also of his kindness, his compassion and—a word that keeps recurring—his wisdom. "Even when he was just a boy he understood things that you'd think even an old man would find it easy to condemn." I do not think these people would have easily recognised the ill, irritable, abstracted, hypochondriac man I knew.

14 He "joined up" as an ordinary soldier out of a characteristically quirky scruple: it wasn't right to enjoy officers' privileges when the Tommies had such a bad time. But he could not stick the communal latrines, the obligatory drinking, the collective visits to brothels, the jokes about girls. So next time he was offered a commission he took it.

15 His childhood and young man's memories, kept fluid, were added to, grew, as living memories do. But his war memories were congealed in stories that he told again and again, with the same words and gestures, in stereotyped phrases. They were anonymous, general, as if they

had come out of a communal war memoir. He met a German in no-man's-land, but both slowly lowered their rifles and smiled and walked away. The Tommies were the salt of the earth, the British fighting men the best in the world. He had never known such comradeship. A certain brutal officer was shot in a sortie[1] by his men, but the other officers, recognising rough justice, said nothing. He had known men intimately who saw the Angels at Mons.[2] He wished he could force all the generals on both sides into the trenches for just one day, to see what the common soldiers endured—*that* would have ended the war at once.

16 There was an undercurrent of memories, dreams, and emotions much deeper, more personal. This dark region in him, fate-ruled, where nothing was true but horror, was expressed inarticulately, in brief, bitter exclamations or phrases of rage, incredulity, betrayal. The men who went to fight in that war believed it when they said it was to end war. My father believed it. And he was never able to reconcile his belief in his country with his anger at the cynicism of its leaders. And the anger, the sense of betrayal, strengthened as he grew old and ill.

17 But in 1914 he was naïve, the German atrocities in Belgium inflamed him, and he enlisted out of idealism, although he knew he would have a hard time. He knew because a fortuneteller told him. (He could be described as uncritically superstitious or as psychically gifted.) He would be in great danger twice, yet not die—he was being protected by a famous soldier who was his ancestor. "And sure enough, later I heard from the Little Aunties that the church records showed we were descended the backstairs way from the Duke of Wellington, or was it Marlborough? Damn it, I forget. But one of them would be beside me all through the war, she said." (He was romantic, not only about this solicitous ghost, but also about being a descendant of the Huguenots, on the strength of the "e" in Tayler; and about "the wild blood" in his veins from a great uncle who, sent unjustly to prison for smuggling, came out of a ten-year sentence and earned it, very efficiently, along the coasts of Cornwall until he died.)

18 The luckiest thing that ever happened to my father, he said, was getting his leg shattered by shrapnel ten days before Passchendaele.[3] His whole company was killed. He knew he was going to be wounded because of the fortuneteller, who had said he would know. "I did not

---

[1] A rapid movement of besieged troops to take the offensive.—Ed.

[2] A Belgian town, site of a World War I battle.—Ed.

[3] A town in Belgium, site of a bloody World War I battle.—Ed.

understand what she meant, but both times in the trenches, first when my appendix burst and I nearly died, and then just before Passchendaele, I felt for some days as if a thick, black velvet pall was settled over me. I can't tell you what it was like. Oh, it was awful, awful, and the second time it was so bad I wrote to the old people and told them I was going to be killed."

19 His leg was cut off at mid-thigh, he was shell-shocked, he was very ill for many months, with a prolonged depression afterwards. "You should always remember that sometimes people are all seething underneath. You don't know what terrible things people have to fight against. You should look at a person's eyes, that's how you tell. . . . When I was like that, after I lost my leg, I went to a nice doctor man and said I was going mad, but he said, don't worry, everyone locks up things like that. You don't know—horrible, horrible, awful things. I was afraid of myself, of what I used to dream. I wasn't myself at all."

20 In the Royal Free Hospital was my mother, Sister McVeagh. He married his nurse which, as they both said often enough (though in different tones of voice), was just as well. That was 1919. He could not face being a bank clerk in England, he said, not after the trenches. Besides, England was too narrow and conventional. Besides, the civilians did not know what the soldiers had suffered, they didn't want to know, and now it wasn't done even to remember "The Great Unmentionable." He went off to the Imperial Bank of Persia, in which country I was born.

21 The house was beautiful, with great stone-floored high-ceilinged rooms whose windows showed ranges of snow-streaked mountains. The gardens were full of roses, jasmine, pomegranates, walnuts. Kermanshalhi[4] he spoke of with liking, but soon they went to Teheran, populous with "Embassy people," and my gregarious mother created a lively social life about which he was irritable even in recollection.

22 Irritableness—that note was first struck here, about Persia. He did not like, he said, "the graft and the corruption." But here it is time to try and describe something difficult—how a man's good qualities can also be his bad ones, or if not bad, a danger to him.

23 My father was honourable—he always knew exactly what that word meant. He had integrity. His "one does not do that sort of thing," his "no, it is *not* right," sounded throughout my childhood and were final for all of us. I am sure it was true he wanted to leave Persia because

[4]A city in western Iran (formerly Persia).—Ed.

of "the corruption." But it was also because he was already unconsciously longing for something freer, because as a bank official he could not let go into the dream-logged personality that was waiting for him. And later in Rhodesia, too, what was best in him was also what prevented him from shaking away the shadows: it was always in the name of honesty or decency that he refused to take this step or that out of the slow decay of the family's fortunes.

24 In 1925 there was leave from Persia. That year in London there was an Empire Exhibition, and on the Southern Rhodesian stand some very fine maize cobs and a poster saying that fortunes could be made on maize at 25/- a bag. So on an impulse, turning his back forever on England, washing his hands of the corruption of the East, my father collected all his capital, £800, I think, while my mother packed curtains from Liberty's, clothes from Harrods,[5] visiting cards, a piano, Persian rugs, a governess and two small children.

25 Soon, there was my father in a cigar-shaped house of thatch and mud on the top of a kopje that overlooked in all directions a great system of mountains, rivers, valleys, while overhead the sky arched from horizon to empty horizon. This was a couple of hundred miles south from the Zambesi,[6] a hundred or so west from Mozambique,[7] in the district of Banket, so called because certain of its reefs were of the same formation as those called *banket* on the Rand. Lomagundi[8]—gold country, tobacco country, maize country—wild, almost empty. (The Africans had been turned off it into reserves.) Our neighbours were four, five, seven miles off. In front of the house . . . no neighbours, nothing; no farms, just wild bush with two rivers but no fences to the mountains seven miles away. And beyond these mountains and bush again to the Portuguese border, over which "our boys" used to escape when wanted by the police for pass or other offences.

26 And then? There was bad luck. For instance, the price of maize dropped from 25/- to 9/- a bag. The seasons were bad, prices bad, crops failed. This was the sort of thing that made it impossible for him ever to "get off the farm," which, he agreed with my mother, was what he most wanted to do.

[5]Both Liberty's and Harrods are British department stores.—Ed.

[6]A river in southeastern Africa that flows to the Indian Ocean.—Ed.

[7]A southeastern African nation that borders Zimbabwe (formerly Southern Rhodesia).—Ed.

[8]A district in Zimbabwe west of Salisbury.—Ed.

27 It was an absurd country, he said. A man could "own" a farm for years that was totally mortgaged to the Government and run from the Land Bank, meanwhile employing half-a-hundred Africans at 12/- a month and none of them knew how to do a day's work. Why, two farm labourers from Europe could do in a day what twenty of these ignorant black savages would take a week to do. (Yet he was proud that he had a name as a just employer, that he gave "a square deal.") Things got worse. A fortuneteller had told him that her heart ached when she saw the misery ahead for my father: this was the misery.

28 But it was my mother who suffered. After a period of neurotic illness, which was a protest against her situation, she became brave and resourceful. But she never saw that her husband was not living in a real world, that he had made a captive of her common sense. We were always about to "get off the farm." A miracle would do it—a sweepstake, a goldmine, a legacy. And then? What a question! We would go to England where life would be normal with people coming in for musical evenings and nice supper parties at the Trocadero after a show. Poor woman, for the twenty years we were on the farm, she waited for when life would begin for her and for her children, for she never understood that what was a calamity for her was for them a blessing.

29 Meanwhile my father sank towards his death (at 61). Everything changed in him. He had been a dandy and fastidious, now he hated to change out of shabby khaki. He had been sociable, now he was misanthropic. His body's disorders—soon diabetes and all kinds of stomach ailments—dominated him. He was brave about his wooden leg, and even went down mine shafts and climbed trees with it, but he walked clumsily and it irked him badly. He greyed fast, and slept more in the day, but would be awake half the night pondering about. . . .

30 It could be gold divining. For ten years he experimented on private theories to do with the attractions and repulsions of metals. His whole soul went into it but his theories were wrong or he was *unlucky*—after all, if he had found a mine he would have had to leave the farm. It could be the relation between the minerals of the earth and of the moon; his decision to make infusions of all the plants on the farm and drink them himself in the interests of science; the criminal folly of the British Government in not realising that the Germans and the Russians were conspiring as Anti-Christ to . . . the inevitability of war because no one would listen to Churchill, but it would be all right because God (by then he was a British Israelite) had destined Britain to rule the world; a prophecy said 10 million dead would surround Jerusalem—how would

the corpses be cleared away?; people who wished to abolish flogging should be flogged; the natives understood nothing but a good beating; hanging must not be abolished because the Old Testament said "an eye for an eye and a tooth for a tooth. . . ."

31 Yet, as this side of him darkened, so that it seemed all his thoughts were of violence, illness, war, still no one dared to make an unkind comment in his presence or to gossip. Criticism of people, particularly of women, made him more and more uncomfortable till at last he burst out with: "It's all very well, but no one has the right to say that about another person."

32 In Africa, when the sun goes down, the stars spring up, all of them in their expected places, glittering and moving. In the rainy season, the sky flashed and thundered. In the dry season, the great dark hollow of night was lit by veld[9] fires: the mountains burned through September and October in chains of red fire. Every night my father took out his chair to watch the sky and the mountains, smoking, silent, a thin shabby fly-away figure under the stars. "Makes you think—there are so many worlds up there, wouldn't really matter if we did blow ourselves up—plenty more where we came from."

33 The Second World War, so long foreseen by him, was a bad time. His son was in the Navy and in danger, and his daughter a sorrow to him. He became very ill. More and more often it was necessary to drive him into Salisbury with him in a coma, or in danger of one, on the back seat. My mother moved him into a pretty little suburban house in town near the hospitals, where he took to his bed and a couple of years later died. For the most part he was unconscious under drugs. When awake he talked obsessively (a tongue licking a nagging sore place) about "the old war." Or he remembered his youth. "I've been dreaming—Lord, to see those horses come lickety-split down the course with their necks stretched out and the sun on their coats and everyone shouting. . . . I've been dreaming how I walked along the river in the mist as the sun was rising. . . . Lord, lord, lord, what a time that was, what good times we all had then, before the old war."

QUESTIONS FOR ANALYSIS AND DISCUSSION

1. Lessing begins by asserting that although stories do not have to be "true," essays do. Both times she puts the word *true* in quotes. What is her point

[9]Open, grassy country characteristic of parts of southern Africa.—Ed.

here? In what sense is a novel true? Not true? In what sense is biography true? Not true? What, in short, is the difference between truth and fact?

2. What is most striking about her father's physical appearance?
3. What feature most distressed her father? What did he do about it? What psychological significance does Lessing find possible in his action?
4. Why, according to Lessing, did her father leave home when he was young? What specific motives does she suggest? What general motive?
5. In what ways did the war "kill" Lessing's father? How did the experience change him?
6. Lessing contrasts her father's accounts of his early life with his accounts of World War I. How did these tales differ? What do these differences reveal about her father?
7. What reason did her father give for leaving Persia and returning to England? What other reasons might be found, in his personality? Deriving from his war experiences?
8. What details of his final years in Africa can be explained by personality? By his early family life? By the war?
9. Describe Lessing as a biographer. What characteristics of her essay make her portrait vivid? What makes them interesting to readers who are not particularly interested in her father?
10. How does Lessing reach and hold an audience for her personal writing? What readers might she be able to count on as part of her audience?

Beauty: When the Other Dancer Is the Self

ALICE WALKER

Alice Walker was born in Georgia in 1944. She graduated from Sarah Lawrence College in 1965 and then obtained grants and fellowships between lecture posts to sustain her writing. First came two volumes of short stories: In Love and Trouble: Stories of Black Women *(1973) and* You Can't Keep a Good Woman Down *(1981). The novel that has made her famous –* The Color Purple *– won both the Pulitzer Prize and the American Book Award in 1983, and became a successful film in 1985. In 1983 Walker published a collection of essays,* In Search of Our Mother's Gardens, *that includes*

"Beauty: When the Other Dancer Is the Self," an essay that first appeared in the May 1983 issue of Ms. *magazine. She now lives in San Francisco and is working on another novel.*

Walker's recurring themes are racism and sexism. She seeks to render the black woman—in her view the most oppressed American—more visible and to celebrate the black woman's strength and endurance. Although she chooses black women as her primary subject, whenever Walker gives us a character (in her fiction) or herself (in her essays) surviving oppression or suffering—and growing—she gives witness to the human potential for beauty that is universal.

1 It is a bright summer day in 1947. My father, a fat, funny man with beautiful eyes and a subversive wit, is trying to decide which of his eight children he will take with him to the county fair. My mother, of course, will not go. She is knocked out from getting most of us ready: I hold my neck stiff against the pressure of her knuckles as she hastily completes the braiding and then beribboning of my hair.

2 My father is the driver for the rich old white lady up the road. Her name is Miss Mey. She owns all the land for miles around, as well as the house in which we live. All I remember about her is that she once offered to pay my mother thirty-five cents for cleaning her house, raking up piles of her magnolia leaves, and washing her family's clothes, and that my mother—she of no money, eight children, and a chronic earache—refused it. But I do not think of this in 1947. I am two and a half years old. I want to go everywhere my daddy goes. I am excited at the prospect of riding in a car. Someone has told me fairs are fun. That there is room in the car for only three of us doesn't faze me at all. Whirling happily in my starchy frock, showing off my biscuit-polished patent-leather shoes and lavender socks, tossing my head in a way that makes my ribbons bounce, I stand, hands on hips, before my father. "Take me, Daddy," I say with assurance; "I'm the prettiest!"

3 Later, it does not surprise me to find myself in Miss Mey's shiny black car, sharing the back seat with the other lucky ones. Does not surprise me that I thoroughly enjoy the fair. At home that night I tell the unlucky ones all I can remember about the merry-go-round, the man who eats live chickens, and the teddy bears, until they say: that's enough, baby Alice. Shut up now, and go to sleep.

4 It is Easter Sunday, 1950. I am dressed in a green, flocked, scalloped-hem dress (handmade by my adoring sister, Ruth) that has its own smooth satin petticoat and tiny hot-pink roses tucked into each scallop. My shoes, new T-strap patent leather, again highly biscuit-polished. I

am six years old and have learned one of the longest Easter speeches to be heard that day, totally unlike the speech I said when I was two: "Easter lilies / pure and white / blossom in / the morning light." When I rise to give my speech I do so on a great wave of love and pride and expectation. People in the church stop rustling their new crinolines. They seem to hold their breath. I can tell they admire my dress, but it is my spirit, bordering on sassiness (womanishness), they secretly applaud.

5 "That girl's a little *mess,*" they whisper to each other, pleased.

6 Naturally I say my speech without stammer or pause, unlike those who stutter, stammer, or, worst of all, forget. This is before the word "beautiful" exists in people's vocabulary, but "Oh, isn't she the *cutest* thing!" frequently floats my way. "And got so much sense!" they gratefully add . . . for which thoughtful addition I thank them to this day.

7 *It was great fun being cute. But then, one day, it ended.*

8 I am eight years old and a tomboy. I have a cowboy hat, cowboy boots, checkered shirt and pants, all red. My playmates are my brothers, two and four years older than I. Their colors are black and green, the only difference in the way we are dressed. On Saturday nights we all go to the picture show, even my mother; Westerns are her favorite kind of movie. Back home, "on the ranch," we pretend we are Tom Mix, Hopalong Cassidy, Lash LaRue (we've even named one of our dogs Lash LaRue); we chase each other for hours rustling cattle, being outlaws, delivering damsels from distress. Then my parents decide to buy my brothers guns. These are not "real" guns. They shoot "BBs," copper pellets my brothers say will kill birds. Because I am a girl, I do not get a gun. Instantly I am relegated to the position of Indian. Now there appears a great distance between us. They shoot and shoot at everything with their new guns. I try to keep up with my bow and arrows.

9 One day while I am standing on top of our makeshift "garage"—pieces of tin nailed across some poles—holding my bow and arrow and looking out toward the fields, I feel an incredible blow in my right eye. I look down just in time to see my brother lower his gun.

10 Both brothers rush to my side. My eye stings, and I cover it with my hand. "If you tell," they say, "we will get a whipping. You don't want that to happen, do you?" I do not. "Here is a piece of wire," says the older brother, picking it up from the roof; "say you stepped on one end of it and the other flew up and hit you." The pain is beginning to start. "Yes," I say. "Yes, I will say that is what happened." If I do not say this is what happened, I know my brothers will find ways to make me wish I had. But now I will say anything that gets me to my mother.

11 Confronted by our parents we stick to the lie agreed upon. They place me on a bench on the porch and I close my left eye while they examine the right. There is a tree growing from underneath the porch that climbs past the railing to the roof. It is the last thing my right eye sees. I watch as its trunk, its branches, and then its leaves are blotted out by the rising blood.

12 I am in shock. First there is intense fever, which my father tries to break using lily leaves bound around my head. Then there are chills: my mother tries to get me to eat soup. Eventually, I do not know how, my parents learn what has happened. A week after the "accident" they take me to see a doctor. "Why did you wait so long to come?" he asks, looking into my eye and shaking his head. "Eyes are sympathetic," he says. "If one is blind, the other will likely become blind too."

13 This comment of the doctor's terrifies me. But it is really how I look that bothers me most. Where the BB pellet struck there is a glob of whitish scar tissue, a hideous cataract, on my eye. Now when I stare at people—a favorite pastime, up to now—they will stare back. Not at the "cute" little girl, but at her scar. For six years I do not stare at anyone, because I do not raise my head.

14 Years later, in the throes of a mid-life crisis, I ask my mother and sister whether I changed after the "accident." "No," they say, puzzled. "What do you mean?"

15 *What do I mean?*

16 I am eight, and, for the first time, doing poorly in school, where I have been something of a whiz since I was four. We have just moved to the place where the "accident" occurred. We do not know any of the people around us because this is a different county. The only time I see the friends I knew is when we go back to our old church. The new school is the former state penitentiary. It is a large stone building, cold and drafty, crammed to overflowing with boisterous, ill-disciplined children. On the third floor there is a huge circular imprint of some partition that has been torn out.

17 "What used to be here?" I ask a sullen girl next to me on our way past it to lunch.

18 "The electric chair," says she.

19 At night I have nightmares about the electric chair, and about all the people reputedly "fried" in it. I am afraid of the school, where all the students seem to be budding criminals.

20 "What's the matter with your eye?" they ask, critically.

21 When I don't answer (I cannot decide whether it was an "accident" or not), they shove me, insist on a fight.

22 My brother, the one who created the story about the wire, comes to my rescue. But then brags so much about "protecting" me, I become sick.

23 After months of torture at the school, my parents decide to send me back to our old community, to my old school. I live with my grandparents and the teacher they board. But there is no room for Phoebe, my cat. By the time my grandparents decide there *is* room, and I ask for my cat, she cannot be found. Miss Yarborough, the boarding teacher, takes me under her wing, and begins to teach me to play the piano. But soon she marries an African—a "prince," she says—and is whisked away to his continent.

24 At my old school there is at least one teacher who loves me. She is the teacher who "knew me before I was born" and bought my first baby clothes. It is she who makes life bearable. It is her presence that finally helps me turn on the one child at the school who continually calls me "one-eyed bitch." One day I simply grab him by his coat and beat him until I am satisfied. It is my teacher who tells me my mother is ill.

25 My mother is lying in bed in the middle of the day, something I have never seen. She is in too much pain to speak. She has an abscess in her ear. I stand looking down on her, knowing that if she dies, I cannot live. She is being treated with warm oils and hot bricks held against her cheek. Finally a doctor comes. But I must go back to my grandparents' house. The weeks pass but I am hardly aware of it. All I know is that my mother might die, my father is not so jolly, my brothers still have their guns, and I am the one sent away from home.

26 "You did not change," they say.

27 *Did I imagine the anguish of never looking up?*

28 I am twelve. When relatives come to visit I hide in my room. My cousin Brenda, just my age, whose father works in the post office and whose mother is a nurse, comes to find me. "Hello," she says. And then she asks, looking at my recent school picture, which I did not want taken, and on which the "glob," as I think of it, is clearly visible, "You still can't see out of that eye?"

29 "No," I say, and flop back on the bed over my book.

30 That night, as I do almost every night, I abuse my eye. I rant and rave at it, in front of the mirror. I plead with it to clear up before

morning. I tell it I hate and despise it. I do not pray for sight. I pray for beauty.

31 "You did not change," they say.

32 I am fourteen and baby-sitting for my brother Bill, who lives in Boston. He is my favorite brother and there is a strong bond between us. Understanding my feelings of shame and ugliness he and his wife take me to a local hospital, where the "glob" is removed by a doctor named O. Henry. There is still a small bluish crater where the scar tissue was, but the ugly white stuff is gone. Almost immediately I become a different person from the girl who does not raise her head. Or so I think. Now that I've raised my head I win the boyfriend of my dreams. Now that I've raised my head I have plenty of friends. Now that I've raised my head classwork comes from my lips as faultlessly as Easter speeches did, and I leave high school as valedictorian, most popular student, and *queen*, hardly believing my luck. Ironically, the girl who was voted most beautiful in our class (and was) was later shot twice through the chest by a male companion, using a "real" gun, while she was pregnant. But that's another story in itself. Or is it?

33 "You did not change," they say.

34 It is now thirty years since the "accident." A beautiful journalist comes to visit and to interview me. She is going to write a cover story for her magazine that focuses on my latest book. "Decide how you want to look on the cover," she says. "Glamorous, or whatever."

35 Never mind "glamorous," it is the "whatever" that I hear. Suddenly all I can think of is whether I will get enough sleep the night before the photography session: if I don't, my eye will be tired and wander, as blind eyes will.

36 At night in bed with my lover I think up reasons why I should not appear on the cover of a magazine. "My meanest critics will say I've sold out," I say. "My family will now realize I write scandalous books."

37 "But what's the real reason you don't want to do this?" he asks.

38 "Because in all probability," I say in a rush, "my eye won't be straight."

39 "It will be straight enough," he says. Then, "Besides, I thought you'd made your peace with that."

40 And I suddenly remember that I have.

41 *I remember:*

42 I am talking to my brother Jimmy, asking if he remembers anything

unusual about the day I was shot. He does not know I consider that day the last time my father, with his sweet home remedy of cool lily leaves, chose me, and that I suffered and raged inside because of this. "Well," he says, "all I remember is standing by the side of the highway with Daddy, trying to flag down a car. A white man stopped, but when Daddy said he needed somebody to take his little girl to the doctor, he drove off."

43 *I remember:*

44 I am in the desert for the first time. I fall totally in love with it. I am so overwhelmed by its beauty. I confront for the first time, consciously, the meaning of the doctor's words years ago: "Eyes are sympathetic. If one is blind, the other will likely become blind too." I realize I have dashed about the world madly, looking at this, looking at that, storing up images against the fading of the light. ***But I might have missed seeing the desert!*** The shock of that possibility—and gratitude for over twenty-five years of sight—sends me literally to my knees. Poem after poem comes—which is perhaps how poets pray.

On Sight

I am so thankful I have seen
The Desert
And the creatures in the desert
And the desert Itself.

The desert has its own moon
Which I have seen
With my own eye.
There is no flag on it.

Trees of the desert have arms
All of which are always up
That is because the moon is up
The sun is up
Also the sky
The stars
Clouds
None with flags.

If there *were* flags, I doubt
the trees would point.
Would you?

45 *But mostly, I remember this:*

46 I am twenty-seven, and my baby daughter is almost three. Since her birth I have worried about her discovery that her mother's eyes are different from other people's. Will she be embarrassed? I think. What will she say? Every day she watches a television program called "Big Blue Marble." It begins with a picture of the earth as it appears from the moon. It is bluish, a little battered-looking, but full of light, with whitish clouds swirling around it. Every time I see it I weep with love, as if it is a picture of Grandma's house. One day when I am putting Rebecca down for her nap, she suddenly focuses on my eye. Something inside me cringes, gets ready to try to protect myself. All children are cruel about physical differences, I know from experience, and that they don't always mean to be is another matter. I assume Rebecca will be the same.

47 But no-o-o-o. She studies my face intently as we stand, her inside and me outside her crib. She even holds my face maternally between her dimpled little hands. Then, looking every bit as serious and lawyerlike as her father, she says, as if it may just possibly have slipped my attention: "Mommy, there's a *world* in your eye." (As in, "Don't be alarmed, or do anything crazy.") And then, gently, but with great interest: "Mommy, where did you *get* that world in your eye?"

48 For the most part, the pain left then. (So what, if my brothers grew up to buy even more powerful pellet guns for their sons and to carry real guns themselves. So what, if a young "Morehouse man" once nearly fell off the steps of Trevor Arnett Library because he thought my eyes were blue.) Crying and laughing I ran to the bathroom, while Rebecca mumbled and sang herself off to sleep. Yes indeed, I realized, looking into the mirror. There *was* a world in my eye. And I saw that it was possible to love it: that in fact, for all it had taught me of shame and anger and inner vision, I *did* love it. Even to see it drifting out of orbit in boredom, or rolling up out of fatigue, not to mention floating back at attention in excitement (bearing witness, a friend has called it), deeply suitable to my personality, and even characteristic of me.

49 That night I dream I am dancing to Stevie Wonder's song "Always" (the name of the song is really "As," but I hear it as "Always"). As I dance, whirling and joyous, happier than I've ever been in my life, another bright-faced dancer joins me. We dance and kiss each other and hold each other through the night. The other dancer has obviously come through all right, as I have done. She is beautiful, whole and free. And she is also me.

QUESTIONS FOR ANALYSIS AND DISCUSSION

1. What organizational pattern does Walker use?
2. Why should this piece be called a personal essay rather than autobiography? How does it differ from autobiography?
3. In what sense is it correct to say that the essay examines one experience?
4. Does Walker tell of her experience because it is common to many of us? Because it is shocking or unusual? Because there are lessons or truths to be gained from it? Her subject is her eye accident; what is her thesis?
5. Walker weaves several issues into her primary subject. Why does she tell us that her family did not think she had changed after her accident? Why mention the desert and include the poem?
6. In the introduction you read that Walker's recurring themes are racism and sexism. Although these issues are not primarily what "Beauty" is about, what passages illustrate that racism and sexism are never entirely out of her vision or her writing?
7. A number of lines throughout the essay are italicized. What do they contribute to the essay?
8. Analyze Walker's style, focusing especially on her sentence patterns and sentence length. What tone does she achieve through her style? What does she gain by the sentence patterns she has selected?

"*Education*"

E. B. WHITE

For a biographical sketch of White, see page 70. The following essay is one he wrote for Harper's *magazine (March 1939) and then collected in* One Man's Meat *(1943).*

Read "Education" with care, examining White's organization, use of examples, and elements of style. From your analysis should emerge an understanding of White's views on education.

1 I have an increasing admiration for the teacher in the country school where we have a third-grade scholar in attendance. She not only undertakes to instruct her charges in all the subjects of the first three grades,

but she manages to function quietly and effectively as a guardian of their health, their clothes, their habits, their mothers, and their snowball engagements. She has been doing this sort of Augean task for twenty years, and is both kind and wise. She cooks for the children on the stove that heats the room, and she can cool their passions or warm their soup with equal competence. She conceives their costumes, cleans up their messes, and shares their confidences. My boy already regards his teacher as his great friend, and I think tells her a great deal more than he tells us.

2 The shift from city school to country school was something we worried about quietly all last summer. I have always rather favored public school over private school, if only because in public school you meet a greater variety of children. This bias of mine, I suspect, is partly an attempt to justify my own past (I never knew anything but public schools) and partly an involuntary defense against getting kicked in the shins by a young ceramist on his way to the kiln. My wife was unacquainted with public schools, never having been exposed (in her early life) to anything more public than the washroom of Miss Winsor's. Regardless of our backgrounds, we both knew that the change in schools was something that concerned not us but the scholar himself. We hoped it would work out all right. In New York our son went to a medium-priced private institution with semi-progressive ideas of education, and modern plumbing. He learned fast, kept well, and we were satisfied. It was an electric, colorful, regimented existence with moments of pleasurable pause and giddy incident. The day the Christmas angel fainted and had to be carried out by one of the Wise Men was educational in the highest sense of the term. Our scholar gave imitations of it around the house for weeks afterward, and I doubt if it ever goes completely out of his mind.

3 His days were rich in formal experience. Wearing overalls and an old sweater (the accepted uniform of the private seminary), he sallied forth at morn accompanied by a nurse or a parent and walked (or was pulled) two blocks to a corner where the school bus made a flag stop. This flashy vehicle was as punctual as death: seeing us waiting at the cold curb, it would sweep to a halt, open its mouth, suck the boy in, and spring away with an angry growl. It was a good deal like a train picking up a bag of mail. At school the scholar was worked on for six or seven hours by half a dozen teachers and a nurse, and was revived on orange juice in mid-morning. In a cinder court he played games supervised by an athletic instructor, and in a cafeteria he ate lunch worked out by a dietitian. He soon learned to read with gratifying facility and

discernment and to make Indian weapons of a semi-deadly nature. Whenever one of his classmates fell low of a fever the news was put on the wires and there were breathless phone calls to physicians, discussing periods of incubation and allied magic.

4 In the country all one can say is that the situation is different, and somehow more casual. Dressed in corduroys, sweatshirt, and short rubber boots, and carrying a tin dinner-pail, our scholar departs at crack of dawn for the village school, two and a half miles down the road, next to the cemetery. When the road is open and the car will start, he makes the journey by motor, courtesy of his old man. When the snow is deep or the motor is dead or both, he makes it on the hoof. In the afternoons he walks or hitches all or part of the way home in fair weather, gets transported in foul. The schoolhouse is a two-room frame building, bungalow type, shingles stained a burnt brown with weather-resistant stain. It has a chemical toilet in the basement and two teachers above stairs. One takes the first three grades, the other the fourth, fifth, and sixth. They have little or no time for individual instruction, and no time at all for the esoteric. They teach what they know themselves, just as fast and as hard as they can manage. The pupils sit still at their desks in class, and do their milling around outdoors during recess.

5 There is no supervised play. They play cops and robbers (only they call it "Jail") and throw things at one another—snowballs in winter, rose hips in fall. It seems to satisfy them. They also construct darts, pinwheels, and "pick-up sticks" (jackstraws), and the school itself does a brisk trade in penny candy, which is for sale right in the classroom and which contains "surprises." The most highly prized surprise is a fake cigarette, made of cardboard, fiendishly lifelike.

6 The memory of how apprehensive we were at the beginning is still strong. The boy was nervous about the change too. The tension, on that first fair morning in September when we drove him to school, almost blew the windows out of the sedan. And when later we picked him up on the road, wandering along with his little blue lunch-pail, and got his laconic report "All right" in answer to our inquiry about how the day had gone, our relief was vast. Now, after almost a year of it, the only difference we can discover in the two school experiences is that in the country he sleeps better at night—and *that* probably is more the air than the education. When grilled on the subject of school-in-country *vs.* school-in-city, he replied that the chief difference is that the day seems to go so much quicker in the country. "Just like lightning," he reported.

QUESTIONS FOR ANALYSIS AND DISCUSSION

1. How is White's essay organized? Describe the organization precisely, indicating the topic of each paragraph.
2. An analysis of organization reveals White's contrast purpose. What, exactly, is he contrasting? (Have an answer that is more precise than "city school vs. country school.")
3. Stating the precise subjects of contrast is essential to understanding White's thesis, since he does not state a thesis in the essay. What is White's main point?
4. One way White reinforces his implied thesis is through organization, but he also uses contrasting details, contrasting sentence patterns, and metaphors to make his attitude clear. Find several examples of contrasting details and of sentences that are similar but importantly varied to highlight the schools' differences. You will want to note the effect, for example, of White's use of active and passive voice. What is the effect of each of the following sentences:

   The dog jumped on the boy. (Active)
   The boy was jumped on by the dog. (Passive)

5. The boy's best-remembered event from his city-school days is the fainting Christmas angel. Why does White give us this detail? What is its significance?
6. Perhaps White's vivid metaphors are most effective in conveying his attitude. Analyze two metaphors, explaining how they express White's view of the city school.
7. Describe the essay's tone. What pose does White adopt in this essay? How serious is his attack on the city school? Is his praise of rural life extreme?

Content to Be in My Place

ELLEN GOODMAN

For a biographical sketch of Goodman, see page 42. Although she does devote some of her columns to political commentary, Goodman also examines personal and social issues through the light of her own experiences, thus turning her newspaper column into a personal essay. "Content to Be in My Place" was syndicated in various newspapers on August 13, 1983.

1 CASCO BAY, Maine–The dirt road by the cottage leads me almost daily into the bushes. I seem unable to pass the raspberries that hang like bright ornaments, final gifts from branches that have turned brown.

2 I reach out for one small handful, easing the fragile fruit from its core. And then I am caught, following the crop, migrating from one bush to another, deep again in the middle of a field.

3 I am not the only worker in this space, just the largest. To the right of me, three bees mine a stalk of goldenrod with the concentration of a road crew working a jackhammer. Nearby, a monarch butterfly lights on one wild flower and then another and another in a flight of indecision. The sounds of insects and birds surround me in a quadraphonic breeze.

4 In most ways, we workers are oblivious to each other, each intent on business. There is enough here for all of us, and we coexist easily.

5 I come to the field for the berries. But also for something rarer, this sense of coexistence. I make a peaceful entrance into the natural order. I am not harnessing it, but am simply in it.

6 I have a sense of well-being here that is rare in my urban world. In the cities and suburbs, people are exempt from most of the rhythms of the world. Perhaps we are hostile to them. We put up screens and windshield wipers. Our air comes conditioned and our days and nights come from the electric company.

7 The corner of the office where I work has no windows. The climate is what they call controlled. I can be there all day without knowing if it's hot or cold outside. I commute in a machine on pavement, following the directions of red and green lights. My work day is determined by a clock that remains the same through all tides, moons and seasons.

8 A friend who is an anthropologist tells me that there are two sorts of cultures. In one, humans feel aloof from nature. The natural world is their raw material, something that may prove useful to them. In the other cultures, humans describe a place for themselves in the natural order. You can tell the so-called advanced civilizations, she says, by how far they have retreated from the earth.

9 Well, I suppose that is true. I suppose we are the civilized people. Our own country was built by nature's conquerers, not coexisters. Our short history is dominated by people who made things–bridges, houses, roads, cars, computers–out of mountains, forests, earth. In our economy the tree is timber, and coal is fuel, and even the river is energy.

10 Here, we are all manufacturers in one subtle way or another. We call ourselves creative only when we recreate nature with our own hands.

We are like gardeners who turn bushes into topiary, photographers who review the world in rectangles, writers who reshape experiences into columns.

11 I live most of the year in this modern urban world. I choose a roof over my head and central heating and a word processor. I am hardly a nature girl. I do not like the place I have been assigned in the mosquito's food chain.

12 Yet there are times when our separation from the rest of the world feels like alienation. There are times when it seems peculiar that we have to travel to special preserves—parks, islands, countrysides, bushes—just to recover a sense of belonging. It's peculiar that we have to leave work and cities in order to see the world for what it is, not for what we can do with it.

13 The small pot by my side soon will be full. My co-workers, still preoccupied with their tasks, won't even notice my departure. Perhaps tonight, in the cottage, I will do what people do, make something—jam—of these raspberries. But right now I am content to be here, in my place.

QUESTIONS FOR ANALYSIS AND DISCUSSION

1. What is the occasion for Goodman's column—that is, what specific experience does she write about?
2. What paragraphs are devoted to Goodman's experience? What details do you find most effective in re-creating that experience?
3. What sentence "turns the corner," announcing the beginning of Goodman's reflections on berry picking in Maine? How can you tell?
4. To develop her reflections, Goodman uses contrast. What two worlds, or more accurately, two ways of behaving in the world, are being contrasted? State, in a sentence or two, the precise point of Goodman's contrast, revising your sentences several times if necessary to be on target. Avoid the simplistic—and inaccurate—statement that she contrasts urban and rural life.
5. To help get question 4 right, list the details that establish the contrast and shape Goodman's point.
6. Although she is contemplating a serious subject, Goodman's humor—whether rendered as a knowing chuckle or biting irony—is never far away. List some examples of her humor in this essay. Is her humor light or biting in this column?
7. How does recognizing the tone of her humor help us understand her attitude toward her subject? Is she exposing a great social ill and demanding

immediate change? If not, how would you describe her purpose? (Compare her stance or pose to White's in "Education.")

8. In paragraph 10, Goodman gives three examples of what we usually call creativity. What do the three examples have in common? What sound observations does Goodman make about writing?

Bobcats

JEFFREY COOPER

To listen to Jeffrey Cooper talk about the Sonoran desert is to believe that he was born under a Saguaro cactus and adopted by a deer family. But Cooper came to the high desert of Arizona by way of California; he was born in Eagle Rock in 1954 and attended both Hayward and Humboldt state universities in Northern California, majoring in English literature and minoring in environmental studies. His knowledge of the desert has come primarily through independent study.

Cooper has been the resident naturalist since 1980 at the Wickenburg Inn, a guest ranch northwest of Phoenix. His tasks include not only maintaining the inn's nature center and conducting guests on nature walks, but also keeping account of and helping to preserve the ranch's abundant wild life, especially its endangered species. Cooper describes part of his task as being an interpreter of the desert. "We do not encounter just the rocks or just the birds," he writes; "we encounter a place composed of many elements. It is the landscape and texture of the place as a whole that interests me—so I attempt to portray the [desert's] totality."

His words aptly describe his essay on bobcats, an essay not about bobcats only but about the total desert environment. Cooper sees himself primarily as a poet but views both his poetry and his essays as "the essential core, the ethical and emotional foundation" of his work as a naturalist. As writers, we can take some comfort from Cooper's assertion that while his poems frequently "walk out of [his] mouth, [his] essays struggle in their birth."

1 The tracks began to disappear as she had started to climb the slope. She seemed to have vanished into the talus.[1] I had entered her interstitial[2] domain and she had become invisible.

---

[1]Sloping rocks at a cliff base.—Ed.

[2]Pertaining to the narrow spaces among the rocks.—Ed.

2 I had first picked up her tracks at the pipe fillstand that drips, forming a small pool. She had come up for water late in the afternoon and then headed back, across familiar ground to become two-inch depressions in the sand where she crossed the arroyo.[3] This is just about where her trail vanished and the story begins. "Creative naturalism."

3 As I paused to listen, I heard a slight cry seemingly up beyond the edge of the escarpment, a sound vaguely resembling the more familiar meow, but hushed. A bark-cough. The bobcat (*Lynx refus*) is normally a nearly silent, shy, reclusive animal. But they are indeed capable of a variety of vocal expressions. Wheezing meows and shrieks; whines and outright screams. Strident, piercing sounds that can stop you dead in your tracks on a moonless night and cause you to recoil in horror as some seemingly terrible travesty is being committed. Bobcat lovemaking. If you are lucky enough to hear it, you will know.

4 They will also make the sounds more familiar to your pet safely curled asleep on the bed at this very moment. It is the latter that this present sound brought to mind.

5 But this animal was no pet. She was struggling in her peculiarly solitary manner to hold her own in a world of increasing hostility. Bobcats are secretive beings, not liking to be disturbed, even by their own kind. And that is getting more difficult as the desert is carved up and served as subdivisions. The all-terrain vehicles violate even the most remote, once sacred, places.

6 Trapping is still popular with some in these parts, the practice of a life-style fiercely clung to even as the resource vanishes. Several thousand in the state of Arizona every year. Nearly 4,000 reported to the Game & Fish Department in 1983. I said *reported.*

7 The other cats have paved the way with their fur. The mountain lion is all but gone from many parts of the desert today. Estimates vary as to their current numbers in Arizona and the rest of the West, but their status has clearly become more precarious in the past few decades. The jaguar, once found as far north as the south rim of the Grand Canyon, appears only as a rare transient from Mexico. The ocelot likewise has disappeared from the state.

8 Just two more of the victims sacrificed. Defined as: a resource, an enemy destroyed, an ancient clan symbol used up as part of the swelling tide of the conquered. The extinct. The used up. Those that came before us. Also gone from Arizona for decades, the wolves, methodically

[3] A small gulch with steep sides and flat floor that carries water during heavy rains but is otherwise dry.—Ed.

hunted, suffered the same fate, the very last one being killed on sacred ground in Araviapa canyon.[4] Yes, trapping is still fairly popular in these parts. I have a shed full of rusting steel leghold traps I would be pleased to show you if you doubt it. I spring and confiscate them whenever encountered. It is illegal, but what they represent in suffering and cruelty surpass this, at least where I walk.

9 If you're doing it to feed your family, then I'm with you, but I've yet to meet a trapper who was. The bulk are engaging in "sport" or hobbies, perceived as necessary to maintain domination, teaching their sons to be Men, Men in the West. What year is this? 1885? Walk around Wickenburg[5] on a Thursday afternoon in August; then you tell me. We certainly keep different clocks. The Romance of the Wild West lives. Davey Crockett and his coonskin cap. Mountain men trapping beaver on the Verde,[6] the Gila.[7] Beaver in the desert? You bet! Before the Bureau of Reclamation and the Army Corps of Engineers poured their concrete into the water and the various impoundments destroyed the critical riverine, riparian[8] habitat. Yes, I guess we can say that trapping is still, for some, favorite fun; to others a savage, archaic thrust of ego. The self-centeredness of perception. We, humanity, so it goes, are at the center of all, and the other lives we find around us, both plant and animal, are there for our use, our disposal. Value is derived from what it can do for us. What is it worth? Multiple Use. Balanced Use. Resource Management.

10 She and her feline kin are no exception to this process.

II.

11 I imagine she had sprung lightly from rock to rock as she made her way up a gentle depression in the cliff face. It is as if when the cliff rose up it sagged a bit and fell back upon itself. As I walk I cause minor rockslides even while trying to be quiet. I am reminded of the words of Joseph Wood Krutch: "Whatever man does or produces, noise seems to be an unavoidable by-product. Perhaps he can, as he now tends to believe, do anything. But he cannot do it quietly." I imagine the ravens floating above me to be laughing at my small form creeping up the cliff.

---

[4]A canyon southeast of Phoenix rich in wildlife. – Ed.

[5]A small town northwest of Phoenix. – Ed.

[6]A river that runs through Phoenix and west to the Colorado River. – Ed.

[7]A river that runs across southern Arizona to the Colorado River. – Ed.

[8]River bank. – Ed.

12 At the top or the edge where it becomes a hill again, covered on the southwest slope with many wonderfully old Saguaro cactuses, there is an ancient Palo Verde tree with some of the bobcat's old feces forming a marking of some kind. There was far too much scat ordered about for this to be simply coincidental. There was a fresh urine spot and the faint smell of cat lingering. I heard nothing as I listened for a clue to where she had gone; then I noticed the fresh scratches on the trunk of the Palo Verde revealing cambium.

13 Suddenly I saw her, not ten meters in front of me just beyond the tree. She was crouching in the brittle bush as if she had just become aware of my presence. Perhaps she had been dozing in the sun, getting the last warmth of the January day. Her dazzling yellow-green eyes focused on mine; we met for a moment. A lifetime of such moments. And then she was gone again. Into the last light, the long rays that exaggerate the desert. In her element she becomes invisible, part of the shades and shadows. An encounter with such a solitary and acutely sensitive animal was the lesson I sought. Now I would leave her to herself for this day and add another piece to the puzzle that is my understanding of *Lynx rufus*, another dimension of diversity of life in the Sonoran[9] desert.

14 In a few days her tracks were covered by eight inches of snow. The desert under an uncommon and mysterious blessing. Some trees heavily weighted broke under the strain. Many broken branches. The trees, mostly Palo Verdes, are not adapted to snowfall of any consequence, and were fully leafed out at the time.

15 Later I found her tracks again. She had sheltered in a small cave protected but with a clear view of the surrounding area. A variety of debris betrayed her prior use or the use of others that had come before for perhaps the same reason. There were several sets of tracks in the ground that would thaw by day and freeze at night. She had traveled back and forth across the top of the sheer cliff as if surveying the whitened desert with a strange bewilderment.

16 Some of the old-timers can't remember such snow in this area. Memories that extend to the beginning of this century. A rather profound occurrence really. I don't think that I have ever heard the desert so quiet; even in the scorching midday sun of summer there is some sound, if not from the heat itself. A hum. You learn to recognize it. But in the snow it was really quiet. The occasional cracking of branches was the

---

[9]Desert that stretches from northwest Mexico, Mexico's Sonora state, into Arizona.—Ed.

only sound. The snow clung to the Saguaros as insulation, which indeed it was, perhaps saving them this time from an early death by freezing. A rare but nonetheless essential part of the desert ecology and the plants' tolerance of extremes. Not only the intense heat and drought, but also the cold of relatively hard frosts. This is why so much of the cactus is found on the southern exposures of the desert ridges and hills. They climb up out of the pools of colder air in the valley bottoms. The rather abrupt vegetational changes in the desert are fascinating; as microenvironmental changes occur, the subtleties and frailties of the desert are exposed. And temperature is one of the important determiners of vegetation patterns. Water or moisture in the soil is the most important regulating factor. It is the basis for life in the desert as for the entire planet. It is on the basis of its general scarcity that we define the desert.

17 This bobcat frequently used the fillstand pool. There were very few if any other permanent sources of water in the four or five square miles she actively used. Within this area she had several dens. I followed her track to the top of a small rise where she had stopped to look and listen, to smell the air and read its messages. She then had ambled, with a peculiar gait like a jackrabbit, down and across the plateau and into the valley beyond. It was nearly dark again, and any movement became part of the shadows, tawny with the last glow of the day. I wished her well and apologized.

QUESTIONS FOR ANALYSIS AND DISCUSSION

1. What is the specific occasion about which Cooper writes?
2. Personal essayists can recount an experience in such a way as to imply a thesis (White, "Education"), or they can describe an occasion and then reflect on it (Goodman, "Content to Be in My Place"). Cooper's organization is more complex than either of these options, for he blends recounting with several passages of reflection. Analyze Cooper's structure, noting specific paragraphs devoted to specific topics, thus: paragraph 1 to . . . : tracking the bobcat, etc.
3. How does Cooper bring these several topics together to create a unified essay?
4. How would you describe Cooper's "voice" in this piece? (Review White's list of some possibilities in his "Foreword" to help you think about the "person" we meet in this essay.)
5. What gives his voice weight? What can you learn about personal essay writing from "Bobcats"?

6. What is Cooper's attitude toward the bobcat? Toward the Sonoran desert? Try writing a single thesis sentence that ties together his several subjects and general attitude.
7. Analyze Cooper's writing style, considering sentence structure and sentence length in particular. What is the effect of his frequent short fragments?
8. Explain and comment on the effectiveness of the metaphor in paragraph 5.
9. Explain Cooper's meaning when he writes in paragraph 13 that "we met for a moment. A lifetime of such moments." Why, at the end of his essay, does he write "I wished her well and apologized"?
10. In what sense do Cooper and Goodman share similar attitudes toward the natural world? How do they differ?

Cyclical Time: Reinventing the Wheel

FLOYD C. STUART

An associate professor of English at Norwich University, Floyd C. Stuart (b. 1940) holds degrees from Fordham and John Carroll universities and the State University of New York at Binghamton. He has published over 100 poems in journals and anthologies and a number of essays in various magazines of both local and national circulation. Both "Cyclical Time," first published in Harper's *in May 1981, and "Only Cows Were Killed"* (Harper's, *May 1982) have been reprinted in college anthologies.*

Stuart has shared some thoughtful, personal remarks about his reasons for writing "Cyclical Time" and his perceptions of the writing process, remarks that can best be described as a brief essay on essay writing. They follow the essay as "Comments."

"Cyclical Time" may test your reading skills more than the other pieces in this chapter, but it will reward that effort.

> *I am learning to ride a bicycle. I have so far succeeded that*
> *I can get on sometimes and go quite a good many rods.*
> *But our wheel has some peculiar perversities.*
> —*David S. Kellogg, M.D.*[1]

[1]From *A Doctor at All Hours,* copyright © 1970 by Allan S. Everest. Published by The Stephen Greene Press, Brattleboro, Vermont.

1 In my middle age a boyhood lust has flared up again – bike riding; solitary cruising through miles of northern New England. For years I sped down our Vermont road with eyes glazed on a spot beyond the windshield, which kept throwing me curves. Now I study the character of pothole and crack, and the highway stretches out with the intimacy of a familiar body. I pedal and pedal, tracing the slow revolution of summer in what lies crushed on asphalt: peepers, salamanders, fat August grasshoppers. One afternoon, precisely on schedule, millions of flying ants hatch, plastering me face to foot like an automobile headlamp. Life is still abundant; I am still the inadvertent murderer.

2 Flat space is scarce here. It kills me to think a hill has a crest I could be reaching even faster. I haven't bent to my circumscribed world with a consistent will, and each trip out I must be broken again to that discipline of having no goal. Hunched over handlebars, I teach myself to look into the little circle of all there is. I see only the next toe stroking in; think nothing beyond this measured gulp of breath. For a time, I savor the world's sparseness.

3 I bicycle sometimes between Roxbury and Montpelier, eighteen miles along a lake bottom. For the whole trip it seems that I can reach out my arms and touch the mountains that formed either shore. Roxbury has been here only since 1781; the lake dates from about 12,000 years before that. The old railroad station, a small red box, is now the town clerk's office. If I face the station, all the rain that falls at my right will flow north, and all the rain that falls at my left will flow south. This is the southern threshold of Lake Roxbury, a lake no early settler ever saw.

4 In front of the station is a slab of polished antique verde the size of a gravestone, a monument to the war dead. The serpentine, dark green veined with buff, was quarried in Roxbury earlier this century. It's even older than Lake Roxbury, and underlay these mountains when they were flat ocean floor.

5 Geologists named Lake Roxbury, discovering it long after it was gone. I whirl the ratchets and wheel of my ten-speed and gaze up through a thousand feet of water. Where clouds should be, I see the bellies of icebergs.

6 The last time cold scraped this country clean, these hills (the highest 2,400 feet) were under two miles of ice. The land sank under the weight (later it sprang back by about four feet to the mile); lee tops of mountains were plucked sheer; heels of ice slipped in groaning jerks down valleys. Two miles above the old frame house and its slant-ceiling

bedrooms, which sleep all the people who make things real for me, was white waste and wind and wind.

7 But when the ice began to go, and these hills became nunataks, mountaintops poking through the glacier–here was the landscape of desolation. It's this jagged, lifeless rock and ice I would keep out when I put my arms around a daughter. This has too much the look of one's own soul.

8 When summers began to melt more than winter snows built up, the glacier grew rotten. Streams burbled along its surface, cascaded off the snout, dumping hills of rubble. Rivers wormed ice tunnels inside. Sitting under a tree, sucking at the tepid water bottle. I see it all so vividly, as if some part of me had been here then, an ice crystal with fierce memory. The narrow lake wound north from the railroad station seven miles to my house in Northfield. Bare hills stood on either side, lichens beginning to grow on them, and at my front porch that sheer white wall, retreating more than it rumbled forward, calved icebergs.

9 Lake Roxbury may have drained dry, but other lakes of the era survive, often strung five or six together on a thread of stream, so we call them "paternoster ponds." Lakes are particularly fragile phenomena, quivering with the last vagary of weather, and fated for an early death in the geologist's sense of time. Our cliché for a lake is a mirror or a face; still water is an emblem of ourselves, transitory, profound, never quite accurately reflecting the world it confronts. A lake sparks ebulliently, gold plate spun in the sun. A cloud passes, and immediately it is a cataracted eye. Peer in: dull green depths, flash of perch–it's like leaning perilously over the edge of a dream.

10 Last summer my friend Roger and I, with our boys, glided onto a glacial lake. We launched his canoe from a small mud beach, but mostly the waterline lacked such subtlety. Heavily wooded mountains hunkered right up to the lake, and in places cliffs without even a toehold struck straight down into the water. We pulled the canoe up on a ledge that rounded out of the lake smooth as a whale's back. Roger showed how we could sit on the side of the ledge as if in a chair and let our legs dangle in the water up to our knees, our toes touching nothing. Then he did something I still don't like. He eased off the rock, faced us at arm's length, bit a block of air, and sank. His bald head in the deepening green water turned yellow, his skin aging suddenly to parchment. He shriveled. He became a wizened head at a cannibal's belt. A gibbering monkey. Refraction wiggled his shoulders like a fish.

11 He never touched bottom. We grew uneasy about his ever getting

back. The old timers outdo one another describing the lengths of sounding line they've unwound here into the lake. If one of them ever finds bottom, he will never tell.

12 Roger returned to us slowly, his jiggly form settling into focus like someone coming back from memory in an old movie. We swam after that, and walked about on the scorching rock. Our feet left queer splotches, fossil tracks of smaller dinosaurs; they faded as we watched.

13 And so I sit beside my bike in the dust of the shoulder below cumulus that one can easily mistake for icebergs. Roger takes his sounding down; I pedal lake bottom, gazing up. Mystery is our ambience. It is not simply puzzle but a condition of being, the nourishing incompleteness we float in, rich ache and consolation of our living. Sometimes one of us bursts to the surface, popeyed, full of a surprise he can hardly tell.

14 One sunny morning I whipped down the Roxbury road, front spokes melting into a saw blade and wind shrilling tunes through the vent holes in my helmet. I banked off the highway onto a plank bridge across the Dog River, which is really a stream, and pulled onto a gravel pit. Roots dangled through the lip of topsoil overhanging the cut. It has taken a dozen millennia to accumulate that inch or two of earth. Below are bands of clay and sand, and in between a strip of gravel. The stones are flattish, smooth, usually oblong. They are imbricated, which means they overlap one another in a tight mosaic. They tilt up slightly, offering their angles of least resistance to a current that lost its impulse eons ago. The evidence of geologists suggests that these imbricated stones were the bed of a subglacial stream that flowed under pressure uphill to the west. When I looked down by my feet, I saw the same paving in the dancing light of the Dog River. Within the distance of a man's height are stream beds thousands of years apart. I excavated a skipping stone from the cut; it sparked five times and sank in its ancient waters.

15 If only it were a matter of a man's height or a few billion light years: but I'll never be able to leap that gap between the sons and daughters I helped make, and the impersonal majesty of geologic space and time. Yet I can cup a 400-million-year-old brachiopod fossil in one hand, and in the other the chin of my living son. What must a man teach his children? You are irreplaceable. And you are, like the rest of us, a typical specimen.

16 Things die; what is more amazing is that in a few ways they stay. The various sandpits I bicycle to are often deltas that were constructed by streams entering Lake Roxbury. The bands of clay, sand, or gravel—from a fraction of an inch to several feet thick—mark old lake beds.

They tilt toward the depths of the valley. Often a stream increased in force, its current licking off layers of former lake floor, until the stream weakened and deposited new sediments at angles to the old.

17 Standing thirty feet up a sand cliff, I dig out a narrow shelf to squat on. The sun beats on my back; sweat bands off my forehead onto my bare toes. Here is a perfect cross section of ripple marks, just like those washboard bumps I've felt in the shallows of living Lake Willoughby. After a little practice with my penknife, I can lay a ripple out in three dimensions. Ghost wind shivers ghost water. In a scalloped band of clay, halfway up the abandoned Northfield dump, lies summer 12,000 years ago, the waltz of air with wave, the exact lilt of reflected light.

18 Ice splits from the glacier snout, flinging up white plumes. No one hears the groaning, like a solid house being crowbarred apart, the rumble of ice dropping like a wall. Night. And in the east—over a treeless, grassless, earthless Turkey Hill—the moon rises, and a herd of placid ice humps duplicate themselves on the mirror of Lake Roxbury. Everything waits.

19 A glacier tends to slip down its trough in fits and starts, plucking rocks or boulders as it goes. On smooth outcrops of ledge near our town swimming pool, you can sees scratches where rocks, held in the fist of the glacier, made for an inch or two their crude marks beside the initials teenagers chip out to immortalize their love. Years ago it was a puzzle how boulders that showed signs of this glacial grinding could be found inside lacustrine deposits. How could rocks that had been frozen in the bottom of the glacier end up between layers of sediment out on the lake floor?

20 In the old Northfield dump there is a steady dribble of boulders, hamsized chunks of angular schist, from a band ten feet up the sandbank. Often the hard, greenish rocks have glacial striations. Geologists know now that they were rafted there, frozen in icebergs that calved into Lake Roxbury. Bit by bit, the scored schist melted out, and tumbled hundreds of feet to the dark lake bottom, stirring up mud bombs. They were buried in sediment. Sometime an ice hunk was entombed in sediment to melt later: the roof of its hole caved in, and the varves—neat strata of lake bed—collapsed in a roil of multicolored sands and clays that today looks like a fossil bomb burst. These, 12,000-year-old dramas without human life are here to see, dry as bone, in the abandoned dump, until the rains come to wash them out.

21 Late April into November, our usual snowless season, I bicycle through ocean, ice field, steamy swamp—my town has been all of these.

What eons give us, we obliterate in a lunge of the bulldozer's bucket. But I am awed by what the mind can reconstruct.

22 Perhaps most of any second is irrevocably lost. Pedaling up a steep gulf, I stop beside the brook that has worn this notch between mountains. The modulations of water over rock are endless from ice clink to birdsong. As I whip down into the next valley, wind strums the metal bike, and insects ping off my helmet, crisp little deaths. But not all is lost. In a gouged-out garbage dump, in sand as dry as any desert's, I hear an ancient rhythm of wind and water. I want to give my children ears to hear it.

23 The bits of country, the few humans we love best are everything to us, and just specks of the whirling galaxies. I am trying to balance unresolvable contradictions, scintillant moment and vast white nonatak of time. But our wheel has some peculiar perversities.

Comments on CYCLICAL TIME: REINVENTING THE WHEEL

FLOYD C. STUART

The official (and partly true) reason I give for writing "Cyclical Time" is that I was going to teach a course called Advanced Composition, and I thought that I should write and publish the kind of informal essay I would require of my students. A simple case of "Professor, put up or shut up."

Perhaps there is a deeper reason why I wrote "Cyclical Time." Over the years, some very diverse things had become important to me: rocks, fossils, and all matters geological; bike riding through the Green Mountains of Vermont, where I live; my own awe at the paradoxical grandeur and insignificance of human beings against the vastness of geological time. Then one day I suspected that my diverse interests and experiences might have interconnections that so far I had missed. I began to write this essay. The act of writing for me is not simply transferring a preconceived notion, a "whole in the head" (atrocious pun intended), onto paper, but is a process of discovering what I think. I mis-see; I mis-write; if I'm lucky, things slowly come clearer. In "Cyclical Time," I wanted to state as accurately as I could the "facts"—of bike riding, of the glacial geology of central Vermont—and at the same time to uncover what those "facts" might signify, what they showed me about my life.

In fits and starts, I make a few acts of faith. One is: follow your interests; no experience is worthless. Another is: forget yourself; do justice to the world "out there," to the little concrete details. Then you "express yourself" and are "original" and "have a style" without worrying about these things.

When I wrote "Cyclical Time," I was talking to myself; I was speaking to my four children, trying to put the right words on a page so that, even after I'm dead, they will still hear a man telling of his love for them and for the world. I meant for you to overhear: it's some of your business.

QUESTIONS FOR ANALYSIS AND DISCUSSION

1. Stuart's essay is more demanding reading than the others in this chapter, yet it still should be classified as a personal essay. Why is it harder to read? Why should it be called a personal essay?
2. Although Stuart does not base his reflections on one occasion or event—as Goodman does, for example—he does use one interest or hobby that generated a repeated event—and presumably ongoing reflections. His hobby is bike riding; what repeated event did his bike riding generate? What study did it lead to?
3. Why is it incorrect to say that the essay is about bike riding? Why is it incorrect to say that it is about the geology of the Roxbury area? What is Stuart's subject?
4. Although Stuart's subject is not—exactly—geology, he uses a number of terms (*verde, subglacial, brachiopod, schist*) that you might need to look up. What does Stuart's word choice tell you about his anticipated audience?
5. What is Stuart's attitude toward the contradictory realities of the human experience? How does the image of the wheel and the concept of cyclical time help to answer the question?
6. How does Stuart develop the idea of cyclical time? Examine all his references to memories and dreams.
7. Stuart begins his essay much as Goodman does—Here I am, in this place, involved in this activity—and both are in sympathy with the "seeing" of Dillard. At what point does Stuart shift from the immediacy of his bike riding experience to other issues? What does the location of the shift tell you about Stuart's primary purpose in this essay?
8. In paragraph 9, Stuart says that we see a lake—still water—as "an emblem of ourselves." What do humans share with lakes, as Stuart reveals in this paragraph?

9. Look at Stuart's description of his friend Roger's submerging in a glacial lake (paragraph 10). Why is he described as "a wizened head at a cannibal's belt," "a gibbering monkey," and a "fish"?
10. Explain in your own words, to someone who has not read "Cyclical Time," the connections between Lake Roxbury's geological history, Stuart, and Stuart's children.

STUDENT ESSAY

ALCOHOL AWARENESS

PENNY M. POTTER

Walking through the halls during Alcohol Awareness Week and listening to the joking and teasing about "getting wasted," I reflected on how different my perception of drinking alcohol is now and what precipitated that change. Growing up, consistently being reinforced by everything from advertising to family to peer pressure, I came to believe several notions about drinking. First, drinking had to be the focus of fun. Second, to drink was to be an adult, a responsible human being in control of one's life. Finally, I thought drinking was harmless. After having been arrested, handcuffed, jailed, and sent to counseling, I changed my mind.

Until my arrest, I never had any reason to believe drinking was anything but a positive form of recreation. From my earliest recollections, drinking was associated with socializing, having fun. My father, replying to my inquiry, explained, "Drinking is how grownups play." Carrying this positive attitude toward drinking, I made it the focus of my fun. Using the excuse that there was nothing to do in a small town in Illinois, my friends and I would sip White Lightning while driving on country roads. Every activity centered around consuming alcohol, tailgating at football games, "flasking" it at concerts, chugging beer at parties. The trend continued as a young adult: having wine with dinner, going to bars after work, going to weekend parties. It became impossible to imagine not drinking and still having fun.

In many cultures, alcohol consumption is a rite of passage into adulthood. Pouring a glass of wine for me at holiday dinners, my parents were indicating I was becoming an adult in their eyes. Drinking in high school, still under my parents' wing, became the forbidden fruit of adulthood. In college, attempting to make the transition to adulthood, my friends and I imitated adult behavior; after-class happy hours mirrored after-work martinis; weekend keg parties mirrored cocktail parties. Drinking became a symbol, a declaration to the world I was grown, adult.

Finally, because drinking had become synonymous with positive recreation, I thought drinking was harmless. In the first place, drinking is legal; Big Brother F.D.A. would clamp down on it if it were bad, like drugs. In the second place, it is not only accepted by society but encouraged through advertising and peer pressure. I thought of socially acceptable as good; therefore, drinking was not bad. In the third place my family and friends drank; surely they would not partake of or encourage a harmful act. By comparing, or rationalizing, I felt safe.

Sitting in the back of the police car, handcuffed, and being searched before I was put in my jail cell wasn't fun. Suspending my right to drive and forcing me to attend their Alcohol Safety Action Program, the courts suddenly made me feel like a child being punished. Gradually, over the three months I attended A.S.A.P., I learned about the many harmful effects of alcohol consumption.

What I had perceived for so long as positive and fun is, I learned, negative and serious. I was astonished to learn the definition of a social drinker: one who consumes two alcoholic beverages per week in a social setting. The counselors pointed out to me that when the consumption of alcohol increases beyond that point, it starts to be associated with recreating and relaxing. When alcohol ceases to be on the sidelines of socializing and becomes synonymous with it, it is the beginning of dependency; at this point, the disease of alcoholism can start.

I became more alcohol aware and started observing the drinking habits of my family and friends. These adults, my drinking peers, were looking less adult and more like children escaping, to varying degrees, the realities of adult problems and situations and using alcohol as their security blanket. The professional, after a tough day at work, has a few cocktails "to unwind." The introvert, being uneasy in social gatherings, has a few drinks "to loosen up." The married person, after fighting with the spouse, goes to a bar "to cool down." I myself learned I was camouflaging low self-esteem and feelings of inadequacy with that security blanket. Albeit understandable, these acts are not adult and responsible ways of handling problems.

Understanding that it is inappropriate to make drinking my social focus and to associate it with adulthood, my perceptions were changing. Learning how harmful drinking is brought me to the full, one-hundred-eighty-degree turn. Frequent consumption is harmful, destructive behavior. Thoughts are jumbled, thinking becomes vague. Alcohol clouds the real problems and anesthetizes the tissues of the body. The worst effects are uncontrollable shakes and loss of liver and pancreatic functions, resulting eventually in death. Alcohol is a drug; it destroys.

Alcohol is like a wild hyena, dogging its prey, nipping at its hind quarters, and finally encircling and devouring the parts of one's life. As with any drug, though, the problem lies not with the substance but with the ignorance of the user.

EXERCISES

1. To practice using details, word choice, and metaphors to express attitude, write a paragraph about an activity you like or dislike without including a direct statement of your feelings. Convey attitude by the way you describe the activity. (White's "Education" is your model.)
2. Compare a person you know to an object, and develop the comparison (metaphor) into a paragraph. Your topic sentence would be: "If _____ were an object, he or she would be a _____. Examine as many characteristics of the object as you can, developing the metaphor to describe several of the person's traits.
3. Joan Didion (see "Why I Write") stresses the importance of writers having pictures in their minds and then shaping them into words, and all the essayists in this chapter demonstrate the effectiveness of vivid detail. Concentrate on finding three pictures: one natural scene, one picture of a person, one brief action scene. To find your pictures, take a walk, look out your window, go to the library or cafeteria. When you have decided on your three pictures, capture each one in no more than two sentences per picture. Prepare three versions of each two-sentence picture—really change the sentences around—and decide which version you prefer. Bring all versions to class, switch papers with a classmate, and get his or her choice of the best versions. Discuss reasons for any differences of opinion.
4. Didion also talks about letting the pictures in your mind determine the best kind of sentence pattern—good advice if you are able to control a variety of patterns. Here are some possible patterns for combining sentences:

   Antithesis: Although children sweeten the day, their loss darkens the night.

   Parallel Structure: Walking makes a relaxed man, jogging makes a healthy man, and running makes a robust man.

   Intro. Verbal Phrase: Swirling through the large oak, the sudden wind signaled the storm's coming.

   Cumulative Sentence: He was one of the great leaders of our time, witty and energetic, inspiring confidence in those around him, offering hope for the future.

   Now combine each of the following groups of sentences into one. Try different patterns until you find the most effective and be able to say why you have selected that pattern as the best. Avoid stringing parts together with "and." (Note: Each group was shaped into one sentence by a writer in this chapter.)

   a. I reach out for one small handful.
      I ease the fragile fruit from its core.

   b. One can find the pearl.
      Still, the pearl may not be sought.

c. I pedal up a steep gulf.
I stop beside the brook that has worn this notch between mountains.

d. Still water is transitory and profound.
It is an emblem of ourselves.
It never quite accurately reflects the world it confronts.

e. And then I am caught, following the crop.
I migrate from one bush to another.
I am deep again in the middle of the field.

f. She conceives their costumes.
She cleans up their messes.
She shares their confidences.

g. Gradually the lights went out in the cedar.
Then the colors died.
Also the cells unflamed and disappeared.

WRITING ASSIGNMENTS

1. Take a walk in the woods, through a park, or by a lake, or bike along a rural road. What did you see? If not Dillard's color-patches, did you experience the presence of nature, observe wildlife, or interact with the natural environment in some way that you want to describe to others? If so, seek to recapture your experience concretely; make readers see what you saw, relive what you lived. Make your essay descriptive, with an implied thesis.
2. Has something happened to you—something as simple as picking berries on vacation or as profound as a serious injury—that warrants reflection? If so, write about the experience and its significance. Give only relevant details of the experience so that you have adequate space for reflection. (Goodman and Cooper are your models.)
3. How well do you "see" someone close to you—a family member, friend, colleague, teacher? Select relevant physical and biographical details to create an interesting and thoughtful portrait of the person. Pay close attention, as Lessing does, to the details that have shaped personality.
4. Human beings often have difficulty living in the present. We build expectations about the future and create memories of the past, with the result that sometimes our fantasies do not mesh with reality. Develop an essay in which you contrast your expectations of an event with the realities of that event. Possible topics include revisiting a childhood home or vacation spot, enrolling in a new school, or trying a sport for the first time. Be sure to think about *why* your expectations did not match reality. The student essay is your model.

Georges Seurat, Sunday Afternoon on the Island of La Grande Jatte, 1884–1886. *Approx. 6′ 9″ × 10′. Art Institute of Chicago* (*Helen Birch Bartlett Memorial Collection*).

CHAPTER 4

SEEING II

FICTION, POETRY, AND THE VISUAL ARTS

The essayist can speak to us in many voices—angry, jolly, sad—or adopt different roles—jester, scold, reformer—just as in our own lives we vary our stance depending on the situation, the issue, and the role we are in—boss, friend, mother, daughter. Still we expect some continuity of personality or consistency of vision in others and ourselves; when they (or we) write, we expect integrity and respond with trust. The shifting of pose or role by the essayist we call *persona*; we find the same shifting by the poet, and we identify this as the poem's *speaker.* In a lyric poem, an expression of thought and feeling, we expect the speaker to present, essentially, the views and vision of the poet. When the poet creates a dramatic or narrative poem, however, the poet uses techniques of fiction, and then we, as readers, must shift our approach to the work.

Consider the differences between Figures 4.1 and 4.2. The essayist may select a persona and then select the language appropriate to that persona to shape the work. But the dramatic poet, short-story writer, novelist, or dramatist creates a speaker who utters the words of the poem in character, or the writer/poet creates a *narrator* who tells the story from his or her perspective. In selecting a persona, the essayist highlights one personality trait, or perhaps one mood. But poets and fiction writers may create characters only slightly, if at all, connected to themselves.

The words have been selected by the writer, but they have been selected to fit the narrator or character who speaks. Thus in Browning's "My Last Duchess" the duke speaks, in character, all the words of the

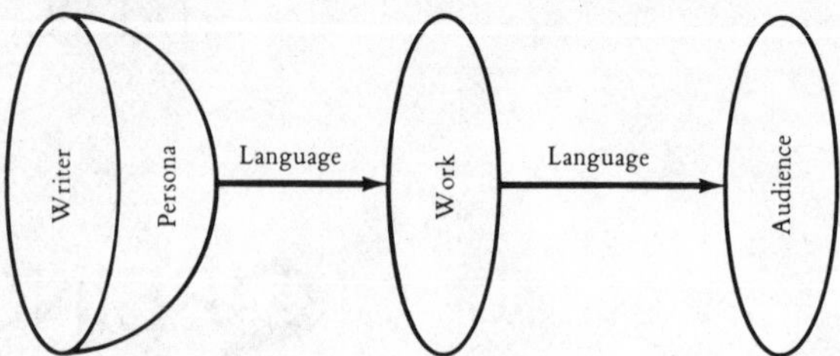

FIGURE 4.1. The Essayist

poem; Browning never was a duke and never had a duchess. More than one literature student, not thinking about an author's creation of character, has made the mistake of referring to the character who narrates Edgar Allan Poe's "Ligeia" as Poe. The result of this mistake is to conclude that Poe kills his wife! Characters love and hate, kill and get killed; their authors may do some, all, or none of these. Fiction writers not only create characters, they also select a narrative *point of view,* the angle of vision from which the story is told. Authors may choose to use an *omniscient* point of view—an all-knowing storyteller. But they may also choose to tell a story from the perspective of one character, as Poe does in "Ligeia," or Twain does in *Adventures of Huckleberry Finn.* Once an author chooses to present a story from the perspective of one character in that story, the writer creates the possibility of a narrator/character who expresses views not those of the author, or of an unreliable narrator, one who does not fully understand other characters, the significance of events, or even himself or herself.

Understanding point of view in literature is essential to accurate reading. Analyzing other elements in a work will also aid understanding. Just as you examine an essay's organization, so you want to analyze a poem's or story's (or painting's) structure (or composition). Lyric poems

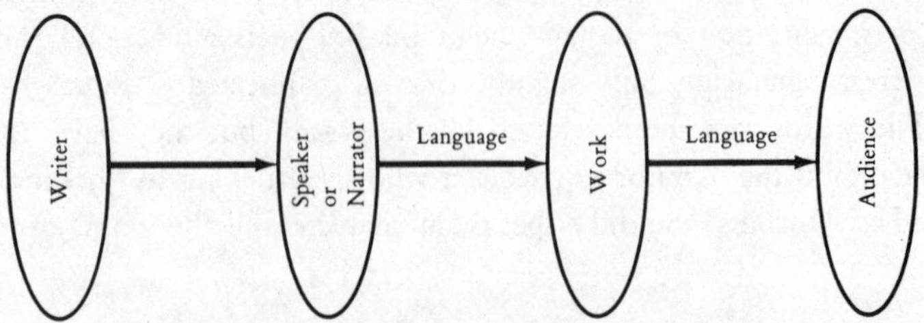

FIGURE 4.2. The Fiction Writer or Dramatic Poet

will employ the same structures found in essays: chronological, spatial, general to particular, particular to general, a list of particulars with an unstated general point, and so forth. In a story we are given a series of events, in time sequence, involving a character or characters. In some stories, episodes are not related to one another but are connected in that they all involve a central character (Mark Twain's *Adventures of Huckleberry Finn,* for example). This kind of plot structure is labeled *episodic.* Other stories present events as causally related: action A by the main character leads to event B, which requires action C by the main character. This kind of plot is called *organic* and can be diagrammed in general terms, as in Figure 4.3.

Figure 4.3 introduces some terms and concepts useful in literary analysis. The story's *exposition* refers to the background details necessary to get the story started; it includes the time and place of the story and traits and relationships of the characters. In Camus's "The Guest," Daru is a schoolmaster living in his schoolhouse in the desert of North Africa, and there are no children in school that day because it has snowed. The *complication* refers to an event; something happens to produce tension or conflict. In "The Guest" Balducci arrives with an Arab prisoner and disrupts Daru's quiet life. Such an event would disrupt anyone's life and cause some *conflict* to be resolved. In some stories, though, the events that take place seem quite ordinary—"uneventful," we might say. Still, for the character in the story they represent a complication because the character is already in conflict, already has problems that make even minor episodes seem alarming. In such stories we recognize that conflict generates complications; in others—Camus's "The Guest"—complications generate conflicts.

Some stories present one major complication leading to a climactic

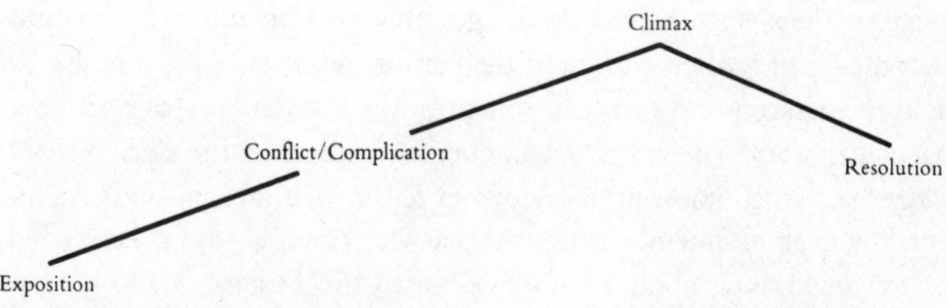

FIGURE 4.3. Organic Plot Structure

moment of decision for the main character; but many actually repeat the pattern, presenting several complications—each with an attempted resolution that generates yet another complication—until we reach the high point of tension, the *climax.* The climax finally generates the story's *resolution* and end. The term *resolution,* in modern literature, can cause readers difficulty because many stories stop abruptly without appearing to have much resolution. This limited resolution is part of the modern writer's view of reality, of lives that go on, with problems remaining unsolved, perhaps unsolvable.

"What is character," Henry James wrote, "but the determination of incident? What is incident but the illustration of character?" These words remind us that fiction requires both plot and character, both events and players in those events. Indeed, this connection is suggested in the close relationship between conflict and complication in plot development. Just as we can generalize about plot structures, as a guide to analysis, so we can generalize about types of character conflicts. First, characters can be in conflict with outside forces; they can struggle against the Arctic cold or against a hostile neighborhood. Second, characters can have a personal conflict, a conflict with another character. In James Thurber's story, Walter Mitty is in conflict with his wife, who bosses and scolds him. Finally, characters can have an internal conflict. They can struggle to choose between conflicting values, goals, or beliefs. Internal conflicts may be the easiest to recognize, but they are frequently the hardest to state. The tendency is to assert only one side of the conflict, to say that character X has a conflict between A and himself—an illogical statement since A is a part of the character, too. Be sure to determine both parts of the conflict—A and B—the desire to win (A) and the desire to be fair (B), for example. Table 4.1 summarizes character conflicts.

Analyzing character is always a challenge because we must infer personality traits from a few words, gestures, and actions. The analysis becomes easier when we know the various techniques authors use to convey character and then can recognize these techniques at work in a particular story. The easiest technique, for authors and readers, is *direct statement.* An all-knowing narrator can tell us that a character is frightened or angry. Remember, though, that we cannot always believe what one character says about another, so when the narrator is also a character, we have no direct statements from the author.

Table 4.1. Types of Character Conflict

TYPE OF CONFLICT	EXAMPLE
With outside forces	
Environmental	American pioneer versus undeveloped West
Social	A newcomer versus the town's expectations of conformity
With other individuals	One woman versus another woman because both love the same man
With oneself (internal)	A boy's dreams of success versus the reality of his failure

Writers frequently use *description* to reveal a character's way of life, personality, and values. Age, physical appearance, dress, and ways of walking or talking are important clues. When Walter Mitty is waiting for his wife, we see him sunk down into a big leather chair. Poor Mitty does not pace or sit upright or flirt with a receptionist.

At least as important as description is a writer's use of *dramatic scenes.* For the playwright and dramatic poet, this is the primary technique; the fiction writer will combine narration and dialogue to show us, in addition to telling us about, the characters. Having more than one character in a story also establishes the possibility of *contrast among characters* as a technique. One of the chief functions of many minor characters is to provide contrast to the main character, thereby revealing the main character's traits. A variation of this technique is found in Mitty's dreams; all the imagined versions of Mitty the victorious stand in contrast to Mitty the ineffectual.

Finally, authors can reveal their characters through associations with other elements in the work. These are indirect, sometimes subtle, techniques. Characters can be given significant names. *Phoenix* Jackson, for example. Characters can be associated with objects: Mitty with his purchases or the duke with his art works. Colors may be used symbolically, as Eudora Welty does in "A Worn Path," and details of setting can convey personality. As you seek to understand character, consider the writer's options for developing character and use your knowledge of technique as a guide to analysis.

Earlier chapters discuss the roles of sentence structure, word choice or diction, and metaphors as tools in shaping style and conveying attitude. When analyzing poetry and fiction, you will need to consider these and other techniques for controlling tone, including sudden shifts in diction, understatement, hyperbole (overstatement), paradox, and irony. When it's pouring outside and you say, "It's a bit damp out," you have used *understatement* to give emphasis to the storm's severity. Understatement can be amusing or serious, even bitter. *Hyperbole* generally ridicules in a light-hearted fashion: "I've told you a million times to brush your teeth!" Your recognition of metaphoric language will help the understanding of *paradox,* for the apparent contradiction of a paradox is usually explained by reading some part of the statement metaphorically rather than literally. Wordsworth's line "The child is father of the man" is nonsense read literally, but insightful when "father" is understood metaphorically. What we are like as children makes us into the adults we become.

Irony, like paradox, involves a kind of contradiction, a tension between what appears to be and what is. By bringing them together, the writer makes us see "what is" more clearly. When you drop by a friend's house and find him in mud-spattered jeans and torn sneakers, you might say, "You look smashing!" You would be using *verbal irony*—saying the opposite of what you mean—to tease your friend. *Dramatic irony* refers to the contrast between what a character says and what we, readers or audience, understand to be the case. Sometimes we have knowledge of other characters or events that the speaker does not have; other times, as in Browning's "My Last Duchess," we understand the character's remarks differently than he intends. This discrepancy arises when the author leads us to a view of the character that is different from the character's view of himself. Finally, in *irony of situation,* the irony lies in the discrepancy between what we expect to happen and what actually happens. When a character flees one town to avoid a problem only to run into the same problem in the next town, that is ironical. There is irony of situation in the conclusion to Camus's "The Guest."

Recognizing metaphoric language, isolating the two elements being compared, and understanding the point and effect of the selected comparison are critical steps in reading both nonfiction and fiction. When analyzing literature, you will want to be careful to distinguish among an image, a symbol, and a metaphor. An *image* re-creates a sense experience;

it describes. A *symbol* is an object (or character or action) that is what it is—an eagle, a chipped tea cup—plus something more—strength and freedom, a less than fully realized social status. A *metaphor* states or implies a comparison between two unlike elements; it explains through comparison. There are various types of metaphors. A metaphor with its connectors (like, as) stated is a *simile.* A comparison of an object or animal to a human being is *personification.* Direct address to a nonhuman is *apostrophe.* (To speak to a rose is to treat it *as* human.) To use a part or detail to represent the whole is *metonomy* (e.g., "The pen is mightier than the sword."). When discussing poetry, you will want to recognize the type of metaphor used and name it correctly in your discussion.

The following passages may help you distinguish among images, symbols, and metaphors.

IMAGE

A gigantic beauty of a stallion, fresh
    and responsive to my carresses,
Head high in the forehead, wide between
    the ears,
Limbs glossy and supple, tail dusting
    the ground,
Eyes full of sparkling wickedness, ears
    finely cut, flexibly moving.

"Song of Myself,"
Walt Whitman

In this passage Whitman presents the image of a horse. We can see and feel the horse and sense the speaker's delight in the horse's beauty and strength.

SYMBOL

The great draught-horses swung past. They were tied head to tail, four of them, and they heaved along to where a lane branched off from the highroad, planting their great hoofs floutingly in the fine black mud, swinging their great rounded haunches sumptuously, and trotting a few sudden steps as they were led into the lane, round the corner. Every movement showed a massive, slumbrous strength, and a stupidity which held them in subjection. The groom at the head looked back, jerking the leading rope. And the cavalcade

Lawrence describes horses being led away from the farm that Mabel and her brothers have lost through bankruptcy. But Lawrence's focus on the horses in the midst of his description of the brothers makes us associate the horses with them, especially Joe. The horses are actually part of the story. They also symbolically represent the animal-like qualities of Joe. They are led away as Joe will be led away into a marriage of convenience.

moved out of sight up the lane, the tail of the last horse, bobbed up tight and stiff, held out taut from the swinging great haunches as they rocked behind the hedges of a motion-like sleep. . . . Joe watched with glazed hopeless eyes. . . . He would marry and go into harness. His life was over, he would be a subject animal now.

"The Horse Dealer's Daughter,"
D. H. Lawrence

METAPHOR

Dickinson is writing about the power of poetry to transport us, by comparing poetry to certain characteristics of ships and horses. Technically she uses similes.

There is no frigate like a book
To take us lands away
Nor any coursers like a page
of prancing poetry.

"There Is No Frigate,"
Emily Dickinson

In the previous pages, many terms and concepts used to discuss literature have been defined and illustrated so that you will have not only strategies for reading literature but language for writing papers about it. In a college literature course, what kinds of papers will you be asked to write? Probably you will not be asked to write the kind you may have written before: the personal response, essentially a personal essay about a reading experience. Usually you will be asked to write either an explication or an analysis. An *explication* seeks to make clear a difficult poem or a complex, significant passage from a longer work. When explicating, you should paraphrase (use your own words; to quote is not to explain) and use simpler sentences than in the original. You will probably write more than in the original, as you paraphrase *and* explain a poem's allusions and metaphors or a passage's symbolic meaning or its significance in understanding the story's theme.

A *literary analysis* can take many forms. You may be asked to analyze one element in a work—for example, the character of Phoenix in "A Worn Path" or the metaphors in Shakespeare's "Sonnet 73." Frequently the analytic assignment will ask you to connect analysis to interpretation, for we analyze the parts in order better to understand the whole. If you are asked to examine (a catch-all verb) Browning's use of irony or Camus's use of setting, your instructor wants you to show how analysis of the irony or of the setting contributes to an understanding of the entire poem or story. A contrast topic also requires analysis; here it is analysis of each work to isolate points of difference. All successful analyses are tied to accurate reading and the use of details from the work to support assertions.

Literary analysis can also incorporate material beyond the particular work. There are many approaches to the reading of literature. One can take a biographical approach, interpreting a poem in the light of what we know about the poet, especially about the experiences and/or mood of the poet at the time the poem was written. Another approach is to place the work in a larger historical context, or a context of literary tradition. We can study Shakespeare's plays in contrast to the earlier sixteenth-century plays known to him and in light of our knowledge of the Elizabethan stage. Some critics choose to read literature from a particular political ideology; others apply their knowledge of psychoanalysis or of myths to the reading of literature. All of these approaches can enrich one's understanding of complex works, but because they require extensive knowledge of fields other than literature, you will need some time to learn to use them well. The key always for you, as a student, is to understand what kind of paper you have been assigned and then to demonstrate a knowledge of the literary work and of the terms and conventions of literary analysis.

The Fiction Writer's Materials

ANNIE DILLARD

For a biographical sketch of Dillard, see page 73. The following excerpt from Living by Fiction *(1982), a study of modern literature, develops some useful concepts about the making—and reading—of literature. Dillard explores, with examples from modern fiction, the relationship between the language of a story and the "world" that language is designed to represent and re-create for the reader. Reading this excerpt will contribute to your understanding of the complex connections among the writer, the work, and the reader that are examined throughout this text.*

1 I have asserted, but not yet defended, the notion that fiction cannot shed the world because its materials are necessarily bits of world. The writer's materials, common sense says, are various characters, places, actions, ideas, and actual or mental objects. The writer's materials are real or imagined phenomena.

2 One could say, however, that the writer's materials are words and the other paraphernalia of language. After all, a writer does not sit at his desk pushing little people and landscapes around. He manipulates words like so many dabs of paint. And who is to say that the words correspond to anything? I want to treat this idea with some respect before I discard it.

3 Language scarcely accounts for things, or for the flux and mystery of experience. If it did, Romantic poets could go about their task with the aplomb of bricklayers. We know that language itself is a selection and abstraction from unknowable flux; the world shades into gradations too fine for speech. A Jerome Bruner[1] study shows that human eyes can distinguish among approximately twenty thousand colors. Yet English, a language rich in color terms, names only a few score of them; some languages name only three or four. Language, like other cognitive structures, is useful for some tasks and worthless for others. I cannot tell you, because I do not know, what my language prevents my knowing. Language is itself like a work of art; it selects, abstracts, exaggerates, and orders. How then could we say that language encloses and signifies phenomena, when language is a fabricated grid someone stuck in a river? Or how can we even say that language communicates by agreed-upon convention, when people personalize symbols so readily, so that a word which means life to me may mean death to you, and we cannot agree?

4 We must grant, then, that words for things miss their marks, or at least, as I see it, obscure things here and there around the edges. And we grant, sighing, that we see through a cultural-linguistic glass darkly, and cannot tell snow from snow. Nevertheless, the plain fact is that language does serve literary purposes adequately.

5 To be quite precise, we must say that a writer's language does not

[1]An experimental psychologist at Oxford, an expert in cognition and the learning process.—Ed.

signify things as they are—because none of us knows things as they are; instead, a writer's language does an airtight job of signifying his *perceptions* of things as they are. The term "salty" may hopelessly confine my perceptions—my sensations—when I taste saltiness, so that I miss a dozen accompanying sensations and taste only saltiness. You suffer the same loss. Well, then, the term "salty," which so dictates how we perceive, at least expresses *what* we perceive, very well, and also communicates it to those afflicted with the same language. Language need not know the world perfectly in order to communicate perceptions adequately.

6 Language actually signifies things transparently, in a way that paint must labor to do. The word "apple" signifies appledom (or our perception of appledom) to all of us, and we will politely suspend our private meanings for the word in order to hear each other out. If I write "apple," I can make you think of a mental apple roughly analogous to the one I have in mind. But I am hard put to make you think of a certain arrangement of alphabet letters or phonemes.[2] The word itself all but vanishes, like Vermeer's[3] paint.

7 The writer, then, composes with mental objects, actual or imagined; he composes with what Poe called "the things and thoughts of time." Dickens drew his materials in *Bleak House* from the breadth of London society and from contemporary British legal usage; it were madness, or quibbling, to say he drew them from a dictionary.

8 The upshot of all this, as I have suggested, is that fiction cannot escape the world as its necessary subject matter. Hence it cannot break with its own traditions, or throw its criticism into crisis, or lose its audience, or move its action entirely to its own surface. Whether a writer writes "grapefruit," or "God," or "freedom," his indispensable subject matter is the world beyond the page. Even when Joyce writes (to cite a familiar example), "Nobirdy aviar soar anywing to eagle it!"[4] This passage does not eliminate referents; it multiplies them.

9 One notable effort to alter the subject matter of fiction—Gertrude Stein's[5]—was an effort to alter the subject matter of language. Her aim

---

[2]Small, basic units of sound.—Ed.

[3]A seventeenth-century Dutch painter.—Ed.

[4]A line from his novel *Finnegans Wake* (1939), a distortion of "Nobody ever saw anything to equal it."—Ed.

[5]An American writer (1874–1946) who lived in Paris and was a central figure among expatriate writers in that city.—Ed.

(like that of Juan Gris,[6] the similarity of whose work to hers she acknowledged) was "exactitude." "A star glide," she wrote, "a frantic sullenness, a single financial grass greediness." "Toasted susie," she wrote, "is my ice cream." Stein's work, and *Finnegans Wake,*[7] come close to vaporizing the world and making of language a genuine stuff. Often Stein's work achieves the unity of a single plane which glitters with a thousand refractions where the words, bound together at the surface, still tilt in every direction toward their referents in the world.

10 Stein's writing brought forth no revolution; neither did *Finnegans Wake.* Literature co-opted them; they joined the canon with scarcely a ripple, and inspired few successors. What Stein did, and what Joyce did in *Finnegans Wake,* was playfully to misread the nature of fiction. Fiction could have moved its arena to its own material surface, to virtually nobody's interest, if fiction's materials had really been words, and if writers had succeeded in detaching the words from their referents. But fiction's materials are bits of world. Fiction's subject matter can indeed move very far in the direction of its own surfaces; but those surfaces are not language surfaces but referential narrative objects. It turned out, then, that *Ulysses,*[8] with its broken narrative surface, indicated a more fruitful and honest modernist direction for fiction.

11 The movement toward the modernist in fiction is one of emphasis. It is a shifting stance, not an outright leap. Just as there has been no sudden shift to abstraction in fiction, because the nature of fiction's materials prevents it, so also there has been no sudden shift to contemporary modernism in fiction, because the nature of everything else prevents it. Before I get to this interesting "everything else," let me make this point. Mere change is not revolution. The contemporary modernists are here, all right, but they did not slay the old guard in their beds. Instead, the old guard liked their looks, invited them in, and exchanged a few tricks with them after dinner.

12 This assertion is controversial. Robert Scholes, in his excellent *Fabulation and Metafiction,* argues at one point that contemporary modernism has replaced traditional fiction. Those who write the old fiction constitute "a small school of neo-naturalists" who write "frantically, headless chickens unaware of the decapitating axe." This is perfectly true, as far

[6]A Spanish painter (1887–1927) who lived in France.—Ed.

[7]A novel by Anglo-Irish writer James Joyce (1882–1941).—Ed.

[8]A novel by James Joyce.—Ed.

as it goes; a purely naturalist fiction today is an absurd relic, like a horseshoe crab, especially if it is, in Scholes's terms, "unaware."

13 But who is unaware? Only undergraduates who try to write without having read. Surely critics are not in the business of berating the ignorant. Woody Allen[9] uses modernist techniques freely; so do television commercials. You can no more avoid either the techniques or the aesthetic they express than you can avoid the Mondrian[10] look at Penney's. If someone out there is writing a purely naturalist fiction, using only nineteenth-century techniques, he is not so much a chicken with his head cut off as a dead horse.

14 The notion of "schools" does not work because neither set of writers constitutes a school. If we admit, as Scholes does, Lawrence Durrell, Bernard Malamud, John Fowles, and Iris Murdoch to the new school—and this is only reasonable—then what have we proved? That the new school has wielded its axe in triumph, or that almost all decent living novelists are capable of using techniques developed sixty years ago?

15 The techniques have been around for centuries, even, if you want to go back to Sterne,[11] and writers are perfectly aware of them. If someone like Saul Bellow does not want to use them, he is not, I think, unaware, or making a last stand; rather, he would prefer not to.* Fiction writers are aiming at eternity, I do believe, and not at each other, and not at the power to determine fiction's direction. And in the house of eternity there are many mansions.

16 Fiction has expanded its borders. Nothing has killed or replaced anything. The old co-opted the new. Everywhere, categories overlap. Even if we name names we get into trouble. There is no such animal as a thoroughgoing, cradle-to-grave contemporary modernist outside France. Pynchon and others describe society; Nabokov, Beckett, and Barth round character; many contemporary modernists imitate the unbroken flow of time; *Ada*[12] brims with emotion; some surrealist work is a bit skimpy on idea; and Borges of late seems to quit the library and hunker instead at a neolithic campfire, bringing fiction full circle to its putative beginnings. As Scholes is pointing out, almost all contemporary

---

[9]An actor and director of contemporary films.—Ed.

[10]A modern Dutch painter (1872–1944) noted for his geometric abstract paintings.—Ed.

[11]An eighteenth-century English novelist.—Ed.

*There are no opposing camps; there is no struggle. Each writer is a one-man camp, unallied and unarmed, a lone bivouac under heaven.

[12]A novel by Nabokov. All writers mentioned in this paragraph are contemporary novelists who break with traditional narrative techniques and use "unrealistic" elements.—Ed.

writers use the new techniques. Where would Frederick Buechner belong? Larry Woiwode? Evan S. Connell, Jr.? Lessing? Garrett's *Death of the Fox*? Updike's *The Centaur*? Grass's *The Tin Drum*?

17 Of course, it is false logic to maintain that where boundaries are blurred, no distinctions exist. Just because no one can specify at which smudge a clean wall becomes a dirty wall, that does not mean there is no difference between a clean wall and a dirty wall. There are abundant differences between naturalist fiction and contemporary modernist fiction. But there are simply too many writers and works of fiction which do excellent things in both categories for anyone to talk about revolution or even opposing schools.

18 If we grant that fiction has changed gradually, we still get to ask why it has not changed wholly. Why is anyone still writing "neo-naturalist" fiction? Why, since everyone can see fiction's direction as plain as day, does anyone fail to follow the pointing finger? How could anyone prefer not to?

19 I have said that the writer is aiming at eternity—at perfecting his art. The writer of traditional fiction may see fiction as a form both solid and open, one which permits him to assault perfection from any intelligent stance without fear of ridicule. (No one is laughing at Saul Bellow, after all.) On the other hand, such a writer may have motives personal as well as theoretical. He may like the world of things. Or he may wish to keep a roof over his head.

20 Fiction, insofar as it is traditional, has a large and paying audience whose tastes serve to keep it traditional. Shall we deny this, or merely deplore it? As Emerson[13] said of the fall of man, "It is very unhappy, but too late to be helped." But, one could find in the fall of man, or even in the mass audience for fiction, a certain grim felicity.

QUESTIONS FOR ANALYSIS AND DISCUSSION

1. What two different assertions can be made about the fiction writer's materials? Which assertion does Dillard agree with?
2. In paragraph 3, Dillard makes some significant statements about what language can and cannot do. Summarize the key points in this paragraph.

---

[13]A nineteenth-century American poet and essayist; chief spokesman for American transcendentalism.—Ed.

3. Explain Dillard's metaphor—we see through a cultural-linguistic glass darkly—in paragraph 4. (Her essay "Seeing" in Chapter 3 may help clarify her point here.)
4. If language fails to signify things as they are, what does a writer's language do? What is the subject matter of fiction?
5. Why are these distinctions important? What happens to the way we read fiction if it is not about elements of the world "out there" but about the words on the page?
6. What did Stein and Joyce accomplish in modern fiction? What did they fail to accomplish?
7. On the basis of your reading of paragraphs 8–11, you can conclude that Stein and Joyce wrote works that are a part of contemporary literature called "modernism." From Dillard's discussion of their works, how would you describe contemporary modernism?
8. What aspects of advertising or Woody Allen films are modernist?
9. By contrast, what are the characteristics of naturalist fiction? Do you know some writers who would fit in this category?
10. Why does Dillard not agree that contemporary modernism has replaced traditional fiction? List all her reasons. Has she convinced you?
11. Since Dillard feels it necessary to defend writers of traditional fiction, some critics must deplore their failure to join the revolution in fiction. Why do some critics disapprove of the traditionalists?
12. Who is Dillard's audience? How do you know? Are you part of her intended audience? If not, what must you do to read this piece with understanding?
13. Whether writing literary analysis or the personal essay, Dillard provides readers with a rich array of metaphors. Find three in this selection and explain each one.

A Worn Path

EUDORA WELTY

With the publication in 1936 of her first two stories, "Death of a Traveling Salesman" and "Magic," Eudora Welty (b. 1909) launched one of the twentieth century's most significant literary careers. Welty was born in Jackson, Mississippi, and except for the years spent earning a B.A. at the University of Wisconsin and studying advertising at Columbia University, she has lived at home in Jackson. In 1941 "A Worn Path" won second prize in the O. Henry short-story contest and was printed in Welty's first collection of short stories, A Curtain of Green. *Additional stories appeared and were brought together in 1980 in* The Collected Stories of Eudora Welty. *Welty has also published several novels, including the Pulitzer Prize–winning* The Optimist's Daughter, *and numerous essays, reviews, and lectures, mostly about the craft of fiction. She has led a quiet, unassuming life, never joining the celebrity cult, and associating with other writers only when they also became friends.*

In much of her writing about fiction, Welty has emphasized creating a sense of place, and indeed she is a master of the art of making pictures out of words, an art she may owe in part to her interest in and talent for photography. Throughout "A Worn Path" Welty makes us see both Phoenix and the path she travels to town. "A Worn Path" is one of Welty's finest stories, and it is also representative of her special marks as a writer: a comic spirit, striking images, a grace of style, and a celebration of the human capacity for love.

1 It was December—a bright frozen day in the early morning. Far out in the country there was an old Negro woman with her head tied in a red rag, coming along a path through the pinewoods. Her name was Phoenix Jackson. She was very old and small and she walked slowly in the dark pine shadows, moving a little from side to side in her steps, with the balanced heaviness and lightness of a pendulum in a grandfather clock. She carried a thin, small cane made from an umbrella, and with this she kept tapping the frozen earth in front of her. This made a grave and persistent noise in the still air, that seemed meditative like the chirping of a solitary little bird.

2 She wore a dark striped dress reaching down to her shoe tops, and an equally long apron of bleached sugar sacks, with a full pocket: all neat and tidy, but every time she took a step she might have fallen over her shoelaces, which dragged from her unlaced shoes. She looked straight ahead. Her eyes were blue with age. Her skin had a pattern all its own of numberless branching wrinkles and as though a whole little tree stood in the middle of her forehead, but a golden color ran underneath, and the two knobs of her cheeks were illumined by a yellow burning under the dark. Under the red rag her hair came down on her neck in the frailest of ringlets, still black, and with an odor like copper.

3 Now and then there was a quivering in the thicket. Old Phoenix said, "Out of my way, all you foxes, owls, beetles, jack rabbits, coons and wild animals! . . . Keep out from under these feet, little bob-whites.

. . . Keep the big wild hogs out of my path. Don't let none of those come running my direction. I got a long way." Under her small black-freckled hand her cane, limber as a buggy whip, would switch at the brush as if to rouse up any hiding things.

4 On she went. The woods were deep and still. The sun made the pine needles almost too bright to look at, up where the wind rocked. The cones dropped as light as feathers. Down in the hollow was the mourning dove–it was not too late for him.

5 The path ran up a hill. "Seem like there is chains about my feet, time I get this far," she said, in the voice of argument old people keep to use with themselves. "Something always take a hold of me on this hill–pleads I should stay."

6 After she got to the top she turned and gave a full, severe look behind her where she had come. "Up through pines," she said at length. "Now down through oaks."

7 Her eyes opened their widest, and she started down gently. But before she got to the bottom of the hill a bush caught her dress.

8 Her fingers were busy and intent, but her skirts were full and long, so that before she could pull them free in one place they were caught in another. It was not possible to allow the dress to tear. "I in the thorny bush," she said. "Thorns, you doing your appointed work. Never want to let folks pass, no sir. Old eyes thought you was a pretty little *green* bush."

9 Finally, trembling all over, she stood free, and after a moment dared to stoop for her cane.

10 "Sun so high!" she cried, leaning back and looking, while the thick tears went over her eyes. "The time getting all gone here."

11 At the foot of this hill was a place where a log was laid across the creek.

12 "Now comes the trial," said Phoenix.

13 Putting her right foot out, she mounted the log and shut her eyes. Lifting her skirt, leveling her cane fiercely before her, like a festival figure in some parade, she began to march across. Then she opened her eyes and she was safe on the other side.

14 "I wasn't as old as I thought," she said.

15 But she sat down to rest. She spread her skirts on the bank around her and folded her hands over her knees. Up above her was a tree in a pearly cloud of mistletoe. She did not dare to close her eyes, and when a little boy brought her a plate with a slice of marble-cake on it she spoke to him. "That would be acceptable," she said. But when she went to take it there was just her own hand in the air.

16 So she left that tree, and had to go through a barbed-wire fence. There she had to creep and crawl, spreading her knees and stretching her fingers like a baby trying to climb the steps. But she talked loudly to herself: she could not let her dress be torn now, so late in the day, and she could not pay for having her arm or her leg sawed off if she got caught fast where she was.

17 At last she was safe through the fence and risen up out in the clearing. Big dead trees, like black men with one arm, were standing in the purple stalks of the withered cotton field. There sat a buzzard.

18 "Who you watching?"

19 In the furrow she made her way along.

20 "Glad this not the season for bulls," she said, looking sideways, "and the good Lord made his snakes to curl up and sleep in the winter. A pleasure I don't see no two-headed snake coming around that tree, where it come once. It took a while to get by him, back in the summer."

21 She passed through the old cotton and went into a field of dead corn. It whispered and shook and was taller than her head. "Through the maze now," she said, for there was no path.

22 Then there was something tall, black, and skinny there, moving before her.

23 At first she took it for a man. It could have been a man dancing in the field. But she stood still and listened, and it did not make a sound. It was as silent as a ghost.

24 "Ghost," she said sharply, "who be you the ghost of? For I have heard of nary death close by."

25 But there was no answer—only the ragged dancing in the wind.

26 She shut her eyes, reached out her hand, and touched a sleeve. She found a coat and inside that an emptiness, cold as ice.

27 "You scarecrow," she said. Her face lighted. "I ought to be shut up for good," she said with laughter. "My senses is gone. I too old. I the oldest people I ever know. Dance, old scarecrow," she said, "while I dancing with you."

28 She kicked her foot over the furrow, and with mouth drawn down, shook her head once or twice in a little strutting way. Some husks blew down and whirled in streamers about her skirts.

29 Then she went on, parting her way from side to side with the cane, through the whispering field. At last she came to the end, to a wagon track where the silver grass blew between the red ruts. The quail were walking around like pullets, seeming all dainty and unseen.

30 "Walk pretty," she said. "This the easy place. This the easy going."

31 She followed the track, swaying through the quiet bare fields, through the little strings of trees silver in their dead leaves, past cabins silver from weather, with the doors and windows boarded shut, all like old women under a spell sitting there. "I walking in their sleep," she said, nodding her head vigorously.

32 In a ravine she went where a spring was silently flowing through a hollow log. Old Phoenix bent and drank. "Sweet-gum makes the water sweet," she said, and drank more. "Nobody know who made this well, for it was here when I born."

33 The track crossed a swampy part where the moss hung as white as lace from every limb. "Sleep on, alligators, and blow your bubbles." Then the track went into the road.

34 Deep, deep the road went down between the high green-colored banks. Overhead the live-oaks met, and it was as dark as a cave.

35 A black dog with a lolling tongue came up out of the weeds by the ditch. She was meditating, and not ready, and when he came at her she only hit him a little with her cane. Over she went in the ditch, like a little puff of milkweed.

36 Down there, her senses drifted away. A dream visited her, and she reached her hand up, but nothing reached down and gave her a pull. So she lay there and presently went to talking. "Old woman," she said to herself, "that black dog come up out of the weeds to stall you off, and now there he sitting on his fine tail, smiling at you."

37 A white man finally came along and found her—a hunter, a young man, with his dog on a chain.

38 "Well, Granny!" he laughed. "What are you doing there?"

39 "Lying on my back like a June-bug waiting to be turned over, mister," she said, reaching up her hand.

40 He lifted her up, gave her a swing in the air, and set her down. "Anything broken, Granny?"

41 "No sir, them old dead weeds is springy enough," said Phoenix, when she had got her breath. "I thank you for your trouble."

42 "Where do you live, Granny?" he asked, while the two dogs were growling at each other.

43 "Away back yonder, sir, behind the ridge. You can't even see it from here."

44 "On your way home?"

45 "No sir, I going to town."

46 "Why, that's too far! That's as far as I walk when I come out myself, and I get something for my trouble." He patted the stuffed bag he carried,

and there hung down a little closed claw. It was one of the bob-whites, with its beak hooked bitterly to show it was dead. "Now you go on home, Granny!"

47 "I bound to go to town, mister," said Phoenix. "The time come around."

48 He gave another laugh, filling the whole landscape. "I know you old colored people! Wouldn't miss going to town to see Santa Claus!"

49 But something held old Phoenix very still. The deep lines in her face went into a fierce and different radiation. Without warning, she had seen with her own eyes a flashing nickel fall out of the man's pocket onto the ground.

50 "How old are you, Granny?" he was saying.

51 "There is no telling, mister," she said, "no telling."

52 Then she gave a little cry and clapped her hands and said, "Git on away from here, dog! Look! Look at that dog!" She laughed as if in admiration. "He ain't scared of nobody. He a big black dog." She whispered, "Sic him!"

53 "Watch me get rid of that cur," said the man. "Sic him, Pete! Sic him!"

54 Phoenix heard the dogs fighting, and heard the man running and throwing sticks. She even heard a gunshot. But she was slowly bending forward by that time, further and further forward, the lids stretched down over her eyes, as if she were doing this in her sleep. Her chin was lowered almost to her knees. The yellow palm of her hand came out from the fold of her apron. Her fingers slid down and along the ground under the piece of money with the grace and care they would have in lifting an egg from under a setting hen. Then she slowly straightened up, she stood erect, and the nickel was in her apron pocket. A bird flew by. Her lips moved. "God watching me the whole time. I come to stealing."

55 The man came back, and his own dog panted about them. "Well, I scared him off that time," he said, and then he laughed and lifted his gun and pointed it at Phoenix.

56 She stood straight and faced him.

57 "Doesn't the gun scare you?" he said, still pointing it.

58 "No, sir, I seen plenty go off closer by, in my day, and for less than what I done," she said, holding utterly still.

59 He smiled, and shouldered the gun. "Well, Granny," he said, "you must be a hundred years old, and scared of nothing. I'd give you a dime if I had any money with me. But you take my advice and stay home, and nothing will happen to you."

60 "I bound to go on my way, mister," said Phoenix. She inclined her head in the red rag. Then they went in different directions, but she could hear the gun shooting again and again over the hill.

61 She walked on. The shadows hung from the oak trees to the road like curtains. Then she smelled wood-smoke, and smelled the river, and she saw a steeple and the cabins on their steep steps. Dozens of little black children whirled around her. There ahead was Natchez shining. Bells were ringing. She walked on.

62 In the paved city it was Christmas time. There were red and green electric lights strung and crisscrossed everywhere, and all turned on in the daytime. Old Phoenix would have been lost if she had not distrusted her eyesight and depended on her feet to know where to take her.

63 She paused quietly on the sidewalk where people were passing by. A lady came along in the crowd, carrying an armful of red-, green- and silver-wrapped presents; she gave off perfume like the red roses in hot summer, and Phoenix stopped her.

64 "Please, missy, will you lace up my shoe?" She held up her foot.

65 "What do you want, Grandma?"

66 "See my shoe," said Phoenix. "Do all right for out in the country, but wouldn't look right to go in a big building."

67 "Stand still then, Grandma," said the lady. She put her packages down on the sidewalk beside her and laced and tied both shoes tightly.

68 "Can't lace 'em with a cane," said Phoenix. "Thank you, missy. I doesn't mind asking a nice lady to tie up my shoe, when I gets out on the street."

69 Moving slowly and from side to side, she went into the big building, and into a tower of steps, where she walked up and around and around until her feet knew to stop.

70 She entered a door, and there she saw nailed up on the wall the document that had been stamped with the gold seal and framed in the gold frame, which matched the dream that was hung up in her head.

71 "Here I be," she said. There was a fixed and ceremonial stiffness over her body.

72 "A charity case, I suppose," said an attendant who sat at the desk before her.

73 But Phoenix only looked above her head. There was sweat on her face, the wrinkles in her skin shone like a bright net.

74 "Speak up, Grandma," the woman said. "What's your name? We must have your history, you know. Have you been here before? What seems to be the trouble with you?"

75 Old Phoenix only gave a twitch to her face as if a fly were bothering her.

76 "Are you deaf?" cried the attendant.

77 But then the nurse came in.

78 "Oh, that's just old Aunt Phoenix," she said. "She doesn't come for herself—she has a little grandson. She makes these trips just as regular as clockwork. She lives away back off the Old Natchez Trace." She bent down. "Well, Aunt Phoenix, why don't you just take a seat? We won't keep you standing after your long trip." She pointed.

79 The old woman sat down, bolt upright in the chair.

80 "Now, how is the boy?" asked the nurse.

81 Old Phoenix did not speak.

82 "I said, how is the boy?"

83 But Phoenix only waited and stared straight ahead, her face very solemn and withdrawn into rigidity.

84 "Is his throat any better?" asked the nurse. "Aunt Phoenix, don't you hear me? Is your grandson's throat any better since the last time you came for the medicine?"

85 With her hands on her knees, the old woman waited, silent, erect and motionless, just as if she were in armor.

86 "You mustn't take up our time this way, Aunt Phoenix," the nurse said. "Tell us quickly about your grandson, and get it over. He isn't dead, is he?"

87 At last there came a flicker and then a flame of comprehension across her face, and she spoke.

88 "My grandson. It was my memory had left me. There I sat and forgot why I made my long trip."

89 "Forgot?" The nurse frowned. "After you came so far?"

90 Then Phoenix was like an old woman begging a dignified forgiveness for waking up frightened in the night. "I never did go to school, I was too old at the Surrender," she said in a soft voice. "I'm an old woman without an education. It was my memory fail me. My little grandson, he is just the same, and I forgot it in the coming."

91 "Throat never heals, does it?" said the nurse, speaking in a loud, sure voice to old Phoenix. By now she had a card with something written on it, a little list. "Yes. Swallowed lye. When was it?—January—two, three years ago—"

92 Phoenix spoke unasked now. "No, missy, he not dead, he just the same. Every little while his throat begin to close up again, and he not able to swallow. He not get his breath. He not able to help himself.

So the time come around, and I go on another trip for the soothing medicine."

93 "All right. The doctor said as long as you came to get it, you could have it," said the nurse. "But it's an obstinate case."

94 "My little grandson, he sit up there in the house all wrapped up, waiting by himself," Phoenix went on. "We is the only two left in the world. He suffer and it don't seem to put him back at all. He got a sweet look. He going to last. He wear a little patch quilt and peep out holding his mouth open like a little bird. I remembers so plain now. I not going to forget him again, no, the whole enduring time. I could tell him from all the others in creation."

95 "All right." The nurse was trying to hush her now. She brought her a bottle of medicine. "Charity," she said, making a check mark in a book.

96 Old Phoenix held the bottle close to her eyes, and then carefully put it into her pocket.

97 "I thank you," she said.

98 "It's Christmas time, Grandma," said the attendant. "Could I give you a few pennies out of my purse?"

99 "Five pennies is a nickel," said Phoenix stiffly.

100 "Here's a nickel," said the attendant.

101 Phoenix rose carefully and held out her hand. She received the nickel and then fished the other nickel out of her pocket and laid it beside the new one. She stared at her palm closely, with her head on one side.

102 Then she gave a tap with her cane on the floor.

103 "This is what come to me to do," she said. "I going to the store and buy my child a little windmill they sells, made out of paper. He going to find it hard to believe there such a thing in the world. I'll march myself back where he waiting, holding it straight up in this hand."

104 She lifted her free hand, gave a little nod, turned around, and walked out of the doctor's office. Then her slow step began on the stairs, going down.

QUESTIONS FOR ANALYSIS AND DISCUSSION

1. What is the story's narrative point of view? From what vantage point does the author tell the story?
2. Phoenix has a difficult journey, for many reasons. List all the obstacles she must overcome and then group them by type of obstacle—that is, physical barriers, etc.

3. Which type of obstacle is most demanding for Phoenix? Which might be most difficult for a different character?
4. Describe Phoenix. What are her dominant character traits?
5. We see Phoenix on her journey to town for medicine; that gives the story its narrative structure or plot. What gives the story its meaning? What is Welty's subject or theme?
6. Why is the journey an appropriate vehicle for Welty's subject? What other journey stories (including novels) do you know? How are they similar to, or different from, "A Worn Path"?
7. Examine Welty's use of colors. What colors dominate? How do they contribute to the story's meaning?
8. Welty also fills her landscape with death and dying. List all the things in the story that are dead or dying. In the midst of our—and the earth's—mutability, what makes this story a hopeful one? What endures?

Is Phoenix Jackson's Grandson Really Dead?

EUDORA WELTY

Reticent, like many writers, when asked to explain her work, Eudora Welty once wrote: "I never saw, as reader or writer, that a finished short story stood in need of any more from the author: for better or worse, there the story is." But because of the many letters she received about Phoenix's grandson, Welty finally decided, in 1974, to respond in the following essay. "Is Phoenix Jackson's Grandson Really Dead?" was then collected with other essays, in 1977, in The Eye of the Story. *In addition to responding to readers' queries, Welty gives us insight into the writer's craft and the values of literature.*

1 A story writer is more than happy to be read by students; the fact that these serious readers think and feel something in response to his work he finds life-giving. At the same time he may not always be able to reply to their specific questions in kind. I wondered if it might clarify something, for both the questioners and myself, if I set down a general reply to the question that comes to me most often in the mail, from

both students and their teachers, after some classroom discussion. The unrivaled favorite is this: "Is Phoenix Jackson's grandson really *dead*?"

2 It refers to a short story I wrote years ago called "A Worn Path," which tells of a day's journey an old woman makes on foot from deep in the country into town and into a doctor's office on behalf of her little grandson; he is at home, periodically ill, and periodically she comes for his medicine; they give it to her as usual, she receives it and starts the journey back.

3 I had not meant to mystify readers by withholding any fact; it is not a writer's business to tease. The story is told through Phoenix's mind as she undertakes her errand. As the author at one with the character as I tell it, I must assume that the boy is alive. As the reader, you are free to think as you like, of course: the story invites you to believe that no matter what happens, Phoenix for as long as she is able to walk and can hold to her purpose will make her journey. The *possibility* that she would keep on even if he were dead is there in her devotion and its single-minded, single-track errand. Certainly the *artistic* truth, which should be good enough for the fact, lies in Phoenix's own answer to that question. When the nurse asks, "He isn't dead, is he?" she speaks for herself: "He still the same. He going to last."

4 The grandchild is the incentive. But it is the journey, the going of the errand, that is the story, and the question is not whether the grandchild is in reality alive or dead. It doesn't affect the outcome of the story or its meaning from start to finish. But it is not the question itself that has struck me as much as the idea, almost without exception implied in the asking, that for Phoenix's grandson to be dead would somehow make the story "better."

5 It's *all right*, I want to say to the students who write to me, for things to be what they appear to be, and for words to mean what they say. It's all right, too, for words and appearances to mean more than one thing—ambiguity is a fact of life. A fiction writer's responsibility covers not only what he presents as the facts of a given story but what he chooses to stir up as their implications; in the end, these implications, too, become facts, in the larger, fictional sense. But it is not all right, not in good faith, for things *not* to mean what they say.

6 The grandson's plight was real and it made the truth of the story, which is the story of an errand of love carried out. If the child no longer lived, the truth would persist in the "wornness" of the path. But his being dead can't increase the truth of the story, can't affect it one way or the other. I think I signal this, because the end of the story has been

reached before old Phoenix gets home again: she simply starts back. To the question "Is the grandson really dead?" I could reply that it doesn't make any difference. I could also say that I did not make him up in order to let him play a trick on Phoenix. But my best answer would be: "*Phoenix* is alive."

7 The origin of a story is sometimes a trustworthy clue to the author—or can provide him with the clue—to its key image; maybe in this case it will do the same for the reader. One day I saw a solitary old woman like Phoenix. She was walking; I saw her, at middle distance, in a winter country landscape, and watched her slowly make her way across my line of vision. That sight of her made me write the story. I invented an errand for her, but that only seemed a living part of the figure she was herself: what errand other than for someone else could be making her go? And her going was the first thing, her persisting in her landscape was the real thing, and the first and the real were what I wanted and worked to keep. I brought her up close enough, by imagination, to describe her face, make her present to the eyes, but the full-length figure moving across the winter fields was the indelible one and the image to keep, and the perspective extending into the vanishing distance the true one to hold in mind.

8 I invented for my character, as I wrote, some passing adventures—some dreams and harassments and a small triumph or two, some jolts to her pride, some flights of fancy to console her, one or two encounters to scare her, a moment that gave her cause to feel ashamed, a moment to dance and preen—for it had to be a *journey*, and all these things belonged to that, parts of life's uncertainty.

9 A narrative line is in its deeper sense, of course, the tracing out of a meaning, and the real continuity of a story lies in this probing forward. The real dramatic force of a story depends on the strength of the emotion that has set it going. The emotional value is the measure of the reach of the story. What gives any such content to "A Worn Path" is not its circumstances but its *subject*: the deep-grained habit of love.

10 What I hoped would come clear was that in the whole surround of this story, the world it threads through, the only certain thing at all is the worn path. The habit of love cuts through confusion and stumbles or contrives its way out of difficulty, it remembers the way even when it forgets, for a dumbfounded moment, its reason for being. The path is the thing that matters.

11 *Her* victory—old Phoenix's—is when she sees the diploma in the doctor's office, when she finds "nailed up on the wall the document that

had been stamped with the gold seal and framed in the gold frame, which matched the dream that was hung up in her head." The return with the medicine is just a matter of retracing her own footsteps. It is the part of the journey, and of the story, that can now go without saying.

12 In the matter of function, old Phoenix's way might even do as a sort of parallel to your way of work if you are a writer of stories. The way to get there is the all-important, all-absorbing problem, and this problem is your reason for undertaking the story. Your only guide, too, is your sureness about your subject, about what this subject is. Like Phoenix, you work all your life to find your way, through all the obstructions and the false appearances and the upsets you may have brought on yourself, to reach a meaning—using inventions of your imagination, perhaps helped out by your dreams and bits of good luck. And finally too, like Phoenix, you have to assume that what you are working in aid of is life, not death.

13 But you would make the trip anyway—wouldn't you?—just on hope.

QUESTIONS FOR ANALYSIS AND DISCUSSION

1. Welty confirms the importance of recognizing point of view. What is the story's point of view? How does that answer the question about Phoenix's grandson?
2. Why is Welty, as a writer, bothered by the question about Phoenix's grandson? (Note that she is bothered for two reasons.)
3. What is the fiction writer's responsibility? What does Welty mean by "artistic truth"? Can her observations apply to all writers?
4. Why do the students who wrote to Welty (and others who didn't write) seem unwilling to let words mean what they say? Are you inclined to read fiction differently from nonfiction? If so, describe the difference.
5. What is the difference between ambiguity and falsity?
6. What did Welty take from experience and what did she invent for "A Worn Path"? If she is in any way representative of fiction writers, what can you observe in general about the process of composing stories?
7. In what ways, for Welty, does Phoenix's journey represent the work of a writer? What similar values does Welty affirm in the story and in her essay?

The Story of an Hour

KATE CHOPIN

Now a highly acclaimed short-story writer, Kate Chopin (1851–1904) enjoyed a decade of publication and popularity from 1890 to 1900, and then critical condemnation followed by sixty years of neglect. Raised in St. Louis by a successful Irish businessman and a mother from an old Creole family, Chopin experienced a Catholic education and a debutante's social world. After marriage, she lived in New Orleans and in a rural plantation section of Louisiana. Like many women writers, she began her writing career after her husband's death, having returned to St. Louis with her six children.

Between 1892 and 1900 Vogue *magazine accepted nineteen of Chopin's stories, and two collections were published:* Bayou Folk *(1894) and* A Night in Acadie *(1897). Depicting Louisiana regional life, Chopin demonstrates a skill with the short story that makes her more than a local colorist of some historical interest. Indeed, the depth of her psychological insight has led to comparisons with Gustave Flaubert and Henry James; it is also what led to strong condemnation with the publication, in 1899, of her short novel* The Awakening. *Chopin portrays religious feelings as sexual sublimation and presents female characters who are frank and free about their sexuality, or struggling for new levels of awareness after years of repression and subservience to traditional roles. "The Story of an Hour" shows us one woman's moment of insight.*

1 Knowing that Mrs. Mallard was afflicted with a heart trouble, great care was taken to break to her as gently as possible the news of her husband's death.

2 It was her sister Josephine who told her, in broken sentences; veiled hints that revealed in half concealing. Her husband's friend Richards was there, too, near her. It was he who had been in the newspaper office when intelligence of the railroad disaster was received, with Brently Mallard's name leading the list of "killed." He had only taken the time to assure himself of its truth by a second telegram, and had hastened to forestall any less careful, less tender friend in bearing the sad message.

3 She did not hear the story as many women have heard the same, with a paralyzed inability to accept its significance. She wept at once, with sudden, wild abandonment, in her sister's arms. When the storm

of grief had spent itself she went away to her room alone. She would have no one follow her.

4 There stood, facing the open window, a comfortable, roomy armchair. Into this she sank, pressed down by a physical exhaustion that haunted her body and seemed to reach into her soul.

5 She could see in the open square before her house the tops of trees that were all aquiver with the new spring life. The delicious breath of rain was in the air. In the street below a peddler was crying his wares. The notes of a distant song which some one was singing reached her faintly, and countless sparrows were twittering in the eaves.

6 There were patches of blue sky showing here and there through the clouds that had met and piled one above the other in the west facing her window.

7 She sat with her head thrown back upon the cushion of the chair, quite motionless, except when a sob came up into her throat and shook her, as a child who has cried itself to sleep continues to sob in its dreams.

8 She was young, with a fair, calm face, whose lines bespoke repression and even a certain strength. But now there was a dull stare in her eyes, whose gaze was fixed away off yonder on one of those patches of blue sky. It was not a glance of reflection, but rather indicated a suspension of intelligent thought.

9 There was something coming to her and she was waiting for it, fearfully. What was it? She did not know; it was too subtle and elusive to name. But she felt it, creeping out of the sky, reaching toward her through the sounds, the scents, the color that filled the air.

10 Now her bosom rose and fell tumultuously. She was beginning to recognize this thing that was approaching to possess her, and she was striving to beat it back with her will—as powerless as her two white slender hands would have been.

11 When she abandoned herself a little whispered word escaped her slightly parted lips. She said it over and over under her breath: "free, free, free!" The vacant stare and the look of terror that had followed it went from her eyes. They stayed keen and bright. Her pulses beat fast, and the coursing blood warmed and relaxed every inch of her body.

12 She did not stop to ask if it were or were not a monstrous joy that held her. A clear and exalted perception enabled her to dismiss the suggestion as trivial.

13 She knew that she would weep again when she saw the kind, tender

hands folded in death; the face that had never looked save with love upon her, fixed and gray and dead. But she saw beyond that bitter moment a long procession of years to come that would belong to her absolutely. And she opened and spread her arms out to them in welcome.

14 There would be no one to live for her during those coming years; she would live for herself. There would be no powerful will bending hers in that blind persistence with which men and women believe they have a right to impose a private will upon a fellow-creature. A kind intention or a cruel intention made the act seem no less a crime as she looked upon it in that brief moment of illumination.

15 And yet she had loved him—sometimes. Often she had not. What did it matter! What could love, the unsolved mystery, count for in face of this possession of self-assertion which she suddenly recognized as the strongest impulse of her being!

16 "Free! Body and soul free!" she kept whispering.

17 Josephine was kneeling before the closed door with her lips to the keyhole, imploring for admission. "Louise, open the door! I beg; open the door—you will make yourself ill. What are you doing, Louise? For heaven's sake open the door."

18 "Go away. I am not making myself ill." No; she was drinking in a very elixir of life through that open window.

19 Her fancy was running riot along those days ahead of her. Spring days, and summer days, and all sorts of days that would be her own. She breathed a quick prayer that life might be long. It was only yesterday she had thought with a shudder that life might be long.

20 She arose at length and opened the door to her sister's importunities. There was a feverish triumph in her eyes, and she carried herself unwittingly like a goddess of Victory. She clasped her sister's waist, and together they descended the stairs. Richards stood waiting for them at the bottom.

21 Some one was opening the front door with a latchkey. It was Brently Mallard who entered, a little travel-stained, composedly carrying his grip-sack and umbrella. He had been far from the scene of accident, and did not even know there had been one. He stood amazed at Josephine's piercing cry; at Richards' quick motion to screen him from the view of his wife.

22 But Richards was too late.

23 When the doctors came they said she had died of heart disease—of joy that kills.

QUESTIONS FOR ANALYSIS AND DISCUSSION

1. Analyze the story's plot structure, using the terms presented in the chapter introduction.
2. What type of character conflict dominates the story? State the opposing elements of the conflict.
3. When Mrs. Mallard goes to her room, she gazes out the window. Consider the details of the scene; what do these details have in common? How do the details help us understand what Mrs. Mallard experiences?
4. Why is it inaccurate to say that Mrs. Mallard did not love her husband?
5. The author James Joyce has described a character's moment of insight or intuition as an "epiphany." What is Mrs. Mallard's epiphany?
6. Are we to agree with the doctor's explanation for Mrs. Mallard's death? What term is appropriate to describe the story's conclusion?

The Secret Life of Walter Mitty

JAMES THURBER

A native of Columbus, Ohio, James Thurber (1894–1962) attended Ohio State University and began his career as a reporter with the Columbus Dispatch. *His success as a humorist, cartoonist, and short-story writer came not in Ohio, however, but in New York City after he met E. B. White and Harold Ross and joined* The New Yorker *staff. In collaboration with White, Thurber in 1929 published his first book,* Is Sex Necessary? *And in 1931, with White's recognition of his talent, Thurber's first cartoons were published in* The New Yorker. *His burlesque autobiography,* My Life and Hard Times, *appeared in 1933; other works, collections of stories and essays and sketches, followed, along with numerous gallery exhibitions of his drawings. Thurber is most widely known, though, for "The Secret Life of Walter Mitty," published in* The New Yorker *in 1939, filmed in 1947, and now anthologized in short-story collections and American literature texts the world over.*

Like Twain's Huck Finn, Thurber's Mitty has assumed a life of his own in American culture. Unfortunately for Mitty, though, he lacks Huck's survival skills. Poor Mitty is laughed at by passersby, dominated by his wife, and intimidated by that modern marvel, the car. Thurber's humor is not bubbling with life but filled with melancholy and a sense of the absurd. His frightened characters struggle unsuccessfully in or retreat from a complex world they can neither understand nor control. Understanding the close connection between comic elements and serious observations, Thurber wrote: "In anything funny you write that isn't close to serious you've missed something along the line."

1 "We're going through!" The Commander's voice was like thin ice breaking. He wore his full-dress uniform, with the heavily braided white cap pulled down rakishly over one cold gray eye. "We can't make it, sir. It's spoiling for a hurricane, if you ask me." "I'm not asking you, Lieutenant Berg," said the Commander. "Throw on the power lights! Rev her up to 8500! We're going through!" The pounding of the cylinders increased: ta-pocketa-pocketa-pocketa-*pocketa-pocketa.* The Commander stared at the ice forming on the pilot window. He walked over and twisted a row of complicated dials. "Switch on No. 8 auxiliary!" he shouted. "Switch on No. 8 auxiliary!" repeated Lieutenant Berg. "Full strength in No. 3 turret!" shouted the Commander. "Full strength in No. 3 turret!" The crew, bending to their various tasks in the huge, hurtling eight-engined Navy hydroplane, looked at each other and grinned. "The Old Man'll get us through," they said to one another. "The Old Man ain't afraid of hell!" . . .

2 "Not so fast! You're driving too fast!" said Mrs. Mitty. "What are you driving so fast for?"

3 "Hmm?" said Walter Mitty. He looked at his wife, in the seat beside him, with shocked astonishment. She seemed grossly unfamiliar, like a strange woman who had yelled at him in a crowd. "You were up to fifty-five," she said. "You know I don't like to go more than forty. You were up to fifty-five." Walter Mitty drove on toward Waterbury in silence, the roaring of the SN202 through the worst storm in twenty years of Navy flying fading in the remote, intimate airways of his mind. "You're tensed up again," said Mrs. Mitty. "It's one of your days. I wish you'd let Dr. Renshaw look you over."

4 Walter Mitty stopped the car in front of the building where his wife went to have her hair done. "Remember to get those overshoes while I'm having my hair done," she said. "I don't need overshoes," said Mitty. She put her mirror back into her bag. "We've been all through that," she said, getting out of the car. "You're not a young man any longer." He raced the engine a little. "Why don't you wear your gloves? Have you lost your gloves?" Walter Mitty reached in a pocket and brought out the gloves. He put them on, but after she had turned and gone into the building and he had driven on to a red light, he took them

off again. "Pick it up, brother!" snapped a cop as the light changed, and Mitty hastily pulled on his gloves and lurched ahead. He drove around the streets aimlessly for a time, and then he drove past the hospital on his way to the parking lot.

5 . . . "It's the millionaire banker, Wellington McMillan," said the pretty nurse. "Yes?" said Walter Mitty, removing his gloves slowly. "Who has the case?" "Dr. Renshaw and Dr. Benbow, but there are two specialists here, Dr. Remington from New York and Dr. Pritchard-Mitford from London. He flew over." A door opened down a long, cool corridor and Dr. Renshaw came out. He looked distraught and haggard. "Hello, Mitty," he said. "We're having the devil's own time with McMillan, the millionaire banker and close personal friend of Roosevelt. Obstreosis of the ductal tract. Tertiary. Wish you'd take a look at him." "Glad to," said Mitty.

6 In the operating room there were whispered introductions: "Dr. Remington, Dr. Mitty. Dr. Pritchard-Mitford, Dr. Mitty." "I've read your book on streptothricosis," said Pritchard-Mitford, shaking hands. "A brilliant performance, sir." "Thank you," said Walter Mitty. "Didn't know you were in the States, Mitty," grumbled Remington. "Coals to Newcastle, bringing Mitford and me up here for a tertiary." "You are very kind," said Mitty. A huge, complicated machine, connected to the operating table, with many tubes and wires, began at this moment to go pocketa-pocketa-pocketa. "The new anesthetizer is giving away!" shouted an intern. "There is no one in the East who knows how to fix it!" "Quiet, man!" said Mitty, in a low, cool voice. He sprang to the machine, which was now going pocketa-pocketa-queep-pocketa-queep. He began fingering delicately a row of glistening dials. "Give me a fountain pen!" he snapped. Someone handed him a fountain pen. He pulled a faulty piston out of the machine and inserted the pen in its place. "That will hold for ten minutes," he said. "Get on with the operation." A nurse hurried over and whispered to Renshaw, and Mitty saw the man turn pale. "Coreopsis has set in," said Renshaw nervously. "If you would take over, Mitty?" Mitty looked at him and at the craven figure of Benbow, who drank, and at the grave, uncertain faces of the two great specialists. "If you wish," he said. They slipped a white gown on him; he adjusted a mask and drew on thin gloves; nurses handed him shining . . .

7 "Back it up, Mac! Look out for that Buick!" Walter Mitty jammed on the brakes. "Wrong lane, Mac," said the parking-lot attendant, looking at Mitty closely. "Gee. Yeh," muttered Mitty. He began cautiously to back out of the lane marked "Exit Only." "Leave her sit there," said

the attendant. "I'll put her away." Mitty got out of the car. "Hey, better leave the key." "Oh," said Mitty, handing the man the ignition key. The attendant vaulted into the car, backed it up with insolent skill, and put it where it belonged.

8 They're so damn cocky, thought Walter Mitty, walking along Main Street; they think they know everything. Once he had tried to take his chains off, outside New Milford, and he had got them wound around the axles. A man had had to come out in a wrecking car and unwind them, a young, grinning garageman. Since then Mrs. Mitty always made him drive to a garage to have the chains taken off. The next time, he thought, I'll wear my right arm in a sling; they won't grin at me then. I'll have my right arm in a sling and they'll see I couldn't possibly take the chains off myself. He kicked at the slush on the sidewalk. "Overshoes," he said to himself, and he began looking for a shoe store.

9 When he came out into the street again, with the overshoes in a box under his arm, Walter Mitty began to wonder what the other thing was his wife had told him to get. She had told him, twice before they set out from their house for Waterbury. In a way he hated these weekly trips to town—he was always getting something wrong. Kleenex, he thought, Squibb's, razor blades? No. Tooth paste, toothbrush, bicarbonate, carborundum, initiative and referendum? He gave it up. But she would remember it. "Where's the what's-its-name?" she would ask. "Don't tell me you forget the what's-its-name." A newsboy went by shouting something about the Waterbury trial.

10 . . . "Perhaps this will refresh your memory." The District Attorney suddenly thrust a heavy automatic at the quiet figure on the witness stand. "Have you ever seen this before?" Walter Mitty took the gun and examined it expertly. "This is my Webley-Vickers 50.80," he said calmly. An excited buzz ran around the courtroom. The Judge rapped for order. "You are a crack shot with any sort of firearms, I believe?" said the District Attorney, insinuatingly. "Objection!" shouted Mitty's attorney. "We have shown that the defendant could not have fired the shot. We have shown that he wore his right arm in a sling on the night of the fourteenth of July." Walter Mitty raised his hand briefly and the bickering attorneys were stilled. "With any known make of gun," he said evenly, "I could have killed Gregory Fitzhurst at three hundred feet *with my left hand.*" Pandemonium broke loose in the courtroom. A woman's scream rose above the bedlam and suddenly a lovely, dark-haired girl was in Walter Mitty's arms. The District Attorney struck at her savagely.

Without rising from his chair, Mitty let the man have it on the point of the chin. "You miserable cur!" . . .

11 "Puppy biscuit," said Walter Mitty. He stopped walking and the buildings of Waterbury rose up out of the misty courtroom and surrounded him again. A woman who was passing laughed. "He said 'Puppy biscuit,' " she said to her companion. "That man said 'Puppy biscuit' to himself." Walter Mitty hurried on. He went into an A.&P., not the first one he came to but a smaller one farther up the street. "I want some biscuit for small, young dogs," he said to the clerk. "Any special brand, sir?" The greatest pistol shot in the world thought a moment. "It says 'Puppies Bark for It' on the box," said Walter Mitty.

12 His wife would be through at the hairdresser's in fifteen minutes, Mitty saw in looking at his watch, unless they had trouble drying it; sometimes they had trouble drying it. She didn't like to get to the hotel first; she would want him to be there waiting for her as usual. He found a big leather chair in the lobby, facing a window, and he put the overshoes and the puppy biscuit on the floor beside it. He picked up an old copy of *Liberty* and sank down into the chair. "Can Germany Conquer the World Through the Air?" Walter Mitty looked at the pictures of bombing planes and of ruined streets.

13 . . . "The cannonading has got the wind up in young Raleigh, sir," said the sergeant. Captain Mitty looked up at him through tousled hair. "Get him to bed," he said wearily, "with the others. I'll fly alone." "But you can't, sir," said the sergeant anxiously. "It takes two men to handle that bomber and the Archies are pounding hell out of the air. Von Richtman's circus is between here and Saulier." "Somebody's got to get that ammunition dump," said Mitty. "I'm going over. Spot of brandy?" He poured a drink for the sergeant and one for himself. War thundered and whined around the dugout and battered at the door. There was a rending of wood and splinters flew through the room. "A bit of a near thing," said Captain Mitty carelessly. "The box barrage is closing in," said the sergeant. "We only live once, Sergeant," said Mitty, with his faint, fleeting smile. "Or do we?" He poured another brandy and tossed it off. "I never see a man could hold his brandy like you, sir," said the sergeant. "Begging your pardon, sir." Captain Mitty stood up and strapped on his huge Webley-Vickers automatic. "It's forty kilometers through hell, sir," said the sergeant. Mitty finished one last brandy. "After all," he said softly, "what isn't?" The pounding of the cannon increased; there was the rat-tat-tatting of machine guns, and from somewhere came the menacing pocketa-pocketa-pocketa of the new flame-throwers. Walter Mitty

walked to the door of the dugout humming "Auprès de Ma Blonde." He turned and waved to the sergeant. "Cheerio!" he said. . . .

14 Something struck his shoulder. "I've been looking all over this hotel for you," said Mrs. Mitty. "Why do you have to hide in this old chair? How did you expect me to find you?" "Things close in," said Walter Mitty vaguely. "What?" Mrs. Mitty said. "Did you get the what's-its-name? The puppy biscuit? What's in that box?" "Overshoes," said Mitty. "Couldn't you have put them on in the store?" "I was thinking," said Walter Mitty. "Does it ever occur to you that I am sometimes thinking?" She looked at him. "I'm going to take your temperature when I get you home," she said.

15 They went out through the revolving doors that made a faintly derisive whistling sound when you pushed them. It was two blocks to the parking lot. At the drugstore on the corner she said, "Wait here for me. I forgot something. I won't be a minute." She was more than a minute. Walter Mitty lighted a cigarette. It began to rain, rain with sleet in it. He stood up against the wall of the drugstore, smoking. . . . He put his shoulders back and his heels together. "To hell with the handkerchief," said Walter Mitty scornfully. He took one last drag on his cigarette and snapped it away. Then, with that faint, fleeting smile playing about his lips, he faced the firing squad; erect and motionless, proud and disdainful, Walter Mitty the Undefeated, inscrutable to the last.

QUESTIONS FOR ANALYSIS AND DISCUSSION

1. Analyze the story's plot structure according to the pattern described in the introduction to the chapter. What other structure dominates the story and is the key to our understanding Mitty?
2. What type of character conflict is central to the story? State the terms of the conflict. What other types of character conflict does Mitty experience?
3. By what techniques does Thurber convey Mitty's character?
4. What do Mitty's dreams have in common? What do they tell us about Mitty?
5. How does Thurber want us to feel about Mitty? Are we to laugh at him? Identify with him? Reject him? Weep with him?
6. What elements in the story are humorous? What makes the story serious, too?

The Guest

ALBERT CAMUS

Albert Camus was born in Mondovi, Algeria, in 1913, of poor, illiterate parents. This was a world he never forgot; but it was a world of warm sun and bright skies that made poverty less painful, standing in sharp contrast, in Camus's perception, to the dark, oppressive slums of industrial cities. Thanks to two teachers who recognized his abilities, Camus was able to attend first the lycée in Algiers and then the university. Suffering periodically from tuberculosis, Camus was rejected for military service in World War II, but he continued his journalistic career with Combat, *an underground publication of the resistance movement in France, and published two works that assured his fame: the novel* The Stranger *(1942) and the philosophical essay "The Myth of Sisyphus" (1941). After the war, Camus lived primarily in Paris and saw his four plays staged. He published two novels,* The Plague *(1947) and* The Fall *(1956); several collections of philosophical essays; and a collection of stories,* Exile and the Kingdom *(1957), from which "The Guest" is taken. In 1957 he was awarded the Nobel Prize in Literature; and then, in 1960, he was killed in an automobile accident. Fortunately for us, Camus accomplished much in his short life. His journalism, active involvement with the staging of his plays, and lecturing abroad when he became famous attest to his love of life and unwillingness to give himself over entirely to the solitude of artistic creation. Many feel that his Nobel Prize, awarded when he was so young, was in honor of the man as well as his works.*

"The Guest" has been called a narrative allegory; certainly it is a philosophical story, depicting Camus's perception that we find ourselves caught in situations that make it difficult to give meaning to our existence, even when we try. But for Camus the absurdity of the human situation was no cause for despair. His own words, from his acceptance speech in Stockholm, affirm life and art:

> *Art is not a solitary enjoyment. It is a means to move great numbers of people by giving them an exquisite image of shared suffering and joy. . . . And he who has chosen the life of an artist—as often occurs—because he believes himself different will soon learn that he can nurture his art and his difference only by avowing his resemblance to all men.*

1 The schoolmaster was watching the two men climb toward him. One was on horseback, the other on foot. They had not yet tackled the

abrupt rise leading to the schoolhouse built on the hillside. They were toiling onward, making slow progress in the snow, among the stones, on the vast expanse of the high, deserted plateau. From time to time the horse stumbled. Without hearing anything yet, he could see the breath issuing from the horse's nostrils. One of the men, at least, knew the region. They were following the trail although it had disappeared days ago under a layer of dirty white snow. The schoolmaster calculated that it would take them half an hour to get onto the hill. It was cold; he went back into the school to get a sweater.

2 He crossed the empty, frigid classroom. On the blackboard the four rivers of France, drawn with four different colored chalks, had been flowing toward their estuaries for the past three days. Snow had suddenly fallen in mid-October after eight months of drought without the transition of rain, and the twenty pupils, more or less, who lived in the villages scattered over the plateaus had stopped coming. With fair weather they would return. Daru now heated only the single room that was his lodging, adjoining the classroom and giving also onto the plateau to the east. Like the class windows, his window looked to the south too. On that side the school was a few kilometers from the point where the plateau began to slope toward the south. In clear weather could be seen the purple mass of the mountain range where the gap opened onto the desert.

3 Somewhat warmed, Daru returned to the window from which he had first seen the two men. They were no longer visible. Hence they must have tackled the rise. The sky was not so dark, for the snow had stopped falling during the night. The morning had opened with a dirty light which had scarcely become brighter as the ceiling of clouds lifted. At two in the afternoon it seemed as if the day were merely beginning. But still this was better than those three days when the thick snow was falling amidst unbroken darkness with little gusts of wind that rattled the double door of the classroom. Then Daru had spent long hours in his room, leaving it only to go to the shed and feed the chickens or get some coal. Fortunately the delivery truck from Tadjid, the nearest village to the north, had brought his supplies two days before the blizzard. It would return in forty-eight hours.

4 Besides, he had enough to resist a siege, for the little room was cluttered with bags of wheat that the administration left as a stock to distribute to those of his pupils whose families had suffered from the drought. Actually they had all been victims because they were all poor. Every day Daru would distribute a ration to the children. They had

missed it, he knew, during these bad days. Possibly one of the fathers or big brothers would come this afternoon and he could supply them with grain. It was just a matter of carrying them over to the next harvest. Now shiploads of wheat were arriving from France and the worst was over. But it would be hard to forget that poverty, that army of ragged ghosts wandering in the sunlight, the plateaus burned to a cinder month after month, the earth shriveled up little by little, literally scorched, every stone bursting into dust under one's foot. The sheep had died then by thousands and even a few men, here and there, sometimes without anyone's knowing.

5 In contrast with such poverty, he who lived almost like a monk in his remote schoolhouse, nonetheless satisfied with the little he had and with the rough life, had felt like a lord with his white-washed walls, his narrow couch, his unpainted shelves, his well, and his weekly provision of water and food. And suddenly this snow, without warning, without the foretaste of rain. This is the way the region was, cruel to live in, even without men—who didn't help matters either. But Daru had been born here. Everywhere else, he felt exiled.

6 He stepped out onto the terrace in front of the schoolhouse. The two men were now halfway up the slope. He recognized the horseman as Balducci, the old gendarme he had known for a long time. Balducci was holding on the end of a rope an Arab who was walking behind him with hands bound and head lowered. The gendarme waved a greeting to which Daru did not reply, lost as he was in contemplation of the Arab dressed in a faded blue jellaba, his feet in sandals but covered with socks of heavy raw wool, his head surmounted by a narrow, short *chèche*. They were approaching. Balducci was holding back his horse in order not to hurt the Arab, and the group was advancing slowly.

7 Within earshot, Balducci shouted: "One hour to do the three kilometers from El Ameur!" Daru did not answer. Short and square in his thick sweater, he watched them climb. Not once had the Arab raised his head. "Hello," said Daru when they got up onto the terrace. "Come in and warm up." Balducci painfully got down from his horse without letting go the rope. From under his bristling mustache he smiled at the schoolmaster. His little dark eyes, deep-set under a tanned forehead, and his mouth surrounded with wrinkles made him look attentive and studious. Daru took the bridle, led the horse to the shed, and came back to the two men, who were now waiting for him in the school. He led them into his room. "I am going to heat up the classroom," he said. "We'll be more comfortable there." When he entered the room again,

Balducci was on the couch. He had undone the rope tying him to the Arab, who had squatted near the stove. His hands still bound, the *chèche* pushed back on his head, he was looking toward the window. At first Daru noticed only his huge lips, fat, smooth, almost Negroid; yet his nose was straight, his eyes were dark and full of fever. The *chèche* revealed an obstinate forehead and, under the weathered skin now rather discolored by the cold, the whole face had a restless and rebellious look that struck Daru when the Arab, turning his face toward him, looked him straight in the eyes. "Go into the other room," said the schoolmaster, "and I'll make you some mint tea." "Thanks," Balducci said. "What a chore! How I long for retirement." And addressing his prisoner in Arabic: "Come on, you." The Arab got up and, slowly, holding his bound wrists in front of him, went into the classroom.

8 With the tea, Daru brought a chair. But Balducci was already enthroned on the nearest pupil's desk and the Arab had squatted against the teacher's platform facing the stove, which stood between the desk and the window. When he held out the glass of tea to the prisoner, Daru hesitated at the sight of his bound hands. "He might perhaps be untied." "Sure," said Balducci. "That was for the trip." He started to get to his feet. But Daru, setting the glass on the floor, had knelt beside the Arab. Without saying anything, the Arab watched him with his feverish eyes. Once his hands were free, he rubbed his swollen wrists against each other, took the glass of tea, and sucked up the burning liquid in swift little sips.

9 "Good," said Daru. "And where are you headed?"

10 Balducci withdrew his mustache from the tea. "Here, son."

11 "Odd pupils! And you're spending the night?"

12 "No. I'm going back to El Ameur. And you will deliver this fellow to Tinguit. He is expected at police headquarters."

13 Balducci was looking at Daru with a friendly little smile.

14 "What's this story?" asked the schoolmaster. "Are you pulling my leg?"

15 "No, son. Those are the orders."

16 "The orders? I'm not . . . " Daru hesitated, not wanting to hurt the old Corsican. "I mean, that's not my job."

17 "What! What's the meaning of that? In wartime people do all kinds of jobs."

18 "Then I'll wait for the declaration of war!"

19 Balducci nodded.

20 "O.K. But the orders exist and they concern you too. Things are

brewing, it appears. There is talk of a forthcoming revolt. We are mobilized, in a way."

21 Daru still had his obstinate look.

22 "Listen, son," Balducci said. "I like you and you must understand. There's only a dozen of us at El Ameur to patrol throughout the whole territory of a small department and I must get back in a hurry. I was told to hand this guy over to you and return without delay. He couldn't be kept there. His village was beginning to stir; they wanted to take him back. You must take him to Tinguit tomorrow before the day is over. Twenty kilometers shouldn't faze a husky fellow like you. After that, all will be over. You'll come back to your pupils and your comfortable life."

23 Behind the wall the horse could be heard snorting and pawing the earth. Daru was looking out the window. Decidedly, the weather was clearing and the light was increasing over the snowy plateau. When all the snow was melted, the sun would take over again and once more would burn the fields of stone. For days, still, the unchanging sky would shed its dry light on the solitary expanse where nothing had any connection with man.

24 "After all," he said, turning around toward Balducci, "what did he do?" And, before the gendarme had opened his mouth, he asked: "Does he speak French?"

25 "No, not a word. We had been looking for him for a month, but they were hiding him. He killed his cousin."

26 "Is he against us?"

27 "I don't think so. But you can never be sure."

28 "Why did he kill?"

29 "A family squabble, I think. One owed the other grain, it seems. It's not at all clear. In short, he killed his cousin with a billhook. You know, like a sheep, *kreezk!*"

30 Balducci made the gesture of drawing a blade across his throat and the Arab, his attention attracted, watched him with a sort of anxiety. Daru felt a sudden wrath against the man, against all men with their rotten spite, their tireless hates, their blood lust.

31 But the kettle was singing on the stove. He served Balducci more tea, hesitated, then served the Arab again, who, a second time, drank avidly. His raised arms made the jellaba fall open and the schoolmaster saw his thin, muscular chest.

32 "Thanks, kid," Balducci said. "And now, I'm off."

33 He got up and went toward the Arab, taking a small rope from his pocket.

34 "What are you doing?" Daru asked dryly.

35 Balducci, disconcerted, showed him the rope.

36 "Don't bother."

37 The old gendarme hesitated. "It's up to you. Of course, you are armed?"

38 "I have my shotgun."

39 "Where?"

40 "In the trunk."

41 "You ought to have it near your bed."

42 "Why? I have nothing to fear."

43 "You're crazy, son. If there's an uprising, no one is safe, we're all in the same boat."

44 "I'll defend myself. I'll have time to see them coming."

45 Balducci began to laugh, then suddenly the mustache covered the white teeth.

46 "You'll have time? O.K. That's just what I was saying. You have always been a little cracked. That's why I like you, my son was like that."

47 At the same time he took out his revolver and put it on the desk.

48 "Keep it; I don't need two weapons from here to El Ameur."

49 The revolver shone against the black paint of the table. When the gendarme turned toward him, the schoolmaster caught the smell of leather and horseflesh.

50 "Listen, Balducci," Daru said suddenly, "every bit of this disgusts me, and first of all your fellow here. But I won't hand him over. Fight, yes, if I have to. But not that."

51 The old gendarme stood in front of him and looked at him severely.

52 "You're being a fool," he said slowly. "I don't like it either. You don't get used to putting a rope on a man even after years of it, and you're even ashamed—yes, ashamed. But you can't let them have their way."

53 "I won't hand him over," Daru said again.

54 "It's an order, son, and I repeat it."

55 "That's right. Repeat to them what I've said to you: I won't hand him over."

56 Balducci made a visible effort to reflect. He looked at the Arab and at Daru. At last he decided.

57 "No, I won't tell them anything. If you want to drop us, go ahead; I'll not denounce you. I have an order to deliver the prisoner and I'm doing so. And now you'll just sign this paper for me."

58 "There's no need. I'll not deny that you left him with me."

59 "Don't be mean with me. I know you'll tell the truth. You're from hereabouts and you are a man. But you must sign, that's the rule."

60 Daru opened his drawer, took out a little square bottle of purple ink, the red wooden penholder with the "sergeant-major" pen he used for making models of penmanship, and signed. The gendarme carefully folded the paper and put it into his wallet. Then he moved toward the door.

61 "I'll see you off," Daru said.

62 "No," said Balducci. "There's no use being polite. You insulted me."

63 He looked at the Arab, motionless in the same spot, sniffed peevishly, and turned away toward the door. "Good-by, son," he said. The door shut behind him. Balducci appeared suddenly outside the window and then disappeared. His footsteps were muffled by the snow. The horse stirred on the other side of the wall and several chickens fluttered in fright. A moment later Balducci reappeared outside the window leading the horse by the bridle. He walked toward the little rise without turning around and disappeared from sight with the horse following him. A big stone could be heard bouncing down. Daru walked back toward the prisoner, who, without stirring, never took his eyes off him. "Wait," the schoolmaster said in Arabic and went toward the bedroom. As he was going through the door, he had a second thought, went to the desk, took the revolver, and stuck it in his pocket. Then, without looking back, he went into his room.

64 For some time he lay on his couch watching the sky gradually close over, listening to the silence. It was this silence that had seemed painful to him during the first days here, after the war. He had requested a post in the little town at the base of the foothills separating the upper plateaus from the desert. There, rocky walls, green and black to the north, pink and lavender to the south, marked the frontier of eternal summer. He had been named to a post farther north, on the plateau itself. In the beginning, the solitude and the silence had been hard for him on these wastelands peopled only by stones. Occasionally, furrows suggested cultivation, but they had been dug to uncover a certain kind of stone good for building. The only plowing here was to harvest rocks. Elsewhere a thin layer of soil accumulated in the hollows would be scraped out to enrich paltry village gardens. This is the way it was: bare rock covered three quarters of the region. Towns sprang up, flourished, then disappeared; men came by, loved one another or fought bitterly, then died. No one in this desert, neither he nor his guest, mattered. And yet, outside this desert neither of them, Daru knew, could have really lived.

65 When he got up, no noise came from the classroom. He was amazed at the unmixed joy he derived from the mere thought that the Arab might have fled and that he would be alone with no decision to make. But the prisoner was there. He had merely stretched out between the stove and the desk. With eyes open, he was staring at the ceiling. In that position, his thick lips were particularly noticeable, giving him a pouting look. "Come," said Daru. The Arab got up and followed him. In the bedroom, the schoolmaster pointed to a chair near the table under the window. The Arab sat down without taking his eyes off Daru.

66 "Are you hungry?"

67 "Yes," the prisoner said.

68 Daru set the table for two. He took flour and oil, shaped a cake in a frying-pan, and lighted the little stove that functioned on bottled gas. While the cake was cooking, he went out to the shed to get cheese, eggs, dates, and condensed milk. When the cake was done he set it on the window sill to cool, heated some condensed milk diluted with water, and beat up the eggs into an omelette. In one of his motions he knocked against the revolver stuck in his right pocket. He set the bowl down, went into the classroom, and put the revolver in his desk drawer. When he came back to the room, night was falling. He put on the light and served the Arab. "Eat," he said. The Arab took a piece of the cake, lifted it eagerly to his mouth, and stopped short.

69 "And you?" he asked.

70 "After you. I'll eat too."

71 The thick lips opened slightly. The Arab hesitated, then bit into the cake determinedly.

72 The meal over, the Arab looked at the schoolmaster. "Are you the judge?"

73 "No, I'm simply keeping you until tomorrow."

74 "Why do you eat with me?"

75 "I'm hungry."

76 The Arab fell silent. Daru got up and went out. He brought back a folding bed from the shed, set it up between the table and the stove, perpendicular to his own bed. From a large suitcase which, upright in a corner, served as a shelf for papers, he took two blankets and arranged them on the camp bed. Then he stopped, felt useless, and sat down on his bed. There was nothing more to do or to get ready. He had to look at this man. He looked at him, therefore, trying to imagine his face bursting with rage. He couldn't do so. He could see nothing but the dark yet shining eyes and the animal mouth.

77 "Why did you kill him?" he asked in a voice whose hostile tone surprised him.

78 The Arab looked away.

79 "He ran away. I ran after him."

80 He raised his eyes to Daru again and they were full of a sort of woeful interrogation. "Now what will they do to me?"

81 "Are you afraid?"

82 He stiffened, turning his eyes away.

83 "Are you sorry?"

84 The Arab stared at him openmouthed. Obviously he did not understand. Daru's annoyance was growing. At the same time he felt awkward and self-conscious with his big body wedged between the two beds.

85 "Lie down there," he said impatiently. "That's your bed."

86 The Arab didn't move. He called to Daru:

87 "Tell me!"

88 The schoolmaster looked at him.

89 "Is the gendarme coming back tomorrow?"

90 "I don't know."

91 "Are you coming with us?"

92 "I don't know. Why?"

93 The prisoner got up and stretched out on top of the blankets, his feet toward the window. The light from the electric bulb shone straight into his eyes and he closed them at once.

94 "Why?" Daru repeated, standing beside the bed.

95 The Arab opened his eyes under the blinding light and looked at him, trying not to blink.

96 "Come with us," he said.

97 In the middle of the night, Daru was still not asleep. He had gone to bed after undressing completely; he generally slept naked. But when he suddenly realized that he had nothing on, he hesitated. He felt vulnerable and the temptation came to him to put his clothes back on. Then he shrugged his shoulders; after all, he wasn't a child and, if need be, he could break his adversary in two. From his bed he could observe him, lying on his back, still motionless with his eyes closed under the harsh light. When Daru turned out the light, the darkness seemed to coagulate all of a sudden. Little by little, the night came back to life in the window where the starless sky was stirring gently. The schoolmaster soon made out the body lying at his feet. The Arab still did not move,

but his eyes seemed open. A faint wind was prowling around the schoolhouse. Perhaps it would drive away the clouds and the sun would reappear.

98 During the night the wind increased. The hens fluttered a little and then were silent. The Arab turned over on his side with his back to Daru, who thought he heard him moan. Then he listened for his guest's breathing, become heavier and more regular. He listened to that breath so close to him and mused without being able to go to sleep. In this room where he had been sleeping alone for a year, this presence bothered him. But it bothered him also by imposing on him a sort of brotherhood he knew well but refused to accept in the present circumstances. Men who share the same rooms, soldiers or prisoners, develop a strange alliance as if, having cast off their armor with their clothing, they fraternized every evening, over and above their differences, in the ancient community of dream and fatigue. But Daru shook himself; he didn't like such musings, and it was essential to sleep.

99 A little later, however, when the Arab stirred slightly, the schoolmaster was still not asleep. When the prisoner made a second move, he stiffened, on the alert. The Arab was lifting himself slowly on his arms with almost the motion of a sleepwalker. Seated upright in bed, he waited motionless without turning his head toward Daru, as if he were listening attentively. Daru did not stir; it had just occurred to him that the revolver was still in the drawer of his desk. It was better to act at once. Yet he continued to observe the prisoner, who, with the same slithery motion, put his feet on the ground, waited again, then began to stand up slowly. Daru was about to call out to him when the Arab began to walk, in a quite natural but extraordinarily silent way. He was heading toward the door at the end of the room that opened into the shed. He lifted the latch with precaution and went out, pushing the door behind him but without shutting it. Daru had not stirred. "He is running away," he merely thought. "Good riddance!" Yet he listened attentively. The hens were not fluttering; the guest must be on the plateau. A faint sound of water reached him, and he didn't know what it was until the Arab again stood framed in the doorway, closed the door carefully, and came back to bed without a sound. Then Daru turned his back on him and fell asleep. Still later he seemed, from the depths of his sleep, to hear furtive steps around the schoolhouse. "I'm dreaming! I'm dreaming!" he repeated to himself. And he went on sleeping.

100 When he awoke, the sky was clear; the loose window let in a cold, pure air. The Arab was asleep, hunched up under the blankets now, his

mouth open, utterly relaxed. But when Daru shook him, he started dreadfully, staring at Daru with wild eyes as if he had never seen him and such a frightened expression that the schoolmaster stepped back. "Don't be afraid. It's me. You must eat." The Arab nodded his head and said yes. Calm had returned to his face, but his expression was vacant and listless.

101 The coffee was ready. They drank it seated together on the folding bed as they munched their pieces of the cake. Then Daru led the Arab under the shed and showed him the faucet where he washed. He went back into the room, folded the blankets and the bed, made his own bed and put the room in order. Then he went through the classroom and out onto the terrace. The sun was already rising in the blue sky; a soft, bright light was bathing the deserted plateau. On the ridge the snow was melting in spots. The stones were about to reappear. Crouched on the edge of the plateau, the schoolmaster looked at the deserted expanse. He thought of Balducci. He had hurt him, for he had sent him off in a way as if he didn't want to be associated with him. He could still hear the gendarme's farewell and, without knowing why, he felt strangely empty and vulnerable. At that moment, from the other side of the schoolhouse, the prisoner coughed. Daru listened to him almost despite himself and then, furious, threw a pebble that whistled through the air before sinking into the snow. That man's stupid crime revolted him, but to hand him over was contrary to honor. Merely thinking of it made him smart with humiliation. And he cursed at one and the same time his own people who had sent him this Arab and the Arab too who had dared to kill and not managed to get away. Daru got up, walked in a circle on the terrace, waited motionless, and then went back into the schoolhouse.

102 The Arab, leaning over the cement floor of the shed, was washing his teeth with two fingers. Daru looked at him and said: "Come." He went back into the room ahead of the prisoner. He slipped a hunting-jacket on over his sweater and put on walking-shoes. Standing, he waited until the Arab had put on his *chèche* and sandals. They went into the classroom and the schoolmaster pointed to the exit, saying: "Go ahead." The fellow didn't budge. "I'm coming," said Daru. The Arab went out. Daru went back into the room and made a package of pieces of rusk, dates, and sugar. In the classroom, before going out, he hesitated a second in front of his desk, then crossed the threshold and locked the door. "That's the way," he said. He started toward the east, followed by the prisoner. But, a short distance from the schoolhouse, he thought he

heard a slight sound behind them. He retraced his steps and examined the surroundings of the house; there was no one there. The Arab watched him without seeming to understand. "Come on," said Daru.

103 They walked for an hour and rested beside a sharp peak of limestone. The snow was melting faster and faster and the sun was drinking up the puddles at once, rapidly cleaning the plateau, which gradually dried and vibrated like the air itself. When they resumed walking, the ground rang under their feet. From time to time a bird rent the space in front of them with a joyful cry. Daru breathed in deeply the fresh morning light. He felt a sort of rapture before the vast familiar expanse, now almost entirely yellow under its dome of blue sky. They walked an hour more, descending toward the south. They reached a level height made up of crumbly rocks. From there on, the plateau sloped down, eastward, toward a low plain where there were a few spindly trees and, to the south, toward outcroppings of rock that gave the landscape a chaotic look.

104 Daru surveyed the two directions. There was nothing but the sky on the horizon. Not a man could be seen. He turned toward the Arab, who was looking at him blankly. Daru held out the package to him. "Take it," he said. "There are dates, bread, and sugar. You can hold out for two days. Here are a thousand francs too." The Arab took the package and the money but kept his full hands at chest level as if he didn't know what to do with what was being given him. "Now look," the schoolmaster said as he pointed in the direction of the east, "there's the way to Tinguit. You have a two-hour walk. At Tinguit you'll find the administration and the police. They are expecting you." The Arab looked toward the east, still holding the package and the money against his chest. Daru took his elbow and turned him rather roughly toward the south. At the foot of the height on which they stood could be seen a faint path. "That's the trail across the plateau. In a day's walk from here you'll find pasturelands and the first nomads. They'll take you in and shelter you according to their law." The Arab had now turned toward Daru and a sort of panic was visible in his expression. "Listen," he said. Daru shook his head: "No, be quiet. Now I'm leaving you." He turned his back on him, took two long steps in the direction of the school, looked hesitantly at the motionless Arab, and started off again. For a few minutes he heard nothing but his own step resounding on the cold ground and did not turn his head. A moment later, however, he turned around. The Arab was still there on the edge of the hill, his arms hanging

now, and he was looking at the schoolmaster. Daru felt something rise in his throat. But he swore with impatience, waved vaguely, and started off again. He had already gone some distance when he again stopped and looked. There was no longer anyone on the hill.

105 Daru hesitated. The sun was now rather high in the sky and was beginning to beat down on his head. The schoolmaster retraced his steps, at first somewhat uncertainly, then with decision. When he reached the little hill, he was bathed in sweat. He climbed it as fast as he could and stopped, out of breath, at the top. The rock-fields to the south stood out sharply against the blue sky, but on the plain to the east a steamy heat was already rising. And in that slight haze, Daru, with heavy heart, made out the Arab walking slowly on the road to prison.

106 A little later, standing before the window of the classroom, the schoolmaster was watching the clear light bathing the whole surface of the plateau, but he hardly saw it. Behind him on the blackboard, among the winding French rivers, sprawled the clumsily chalked-up words he had just read: "You handed over our brother. You will pay for this." Daru looked at the sky, the plateau, and, beyond, the invisible lands stretching all the way to the sea. In this vast landscape he had loved so much, he was alone.

QUESTIONS FOR ANALYSIS AND DISCUSSION

1. Characterize Daru. What are his values? What are his attitudes toward his work? The landscape around his school/home?
2. What is the relationship between Daru and Balducci? What conflict does Daru create for him? What decision does Balducci make to resolve his conflict?
3. Daru experiences a variety of attitudes toward the Arab; describe them.
4. What choice does Daru offer the Arab? What choice does the Arab make? Why?
5. Insofar as the Arab represents everyman, what comment is Camus making about us?
6. Examine Camus's detailed descriptions of his North African setting. What elements of the setting take on symbolic meaning? Is it appropriate, and helpful, to depict the setting as another character in the story?
7. What is tragic about the chalkboard note? What is absurd about it?
8. In a paragraph, state the story's dominant meaning or theme.

The Magic Barrel

BERNARD MALAMUD

The son of Russian-Jewish immigrant grocers in Brooklyn, Bernard Malamud (1914–1986) is one of the most popular of contemporary writers who has also been praised by critics and is regularly anthologized in literature texts. With degrees from City College of New York and Columbia University, Malamud combined teaching and writing, first at Oregon State and then at Bennington College in Vermont. Three of his novels have been made into films: The Natural *(1952),* The Assistant *(1957), and* The Fixer *(1966; winner of the National Book Award and Pulitzer Prize). Other novels include* A New Life *(1961),* Pictures of Fedelman *(1969),* Dubin's Lives *(1977), and* God's Grace *(1982). Although he became a successful novelist, Malamud did not stop working in the less lucrative short-story format. He has published two collections:* The Magic Barrel *(1958), from which the following story comes, and* Idiot's First *(1963).*

It is easy to say that Malamud writes about Jewish-Americans: "Jews are absolutely the very stuff of drama," Malamud wrote. But we cannot dismiss his works as limited regional or cultural portraits. His narratives move toward the symbolic and mystical, and his characters, revealing not only their failings but their decency and courage, become all of us. "My work," Malamud has said, "all of it, is an idea of dedication to the human. If you do not respect man, you cannot respect my work." Critical judgment in the next century will mark Malamud as one of America's most universal and enduring writers.

1 Not long ago there lived in uptown New York, in a small, almost meager room, though crowded with books, Leo Finkle, a rabbinical student in the Yeshivah University. Finkle, after six years of study, was to be ordained in June and had been advised by an acquaintance that he might find it easier to win himself a congregation if he were married. Since he had no present prospects of marriage, after two tormented days of turning it over in his mind, he called in Pinye Salzman, a marriage broker whose two-line advertisement he had read in the *Forward.*

2 The matchmaker appeared one night out of the dark fourth-floor hallway of the graystone rooming house where Finkle lived, grasping a black, strapped portfolio that had been worn thin with use. Salzman,

who had been long in the business, was of slight but dignified build, wearing an old hat, and an overcoat too short and tight for him. He smelled frankly of fish, which he loved to eat, and although he was missing a few teeth, his presence was not displeasing, because of an amiable manner curiously contrasted with mournful eyes. His voice, his lips, his wisp of beard, his bony fingers were animated, but give him a moment of repose and his mild blue eyes revealed a depth of sadness, a characteristic that put Leo a little at ease although the situation, for him, was inherently tense.

3 He at once informed Salzman why he had asked him to come, explaining that his home was in Cleveland, and that but for his parents, who had married comparatively late in life, he was alone in the world. He had for six years devoted himself almost entirely to his studies, as a result of which, understandably, he had found himself without time for a social life and the company of young women. Therefore he thought it the better part of trial and error—of embarrassing fumbling—to call in an experienced person to advise him on these matters. He remarked in passing that the function of the marriage broker was ancient and honorable, highly approved in the Jewish community, because it made practical the necessary without hindering joy. Moreover, his own parents had been brought together by a matchmaker. They had made, if not a financially profitable marriage—since neither had possessed any worldly goods to speak of—at least a successful one in the sense of their everlasting devotion to each other. Salzman listened in embarrassed surprise, sensing a sort of apology. Later, however, he experienced a glow of pride in his work, an emotion that had left him years ago, and he heartily approved of Finkle.

4 The two went to their business. Leo had led Salzman to the only clear place in the room, a table near a window that overlooked the lamp-lit city. He seated himself at the matchmaker's side but facing him, attempting by an act of will to suppress the unpleasant tickle in his throat. Salzman eagerly unstrapped his portfolio and removed a loose rubber band from a thin packet of much-handled cards. As he flipped through them, a gesture and sound that physically hurt Leo, the student pretended not to see and gazed steadfastly out the window. Although it was still February, winter was on its last legs, signs of which he had for the first time in years begun to notice. He now observed the round white moon, moving high in the sky through a cloud menagerie, and watched with half-open mouth as it penetrated a huge hen, and dropped out of her like an egg laying itself. Salzman, though pretending through

eyeglasses he had just slipped on, to be engaged in scanning the writing on the cards, stole occasional glances at the young man's distinguished face, noting with pleasure the long, severe scholar's nose, brown eyes heavy with learning, sensitive yet ascetic lips, and a certain, almost hollow quality of the dark cheeks. He gazed around at shelves upon shelves of books and let out a soft, contented sigh.

5 When Leo's eyes fell upon the cards, he counted six spread out in Salzman's hand.

6 "So few?" he asked in disappointment.

7 "You wouldn't believe me how much cards I got in my office," Salzman replied. "The drawers are already filled to the top, so I keep them now in a barrel, but is every girl good for a new rabbi?"

8 Leo blushed at this, regretting all he had revealed of himself in a curriculum vitae he had sent to Salzman. He had thought it best to acquaint him with his strict standards and specifications, but in having done so, felt he had told the marriage broker more than was absolutely necessary.

9 He hesitantly inquired, "Do you keep photographs of your clients on file?"

10 "First comes family, amount of dowry, also what kind of promises," Salzman replied, unbuttoning his tight coat and settling himself in the chair. "After comes pictures, rabbi."

11 "Call me Mr. Finkle. I'm not yet a rabbi."

12 Salzman said he would, but instead called him doctor, which he changed to rabbi when Leo was not listening too attentively.

13 Salzman adjusted his horn-rimmed spectacles, gently cleared his throat and read in an eager voice the contents of the top card:

14 "Sophie P. Twenty-four years. Widow one year. No children. Educated high school and two years college. Father promises eight thousand dollars. Has wonderful wholesale business. Also real estate. On the mother's side comes teachers, also one actor. Well known on Second Avenue."

15 Leo gazed up in surprise. "Did you say a widow?"

16 "A widow don't mean spoiled, rabbi. She lived with her husband maybe four months. He was a sick boy she made a mistake to marry him."

17 "Marrying a widow has never entered my mind."

18 "This is because you have no experience. A widow, especially if she is young and healthy like this girl, is a wonderful person to marry. She will be thankful to you the rest of her life. Believe me, if I was looking now for a bride, I would marry a widow."

19 Leo reflected, then shook his head.

20 Salzman hunched his shoulders in an almost imperceptible gesture of disappointment. He placed the card down on the wooden table and began to read another:

21 "Lily H. High school teacher. Regular. Not a substitute. Has savings and new Dodge car. Lived in Paris one year. Father is successful dentist thirty-five years. Interested in professional man. Well Americanized family. Wonderful opportunity."

22 "I knew her personally," said Salzman. "I wish you could see this girl. She is a doll. Also very intelligent. All day you could talk to her about books and theyater and what not. She also knows current events."

23 "I don't believe you mentioned her age?"

24 "Her age?" Salzman said, raising his brows. "Her age is thirty-two years."

25 Leo said after a while, "I'm afraid that seems a little too old."

26 Salzman let out a laugh. "So how old are you, rabbi?"

27 "Twenty-seven."

28 "So what is the difference, tell me, between twenty-seven and thirty-two? My own wife is seven years older than me. So what did I suffer?—Nothing. If Rothschild's a daughter wants to marry you, would you say on account her age, no?"

29 "Yes," Leo said dryly.

30 Salzman shook off the no in the yes. "Five years don't mean a thing. I give you my word that when you will live with her for one week you will forget her age. What does it mean five years—that she lived more and knows more than somebody who is younger? On this girl, God bless her, years are not wasted. Each one that it comes makes better the bargain."

31 "What subject does she teach in high school?"

32 "Languages. If you heard the way she speaks French, you will think it is music. I am in the business twenty-five years, and I recommend her with my whole heart. Believe me, I know what I'm talking, rabbi."

33 "What's on the next card?" Leo said abruptly.

34 Salzman reluctantly turned up the third card:

35 "Ruth K. Nineteen years. Honor student. Father offers thirteen thousand cash to the right bridegroom. He is a medical doctor. Stomach specialist with marvelous practice. Brother in law owns own garment business. Particular people."

36 Salzman looked as if he had read his trump card.

37 "Did you say nineteen?" Leo asked with interest.

38 "On the dot."

39 "Is she attractive?" He blushed. "Pretty?"

40 Salzman kissed his finger tips. "A little doll. On this I give you my word. Let me call the father tonight and you will see what means pretty."

41 But Leo was troubled. "You're sure she's that young?"

42 "This I am positive. The father will show you the birth certificate."

43 "Are you positive there isn't something wrong with her?" Leo insisted.

44 "Who says there is wrong?"

45 "I don't understand why an American girl her age should go to a marriage broker."

46 A smile spread over Salzman's face.

47 "So for the same reason you went, she comes."

48 Leo flushed. "I am pressed for time."

49 Salzman, realizing he had been tactless, quickly explained. "The father came, not her. He wants she should have the best, so he looks around himself. When we will locate the right boy he will introduce him and encourage. This makes a better marriage than if a young girl without experience takes for herself. I don't have to tell you this."

50 "But don't you think this young girl believes in love?" Leo spoke uneasily.

51 Salzman was about to guffaw but caught himself and said soberly, "Love comes with the right person, not before."

52 Leo parted dry lips but did not speak. Noticing that Salzman had snatched a glance at the next card, he cleverly asked, "How is her health?"

53 "Perfect," Salzman said, breathing with difficulty. "Of course, she is a little lame on her right foot from an auto accident that it happened to her when she was twelve years, but nobody notices on account she is so brilliant and also beautiful."

54 Leo got up heavily and went to the window. He felt curiously bitter and upbraided himself for having called in the marriage broker. Finally, he shook his head.

55 "Why not?" Salzman persisted, the pitch of his voice rising.

56 "Because I detest stomach specialists."

57 "So what do you care what is his business? After you marry her do you need him? Who says he must come every Friday night in your house?"

58 Ashamed of the way the talk was going, Leo dismissed Salzman, who went home with heavy, melancholy eyes.

59 Though he had felt only relief at the marriage broker's departure,

Leo was in low spirits the next day. He explained it as arising from Salzman's failure to produce a suitable bride for him. He did not care for his type of clientele. But when Leo found himself hesitating whether to seek out another matchmaker, one more polished than Pinye, he wondered if it could be—his protestations to the contrary, and although he honored his father and mother—that he did not, in essence, care for the matchmaking institution? This thought he quickly put out of mind yet found himself still upset. All day he ran around in the woods—missed an important appointment, forgot to give out his laundry, walked out of a Broadway cafeteria without paying and had to run back with the ticket in his hand; had even not recognized his landlady in the street when she passed with a friend and courteously called out, "A good evening to you, Doctor Finkle." By nightfall, however, he had regained sufficient calm to sink his nose into a book and there found peace from his thoughts.

60 Almost at once there came a knock on the door. Before Leo could say enter, Salzman, commercial cupid, was standing in the room. His face was gray and meager, his expression hungry, and he looked as if he would expire on his feet. Yet the marriage broker managed, by some trick of the muscles, to display a broad smile.

61 "So good evening. I am invited?"

62 Leo nodded, disturbed to see him again, yet unwilling to ask the man to leave.

63 Beaming still, Salzman laid his portfolio on the table. "Rabbi, I got for you tonight good news."

64 "I've asked you not to call me rabbi. I'm still a student."

65 "Your worries are finished. I have for you a first-class bride."

66 "Leave me in peace concerning this subject." Leo pretended lack of interest.

67 "The world will dance at your wedding."

68 "Please, Mr. Salzman, no more."

69 "But first must come back my strength," Salzman said weakly. He fumbled with the portfolio straps and took out of the leather case an oily paper bag, from which he extracted a hard, seeded roll and a small, smoked white fish. With a quick motion of his hand he stripped the fish out of its skin and began ravenously to chew. "All day in a rush," he muttered.

70 Leo watched him eat.

71 "A sliced tomato you have maybe?" Salzman hesitantly inquired.

72 "No."

73 The marriage broker shut his eyes and ate. When he had finished he carefully cleaned up the crumbs and rolled up the remains of the fish, in the paper bag. His spectacled eyes roamed the room until he discovered, amid some piles of books, a one-burner gas stove. Lifting his hat he humbly asked, "A glass tea you got, rabbi?"

74 Conscience-stricken, Leo rose and brewed the tea. He served it with a chunk of lemon and two cubes of lump sugar, delighting Salzman.

75 After he had drunk his tea, Salzman's strength and good spirits were restored.

76 "So tell me, rabbi," he said amiably, "you considered some more the three clients I mentioned yesterday?"

77 "There was no need to consider."

78 "Why not?"

79 "None of them suits me."

80 "What then suits you?"

81 Leo let it pass because he could give only a confused answer.

82 Without waiting for a reply, Salzman asked, "You remember this girl I talked to you—the high school teacher?"

83 "Age thirty-two?"

84 But, surprisingly, Salzman's face lit in a smile. "Age twenty-nine."

85 Leo shot him a look. "Reduced from thirty-two?"

86 "A mistake," Salzman avowed. "I talked today with the dentist. He took me to his safety deposit box and showed me the birth certificate. She was twenty-nine years last August. They made her a party in the mountains where she went for her vacation. When her father spoke to me the first time I forgot to write the age and I told you thirty-two, but now I remember this was a different client, a widow."

87 "The same one you told me about? I thought she was twenty-four?"

88 "A different. Am I responsible that the world is filled with widows?"

89 "No, but I'm not interested in them, nor for that matter, in school teachers."

90 Salzman pulled his clasped hands to his breast. Looking at the ceiling he devoutly exclaimed, "Yiddishe kinder, what can I say to somebody that he is not interested in high school teachers? So what then you are interested?"

91 Leo flushed but controlled himself.

92 "In what else will you be interested," Salzman went on, "if you not interested in this fine girl that she speaks four languages and has personally in the bank ten thousand dollars? Also her father guarantees further twelve thousand. Also she has a new car, wonderful clothes,

talks on all subjects, and she will give you a first-class home and children. How near do we come in our life to paradise?"

93 "If she's so wonderful, why wasn't she married ten years ago?"

94 "Why?" said Salzman with a heavy laugh. "—Why? Because she is *partikiler.* This is why. She wants the *best.*"

95 Leo was silent, amused at how he had entangled himself. But Salzman had aroused his interest in Lily H., and he began seriously to consider calling on her. When the marriage broker observed how intently Leo's mind was at work on the facts he had supplied, he felt certain they would soon come to an agreement.

96 Late Saturday afternoon, conscious of Salzman, Leo Finkle walked with Lily Hirschorn along Riverside Drive. He walked briskly and erectly, wearing with distinction the black fedora he had that morning taken with trepidation out of the dusty hat box on his closet shelf, and the heavy black Saturday coat he had thoroughly whisked clean. Leo also owned a walking stick, a present from a distant relative, but quickly put temptation aside and did not use it. Lily, petite and not unpretty, had on something signifying the approach of spring. She was au courant, animatedly, with all sorts of subjects, and he weighed her words and found her surprisingly sound—score another for Salzman, whom he uneasily sensed to be somewhere around, hiding perhaps high in a tree along the street, flashing the lady signals with a pocket mirror; or perhaps a cloven-hoofed Pan, piping nuptial ditties as he danced his invisible way before them, strewing wild buds on the walk and purple grapes in their path, symbolizing fruit of a union, though there was of course still none.

97 Lily startled Leo by remarking, "I was thinking of Mr. Salzman, a curious figure, wouldn't you say?"

98 Not certain what to answer, he nodded.

99 She bravely went on, blushing. "I for one am grateful for his introducing us. Aren't you?"

100 He courteously replied, "I am."

101 "I mean," she said with a little laugh—and it was all in good taste, or at least gave the effect of being not in bad—"do you mind that we came together so?"

102 He was not displeased with her honesty, recognizing that she meant to set the relationship aright, and understanding that it took a certain amount of experience in life, and courage, to want to do it quite that way. One had to have some sort of past to make that kind of beginning.

103 He said that he did not mind. Salzman's function was traditional and honorable—valuable for what it might achieve, which, he pointed out, was frequently nothing.

104 Lily agreed with a sigh. They walked on for a while and she said after a long silence, again with a nervous laugh, "Would you mind if I asked you something a little bit personal? Frankly, I find the subject fascinating." Although Leo shrugged, she went on half embarrassedly, "How was it that you came to your calling? I mean was it a sudden passionate inspiration?"

105 Leo, after a time, slowly replied, "I was always interested in the Law."

106 "You saw revealed in it the presence of the Highest?"

107 He nodded and changed the subject. "I understand that you spent a little time in Paris, Miss Hirschorn?"

108 "Oh, did Mr. Salzman tell you, Rabbi Finkle?" Leo winced but she went on, "It was ages ago and almost forgotten. I remember I had to return for my sister's wedding."

109 And Lily would not be put off. "When," she asked in a trembly voice, "did you become enamored of God?"

110 He stared at her. Then it came to him that she was talking not about Leo Finkle, but of a total stranger, some mystical figure, perhaps even passionate prophet that Salzman had dreamed up for her—no relation to the living or dead. Leo trembled with rage and weakness. The trickster had obviously sold her a bill of goods, just as he had him, who'd expected to become acquainted with a young lady of twenty-nine, only to behold, the moment he laid eyes upon her strained and anxious face, a woman past thirty-five and aging rapidly. Only his self control had kept him this long in her presence.

111 "I am not," he said gravely, "a talented religious person," and in seeking words to go on, found himself possessed by shame and fear. "I think," he said in a strained manner, "that I came to God not because I loved Him, but because I did not."

112 This confession he spoke harshly because its unexpectedness shook him.

113 Lily wilted. Leo saw a profusion of loaves of bread go flying like ducks over his head, not unlike the winged loaves by which he had counted himself to sleep last night. Mercifully, then, it snowed, which he would not put past Salzman's machinations.

114 He was infuriated with the marriage broker and swore he would throw him out of the room the minute he reappeared. But Salzman did

not come that night, and when Leo's anger had subsided, an unaccountable despair grew in its place. At first he thought this was caused by his disappointment in Lily, but before long it became evident that he had involved himself with Salzman without a true knowledge of his own intent. He gradually realized—with an emptiness that seized him with six hands—that he had called in the broker to find him a bride because he was incapable of doing it himself. This terrifying insight he had derived as a result of his meeting and conversation with Lily Hirschorn. Her probing questions had somehow irritated him into revealing—to himself more than her—the true nature of his relationship to God, and from that it had come upon him, with shocking force, that apart from his parents, he had never loved anyone. Or perhaps it went the other way, that he did not love God so well as he might, because he had not loved man. It seemed to Leo that his whole life stood starkly revealed and he saw himself for the first time as he truly was—unloved and loveless. This bitter but somehow not fully unexpected revelation brought him to a point of panic, controlled only by extraordinary effort. He covered his face with his hands and cried.

115 The week that followed was the worst of his life. He did not eat and lost weight. His beard darkened and grew ragged. He stopped attending seminars and almost never opened a book. He seriously considered leaving the Yeshivah, although he was deeply troubled at the thought of the loss of all his years of study—saw them like pages torn from a book, strewn over the city—and at the devastating effect of this decision upon his parents. But he had lived without knowledge of himself, and never in the Five Books and all the Commentaries—mea culpa—had the truth been revealed to him. He did not know where to turn, and in all this desolating loneliness there was no *to whom,* although he often thought of Lily but not once could bring himself to go downstairs and make the call. He became touchy and irritable, especially with his landlady, who asked him all manner of personal questions; on the other hand, sensing his own disagreeableness, he waylaid her on the stairs and apologized abjectly, until mortified, she ran from him. Out of this, however, he drew the consolation that he was a Jew and that a Jew suffered. But gradually, as the long and terrible week drew to a close, he regained his composure and some idea of purpose in life: to go on as planned. Although he was imperfect, the ideal was not. As for his quest of a bride, the thought of continuing afflicted him with anxiety and heartburn, yet perhaps with this new knowledge of himself he would be more successful than in the past. Perhaps love would now come to him and a bride to that love. And for this sanctified seeking who needed a Salzman?

116 The marriage broker, a skeleton with haunted eyes, returned that very night. He looked, withal, the picture of frustrated expectancy—as if he had steadfastly waited the week at Miss Lily Hirschorn's side for a telephone call that never came.

117 Casually coughing, Salzman came immediately to the point: "So how did you like her?"

118 Leo's anger rose and he could not refrain from chiding the matchmaker: "Why did you lie to me, Salzman?"

119 Salzman's pale face went dead white, the world had snowed on him.

120 "Did you not state that she was twenty-nine?" Leo insisted.

121 "I give you my word—"

122 "She was thirty-five, if a day. *At least* thirty-five."

123 "Of this don't be too sure. Her father told me—"

124 "Never mind. The worst of it was that you lied to her."

125 "How did I lie to her, tell me?"

126 "You told her things about me that weren't true. You made me out to be more, consequently less than I am. She had in mind a totally different person, a sort of semimystical Wonder Rabbi."

127 "All I said, you was a religious man."

128 "I can imagine."

129 Salzman sighed. "This is my weakness that I have," he confessed. "My wife says to me I shouldn't be a salesman, but when I have two fine people that they would be wonderful to be married, I am so happy that I talk too much." He smiled wanly. "This is why Salzman is a poor man."

130 Leo's anger left him. "Well, Salzman, I'm afraid that's all."

131 The marriage broker fastened hungry eyes on him.

132 "You don't want any more a bride?"

133 "I do," said Leo, "but I have decided to seek her in a different way. I am no longer interested in an arranged marriage. To be frank, I now admit the necessity of premarital love. That is, I want to be in love with the one I marry."

134 "Love?" said Salzman astounded. After a moment he remarked, "For us, our love is our life, not for the ladies. In the ghetto they—"

135 "I know, I know," said Leo. "I've thought of it often. Love, I have said to myself, should be a by-product of living and worship rather than its own end. Yet for myself I find it necessary to establish the level of my need and fulfill it."

136 Salzman shrugged but answered, "Listen, rabbi, if you want love, this I can find for you also. I have such beautiful clients that you will love them the minute your eyes will see them."

137 Leo smiled unhappily. "I'm afraid you don't understand."

138 But Salzman hastily unstrapped his portfolio and withdrew a manila packet from it.

139 "Pictures," he said, quickly laying the envelope on the table.

140 Leo called after him to take the pictures away, but as if on the wings of the wind, Salzman had disappeared.

141 March came. Leo had returned to his regular routine. Although he felt not quite himself yet—lacked energy—he was making plans for a more active social life. Of course it would cost something, but he was an expert in cutting corners; and when there were no corners left he would make circles rounder. All the while Salzman's pictures had lain on the table, gathering dust. Occasionally as Leo sat studying, or enjoying a cup of tea, his eyes fell on the manila envelope, but he never opened it.

142 The days went by and no social life to speak of developed with a member of the opposite sex—it was difficult, given the circumstances of his situation. One morning Leo toiled up the stairs to his room and stared out the window at the city. Although the day was bright his view of it was dark. For some time he watched the people in the street below hurrying along and then turned with a heavy heart to his little room. On the table was the packet. With a sudden relentless gesture he tore it open. For a half-hour he stood by the table in a state of excitement, examining the photographs of the ladies Salzman had included. Finally, with a deep sigh he put them down. There were six, of varying degrees of attractiveness, but look at them long enough and they all became Lily Hirschorn: all past their prime, all starved behind bright smiles, not a true personality in the lot. Life, despite their frantic yoohooings, had passed them by; they were pictures in a brief case that stank of fish. After a while, however, as Leo attempted to return the photographs into the envelope, he found in it another, a snapshot of the type taken by a machine for a quarter. He gazed at it a moment and let out a cry.

143 Her face deeply moved him. Why, he could at first not say. It gave him the impression of youth—spring flowers, yet age—a sense of having been used to the bone, wasted; this came from the eyes, which were hauntingly familiar, yet absolutely strange. He had a vivid impression that he had met her before, but try as he might he could not place her although he could almost recall her name, as if he had read it in her own handwriting. No, this couldn't be; he would have remembered her. It was not, he affirmed, that she had an extraordinary beauty—no, though her face was attractive enough; it was that *something* about her moved him. Feature for feature, even some of the ladies of the photographs could do

better; but she leaped forth to his heart—and *lived,* or wanted to—more than just wanted, perhaps regretted how she had lived—had somehow deeply suffered: it could be seen in the depths of those reluctant eyes, and from the way the light enclosed and shone from her, and within her, opening realms of possibility: this was her own. Her he desired. His head ached and eyes narrowed with the intensity of his gazing, then as if an obscure fog had blown up in the mind, he experienced fear of her and was aware that he had received an impression, somehow, of evil. He shuddered, saying softly, it is thus with us all. Leo brewed some tea in a small pot and sat sipping it without sugar, to calm himself. But before he had finished drinking, again with excitement he examined the face and found it good: good for Leo Finkle. Only such a one could understand him and help him seek whatever he was seeking. She might, perhaps, love him. How she had happened to be among the discards in Salzman's barrel he could never guess, but he knew he must urgently go find her.

144 Leo rushed downstairs, grabbed up the Bronx telephone book, and searched for Salzman's home address. He was not listed, nor was his office. Neither was he in the Manhattan book. But Leo remembered having written down the address on a slip of paper after he had read Salzman's advertisement in the "personals" column of the *Forward.* He ran up to his room and tore through his papers, without luck. It was exasperating. Just when he needed the matchmaker he was nowhere to be found. Fortunately Leo remembered to look in his wallet. There on a card he found his name written and a Bronx address. No phone number was listed, the reason—Leo now recalled—he had originally communicated with Salzman by letter. He got on his coat, put a hat on over his skull cap and hurried to the subway station. All the way to the far end of the Bronx he sat on the edge of his seat. He was more than once tempted to take out the picture and see if the girl's face was as he remembered it, but he refrained, allowing the snapshot to remain in his inside coat pocket, content to have her so close. When the train pulled into the station he was waiting at the door and bolted out. He quickly located the street Salzman had advertised.

145 The building he sought was less than a block from the subway, but it was not an office building, nor even a loft, nor a store in which one could rent office space. It was a very old tenement house. Leo found Salzman's name in pencil on a soiled tag under the bell and climbed three dark flights to his apartment. When he knocked, the door was opened by a thin, asthmatic, gray-haired woman, in felt slippers.

146 "Yes?" she said, expecting nothing. She listened without listening.

He could have sworn he had seen her, too, before but knew it was an illusion.

147 "Salzman–does he live here? Pinye Salzman," he said, "the matchmaker?"

148 She stared at him a long minute. "Of course."

149 He felt embarrassed. "Is he in?"

150 "No." Her mouth, though left open, offered nothing more.

151 "The matter is urgent. Can you tell me where his office is?"

152 "In the air." She pointed upward.

153 "You mean he has no office?" Leo asked.

154 "In his socks."

155 He peered into the apartment. It was sunless and dingy, one large room divided by a half-open curtain, beyond which he could see a sagging metal bed. The near side of a room was crowded with rickety chairs, old bureaus, a three-legged table, racks of cooking utensils, and all the apparatus of a kitchen. But there was no sign of Salzman or his magic barrel, probably also a figment of the imagination. An odor of frying fish made Leo weak to the knees.

156 "Where is he?" he insisted. "I've got to see your husband."

157 At length she answered, "So who knows where he is? Every time he thinks a new thought he runs to a different place. Go home, he will find you."

158 "Tell him Leo Finkle."

159 She gave no sign she had heard.

160 He walked downstairs, depressed.

161 But Salzman, breathless, stood waiting at his door.

162 Leo was astounded and overjoyed. "How did you get here before me?"

163 "I rushed."

164 "Come inside."

165 They entered. Leo fixed tea, and a sardine sandwich for Salzman. As they were drinking he reached behind him for the packet of pictures and handed them to the marriage broker.

166 Salzman put down his glass and said expectantly, "You found somebody you like?"

167 "Not among these."

168 The marriage broker turned away.

169 "Here is the one I want." Leo held forth the snapshot.

170 Salzman slipped on his glasses and took the picture into his trembling hand. He turned ghastly and let out a groan.

171 "What's the matter?" cried Leo.

172 "Excuse me. Was an accident this picture. She isn't for you."

173 Salzman frantically shoved the manila packet into his portfolio. He thrust the snapshot into his pocket and fled down the stairs.

174 Leo, after momentary paralysis, gave chase and cornered the marriage broker in the vestibule. The landlady made hysterical outcries but neither of them listened.

175 "Give me back the picture, Salzman."

176 "No." The pain in his eyes was terrible.

177 "Tell me who she is then."

178 "This I can't tell you. Excuse me."

179 He made to depart, but Leo, forgetting himself, seized the matchmaker by his tight coat and shook him frenziedly.

180 "Please," sighed Salzman. "*Please.*"

181 Leo ashamedly let him go. "Tell me who she is," he begged. "It's very important for me to know."

182 "She is not for you. She is a wild one—wild, without shame. This is not a bride for a rabbi."

183 "What do you mean wild?"

184 "Like an animal. Like a dog. For her to be poor was a sin. This is why to me she is dead now."

185 "In God's name, what do you mean?"

186 "Her I can't introduce to you," Salzman cried.

187 "Why are you so excited?"

188 "Why, he asks," Salzman said, bursting into tears. "This is my baby, my Stella, she should burn in hell."

189 Leo hurried up to bed and hid under the covers. Under the covers he thought his life through. Although he soon fell asleep he could not sleep her out of his mind. He woke, beating his breast. Though he prayed to be rid of her, his prayers went unanswered. Through days of torment he endlessly struggled not to love her; fearing success, he escaped it. He then concluded to convert her to goodness, himself to God. The idea alternately nauseated and exalted him.

190 He perhaps did not know that he had come to a final decision until he encountered Salzman in a Broadway cafeteria. He was sitting alone at a rear table, sucking the bony remains of a fish. The marriage broker appeared haggard, and transparent to the point of vanishing.

191 Salzman looked up at first without recognizing him. Leo had grown a pointed beard and his eyes were weighted with wisdom.

192 "Salzman," he said, "love has at last come to my heart."

193 "Who can love from a picture?" mocked the marriage broker.

194 "It is not impossible."

195 "If you can love her, then you can love anybody. Let me show you some new clients that they just sent me their photographs. One is a little doll."

196 "Just her I want," Leo murmured.

197 "Don't be a fool, doctor. Don't bother with her."

198 "Put me in touch with her, Salzman," Leo said humbly. "Perhaps I can be of service."

199 Salzman had stopped eating and Leo understood with emotion that it was now arranged.

200 Leaving the cafeteria, he was, however, afflicted by a tormenting suspicion that Salzman had planned it all to happen this way.

201 Leo was informed by letter that she would meet him on a certain corner, and she was there one spring night, waiting under a street lamp. He appeared, carrying a small bouquet of violets and rosebuds. Stella stood by the lamp post, smoking. She wore white with red shoes, which fitted his expectations, although in a troubled moment he had imagined the dress red, and only the shoes white. She waited uneasily and shyly. From afar he saw that her eyes—clearly her father's—were filled with desperate innocence. He pictured, in her, his own redemption. Violins and lit candles revolved in the sky. Leo ran forward with flowers outthrust.

202 Around the corner, Salzman, leaning against a wall, chanted prayers for the dead.

QUESTIONS FOR ANALYSIS AND DISCUSSION

1. List all details that give the story a fantasy or fairy-tale quality. Look especially at words that describe Salzman.
2. List all details that make the story realistic, that provide local color.
3. How does Malamud fuse fantasy elements and realistic details into a unified story?
4. Although Leo Finkle's problem is serious enough, there are many comic elements in the story; note them. What do these comic elements suggest to you about Malamud's view of life?
5. What does the name *Stella* mean? Why does the author dress her in white with red shoes? Why did Leo imagine her wearing a red dress and white shoes?
6. What is the magic of the magic barrel? How is Salzman truly a magician? How has Leo changed?

Report

DONALD BARTHELME

Born in Philadelphia in 1931, Donald Barthelme now lives in New York City. He held positions as newspaper reporter and managing editor of an art and literature review before choosing to be a full-time writer. A regular contributor of short fiction to The New Yorker, *Barthelme now has several collections of stories and a number of novels to his credit. His novels include* Snow White *(1967),* The Dead Father *(1975), and* Paradise *(1986). He also has a children's book,* The Slightly Irregular Fire Engine *(1971). Barthelme has won both a National Book Award and a Guggenheim Fellowship. "Report" was published in 1968 in the collection* Unspeakable Practices, Unnatural Acts.

Many reviewers have applauded Barthelme as an important writer seeking new forms in fiction. He has experimented with alternating narrators and a disruption of narrative line; he successfully uses an exaggerated wit and playfulness. Many of these techniques are what Dillard has in mind when she discusses, in "The Fiction Writer's Materials," the new directions in current fiction. In "Report," Barthelme reveals his essentially comic vision of a hysterical world.

1 Our group is against the war. But the war goes on. I was sent to Cleveland to talk to the engineers. The engineers were meeting in Cleveland. I was supposed to persuade them not to do what they are going to do. I took United's 4:45 from LaGuardia arriving in Cleveland at 6:13. Cleveland is dark blue at that hour. I went directly to the motel, where the engineers were meeting. Hundreds of engineers attended the Cleveland meeting. I noticed many fractures among the engineers, bandages, traction. I noticed what appeared to be fracture of the carpal scaphoid in six examples. I noticed numerous fractures of the humeral shaft, of the os calcis, of the pelvic girdle. I noticed a high incidence of clay-shoveler's fracture. I could not account for these fractures. The engineers were making calculations, taking measurements, sketching on the blackboard, drinking beer, throwing bread, buttonholing employers, hurling glasses into the fireplace. They were friendly.

2 They were friendly. They were full of love and information. The chief engineer wore shades. Patella in Monk's traction, clamshell fracture

by the look of it. He was standing in a slum of beer bottles and microphone cable. "Have some of this chicken à la Isambard Kingdom Brunel the Great Ingineer," he said. "And declare who you are and what we can do for you. What is your line, distinguished guest?"

3 "Software," I said. "In every sense. I am here representing a small group of interested parties. We are interested in your thing, which seems to be functioning. In the midst of so much dysfunction, function is interesting. Other people's things don't seem to be working. The State Department's thing doesn't seem to be working. The UN's thing doesn't seem to be working. The democratic left's thing doesn't seem to be working. Buddha's thing—"

4 "Ask us anything about our thing, which seems to be working," the chief engineer said. "We will open our hearts and heads to you, Software Man, because we want to be understood and loved by the great lay public, and have our marvels appreciated by that public, for which we daily unsung produce tons of new marvels each more life-enhancing than the last. Ask us anything. Do you want to know about evaporated thin-film metallurgy? Monolithic and hybrid integrated-circuit processes? The algebra of inequalities? Optimization theory? Complex high-speed micro-miniature closed and open loop systems? Fixed variable mathematical cost searches? Epitaxial deposition of semiconductor materials? Gross interfaced space gropes? We also have specialists in the cuckoo-flower, the doctorfish, and the dumdum bullet as these relate to aspects of today's expanding technology, and they do in the damnedest ways."

5 I spoke to him then about the war. I said the same things people always say when they speak against the war. I said that the war was wrong. I said that large countries should not burn down small countries. I said that the government had made a series of errors. I said that these errors once small and forgivable were now immense and unforgivable. I said that the government was attempting to conceal its original errors under layers of new errors. I said that the government was sick with error, giddy with it. I said that ten thousand of our soldiers had already been killed in pursuit of the government's errors. I said that tens of thousands of the enemy's soldiers and civilians had been killed because of various errors, ours and theirs. I said that we are responsible for errors made in our name. I said that the government should not be allowed to make additional errors.

6 "Yes, yes," the chief engineer said, "there is doubtless much truth in what you say, but we can't possibly *lose* the war, can we? And stopping is losing, isn't it? The war regarded as a process, stopping regarded as an

abort? We don't know *how* to lose a war. That skill is not among our skills. Our array smashes their array, that is what we know. That is the process. That is what is.

7 "But let's not have any more of this dispiriting downbeat counterproductive talk. I have a few new marvels here I'd like to discuss with you just briefly. A few new marvels that are just about ready to be gaped at by the admiring layman. Consider for instance the area of realtime online computer-controlled wish evaporation. Wish evaporation is going to be crucial in meeting the rising expectations of the world's peoples, which are as you know rising entirely too fast."

8 I noticed then distributed about the room a great many transverse fractures of the ulna. "The development of the pseudo-ruminant stomach for underdeveloped peoples," he went on, "is one of our interesting things you should be interested in. With the pseudo-ruminant stomach they can chew cuds, that is to say, eat grass. Blue is the most popular color worldwide and for that reason we are working with certain strains of your native Kentucky *Poa pratensis,* or bluegrass, as the staple input for the p/r stomach cycle, which would also give a shot in the arm to our balance-of-payments thing don't you know. . . ." I noticed about me then a great number of metatarsal fractures in banjo splints. "The kangaroo initiative . . . eight hundred thousand harvested last year . . . highest percentage of edible protein of any herbivore yet studied . . ."

9 "Have new kangaroos been planted?"

10 The engineer looked at me.

11 "I intuit your hatred and jealousy of our thing," he said. "The ineffectual always hate our thing and speak of it as antihuman, which is not at all a meaningful way to speak of our thing. Nothing mechanical is alien to me," he said (amber spots making bursts of light in his shades), "because I am human, in a sense, and if I think it up, then 'it' is human too; whatever 'it' may be. Let me tell you, Software Man, we have been damned forbearing in the matter of this little war you declare yourself to be interested in. Function is the cry, and our thing is functioning like crazy. There are things we could do that we have not done. Steps we could take that we have not taken. These steps are, regarded in a certain light, the light of our enlightened self-interest, quite justifiable steps. We could, of course, get irritated. We could, of course, *lose patience.*

12 "We could, of course, release thousands upon thousands of self-powered crawling-along-the-ground lengths of titanium wire eighteen inches long with a diameter of .0005 centimeters (that is to say, invisible) which, scenting an enemy, climb up his trouser leg and wrap themselves

around his neck. We have developed those. They are within our capabilities. We could, of course, release in the arena of the upper air our new improved pufferfish toxin which precipitates an identity crisis. No special technical problems there. That is almost laughably easy. We could, of course, place up to two million maggots in their rice within twenty-four hours. The maggots are ready, massed in secret staging areas in Alabama. We have hypodermic darts capable of piebalding the enemy's pigmentation. We have rots, blights, and rusts capable of attacking his alphabet. Those are dandies. We have a hut-shrinking chemical which penetrates the fibers of the bamboo, causing it, the hut, to strangle its occupants. This operates only after 10 P.M., when people are sleeping. Their mathematics are at the mercy of a suppurating surd we have invented. We have a family of fishes trained to attack their fishes. We have the deadly testicle-destroying telegram. The cable companies are coöperating. We have a green substance that, well, I'd rather not talk about. We have a secret word that, if pronounced, produces multiple fractures in all living things in an area the size of four football fields."

13 "That's why—"

14 "Yes. Some damned fool couldn't keep his mouth shut. The point is that the whole structure of enemy life is within our power to *rend, vitiate, devour,* and *crush.* But that's not the interesting thing."

15 "You recount these possibilities with uncommon relish."

16 "Yes, I realize that there is too much relish here. But *you* must realize that these capabilities represent in and of themselves highly technical and complex and interesting problems and hurdles on which our boys have expended many thousands of hours of hard work and brilliance. And that the effects are often grossly exaggerated by irresponsible victims. And that the whole thing represents a fantastic series of triumphs for the multi-disciplined problem-solving team concept."

17 "I appreciate that."

18 "We *could* unleash all this technology at once. You can imagine what would happen then. But that's not the interesting thing."

19 "What is the interesting thing?"

20 "The interesting thing is that we have a *moral sense.* It is on punched cards, perhaps the most advanced and sensitive moral sense the world has ever known."

21 "Because it is on punched cards?"

22 "It considers all considerations in endless and subtle detail," he said. "It even quibbles. With this great new moral tool, how can we go wrong?

I confidently predict that, although we *could* employ all this splendid new weaponry I've been telling you about, ***we're not going to do it.***"

23 "We're not going to do it?"

24 I took United's 5:44 from Cleveland arriving at Newark at 7:19. New Jersey is bright pink at that hour. Living things move about the surface of New Jersey at that hour molesting each other only in traditional ways. I made my report to the group. I stressed the friendliness of the engineers. I said, It's all right. I said, We have a moral sense. I said, ***We're not going to do it.*** They didn't believe me.

QUESTIONS FOR ANALYSIS AND DISCUSSION

1. The story begins and ends with simple, direct statements of the narrator's flights to and from Cleveland. In addition to providing a beginning and end to this brief "report," what is accomplished by these passages? How do they contrast with the rest of the story?
2. How does the chief engineer account for the many fractures? What else is suggested by the many broken bones and splints? What is gained by the use of so much medical terminology?
3. One could label the medical terms as jargon. What other types of jargon are spoken in the story?
4. The narrator is a software specialist. What is software? What is the opposite of software? What does this contrast suggest that is relevant to the story?
5. When the chief engineer asserts that the engineers have a moral sense, he seems quite serious—and pleased. How are we to understand his claim to a moral sense? What details about the moral sense help make the author's attitude clear to us?
6. What particular war is the occasion for this story?
7. How does Barthelme's satire keep the story from being dated? Or, how does the world keep Barthelme's satire from being dated?

A COLLECTION OF POEMS

The following ten poems, four from British poets, six from American poets, offer a brief opportunity for some close reading and analysis of poetic techniques. These works also illustrate a sampling of poetic forms, providing you with a chance to review some key poetic terms. Two of the poems are sonnets. Remember that a *sonnet* consists of fourteen lines of iambic pentameter (five iambic feet, each one composed of one unstressed followed by one stressed syllable), but the rhyme scheme can vary somewhat. Browning's *dramatic monologue* (a speaker/character says all the lines but another person is present, listening to the speaker) is written in *couplets,* two rhyming lines with the same metrical pattern (pattern of stressed and unstressed syllables). The other poems employ several stanza forms or are written in *free verse,* verse without a regular metrical pattern.

Some of the poets will be familiar to you. William Shakespeare (1564–1616), actor, dramatist, and country gentleman in his last years, also wrote 126 sonnets that were first published, probably without his knowledge or approval, in 1609. Although many focus on separation, death, and weariness, others assert the value of love and its endurance. In his best sonnets, Shakespeare perfectly controls tone and gives us richly suggestive metaphors.

Although some readers are annoyed by John Donne's (1572–1631) complex word order and at times tasteless metaphors, many find this seventeenth-century poet's cleverness a delight and his debunking of romantic love poetry an appropriate challenge to the "ruby lips" and "rosy cheeks" of his day's less original love poems. In "The Flea" the speaker's verbal assault on the lady attests to his energy and desire, if not to his romantic nature. For our purposes, the poem provides practice in the active reading required to imagine the scene that Donne presents entirely through the words of one speaker.

Robert Browning (1812–1889), first considered a minor light made famous by his marriage to Elizabeth Barrett Browning, has now emerged as the more highly valued of the two, perhaps because his poetry looks forward to contemporary styles, structures, and themes. A Londoner who spent his married years in Italy and drew on the Italian landscape and history for many works, Browning's colloquial and sometimes discordant style resembles the novelists of his time (Dickens, Eliot) more than the poets (Tennyson, Arnold). Browning was interested in our deviousness and hidden motives, and he established the dramatic monologue as an important poetic form.

Born on a farm on Long Island, New York, Walt Whitman (1819–1892) was a newspaperman, teacher, and most important, a poet. In his collection of poems, *Leaves of Grass,* first published in 1855 and added to through nine editions until his death, Whitman gives romantic, energetic expression to America's growth and to his vision of transcendental unity, the oneness of nature and spirit. His poetry was not widely read during his life, although he achieved increasing critical recognition. Whitman rejected traditional poetic forms for a rhythmic free verse, and he wrote openly of sex. Both his verse and his subjects, if not his romanticism, have found favor with modern readers.

If America had a poet laureate, the honor in the twentieth century would have been given to Robert Frost (1874–1963), the New England farmer and teacher whose poetry was first published and reviewed favorably in England but who returned home to win four Pulitzer Prizes for his collections, receive honorary degrees, and read his poetry at John Kennedy's inauguration. Frost's poems are accessible to most readers both for their folksy subjects and conversational diction. But his lines are always more controlled than casual conversation, and his use of ordinary activities can distract readers from recognizing a complex and subtle response to nature as symbol.

One of the most promising of modern English poets, Wilfred Owen (1893–1918) was killed near the end of World War I. His poems, many inspired by his war experiences, were collected and published after his death by the poet Siegfried Sassoon. Owen's compassionate, ironic poems deplore the waste of war; his use of imperfect rhymes and flexible stanza patterns reveals his willingness to adapt traditional forms rather than break from tradition as Whitman did.

Like many American writers, Langston Hughes (1902–1967) came from the Middle West to New York, lived and worked in Europe, and then returned to America to a career of writing. He was a journalist, fiction writer, and poet, and author of more than sixty books. He was also the first black American to become a successful professional writer. At mid-century, he was an important voice for black culture in America.

Another black American, Gwendolyn Brooks (b. 1917), was born in Kansas but has lived most of her life in Chicago. She has taught poetry writing at many colleges, and has received honorary degrees and awards for her poetry. She is the first black author to win a Pulitzer Prize, awarded in 1950 for *Annie Allen,* a three-part verse narrative. Although her primary subjects have been poor urban blacks, her vivid portraits of suffering, her concentration on the details of ordinary lives, and her compassionate detachment give her subjects universal significance.

An easterner and son of a Presbyterian minister, W. S. (William Stanley) Merwin (b. 1927) grew up in New Jersey and Pennsylvania, graduated from Princeton and has worked as a tutor and translator of Spanish and French classics in addition to writing poetry. He also has won a Pulitzer Prize, for his 1971 collection of poems, *The Carrier of Ladders.* Although his subjects are numerous, Merwin's repeated concerns are with our destruction of nature, our alienation from the environment, our abuses of technology. His sparse style places him in the poetic tradition of Emerson and Dickinson.

The brilliant and sadly abbreviated life of Sylvia Plath (1932–1963) has fascinated the many readers of her autobiographical novel *The Bell Jar.* Although probably more readers know Plath for her novel, most critics regard her several volumes of poetry as her most mature and creative work. Even though she moved to a more direct style of "spoken language" in her last poems, Plath's style remains more formal than Brooks's. Less terse and objective than either Brooks or Merwin, Plath exemplifies the modern confessional poet, the writer who offers his or her personal, private world as subject matter and asserts the process of self-exploration as a condition of modern times.

In speaking of his own poems, Frost said, "I'm always saying something that's just on the edge of something more," an observation that can be made about most poems.

WILLIAM SHAKESPEARE
Sonnet 73

That time of year thou mayst in me behold
When yellow leaves, or none, or few, do hang
Upon those boughs which shake against the cold,
Bare ruined choirs where late the sweet birds sang.
In me thou see'st the twilight of such day
As after sunset fadeth in the west,
Which by and by black night doth take away,
Death's second self, that seals up all in rest.
In me thou see'st the glowing of such fire
That on the ashes of his youth doth lie,
As the deathbed whereon it must expire,
Consumed with that which it was nourished by.
  This thou perceivest, which makes thy love more strong,
  To love that well which thou must leave ere long.

QUESTIONS FOR ANALYSIS AND DISCUSSION

1. Determine the rhyme scheme for the English (or Shakespearean) sonnet. (Use letters, beginning with "a," to mark the pattern, a new letter for each new sound.)
2. What structure, or grouping by lines, is suggested by the rhyme scheme? How does Shakespeare use this structure?
3. To what does the speaker compare himself in each quatrain (set of four lines)? Paraphrase the last two lines.
4. What is effective about the ordering of the three metaphors?
5. What attitude toward growing old does the speaker convey through the selection and ordering of the metaphors?

JOHN DONNE

The Flea

Mark but this flea, and mark in this
How little that which thou deny'st me is;
It sucked me first, and now sucks thee,
And in this flea our two bloods mingled be;
Thou know'st that this cannot be said
A sin, nor shame, nor loss of maidenhead;
    Yet this enjoys before it woo,
    And pampered swells with one blood made of two,
    And this, alas, is more than we would do.

Oh stay, three lives in one flea spare,
Where we almost, yea, more than married are.
This flea is you and I, and this
Our marriage bed and marriage temple is;
Though parents grudge, and you, we are met
And cloistered in these living walls of jet.
    Though use make you apt to kill me,
    Let not to that, self-murder added be,
    And sacrilege, three sins in killing three.

Cruel and sudden, hast thou since
Purpled thy nail in blood of innocence?
Wherein could this flea guilty be,
Except in that drop which it sucked from thee?

Yet thou triumph'st and say'st that thou
Find'st not thyself, nor me the weaker now.
'Tis true. Then learn how false fears be:
Just so much honor, when thou yield'st to me,
Will waste, as this flea's death took life from thee.

QUESTIONS FOR ANALYSIS AND DISCUSSION

1. Describe the situation presented in the poem. Who is speaking? To whom? Under what circumstances?
2. What happens between stanza 1 and stanza 2? Between stanza 2 and stanza 3? (Why is her nail "purpled"?)
3. Summarize the speaker's arguments. What does he hope to gain by his clever use of the flea?
4. From the arguments and the tone in which the speaker presents them—and the lady's actions—how would you describe her response to the speaker?

ROBERT BROWNING

My Last Duchess[1]
Ferrara

That's my last Duchess painted on the wall,
Looking as if she were alive. I call
That piece a wonder, now: Fra Pandolf's[2] hands
Worked busily a day, and there she stands.
Will't please you sit and look at her? I said
"Fra Pandolf" by design, for never read
Strangers like you that pictured countenance,
The depth and passion of its earnest glance,
But to myself they turned (since none puts by
The curtain I have drawn for you, but I)
And seemed as they would ask me, if they durst,
How such a glance came there; so, not the first

[1]Browning is probably drawing on the life of Alfonso II, duke of Ferrara; the duke's first wife died after three years of marriage, and he then negotiated to marry a niece of the count of Tyrol.—Ed.

[2]An imaginary painter.—Ed.

Are you to turn and ask thus. Sir, 'twas not
Her husband's presence only, called that spot
Of joy into the Duchess' cheek: perhaps
Fra Pandolf chanced to say "Her mantle laps
Over my lady's wrist too much," or "Paint
Must never hope to reproduce the faint
Half-flush that dies along her throat": such stuff
Was courtesy, she thought, and cause enough
For calling up that spot of joy. She had
A heart—how shall I say?—too soon made glad,
Too easily impressed; she liked whate'er
She looked on, and her looks went everywhere.
Sir, 'twas all one! My favor at her breast,
The dropping of the daylight in the West,
The bough of cherries some officious fool
Broke in the orchard for her, the white mule
She rode with round the terrace—all and each
Would draw from her alike the approving speech,
Or blush, at least. She thanked men—good! but thanked
Somehow—I know not how—as if she ranked
My gift of a nine-hundred-years-old name
With anybody's gift. Who'd stoop to blame
This sort of trifling? Even had you skill
In speech—(which I have not)—to make your will
Quite clear to such an one, and say, "Just this
Or that in you disgusts me; here you miss,
Or there exceed the mark"—and if she let
Herself be lessoned so, nor plainly set
Her wits to yours, forsooth, and made excuse
—E'en then would be some stooping; and I choose
Never to stoop. Oh sir, she smiled, no doubt,
Whene'er I passed her; but who passed without
Much the same smile? This grew; I gave commands;
Then all smiles stopped together. There she stands
As if alive. Will't please you rise? We'll meet
The company below, then. I repeat,
The Count your master's known munificence
Is ample warrant that no just pretense
Of mine for dowry will be disallowed;
Though his fair daughter's self, as I avowed

At starting, is my object. Nay, we'll go
Together down, sir. Notice Neptune, though,
Taming a sea horse, thought a rarity,
Which Claus of Innsbruck[3] cast in bronze for me!

QUESTIONS FOR ANALYSIS AND DISCUSSION

1. Who speaks the words of the poem? To whom are they addressed? Where is the speaker?
2. What is happening? Why is the duke addressing this person?
3. What facts do we learn about the last duchess? What is the duke's attitude? How reliable is his reporting?
4. As he speaks, what does the duke reveal to us about himself? Does he expect us to perceive his personality as we do? What literary term do we use for this situation?
5. Why does the poem begin and end with the duke pointing to an art work?

WALT WHITMAN

When I Heard the Learn'd Astronomer

When I heard the learn'd astronomer,
When the proofs, the figures, were ranged in columns before me,
When I was shown the charts and diagrams, to add, divide, and
    measure them,
When I sitting heard the astronomer where he lectured with
    much applause in the lecture-room,
How soon unaccountable I became tired and sick,
Till rising and gliding out I wandered off by myself,
In the mystical moist night-air, and from time to time,
Looked up in perfect silence at the stars.

QUESTIONS FOR ANALYSIS AND DISCUSSION

1. Note that the poem is one sentence. What is the main clause that the four "when" clauses and one "how" clause lead up to?
2. What does the speaker do? What is the situation of the poem?

[3] An imaginary sculptor. The count of Tyrol's capital was at Innsbruck. – Ed.

3. How would you have described the tone of line 1 before reading the rest of the poem? Having completed the poem, how would you describe the speaker's attitude to "the learn'd astronomer"?
4. What kind of word choice dominates the first four lines? How does it contrast to "the mystical moist night-air"?
5. What attitude toward science does the poem convey? What attitude toward nature?

ROBERT FROST
Desert Places

Snow falling and night falling fast, oh, fast
In a field I looked into going past,
And the ground almost covered smooth in snow,
But a few weeds and stubble showing last.

The woods around it have it—it is theirs.
All animals are smothered in their lairs.
I am too absent-spirited to count;
The loneliness includes me unawares.

And lonely as it is that loneliness
Will be more lonely ere it will be less—
A blanker whiteness of benighted snow
With no expression, nothing to express.

They cannot scare me with their empty spaces
Between stars—on stars where no human race is.
I have it in me so much nearer home
To scare myself with my own desert places.

QUESTIONS FOR ANALYSIS AND DISCUSSION

1. What is the poem's situation? Where is the speaker? What does he observe?
2. What is the speaker's connection to the woods, the animals, the snow?
3. The speaker describes the scene as lonely and becoming more lonely; why will it be more lonely?
4. What image, then, represents the greatest loneliness?
5. The empty, expressionless space of the snow-covered ground leads the speaker to what reflection? What is more frightening than physical loneliness?
6. Why is it appropriate to say that "Desert Places" is not a nature poem?

WILFRED OWEN

Dulce Et Decorum Est

Bent double, like old beggars under sacks,
Knock-kneed, coughing like hags, we cursed through sludge,
Till on the haunting flares we turned our backs
And towards our distant rest began to trudge.
Men marched asleep. Many had lost their boots
But limped on, blood-shod. All went lame; all blind;
Drunk with fatigue; deaf even to the hoots
Of tired, outstripped Five-Nines that dropped behind.

Gas! Gas! Quick, boys!—An ecstasy of fumbling,
Fitting the clumsy helmets just in time;
But someone still was yelling out and stumbling
And flound'ring like a man in fire or lime . . .
Dim, through the misty panes and thick green light,
As under a green sea, I saw him drowning.

In all my dreams, before my helpless sight,
He plunges at me, guttering, choking, drowning.

If in some smothering dreams you too could pace
Behind the wagon that we flung him in,
And watch the white eyes writhing in his face,
His hanging face, like a devil's sick of sin;
If you could hear, at every jolt, the blood
Come gargling from the froth-corrupted lungs,
Obscene as cancer, bitter as the cud
Of vile, incurable sores on innocent tongues,—
My friend, you would not tell with such high zest
To children ardent for some desperate glory,
The old Lie: Dulce et decorum est
Pro patria mori.[1]

QUESTIONS FOR ANALYSIS AND DISCUSSION

1. Who is the speaker? What is his situation?
2. How does the speaker's shift in pronoun use ("we," "I," "you") give structure to the poem? What is the effect of these shifts?

[1]Sweet and befitting it is to die for one's country.—Ed.

3. What images are especially moving for you? What do many of the images depict?
4. Find and explain three metaphors.
5. Owen uses several patterns of alliteration (repetition of an initial consonant). Examine the words beginning with *d* and those beginning with *g*. What is the effect of connecting each group of words? (Note that *dulce* and *decorum* are also part of this alliterative pattern.)
6. What attitude toward war emerges from the images and situation of the poem?
7. Why does Owen use the Latin quote for his title and conclusion? How is it a lie?

LANGSTON HUGHES
Dream Deferred

What happens to a dream deferred?

Does it dry up
like a raisin in the sun?
Or fester like a sore—
And then run?
Does it stink like rotten meat?
Or crust and sugar over—
like a syrupy sweet?

Maybe it just sags
like a heavy load.

Or does it explode?

QUESTIONS FOR ANALYSIS AND DISCUSSION

1. Describe the poem's structure.
2. Identify and explain each simile.
3. Which line is a metaphor? Explain it. Why is it effective?
4. What do the similes have in common?
5. What is Hughes's attitude toward deferred dreams, or unfulfilled goals?
6. What social comment might the poem be making?

GWENDOLYN BROOKS
from *The Womanhood*
from *"the children of the poor"*

2

What shall I give my children? who are poor,
Who are adjudged the leastwise of the land,
Who are my sweetest lepers, who demand
No velvet and no velvety velour;
But who have begged me for a brisk contour,
Crying that they are quasi, contraband
Because unfinished, graven by a hand
Less than angelic, admirable or sure.
My hand is stuffed with mode, design, device.
But I lack access to my proper stone.
And plenitude of plan shall not suffice
Nor grief nor love shall be enough alone
To ratify my little halves who bear
Across an autumn freezing everywhere.

QUESTIONS FOR ANALYSIS AND DISCUSSION

1. What type of lyric poem is this? (Compare it to Shakespeare's poem in this collection.)
2. After comparing Brooks and Shakespeare, can you provide a general definition for this type of poem? (Consider length, meter, and rhyme.)
3. Who is speaking? How does the speaker feel about the children? (Consider word choice and tone.)
4. What does the speaker have to give the children? Why does she lack "access to . . . proper stone"? What do you take "proper stone" to mean?
5. List the words and phrases that describe the children. How do these words create accurate, vivid portraits of poor children?
6. Trace Brooks's use of repeated sounds in the poem (e.g., "leastwise," "land," "lepers"). What does this technique accomplish?

W. S. MERWIN
Tool

If it's invented it will be used

maybe not for some time

then all at once
a hammer rises from under a lid
and shakes off its cold family

its one truth is stirring in its head
order order saying

and a surprised nail leaps
into darkness
that a moment before had been nothing

waiting
for the law

QUESTIONS FOR ANALYSIS AND DISCUSSION

1. The poem's first line is a generalization. What is its relationship to the rest of the poem?
2. The hammer "rises" and "shakes" and has a truth "stirring in its head." What does Merwin gain by personifying the hammer?
3. Is the nail also personified? How do you know?
4. What is "the law" the nail has been waiting for?
5. What larger social or political comment does the poem suggest?

SYLVIA PLATH
Mirror

I am silver and exact. I have no preconceptions.
Whatever I see I swallow immediately
Just as it is, unmisted by love or dislike.
I am not cruel, only truthful—
The eye of a little god, four-cornered.
Most of the time I meditate on the opposite wall.
It is pink, with speckles. I have looked at it so long
I think it is a part of my heart. But it flickers.
Faces and darkness separate us over and over.

Now I am a lake. A woman bends over me,
Searching my reaches for what she really is.
Then she turns to those liars, the candles or the moon.
I see her back, and reflect it faithfully.

She rewards me with tears and an agitation of hands.
I am important to her. She comes and goes.
Each morning it is her face that replaces the darkness.
In me she has drowned a young girl, and in me an old woman
Rises toward her day after day, like a terrible fish.

QUESTIONS FOR ANALYSIS AND DISCUSSION

1. What, according to the mirror, are its chief characteristics?
2. What characteristics actually come to dominate, as we read through the poem? What does the mirror *do* to what it sees? What is its relationship to the wall? To the woman?
3. A lake is like a mirror in that it reflects; how, for Plath, is a mirror like a lake?
4. What is the woman searching for? How does "looking into a mirror" provide an appropriate, and interesting, action to represent that search?
5. What associations do you make with the "terrible fish"? Is this primarily a negative comparison? Is it exclusively negative?

STUDENT ESSAY

A VIEW OF WAR'S HORRORS

CLARK MARTIN

Most of us would agree that war is a terrible result of the failure of one people to reason with another. When a war occurs, all citizens of the nations that are fighting, if not the world, are involved in some way. Francisco Goya's painting, *The Third of May, 1808*, effectively conveys his feeling of disgust at the horrors of war, particularly the involvement of innocent civilians in warfare.

At first glance, the viewer's eyes are drawn to the figure in the white shirt, just to the left of center. If not immediately attracted by the brightness of the garment itself, one's gaze moves from the center down the shining barrels of the muskets to the figure. The white shirt, in addition to attracting our attention, symbolizes the innocence of those before the firing squad. The man's face, besides the obvious mask of terror, looks puzzled. His arms, flung upward to either side, reflect his inability to comprehend fully what is happening and in themselves appear to ask "Why?"

Two of the figures kneeling with the innocent man represent the other predominant feelings of the horde of doomed peasants. One man glares at his executioners, thrusting his chin forward and clenching his fists. His posture reveals defiance. The monk, kneeling with hands clasped in prayer, begs for mercy.

Francisco Goya, The Third of May, 1808, 1814. *Museo del Prado, Madrid.*
Goya's famous painting depicts a firing squad of French soldiers, who were stationed in Madrid as part of Napoleon's conquest of Spain, executing Spaniards believed to have participated in an uprising against the French.

Immediately below and in front of the three figures just discussed are the victims of a previous volley. Goya has spared no crimson shades in his detailed treatment of this carnage, appealing to our basic human feelings when we are confronted with the sight of blood. The shock value is only too apparent, especially in the way the blood contrasts with the ground and the bright figure nearby.

Following the flow of blood down the slope toward the lantern, one's gaze comes to the feet of a man leading the column of approaching peasants. He, like those behind him, bows his head and covers his eyes, unable to witness his fate. These figures accent the repulsiveness of the entire scene by mirroring our desire to shield our own eyes from it. We have also taken note, if only subconsciously, that none of the victims-to-be is armed or has any semblance of a uniform to indicate that they are combatants in the struggle.

Cutting across the column of approaching peasants are the fixed bayonets of the rifles, which lead our eyes back to the right in a study of the firing squad. The squad embodies both the senselessness and coldness of the act. The barrels are aligned with one another almost perfectly, as are the feet of the riflemen, suggesting a machine-like precision and indifference to the proceedings. Goya has also managed to hide the faces of the soldiers composing the firing squad, thereby depersonalizing them further, stealing away any hope we may have of their ability either to justify what they are doing or to feel guilt.

An overview of the remainder of the painting shows a lack of detail, except for the distant city walls; this accents the foreground and lends a feeling of finality to the scene. Goya's use of brown, normally a warm color, is dismal in its combination with varying shades of gray. The starless sky falls on the area like a shroud, revealing little beyond the close horizon.

Goya's treatment of the fall of Madrid, depicted in the massacre of innocent civilians, is a moving statement on the fearful capacities of humankind for inhuman acts. Sadly, the power of Goya's brush has not prevented recurrences—at Guernica, Auschwitz, and My Lai.

EXERCISES

1. Select the correct literary term to identify each of the following uses of language, then explain the passage.

   a. she woke sometimes to feel the daylight coming
   like a relentless milkman up the stairs.

   ADRIENNE RICH

   b. The hand that signed the treaty bred a fever,
   And famine grew, and locusts came;
   Great is the hand that holds dominion over
   Man by a scribbled name.

   DYLAN THOMAS

   c. Life's but a walking shadow, a poor player
   That struts and frets his hour upon the stage
   And then is heard no more. . . .

   WILLIAM SHAKESPEARE

   d. "Yes; quaint and curious war is!
   You shoot a fellow down
   You'd treat if met where any bar is,
   Or help to half-a-crown."

   THOMAS HARDY

e. Take me to you [God], imprison me, for I
Except you enthrall me, never shall be free,
Nor ever chaste, except you ravish me.

JOHN DONNE

f. Busy old fool, unruly Sun,
Why dost thou thus
Through windows and through curtains call on us?

JOHN DONNE

g. The grave's a fine and private place,
But none, I think, do there embrace.

ANDREW MARVELL

h. Love, all alike, no season knows, nor clime,
Nor hours, days, months, which are the rags of time.

JOHN DONNE

i. Like a poem poorly written
We are verses out of rhythm
Couplets out of rhyme.

PAUL SIMON

2. Explicate the following sonnet by William Shakespeare, combining paraphrasing of the lines and explanation of the figurative language.

Sonnet 18

Shall I compare thee to a summer's day?
Thou art more lovely and more temperate:
Rough winds do shake the darling buds of May,
And summer's lease hath all too short a date:
Sometimes too hot the eye of heaven shines,
And often is his gold complexion dimmed;
And every fair from fair sometime declines,
By chance, or nature's changing course untrimmed;
But thy eternal summer shall not fade,
Nor lose possession of that fair thou owest;
Nor shall death brag thou wander'st in his shade,
When in eternal lines to time thou growest.
So long as men can breathe, or eyes can see,
So long lives this, and this gives life to thee.

3. Flowers are important in each of the following poems. Which poet presents his as an *image*, which as a *metaphor*, and which as a *symbol*? Explain the

metaphoric use: what is being compared to the flowers and what point is being made? Explain the symbolic use: what does the flower come to represent?

a. PAUL LAWRENCE DUNBAR (1872–1906)

Promise

I grew a rose within a garden fair,
And, tending it with more than loving care,
I thought how, with the glory of its bloom,
I should the darkness of my life illume;
And, watching, ever smiled to see the lusty bud
Drink freely in the summer sun to tinct its blood.

My rose began to open, and its hue
Was sweet to me as to it sun and dew;
I watched it taking on its ruddy flame
Until the day of perfect blooming came,
Then hasted I with smiles to find it blushing red—
Too late! Some thoughtless child has plucked my rose and fled!

b. WILLIAM WORDSWORTH (1770–1850)

I Wandered Lonely as a Cloud

I wandered lonely as a cloud
That floats on high o'er vales and hills,
When all at once I saw a crowd,
A host, of golden daffodils;
Beside the lake, beneath the trees,
Fluttering and dancing in the breeze.

Continuous as the stars that shine
And twinkle on the milky way,
They stretched in never-ending line
Along the margin of a bay:
Ten thousand saw I at a glance,
Tossing their heads in sprightly dance.

The waves beside them danced; but they
Outdid the sparkling waves in glee;
A poet could not but be gay,
In such a jocund company;
I gazed—and gazed—but little thought
What wealth the show to me had brought:

For oft, when on my couch I lie
In vacant or in pensive mood,
They flash upon that inward eye
Which is the bliss of solitude;
And then my heart with pleasure fills,
And dances with the daffodils.

c. ROBERT HERRICK (1591–1674)

To Daffodils

Fair daffodils, we weep to see
    You haste away so soon;
As yet the early-rising sun
    Has not attained his noon.
        Stay, stay,
    Until the hasting day
        Has run
    But to the even-song;
And, having prayed together, we
    Will go with you along.

We have short time to stay, as you;
    We have as short a spring,
As quick a growth to meet decay,
    As you, or anything.
        We die
    As your hours do, and dry
        Away
    Like to the summer's rain;
Or as the pearls of morning's dew.
    Ne'er to be found again.

WRITING ASSIGNMENTS

(Note: When preparing any one of these assignments, remember that literary analysis and interpretation is directed to readers who have read the work but may not have the work in front of them. Do not summarize, but do provide details from the work as evidence for your assertions.)

1. Explain how Camus uses setting symbolically in "The Guest" to convey the story's theme, or explain how Welty uses setting to convey Phoenix Jackson's character. Whichever story you select to analyze, examine details of setting closely and refer to them in your paper.

2. Analyze Thurber's techniques for portraying the character of Walter Mitty. Make sure that you explain Mitty's dominant traits, but also explain how we know them, how Thurber reveals character to us.
3. Select one of the paintings reproduced in this text, find a color reproduction in your library's art books collection, and analyze the work to explain the artist's attitude toward his subject. Organize thoughtfully and use spatial terms ("in the foreground," "to the left of the main figure," etc.) to guide your reader.
4. Contrast the attitudes toward nature in Whitman's "When I Heard the Learn'd Astronomer" and Frost's "Desert Places." Some subtle distinctions are needed here. Consider, especially, each poet's view of the human response to nature.
5. Contrast attitudes toward war in Owen's "Dulce Et Decorum Est" and the following poem by Walt Whitman. Show how the images in each poem convey each poet's views.

Cavalry Crossing a Ford

A line in long array where they wind betwixt green islands,
They take a serpentine course, their arms flash in the sun—
    hark to the musical clank,
Behold the silvery river, in it the splashing horses loitering
    stop to drink,
Behold the brown-faced men, each group, each person a picture,
    the negligent rest on the saddles,
Some emerge on the opposite bank, others are just entering the
    ford—while,
Scarlet and blue and snowy white,
The guidon flags flutter gayly in the wind.

Eugène Delacroix, Liberty Leading the People, 1830. *Approx.* 10′ 8″ × 8′ 6″. *Louvre, Paris. Giraudon/Art Resource.*

CHAPTER 5

WRITINGS FROM HISTORY, GOVERNMENT, AND PHILOSOPHY

Doris Lessing says, at the beginning of her essay on her father (Chapter 3), that she has written about him before in her novels, but now what she writes has to be "true." In her remarks Lessing separates the "made-up" characters of her fiction from the "true" portrait expected in a biographical sketch. She may use her father in the shaping of characters for her stories, but none *are* her father; they are transformed in the creating of fiction. The characters of fiction are made up; the character that emerges in a biography or the characters in a history book are or were actual people whose "true" personalities it is the task of the biographer or historian to capture in words. The distinction between "true" and "fictional" is a tricky one, however. On the one hand, we do test the truth of fictional characters against our knowledge of people and sometimes declare that a novelist's characters aren't true, that is, they are not believable. On the other hand, biographers and historians cannot guarantee to give us the true Henry VIII or the true George Washington; they can only portray these figures as they understand them after studying available sources.

Historians seek to tell us about the past what journalists seek to tell us about the present: who did what, where, when—and why. What, then, makes history different from journalism? First, the historian is not an eyewitness and must make an intellectual leap over time and cultural differences. Second, the sources available to historians are incomplete and at times contradictory. Conflicting reports must be reconciled; inferences must be made about missing links; and judgments must be made first about the reliability of sources and then about the relative significance of events. The truth we perceive to be in a historical account is in part a matter of the judgment we make about the historian's reliability and quality of thinking.

History is not only filtered through the training of a particular scholar; it is also filtered through the writer's particular purpose and, in varying degrees, through the writer's particular ideology. A high school American history text will not provide the same understanding of the Civil War as a six-volume study of the war. The briefer, simpler account is in some sense less "true" than the longer, more complex account. Similarly, a highly readable biography of Henry VIII for a popular audience will give us a somewhat different portrait of England's king than we would find in a scholarly, heavily documented biography. Audience, as noted in previous chapters, will affect a writer's choice of style, content, and conventions. Finally, some historians write from a precise ideological perspective. They may see cycles or other patterns in the stream of human events, or they may see events of the past as justification for some current policy. A Marxist historian's account of America's Depression years will be different from that of a historian embracing a free-market economic policy. Figure 5.1 summarizes these observations about the historian's stance.

The connections between history and philosophy are significant. First, we have observed that a historian's political or economic philosophy will, to some extent, shape her perception of historical events; certainly her analyses of cause will be affected. Second, philosophers, like

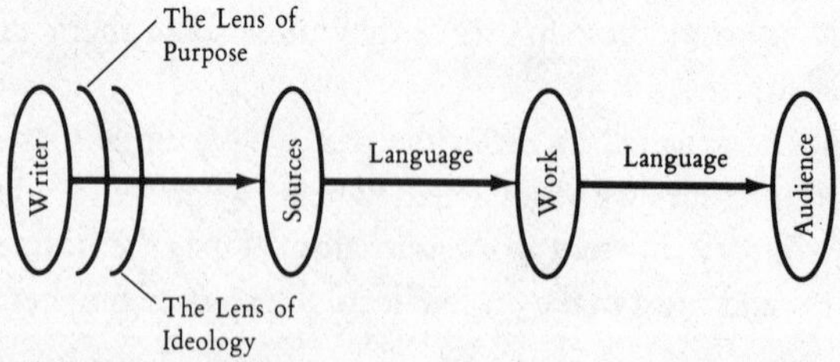

FIGURE 5.1 The Historian's Stance

historians, need facts; a philosopher is unlikely to write much that is meaningful to others if he has remained uneducated and reclusive during his life. A philosopher needs knowledge of the physical universe, of history, of human behavior, if he is to prepare a system of thought meaningful to others. For philosophy is not an odd assortment of notions; it is a systematic answer to one or more key questions we ask about the nature and meaning of life. Third, one of the ways we study philosophy in college is by historical survey. In any age, the literature, the art and music, and the philosophy of that time both reflect and shape the events of that time. We separate these fields of study to organize a university; but we should not lose sight of their "family" connections.

Philosophy and history connect closely in the study of government, in political theory. The cornerstone of Plato's philosophy is the *Republic*, a study of the ideal state; Aristotle, who wanted to organize all philosophical thought, wrote about politics as well as metaphysics and ethics. One major branch of philosophical inquiry since their time has covered, to quote Barbara Tuchman, "the major issues of ethics, sovereignty, the social contract, the rights of man, the corruption of power, the balance between freedom and order." Tuchman, in her second essay in this chapter, would add to these a study of governmental folly, an inquiry into the causes for failures in government. Walter Lippmann more traditionally examines issues of freedom and order, specifically freedom of speech and censorship. Shifting the focus from the functioning of government to the role of the citizen, Charles Krauthammer and Amitai Etzioni examine the issues of right judgment and duty to others.

Given the structuring of academic disciplines, students can study political theory as a part of the history of philosophy—since major philosophers from Plato to Marx write about the state; or students can focus on political theory in government courses and examine the history of ideas in literature, art, and history courses as well.

Within the discipline of philosophy, further divisions of inquiry are made and provide some terms and types of questions useful to your study. The most sweeping philosophical study is *metaphysics*, an inquiry into the ultimate nature of existence and reality. Metaphysics seeks to define the nature of the universe and the nature and purpose of human existence. Albert Camus's essay, "The Myth of Sisyphus," although not providing a complete metaphysics, addresses these large issues of who we are and what, if anything, is meaningful in our existence. Closely related to metaphysical discussion is the study of *how* we know or experience the world. This branch of philosophy, *epistemology,* has become, for modern philosophers, the starting point of inquiry. Is all knowledge subjective? Can we really know anything beyond our own sense experiences? Is there anything beyond them to know?—this is the question that connects epistemology and metaphysics. If epistemology poses the philosophical questions of modern psychology, education, and literary theory, then metaphysics poses the philosophical questions of modern science. It is not surprising to find scientists and mathematicians also engaging in complex philosophical inquiry. Bertrand Russell's works demonstrate the close connections among mathematics, abstract logic, and metaphysics. Finally, the branch of philosophy most widely discussed, at least among nonspecialists, is *ethics,* the study of values, or right and wrong conduct. We could categorize the essays of Krauthammer and Etzioni as being ethical studies as well as political inquiries, for right conduct cannot be discussed for long outside a social context. It helps to read a philosophical work with an understanding of the key questions being addressed in it, so that the writer's answers can be evaluated in the light of other possible answers to those same questions.

The academic study of history, government, and philosophy requires students to demonstrate a knowledge of facts, an understanding of terms, and an ability to explain concepts. One cannot usefully debate the effects of America's involvement in Southeast Asia without the facts: a history of the area; a history of American foreign policy; the values, Arthur Schlesinger would argue, that shape our foreign policy decisions; the concept of the domino theory. One cannot contrast the ideal states of Plato and Aristotle without knowing, in detail, what each philosopher has written. You can expect, then, to read extensively and to be tested on details: What is the Magna Carta? Who commanded the Union army? Explain the domino theory. Explain how the guardians will be chosen and trained in Plato's *Republic.* You will need to summarize, explicate, or define with precision. In more complex essay topics, these same skills will be combined. Consider the following paper topic for a political anthropology course: "Debate: 'Aristocracy is a more primitive form of government than democracy.' " What will you need to respond? Good definitions of "aristocracy" and "democracy"; detailed knowledge of specific primitive governments to use as illustration; control of contrast structure.

You will find that study in these fields cannot be undertaken without the support of the library. You will need to use the library's book and periodical collections to expand textbook readings and provide useful analyses and opposing viewpoints. And you will come to rely on reference materials as guides to sources and for direct help with the task of identifying people, places, and terms. A quick glance through the first two essays in this chapter will reveal the vast number of specific references found in writings from history. The exercises and writing assignments that complete this chapter will help sharpen your research skills and provide opportunities for writing history, defining terms, and debating issues.

In Search of History

BARBARA W. TUCHMAN

A native of New York City, Barbara Wertheim Tuchman (b. 1912) began her career, after graduating from Radcliffe, as editorial assistant and then correspondent for the Nation. *Tuchman has held other journalistic positions and many visiting lectureships but she is best known for her eight historical studies. Two of her books have won Pulitzer Prizes:* The Guns of August *(1962), a study of the first month of World War I, and* Stilwell and the American Experience in China *(1971). Other works include* The Zimmermann Telegram *(1958);* A Distant Mirror: The Calamitous Fourteenth Century *(1978); and most recently,* The March of Folly *(1984). Tuchman's books have been translated into many languages, and she has been recognized with numerous honorary degrees.*

Tuchman sees herself as a writer whose subjects are historical, rather than as a historian—at least in a scholarly sense. Her books are written for a nonspecialist audience, not other historians. To write a good "story," Tuchman draws on the novelist's sense of timing and the journalist's eye for visual detail; but as she explains, her studies are always true: no characters or events are invented.

The following essay, first delivered as the Phi Beta Kappa address at Radcliffe in May 1963, was published in 1981 in a collection titled Practicing History. *In her essay, Tuchman examines the historian's tasks, distinguishes between fiction and history, gives advice for preparing researched works, and conveys her enthusiasm for the study of history.*

1 History began to exert its fascination upon me when I was about six, through the medium of the Twins series by Lucy Fitch Perkins.[1] I became absorbed in the fortunes of the Dutch Twins; the Twins of the American Revolution, who daringly painted the name *Modeerf*, or "freedom" spelled backward, on their row boat; and especially the Belgian Twins, who suffered under the German occupation of Brussels in 1914.

2 After the Twins, I went through a G. A. Henty[2] period and bled with Wolfe in Canada. Then came a prolonged Dumas[3] period, during which I became so intimate with the Valois kings, queens, royal mistresses, and various Ducs de Guise that when we visited the French *châteaux* I was able to point out to my family just who had stabbed whom in which room. Conan Doyle's[4] *The White Company* and, above all, Jane Porter's[5] *The Scottish Chiefs* were the definitive influence. As the noble Wallace, in tartan and velvet tam, I went to my first masquerade party, stalking in silent tragedy among the twelve-year-old Florence Nightingales and Juliets. In the book the treachery of the Countess of Mar, who betrayed Wallace, carried a footnote that left its mark on me. "The crimes of this wicked woman," it said darkly, "are verified by history."

3 By the time I reached Radcliffe, I had no difficulty in choosing a field of concentration, although it turned out to be History and Lit rather than pure history. I experienced at college no moment of revelation that determined me to write historical narrative. When that precise moment occurred I cannot say; it just developed and there was a considerable time lag. What Radcliffe *did* give me, however, was an *impetus* (not to mention an education, but I suppose that goes without saying). Part of the impetus came from great courses and great professors. Of the

---

[1]American author (1865–1937) of several children's books, including *The Dutch Twins* and *The French Twins*, stories designed to create understanding of different cultures. —Ed.

[2]A nineteenth-century author of twelve novels, some historical and some set in distant countries. —Ed.

[3]A nineteenth-cenutry French dramatist and novelist. —Ed.

[4]A British detective-story writer (1859–1930). —Ed.

[5]A Scottish author (1776–1850) of two popular novels, *The Scottish Chiefs* and *Thaddeus of Warsaw*. —Ed.

three to which I owe most, two, curiously enough, were in literature rather than history. They were Irving Babbitt's Comp Lit 11 and John Livingston Lowes's English 72, which included his spectacular tour de force on the origins of "The Ancient Mariner" and "Kubla Khan."[6] He waved at Wordsworth, bowed briefly to Keats and Shelley, and really let himself go through twelve weeks of lectures, tracing the sources of Coleridge's imagery, and spending at least a week on the fatal apparition of the person from Porlock. What kept us, at least me, on the edge of my seat throughout this exploit was Lowes's enthusiasm for his subject.

4 This quality was the essence, too, of Professor C. H. McIlwain's Constitutional History of England, which came up as far as Magna Carta. It did not matter to McIlwain, a renowned scholar and historian, that only four of us were taking his course, or that he had already given it at Harvard and had to come over to repeat it to us (yes, that was the quaint custom of the time). It did not matter because McIlwain was conducting a passionate love affair with the laws of the Angles and the articles of the Charter, especially, as I remember, Article 39. Like any person in love, he wanted to let everyone know how beautiful was the object of his affections. He had white hair and pink cheeks and the brightest blue eyes I ever saw, and though I cannot remember a word of Article 39, I do remember how his blue eyes blazed as he discussed it and how I sat on the edge of my seat then too, and how, to show my appreciation, I would have given anything to write a brilliant exam paper, only to find that half the exam questions were in Anglo-Saxon, about which he had neglected to forewarn us. That did not matter either, because he gave all four of us A's anyway, perhaps out of gratitude for our affording him another opportunity to talk about his beloved Charter.

5 Professor Babbitt, on the other hand, being a classicist and anti-romantic, frowned on enthusiasm. But his contempt for zeal was so zealous, so vigorous and learned, pouring out in a great organ fugue of erudition, that it amounted to enthusiasm in the end and held not only me, but all his listeners, rapt.

6 Although I did not know it or formulate it consciously at the time, it is this quality of being in love with your subject that is indispensable for writing good history—or good anything, for that matter. A few months ago when giving a talk at another college, I was invited to meet the faculty and other guests at dinner. One young member of the

---

[6]Poems by Samuel Taylor Coleridge. Wordsworth, Keats, Shelley, and Coleridge are all British poets of the Romantic period.—Ed.

History Department who said he envied my subject in *The Guns of August* confessed to being bogged down and brought to a dead stop halfway through his doctoral thesis. It dealt, he told me, with an early missionary in the Congo who had never been "done" before. I asked what was the difficulty. With a dreary wave of his cocktail he said, "I just don't like him." I felt really distressed and depressed—both for him and for the conditions of scholarship. I do not know how many of you are going, or will go, to graduate school, but when you come to write that thesis on, let us say, "The Underwater Imagery Derived from the Battle of Lepanto in the Later Poetic Dramas of Lope de Vega," I hope it will be because you care passionately about this imagery rather than because your department has suggested it as an original subject.

7 In the process of doing my own thesis—not for a Ph.D., because I never took a graduate degree, but just my undergraduate honors thesis—the single most formative experience in my career took place. It was not a tutor or a teacher or a fellow student or a great book or the shining example of some famous visiting lecturer—like Sir Charles Webster, for instance, brilliant as he was. It was the stacks at Widener.[7] They were *my* Archimedes'[8] bathtub, my burning bush, my dish of mold where I found my personal penicillin. I was allowed to have as my own one of those little cubicles with a table under a window, queerly called, as I have since learned, carrels, a word I never knew when I sat in one. Mine was deep in among the 942s (British History, that is) and I could roam at liberty through the rich stacks, taking whatever I wanted. The experience was marvelous, a word I use in its exact sense meaning full of marvels. The happiest days of my intellectual life, until I began writing history again some fifteen years later, were spent in the stacks at Widener. My daughter Lucy, class of '61, once said to me that she could not enter the labyrinth of Widener's stacks without feeling that she ought to carry a compass, a sandwich, and a whistle. I too was never altogether sure I could find the way out, but I was blissful as a cow put to graze in a field of fresh clover and would not have cared if I had been locked in for the night.

8 Once I stayed so late that I came out after dark, long after the dinner hour at the dorm, and found to my horror that I had only a nickel in my purse. The weather was freezing and I was very hungry. I could

[7]Main library at Harvard University.—Ed.

[8]A Greek mathematician, physicist, and inventor (287?–212 B.C.). Tuchman's sentence gives examples of invention, discovery, and insight.—Ed.

not decide whether to spend the nickel on a chocolate bar and walk home in the cold or take the Mass Avenue trolley and go home hungry. This story ends like "The Lady or the Tiger," because although I remember the agony of having to choose, I cannot remember how it came out.

9 My thesis, the fruit of those hours in the stacks, was my first sustained attempt at writing history. It was called "The Moral Justification for the British Empire," an unattractive title and, besides, inaccurate, because what I meant was the moral *justifying* of empire by the imperialists. It was for me a wonderful and terrible experience. Wonderful because finding the material, and following where it led, was constantly exciting and because I was fascinated by the subject, which I had thought up for myself—much to the disapproval of my tutor, who was in English Lit, not History, and interested only in Walter Pater—or was it Walter Savage Landor?[9] Anyway, it was *not* the British Empire, and since our meetings were consequently rather painfully uncommunicative, I think he was relieved when I took to skipping them.

10 The experience was terrible because I could not make the piece sound, or rather read, the way I wanted it to. The writing fell so far short of the ideas. The characters, who were so vivid inside my head, seemed so stilted when I got them on paper. I finished it, dissatisfied. So was the department: "Style undistinguished," it noted. A few years ago, when I unearthed the thesis to look up a reference, that impression was confirmed. It reminded me of *The Importance of Being Earnest,* when Cecily says that the letters she wrote to herself from her imaginary fiancé when she broke off their imaginary engagement were so beautiful and so badly spelled she could not reread them without crying. I felt the same way about my thesis: so beautiful—in intent—and so badly written. Enthusiasm had not been enough; one must also know how to use the language.

11 One learns to write, I have since discovered, in the practice thereof. After seven years' apprenticeship in journalism I discovered that an essential element for good writing is a good ear. One must *listen* to the sound of one's own prose. This, I think, is one of the failings of much American writing. Too many writers do not listen to the sound of their own words. For example, listen to this sentence from the organ of my own discipline, the *American Historical Review*: "His presentation is not vitiated historically by efforts at expository simplicity." In one short sentence five long Latin words of four or five syllables each. One has to

[9] Minor nineteenth-century British poets.—Ed.

read it three times over and take time out to think, before one can even make out what it means.

12 In my opinion, short words are always preferable to long ones; the fewer syllables the better, and monosyllables, beautiful and pure like "bread" and "sun" and "grass," are the best of all. Emerson, using almost entirely one-syllable words, wrote what I believe are among the finest lines in English:

By the rude bridge that arched the flood,
Their flag to April's breeze unfurled,
Thy Naiad airs have brought me home
And fired the shot heard round the world.

Out of twenty-eight words, twenty-four are monosyllables. It is English at its purest, though hardly characteristic of its author.

13 Or take this:

On desperate seas long wont to roam,
Thy hyacinth hair, thy classic face,
Here once the embattled farmers stood
To the glory that was Greece
And the grandeur that was Rome.

Imagine how it must feel to have composed those lines! Though coming from a writer satisfied with the easy rhythms of "The Raven" and "Annabel Lee," they represent, I fear, a fluke. To quote poetry, you will say, is not a fair comparison. True, but what a lesson those stanzas are in the sound of words! What superb use of that magnificent instrument that lies at the command of all of us—the English language. Quite by chance both practitioners in these samples happen to be Americans, and both, curiously enough, writing about history.

14 To write history so as to enthrall the reader and make the subject as captivating and exciting to him as it is to me has been my goal since that initial failure with my thesis. A prerequisite, as I have said, is to be enthralled one's self and to feel a compulsion to communicate the magic. Communicate to whom? We arrive now at the reader, a person whom I keep constantly in mind. Catherine Drinker Bowen[10] has said that she writes her books with a sign pinned up over her desk asking, "Will the reader turn the page?"

[10]An American biographer (1897–1973).—Ed.

15 The writer of history, I believe, has a number of duties *vis-à-vis* the reader, if he wants to keep him reading. The first is to distill. He must do the preliminary work for the reader, assemble the information, make sense of it, select the essential, discard the irrelevant—above all, discard the irrelevant—and put the rest together so that it forms a developing dramatic narrative. Narrative, it has been said, is the lifeblood of history. To offer a mass of undigested facts, of names not identified and places not located, is of no use to the reader and is simple laziness on the part of the author, or pedantry to show how much he has read. To discard the unnecessary requires courage and also extra work, as exemplified by Pascal's[11] effort to explain an idea to a friend in a letter which rambled on for pages and ended, "I am sorry to have wearied you with so long a letter but I did not have time to write you a short one." The historian is continually being beguiled down fascinating byways and sidetracks. But the art of writing—the test of the artist—is to resist the beguilement and cleave to the subject.

16 Should the historian be an artist? Certainly a conscious art should be part of his equipment. Macaulay[12] describes him as half poet, half philosopher. I do not aspire to either of these heights. I think of myself as a storyteller, a narrator, who deals in true stories, not fiction. The distinction is not one of relative values; it is simply that history interests me more than fiction. I agree with Leopold von Ranke, the great nineteenth-cenutry German historian, who said that when he compared the portrait of Louis XI in Scott's *Quentin Durward*[13] with the portrait of the same king in the memoirs of Philippe de Comines, Louis' minister, he found "the truth more interesting and beautiful than the romance."

17 It was Ranke, too, who set the historian's task: to find out *wie es eigentlich gewesen ist,* what really happened, or, literally, how it really was. His goal is one that will remain forever just beyond our grasp for reasons I explained in a "Note on Sources" in *The Guns of August* (a paragraph that no one ever reads but *I* think is the best thing in the book). Summarized, the reasons are that we who write about the past were not there. We can never be certain that we have recaptured it as it really was. But the least we can do is to stay within the evidence.

18 I do not invent anything, even the weather. One of my readers told me he particularly liked a passage in *The Guns* which tells how the

[11]A French philosopher and mathematician (1623–1662).—Ed.

[12]An English historian, author, and statesman (1800–1859).—Ed.

[13]A romantic novel by English author Sir Walter Scott (1771–1832).—Ed.

British Army landed in France and how on that afternoon there was a sound of summer thunder in the air and the sun went down in a blood-red glow. He thought it an artistic touch of doom, but the fact is it was true. I found it in the memoirs of a British officer who landed on that day and heard the thunder and saw the blood-red sunset. The art, if any, consisted only in selecting it and ultimately using it in the right place.

19 Selection is what determines the ultimate product, and that is why I use material from primary sources only. My feeling about secondary sources is that they are helpful but pernicious. I use them as guides at the start of a project to find out the general scheme of what happened, but I do not take notes from them because I do not want to end up simply rewriting someone else's book. Furthermore, the facts in a secondary source have already been pre-selected, so that in using them one misses the opportunity of selecting one's own.

20 I plunge as soon as I can into the primary sources: the memoirs and the letters, the generals' own accounts of their campaigns, however tendentious, not to say mendacious, they may be. Even an untrustworthy source is valuable for what it reveals about the personality of the author, especially if he is an actor in the events, as in the case of Sir John French,[14] for example. Bias in a primary source is to be expected. One allows for it and corrects it by reading another version. I try always to read two or more for every episode. Even if an event is not controversial, it will have been seen and remembered from different angles of view by different observers. If the event *is* in dispute, one has extra obligation to examine both sides. As the lion in Aesop[15] said to the Man, "There are many statues of men slaying lions, but if only the lions were sculptors there might be quite a different set of statues."

21 The most primary source of all is unpublished material: private letters and diaries or the reports, orders, and messages in government archives. There is an immediacy and intimacy about them that reveals character and makes circumstances come alive. I remember Secretary of State Robert Lansing's[16] desk diary, which I used when I was working on *The Zimmermann Telegram.* The man himself seemed to step right out from his tiny neat handwriting and his precise notations of every visitor and each subject discussed. Each day's record opened and closed with the Secretary's time of arrival and departure from the office. He

---

[14]An English field marshal in World War I.—Ed.

[15]A Greek writer of fables (620?–560?B.C.).—Ed.

[16]Secretary of state from 1915 to 1920.—Ed.

even entered the time of his lunch hour, which invariably lasted sixty minutes: "Left at 1:10; returned at 2:10." Once, when he was forced to record his morning arrival at 10:15, he added, with a worried eye on posterity, "Car broke down."

22 Inside the National Archives even the memory of Widener paled. Nothing can compare with the fascination of examining material in the very paper and ink of its original issue. A report from a field agent with marginal comments by the Secretary of War, his routing directions to State and Commerce, and the scribbled initials of subsequent readers can be a little history in itself. In the Archives I found the original decode of the Zimmermann Telegram, which I was able to have declassified and photostated for the cover of my book.

23 Even more immediate is research on the spot. Before writing *The Guns* I rented a little Renault and in another August drove over the battle areas of August 1914, following the track of the German invasion through Luxembourg, Belgium, and northern France. Besides obtaining a feeling of the geography, distances, and terrain involved in military movements, I saw the fields ripe with grain which the cavalry would have trampled, measured the great width of the Meuse at Liège,[17] and saw how the lost territory of Alsace looked to the French soldiers who gazed down upon it from the heights of the Vosges.[18] I learned the discomfort of the Belgian *pavé*[19] and discovered, in the course of losing my way almost permanently in a tangle of country roads in a hunt for the house that had been British Headquarters, why a British motorcycle dispatch rider in 1914 had taken three hours to cover twenty-five miles. Clearly, owing to the British officers' preference for country houses, he had not been able to find Headquarters either. French army commanders, I noticed, located themselves in *towns,* with railroad stations and telegraph offices.

23 As to the mechanics of research, I take notes on four-by-six index cards, reminding myself about once an hour of a rule I read long ago in a research manual, "Never write on the back of anything." Since copying is a chore and a bore, use of the cards, the smaller the better, forces one to extract the strictly relevant, to distill from the very beginning, to pass the material through the grinder of one's own mind, so to speak. Eventually, as the cards fall into groups according to subject or person or

[17]The Meuse River at the Belgian city of Liège.—Ed.

[18]A mountain range in eastern France.—Ed.

[19]Unevenly paved roadways.—Ed.

chronological sequence, the pattern of my story will emerge. Besides, they are convenient, as they can be filed in a shoebox and carried around in a pocketbook. When ready to write I need only take along a packet of them, representing a chapter, and I am equipped to work anywhere; whereas if one writes surrounded by a pile of books, one is tied to a single place, and furthermore likely to be too much influenced by other authors.

25 The most important thing about research is to know when to stop. How does one recognize the moment? When I was eighteen or thereabouts, my mother told me that when out with a young man I should always leave a half-hour before I wanted to. Although I was not sure how this might be accomplished, I recognized the advice as sound, and exactly the same rule applies to research. One must stop *before* one has finished; otherwise, one will never stop and never finish. I had an object lesson in this once in Washington at the Archives. I was looking for documents in the case of Perdicaris, an American—or supposed American—who was captured by Moroccan brigands in 1904. The Archives people introduced me to a lady professor who had been doing research in United States relations with Morocco all her life. She had written her Ph.D. thesis on the subject back in, I think, 1936, and was still coming for six months each year to work in the Archives. She was in her seventies and, they told me, had recently suffered a heart attack. When I asked her what year was her cut-off point, she looked at me in surprise and said she kept a file of newspaper clippings right up to the moment. I am sure she knew more about United States–Moroccan relations than anyone alive, but would she ever leave off her research in time to write that definitive history and tell the world what she knew? I feared the answer. Yet I know how she felt. I too feel compelled to follow every lead and learn everything about a subject, but fortunately I have an even more overwhelming compulsion to see my work in print. That is the only thing that saves me.

26 Research is endlessly seductive; writing is hard work. One has to sit down on that chair and think and transform thought into readable, conservative, interesting sentences that both make sense and make the reader turn the page. It is laborious, slow, often painful, sometimes agony. It means rearrangement, revision, adding, cutting, rewriting. But it brings a sense of excitement, almost of rapture; a moment on Olympus. In short, it is an act of creation.

27 I had of course a tremendous head start in having for *The Guns of August* a spectacular subject. The first month of the First World War, as

Winston Churchill said, was "a drama never surpassed." It has that heroic quality that lifts the subject above the petty and that is necessary to great tragedy. In the month of August 1914 there was something looming, inescapable, universal, that involved us all. Something in that awful gulf between perfect plans and fallible men that makes one tremble with a sense of "There but for the Grace of God go we."

28 It was not until the end, until I was actually writing the Epilogue, that I fully realized all the implications of the story I had been writing for two years. Then I began to feel I had not done it justice. But now it was too late to go back and put in the significance, like the girl in the writing course whose professor said now they would go back over her novel and put in the symbolism.

29 One of the difficulties in writing history is the problem of how to keep up suspense in a narrative whose outcome is known. I worried about this a good deal at the beginning, but after a while the actual process of writing, as so often happens, produced the solution. I found that if one writes *as of the time,* without using the benefit of hindsight, resisting always the temptation to refer to events still ahead, the suspense will build itself up naturally. Sometimes the temptation to point out to the reader the significance of an act or event in terms of what later happened is almost irresistible. But I tried to be strong. I went back and cut out all references but one of the Battle of the Marne, in the chapters leading up to the battle. Though it may seem absurd, I even cut any references to the ultimate defeat of Germany. I wrote as if I did not know who would win, and I can only tell you that the method worked. I used to become tense with anxiety myself, as the moments of crisis approached. There was Joffre, for instance, sitting under the shade tree outside Headquarters, all that hot afternoon, considering whether to continue the retreat of the French armies to the Seine or, as Gallieni is pleading, turn around now and counterattack at the Marne.[20] The German right wing is sliding by in front of Paris, exposing its flank. The moment is escaping. Joffre still sits and ponders. Even though one knows the outcome, the suspense is almost unbearable, because one knows that if he had made the wrong decision, you and I might not be here today—or, if we were, history would have been written by others.

30 This brings me to a matter currently rather moot—the nature of

---

[20]Joffre and Gallieni were French generals. They had to decide whether to retreat to the Seine River, which runs through central France, or to fight the German army at the Marne River in northeastern France. The Allies did fight at the Marne, early in September 1914.—Ed.

history. Today the battle rages, as you know, between the big thinkers or Toynbees or systematizers on the one hand and the humanists, if I may so designate them – using the word to mean concerned with human nature, not with the humanities – on the other. The genus Toynbee[21] is obsessed and oppressed by the need to find an explanation for history. They arrange systems and cycles into which history must be squeezed so that it will come out evenly and have pattern and a meaning. When history, wickedly disobliging, pops up in the wrong places, the systematizers hurriedly explain any such aberrant behavior by the climate. They need not reach so far; it is a matter of people. As Sir Charles Oman, the great historian of the art of war, said some time ago, "The human record is illogical . . . and history is a series of happenings with no inevitability about it."

31 Prefabricated systems make me suspicious and science applied to history makes me wince. The nearest anyone has come to explaining history is, I think, Leon Trotsky,[22] who both made history and wrote it. Cause in history, he said, "refracts itself through a natural selection of accidents." The more one ponders that statement the more truth one finds. More recently an anonymous reviewer in the *Times Literary Supplement* disposed of the systematizers beyond refute. "The historian," he said, "who puts his system first can hardly escape the heresy of preferring the facts which suit his system best." And he concluded, "Such explanation as there is must arise in the mind of the reader of history." That is the motto on my banner.

32 To find out what happened in history is enough at the outset without trying too soon to make sure of the "why." I believe it is safer to leave the "why" alone until after one has not only gathered the facts but arranged them in sequence; to be exact, in sentences, paragraphs, and chapters. The very process of transforming a collection of personalities, dates, gun calibers, letters, and speeches into a narrative eventually forces the "why" to the surface. It will emerge of itself one fine day from the story of what happened. It will suddenly appear and tap one on the shoulder, but not if one chases after it first, *before* one knows what happened. Then it will elude one forever.

---

[21]The type of historian who, like the British historian Arnold Toynbee, sees large patterns or cycles in history. – Ed.

[22]A Russian revolutionary leader and writer; he was minister of war from 1918 to 1925. – Ed.

33 If the historian will submit himself *to* his material instead of trying to impose himself *on* his material, then the material will ultimately speak to him and supply the answers. It has happened to me more than once. In somebody's memoirs I found that the Grand Duke Nicholas wept when he was named Russian Commander-in-Chief in 1914, because, said the memoirist, he felt inadequate for the job. That sounded to me like one of those bits of malice one has to watch out for in contemporary observers; it did not ring true. The Grand Duke was said to be the only "man" in the royal family; he was known for his exceedingly tough manners, was admired by the common soldier and feared at court. I did not believe he felt inadequate, but then why should he weep? I could have left out this bit of information, but I did not want to. I wanted to find the explanation that would make it fit. (Leaving things out because they do not fit is writing fiction, not history.) I carried the note about the Grand Duke around with me for days, worrying about it. Then I remembered other tears. I went through my notes and found an account of Churchill weeping and also Messimy, the French War Minister. All at once I understood that it was not the individuals but the *times* that were the stuff for tears. My next sentence almost wrote itself: "There was an aura about 1914 that caused those who sensed it to shiver for mankind." Afterward I realized that this sentence expressed why I had wanted to write the book in the first place. The "why," you see, had emerged all by itself.

34 The same thing happened with Joffre's battle order on the eve of the Marne. I had intended to make this my climax, a final bugle call, as it were. But the order was curiously toneless and flat and refused utterly to rise to the occasion. I tried translating it a dozen different ways, but nothing helped. I grew really angry over that battle order. Then, one day, when I was rereading it for the twentieth time, it suddenly spoke. I discovered that its very flatness *was* its significance. Now I was able to quote it at the end of the last chapter and add, "It did not shout 'Forward!' or summon men to glory. After the first thirty days of war in 1914, there was a premonition that little glory lay ahead."

35 As, in this way, the explanation conveys itself to the writer, so will the implications or meaning for our time arise in the mind of the reader. But such lessons, if present and valid, must emerge from the material, not the writer. I did not write to instruct but to tell a story. The implications are what the thoughtful reader himself takes out of the book. This is as it should be, I think, because the best book is a collaboration between author and reader.

QUESTIONS FOR ANALYSIS AND DISCUSSION

1. What did Tuchman gain from her early reading?
2. What did she gain from Professors Babbitt, Lowes, and McIlwain?
3. What, according to Tuchman, is indispensable for writing well?
4. What else is indispensable? What piece of her writing taught Tuchman this lesson?
5. How do we learn to write? How can we improve our writing?
6. What tasks must the historian perform for the reader?
7. Why will the historian never be able to know what really happened?
8. What is the historian's art? What must the historian not do?
9. What does Tuchman feel she gains by visiting the sites of her books?
10. Tuchman gives good advice to researchers on the use of index cards; why use cards?
11. Tuchman says that "writing is hard work." If it is such agony, why does she do it?
12. What is Tuchman's argument against fitting history into systems or cycles? What is the best way to discover why things happened, or what they mean? Do you agree? Why or why not?
13. Tuchman says that the best writing uses short words. Does she follow her own advice? What makes her writing challenging to a reader?
14. Given her many references, what can you conclude about her anticipated audience?

An Inquiry into the Persistence of Unwisdom in Government

BARBARA W. TUCHMAN

For a biographical sketch of Tuchman, see p. 215. In "An Inquiry into the Persistence of Unwisdom in Government," first published in Esquire *in May 1980, we see Tuchman practicing her art. She demonstrates her wealth of knowledge, illustrating unwisdom in government in ancient times (the Trojan War), in the American Revolution, and in American involvement in Vietnam. This essay also demonstrates her current interest in drawing a thesis from historical study, an interest first revealed in* A Distant Mirror, *her study of the calamitous fourteenth century. In the following essay, Tuchman generalizes about the nature and causes of folly in government and illustrates that folly with some of the all too numerous examples from history. Presumably, Tuchman believes, an understanding of folly can lead to avoiding it in the future, a hopeful view that serves as the controlling idea in Tuchman's latest book,* The March of Folly. *This essay, in an expanded form, serves as the first chapter of* The March of Folly.

1 A problem that strikes one in the study of history, regardless of period, is why man makes a poorer performance of government than of almost any other human activity. In this sphere, wisdom—meaning judgment acting on experience, common sense, available knowledge, and a decent appreciation of probability—is less operative and more frustrated than it should be. Why do men in high office so often act contrary to the way that reason points and enlightened self-interest suggests? Why does intelligent mental process so often seem to be paralyzed?

2 Why, to begin at the beginning, did the Trojan authorities drag that suspicious-looking wooden horse inside their gates? Why did successive ministries of George III—that "bundle of imbecility," as Dr. Johnson[1] called them collectively—insist on coercing rather than conciliating the Colonies though strongly advised otherwise by many counselors? Why did Napoleon and Hitler invade Russia? Why did the kaiser's[2] government resume unrestricted submarine warfare in 1917 although explicitly warned that this would bring in the United States and that American belligerency would mean Germany's defeat? Why did Chiang Kai-shek[3] refuse to heed any voice of reform or alarm until he woke up to find that his country had slid from under him? Why did Lyndon Johnson, seconded by the best and the brightest, progressively involve this nation in a war both ruinous and halfhearted and from which nothing but bad for our side resulted? Why does the present Administration[4] continue to avoid introducing effective measures to reduce the wasteful consumption of oil while members of OPEC follow a price policy that must bankrupt their customers? How is it possible that the

---

[1]An eighteenth-century British writer.—Ed.

[2]Kaiser Wilhelm (1859–1941), emperor of Germany.—Ed.

[3]A Chinese general and political leader (1886?–1975); president of China from 1948 until the Mao revolution in 1949; president of "Nationalist China" (Taiwan) from 1950 to 1975.—Ed.

[4]The Carter administration.—Ed.

Central Intelligence Agency, whose function it is to provide, at taxpayers' expense, the information necessary to conduct a realistic foreign policy, could remain unaware that discontent in a country crucial to our interests was boiling up to the point of insurrection and overthrow of the ruler upon whom our policy rested? It has been reported that the CIA was ordered *not* to investigate the opposition to the shah of Iran in order to spare him any indication that we took it seriously, but since this sounds more like the theater of the absurd than like responsible government, I cannot bring myself to believe it.

3 There was a king of Spain once, Philip III, who is said to have died of a fever he contracted from sitting too long near a hot brazier, helplessly overheating himself because the functionary whose duty it was to remove the brazier when summoned could not be found. In the late twentieth century, it begins to appear as if mankind may be approaching a similar stage of suicidal incompetence. The Italians have been sitting in Philip III's hot seat for some time. The British trade unions, in a lunatic spectacle, seem periodically bent on dragging their country toward paralysis, apparently under the impression that they are separate from the whole. Taiwan was thrown into a state of shock by the United States' recognition of the People's Republic of China because, according to one report, in the seven years since the Shanghai Communiqué, the Kuomintang rulers of Taiwan had "refused to accept the new trend as a reality."

4 Wooden-headedness is a factor that plays a remarkably large role in government. Wooden-headedness consists of assessing a situation in terms of preconceived, fixed notions while ignoring or rejecting any contrary signs. It is acting according to wish while not allowing oneself to be confused by the facts.

5 A classic case was the French war plan of 1914, which concentrated everything on a French offensive to the Rhine, leaving the French left flank from Belgium to the Channel virtually unguarded. This strategy was based on the belief that the Germans would not use reserves in the front line and, without them, could not deploy enough manpower to extend their invasion through the French left. Reports by intelligence agents in 1913 to the effect that the Germans were indeed preparing their reserves for the front line in case of war were resolutely ignored because the governing spirits in France, dreaming only of their own offensive, did not want to believe in any signals that would require them to strengthen their left at the expense of their march to the Rhine. In the event, the Germans could and did extend themselves around the

French left with results that determined a long war and its fearful consequences for our century.

6 Wooden-headedness is also the refusal to learn from experience, a form in which fourteenth-century rulers were supreme. No matter how often and obviously devaluation of the currency disrupted the economy and angered the people, French monarchs continued to resort to it whenever they were desperate for cash until they provoked insurrection among the bourgeoisie. No matter how often a campaign that depended on living off a hostile country ran into want and even starvation, campaigns for which this fate was inevitable were regularly undertaken.

7 Still another form is identification of self with the state, as currently exhibited by the ayatollah Khomeini. No wooden-headedness is so impenetrable as that of a religious zealot. Because he is connected with a private wire to the Almighty, no idea coming in on a lesser channel can reach him, which leaves him ill equipped to guide his country in its own best interests.

8 Philosophers of government ever since Plato[5] have devoted their thinking to the major issues of ethics, sovereignty, the social contract, the rights of man, the corruption of power, the balance between freedom and order. Few—except Machiavelli,[6] who was concerned with government as it is, not as it should be—bothered with mere folly, although this has been a chronic and pervasive problem. "Know, my son," said a dying Swedish statesman in the seventeenth century, "with how little wisdom the world is governed." More recently, Woodrow Wilson warned, "In public affairs, stupidity is more dangerous than knavery."

9 Stupidity is not related to type of regime; monarchy, oligarchy, and democracy produce it equally. Nor is it peculiar to nation or class. The working class as represented by the Communist governments functions no more rationally or effectively in power than the aristocracy or the bourgeoisie, as has notably been demonstrated in recent history. Mao Tse-tung may be admired for many things, but the Great Leap Forward, with a steel plant in every backyard, and the Cultural Revolution were exercises in unwisdom that greatly damaged China's progress and stability, not to mention the chairman's reputation. The record of the Russian proletariat in power can hardly be called enlightened, although after

---

[5]A Greek philosopher (427–347 B.C.).—Ed.

[6]An Italian statesman and philosopher (1469–1527); author of *The Prince*.—Ed.

sixty years of control it must be accorded a kind of brutal success. If the majority of Russians are better off now than before, the cost in cruelty and tyranny has been no less and probably greater than under the czars.

10 After the French Revolution, the new order was rescued only by Bonaparte's military campaigns, which brought the spoils of foreign wars to fill the treasury, and subsequently by his competence as an executive. He chose officials not on the basis of origin or ideology but on the principle of "*la carrière ouverte aux talents*"[7]—the said talents being intelligence, energy, industry, and obedience. That worked until the day of his own fatal mistake.

11 I do not wish to give the impression that men in office are incapable of governing wisely and well. Occasionally, the exception appears, rising in heroic size above the rest, a tower visible down the centuries. Greece had her Pericles,[8] who ruled with authority, moderation, sound judgment, and a certain nobility that imposes natural dominion over others. Rome had Caesar, a man of remarkable governing talents, although it must be said that a ruler who arouses opponents to resort to assassination is probably not as smart as he ought to be. Later, under Marcus Aurelius and the other Antonines,[9] Roman citizens enjoyed good government, prosperity, and respect for about a century. Charlemagne was able to impose order upon a mass of contending elements, to foster the arts of civilization no less than those of war, and to earn a prestige supreme in the Middle Ages—probably not equaled in the eyes of contemporaries until the appearance of George Washington.

12 Possessor of an inner strength and perseverance that enabled him to prevail over a sea of obstacles, Washington was one of those critical figures but for whom history might well have taken a different course. He made possible the physical victory of American independence, while around him, in extraordinary fertility, political talent bloomed as if touched by some tropical sun. For all their flaws and quarrels, the Founding Fathers, who established our form of government, were, in the words of Arthur Schlesinger, Sr., "the most remarkable generation of public men in the history of the United States or perhaps of any other nation." It is worth noting the qualities Schlesinger ascribes to them: They were fearless, high-principled, deeply versed in ancient and modern political thought, astute and pragmatic, unafraid of experiment, and—this is

---

[7]A French expression meaning "tools to those who can handle them."—Ed.

[8]An Athenian statesman of the fifth century B.C.—Ed.

[9]Second-century A.D. Roman emperors.—Ed.

significant—"convinced of man's power to improve his condition through the use of intelligence." That was the mark of the Age of Reason that formed them, and though the eighteenth century had a tendency to regard men as more rational than they in fact were, it evoked the best in government from these men.

13 For our purposes, it would be invaluable if we could know what produced this burst of talent from a base of only two million inhabitants. Schlesinger suggests some contributing factors: wide diffusion of education, challenging economic opportunities, social mobility, training in self-government—all these encouraged citizens to cultivate their political aptitudes to the utmost. Also, he adds, with the Church declining in prestige and with business, science, and art not yet offering competing fields of endeavor, statecraft remained almost the only outlet for men of energy and purpose. Perhaps the need of the moment—the opportunity to create a new political system—is what brought out the best.

14 Not before or since, I believe, has so much careful and reasonable thinking been invested in the creation of a new political system. In the French, Russian, and Chinese revolutions, too much class hatred and bloodshed were involved to allow for fair results or permanent constitutions. The American experience was unique, and the system so far has always managed to right itself under pressure. In spite of accelerating incompetence, it still works better than most. We haven't had to discard the system and try another after every crisis, as have Italy and Germany, Spain and France. The founders of the United States are a phenomenon to keep in mind to encourage our estimate of human possibilities, but their example, as a political scientist has pointed out, is "too infrequent to be taken as a basis for normal expectations."

15 The English are considered to have enjoyed reasonably benign government during the eighteenth and nineteenth centuries, except for their Irish subjects, debtors, child laborers, and other unfortunates in various pockets of oppression. The folly that lost the American colonies reappeared now and then, notably in the treatment of the Irish and the Boers,[10] but a social system can survive a good deal of folly when circumstances are historically favorable or when it is cushioned by large resources, as in the heyday of the British Empire, or absorbed by sheer

[10]South Africans of Dutch extraction, whom the British fought for control of South Africa 1899–1902.—Ed.

size, as in this country during our period of expansion. Today there are no more cushions, which makes folly less affordable.

16 Elsewhere than in government, man has accomplished marvels: invented the means in our time to leave the world and voyage to the moon; in the past, harnessed wind and electricity, raised earthbound stone into soaring cathedrals, woven silk brocades out of the spinnings of a worm, composed the music of Mozart and the dramas of Shakespeare, classified the forms of nature, penetrated the mysteries of genetics. Why is he so much less accomplished in government? What frustrates, in that sphere, the operation of the intellect? Isaac Bashevis Singer,[11] discoursing as a Nobel laureate on mankind, offers the opinion that God had been frugal in bestowing intellect but lavish with passions and emotions. "He gave us," Singer says, "so many emotions and such strong ones that every human being, even if he is an idiot, is a millionaire in emotions."

17 I think Singer has made a point that applies to our inquiry. What frustrates the workings of intellect is the passions and the emotions: ambition, greed, fear, face-saving, the instinct to dominate, the needs of the ego, the whole bundle of personal vanities and anxieties.

18 Reason is crushed by these forces. If the Athenians out of pride and overconfidence had not set out to crush Sparta for good but had been content with moderate victory, their ultimate fall might have been averted. If fourteenth-century knights had not been obsessed by the idea of glory and personal prowess, they might have defeated the Turks at Nicopolis with incalculable consequence for all of Eastern Europe. If the English, 200 years ago, had heeded Chatham's[12] knocking on the door of what he called "this sleeping and confounded Ministry" and his urgent advice to repeal the Coercive Acts[13] and withdraw the troops before the "inexpiable drop of blood is shed in an impious war with a people contending in the great cause of publick liberty" or, given a last chance, if they had heeded Edmund Burke's[14] celebrated plea for conciliation and his warning that it would prove impossible to coerce a "fierce people" of their own pedigree, we might still be a united people bridging the Atlantic, with incalculable consequence for the history of the West.

[11] A Jewish-American novelist and short-story writer (b. 1904); winner of the Nobel Prize in Literature in 1978. —Ed.

[12] William Pitt, first earl of Chatham (1708–1788), opposed British treatment of the American colonies. —Ed.

[13] Laws passed in Britain in 1774 designed to close the port of Boston after the Boston Tea Party. —Ed.

[14] An eighteenth-century British statesman and writer. —Ed.

It did not happen that way, because king and Parliament felt it imperative to affirm sovereignty over arrogant colonials. The alternative choice, as in Athens and medieval Europe, was close to psychologically impossible.

19 In the case we know best—the American engagement in Vietnam—fixed notions, preconceptions, wooden-headed thinking, and emotions accumulated into a monumental mistake and classic humiliation. The original idea was that the lesson of the failure to halt fascist aggression during the appeasement era[15] dictated the necessity of halting the so-called aggression by North Vietnam, conceived to be the spearhead of international communism. This was applying the wrong model to the wrong facts, which would have been obvious if our policy makers had taken into consideration the history of the people on the spot instead of charging forward wearing the blinders of the cold war.

20 The reality of Vietnamese nationalism, of which Ho Chi Minh had been the standard-bearer since long before the war, was certainly no secret. Indeed, Franklin Roosevelt had insisted that the French should not be allowed to return after the war, a policy that we instantly abandoned the moment the Japanese were out. Ignoring the Vietnamese demand for self-government, we first assisted the return of the French, and then, when, incredibly, they had been put to rout by the native forces, we took their place, as if Dien Bien Phu[16] had no significance whatever. Policy founded upon error multiplies, never retreats. The pretense that North versus South Vietnam represented foreign aggression was intensified. If Asian specialists with knowledge of the situation suggested a reassessment, they were not persuasive. As a Communist aggressor, Hanoi was presumed to be a threat to the United States, yet the vital national interest at stake, which alone may have justified belligerency, was never clear enough to sustain a declaration of war.

21 A further, more fundamental error confounded our policy. This was the nature of the client. In war, as any military treatise or any soldier who has seen active service will tell you, it is essential to know the nature—that is, the capabilities *and* intentions—of the enemy and no less so of an ally who is the primary belligerent. We fatally underestimated the one and foolishly overestimated the other. Placing reliance on, or hope in, South Vietnam was an advanced case of wooden-headedness. Improving

---

[15]The period before World War II, when German aggression was ignored in the desire for peace.—Ed.

[16]The town in North Vietnam where French forces were defeated in 1954.—Ed.

on the Bourbons,[17] who forgot nothing and learned nothing, our policy makers forgot everything and learned nothing. The oldest lesson in history is the futility and, often, fatality of foreign interference to maintain in power a government unwanted or hated at home. As far back as 500 B.C., Confucius stated, "Without the confidence of the people, no government can stand," and political philosophers have echoed him down through the ages. What else was the lesson of our vain support of Chiang Kai-shek, within such recent experience? A corrupt or oppressive government may be maintained by despotic means but not for long, as the English occupiers of France learned in the fifteenth century. The human spirit protests and generates a Joan of Arc, for people will not passively endure a government that is in fact unendurable.

22 The deeper we became involved in Vietnam during the Johnson era, the greater grew the self-deception, the lies, the false body counts, the cheating on Tonkin Gulf, the military mess, domestic dissent, and all those defensive emotions in which, as a result, our leaders became fixed. Their concern for personal ego, public image, and government status determined policy. Johnson was not going to be the first President to preside over defeat; generals could not admit failure nor civilian advisers risk their jobs by giving unpalatable advice.

23 Males, who so far in history have managed government, are obsessed with potency, which is the reason, I suspect, why it is difficult for them to admit error. I have rarely known a man who, with a smile and a shrug, could easily acknowledge being wrong. Why not? *I* can, without any damage to self-respect. I can only suppose the difference is that deep in their psyches, men somehow equate being wrong with being impotent. For a Chief of State, it is almost out of the question, and especially so for Johnson and Nixon, who both seem to me to have had shaky self-images. Johnson's showed in his deliberate coarseness and compulsion to humiliate others in crude physical ways. No self-confident man would have needed to do that. Nixon was a bundle of inferiorities and sense of persecution. I do not pretend to be a psychohistorian, but in pursuit of this inquiry, the psychological factors must be taken into account. Having no special knowledge of Johnson and Nixon, I will not pursue the question other than to say that it was our misfortune during the Vietnam period to have had two Presidents who lacked the self-confidence for a change of course, much less for a grand withdrawal. "Magnanimity in politics," said Edmund Burke, "is not seldom the truest wisdom, and a great Empire and little minds go ill together."

---

[17]The last royal family to rule in France before the French Revolution in 1792.—Ed.

24 An essential component of that "truest wisdom" is the self-confidence to reassess. Congressman Morris Udall made this point in the first few days after the nuclear accident at Three Mile Island. Cautioning against a hasty decision on the future of nuclear power, he said, "We have to go back and reassess. There is nothing wrong about being optimistic or making a mistake. The thing that is wrong, as in Vietnam, is *persisting* in a mistake when you see you are going down the wrong road and are caught in a bad situation."

25 The test comes in recognizing when persistence has become a fatal error. A prince, says Machiavelli, ought always to be a great asker and a patient hearer of truth about those things of which he has inquired, and he should be angry if he finds that anyone has scruples about telling him the truth. Johnson and Nixon, as far as an outsider can tell, were not great askers; they did not want to hear the truth or to face it. Chiang Kai-shek knew virtually nothing of real conditions in his domain because he lived a headquarters life amid an entourage all of whom were afraid to be messengers of ill report. When, in World War I, a general of the headquarters staff visited for the first time the ghastly landscape of the Somme,[18] he broke into tears, saying, "If I had known we sent men to fight in that, I could not have done it." Evidently he was no great asker either.

26 Neither, we now know, was the shah of Iran. Like Chiang Kai-shek, he was isolated from actual conditions. He was educated abroad, took his vacations abroad, and toured his country, if at all, by helicopter.

27 Why is it that the major clients of the United States, a country founded on the principle that government derives its just powers from the consent of the governed, tend to be unpopular autocrats? A certain schizophrenia between our philosophy and our practice afflicts American policy, and this split will always make the policy based on it fall apart. On the day the shah left Iran, an article summarizing his reign said that "except for the generals, he has few friends or allies at home." How useful to us is a ruler without friends or allies at home? He is a kind of luftmensch,[19] no matter how rich or how golden a customer for American business. To attach American foreign policy to a ruler who does not have the acceptance of his countrymen is hardly intelligent. By now, it seems to me, we might have learned that. We must understand conditions—and by conditions, I mean people and history—

[18]A muddy marshland area of northern France near the English Channel.—Ed.

[19]German for "airhead."—Ed.

on the spot. Wise policy can only be made on the basis of *informed*, not automatic, judgments.

28 When it has become evident to those associated with it that a course of policy is pointed toward disaster, why does no one resign in protest or at least for the peace of his own soul? They never do. In 1917, the German chancellor Bethmann-Hollweg pleaded desperately against the proposed resumption of unrestricted submarine warfare, since, by bringing in the United States, it would revive the Allies' resources, their confidence in victory, and their will to endure. When he was overruled by the military, he told a friend who found him sunk in despair that the decision meant "*finis Germaniae.*" When the friend said simply, "You should resign," Bethmann said he could not, for that would sow dissension at home and let the world know he believed Germany would fail.

29 This is always the refuge. The officeholder tells himself he can do more from within and that he must not reveal division at the top to the public. In fact if there is to be any hope of change in a democratic society, that is exactly what he must do. No one of major influence in Johnson's circle resigned over our Vietnam policy, although several, hoping to play it both ways, hinted their disagreement. Humphrey, waiting for the nod, never challenged the President's policy, although he campaigned afterward as an opponent of the war. Since then, I've always thought the adulation given to him misplaced.

30 Basically, what keeps officeholders attached to a policy they believe to be wrong is nothing more nor less, I believe, than the lure of office, or Potomac fever. It is the same whether the locus is the Thames or the Rhine or, no doubt, the Nile. When Herbert Lehman ran for a second term as senator from New York after previously serving four terms as governor, his brother asked him why on earth he wanted it. "Arthur," replied the senator, "after you have once ridden behind a motorcycle escort, you are never the same again."

31 Here is a clue to the question of why our performance in government is worse than in other activities: because government offers power, excites that lust for power, which is subject to emotional drives—to narcissism, fantasies of omnipotence, and other sources of folly. The lust for power, according to Tacitus,[20] "is the most flagrant of all the passions" and cannot really be satisfied except by power over others. Business offers a kind of power but only to the very successful at the very top, and even

[20]A Roman historian (C.A.D.55–C.120).—Ed.

they, in our day, have to play it down. Fords and Du Ponts, Hearsts and Pulitzers nowadays are subdued, and the Rockefeller who most conspicuously wanted power sought it in government. Other activities—in sports, science, the professions, and the creative and performing arts—offer various satisfactions but not the opportunity for power. They may appeal to status seeking and, in the form of celebrity, offer crowd worship and limousines and recognition by headwaiters, but these are the trappings of power, not the essence. Of course, mistakes and stupidities occur in nongovernmental activities too, but since these affect fewer people, they are less noticeable than they are in public affairs. Government remains the paramount field of unwisdom because it is there that men seek power over others—and lose it over themselves.

32 There are, of course, other factors that lower competence in public affairs, among them the pressure of overwork and overscheduling; bureaucracy, especially big bureaucracy; the contest for votes that gives exaggerated influence to special interests and an absurd tyranny to public opinion polls. Any hope of intelligent government would require that the persons entrusted with high office should formulate and execute policy according to their best judgment and the best knowledge available, not according to every breeze of public opinion. But reelection is on their minds, and that becomes the criterion. Moreover, given schedules broken down into fifteen-minute appointments and staffs numbering in the hundreds and briefing memos of never less than thirty pages, policy makers never have time to *think*. This leaves a rather important vacuum. Meanwhile, bureaucracy rolls on, impervious to any individual or cry for change, like some vast computer that when once penetrated by error goes on pumping it out forever.

33 Under the circumstances, what are the chances of improving the conduct of government? The idea of a class of professionals trained for the task has been around ever since Plato's *Republic*. Something of the sort animates, I imagine, the new Kennedy School of Government at Harvard. According to Plato, the ruling class in a just society should be men apprenticed to the art of ruling, drawn from the rational and the wise. Since he acknowledged that in natural distribution these are few, he believed they would have to be eugenically bred and nurtured. Government, he said, was a special art in which competence, as in any other profession, could be acquired only by study of the discipline and could not be acquired otherwise.

34 Without reference to Plato, the Mandarins of China were trained, if not bred, for the governing function. They had to pass through years

of study and apprenticeship and weeding out by successive examinations, but they do not seem to have developed a form of government much superior to any other, and in the end, they petered out in decadence and incompetence.

35 In seventeenth-century Europe, after the devastation of the Thirty Years' War, the electors of Brandenburg, soon to be combined with Prussia, determined to create a strong state by means of a disciplined army and a trained civil service. Applicants for the civil positions, drawn from commoners in order to offset the nobles' control of the military, had to complete a course of study covering political theory, law and legal philosophy, economics, history, penology, and statutes. Only after passing through various stages of examination and probationary terms of office did they receive definitive appointments and tenure and opportunity for advancement. The higher civil service was a separate branch, not open to promotion from the middle and lower levels.

36 The Prussian system proved so effective that the state was able to survive both military defeat by Napoleon in 1807 and the revolutionary surge of 1848. By then it had begun to congeal, losing many of its most progressive citizens in emigration to America; nevertheless, Prussian energies succeeded in 1871 in uniting the German states in an empire under Prussian hegemony. Its very success contained the seed of ruin, for it nourished the arrogance and power hunger that from 1914 through 1918 was to bring it down.

37 In England, instead of responding in reactionary panic to the thunders from the Continent in 1848, as might have been expected, the authorities, with commendable enterprise, ordered an investigation of their own government practices, which were then the virtually private preserve of the propertied class. The result was a report on the need for a permanent civil service to be based on training and specialized skills and designed to provide continuity and maintenance of the long view as against transient issues and political passions. Though heavily resisted, the system was adopted in 1870. It has produced distinguished civil servants but also Burgess, Maclean, Philby, and the fourth man.[21] The history of British government in the last 100 years suggests that factors other than the quality of its civil service determine a country's fate.

38 In the United States, civil service was established chiefly as a barrier to patronage and the pork barrel rather than in search of excellence. By 1937, a presidential commission, finding the system inadequate,

---

[21]British civil servants who were exposed in the 1970s as Russian spies. — Ed.

urged the development of a "real career service . . . requiring personnel of the highest order, competent, highly trained, loyal, skilled in their duties by reason of long experience, and assured of continuity." After much effort and some progress, that goal is still not reached, but even if it were, it would not take care of elected officials and high appointments —that is, of government at the top.

39 I do not know if the prognosis is hopeful or, given the underlying emotional drives, whether professionalism is the cure. In the Age of Enlightenment, John Locke[22] thought the emotions should be controlled by intellectual judgment and that it was the distinction and glory of man to be able to control them. As witnesses of the twentieth century's record, comparable to the worst in history, we have less confidence in our species. Although professionalism can help, I tend to think that fitness of character is what government chiefly requires. How that can be discovered, encouraged, and brought into office is the problem that besets us.

40 No society has yet managed to implement Plato's design. Now, with money and image-making manipulating our elective process, the chances are reduced. We are asked to choose by the packaging, yet the candidate seen in a studio-filmed spot, sincerely voicing lines from the TelePrompTer, is not the person who will have to meet the unrelenting problems and crucial decisions of the Oval Office. It might be a good idea if, without violating the First Amendment, we could ban all paid political commercials and require candidates (who accept federal subsidy for their campaigns) to be televised live only.

41 That is only a start. More profound change must come if we are to bring into office the kind of person our form of government needs if it is to survive the challenges of this era. Perhaps rather than educating officials according to Plato's design, we should concentrate on educating the electorate—that is, ourselves—to look for, recognize, and reward character in our representatives and to reject the ersatz.

QUESTIONS FOR ANALYSIS AND DISCUSSION

1. Tuchman begins by offering a definition of wisdom. State her definition in your own words. Do you agree with this definition?

[22]A seventeenth-century English philosopher.—Ed.

2. How does Tuchman define unwisdom or wooden-headedness? (See paragraphs 5, 6, and 7.)
3. From Tuchman's examples of unwisdom in paragraphs 2, 3, 5, 6, and 7, what can you conclude to be the characteristics of governmental folly that Tuchman is interested in? What, according to Tuchman, is not a factor in folly? (See paragraph 9.)
4. What is Tuchman's primary purpose in this essay? To prove that her examples from history represent unwisdom? To determine the causes of unwisdom? To define unwisdom?
5. If Tuchman's purpose is not proving folly in her examples, then her examples need to be generally agreed on as models of unwisdom. Judging from her summaries of events and your knowledge of history, do you concur with Tuchman?
6. What point does Tuchman establish in paragraphs 11 through 15? Why does she include this section?
7. What question does Tuchman raise in paragraph 16? What is one answer to the question?
8. Why, according to Tuchman, do male leaders have particular difficulty admitting to error and changing policy? What American presidents illustrate her point? Do you agree with her assessment? Why or why not?
9. If you believe that women have as much difficulty as men admitting to error, do you agree with Tuchman that self-confidence is an important trait for leaders? If so, how do we "test" for this trait in candidates for office? Any suggestions?
10. What, according to Tuchman, should leaders opposed to a government's policy do? Why do few office holders act as they should when their government perpetuates folly?
11. Tuchman has asserted that emotions in general drown reason and lead to folly. What particular emotion or drive leads to the enormous display of unwisdom in government?
12. What suggestions have been offered in the past for improving the performance of government? How well have they worked?
13. What does Tuchman think is the key? What specific suggestions does she offer for implementing her solution? Can you make other specific suggestions?

Foreign Policy and the American Character

ARTHUR SCHLESINGER, JR.

Respected historian, successful author, and adviser to presidents, Arthur Schlesinger, Jr. (b. 1917) is the Albert Schweitzer Professor in the Humanities at the City University of New York. A native of Columbus, Ohio, and son of the historian Arthur Schlesinger, he was educated at Harvard, taught at Harvard, was special assistant to Presidents Kennedy and Johnson, and has been at CUNY since 1966. Schlesinger is the author of numerous books and articles, many of which have won major awards, and all of which are valued both for the scholarship they reflect and for the quality of writing they sustain. His three-volume The Age of Roosevelt *is recognized as a standard study of the period. His* The Age of Jackson *(1946) and his John F. Kennedy biography* A Thousand Days *(1965) won Pulitzer Prizes; both* A Thousand Days *and* Robert Kennedy and His Times *(1978) won National Book Awards. While serving as presidential adviser, Schlesinger helped formulate the New Frontier and Great Society reform policies. His most recent book is* The Cycles of American History *(1986).*

"Foreign Policy and the American Character," adapted from the Cyril Foster Lecture delivered at Oxford University in May 1983, was published in the fall 1983 issue of Foreign Affairs. *In this article Schlesinger argues that there is an American character and that it affects our foreign policy decisions, often in unfortunate ways.*

1 Foreign policy is the face a nation wears to the world. The minimal motive is the same for all states—the protection of national integrity and interest. But the manner in which a state practices foreign policy is greatly affected by national peculiarities.

2 The United States is not exempt from these unimpeachable generalities. As Henry James,[1] an early American specialist in international relations, once put it, "It's a complex fate, being an American." The American character is indeed filled with contradiction and paradox. So, in consequence, is American foreign policy. No paradox is more persistent

[1] A nineteenth-century American novelist who spent most of his adult life in Europe.—Ed.

than the historic tension in the American soul between an addiction to experiment and a susceptibility to ideology.

3 On the one hand, Americans are famous for being a practical people, preferring fact to theory, finding the meaning of propositions in results, regarding trial and error, not deductive logic, as the path to truth. "In no country in the civilized world," wrote Tocqueville,[2] "is less attention paid to philosophy than in the United States." And when Americans developed a distinctive philosophy, it was of course the pragmatism of William James.[3] James perceived a pluralist universe where men can discover partial and limited truths—truths that work for them—but where no one can gain an absolute grip on ultimate truth. He stood against monism—the notion that the world can be understood from a single point of view. He stood against the assumption that all virtuous principles are in the end reconcilable; against faith in a single body of unified dogma; in short, against the delusions of ideology.

4 Yet at the same time that Americans live by experiment, they also show a recurrent vulnerability to spacious generalities. This is not altogether surprising. The American colonists, after all, were nurtured on one of the most profound and exacting ideologies ever devised—the theology of Calvin—and they passed on to their descendants a certain relish in system and abstraction. The ideas of the Americans, as Tocqueville found in the 1830s, "are all either extremely minute and clear or extremely general and vague." The Calvinist cast of mind saw America as the redeemer nation. It expressed itself in the eighteenth century in Jonathan Edwards'[4] theology of Providence, in the nineteenth century in John Calhoun's[5] theology of slavery, in the twentieth century in Woodrow Wilson's vision of world order and in John Foster Dulles'[6] summons to a holy war against godless communism. The propensity to ideology explains too why the theory of American internal society as expounded by some Americans—the theory of America as the triumph of immaculate and sanctified private enterprise—differs so sharply from the reality of continual government intervention in economic life.

---

[2]A nineteenth-century French statesman and traveler in America; author of *Democracy in America*.—Ed.

[3]A nineteenth-century philosopher and psychologist; brother of Henry James.—Ed.

[4]A Puritan clergyman and theologian.—Ed.

[5]U.S. senator from South Carolina; vice president from 1825 to 1832.—Ed.

[6]A U.S. statesman (1888–1959); secretary of state from 1953 to 1959.—Ed.

5 This tension between experiment and ideology offers one way of looking at the American experience in world affairs. The Founding Fathers were hard-headed and clear-sighted men. They believed that states responded to specific national interests—and were morally obliged to do so, if there were to be regularity and predictability in international affairs. "No nation," observed George Washington, "is to be trusted farther than it is bound by its interest." They understood, moreover, that the preservation of American independence depended on the maintenance of a balance of power in Europe. "It never could be our interest," wrote John Adams, "to unite with France in the destruction of England. . . . On the other hand, it could never be our duty to unite with Britain in too great a humiliation of France."

6 The Jeffersonians, though sentimentally inclined to favor France against Britain, were equally hard-headed when national interest intervened. "We shall so take our distance between the two rival nations," wrote Thomas Jefferson in 1802, "as, remaining disengaged till necessity compels us, we may haul finally to the enemy of that which shall make it necessary." And in 1814, with Britain waging war against America as well as France, indeed seven months before the British captured Washington and burned the White House, Jefferson watched Napoleon's European victories with concern. "It cannot be to our interest that all Europe should be reduced to a single monarchy," he wrote. "Were he again advanced to Moscow, I should again wish him such disaster as would prevent his reaching Petersburg. And were the consequences even to be the longer continuance of our war, I would rather meet them than see the whole force of Europe wielded by a single hand." In these arresting words Jefferson defined the national interest that explains American intervention in two world wars as well as in the present cold war.

7 I do not imply that the Founding Fathers were devoid of any belief in a special mission for the United States. It was precisely to protect that mission that they wished to preserve the balance of power in Europe. They hoped that the American experiment would in time redeem the world. But they did not suppose that the young republic had attained, in Alexander Hamilton's words, "an exemption from the imperfections, weaknesses, and evils incident to society in every shape." Hamilton urged his countrymen instead "to adopt as a practical maxim for the direction of our political conduct that we, as well as the other inhabitants of the globe, are yet remote from the happy empire of perfect wisdom and perfect virtue." If America was to redeem the world, it would do so by perfecting its own institutions, not by moving into other countries and

setting things straight; by example, not by intervention. "She goes not abroad in search of monsters to destroy," said John Quincy Adams. If ever she did, "The fundamental maxims of her policy would insensibly change from liberty to force. . . . She might become the dictatress of the world. She would no longer be the ruler of her own spirit."

8 The realism of the revolutionary generation was founded in the harsh requirements of a struggle for precarious independence. It was founded too in rather pessimistic conceptions of human nature and history. History taught the Founding Fathers to see the American republic itself as a risky and doubtful experiment. And the idea of experiment, by directing attention to the relation between actions and consequences in specific contexts, implied a historical approach to public affairs. Yet–another paradox–the role of the Founding Fathers was to annul history for their descendants. "We have it in our power," cried Tom Paine, "to begin the world all over again"–a proposition quoted, by the way, by President Reagan in his recent address to the evangelicals at Orlando. Once the Founders had done their work, history could start again on a new foundation and in American terms.

9 So the process began of an American withdrawal from secular history–or rather of an American entry into what Dean Acheson[7] once called "a cocoon of history." This process was sustained by the fact that the men and women who populated the new world were in revolt against their own histories. It was sustained, too, by the simultaneous withdrawal of the American state from the power embroilments of the old world. The realism of the revolutionary generation faded away in the century from Waterloo to Sarajevo when the European balance of power was maintained without American intervention. As the historical consciousness thinned out, ideology flowed into the vacuum. The very idea of power politics became repellent. The exemption from the European scramble nourished the myth of American innocence and the doctrine of American righteousness.

10 When America rejoined the scramble in 1898, it did so with an exalted conviction of its destiny as a redeemer nation, and no longer by example alone. The realist tradition by no means vanished. So William James protested the messianic delusion: "Angelic impulses and predatory lusts divide our heart exactly as they divide the heart of other countries." But this was for a season a minority view. When the United States entered the First World War for traditional balance-of-power reasons,

[7]A U.S. statesman; secretary of state from 1949 to 1953.–Ed.

Woodrow Wilson could not bring himself to admit the national interest in preventing the whole force of Europe from being wielded by a single hand. Instead he made himself the prophet of a world beyond power politics where the bad old balance of power would give way to a radiant new community of power. And he insisted on the providential appointment of the United States as "the only idealistic nation in the world," endowed with "the infinite privilege of fulfilling her destiny and saving the world."

11 So two strains have competed for the control of American foreign policy: one empirical, the other dogmatic; one viewing the world in the perspective of history, the other in the perspective of ideology; one supposing that the United States is not entirely immune to the imperfections, weaknesses and evils incident to all societies, the other regarding the United States as indeed the happy empire of perfect wisdom and perfect virtue, commissioned to save all mankind.

12 This schematic account does not do justice to the obvious fact that any American President, in order to command assent for his policies, must appeal to both reality and ideology—and that, to do this effectively, Presidents must combine the two strains not only in their speeches but in their souls. Franklin Roosevelt, the disciple at once of Admiral Mahan[8] and of President Wilson, was supreme in marrying national interest to idealistic hope, though in the crunch interest always came first. Most postwar Presidents—Truman, Eisenhower, Kennedy, even Nixon—shared a recognition, alert or grudging, of the priority of power politics over ideology.

13 The competition between realism and ideology was complicated, however, by two developments: by the fact that the United States in the twentieth century became a great power; and by the fact that the balance of power in the twentieth century faced the gravest possible threats. There was in 1940 a very real monster to destroy and after 1945 another very real monster to contain. These threats demanded U.S. intervention abroad and brought the tradition of isolationism to a permanent end. But the growth of American power also confirmed the messianism of those who believed in America's divine appointment. And the fact that there were a couple of real monsters roaming the world encouraged a fearful tendency to look everywhere for new monsters to destroy.

---

[8]President of the Naval War College and author of several books on the influence of sea power that gave justification to a build-up of navies in the twentieth century.—Ed.

II

14 The present Administration represents a mighty comeback of the messianic approach to foreign policy. "I have always believed," President Reagan said last November, "that this anointed land was set apart in an uncommon way, that a divine plan placed this great continent here between the oceans to be found by people from every corner of the earth who had a special love of faith and freedom." The Reagan Administration sees the world through the prism not of history but of ideology. The convictions that presently guide American foreign policy are twofold: that the United States is infinitely virtuous and that the Soviet Union is infinitely wicked.

15 The Soviet Union, Mr. Reagan has proclaimed, is an "evil empire," "the focus of evil in the modern world." Everything follows by deductive logic from this premise. The world struggle is "between right and wrong and good and evil." When there is evil loose in the world, "we are enjoined by scripture and the Lord Jesus to oppose it with all our might." Negotiation with evil is futile if not dangerous. The Soviet Union is forever deceitful and treacherous. The Soviet leaders erect lying and cheating into a philosophy and are personally responsible for the world's manifold ills. "Let us not delude ourselves," Mr. Reagan has said. "The Soviet Union underlies all the unrest that is going on. If they weren't engaged in this game of dominos, there wouldn't be any hot spots in the world." Not content with the orchestration of crisis in the Third World, the Soviet Union, once it acquires a certain margin of numerical superiority in warheads, can well be expected to launch a surprise nuclear attack on American targets. Safety lies only in the establishment of unequivocal military dominance by the United States, including a first-strike capability. If this means a nuclear arms race, that is Moscow's fault, not Washington's, because America's heart is pure. In any event nuclear weapons are usable and nuclear wars are winnable. We shall prevail.

16 The seizure of foreign policy by a boarding-party of ideologues invites a host of dangers. Most of all you tend to get things wrong. Where the empirical approach sees the present as emerging from the past and preparing for the future, ideology is counter-historical. Its besetting sin is to substitute models for reality. No doubt the construction of models—logically reticulated, general principles leading inexorably to particular outcomes—is an exercise that may help in the delineation of problems—but not when artificial constructs are mistaken for

descriptions of the real world. This is what Alfred North Whitehead[9] called "the fallacy of misplaced concreteness," and it explains why ideology infallibly gets statesmen into trouble, later if not sooner. The error of ideology is to prefer essence to existence, and the result, however gratifying logically and psychologically, undermines the reality principle itself.

17 Ideology withdraws problems from the turbulent stream of change and treats them in splendid abstraction from the whirl and contingency of life. So ideology portrays the Soviet Union as an unalterable monolith, immune to historical vicissitude and permutation, its behavior determined by immutable logic, the same yesterday, today and tomorrow; Sunday, Monday and always. We are forever in 1950, with a crazed Stalin reigning in the Kremlin and commanding an obedient network of communist parties and agents around the planet. In the light of ideology, the Soviet Union becomes a fanatic state carrying out with implacable zeal and cunning a master plan of world dominion.

18 Perhaps this is all so. But others may see rather a weary, dreary country filled with cynicism and corruption, beset by insuperable problems at home and abroad, lurching uncertainly from crisis to crisis. The Soviet leadership, three quarters of a century after the Bolshevik revolution, cannot provide the people with elementary items of consumer goods. It cannot rely on the honesty of bureaucrats or the loyalty of scientists and writers. It confronts difficult ethnic challenges as the non-Russians in the Soviet Union, so miserably underrepresented in the organs of power, begin to outnumber the Russians. Every second child born this year in the Soviet Union will be a Muslim. Abroad, the Soviet Union faces hostile Chinese on its eastern frontier and restless satellites on the west, while to the south the great Red Army after three and a half years still cannot defeat ragged tribesmen fighting bravely in the hills of Afghanistan.

19 I don't want to overdo the picture of weakness. The Soviet Union remains a powerful state, with great and cruel capacity to repress consumption and punish dissent and with an apparent ability to do at least one thing pretty well, which is to build nuclear missiles. But there is enough to the reality of Soviet troubles to lead even the ideologues in Washington to conceive Soviet Russia as a nation at once so robust that it threatens the world and so frail that a couple of small pushes will shove its ramshackle economy into collapse.

---

[9]An English mathematician and philosopher (1861–1947).—Ed.

20 The Soviet Union of course is ideological too, even if its ideology has got a little shopworn and ritualistic over the long years. It too sees the enemy as unchanging and unchangeable, a permanently evil empire vitiated through eternity by the original sin of private property. Each regime, reading its adversary ideologically rather than historically, deduces act from imputed essence and attributes purpose, premeditation and plan where less besotted analysts would raise a hand for improvisation, accident, chance, ignorance, negligence and even sheer stupidity. We arrive at the predicament excellently described by Henry Kissinger: "The superpowers often behave like two heavily armed blind men feeling their way around a room, each believing himself in mortal peril from the other whom he assumes to have perfect vision. . . . Each tends to ascribe to the other a consistency, foresight, and coherence that its own experience belies. Of course, over time, even two blind men can do enormous damage to each other, not to speak of the room."

21 By construing every local mess as a test of global will, ideology raises stakes in situations that cannot be easily controlled and threatens to transmute limited into unlimited conflicts. Moreover, ideology, if pursued to the end, excludes the thought of accommodation or coexistence. Mr. Reagan has instructed us that we must oppose evil "with all our might." How now can we compromise with evil without losing our immortal soul? Ideology summons the true believer to a *jihad,* a crusade of extermination against the infidel.

22 The Russians are in no position to complain about such language. It has been more or less their own line since 1917. Reagan is simply paraphrasing Khrushchev: "We will bury you." Still the holy war has always represented a rather drastic approach to human affairs. It seems singularly unpromising in the epoch of nuclear weapons. And the irony is that, while Soviet ideology has grown tired, cynical and venal, the new American crusade is fresh and militant; and the Washington ideologues thereby present the Kremlin with an unearned and undeserved opportunity to appear reasonable and prudent. In particular, the American dash into ideology promotes a major Soviet objective, the turning away of Western Europe from the alliance with the United States.

23 Having suggested the current domination of American foreign policy by ideology, let me add that this domination is far from complete. Mr. Reagan's world view is not necessarily shared even by all members of his own Administration. It is definitely not shared by the Republican leadership in Congress. In general, it has been more vigorously translated into rhetoric than into policy. The suspicion has even arisen that

Mr. Reagan's more impassioned ideological flights are only, in Wendell Willkie's[10] old phrase, "campaign oratory," pap for right-wing zealots to conceal the Administration's covert creep to the center in domestic affairs. And the prospect of a presidential election next year [1984] creates a compelling political need for the Administration to attend to public opinion—a concern that may be a force for restraint in Central America and that could conceivably drive the Administration into arms control negotiations well before November 1984. Still, Mr. Reagan is not a cynical man, and, whatever the tactical function of his speeches, they must also in some sense express sincere convictions.

24 The greater restraint on ideology comes from the nature of foreign policy itself. The realism of the Founding Fathers sprang from the ineluctable character of international relations. National interest in the end must set limits on messianic passions. This fact explains the Administration's tendency to march up the ideological hill and then march down again, as in the case of the pipeline embargo. For the United States does not have the power, even if it had the wisdom, to achieve great objectives in the world by itself. Because this is so, a responsible foreign policy requires the cooperation of allies, and allies therefore have it within their power to rein in American messianism.

25 The pipeline embargo is only one example of the modification of ideology by interest. Ideology favors a blank check for Menachem Begin[11] in Israel, but interest argues for the comprehensive approach to a Middle Eastern settlement that Reagan set forth on September 1, 1982, in the most impressive speech of his presidency. Ideology calls for the support of Taiwan at the expense of mainland China. Interest argues against policies tending to unite Chinese and Soviet communism. Ideology calls for the support of South Africa against black Africa. Interest argues against a course that leaves black Africa no friends but the Soviet Union. Ideology calls for the excommunication of socialist regimes. Interest sees benefits in cheerful relations with France, Spain, Italy, Portugal, Greece and Sweden. Ideology calls for chastisement of the debtor nations in the Third World. Interest leads to an additional $8.4-billion contribution to the International Monetary Fund.

III

26 Yet there remain sectors of policy where ideology still holds sway. One, for the season at least, is Central America. No one can be too sure

[10]A twentieth-century American executive, lawyer, and political leader.—Ed.

[11]Prime minister of Israel from 1977 to 1983.—Ed.

over the longer run because the Administration has marched up and down this particular hill more than once in the last two years. During the vicariate of General Haig,[12] insurgency in Central America was deemed a major Soviet challenge demanding a mighty American response. Then, in the first tranquilizing days of Secretary Shultz, the impression was allowed to spread that perhaps the troubles had ample local origins and, despite allegations of extracontinental instigation, might be amenable to local remedies. Subsequently Secretary Shultz caught the ideological flu, and by mid-1983 we were back at the global test of will.

27 Unquestionably the United States is facing tough problems in Central America. Nor does it meet the problems to observe that they are, in some part, of American creation. Twenty years ago the Alliance for Progress set out to deal with poverty and oligarchy in Central America. But the Alliance changed its character after the death of President Kennedy, and American policy abandoned concern with social change. When revolution predictably erupted in Central America, ideology rejected the notion of local origins and decreed that the Russians were back at their old game of dominos.

28 Ideology, it should be noted, offers a field day for self-fulfilling prophecies. If you shape rhetoric and policy to what you regard as a predestined result, chances are that you will get the result you predestine. Having decided a priori that the Nicaraguan revolution was a Soviet-Cuban conspiracy, Washington gave the Sandinistas little alternative but to seek support from the Cubans and Russians. The French wanted to sell Nicaragua arms and send in a military mission. Washington, instead of welcoming a democratic presence that would have been reliably alert to Soviet deviltry, exploded in indignation. When the CIA does its best to overthrow the government in Managua, we express unseemly shock that this government dare take measures to defend itself. Maybe it would have happened anyway, but the ideological policy makes insurgent anti-Americanism inevitable.

29 The present Washington disposition is to raise the stakes and to militarize the remedy. We are trying to provide the government of El Salvador with sufficient military aid to defeat the insurgency and to provide the insurgency in Nicaragua with sufficient military aid to defeat the government. If we don't act to stop Marxism in Central America, the argument runs, dominos will topple, and the Soviet Union will

[12]Secretary of state from 1981 to 1982.—Ed.

establish a bridgehead in the center of the Western Hemisphere. "Our credibility would collapse," Mr. Reagan has said, "our alliances would crumble, and the safety of our homeland would be in jeopardy." In April 1983 he denied any "thought of sending American combat troops to Central America." By June the thought had occurred, and he now cautioned, "Presidents never say never."

30 Other views are possible. The historian is bound to note that unilateral military action by the United States in Latin America is nearly always a mistake. Another by-product of ideology, along with the self-fulfilling prophecy, is the conviction that the anointed country, whether the United States these days or the Soviet Union in all days, understands the interests of other countries better than they understand their own interests. So in 1967 President Johnson sent Clark Clifford on an Asian tour, charging him to get the states of the South East Asia Treaty Organization to increase their contributions to the forces fighting communism in Vietnam. Clifford was astonished to discover that other Asian countries, though considerably more exposed to the danger, took it less tragically than the United States did and saw no need to increase their contributions. When he thereafter became Secretary of Defense, Clifford did his best to wind down American participation in the war.

31 If a Marxist Nicaragua (population 2.7 million) or El Salvador (population 4.5 million) is a threat to the Hemisphere, it is a more dire threat to Mexico, to Costa Rica, to Panama, to Venezuela, to Colombia than it is to the United States. These nations are closer to the scene and more knowledgeable about it; they are a good deal more vulnerable politically, economically and militarily than the United States; and they are governed by men just as determined as those in Washington to resist their own overthrow. When Latin American countries don't see the threat as apocalyptically as we do, only ideology can conclude with divine assurance that they are wrong and we are right. Are we really so certain that we understand *their* world better than they do?

32 In any event, ideology is a sure formula for hypocrisy, if not for disaster. Mr. Reagan says righteously that we will not "protect the Nicaraguan government from the anger of its own people." A fine sentiment —but why does it not apply equally to the government of El Salvador? Why do we condemn Nicaragua for postponing elections until 1985 while we condone Chile, which postpones elections till 1989? Would the Administration display the same solicitude for elections and rights in Nicaragua if the Somozas were still running things?

33 Ideology insists on the inflation of local troubles into global crises.

National interest would emphasize the indispensability of working with Latin Americans who know the territory far better than we do and without whose support we cannot succeed. Let Mexico, Venezuela, Colombia and Panama—the so-called Contadora Group—take the lead, and back them to the hilt. Only if all agree on the nature of the response will intervention do the United States more good than harm in the Hemisphere. If it is too late for a negotiated settlement and our Latin friends reject military intervention, then we may have to resign ourselves to turmoil in Central America for some time to come—turmoil beyond our power to correct and beyond our wisdom to cure.

IV

34 Another sector where ideology still controls policy in Washington is, alas, the most grave and menacing of all—the nuclear arms race. It is in this field that the substitution of models for reality has the most baneful effect. War games these days are played by general staffs with such intensity that they come to be taken not as speculations but as predictions. The higher metaphysics of deterrence, by concentrating on the most remote contingencies, such as a Soviet first strike against the United States or a surprise invasion of Western Europe, makes such improbable events suddenly the governing force in budgetary, weapons and deployment decisions. History shows the Soviet Union to be generally cautious about risking direct military encounters with the United States; but ideology abolishes history. Reality evaporates in the hallucinatory world where strategic theologians calculate how many warheads can be balanced on the head of a pin. Little seems to me more dangerous than the current fantasy of controlled and graduated nuclear war, with generals calibrating nuclear escalation like grand masters at the chessboard. Let us not be bamboozled by models. Once the nuclear threshold is breached, the game is over.

35 I do not dismiss the Soviet Union as a military threat. We have noted that one thing Russia apparently does well is to build nuclear missiles. But we must keep things in proportion. Ideology, here as elsewhere, encourages exaggeration. Moreover, the professional duty of generals is to guarantee the safety of their countries; and the professional instinct of generals is to demand enough to meet every conceivable contingency. As old Lord Salisbury once wrote, "If you believe the doctors, nothing is wholesome; if you believe the theologians, nothing

is innocent; if you believe the soldiers, nothing is safe."[13] Like ideology, defense budgets need ever more menacing enemies.

36 In Washington Pentagon officials take masochistic pleasure at regular intervals in declaring that the Soviet Union is now stronger than the United States. These recurrent Pentagon panics, ably recalled by Robert H. Johnson in the Spring 1983 issue of this journal, range from the "missile gap," promulgated by the Gaither Report 25 years ago, to the "window of vulnerability," announced by Secretary of Defense Weinberger in 1981 and slammed shut by the Scowcroft Commission in 1983. One doubts that defense officials really believe their own lamentations; at least, I have never heard any of them offering to trade in the American for the Soviet defense establishment. When asked in Congress recently whether he would exchange places with his Soviet counterpart, the chairman of the American Joint Chiefs of Staff replied succinctly, "Not on your life." The ideologues achieve their dire effects by selective counting–by comparing theater nuclear weapons, for example, and omitting American superiority in the invulnerable sea-based deterrent. I would not take the lamentations too seriously, especially around budget time.

37 The irony is that the Pentagon and the Soviet Defense Ministry prosper symbiotically. There is no greater racket in the world today than generals claiming the other side is ahead in order to get bigger budgets for themselves. This tacit collusion, based on a common vested interest in crisis, remains a major obstacle in the search for peace. As President Kennedy remarked to Norman Cousins, the editor of the *Saturday Review*, in the spring of 1963, "Mr. Khrushchev and I occupy approximately the same political positions inside our governments. He would like to prevent a nuclear war but is under severe pressure from his hard-line crowd, which interprets every move in that direction as appeasement. I've got similar problems. . . . The hard-liners in the Soviet Union and the United States feed on one another."

38 The existence of Soviet military might obviously requires effective counterbalance. It requires nuclear deterrence capable of retaliation against a first strike, and this the West has. It also requires conventional force capable of discouraging Soviet aspirations in Europe, and this the West may presently lack. The need is to remove European defense from the delusion of rescue through limited nuclear war. The European democracies must understand that reliance on the bomb to save Europe

[13]Famous quotation from a letter to Lord Lytton, viceroy of India, in 1877.–Ed.

no longer makes sense in the age of nuclear stand-off. However destructive conventional war can be in modern times, it is infinitely less destructive than nuclear war would be. And the sure way to make the improbability of a Soviet attack across the rebellious satellites on Western Europe even more improbable is to leave no doubt that the costs, even without nuclear response, would be intolerably high. This lies within the power of the European democracies to do.

V

39 But what of the bomb itself? For we live today in a situation without precedent—a situation that transcends all history and threatens the end of history. I must confess that I have come late to this apocalyptic view of the future. To set limits on the adventures of the human mind has always seemed—still seems—the ultimate heresy, the denial of humanity itself. But we always recognized that freedom involves risk, and the free mind in our time has led us to the edge of the Faustian[14] abyss. "Man has mounted science, and is now run away with," Henry Adams[15] wrote more than a century ago. "Some day science may have the existence of mankind in its power, and the human race commit suicide by blowing up the world."

40 I had always supposed that, with the nuclear genie out of the bottle, the prospect of the suicide of the human race would have a sobering effect on those who possessed the tragic power to initiate nuclear war. For most of the nuclear age this supposition has been roughly true. Statesmen have generally understood, as President Kennedy said in 1961, "Mankind must put an end to war or war will put an end to mankind." I saw how after the Cuban missile crisis a shaken Kennedy—and a shaken Khrushchev, too—moved swiftly toward a ban on nuclear testing and a systematic reduction of international acrimony.

41 I no longer have much confidence in the admonitory effect of the possession of nuclear weapons. The curse of ideology is that as it impoverishes our sense of reality, it impoverishes our imagination, too. It enfeebles our capacity to visualize the Doomsday horror. It inhibits us from confronting the awful possibility we can no longer deny: the extermination of sentient life on this planet.

42 Under the hypnosis of doctrine, ideologues in Washington today

---

[14]Faustus sold his soul to the devil in exchange for knowledge and power.—Ed.

[15]An American historian and writer (1838–1918); grandson of John Quincy Adams.—Ed.

plainly see an unlimited nuclear arms race not as an appalling threat to the survival of humanity, but simply as a fine way to do the Russians in. Either they will try to keep up with us, which will wreck their economy, or they will fail to keep up, which will give us the decisive military advantage. To have an arms control agreement, they believe, would be to renounce our most potent weapon against the empire of evil.

43 I continue to find it hard to suppose that either superpower would deliberately embark on nuclear war *ab initio.* But it is not hard to foresee a nuclear overreaction to the frustration or embarrassment of defeat in conventional warfare. It is still easier, with 50,000 warheads piling up in the hands of the superpowers and heaven knows how many more scattered or hidden or incipient in other hands, to foresee nuclear war precipitated by terrorists, or by madness, or by accident, or by misreading the flashes on a radar screen.

44 The stake is too great to permit this horror to grow. For the stake is supreme: it is the fate of humanity itself. Let me say at once that the answer to the nightmare cannot conceivably be unilateral nuclear disarmament. The likely result of unilateral nuclear disarmament by the West would not be to prompt the Soviet leadership to do likewise but to place the democratic world at the mercy of Soviet communism. History offers abundant proof that mercy is not a salient characteristic of any communist regime.

45 Neither the arms race nor unilateral disarmament therefore holds out hope. What we must do rather is to revive the vanishing art of diplomacy. American officials these days like to strike Churchillian poses. They remind one of Mark Twain's response when his wife tried to cure him of swearing by loosing a string of oaths herself: "You got the words right, Livy, but you don't know the tune." Our road-company Churchills lack one of the things that made Churchill great: his power of historical discrimination.

46 "Those who are prone by temperament and character," Churchill wrote in *The Gathering Storm,* "to seek sharp and clear-cut solutions of difficult and obscure problems, who are ready to fight whenever some challenge comes from a foreign Power, have not always been right. On the other hand, those whose inclination is . . . to seek patiently and faithfully for peaceful compromise are not always wrong. On the contrary, in the majority of instances they may be right, not only morally but from a practical standpoint." So, in the spirit of Churchill, let us not prematurely abandon the quest for peaceful compromise.

47 The reciprocal and verifiable nuclear freeze on the production,

testing and deployment of nuclear weapons and delivery vehicles is backed today, according to polls, by more than 80 percent of Americans. The freeze is the most promising beginning, or so it seems to me. More must come. A joint Soviet-NATO command post, where each side could monitor the other side's radar screens and to which all war rumors would go for resolution, would do much to reduce the chances of accidental nuclear war. Deep cuts in nuclear stockpiles must follow, perhaps by each superpower delivering an equal number of nuclear weapons of its own choice for destruction by an international authority, a procedure that would minimize the theoretically destabilizing effect of reduction by fixed categories. Mankind has no choice but to find ways to crawl back from the edge of the Faustian abyss and to move toward the extinction of the nuclear race; better this, with all its difficulties, than the extinction of the human race.

VI

48 What the world needs to bring this about is above all deliverance from ideology. This is not to suggest for a moment any symmetry between the United States and the Soviet Union. In the United States, ideology is a lurking susceptibility, a periodic fling, fooling some of the people some of the time but profoundly alien to the Constitution and to the national spirit. Washington's current ideological commotion is the result, not of popular demand or mandate, but of the superficial fact that in 1980 the voters, unable to abide the thought of four more years of what they had, had Reagan as the only practical alternative.

49 In the Soviet Union ideology remains the heart of the matter. It is not a susceptibility but a compulsion, inscribed in sacred texts and enforced by all the brutal machinery of a still vicious police state. Yet even in the Soviet Union one senses an erosion of the old ideological intensity until a good deal of what remains is simply a vocabulary in which Soviet leaders are accustomed to speak. Let not a spurt of American ideologizing breathe new life into the decadent Soviet ideology, especially by legitimizing the Russian fear of an American crusade aimed at the destruction of Russian society.

50 In the end, ideology runs against the grain of American democracy. Popular elections, as the Founding Fathers saw long ago, supply the antidote to the fanaticism of abstract propositions. High-minded Americans have recently taken to calling for a single six-year presidential term on the ground that Presidents, not having to worry about reelection,

would thereby be liberated to make decisions for the good of the republic. This assumes that the less a President takes public opinion into account, the better a President he will be—on reflection, a rather antidemocratic assumption. In the instant case, the best things Mr. Reagan has done—his belated concern about racial justice, about the environment and natural resources, about hunger, about women, about arms control—have all been under the pressure of the 1984 election. He might never have cared if he had had a single six-year term. It may well be that Presidents do a better job when politics requires them to respond to popular needs and concerns than they would if constitutionally empowered to ignore popular needs and concerns for the sake of ideological gratification.

51 Ideology is the curse of public affairs because it converts politics into a branch of theology and sacrifices human beings on the altar of abstractions. "To serene Providence," Winston Churchill wrote an American politician nearly 90 years ago, "a couple of generations of trouble and distress may seem an insignificant thing. . . . Earthly Governments, however, are unable to approach questions from the same standpoint. Which brings me to the conclusion that the duty of governments is to be first of all practical. I am for makeshifts and expediency. I would like to make the people who live on this world at the same time as I do better fed and happier generally. If incidentally I benefit posterity—so much the better—but I would not sacrifice my own generation to a principle—however high—or a truth however great."

52 In this humane spirit we may save not only our generation but posterity, too.

QUESTIONS FOR ANALYSIS AND DISCUSSION

1. What is Schlesinger's subject?
2. According to Schlesinger, what is the American character? What tension dominates the American soul and affects our foreign policy?
3. What seem to be the historical sources for these two conflicting elements in the American character?
4. List three of Schlesinger's examples of American foreign policy actions based on pragmatic self-interest. List three examples of decisions either based on or justified by ideology.
5. When foreign policy decisions are made on or justified by ideology, what is America's ideological position? What is our view of ourselves and the world?

6. Which element of the American character dominates current foreign policy decisions? Does Schlesinger approve or not? Do you approve or not? Why?
7. What are the three major areas of foreign policy decisions currently facing American government? Summarize Schlesinger's suggestions for strategies in each area.
8. Analyze the structure of the article. How does Schlesinger build his argument?
9. What is Schlesinger's primary purpose in writing this article? Who is his audience?
10. Has he been successful in achieving his purpose with you? Why or why not?

The Indispensable Opposition

WALTER LIPPMANN

A syndicated columnist for over thirty-five years, Walter Lippmann (1889–1974) has been called the father of political columnists. Lippmann graduated from Harvard in 1909, did some graduate study, and began his career as an associate editor in 1914 with the inception of the New Republic. *He then moved to the* New York World *as editor and director of the editorial page. In an amazing career, Lippmann wrote twenty-one books, won two Pulitzer Prizes for his columns, was awarded nineteen honorary degrees, advised presidents from Wilson to Nixon, and was given the presidential Medal of Honor: all of these accomplishments in addition to writing columns that defined the genre and set the standard for our times. Among his many books are* Liberty and the Press *(1920),* Public Opinion *(1922), and* Men of Destiny *(1927), three works that address—in whole or in part—the role of the journalist and the issues surrounding censorship.* The Public Philosophy *(1955) argues for a just prudence for the public good, a philosophy that can be called elitist.*

Lippmann also addressed First Amendment issues of free speech and censorship in many of his columns and in articles in popular magazines. "The Indispensable Opposition" was published in the August 1939 issue of Atlantic Monthly.

1

1 Were they pressed hard enough, most men would probably confess that political freedom—that is to say, the right to speak freely and to act in opposition—is a noble ideal rather than a practical necessity. As the case for freedom is generally put to-day, the argument lends itself to this feeling. It is made to appear that, whereas each man claims his freedom as a matter of right, the freedom he accords to other men is a matter of toleration. Thus, the defense of freedom of opinion tends to rest not on its substantial, beneficial, and indispensable consequences, but on a somewhat eccentric, a rather vaguely benevolent, attachment to an abstraction.

2 It is all very well to say with Voltaire,[1] 'I wholly disapprove of what you say, but will defend to the death your right to say it,' but as a matter of fact most men will not defend to the death the rights of other men: if they disapprove sufficiently what other men say, they will somehow suppress those men if they can.

3 So, if this is the best that can be said for liberty of opinion, that a man must tolerate his opponents because everyone has a 'right' to say what he pleases, then we shall find that liberty of opinion is a luxury, safe only in pleasant times when men can be tolerant because they are not deeply and vitally concerned.

4 Yet actually, as a matter of historic fact, there is a much stronger foundation for the great constitutional right of freedom of speech, and as a matter of practical human experience there is a much more compelling reason for cultivating the habits of free men. We take, it seems to me, a naïvely self-righteous view when we argue as if the right of our opponents to speak were something that we protect because we are magnanimous, noble, and unselfish. The compelling reason why, if liberty of opinion did not exist, we should have to invent it, why it will eventually have to be restored in all civilized countries where it is now suppressed, is that we must protect the right of our opponents to speak because we must hear what they have to say.

5 We miss the whole point when we imagine that we tolerate the freedom of our political opponents as we tolerate a howling baby next door, as we put up with the blasts from our neighbor's radio because we are too peaceable to heave a brick through the window. If this were all there is to freedom of opinion, that we are too good-natured or too timid

---

[1]Pen name of François Marie Arouet, an eighteenth-century French philosopher, dramatist, and essayist.—Ed.

to do anything about our opponents and our critics except to let them talk, it would be difficult to say whether we are tolerant because we are magnanimous or because we are lazy, because we have strong principles or because we lack serious convictions, whether we have the hospitality of an inquiring mind or the indifference of an empty mind. And so, if we truly wish to understand why freedom is necessary in a civilized society, we must begin by realizing that, because freedom of discussion improves our own opinions, the liberties of other men are our own vital necessity.

6 We are much closer to the essence of the matter, not when we quote Voltaire, but when we go to the doctor and pay him to ask the most embarrassing questions and to prescribe the most disagreeable diet. When we pay the doctor to exercise complete freedom of speech about the cause and cure of our stomachache, we do not look upon ourselves as tolerant and magnanimous, and worthy to be admired by ourselves. We have enough common sense to know that if we threaten to put the doctor in jail because we do not like the diagnosis and the prescription it will be unpleasant for the doctor, to be sure, but equally unpleasant for our own stomachache. That is why even the most ferocious dictator would rather be treated by a doctor who was free to think and speak the truth than by his own Minister of Propaganda. For there is a point, the point at which things really matter, where the freedom of others is no longer a question of their right but of our need.

7 The point at which we recognize this need is much higher in some men than in others. The totalitarian rulers think they do not need the freedom of an opposition: they exile, imprison, or shoot their opponents. We have concluded on the basis of practical experience, which goes back to Magna Carta and beyond, that we need the opposition. We pay the opposition salaries out of the public treasury.

8 In so far as the usual apology for freedom of speech ignores this experience, it becomes abstract and eccentric rather than concrete and human. The emphasis is generally put on the right to speak, as if all that mattered were that the doctor should be free to go out into the park and explain to the vacant air why I have a stomachache. Surely that is a miserable caricature of the great civic right which men have bled and died for. What really matters is that the doctor should tell *me* what ails me, that I should listen to him; that if I do not like what he says I should be free to call in another doctor; and that then the first doctor should have to listen to the second doctor; and that out of all the speaking and listening, the give-and-take of opinions, the truth should be arrived at.

9 This is the creative principle of freedom of speech, not that it is a system for the tolerating of error, but that it is a system for finding the truth. It may not produce the truth, or the whole truth all the time, or often, or in some cases ever. But if the truth can be found, there is no other system which will normally and habitually find so much truth. Until we have thoroughly understood this principle, we shall not know why we must value our liberty, or how we can protect and develop it.

2

10 Let us apply this principle to the system of public speech in a totalitarian state. We may, without any serious falsification, picture a condition of affairs in which the mass of the people are being addressed through one broadcasting system by one man and his chosen subordinates. The orators speak. The audience listens but cannot and dare not speak back. It is a system of one-way communication; the opinions of the rulers are broadcast outwardly to the mass of the people. But nothing comes back to the rulers from the people except the cheers; nothing returns in the way of knowledge of forgotten facts, hidden feelings, neglected truths, and practical suggestions.

11 But even a dictator cannot govern by his own one-way inspiration alone. In practice, therefore, the totalitarian rulers get back the reports of the secret police and of their party henchmen down among the crowd. If these reports are competent, the rulers may manage to remain in touch with public sentiment. Yet that is not enough to know what the audience feels. The rulers have also to make great decisions that have enormous consequences, and here their system provides virtually no help from the give-and-take of opinion in the nation. So they must either rely on their own institution, which cannot be permanently and continually inspired, or, if they are intelligent despots, encourage their trusted advisers and their technicians to speak and debate freely in their presence.

12 On the walls of the houses of Italian peasants one may see inscribed in large letters the legend, 'Mussolini[2] is always right.' But if that legend is taken seriously by Italian ambassadors, by the Italian General Staff, and by the Ministry of Finance, then all one can say is heaven help Mussolini, heaven help Italy, and the new Emperor of Ethiopia.[3]

---

[2]Premier of fascist Italy 1922–1943.—Ed.

[3]The Italians invaded Ethiopia in 1935 and occupied it until 1941, deposing Haile Selassie and making King Victor Emanuel of Italy the emperor.—Ed.

13 For at some point, even in a totalitarian state, it is indispensable that there should exist the freedom of opinion which causes opposing opinions to be debated. As time goes on, that is less and less easy under a despotism; critical discussion disappears as the internal opposition is liquidated in favor of men who think and feel alike. That is why the early successes of despots, of Napoleon I[4] and of Napoleon III,[5] have usually been followed by an irreparable mistake. For in listening only to his yes men—the others being in exile or in concentration camps, or terrified—the despot shuts himself off from the truth that no man can dispense with.

14 We know all this well enough when we contemplate the dictatorships. But when we try to picture our own system, by way of contrast, what picture do we have in our minds? It is, is it not, that anyone may stand up on his own soapbox and say anything he pleases, like the individuals in Kipling's[6] poem who sit each in his separate star and draw the Thing as they see it for the God of Things as they are. Kipling, perhaps, could do this, since he was a poet. But the ordinary mortal isolated on his separate star will have an hallucination, and a citizenry declaiming from separate soapboxes will poison the air with hot and nonsensical confusion.

15 If the democratic alternative to the totalitarian one-way broadcasts is a row of separate soapboxes, then I submit that the alternative is unworkable, is unreasonable, and is humanly unattractive. It is above all a false alternative. It is not true that liberty has developed among civilized men when anyone is free to set up a soapbox, is free to hire a hall where he may expound his opinions to those who are willing to listen. On the contrary, freedom of speech is established to achieve its essential purpose only when different opinions are expounded in the same hall to the same audience.

16 For, while the right to talk may be the beginning of freedom, the necessity of listening is what makes the right important. Even in Russia and Germany a man may still stand in an open field and speak his mind. What matters is not the utterance of opinions. What matters is the confrontation of opinions in debate. No man can care profoundly that every fool should say what he likes. Nothing has been accomplished if the wisest man proclaims his wisdom in the middle of the Sahara Desert.

---

[4]A French general; emperor of France 1804–1815.—Ed.

[5]President of France 1848–1852; emperor 1852–1870.—Ed.

[6]A British author (1865–1936) best known for his *Just-So Stories* and *The Jungle Book*.—Ed.

This is the shadow. We have the substance of liberty when the fool is compelled to listen to the wise man and learn; when the wise man is compelled to take account of the fool, and to instruct him; when the wise man can increase his wisdom by hearing the judgment of his peers.

17 That is why civilized men must cherish liberty—as a means of promoting the discovery of truth. So we must not fix our whole attention on the right of anyone to hire his own hall, to rent his own broadcasting station, to distribute his own pamphlets. These rights are incidental; and though they must be preserved, they can be preserved only by regarding them as incidental, as auxiliary to the substance of liberty that must be cherished and cultivated.

18 Freedom of speech is best conceived, therefore, by having in mind the picture of a place like the American Congress, an assembly where opposing views are represented, where ideas are not merely uttered but debated, or the British Parliament, where men who are free to speak are also compelled to answer. We may picture the true condition of freedom as existing in a place like a court of law, where witnesses testify and are cross-examined, where the lawyer argues against the opposing lawyer before the same judge and in the presence of one jury. We may picture freedom as existing in a forum where the speaker must respond to questions; in a gathering of scientists where the data, the hypothesis, and the conclusion are submitted to men competent to judge them; in a reputable newspaper which not only will publish the opinions of those who disagree but will reëxamine its own opinion in the light of what they say.

19 Thus the essence of freedom of opinion is not in mere toleration as such, but in the debate which toleration provides: it is not in the venting of opinion, but in the confrontation of opinion. That this is the practical substance can readily be understood when we remember how differently we feel and act about the censorship and regulation of opinion purveyed by different media of communication. We find then that, in so far as the medium makes difficult the confrontation of opinion in debate, we are driven towards censorship and regulation.

20 There is, for example, the whispering campaign, the circulation of anonymous rumors by men who cannot be compelled to prove what they say. They put the utmost strain on our tolerance, and there are few who do not rejoice when the anonymous slanderer is caught, exposed, and punished. At a higher level there is the moving picture, a most powerful medium for conveying ideas, but a medium which does not permit debate. A moving picture cannot be answered effectively by another moving picture; in all free countries there is some censorship of

the movies, and there would be more if the producers did not recognize their limitations by avoiding political controversy. There is then the radio. Here debate is difficult; it is not easy to make sure that the speaker is being answered in the presence of the same audience. Inevitably, there is some regulation of the radio.

21 When we reach the newspaper press, the opportunity for debate is so considerable that discontent cannot grow to the point where under normal conditions there is any disposition to regulate the press. But when newspapers abuse their power by injuring people who have no means of replying, a disposition to regulate the press appears. When we arrive at Congress we find that, because the membership of the House is so large, full debate is impracticable. So there are restrictive rules. On the other hand, in the Senate, where the conditions of full debate exist, there is almost absolute freedom of speech.

22 This shows us that the preservation and development of freedom of opinion are not only a matter of adhering to abstract legal rights, but also, and very urgently, a matter of organizing and arranging sufficient debate. Once we have a firm hold on the central principle, there are many practical conclusions to be drawn. We then realize that the defense of freedom of opinion consists primarily in perfecting the opportunity for an adequate give-and-take of opinion; it consists also in regulating the freedom of those revolutionists who cannot or will not permit or maintain debate when it does not suit their purposes.

23 We must insist that free oratory is only the beginning of free speech; it is not the end, but a means to an end. The end is to find the truth. The practical justification of civil liberty is not that self-expression is one of the rights of man. It is that the examination of opinion is one of the necessities of man. For experience tells us that it is only when freedom of opinion becomes the compulsion to debate that the seed which our fathers planted has produced its fruit. When that is understood, freedom will be cherished not because it is a vent for our opinions but because it is the surest method of correcting them.

24 The unexamined life, said Socrates,[7] is unfit to be lived by man. This is the virtue of liberty, and the ground on which we may best justify our belief in it, that it tolerates error in order to serve the truth. When men are brought face to face with their opponents, forced to listen and learn and mend their ideas, they cease to be children and savages

[7]An Athenian philosopher (469?–399 B.C.) whose debates are contained in Plato's works. – Ed.

and begin to live like civilized men. Then only is freedom a reality, when men may voice their opinions because they must examine their opinions.

3

25 The only reason for dwelling on all this is that if we are to preserve democracy we must understand its principles. And the principle which distinguishes it from all other forms of government is that in a democracy the opposition not only is tolerated as constitutional but must be maintained because it is in fact indispensable.

26 The democratic system cannot be operated without effective opposition. For, in making the great experiment of governing people by consent rather than by coercion, it is not sufficient that the party in power should have a majority. It is just as necessary that the party in power should never outrage the minority. That means that it must listen to the minority and be moved by the criticisms of the minority. That means that its measures must take account of the minority's objections, and that in administering measures it must remember that the minority may become the majority.

27 The opposition is indispensable. A good statesman, like any other sensible human being, always learns more from his opponents than from his fervent supporters. For his supporters will push him to disaster unless his opponents show him where the dangers are. So if he is wise he will often pray to be delivered from his friends because they will ruin him. But, though it hurts, he ought also to pray never to be left without opponents; for they keep him on the path of reason and good sense.

28 The national unity of a free people depends upon a sufficiently even balance of political power to make it impracticable for the administration to be arbitrary and for the opposition to be revolutionary and irreconcilable. Where that balance no longer exists, democracy perishes. For unless all the citizens of a state are forced by circumstances to compromise, unless they feel that they can affect policy but that no one can wholly dominate it, unless by habit and necessity they have to give and take, freedom cannot be maintained.

QUESTIONS FOR ANALYSIS AND DISCUSSION

1. Why is the opposition indispensable? What is Lippmann's central argument for freedom of speech?

2. What *type* of argument is this? That is, instead of arguing for freedom of speech because it is the good or humane position, Lippmann argues from what principle?
3. Why must opposing views be given expression? What is gained by this?
4. What was Magna Carta? Why does Lippmann make reference to it?
5. For Lippmann, freedom of speech must mean more than addressing the trees in a park; who must hear all views? In what situation does genuine freedom of speech flourish?
6. Why does the despot silence all opposition? How would Tuchman explain this example of unwisdom?
7. List Lippmann's examples of environments in which freedom of speech truly exists.
8. Why are there few environments in which we find absolute freedom of speech?
9. What is Lippmann's argument for some rules and restrictions to absolute freedom? Can his discussion be seen as an argument in favor of some forms of censorship? Do you agree with his restrictions? Why or why not?
10. What, for Lippmann, is the virtue of liberty? What does it allow men and women to become?
11. Why is freedom of speech indispensable to democracy?
12. What events in 1939 may have spurred Lippmann to write this article? What current events here and abroad continue to make it relevant?
13. Lippmann's essay is philosophical and abstract, but not without details or examples. If Lippmann's writing is typical of philosophical argument, what *type* of example can you expect?
14. Analyze Lippmann's sentence structure. What sentence pattern does he use effectively for key assertions or summary statements?

On Moral Equivalence

CHARLES KRAUTHAMMER

One of today's most penetrating—and uniquely trained—political thinkers and writers is Charles Krauthammer (b. 1950). After graduating, with honors, from Canada's McGill University and studying political theory at Oxford, Krauthammer decided to become a doctor and entered Harvard Medical School.

He graduated in 1975 and went on to a residency in psychiatry at Boston's Massachusetts General Hospital. Board certified in psychiatry and neurology, Krauthammer has been senior editor of the New Republic *since 1981, a* Time *magazine essayist since 1983, and a syndicated columnist since 1985. As Krauthammer observes, "when one makes as circuitous a journey as I have from political study to medicine to psychiatry to writing, one is expected to offer some explanation." At times tempted to encourage would-be columnists to prepare by attending medical school, Krauthammer credits medical training for the organizational skills evident in his thinking and writing, but admits that he was drawn to medicine because it seemed to offer both moral and intellectual certainty not found in the world of politics. In addition to discovering the naïveté of this view, Krauthammer also discovered that medicine is a confining career and that he had never lost his love of politics.*

Krauthammer explains, in the introduction to his collection of essays Cutting Edges *(1985), his several purposes in writing:*

> *1) to offer a skeptical survey of the myths and fads which periodically wash over our culture in waves of enthusiasm, leaving confusion, and some amusement, in their wake; . . .*
> *2) to conduct a critical—clinical perhaps—inquiry into those political and moral questions of inescapable ambiguity . . . which demand illumination rather than solution; . . . and*
> *3) to apply to much of the rest of the political universe . . . a political philosophy of liberal internationalism.*

"On Moral Equivalence," reprinted in Cutting Edges, *was first published as a* Time *essay on July 9, 1984. After reading the essay and Krauthammer's further comments on its writing, which follow, decide which of his purposes dominates in this sample of his political thinking.*

1 "If he does really think that there is no distinction between virtue and vice," warns Dr. Samuel Johnson,[1] "why, sir, when he leaves our house let us count our spoons." Judging by the recent pronouncements of some of our leaders, it is time to start husbanding spoons. Not that anyone in public life denies that there are moral distinctions to be made; but there seems to be a growing unwillingness—or is it an inability?—to make them, even the most simple.

2 Consider the case of another wise and respected doctor, Dr. Seuss. His latest epic, *The Butter Battle Book*, is a parable of the nuclear age. Two peoples, the Yooks and the Zooks, find themselves in such fierce—

[1]An eighteenth-century British poet, critic, lexicographer, and social commentator.—Ed.

and pointless—confrontation that each is ready to drop the fatal Bitsy Big-Boy Bomberoo on the other. They are very similar, these Yooks and Zooks. They seem to differ in only one way: one side takes its bread butter-side up, the other butter-side down.

3 Yooks, Zooks. East, West. Butter-side up, butter-side down. What's the difference? cries the good Dr. Seuss in a plea predictably hailed for its sanity by everyone from Art Buchwald[2] ("must reading") to Ralph Nader[3] ("a bundle of wisdom in a small package"). Now is it really necessary to observe that in this world, as opposed to Dr. Seuss's cuddly creation, what divides Yooks and Zooks is democracy and constitutional government, among other conventions? The principal reason Yooks insist on arming themselves is that the Zooks of this planet have the unfortunate tendency to build gulags (for export too) and to stockpile those nasty intercontinental ballistic Bomberoos.

4 The allergy to elementary distinctions is not confined to child educators and their admirers. It also turns up on the political front, even among presidential candidates. For example, when Louis Farrakhan[4] publicly threatened the life of the *Washington Post* reporter who had disclosed Jesse Jackson's "Hymie" slur, Jackson characterized the episode as a "conflict" between "two very able professionals caught in a cycle that could be damaging to their careers."

5 This is the language of moral equivalence. "Two professionals"—each guy just doing his job—cleverly places the two men on the same moral plane. "Caught"—passive victims, both men done to and not doing—neatly removes any notion of guilt or responsibility. "In a cycle"—no beginning and no end—insinuates an indeterminateness in the relationship between the two men: Someone may have started this, but who can tell and what does it matter? (Nor is this the first time Jackson has pressed the cycle image into dubious service. Remember his "cycle of pain" in Lebanon, as if Navy Lieut. Robert Goodman, the flyer for the American peace-keeping force that had lost more than 250 men to terrorist attack, and President Hafez Assad, who had at least acquiesced in that attack, were equal partners in crime?) Having framed the issue in these terms, Jackson proceeded to the logical conclusion: he proposed a meeting between Farrakhan and the reporter, offering himself as mediator.

---

[2]A contemporary syndicated columnist of social and political satire.—Ed.

[3]A contemporary lawyer, speaker, and consumer advocate.—Ed.

[4]The leader of one faction of the Black Muslim movement in the United States, the faction most actively committed to black separatism and black supremacy.—Ed.

6 What was most disturbing about this affair was not the excesses of an extremist, but how his candidate parsed the problem, and worse, how uncritically that rendering was received. That Jackson's peculiar moral logic should have gone virtually unchallenged among his Democratic rivals (they criticized Farrakhan's death threats instead—a victory of discretion over valor) is an index of just how unserious about moral distinctions we have become. As conservative economist Thomas Sowell put it, the inability to make moral distinctions is the AIDS of the intellectuals: an acquired immune deficiency syndrome. It certainly is not inborn. Children can make elementary distinctions between, say, threatener and threatened. Moral blindness of this caliber requires practice. It has to be learned.

7 We learn it in several ways. One arrives at much of the currently fashionable agnosticism about the cold war (the inability to tell Yooks from Zooks because of nukes) through world-weariness. After forty years of long twilight struggle, one feels one has had enough. And when the easy distinctions become too much, the hard ones, like choosing one group of guerrillas over another in a murky Third World struggle, become intolerable. Thus, that facile evasion now elevated to the status of wisdom, that one man's terrorist is another man's freedom fighter. "Who goes there, friend or foe?" asks Uncle Sam of a Central American revolutionary in a recent cartoon. "I am a rebel trying to overthrow my government through murder, mayhem and terrorism," he replies. "That doesn't answer my question," responds Uncle Sam, the implication being that there is something arbitrary about supporting one set of guerrillas (Nicaragua) and not another (El Salvador).

8 Is there? Pol Pot, Jonas Savimbi, Edén Pastora Gómez[5] and an assortment of Salvadoran Marxist-Leninists have taken up arms against their respective governments. Is there nothing to choose between them? If one is serious about the issue, one has to ask how they fight: Bombs on school buses? Mines in harbors? Or attacks on the other side's military? They all differ qualitatively and—forgive the piety—morally. One is also obliged to ask about goals: to sort out the totalitarians from the democrats, and when one really encounters them (Grenada, for example), to call thugs, thugs. The pox-on-all-their-houses sentiment is not just traditional American isolationism making a comeback. It is moral exhaustion, an abdication of the responsibility to distinguish between shades of gray. The usual excuse is that the light has grown pale; the real problem is a glaze in the eye of the beholder.

---

[5]Three revolutionary leaders, a Cambodian, an Angolan, and a Nicaraguan Contra.—Ed.

9 Another mode of unlearning moral distinctions is through an excess of empathy. The claim is that we must not judge before we fully understand. "Context," protested Jackson, arguing that one must first put Farrakhan's threats in the context of the Black Muslim's apocalyptic language and his history (like his good deeds combating drug abuse). But this is to confuse moral analysis with psychotherapy. Treating people seriously, that is, as adults—whatever their history, their culture, their unconscious drives—means judging what people do and say, not what they intend or feel. To defer judgment pending full understanding is to ensure that we will make no judgments at all.

10 Not that psychological insight and moral judgment are mutually exclusive. John le Carré[6] is extraordinarily skillful at showing the psychological affinity between the British master spy Smiley and his KGB nemesis Karla. But in the end, there is no mistaking Le Carré's view of the worthiness of their respective enterprises. One can understand and still judge, so long as one is not tempted to understand everything.

11 Finally, perhaps the deepest cause of moral confusion is the state of language itself, language that has been bleached of its moral distinctions, turned neutral, value-free, "nonjudgmental." When that happens, moral discourse becomes difficult, moral distinctions impossible and moral debate incomprehensible. If abortion is simply "termination of pregnancy," the moral equivalent of, say, removing a tumor, how to account for a movement of serious people dedicated to its abolition? If homosexuality is merely a "sexual preference"—if a lover's sex is as much a matter of taste as say, haircolor (or having it butter-side up or butter-side down)—then why the to-do over two men dancing together at Disneyland? But there is a fuss, because there is a difference. One can understand neither with language that refuses to make distinctions.

12 Why, after all, say "single-parent family" when we mean fatherless home? (Single, male-headed households are a small minority of the single-parent family group.) The descriptive, and sympathetic, "fatherless" acknowledges that something is missing; the ostentatiously neutral "single-parent family" would have us believe that the distinction between a single- and a double-—why not a triple?—parent household is entirely statistical.

13 Using unflattened, living language does not commit one to an anti-abortion, anti-gay or anti-welfare position. One can argue forcefully for

[6]A contemporary writer, author of several spy novels with British spy Smiley as the main character.—Ed.

free choice in abortion, rights for homosexuals and aid to fatherless families without pretending that the issues here are merely clinical, aesthetic or statistical. They are moral too. But to make, or even follow, moral arguments, we need language that has not yet obliterated any trace of distinctions.

14 And yet the language of moral equivalence has become routine. Calling something the moral equivalent of war, for example, is a favorite Presidential technique for summoning the nation to a cause. That metaphor, coined by William James,[7] was last pressed into service by Jimmy Carter to gird us for the energy crisis. Before that, we have had wars on poverty, crime, cancer and even war itself (World War I). Now, Mr. Carter knew that turning down thermostats and risking lives in combat make vastly different claims on the citizenry. Indeed, he sought to exploit that disproportion to rally the nation to the unglamorous task of conserving energy. The idea was to make the notion of conserving energy more important. What went unconsidered was what that kind of linguistic maneuver does to the idea of going to war. The problem with summoning a great moral theme in the service of a minor one—the problem with declaring moral equivalance when it does not exist—is what that does to the *great* idea. In a dangerous world Americans might some day be called upon to go to war, and if that happens, the difference between reaching for a thermostat and reaching for a gun will become painfully apparent.

15 The trouble with blurring moral distinctions, even for the best of causes, is that it can become a habit. It is a habit we can ill afford, since the modern tolerance for such distinctions is already in decline. Some serious ideas are used so promiscuously in the service of so many causes that they have lost all their power. Genocide, for example, has been used to describe almost every kind of perceived injustice, from Vietnam to pornography to Third World birth control. A new word, holocaust, has to be brought in as a substitute. But its life before ultimate trivialization will not be long. Only recently a financial commentator on PBS, referring to a stock-market drop, spoke of the holocaust year of 1981. The host did not blink.

16 Counted your spoons lately?

---

[7]A nineteenth-century psychologist, philosopher, and writer.—Ed.

Comments on ON MORAL EQUIVALENCE

CHARLES KRAUTHAMMER

I came to write this article on moral equivalence the same way I come to write most articles. Certain events in the world strike me as either odd or wrong. When enough of them occur at once, and when I can see some connection between them, I am prompted to address the underlying issue. Here, for example, the connection between the words of Jesse Jackson and those of Doctor Seuss became immediately apparent. At that point, other events also illustrating this idea of moral equivalence came to mind. The rest was commentary.

I came to writing by way of politics. I am interested in what politics does, i.e., the authoritative allocation of values. And I saw that my way to influence political debate lay in writing. Accordingly, most of my writing is about politics and, precisely, about the ideas that underlie our political life. I write not so much about what is happening in Washington, as what I think is happening beneath that produces what happens in Washington. Not that I am a mere observer. I have a certain ideological view which I try to promote rather openly in my pieces. I try, at the same time, to understand the opposition and to present its case as strongly as I can.

I am, however, not a theorist. I find criticism easier, and safer. Marx, for example, was the greatest social theorist of the modern era, and the wreckage of human lives that his theories have occasioned might have appalled even him. It certainly appalls me. My mission is modest. Not to change the world, but to understand a little of it. And, perhaps, every once in a while, as Tom Stoppard puts it, to give it a bit of a nudge.

QUESTIONS FOR ANALYSIS AND DISCUSSION

1. What contemporary issue does Krauthammer examine in this essay?
2. What is his attitude toward the issue—or what is his thesis?
3. What specific examples does Krauthammer offer to demonstrate our current inability to make moral distinctions? Do you agree that the two examples illustrate moral equivalence? If not, why not?
4. Where, according to Krauthammer, does moral blindness "come from"?
5. State, in your own words, the three ways we unlearn moral distinctions.

6. What does Krauthammer consider to be the chief cause of moral equivalence? How might you have guessed this if Krauthammer had not said so at the beginning of paragraph 11?
7. Do you accept Krauthammer's three causes? Do you think there are others?
8. To the extent that you are disinclined to make moral distinctions, which cause has most influenced your moral neutrality? How do you think you learned, over time, this neutrality? If you are inclined to make moral distinctions, to what do you attribute your avoidance of the trend to moral neutrality?
9. Krauthammer says that to treat people as adults is to judge their actions, not their intentions or feelings. What do you think about this idea? This distinction has for a long time been central to what important social institution?
10. Analyze Krauthammer's style. What techniques does he use to make his style informal and his tone reasonably light (considering the seriousness of his subject)? What does his choice of style and tone tell us about his awareness of audience?

Duty: The Forgotten Virtue

AMITAI ETZIONI

An internationally renowned sociologist, Amitai Etzioni (b. 1929) was born in Cologne, Germany, and earned his Ph.D. at the University of California at Berkeley. Etzioni taught in the sociology department at Columbia University for many years before becoming, in 1980, University Professor at George Washington University. He is also director of the Center for Policy Research and the author of numerous books and articles. Among the many books he has published are Modern Organizations *(1964),* Studies in Social Change *(1966), and* Anatomies of America: Sociological Perspectives *(1969). Etzioni also writes monthly columns for* Human Behavior *and* Psychology Today. *In addition to works on social change and organizations, two of his favorite subjects, Etzioni has recently published* Capital Corruption: A New Attack on American Democracy *(1984). This study of the corrupting influence of special interest money on the political system grew out of his experience as a White House adviser.*

Like Charles Krauthammer, Etzioni examines our times and finds something missing; for Etzioni it is the concept of duty. The following article on this forgotten virtue was printed in the March 9, 1986, issue of the Washington Post.

1 Air accidents can be viewed as random tests of the extent to which those responsible for keeping airplanes flying are doing their duty.

2 For example, the crew of an American Airlines plane recently tried to land it three times, in low visibility, with 124 people aboard, in Harlingen, Tex. On the third pass, they hit two sets of runway approach lights four feet off the ground. The collision was severe enough to deploy some oxygen masks in the passenger cabin and knock ceiling panels loose. Yet after the plane regained altitude and landed safely in San Antonio, other crews took it to Dallas-Fort Worth and then on to Denver where damage to the exterior of the plane was discovered and the plane taken out of service.

3 One may view this as nothing more than an isolated incident of questionable judgment, but there is some evidence to suggest that Americans—always ambivalent about their duties—have been particularly loath to live up to their responsibilities in recent years.

4 A survey of young Americans found that most rank trial by jury high among their rights. However, few indicated a willingness to serve on a jury.

5 Patriotism is reported to be in vogue. However, Americans would rather pay volunteers to serve in the military than support a draft in which all would share the burden.

6 A survey conducted by H & R Block shows that Americans favor a flat tax. However, that support is offered on one troubling condition: that the respondent's favorite loophole not be closed.

7 These observations led me to ask my class at The George Washington University what the term "duty" brought to their mind. They responded uneasily. They felt that people ought to be free to do what *they* believe in. Duties are imposed, alien, authoritarian—what the principal, the curriculum committee, the society, "they," want you to do.

8 I responded with a little impassioned address about the common good: If everyone goes to the forest and fells a tree, soon the hillsides will be denuded. We cannot rely on the fact that once we are out of trees, people will recognize the need to plant new ones; it takes years for trees to grow. Hence, we must, I explained, expect members of society to plant some trees now, invest in the infrastructure, trim the deficit, etc., so that the next generation will have a forest, a thriving economy, a future. We must balance the desire to focus on one's own interests with some obligation to the commons. True, duties are not fun, *otherwise*

there would be no need to impose them. But a civil society cannot do without them.

9 Well, the students reflected aloud; they understood where I was coming from. Okay, they said, maybe there was room for duty, but—compliance ought to be voluntary, they insisted. I felt I had failed them; I never got the point across.

10 Americans have never been very duty-bound. The country was created by people who escaped duties imposed by authoritarian monarchies and dogmatic churches. And the ethos of the pioneers was of striking out on one's own—even if, as a matter of fact, settlement was carried out by groups very much dependent on one another.

11 But over the last decades the need for duty to the commons has grown as the supply diminished. Consider:

12 *Demand Side.* Practically no one expects that America can do without *some* defense. The problem is that defense requires a *continuous* willingness to dedicate resources to national security that might otherwise be used to enhance one's standard of living. As obvious as this may seem, the fact is that Americans have found it very difficult to sustain such a commitment. The defense budget typically reflects cycles of neglect followed by hysterical reactions to some real or alleged crisis. There is no well-grounded commitment.

13 On the domestic front, voluntarism is now supposed to replace many government services. Anyone who points to the limits of such an approach is immediately suspect of being an old-time liberal, a champion of big government. But this simple-minded dichotomy—do things privately *or* via the government—conceals the real issue: What duties to the commons *should* the government impose?

14 Most would include, aside from defense, support for basic and medical research, some environmental protection, public education and services for the deserving poor. But today these obligations to the commons are left without a moral underpinning. Most do not subscribe to a social philosophy which endorses these commitments. Instead, we celebrate *laissez faire* and a generation rich in Me-ism.

15 *Supply Side.* Americans are hardly enamored with the notion that they have duties to the social weal. They find escape in an odd concoction: a misapplication of Adam Smith[1] mixed with surging libertarianism, pop psychology and a dash of liberation theory.

---

[1]An eighteenth-century Scottish economist who argued, in *The Wealth of Nations,* that wealth would increase if government eliminated restrictive regulations. But Smith did not advocate total laissez faire.—Ed.

16 Americans have been brought up on a highly simplified notion of the invisible hand: Everybody goes out and tries to "maximize" himself – and the economy thrives for all. There is no need to curb self-interest, even greed; it is the propellant that fires up economies.

17 Now the reach of the invisible hand has been extended to wholly new spheres. Antismoking campaigns, pro-seatbelt moves, Social Security, environmental protection and employee safety are said to work best without "coercion" – if people are left to their own devices.

18 In this rejection of any sense that we have duties to each other, we gloss over the consequences to innocent bystanders of such a free-for-all, it's-up-to-you-Jack attitude. These range from the effect on children of those who choose not to buy insurance, to the neglect of "public goods" – goods we all need but no one is individually entrusted with procuring (e.g, highways).

19 Pop psychology is still with us. It argues that everyone ought to focus on his or her own growth. Society and its duties are viewed as standing in the way of self-fulfillment.

20 Pollster Daniel Yankelovich estimated that in the late 1970s, 17 percent of Americans were deeply committed to a philosophy of self-fulfillment and another 63 percent subscribed to it in varying degrees. These people said they "spend a great deal of time thinking about myself" and "satisfactions come from shaping oneself rather than from home and family life." They had a strong need for excitement and sensation and tended to feel free to look, live and act however they wanted, even if this violated others' concepts of what is proper.

21 The significance of this is that the escape from duty reaches beyond neglect of the community's needs to the neglect of one's immediate family.

22 Last but not least are the interest groups which elevate Me-ism to a group level. True, lobbies have been around since the founding of the Republic. But in recent years their power has increased sharply. And the consequence is that service to each interest group is easily put above a concern for the general welfare.

23 How do we redress the balance between the "I" and the "We" – so that we enhance the sense of duty?

24 There obviously are no simple solutions, but schools could help. They could change their civics courses from teaching that the government has three branches and the Supreme Court nine members (and so on), and instead promote civility. However, since most schools are overworked and underfunded, they are unlikely to do much.

25 More may be achieved if the issue is put on the agenda of the nationwide town-hall meetings we are, in effect, constantly conducting. The subjects vary, from civil rights to environmental protection to deficit reduction. However, the process is the same: Triggered by a leading book (such as "Silent Spring"[2]), a series of reports in leading newspapers or on television (e.g., on Vietnam), or by commissions (on education), we turn our collective attention to an issue. We debate it at length.

26 At first it seems nothing happens, but gradually a new consensus arises that affects people's behavior. We agree to pollute less or drink less; we exercise more; we become more sensitive to the rights of minorities or women.

27 The issue of our social obligations as Americans—our duties—is overdue for such a treatment. Meanwhile, we each ought to examine ourselves: What have you done for your community lately?

QUESTIONS FOR ANALYSIS AND DISCUSSION

1. What is the purpose of the first six paragraphs?
2. Compare Etzioni's opening to Krauthammer's; how are they similar? What can you learn from these writers about ways to begin essays on controversial topics?
3. What was the response of Etzioni's students to the concept of duty?
4. What is Etzioni's attitude toward duty?
5. Etzioni asserts that Americans have never been strongly motivated by a sense of duty. State, in your own words, the specific examples he gives to illustrate our current lack of a sense of duty.
6. What are some of the contemporary sources of values and ideas that run counter to our developing a sense of duty? To what extent are the causes Etzioni finds similar to those Krauthammer finds for moral relativism?
7. According to Etzioni, what is the dominant value among Americans today? Do you agree? Why or why not? What evidence can you offer to support your view?
8. Etzioni suggests that interest groups, so active in politics today, are a kind of "Me-ism." How is this a useful way to understand these groups?
9. What three solutions does Etzioni offer to "enhance the sense of duty"? Which does he think is most likely to bring about change?

---

[2] A study of abuses to the environment by chemical pollutants in the air and water supply, written by biologist and author Rachel Carson.—Ed.

10. In what ways do Etzioni's actions contribute to each of the three kinds of solutions? What does this suggest to you about the power of language?
11. Analyze Etzioni's organization. What does he do first? Second? Third?

The Myth of Sisyphus

ALBERT CAMUS

For a biographical sketch of Camus, see p. 157. Camus was a philosopher as well as a fiction writer, and he may indeed be best known for his philosophical essay, reprinted here, "The Myth of Sisyphus." The essay was first published in 1942, the same year in which his famous short novel The Stranger *was published. Both works—one fiction, one nonfiction—examine the concept of the absurd, of a universe without meaning. Both Meursault in* The Stranger *and Sisyphus are absurd figures expected to behave purposefully in a universe that cannot provide a definition of purposeful. In his essay Camus makes clear that life is, nevertheless, worth the effort it takes to live it. We are to imagine, Camus tells us, that Sisyphus is happy.*

1 The gods had condemned Sisyphus to ceaselessly rolling a rock to the top of a mountain, whence the stone would fall back of its own weight. They had thought with some reason that there is no more dreadful punishment than futile and hopeless labor.

2 If one believes Homer, Sisyphus was the wisest and most prudent of mortals. According to another tradition, however, he was disposed to practice the profession of highwayman. I see no contradiction in this. Opinions differ as to the reasons why he became the futile laborer of the underworld. To begin with, he is accused of a certain levity in regard to the gods. He stole their secrets. Ægina, the daughter of Æsopus, was carried off by Jupiter. The father was shocked by that disappearance and complained to Sisyphus. He, who knew of the abduction, offered to tell about it on condition that Æsopus would give water to the citadel of Corinth. To the celestial thunderbolts he preferred the benediction of water. He was punished for this in the underworld. Homer tells us also that Sisyphus had put Death in chains. Pluto could not endure the sight of his deserted, silent empire. He dispatched the god of war, who liberated Death from the hands of her conqueror.

3 It is also said that Sisyphus, being near to death, rashly wanted to test his wife's love. He ordered her to cast his unburied body into the middle of the public square. Sisyphus woke up in the underworld. And there, annoyed by an obedience so contrary to human love, he obtained from Pluto permission to return to earth in order to chastise his wife. But when he had seen again the face of this world, enjoyed water and sun, warm stones and the sea, he no longer wanted to go back to the infernal darkness. Recalls, signs of anger, warnings were of no avail. Many years more he lived facing the curve of the gulf, the sparkling sea, and the smiles of earth. A decree of the gods was necessary. Mercury came and seized the impudent man by the collar and, snatching him from his joys, led him forcibly back to the underworld, where his rock was ready for him.

4 You have already grasped that Sisyphus is the absurd hero. He *is*, as much through his passions as through his torture. His scorn of the gods, his hatred of death, and his passion for life won him that unspeakable penalty in which the whole being is exerted toward accomplishing nothing. This is the price that must be paid for the passions of this earth. Nothing is told us about Sisyphus in the underworld. Myths are made for the imagination to breathe life into them. As for this myth, one sees merely the whole effort of a body straining to raise the huge stone, to roll it and push it up a slope a hundred times over; one sees the face screwed up, the cheek tight against the stone, the shoulder bracing the clay-covered mass, the foot wedging it, the fresh start with arms outstretched, the wholly human security of two earth-clotted hands. At the very end of his long effort measured by skyless space and time without depth, the purpose is achieved. Then Sisyphus watches the stone rush down in a few moments toward that lower world whence he will have to push it up again toward the summit. He goes back down to the plain.

5 It is during that return, that pause, that Sisyphus interests me. A face that toils so close to stones is already stone itself! I see that man going back down with a heavy yet measured step toward the torment of which he will never know the end. That hour like a breathing-space which returns as surely as his suffering, that is the hour of consciousness. At each of those moments when he leaves the heights and gradually sinks toward the lairs of the gods, he is superior to his fate. He is stronger than his rock.

6 If this myth is tragic, that is because its hero is conscious. Where would his torture be, indeed, if at every step the hope of succeeding upheld him? The workman of today works every day in his life at the same tasks, and this fate is no less absurd. But it is tragic only at the rare

moments when it becomes conscious. Sisyphus, proletarian of the gods, powerless and rebellious, knows the whole extent of his wretched condition: it is what he thinks of during his descent. The lucidity that was to constitute his torture at the same time crowns his victory. There is no fate that cannot be surmounted by scorn.

7 If the descent is thus sometimes performed in sorrow, it can also take place in joy. This word is not too much. Again I fancy Sisyphus returning toward his rock, and the sorrow was in the beginning. When the images of earth cling too tightly to memory, when the call of happiness becomes too insistent, it happens that melancholy rises in man's heart: this is the rock's victory, this is the rock itself. The boundless grief is too heavy to bear. These are our nights of Gethsemane.[1] But crushing truths perish from being acknowledged. Thus, Œdipus[2] at the outset obeys fate without knowing it. But from the moment he knows, his tragedy begins. Yet at the same moment, blind and desperate, he realizes that the only bond linking him to the world is the cool hand of a girl. Then a tremendous remark rings out: "Despite so many ordeals, my advanced age and the nobility of my soul make me conclude that all is well." Sophocles' Œdipus, like Dostoevsky's Kirilov,[3] thus gives the recipe for the absurd victory. Ancient wisdom confirms modern heroism.

8 One does not discover the absurd without being tempted to write a manual of happiness. "What! by such narrow ways—?" There is but one world, however. Happiness and the absurd are two sons of the same earth. They are inseparable. It would be a mistake to say that happiness necessarily springs from the absurd discovery. It happens as well that the feeling of the absurd springs from happiness. "I conclude that all is well," says Œdipus, and that remark is sacred. It echoes in the wild and limited universe of man. It teaches that all is not, has not been, exhausted. It drives out of this world a god who had come into it with dissatisfaction and a preference for futile sufferings. It makes of fate a human matter, which must be settled among men.

---

[1]A garden east of Jerusalem in which Jesus prayed to be released from the suffering and death to come.—Ed.

[2]The tragic hero in the plays *Oedipus the King* and *Oedipus at Colonus* by Sophocles, Greek dramatist of the fifth century B.C. Discovering that he has killed his father and married his mother, Oedipus blinds himself and is led by his daughter Antigone.—Ed.

[3]A character in *The Possessed,* a rebellious atheist who decides to commit suicide to avoid his fate of death.—Ed.

9 All Sisyphus' silent joy is contained therein. His fate belongs to him. His rock is his thing. Likewise, the absurd man, when he contemplates his torment, silences all the idols. In the universe suddenly restored to its silence, the myriad wondering little voices of the earth rise up. Unconscious, secret calls, invitations from all the faces, they are the necessary reverse and price of victory. There is no sun without shadow, and it is essential to know the night. The absurd man says yes and his effort will henceforth be unceasing. If there is a personal fate, there is no higher destiny, or at least there is but one which he concludes is inevitable and despicable. For the rest, he knows himself to be the master of his days. At that subtle moment when man glances backward over his life, Sisyphus returning toward his rock, in that slight pivoting he contemplates that series of unrelated actions which becomes his fate, created by him, combined under his memory's eye and soon sealed by his death. Thus, convinced of the wholly human origin of all that is human, a blind man eager to see who knows that the night has no end, he is still on the go. The rock is still rolling.

10 I leave Sisyphus at the foot of the mountain! One always finds one's burden again. But Sisyphus teaches the higher fidelity that negates the gods and raises rocks. He too concludes that all is well. This universe henceforth without a master seems to him neither sterile nor futile. Each atom of that stone, each mineral flake of that night-filled mountain, in itself forms a world. The struggle itself toward the heights is enough to fill a man's heart. One must imagine Sisyphus happy.

QUESTIONS FOR ANALYSIS AND DISCUSSION

1. There are several explanations for Sisyphus's punishment, several ways that he is supposed to have angered the gods. What do his actions have in common?
2. Why does Camus consider Sisyphus a hero?
3. Why did the gods choose Sisyphus's particular form of punishment? How does Sisyphus rise above his punishment?
4. Why is this myth tragic? What is required to make it tragic?
5. What, for Camus, does the rock symbolize? How do we become victorious over our burden?
6. Who, for Camus, controls, or should be perceived to control, a person's life? What is required to see one's life as "neither sterile nor futile"? How does this lead to happiness?
7. To draw elements of Camus's philosophy from his analysis of this myth, consider how Camus would answer the following questions:

a. What is the nature of the universe?
b. Is there a god (or gods)?
c. What controls or shapes a person's life?
d. What is the purpose of human life?
e. What gives life meaning?
f. What, then, is good?

8. Do you agree with some, all, or none of Camus's answers to these questions? Can you give reasons for your agreement/disagreement?

A Free Man's Worship

BERTRAND RUSSELL

Mathematician, philosopher, and social activist, Bertrand Russell (1872–1970) was born in Trelleck, Wales, and educated at Cambridge, first in mathematics, then in philosophy. Between periods of lecturing at Trinity College, Cambridge, Russell traveled in Europe, Russia, and China, and lectured many times in the United States. Russell actively opposed World War I and, later, nuclear proliferation. His best political writing appears in Principles of Social Reconstruction, *published in 1916.*

If his political positions were not always universally esteemed, his philosophical reputation has remained secure, from his earliest lectures and books until the present. One biographer has written that "no one had had a more fundamental and persistent effect on the course of academic, technical philosophy in the English-speaking world than Russell did." He not only influenced students of philosophy; he also wrote in a clear expository style for the nonspecialist. The most important of his books for philosophers was The Principles of Mathematics *(1930). His best nonscholarly works include* A History of Western Philosophy, *a great success in Europe and America on its publication in 1945, and* Relativity *(1925), an account of what was then the newest work in physics. Other widely read works of Russell's are* On Education *(1926),* Education and the Social Order *(1932),* Religion and Science *(1935), and two collections of essays,* The Problems of Philosophy *(1912) and* Mysticism and Logic *(1918).*

The following essay, described as Russell's "declaration of cosmic defiance," was first published in the Independent Review *in December 1903 and then reprinted in* Mysticism and Logic.

1 To Dr. Faustus in his study Mephistopheles[1] told the history of the Creation, saying:

2 "The endless praises of the choirs of angels had begun to grow wearisome; for, after all, did he not deserve their praise? Had he not given them endless joy? Would it not be more amusing to obtain undeserved praise, to be worshipped by beings whom he tortured? He smiled inwardly, and resolved that the great drama should be performed.

3 "For countless ages the hot nebula whirled aimlessly through space. At length it began to take shape, the central mass threw off planets, the planets cooled, boiling seas and burning mountains heaved and tossed, from black masses of cloud hot sheets of rain deluged the barely solid crust. And now the first germ of life grew in the depths of the ocean, and developed rapidly in the fructifying warmth into vast forest trees, huge ferns springing from the damp mold, sea monsters breeding, fighting, devouring, and passing away. And from the monsters, as the play unfolded itself, Man was born, with the power of thought, the knowledge of good and evil, and the cruel thirst for worship. And Man saw that all is passing in this mad, monstrous world, that all is struggling to snatch, at any cost, a few brief moments of life before Death's inexorable decree. And Man said: 'There is a hidden purpose, could we but fathom it, and the purpose is good; for we must reverence something, and in the visible world there is nothing worthy of reverence.' And Man stood aside from the struggle, resolving that God intended harmony to come out of chaos by human efforts. And when he followed the instincts which God had transmitted to him from his ancestry of beasts of prey, he called it Sin, and asked God to forgive him. But he doubted whether he could be justly forgiven, until he invented a divine Plan by which God's wrath was to have been appeased. And seeing the present was bad, he made it yet worse, that thereby the future might be better. And he gave God thanks for the strength that enabled him to forgo even the joys that were possible. And God smiled; and when he saw that Man had become perfect in renunciation and worship, he sent another sun through the sky, which crashed into Man's sun; and all returned again to nebula.

4 " 'Yes,' he murmured, 'it was a good play; I will have it performed again.' "

5 Such, in outline, but even more purposeless, more void of meaning, is the world which Science presents for our belief. Amid such a world, if

[1]One of the seven chief devils, the one conjured by Faustus and the one to whom he sells his soul for knowledge and power. – Ed.

anywhere, our ideals henceforward must find a home. That Man is the product of causes which had no prevision of the end they were achieving; that his origin, his growth, his hopes and fears, his loves and his beliefs, are but the outcome of accidental collocations of atoms; that no fire, no heroism, no intensity of thought and feeling, can preserve an individual life beyond the grave; that all the labours of the ages, all the devotion, all the inspiration, all the noonday brightness of human genius, are destined to extinction in the vast death of the solar system, and that the whole temple of Man's achievement must inevitably be buried beneath the débris of a universe in ruins—all these things, if not quite beyond dispute, are yet so nearly certain, that no philosophy which rejects them can hope to stand. Only within the scaffolding of these truths, only on the firm foundation of unyielding despair, can the soul's habitation henceforth be safely built.

6 How, in such an alien and inhuman world, can so powerless a creature as Man preserve his aspirations untarnished? A strange mystery it is that Nature, omnipotent but blind, in the revolutions of her secular hurryings through the abysses of space, has brought forth at last a child, subject still to her power, but gifted with sight, with knowledge of good and evil, with the capacity of judging all the works of his unthinking Mother. In spite of Death, the mark and seal of the parental control, Man is yet free, during his brief years, to examine, to criticise, to know, and in imagination to create. To him alone, in the world with which he is acquainted, this freedom belongs; and in this lies his superiority to the resistless forces that control his outward life.

7 The savage, like ourselves, feels the oppression of his impotence before the powers of Nature; but having in himself nothing that he respects more than Power, he is willing to prostrate himself before his gods, without inquiring whether they are worthy of his worship. Pathetic and very terrible is the long history of cruelty and torture, of degradation and human sacrifice, endured in the hope of placating the jealous gods: surely, the trembling believer thinks, when what is most precious has been freely given, their lust for blood must be appeased, and more will not be required. The religion of Moloch[2]—as such creeds may be generically called—is in essence the cringing submission of the slave, who dare not, even in his heart, allow the thought that his master deserves no adulation. Since the independence of ideals is not yet acknowledged, Power may be freely worshipped, and receive an unlimited respect, despite its wanton infliction of pain.

---

[2]A deity whose worship required the sacrificing of children.—Ed.

8 But gradually, as morality grows bolder, the claim of the ideal world begins to be felt; and worship, if it is not to cease, must be given to gods of another kind than those created by the savage. Some, though they feel the demands of the ideal, will still consciously reject them, still urging that naked Power is worthy of worship. Such is the attitude inculcated in God's answer to Job[3] out of the whirlwind: the divine power and knowledge are paraded, but of the divine goodness there is no hint. Such also is the attitude of those who, in our own day, base their morality upon the struggle for survival, maintaining that the survivors are necessarily the fittest. But others, not content with an answer so repugnant to the moral sense, will adopt the position which we have become accustomed to regard as specially religious, maintaining that, in some hidden manner, the world of fact is really harmonious with the world of ideals. Thus Man creates God, all-powerful and all-good, the mystic unity of what is and what should be.

9 But the world of fact, after all, is not good; and, in submitting our judgment to it, there is an element of slavishness from which our thoughts must be purged. For in all things it is well to exalt the dignity of Man, by freeing him as far as possible from the tyranny of non-human Power. When we have realised that Power is largely bad, that man, with his knowledge of good and evil, is but a helpless atom in a world which has no such knowledge, the choice is again presented to us: Shall we worship Force, or shall we worship Goodness? Shall our God exist and be evil, or shall he be recognised as the creation of our own conscience?

10 The answer to this question is very momentous, and affects profoundly our whole morality. The worship of Force, to which Carlyle[4] and Nietzsche[5] and the creed of Militarism have accustomed us, is the result of failure to maintain our own ideals against a hostile universe: it is itself a prostrate submission to evil, a sacrifice of our best to Moloch. If strength indeed is to be respected, let us respect rather the strength of those who refuse that false "recognition of facts" which fails to recognise that facts are often bad. Let us admit that, in the world we know, there are many things that would be better otherwise, and that the ideals to which we do and must adhere are not realised in the realm of matter.

---

[3]A figure in the Old Testament who questioned the ways of God; God answered out of the whirlwind to display his power to Job.—Ed.

[4]A nineteenth-century Scottish essayist and historian.—Ed.

[5]A nineteenth-century German philosopher who stressed that the will to power motivates both individuals and society.—Ed.

Let us preserve our respect for truth, for beauty, for the ideal of perfection which life does not permit us to attain, though none of these things meet with the approval of the unconscious universe. If Power is bad, as it seems to be, let us reject it from our hearts. In this lies Man's true freedom: in determination to worship only the God created by our own love of the good, to respect only the heaven which inspires the insight of our best moments. In action, in desire, we must submit perpetually to the tyranny of outside forces; but in thought, in aspiration, we are free, free from our fellow-men, free from the petty planet on which our bodies impotently crawl, free even, while we live, from the tyranny of death. Let us learn, then, that energy of faith which enables us to live constantly in the vision of the good; and let us descend, in action, into the world of fact, with that vision always before us.

11 When first the opposition of fact and ideal grows fully visible, a spirit of fiery revolt, of fierce hatred of the gods, seems necessary to the assertion of freedom. To defy with Promethean[6] constancy a hostile universe, to keep its evil always in view, always actively hated, to refuse no pain that the malice of Power can invent, appears to be the duty of all who will not bow before the inevitable. But indignation is still a bondage, for it compels our thoughts to be occupied with an evil world; and in the fierceness of desire from which rebellion springs there is a kind of self-assertion which it is necessary for the wise to overcome. Indignation is a submission of our thoughts, but not of our desires; the Stoic freedom in which wisdom consists is found in the submission of our desires, but not of our thoughts. From the submission of our desires springs the virtue of resignation; from the freedom of our thoughts springs the whole world of art and philosophy, and the vision of beauty by which, at last, we half reconquer the reluctant world. But the vision of beauty is possible only to unfettered contemplation, to thoughts not weighted by the load of eager wishes; and thus Freedom comes only to those who no longer ask of life that it shall yield them any of those personal goods that are subject to the mutations of Time.

12 Although the necessity of renunciation is evidence of the existence of evil, yet Christianity, in preaching it, has shown a wisdom exceeding that of the Promethean philosophy of rebellion. It must be admitted that, of the things we desire, some, though they prove impossible, are yet real goods; others, however, as ardently longed for, do not form part of a fully purified ideal. The belief that what must be renounced is bad,

---

[6]Prometheus defied the gods of Olympus and stole fire to give to man.—Ed.

though sometimes false, is far less often false than untamed passion supposes; and the creed of religion, by providing a reason for proving that it is never false, has been the means of purifying our hopes by the discovery of many austere truths.

13 But there is in resignation a further good element: even real goods, when they are unattainable, ought not to be fretfully desired. To every man comes, sooner or later, the great renunciation. For the young, there is nothing unattainable; a good thing desired with the whole force of a passionate will, and yet impossible, is to them not credible. Yet, by death, by illness, by poverty, or by the voice of duty, we must learn, each one of us, that the world was not made for us, and that, however beautiful may be the things we crave, Fate may nevertheless forbid them. It is the part of courage, when misfortune comes, to bear without repining the ruin of our hopes, to turn away our thoughts from vain regrets. This degree of submission to Power is not only just and right: it is the very gate of wisdom.

14 But passive renunciation is not the whole of wisdom; for not by renunciation alone can we build a temple for the worship of our own ideals. Haunting foreshadowings of the temple appear in the realm of imagination, in music, in architecture, in the untroubled kingdom of reason, and in the golden sunset magic of lyrics, where beauty shines and glows, remote from the touch of sorrow, remote from the fear of change, remote from the failures and disenchantments of the world of fact. In the contemplation of these things the vision of heaven will shape itself in our hearts, giving at once a touchstone to judge the world about us, and an inspiration by which to fashion to our needs whatever is not incapable of serving as a stone in the sacred temple.

15 Except for those rare spirits that are born without sin, there is a cavern of darkness to be traversed before that temple can be entered. The gate of the cavern is despair, and its floor is paved with the gravestones of abandoned hopes. There Self must die; there the eagerness, the greed of untamed desire must be slain, for only so can the soul be freed from the empire of Fate. But out of the cavern the Gate of Renunciation leads again to the daylight of wisdom, by whose radiance a new insight, a new joy, a new tenderness, shine forth to gladden the pilgrim's heart.

16 When, without the bitterness of impotent rebellion, we have learnt both to resign ourselves to the outward rule of Fate and to recognise that the non-human world is unworthy of our worship, it becomes possible at last so to transform and refashion the unconscious universe, so to

transmute it in the crucible of imagination, that a new image of shining gold replaces the old idol of clay. In all the multiform facts of the world – in the visual shapes of trees and mountains and clouds, in the events of the life of man, even in the very omnipotence of Death – the insight of creative idealism can find the reflection of a beauty which its own thoughts first made. In this way mind asserts its subtle mastery over the thoughtless forces of Nature. The more evil the material with which it deals, the more thwarting to untrained desire, the greater is its achievement in inducing the reluctant rock to yield up its hidden treasures, the prouder its victory in compelling the opposing forces to swell the pageant of its triumph. Of all the arts, Tragedy is the proudest, the most triumphant; for it builds its shining citadel in the very centre of the enemy's country, on the very summit of his highest mountain; from its impregnable watch-towers, his camps and arsenals, his columns and forts, are all revealed; within its walls the free life continues, while the legions of Death and Pain and Despair, and all the servile captains of tyrant Fate, afford the burghers of that dauntless city new spectacles of beauty. Happy those sacred ramparts, thrice happy the dwellers on that all-seeing eminence. Honour to those brave warriors who, through countless ages of warfare, have preserved for us the priceless heritage of liberty, and have kept undefiled by sacrilegious invaders the home of the unsubdued.

17 But the beauty of Tragedy does but make visible a quality which, in more or less obvious shapes, is present always and everywhere in life. In the spectacle of Death, in the endurance of intolerable pain, and in the irrevocableness of a vanished past, there is a sacredness, an overpowering awe, a feeling of the vastness, the depth, the inexhaustible mystery of existence, in which, as by some strange marriage of pain, the sufferer is bound to the world by bonds of sorrow. In these moments of insight, we lose all eagerness of temporary desire, all struggling and striving for petty ends, all care for the little trivial things that, to a superficial view, make up the common life of day by day; we see, surrounding the narrow raft illumined by the flickering light of human comradeship, the dark ocean on whose rolling waves we toss for a brief hour; from the great night without, a chill blast breaks in upon our refuge; all the loneliness of humanity amid hostile forces is concentrated upon the individual soul, which must struggle alone, with what of courage it can command, against the whole weight of a universe that cares nothing for its hopes and fears. Victory, in this struggle with the powers of darkness, is the true baptism into the glorious company of heroes, the true initiation

into the overmastering beauty of human existence. From that awful encounter of the soul with the outer world, enunciation, wisdom, and charity are born; and with their birth a new life begins. To take into the inmost shrine of the soul the irresistible forces whose puppets we seem to be—Death and change, the irrevocableness of the past, and the powerlessness of man before the blind hurry of the universe from vanity to vanity—to feel these things and know them is to conquer them.

18 This is the reason why the Past has such magical power. The beauty of its motionless and silent pictures is like the enchanged purity of late autumn, when the leaves, though one breath would make them fall, still glow against the sky in golden glory. The Past does not change or strive; like Duncan,[7] after life's fitful fever it sleeps well; what was eager and grasping, what was petty and transitory, has faded away, the things that were beautiful and eternal shine out of it like stars in the night. Its beauty, to a soul not worthy of it, is unendurable; but to a soul which has conquered Fate it is the key of religion.

19 The life of Man, viewed outwardly, is but a small thing in comparison with the forces of Nature. The slave is doomed to worship Time and Fate and Death, because they are greater than anything he finds in himself, and because all his thoughts are of things which they devour. But, great as they are, to think of them greatly, to feel their passionless splendour, is greater still. And such thought makes us free men; we no longer bow before the inevitable in Oriental subjection, but we absorb it, and make it a part of ourselves. To abandon the struggle for private happiness, to expel all eagerness of temporary desire, to burn with passion for eternal things—this is emancipation, and this is the free man's worship. And this liberation is effected by a contemplation of Fate: for Fate itself is subdued by the mind which leaves nothing to be purged by the purifying fire of Time.

20 United with his fellow-men by the strongest of all ties, the tie of a common doom, the free man finds that a new vision is with him always, shedding over every daily task the light of love. The life of Man is a long march through the night, surrounded by invisible foes, tortured by weariness and pain, towards a goal that few can hope to reach, and where none may tarry long. One by one, as they march, our comrades vanish from our sight, seized by the silent orders of omnipotent Death. Very brief is the time in which we can help them, in which their happiness or misery is decided. Be it ours to shed sunshine on their path, to lighten

---

[7]A king of Scotland; killed by Macbeth in Shakespeare's play.—Ed.

their sorrows by the balm of sympathy, to give them the pure joy of a never-tiring affection, to strengthen failing courage, to instil faith in hours of despair. Let us not weigh in grudging scales their merits and demerits, but let us think only of their need—of the sorrows, the difficulties, perhaps the blindnesses, that make the misery of their lives; let us remember that they are fellow-sufferers in the same darkness, actors in the same tragedy with ourselves. And so, when their day is over, when their good and their evil have become eternal by the immortality of the past, be it ours to feel that, where they suffered, where they failed, no deed of ours was the cause; but wherever a spark of the divine fire kindled in their hearts, we were ready with encouragement, with sympathy, with brave words in which high courage glowed.

21 Brief and powerless is Man's life; on him and all his race the slow, sure doom falls pitiless and dark. Blind to good and evil, reckless of destruction, omnipotent matter rolls on its relentless way; for Man, condemned to-day to lose his dearest, to-morrow himself to pass through the gate of darkness, it remains only to cherish, ere yet the blow falls, the lofty thoughts that ennoble his little day; disdaining the coward terrors of the slave of Fate, to worship at the shrine that his own hands have built; undismayed by the empire of chance, to preserve a mind free from the wanton tyranny that rules his outward life; proudly defiant of the irresistible forces that tolerate, for a moment, his knowledge and his condemnation, to sustain alone, a weary but unyielding Atlas,[8] the world that his own ideals have fashioned despite the trampling march of unconscious power.

QUESTIONS FOR ANALYSIS AND DISCUSSION

1. What does Russell accomplish by having Mephistopheles give the account of Creation, an account that includes the death of the earth and the figure of a powerful but cynical, unloving God?
2. What is the relationship between Mephistopheles's account and science's account of the origins, meaning, and end of existence? What is Russell's attitude toward this account?
3. What are man's distinct traits? What is it that man cannot do? Compare Russell's concept of man's freedom with Camus's; how are they similar?

[8]Brother of Prometheus, condemned to support the sky on his shoulders; thus anyone bearing a heavy load.—Ed.

4. What kind of God, according to Russell, does the savage worship? Why does Russell reject the savage's concept of God?
5. Russell also rejects transcendental religious beliefs that assert the "unity of what is and what should be." Why?
6. What kind of God, then, should we worship? What is the source of this God? What traits do we ascribe to this God?
7. Paragraph 12 demands especially careful reading. Explicate the paragraph, making sure that you explain what is to be renounced and why renunciation is superior to rebellion.
8. Russell develops a metaphor in paragraphs 13, 14, and 15. Explain the parts of the metaphor—what items are being compared? Then explain Russell's point about obtaining wisdom.
9. A second metaphor is developed in paragraph 16; what is the citadel? Who are the enemies? What do the warriors preserve? What is the victory? Explain the metaphor.
10. Explain, in your own words, "the free man's worship."
11. The free man finds not only a new vision but a guide to his relations with others. Explain Russell's ethics as he presents it in paragraph 20.
12. Analyze Russell's style. Which element of style—word choice, sentence structure, metaphors, etc.—strikes you as dominant, creating the tone of high seriousness and demanding the greatest attention? Explain your answer.

STUDENT ESSAY

THE QUEST FOR WISDOM

KEVIN HITE

Knowledge of the universe bestows awesome power. To understand the secrets of atoms and galaxies is to become like the gods. We can fly our steel chariots to the moon, light the fires of the stars, and perhaps someday create the spark of human life. Whether we use these abilities for the betterment of humanity or for the devastation of our planet is entirely a matter of our own free choice. It is a matter of wisdom.

As scientists search for and uncover more and more knowledge, we must be prepared to balance the new information with wisdom. So far, the world has done a somewhat imperfect job of this balancing act. We have precious little excuse for thinking we can teach our children wisdom when our own record is filled with dumb stunts beyond the wildest fears of even our own ancestors. What is this balance called wisdom? One dictionary defines wisdom as "common sense." Yet, Thoreau asks, "Why level downward to our dullest perception always, and praise that a common sense"? Perhaps wisdom is an uncommon sense, and instead of dull perception, maybe awareness is required.

Wisdom is often used in two senses. First, it is contrasted with ignorance. The wise person is one who knows and therefore is not ignorant. This meaning, however, does not help one distinguish knowledge from wisdom. For example, scientists replace ignorance with knowledge. However, they may use this knowledge unwisely, thereby harming themselves, others, or the environment. In the second sense, wisdom is contrasted with foolishness. The wise person is one who has sound judgment and therefore is not foolish. The fool, as we have seen, may be a scientist with a great deal of knowledge about various matters of fact but lacking the balance and insight that are needed for proper judgment. This meaning points in the right direction, though more detail is required for a better understanding of wisdom.

Scientists employ reason and evidence as means to the discovery of knowledge. The faith of the philosopher, like that of the scientist, is that inquiry is worthwhile. Inquiry is the beginning of wisdom. Just as knowledge unfolds the laws of nature, wisdom directs and integrates a person's actions with these laws. Since one's actions are based on one's thoughts, and one's thoughts are based on one's existence, wisdom is the awareness of how these three fields of life interrelate. This sort of awareness can be compared to an "uncommon sense" of ecology.

To understand wisdom, one should first be aware of existence or the environment. This is everything. It is the big living room which all of us share; it is all around us and extends farther than our limited sight. The environment is our system of interactions. The integration and regulation of any system, whether it be a single cell, a society, or the universe, demands the coexistence and harmonizing of conflicting values and principles. The highly refined human nervous system is an example of such a system. It is characterized by the integration of contrasting values: great diversity on the level of anatomy, order and unity on the level of function. On this most basic level of the environment, whether it be our nervous system or the earth's hydrosphere, there is a quality of maintenance and stability that is often silent. This is the foundation of wisdom and underlies the more obvious levels of thought and action.

Thought, speech, and action, the voluntary modes of our nervous system, can be discriminatively directed toward the expansion and progress of the individual. When these voluntary thoughts and actions maintain the homeostasis of our environment, and natural law is not violated, then we operate in the mode of wisdom. From the perspective of planetary ecology, one may consider how the interactions arising from the rapid expansion of world population and its resulting problems have come about due to lack of wisdom.

In further analysis of wisdom, one may see that wisdom involves knowledge, but knowledge of a special kind. For there is a difference between a person who is wise and a person who is merely knowledgeable. This difference lies in the possession of awareness of the nature of life.

Back to the big living room: we are confronting the industrial dragon that belches rockets from the front end and hydrocarbon gas from the other end. We can discourse one way or another about the spiritual side of wisdom, and our ideas are open to debate. But on the physical side, we see evidence everywhere that our environment is being systematically ravaged. Is this smart ecology? Is this wisdom?

In the *Apology*, Socrates expresses the fundamental conviction of all true philosophers: "The unexamined life," he declares, "is not worth living." Indeed, inquiry is only the beginning. For wisdom should be concerned with the living, intimate, human sort of knowledge that will lead to a life characterized by truth, progress, and harmony with the environment. We can certainly appreciate the words of Socrates only if we, too, engage in the quest for wisdom.

EXERCISES

1. There are twenty-two footnotes to Tuchman's "In Search of History" and twenty-two to her "Inquiry into the Persistence of Unwisdom in Government." To begin to develop a sense of available and useful reference works, select one of Tuchman's essays and for each footnote list *one source* for obtaining the information it contains. There will, of course, be more than one possible answer, but try to be a smart researcher, using the simplest or most readily available sources first. You may have some reference works in your own book collection. Other notes will require your use of the library's reference collection.
2. If you wanted to pursue a study of Camus or read for a paper on censorship, your first step should be to collect a bibliography, a list of sources on your subject. For a large project, your next step should be to skim available sources to see what each contains and is useful for. Some scholars prepare bibliographies for us, sometimes grouping works by broad categories, other times annotating (briefly commenting on) each source. Both types of bibliographies can be useful.

   a. Prepare an extensive bibliography for one of the following topics, grouping items into logical categories such as articles, books, chapters/sections from reference works; or works by the writer, biographies of the writer, books about the writer, etc.

Albert Camus
Bertrand Russell
existentialism
censorship
World War I
Greek mythology
positivism

b. Prepare a brief annotated bibliography of recent articles on one of the following topics. Make your annotations no more than two or three sentences on each article, focusing on what the article contains, not what it says; that is, on what a researcher would find useful in it.

censorship
the Vietnam War
the Black Muslim movement in America
the domino theory
the "Me" decade

3. If you were Barbara Tuchman about to embark on a history of your family, your hometown, or your college, how would you plan your research? Select one of these topics for your "history" and brainstorm about the research task. List all the sources or types of sources you can think of that might be useful to prepare your history. Remember that many of your sources will not be books in a library but what are called primary sources.

WRITING ASSIGNMENTS

1. Defining terms is essential for both the historian and the philosopher. Defining a controversial or complex concept can become part of philosophical inquiry. In a 500-word essay, offer your definition of one of the following terms:

   wisdom
   liberty
   pornography
   duty
   patriotism

   The student essay in the chapter is your model, but if you choose to write about wisdom, be sure not to copy from the model.

2. In a 500- to 600-word essay, enter into the ongoing debate on one of the issues stated below. If you refer to or quote from Lippmann, Krauthammer, Etzioni, or other writers you have read, give credit informally ("As Walter Lippmann observes in 'The Indispensable Opposition,' . . .") but be sure to give credit. Have a precise thesis and establish the limits and focus of your argument.

   a. The censorship of pornographic materials
   b. The removal from high-school libraries of books offensive to some students and/or parents

c. Mandatory national service (to include service in Peace Corps and Vista programs as well as in the armed forces)
d. The need in America for a "We decade"
e. The appropriateness of moral relativism
f. The dangers of single-issue politics

3. Using the results of your brainstorming exercise (see question 3 on p. 296), do the research necessary and prepare a 1,000-word history of your family, town, or college from as far back as you can go up to the present. Write as a historian, using the third person (even when placing yourself in your family history), as if you were preparing a chapter for a history book.

Mrs. Kennedy and Caroline Say Farewell. (*Bob Gomel/Life Magazine*, © 1963, *Time, Inc.*)

CHAPTER 6

JOURNALISM

INVESTIGATIVE, EDITORIAL, SATIRIC, LITERARY

If history is the story of facts, of things done in the past—unlike fiction, which is the story of things made up—what is journalism? Where does it fit into the picture? If by journalism we mean the relaying of news, whether by television, radio, or print, then journalism is also the story of facts, but of recent facts, of things just done. Few histories are written by eyewitnesses; historians who do write contemporary history are rarely participants in the major events of their time. By contrast, many journalists are witnesses to the events they write about, or arrive shortly after an event begins to unfold, to interview those who were present from the beginning. Journalists are supported by the wire services, sources for corroborating facts, and by film, another reasonably objective witness. Thus, although journalists lose the reflective vantage point of the historian, they gain an immediacy, a closeness to the facts, that acts as a safeguard against distortion. Further, the stance expected by those who read the news is objectivity, a *reporting,* not a retelling and embellishing of events. News reporters, then, stand closer to scientists than to novelists; their task is to get the facts and present them accurately.

If only defining journalism were this simple! We know, however, that the term *journalism* refers to an array of writing purposes and formats (and styles), for the term today must include the weekly news magazines and the nightly television newscasts in addition to the city dailies and community weeklies. Consider, for example, the contents of just one of these journalistic packages—the city daily paper. The daily paper not only reports the day's events locally, nationally, and worldwide; it also analyzes and comments on those events; provides profiles of people who make the news; is our chief guide for shopping, from food to furs; and tells us what movies to see and books to read. A wondrous instrument for daily living, and we have come to expect much from it.

We need to add, then, to our initial discussion of news reporting an analysis of the many types of writing to be found under the umbrella term *journalism*. And we need to observe how the newsmagazines and television news shows vary these types to fit their particular formats. First, there is the standard *news article* that reports an event and answers the traditional questions: who, what, where, when, and (sometimes) why. In the news article, readers expect to find the facts, whatever facts can be known on a given day.

In addition to news articles, we find articles labeled *news analysis*. These articles examine a major event (generally referred to as "hard" news), providing background information and analysis of both causes and consequences. Feature articles also give background and analysis, but this term is usually reserved for "soft" news, for studies of people or places in the news, not for topics of war and peace, congressional action, or the inflation rate. Blaine Harden's "How Not to Aid African Nomads" is an example of a feature article. Another related term, *investigative reporting*, refers to a long-term study of a social problem (e.g., an inner city drug ring) or a political controversy (e.g., the *Washington Post*'s investigation of Watergate). The results of an ongoing investigation may be presented in a series of articles (or TV segments) or in one long feature piece. One could also describe Harden's piece as investigative reporting.

Shorter than a news article, less detailed in their analysis than a feature, and more clearly argumentative are the *editorials* and *op-ed* (opposite-the-editorials) articles—usually the columns of syndicated journalists, sometimes the work of free-lance writers. The unsigned editorials, written by members of the paper's editorial board, are brief, persuasive pieces on issues from the current governor's race to no-turn-on-red driving regulations. The op-ed articles are somewhat longer and more developed essays, sometimes on current political controversies, sometimes on social and moral issues. Some of the best essay writing today can be found on the op-ed page; these columnists are generalists, philosophers and social commentators who both analyze and reflect on our times. You have read two of Ellen Goodman's columns in earlier chapters and a *Time* essay by Charles Krauthammer. The columnists are further represented in this chapter by Joseph Kraft. The creations of the paper's cartoonist also appear on the editorial page, for the cartoon is a visual editorial.

Newspapers and newsmagazines alike divide their content into sections, with the most important world and national news up front. Newspapers give front-page coverage to important local news, too; but big-city papers may also have a separate local news section. A newspaper's editorials are usually at the end of the first section; by contrast, the few "editorials" run by a newsmagazine (e.g., the *Time* essay or Meg Greenfield's commentary in *Newsweek*) are found at the back. The television news shows also occasionally include a commentary segment. The other three subjects given considerable space in newspapers are life-style topics, business, and sports. The newsmagazines also have business and life-style sections, but they give little coverage to sports, compared to newspapers. The same can be said of network newscasts; local television shows include a sports segment, but only really big or significant sports events will be covered by the national news shows.

This chapter begins with a lengthy excerpt from sociologist Herbert Gans's study of newsmagazines and the TV nightly news. By extension, his analysis applies to newspapers as well. Indeed Gans makes clear that for journalists (and perhaps for readers, too) the standard of excellence is the *New York Times.* (Other editors often make story selections based on whether or not it's in the *Times.*) Throughout his study, Gans speaks of the news *story,* and in the excerpt he explains the guidelines for selecting stories. Reporters are urged to "go out and get the story." This use of the term *story* has had profound effects on the writing of news articles and, as we have seen in previous chapters, on our reading of printed matter.

As Gans explains, news is shaped into a pattern that resembles a fictional narrative, the writing for which the term *story* used to be reserved. Gans observes three similarities between news articles and fiction. First, reporters generally use time sequence or *chronology* as an organizing principle, just as fiction writers and historians do. Second, the news event is presented as a *conflict,* or several intertwined conflicts. Conflicts, within a character, between characters, or between the main character and society, are of course key techniques for the fiction writer. Conflict creates suspense or tension and makes us want to read on. And we read on to find some *resolution* of the conflict, or some "peg" or point to the story, whether stated or implied. Since life's events are not always so neatly structured into conflict/resolution patterns, journalists, anxious to give their articles structure, sometimes resort to speculation about possible conflicts. The State Department issues a statement about the Middle East, the journalist reports. How will Libya respond? How will our friends in the Middle East react? What about our NATO allies? Tune in tomorrow for the exciting sequel! Perhaps an overstatement, but as Roger Rosenblatt points out in the chapter's second article, to the extent that news stories are structured, they may not be accurately reflecting the random events of a seemingly chaotic universe. Certainly we can wonder if the journalist is too close to today's events to see a pattern that might develop over time, a pattern the historian can better assess. Perhaps at times the term *story* applies to news articles in ways journalists do not intend.

The use of the expression *news story* does not seem to have affected readers' expectations of finding "the facts" or "the truth" in news reporting. Although some readers today have become thoroughly cynical and assert that we shouldn't believe anything we read—or hear on the nightly news—most do expect to find an accurate reporting of events and indeed may not be alert to the story structure of news articles and its possible distortion of events. But use of the term *story* seems to have had a subtle effect on readers in that many now refer to all printed works in prose as stories. The result is that students in an American literature course, for example, refer to Puritan diaries, Franklin's *Autobiography*, and Paine's political essay *Common Sense* as "stories," when in fact they will not read a traditional story (fiction) until they reach the short stories of Edgar Allan Poe.

The careless use of *story* to refer to both fiction and many kinds of nonfiction writing is a problem, because we read with greater appreciation and analyze with greater accuracy when we place ourselves in the proper reading context and ask useful questions about the material. Fiction makes up a story; a news article is supposed to report, accurately and objectively, an event that actually took place. We may ask a friend if Poe tells a good story; we would not ask if the *New York Times* tells a good story. Our expectations and demands of fiction writers and journalists are different; we will keep those differences in mind if we use terms accurately, reserving *story* for fiction and labeling appropriately the various kinds of journalistic writing.

To complicate matters further, we have today a new kind of journalistic writing that consciously and purposely blends and unites the traditional forms of fiction and journalism. The label coined to refer to these works (both articles and books) is *literary journalism.* In his anthology *The Literary Journalists,* Norman Sims lists four traits of literary journalism: accuracy, structure, immersion, and voice. The demand that there be facts makes these authors more closely related to journalists than to fiction writers. In her account of a trip to El Salvador, Joan Didion does not make up a country or characters; she wants us to understand what life there is really like. But Didion is also a storyteller; she renders her experience in a vivid, tension-filled drama that rivets our attention. The literary journalists most clearly break with the journalist's tradition of objectivity in their immersion in the subject and presentation of it through a distinct personal voice. Speaking in the first person, revealing feelings and attitudes, the literary journalists frequently write with the fervor of the personal essayist. If this new category helps us be aware of important characteristics in some of today's best nonfiction writing, then the label serves a purpose—so long as we remember that literary journalism still fits into the broader category of nonfiction rather than fiction.

No discussion of journalism is complete without raising the question of bias. For all the emphasis journalists place on accuracy, fairness, and an objective stance, we know that writing cannot but reflect the writer's perceptions, values, and understanding of the subject. The way stories are selected and the conflicts they are perceived to contain—the subject of Gans's study—form a kind of bias basic to journalistic writing. Additionally, specific news sources may have a particular political bias that is revealed in several ways.

In the Autumn 1965 issue of *Journalism Quarterly,* journalism professor John C. Merrill published a study of *Time* magazine's techniques for slanting or subjectivizing news coverage. Merrill found that *Time* consistently presented a negative image of Truman, a positive image of Eisenhower, and a generally neutral image of Kennedy—but more positive after his death than before. *Time* created its slanted portraits by use of six kinds of bias: attribution, adjective, adverb, contextual, photographic, and outright opinion. The first three we can recognize as specific forms of connotative word choice (e.g., The scowling president snapped angrily.) Contextual bias includes story selection and structure—the subject of Gans's article; it is the reporter's specific selection and arrangement of material. Sometimes reporters express opinion by proclaiming, without evidence, that the nation or the world believes or feels a particular way (e.g., A saddened nation weeps today for its assassinated leader). The photographs selected to accompany an article also tell a story; they can show us, for instance, a confident or a clumsy president.

Although some of you may choose a journalism career, many more will take courses in communications and the social sciences to support a variety of degree programs. Thus most of the assignments in this chapter call for the analytic paper so central to academic writing. You can also try travel writing and some primary research. The exercises concentrate on word choice, the building blocks of bias or slant. Your comparative analysis of articles from different sources covering the same event will likely reveal subtle but at times significant differences. This should not be surprising, for the words we select not only report our experience, they shape our understanding of that experience. Words mold a particular reality out of a loose collection of facts, impressions, and thoughts. If journalists have power, it is in part because they work with words, the most powerful tool we have.

Selecting the News: Story Suitability

HERBERT J. GANS

Born in Germany in 1927, Herbert J. Gans became a U.S. citizen in 1945. He was educated at the University of Chicago and the University of Pennsylvania (Ph.D.) and worked in city and regional planning and urban studies before going to Columbia University's sociology department in 1971. He continued his work in urban studies as a consultant to numerous planning agencies and as a research fellow at the Center for Policy Research. He has authored or contributed to many books and articles, including Popular Culture and High Culture *(1974) and* The Urban Villagers (1962; rev. ed. 1982). Deciding What's News *(1979), from which the following excerpt is taken, won the National Association of Educational Broadcasters Book Award in 1980.*

Gans's approach to sociological studies has been to use the fieldwork or participant/observer method; his interest has been to reveal errors in generally held views, to debunk social myths. Thus when writing Deciding What's News, *he spent several months visiting the studios and offices of CBS, NBC,* Newsweek, *and* Time, *watching the journalists at work, talking with them about story decisions, and observing editorial meetings. What myths about journalism need correcting? It seems there are several. First, Gans feels that journalists are really much like most college-educated, upper-middle-class urban Americans and hold typically American social ideas and values. Second, Gans observes that indeed the "rules" of this profession—as in any profession—stem from values; journalists have an ideology even though they may describe themselves as objective and nonideological. And third, because journalists talk mostly to people like themselves—the individuals they write about, their sources, each other—the news they present appears much the same however the world may change. Gans's study is filled with information that helps us understand how the news is selected and shaped, whether for TV nightly news shows or for the weekly newsmagazines. The questions that follow, primarily about content, will guide your study of Gans's key points about story selection.*

1 *The New York Times* announces every day that it contains "All the News That's Fit to Print." The wording is arrogant, but the phrase makes the point that the news consists of suitable stories. To determine story suitability, journalists employ a large number of suitability considerations, all of which are interrelated. These can be divided into three categories: substantive considerations judge story content and the newsworthiness of what sources supply; product considerations evaluate the "goodness" of stories; and competitive considerations test stories for their ability to serve in the continuing rivalry among news organizations to provide the most suitable news.

2 I distinguish among the various suitability considerations to emphasize that story selection involves more than story content. This is not accidental, for if story selectors had to rely solely on substantive considerations, they would need many hundreds, and in ranked order, to be able to choose stories from the mass and variety of available ones. Indeed, many suitability considerations are of the exclusionary type; they exist to help story selectors cope with the oversupply of available

news. They are also relational: on a "slow news day," story selectors may use stories they would ordinarily dismiss, though never happily so.

SUBSTANTIVE CONSIDERATIONS

3 Story suggesters and selectors begin with substantive considerations. Stories are bought and sold on the basis of their content summaries; once they enter the story list, the summaries are condensed further, to four-to-six word labels. In this way, story selectors always remain aware of story content.

4 Substantively, stories can be either "important" or "interesting," the ideal being an important story that is also interesting. All journalists learn to distinguish these qualities in stories, but in and of themselves, the two terms are meaningless. Since an actor or activity can be important to some sectors of America but not to others, or of interest to some while boring to others, importance and interest are not useful considerations until they acquire subjects and objects which indicate to whom and for whom a particular story is important and/or interesting, and by what criteria. When story selectors apply substantive considerations, they do so in terms of subjects and objects, thereby making the considerations operational.

Story Importance

5 Importance judgments are applied to both actors and activities; for domestic news, to be discussed here, the judgments are usually determined by four considerations. Stories become important by satisfying one, and increase in importance with every additional one they satisfy.

6 1. *Rank in governmental and other hierarchies.* The federal government and its activities are always important, but the higher an actor is in the governmental hierarchy, the more his or her activities are of importance. Although this consideration endows the government and its hierarchy with journalistic legitimation and has numerous ideological implications, it exists for very practical reasons. National news media cannot report all stories that affect the nation or the national audience they serve; consequently, they need an exclusionary consideration that automatically limits the number of suitable stories.

7 Of course, journalists could attribute importance to other national hierarchies: those based on power, wealth, or prestige. These are difficult to identify or to agree upon, however. The governmental hierarchy

is visible and nicely rank-ordered, which facilitates journalists in making importance judgments. Equally relevant, it is widely accepted as a symbol of the nation.

8 It goes without saying that the president is most important. In the past, the newsmagazines ran a special subsection informally titled "The President's Week"; and although it has been eliminated, much of the president's week is still reported. One summer, when the president was on vacation and was clearly not minding the ship of state, a top editor decided to break with tradition and omit the customary weekly picture of the chief executive. Although his assistants supported his decision, he later changed his mind.

9 Journalists do not slavishly follow the governmental hierarchy below the presidency; for instance, the Speaker of the House is not important solely by virtue of his being fourth in line of succession. He and other federal officials are judged by the extent to which they affect, change, or oppose the president's policies, or affect the nation or the lives of other Americans. On a slow news day, even a minor official can become newsworthy by proposing a new policy or making a dramatic statement; but story selectors may wait until the last moment before reporting it in the hope that a more important story will suddenly break.

10 Actors outside the governmental hierarchy are harder to evaluate, since journalists have no easy way of determining whether the head of one corporation is more newsworthy than the head of another when both do or say the same thing. This is one reason why nongovernment officials appear in the news less often. Another, perhaps more significant reason is their sheer number: there are so many corporate heads that journalists cannot report on more than a small fraction at best; consequently, they need quickly and easily applied exclusionary judgments.

11 The most efficient criterion is, once more, the governmental hierarchy. Nongovernmental leaders who come into contact, and particularly into conflict, with that hierarchy become important. Moreover, the higher their governmental contact, the greater their importance. When corporate heads attack a presidential policy, they are more likely to appear in the news than when they challenge the administrative regulation of a lowly government agency. All other things being equal, their general visibility and the size of their organizations are also taken into account; leaders of larger or more prestigious organizations outrank those of smaller or less prestigious ones.

12 Although this importance consideration overlaps with the source consideration that encourages the use of authoritative officials, it does

not simply rationalize the choice of sources but functions as a separate component of news judgment. That the two coincide only facilitates and accelerates story selection.

13 2. *Impact on the nation and the national interest.* What affects the nation—its interests and its well-being—is a complex question which can be answered in many ways, but journalists resort to answers that enable them to make fast story-selection judgments.

14 In the case of foreign news, the solution is easy: America is a unit as it deals with other nations, and American citizens or organizations overseas become representatives of that unit when their constitutional rights are threatened. In fact, journalists often follow American foreign policy in selecting foreign news because it supplies a quick and easy importance consideration and because no other equally efficient model is available. This solution also discourages State Department criticism. While journalists do not generally make story choices to minimize government criticism, they gain nothing by unnecessarily provoking official criticism. They know that their audience is not particularly interested in foreign news and would be unlikely to support them if the government chose to attack the news media for harming the national interest.

15 The criteria that can easily be applied to foreign news, however, do not suit the domestic scene, for the nation cannot often be treated as a unit. Nor is there an efficient way to determine whether and in what ways domestic actors and activities express the national interest. (This is an additional reason why the president is thought to represent the nation.) Story selectors assign importance to activities which are carried out by the entire nation, such as voting; and those which are carried out in behalf of the nation, such as space exploration and national anniversaries.

16 Because elections and anniversaries occur only periodically, journalists need more frequent domestic news, which they find in actors and activities that express, represent, or affect the nation's values. They do not have a list of national values, however; nor do they have time to decide which of the values constantly pressed on them by sources are truly national. Instead, story selectors fasten on the laws of the land, which are beyond argument most of the time and can be construed as official national values. But in the process, they add the enduring news values that they assume to be national values as well: ethnocentrism, altruistic democracy, responsible capitalism, small-town pastoralism, individualism, moderatism, the preservation of social order, and the need for national leadership.

17 Hundreds of magazine pages and hours of air time would be needed if story selectors were to report every actor or activity expressing these values. Instead, they apply an exclusionary consideration that is virtually part of the definition of news; national values become important only when they are threatened or violated. The role of journalists is to report, in the words of one top producer, "when things go awry, when institutions are not functioning normally." This definition of news awards importance to a wide variety of natural, social, and moral disorder stories.

18 A finding that institutions are not functioning normally requires standards of institutional normality and abnormality, which can be set either on empirical grounds, value grounds, or both. Political patronage jobs may be awarded frequently enough to be viewed as empirically normal, and they may be evaluated as normal by heads of political organizations but abnormal by political reformers. Story selectors, having neither the time nor inclination to debate standards of normality, rely upon their own expectations about what is, and should be, normal, often mixing the two.[1] These expectations, in turn, involve reality and value judgments that journalists make intuitively, but they are particularly guided by the enduring values which suggest what ought to be normal. Accordingly, patronage remains abnormal, and therefore newsworthy.

19 Many more instances of abnormality occur, however, than can possibly be considered important news. Consequently, story selectors apply a further exclusionary consideration, which regards the rank and power of those acting abnormally. High public officials who engage in abnormal behavior that violates national values are always important news, but lesser Americans who do so must concurrently threaten or engage in conflict or violence. Likewise, high officials make important news when they disagree, but lesser Americans must resort to protest;[2] and the more highly ranked the target of protest or violence, the more important the story becomes. This is why the assassination of a president is the biggest story journalists can conceive, at least in a nation in which revolution is an unlikely prospect.

---

[1]The expectations sometimes include a historical component when journalists assume that the present abnormality was preceded by a past normality. In this process, they stipulate an ideal past, if only to make today's abnormality new and thus news.

[2]Because television has little room for foreign news, and the magazines must cover the entire globe, both news media use an even more limited exclusionary consideration: in all but the most important allied or Communist countries, governmental change is newsworthy only when it involves violent protest.

20 Protest, especially the violent kind, is an easily applied indicator of abnormality, whether the abnormality resides in the protesters or the target of protest. But since considerations are always relational, indicators change in importance depending on the supply of available news. During the late 1960s, when protest stories were plentiful, story selectors often ignored peaceful protests. During the 1970s, when they became scarcer, protest of any kind once more became a prime indicator of importance; sometimes, new issues did not become important until protest erupted. Medical malpractice developed into important national news only after doctors resorted to demonstrations for the first time. When New York City was threatened with default in 1975, a scheduled mass protest by municipal employees persuaded one top editor to put the default story on the cover; but when the demonstration was called off, the cover story was postponed.

21 Although the violation of national values is most newsworthy when it involves national institutions, the number of such institutions is limited. Consequently, journalists apply an inclusionary consideration in which they nationalize various institutions and symbolic complexes. As a result, even the smallest locality can generate important national news. In 1975, the decision by a tiny California county to drop out of state and national welfare programs appeared in several national news media because it represented an initiative against Big Government. That same year, when five children living in the ghetto of a small southern town died because the city had failed to spray the area against mosquitoes, a top producer told the reporter who suggested it that "you don't even have to sell me."

22 3. *Impact on large numbers of people.* The most important story of all is one that affects every American. The assassination or attempted assassination of an American president is such a story because it is thought to touch the entire population. But such news is rare; consequently, journalists assign importance to stories that affect large numbers; and the larger the number, the more important is the story. During the stagflation of the early 1970s, for example, story selectors paid more attention to inflation than to unemployment; at the start of the energy crisis, they gave more play to gasoline shortages and price increases than to other ramifications of the crisis.

23 Lacking data about how many people are affected by an event, journalists make impressionistic judgments. One indicator is their perception of the population, which is derived in part from the people they know best. One newsmagazine often evaluated stories by the extent to which they were thought to affect "our kinds of people," the well-educated

upper middle-class to which journalists belong and which is a major constituency in the magazine readership.

24 A second indicator is the number of people who might eventually be affected. Stories about floods, forest fires, and epidemics become important news, because even if the number of victims is small, the thought that a similar disaster could strike almost anywhere will affect a much larger number of people. A related third indicator assumes a similarity of interests among large sectors of the population. Television producers look for stories relevant to old people, assuming interest on the part of the many older viewers in the audience; thus, a story about a new welfare program for rural old people was deemed important for the urban aged as well.

25 A final indicator applies journalistic values directly. Perceiving America as a unit, journalists believe that people ought to be interested in important news because they should be informed citizens, even if the news does not directly affect them. The national news media continue to report foreign news for this reason alone, even though journalists know that many viewers and readers do not pay close attention to it.

26 4. *Significance for the past and future.* News about the American past is usually important, but it can be dealt with easily by keeping track of anniversaries. The future significance of today's news is more important; but because it is more difficult to assess it, journalists may disagree. When, in 1977, James Schlesinger, then a presidential assistant, testified before a Senate committee about the president's proposal to create a Department of Energy, one network's Washington bureau felt that his testimony "didn't amount to anything"; but the other networks decided that his prediction of future energy shortages was important because they could affect the lives of many people.[3]

27 Prediction is risky, and it is generally eschewed because an incorrect guess impairs the journalists' credibility. Nor do journalists see their role as writers of history; but at the same time, they do not want to be accused later of having ignored events which, in retrospect, ultimately achieved historical significance. This is why they assign importance to record-breaking events and to firsts. Both are easily applied indicators. Firsts are also automatically novel and therefore news almost by definition. The first presidential primary remains important news despite its ambiguous role in, and meaning for, the presidential nomination process.[4]

---

[3]Eric Levin, "How the Networks Decide What Is News," *TV Guide,* 2 July 1977, pp. 4–10, quote at p. 6.

[4]Michael J. Robinson, "The TV Primaries," *Wilson Quarterly* 1 (Spring 1977): 80–83.

Variability in Importance Judgments

28 In the final analysis, importance judgments are made by individuals or small groups; and even if all are journalists, their assessments, particularly in estimating the future significance of a story, will inevitably differ at times. Also, because importance considerations are general but must be applied to specific stories, individual story selectors may arrive at different conclusions as they proceed from the general to the specific.

29 Moreover, inasmuch as story selectors are competing against their peers at another network or magazine, they may assign news higher importance on the basis of product or competitive considerations, although usually these judgments affect the emphasis given a story rather than its inclusion or exclusion. If a news program or magazine has particularly exciting film or still pictures, or an interview with a high official, the story may be given more importance; and its priority will be further increased if the story is an exclusive. Organizational factors also come into play. If an anchorperson argues strongly for the importance of a story, executive producers may not want to disagree. CBS News has, over the years, given more play to space exploration because Walter Cronkite is an enthusiastic space buff.

30 At times, story selectors react simply like the people and the members of nation and society that they always are. In the spring of 1975, for example, *Newsweek* decided to run a cover about Ted Kennedy as a possible presidential candidate, partly because the top editors felt the current list of hopefuls was undramatic and they wanted to add some excitement to the race. But the need for excitement was also journalistic, for little important domestic news that could excite the journalists was available at the time, and they were remembering the good old days of Watergate, which had been an unusually exciting period in every newsroom. . . .

Interesting Stories

31 Important stories are sometimes called necessities, signifying the extent to which their selection is obligatory. Interesting stories are, prototypically, "people stories." A top producer, himself a space buff, bemoaned the end of space stories during the Apollo-Soyuz linkup in 1975 and rejected those on the exploration of Mars then already in the works, because "that's with robots; I want men there."

32 Interesting stories are used for two reasons. First, important news is often "bad" and must be balanced by interesting stories which either

report "good" news or are light. In addition, interesting stories are timeless, so that they can be used when last-minute replacements are needed.

33 If an interesting story evokes the enthusiasm of story selectors, it is assumed that it will also interest the audience. As a result, journalists do not think about the audience when selecting interesting stories any more than when selecting important ones. The choice of interesting stories is usually a group decision; and if anyone thinks that a story is "boring," it is not likely to remain on the list, unless a top producer or editor announces decisively that he likes it. Because the selection is based on shared personal reactions, it is not governed by considerations; rather, story selectors gravitate toward a handful of story types.

34 1. *People stories.* These feature ordinary people acting or being acted upon in unusual situations, and public officials acting in unofficial ways or behaving "like people rather than politicians." Thus, the news media always report on the president when he performs in a familial or private capacity, thereby allowing the public a glimpse at his private persona, even if it is created or made visible for public consumption. For much the same reason, the private activities of the president's family are also regularly newsworthy.[5]

35 2. *Role reversals.* Most people stories are actually what journalists call man-bites-dog stories; they are often humorous features about people who depart from expected roles, such as a college professor who becomes a janitor upon retirement. Role reversals can be serious, too, depicting "hard-core" criminals who go straight or juvenile delinquents who become involved in community development projects. A story about the president's private activities is interesting precisely because politicians are rarely thought to behave "like people."

36 3. *Human-interest stories.* These are people stories in which ordinary people undergo an unusual experience that evokes audience sympathy, pity, or admiration, such as victims of tragic illnesses or people who act heroically in disasters.[6] Story selectors choose

---

[5]In 1975, the same journalists who were uneasy about President Ford's performance in the White House and embarrassed about his physical clumsiness were also enthusiastic about Susan Ford's work as a photographer.

[6]Helen M. Hughes, *News and the Human Interest Story* (Chicago: University of Chicago Press, 1940).

them because they expect the audience to "identify" with a victim or hero; nonetheless, they themselves are often moved.[7]

37 4. *Exposé anecdotes.* These report, and by implication condemn, actors and activities which story selectors dislike, usually because they violate the enduring values. Lowly public officials who behave like callous bureaucrats or invade people's privacy, members of the business community who desecrate wildernesses, and malfunctioning computers are favorite journalistic villains. *Time*'s Americana section, a page of short items in the Nation section, sometimes uses these anecdotes as miniature editorials.

38 5. *Hero stories.* Ordinary people who overcome these villains are ready subjects for interesting stories; so are amateur and professional adventurers who climb a previously unclimbed mountain or set an endurance record, thus showing that human beings can overcome nature without hurting it. Charles Kuralt likes to find harmless eccentrics who flout social pressure toward conformity and offer testimony to the continued resilience of individualism.

39 6. *"Gee-whiz" stories.* This is a residual category that includes all stories which evoke surprise. Although role reversals and hero stories are sometimes labeled gee-whiz stories, these stories are, typically, reports of unusual fads, cults, and distinctive vocations or avocations. One producer defined the genre as "an extraordinary, unusual, but not terribly important item; a story we had one night of a hen laying green eggs."

40 The selection of interesting stories is free of the tensions and costs that surround important stories. Story selectors cannot be criticized for having missed an interesting one; in fact, because access to them is often a matter of luck, the reporter who is in the right place at the right time can scoop the competition. Reporters who are adept at unearthing interesting stories are therefore held in high regard, especially if they can dig up the humorous ones with which top producers like to end their news programs. These are highly prized, and occasionally executive producers are so excited about them that they will personally edit them, leaving

[7]Like local journalists, national story selectors choose human-interest stories from time to time in order to invite financial help to the victim from the audience. Although objectivity and detachment are violated in the process, journalists are always pleased when audience contributions roll in, because they feel they are helping and because the response indicates that the audience is paying attention to the news.

the important news stories to subordinates for more than an hour. The morale in the newsroom always rises when a good, humorous "closer" is available, and even more so when the journalists discover later that the competing network had to end its show with a serious feature.

PRODUCT CONSIDERATIONS

41 Suitable news is, among other things, a product, and journalists want to come up with good stories. "Good" is a simple word, but the "goodness" of a story is judged in several ways. Stories must fit the particular requirements of each news medium, as well as the format within which the news is presented. (*The New York Times* also contains all the news that fits the print medium.) In addition, journalists aim for several kinds of novelty and quality, and they want to provide a balanced product. These product considerations are applied to every story, but the less important a story, the more product considerations enter into news judgment. They also allow story selectors to choose between stories of equal substantive merit; and because these considerations have built-in devices to attract the audience, journalists are thus relieved from having to think about it.

QUESTIONS FOR ANALYSIS AND DISCUSSION

1. On the basis of what three considerations are stories selected? Why does Gans emphasize that there are three considerations?
2. When story content is being evaluated, what two broad judgments will be considered? What is the ideal story content?
3. Story importance is determined by judging actors and activities according to what four considerations? What does Gans stress about story selection regardless of the consideration used? What prevailing reality of a daily paper or weekly newsmagazine echoes throughout his analysis?
4. How do journalists seem to define the national interest? What values do they assume to be national ones? Do you think they are right? Do you have any evidence?
5. In what kind of news story do considerations of rank, national interest, and national values come together?
6. When journalists consider an event's impact on large numbers of people, what kinds of people are frequently used as a "weather vane"?
7. What kinds of events are usually considered newsworthy, almost by definition?

8. Why are interesting stories selected? Who decides what is interesting?
9. State briefly, in your own words, the six types of interesting stories. Which news medium is especially anxious to find light, interesting stories?
10. What does Gans mean by product consideration?
11. What, in your view, is the most important information about story selection in Gans's study? Why?
12. What specifics of format in Gans's work aid in his presentation?
13. How would you characterize Gans's style of writing? Given Gans's style, what seems to be his primary purpose in writing? What kind of reader does he assume he has?

Journalism and the Larger Truth

ROGER ROSENBLATT

A native New Yorker who graduated from New York University, Roger Rosenblatt (b. 1940) went on to obtain both an M.A. and a Ph.D. from Harvard University and to study, as a Fulbright scholar, at Trinity College, Dublin. For six years he taught English and American literature at Harvard and was Harvard's youngest-ever house master. Moving to Washington, Rosenblatt became education director of the National Endowment for the Humanities, then literary editor of the New Republic, *then a columnist for the* Washington Post. *He returned to New York to join* Time *magazine, first as an associate editor and then, in December 1980, as a senior writer. Rosenblatt's career gives witness to the close connections between the worlds of academia, politics, and journalism, an observation Gans makes in his study* Deciding What's News.

During his academic years, Rosenblatt wrote the study Black Fiction *(1974), and during his journalistic years, the award-winning* Children at War *(1983). Many of his essays, ranging from politics to social events to art, have won awards. In the* Time *essay reprinted here, published July 2, 1984, Rosenblatt takes a firm stand on the issue of a journalist's altering facts to create a more effective story or to demonstrate a larger truth.*

1 When journalists hear journalists claim a "larger truth," they really ought to go for their pistols. *The New Yorker*'s Alastair Reid[1] said the

[1]*New Yorker* staff writer who defended his revelation at a seminar that his nonfiction articles about Spain contain fictional embellishments.—Ed.

holy words last week: "A reporter might take liberties with the factual circumstances to make the larger truth clear." O large, large truth. Apparently Mr. Reid believes that imposing a truth is the same as arriving at one. Illogically, he also seems to think that truths may be disclosed through lies. But his error is more fundamental still in assuming that large truth is the province of journalism in the first place. The business of journalism is to present facts accurately—Mr. Reid notwithstanding. Those seeking something larger are advised to look elsewhere.

2 For one thing, journalism rarely sees the larger truth of a story because reporters are usually chasing quite small elements of information. A story, like a fern, only reveals its final shocking shape in stages. Journalism also reduces most of the stories it deals with to political considerations. Matters are defined in terms of where power lies, who opposes whom or what, where the special interests are. As a result, the larger truth of a story is often missed or ignored. By its nature, political thought limits speculative thought. Political realities themselves cannot be grasped by an exclusively political way of looking at things.

3 Then, too, journalism necessarily deals with discontinuities. One has never heard of the Falkland Islands.[2] Suddenly the Falklands are the center of the universe; one knows all there is to know about "kelpers" and Port Stanley; sheep jokes abound. In the end, as at the beginning, no one really knows anything about the Falkland Islands other than the war that gave it momentary celebrity—nothing about the people in the aftermath of the war, their concerns, isolation, or their true relationship to Argentina and Britain. Discontinuities are valuable because they point up the world's variety as well as the special force of its isolated parts. But to rely on them for truth is to lose one's grip on what is continuous and whole.

4 Journalism looks to where the ball is, and not where it is not. A college basketball coach, trying to improve the performance of one of his backcourt men, asked the player what he did when he practiced on his own. "Dribble and shoot," came the reply. The coach then asked the player to add up the total time he dribbled and shot during a scrimmage game, how many minutes he had hold of the ball. "Three minutes in all," came the reply. "That means," said the coach, "that you practice what you do in three minutes out of 40 in a game." Which means in turn that for every player, roughly 37 out of a possible 40 minutes are played away from the ball.

---

[2]Islands near Argentina fought over by Britain and Argentina in 1982. They remain a part of the United Kingdom.—Ed.

5 Journalism tends to focus on the poor when the poor make news, usually dramatic news like a tenement fire or a march on Washington. But the poor are poor all the time. It is not journalism's ordinary business to deal with the unstartling normalities of life. Reporters need a *story,* something shapely and elegant. Poverty is disorderly, anticlimactic and endless. If one wants truth about the poor, one must look where the ball is not.

6 Similarly, journalism inevitably imposes forms of order on both the facts in a story and on the arrangement of stories itself. The structures of magazines and newspapers impose one kind of order; radio and television another, usually sequential. But every form journalism takes is designed to draw the public's attention to what the editors deem most important in a day's or week's events. This naturally violates the larger truth of a chaotic universe. Oddly, the public often contributes its own hierarchical arrangements by dismissing editors' discriminations and dwelling on the story about the puppy on page 45 instead of the bank collapse on Page One. The "truth" of a day's events is tugged at from all sides.

7 Finally, journalism often misses the truth by unconsciously eroding one's sympathy with life. A seasoned correspondent in Evelyn Waugh's maliciously funny novel *Scoop* lectures a green reporter. "You know," he says, "you've got a lot to learn about journalism. Look at it this way. News is what a chap who doesn't care much about anything wants to read." The matter is not a laughing one. A superabundance of news has the benumbing effect of mob rule on the senses. Every problem in the world begins to look unreachable, unimprovable. What could one lone person possibly accomplish against a constant and violent storm of events that on any day include a rebellion of Sikhs, a tornado in Wisconsin, parents pleading for a healthy heart for their child? Sensibilities, overwhelmed, eventually grow cold; and therein monsters lie. Nobody wants to be part of a civilization that reads the news and does not care about it. Certainly no journalist wants that.

8 If one asks, then, where the larger truth is to be sought, the answer is where it has always been: in history, poetry, art, nature, education, conversation; in the tunnels of one's own mind. People may have come to expect too much of journalism. Not of journalism at its worst; when one is confronted with lies, cruelty and tastelessness, it is hardly too much to expect better. But that is not a serious problem because lies, cruelty and tastelessness are the freaks of the trade, not the pillars. The trouble is that people have also come to expect too much of journalism

at its best, because they have invested too much power in it, and in so doing have neglected or forfeited other sources of power in their lives. Journalists appear to give answers, but essentially they ask a question: What shall we make of this? A culture that would rely on the news for truth could not answer that question because it already would have lost the qualities of mind that make the news worth knowing.

9 If people cannot rely on the news for facts, however, then journalism has no reason for being. Alastair Reid may have forgotten that the principal reason journalists exist in society is that people have a need to be informed of and comprehend the details of experience. "The right to know and the right to be are one," wrote Wallace Stevens[3] in a poem about Ulysses. The need is basic, biological. In that sense, everyone is a journalist, seeking the knowledge of the times in order to grasp the character of the world, to survive in the world, perhaps to move it. Archimedes[4] said he could move the world as long as he had a long enough lever. He pointed out, too, that he needed a ground to stand on.

QUESTIONS FOR ANALYSIS AND DISCUSSION

1. Alastair Reid's assertion that journalists may alter the facts in a report to get at a larger truth is Rosenblatt's occasion for writing. What three objections does Rosenblatt have to journalists taking liberties with the facts?
2. One of his three objections becomes Rosenblatt's thesis. What is his thesis?
3. Rosenblatt offers six reasons in support of his thesis. Restate, in your own words, each of the six reasons, spotting each new reason by finding the reading clues announcing a transition to another point.
4. Rosenblatt's essay has a clear, simple, classic organization. Analyze the essay's structure, noting the function of each paragraph.
5. Rosenblatt devotes two paragraphs to his fourth reason, developing it in part by using a comparison or analogy with basketball. Explain the point of the analogy.
6. If journalism cannot give us the truth, where, then, should we look for the truth? Why? Do you agree with Rosenblatt?
7. Judging from the distinction he draws between the facts of journalism and the truth of literature, for example, what does Rosenblatt seem to mean by "truth"?
8. If journalists impose (or find) an order in their "stories," isn't that the process

[3]An American poet (1879–1955).—Ed.

[4]A Greek mathematician (287?–212 B.C.) known for his mechanical inventions.—Ed.

of seeing a larger meaning in events? Isn't that to find some truth to these events that will eventually become a part of history, or a source for literature and art? Why, according to Rosenblatt, is the journalist's order not going to give us the truth?

9. Do you think Rosenblatt is accurate when he observes that we now expect too much of journalism? Does journalism have too much power? In what ways does it have power?

The Sports Craze

JOSEPH KRAFT

A graduate of Columbia University, Joseph Kraft (1924–1986) began his career as an editorial writer at the Washington Post *in 1951. He also worked for the* New York Times *and* Harper's, *and then became a syndicated columnist in 1965. Like many in his field, Kraft's experiences as a journalist led to several books:* The Struggle for Algeria *(1961),* Profiles in Power: A Washington Insight *(1966), and* The Chinese Difference *(1973).*

Kraft almost always kept his columns focused on current political issues, but his penetrating analysis revealed his breadth of knowledge and perspective. "The Sports Craze," syndicated on September 15, 1985, reveals Kraft's knowledge of social history and his broad perspective on our times. Pay attention to the column's structure and the relationship between details and general statements.

1 Pete Rose, Joe Montana, John McEnroe and Larry Bird surpass Ruth, Tilden, Dempsey and Bobby Jones in technique, speed, power, crowd appeal and cash flow. The '80s have replaced the '20s as the Golden Age of American sport.

2 But the sports craze common to the two eras denotes a deeper harmony. The '80s resemble the '20s in many other ways, and a comparison helps to define the spirit of our times.

3 A waning of common purpose set the stage in each case. Just before the turn of the century the sense of national destiny quickened. The war with Spain was one sign, and the building of the Panama Canal another. Theodore Roosevelt's Progressivism and Woodrow Wilson's New Freedom both featured what Herbert Croly called the "promise of American Life." World War I, and Wilson's call to make the world "safe for democracy," enhanced the sense of mission.

4 With victory came disillusionment. A provincial backlash fastened Prohibition on the nation and fostered a vogue for religious quackery. Sophisticates in the great cities turned away from larger national goals to the comforts of individual success and good living.

5 Financial speculation was one, highly approved, form of self-assertion. Making whoopee at speak-easies and country clubs was another. Gangsters enjoyed a vogue as stars who gave thrills. The great figures of sport combined personal achievement with a certain insouciance.[1] They joked and jested. They were innocent heroes who had fun. It figured that they would be wiped out by the Great Depression.

6 A deeper and more enduring national cohesion was born of World War II and the Cold War that followed. The challenge joined Americans together, first to defeat foreign enemies and then in a new burst of creative activity.

7 International institutions were established to maintain the strength of the Atlantic nations and to minimize the danger of world depression. An American brand of welfare state—mixing public and private power and cooperation between business and labor—was invented. The Republicans under Eisenhower consolidated the innovations of Roosevelt and Truman. Science and industry flourished. Great strides were made in eliminating racial discrimination. American painting, poetry, dance and drama made New York the artistic capital of the world. It was possible, in the supposedly stultifying conformity of the '50s, to be a critic without breaking windows.

8 The assassination of Kennedy brought to power a series of leaders who never could have been elected president on their own. They strained to please, and their excesses accelerated the breakdown of national purpose that was, in any case, losing its cohesive force.

9 Me-ism, the emancipation of self, marked the later '60s and '70s. Political controversy became invidious—for the rights of minorities, or feminists or gays—and thus took on a quality poisonous to national fellowship. Many people simply dropped out or withdrew. The great symbols of that process were the hippie communes and the drug culture. Marijuana was a turn-off.

10 Inflation confirmed the impression that national authority was inept. It gave license to greed and made heroes of the successful wheeler-dealers in securities, commodities and real estate. A new army of *arrivistes*[2] arose and found its legitimization in the Reagan presidency. It

[1]Carefree indifference.—Ed.

[2]Those who have recently acquired wealth and status.—Ed.

has attacked as "the problem" the governmental institutions that used to be the focus of common aspiration. Its message is "get rich." In that sense, we are back in the 1920s today.

11 Vietnam provides one break in the analogy. To be sure, the war worked to heap new contempt on established national institutions. It swelled the ranks of the alienated and gave a cause to those who wanted to protest anyhow. But many Americans who fought in the war prevailed over harsh circumstance by individual toughness. Out of that experience there was born the cult of the body which has, in turn, yielded the craze for sports.

12 A furious, obsessive quality distinguishes the great athletes of today. Their skills are superhuman, and their endurance is phenomenal. They have been pointing toward championship competition since their earliest years. They practice all the time. They pit themselves against the odds and will do anything to win. They play dirty. They talk and act tough. Some pump themselves up with drugs—not marijuana, which is for dropouts, but cocaine, which imparts a high. They go for world records and very big bucks.

13 As performers, they are truly awesome. For they personify individualism in a materialist age. They validate the proposition that by steely resolve and digging deep into reserves of nerve, energy and will, a person can change the structure of things. A champion can take on the world and win.

14 No one can be clear as to how the current chapter will end. Forecasting another great crash is like predicting a return to flagpole-sitting. But the élan[3] of the present is based on illusion. Confidence cannot change everything, nor can buoyant leadership. Generals matter, but armies make the big difference. So if Americans are lucky, we will rediscover a sense of social purpose before we are again threatened by a supreme danger.

QUESTIONS FOR ANALYSIS AND DISCUSSION

1. Kraft expects his readers to recognize the people mentioned in paragraph 1. Check appropriate reference sources for any you don't know. (The first four are 1980s athletes; the second four are 1920s athletes.)
2. Kraft's comparison makes many points in a brief space and thus warrants careful analysis. Make a list of each point of comparison between the 1920s and the 1980s.

[3]Dash, ardor, enthusiasm.—Ed.

3. Kraft asserts in paragraph 8 that Kennedy's death resulted in a series of presidents who would not otherwise have been elected. List the presidents Kraft has in mind. Do you think most will go down in history as average or worse—much like the presidents between Wilson and FDR?
4. How do the sports heroes of the 1980s differ from those of the 1920s? What traits characterize today's sports figures? How do they "personify individualism in a materialist age"?
5. Kraft observes that in the 1920s there was a "provincial backlash" that resulted in Prohibition and a "vogue for religious quackery." What 1980s parallels in moral and religious activities might Kraft have mentioned?
6. What specific elements of the 60s and 70s contributed to a breakdown of national cohesion?
7. After reading the first two paragraphs, how would you state Kraft's thesis? When his final paragraph is added, what do we understand to be the larger purpose of his comparison? What does Kraft want to see in America?
8. Using Kraft's piece as representative, what can you conclude about the role of evidence in an editorial column? How much evidence can readers expect? How will it be developed?
9. Do you agree with Kraft that we have a problem? If so, do you have any suggestions for strengthening national cohesion? If you do not agree with Kraft, how would you refute his views?

PAT OLIPHANT

Born "down under" and now a United States citizen, Pat Oliphant (b. 1936) began his journalism career as a copyboy for the Adelaide News *in Australia and became its cartoonist when he was twenty. His career in America began in 1964 at the* Denver Post *and continued later at the old* Washington Star. *Now, still living in the Washington, D.C., area, Oliphant has his cartoons syndicated in over 500 newspapers in this country, and in Paris, Bangkok, and Tokyo as well, and they have been compiled into eight books. Oliphant's cartoons have won numerous awards, including a Pulitzer Prize, and he was chosen best cartoonist of 1984 by readers of the* Washington Journalism Review.

Recognizing that his cartoons do distress readers at times, especially when he satirizes their religion, Oliphant still believes strongly in hard-hitting political satire. He is concerned that conservative times may discourage papers from risking controversy; he also worries that young people are not learning enough history and literature to have a reading context for cartoons that turn on allusions and metaphors.

When analyzing political cartoons, you should answer these questions:

1. *What is the work's central idea?*
2. *What visual details establish its point?*
3. *What makes the cartoon funny?*

"CLASS WILL CONFINE ITS STYLE OF CLASSROOM PRAYER TO THE NORMAL, PROPER, ACCEPTED, CONSERVATIVE, ALL-AMERICAN, RIGHT-WING CHRISTIAN VARIETY!"

Made in Heaven

LEIGH MONTVILLE

A graduate of the University of Connecticut with a major in English, Leigh Montville (b. 1943) says that he always wanted to be a sports journalist. He began his journalism career by working on his college paper—as sports editor in his sophomore and junior years, and as editor-in-chief in his senior year. His first paying job was as a sports reporter for the New Haven Journal-Courier; *he then moved to the Boston* Globe, *where he has been working and writing for—in his words—"a thousand years" (actually eighteen). Montville has a dual existence at the* Globe, *writing a sports column during the week and a general column of social commentary in the magazine section of the Sunday* Globe. *Winner of a Headliner award for his columns, Montville is represented here by one of his Sunday columns, first printed May 15, 1983.*

Montville sees as the key difference between his weekday and Sunday columns the role of facts. His sports reporting and analysis must be connected to the facts and contain facts; the danger is in having too many facts and then not seeing what they mean. By contrast, his Sunday columns, he says, come out of his head; that is, his observations can be imaginatively shaped, presented one week as a character speaking, another in the format of a warning label, another (as in "Made in Heaven") as a fable.

1 And in the spring of one year in the sixth millennium of Creation, the Lord became bored. He watched the long line of human beings heading toward the world and knew He had to make some changes. Just to stay awake.

2 He had an idea.

3 "Put a tiny alligator on the left breast of every human who leaves the shop for the next week," He bellowed to his angels. "And make it snappy."

4 "An alligator?" the angels asked.

5 "An alligator," the Lord said. "Now."

6 The angels hurried to work. A change like this hadn't happened in a long time, not since the Lord requested redheads and peroxide blondes. An alligator . . . an alligator. One of the angels drew a stencil and the others began the work.

7 "Do you think He wants the alligator above or below the nipple?" one angel asked.

8 "We'll try a few spots," a second angel replied. "We'll see what works best."

9 The final choice was slightly above the left nipple. Thousands, then millions of people were sent to the world with the little alligators upon their breasts. The angels watched with horror. The Lord watched with renewed interest. He found that He was pleased.

10 "Look at that, will you?" He said. "Man seems to like having a little alligator above his left breast. Look how proud he is. He parades around with confidence he never had before."

11 Sure enough, race and creed and ethnic origin made no difference. The people who wore the alligator were the most confident on the

planet. They admired each other's alligators. They pitied the poor folk who did not have alligators.

12 "Let us try this," the Lord said. "Let us keep making alligators, but on Tuesdays and Thursdays, perhaps, let's produce people with a little polo player on the left breast."

13 "A polo player, Lord?" the angels asked.

14 "Just do what I ask," the Lord said.

15 The appearance of people with polo players above their left breasts seemed to be as exciting as the appearance of the people with alligators. The Lord laughed as He watched everyone admiring everyone else. He wanted to see more.

16 "Let us make people with little penguins above their left breasts," He told the angels. "Let us make some people with a fox in that spot. A tiger. A hand making a signal with the index finger and thumb. Every now and then, too, make some people with the word 'Rugger' across the right biceps."

17 The new diversity soon dominated the world. Virtually everyone under age 58 bore an insignia or name above the left breast. Humankind viewed these changes as blessings supplied by a Benevolent Being.

18 "You are a genius, Lord," the angels said.

19 "I have only begun," the Lord replied.

20 He turned his attention now to the right buttock. He thought and thought, searching for the right expression. He decided upon names.

21 "Names, Lord?" the angels asked.

22 "Take these down," the Lord said in a flash of inspiration. "Calvin Klein. Gloria Vanderbilt. Sasson. Sergio Valenti. Lee. And . . . let me think . . . yes, Jordache."

23 The names on the right buttock were at least as successful as the animals above the left breast. Some names were printed. Some were written in script. People looked each other over, fore and aft, and cooed at the different markings.

24 "Love your alligator," one of them would say to a complete stranger. "And love your Sergio Valenti, too."

25 "Wonderful, Lord," the angels said. "Man has not been so interested in his surroundings for a long time."

26 "Take out your pads," the Lord said. "There is more work to do."

27 He now turned his attention to feet. He ordered some feet to be made with three stripes down the sides. He ordered other feet made with two stripes. With stars. He ordered feet made with little green tabs

with the word "Bass" or "Dexter" written on the tabs. He ordered feet made with metal plates on the side that read "Candie's."

28 "Feet may be the ultimate," the Lord said. "I have a hunch we haven't seen anything, compared to what will happen with feet."

29 He was right again, of course. The designs on the feet were the best of all. People boasted about their feet. People admired each other's feet. To walk down the street with an animal on the left breast, a name on the right buttock, and swirls on the feet was to be as close to heaven as possible.

30 "I am pleased," the Lord said as he sat upon a cloud and watched the activity. "I am very, very pleased."

31 The angels were pleased because He was pleased. They stood in a line and awaited orders. There was nary a waver when the Lord decreed that some people should now be made with little plugs in their ears that played Top 40 music all day long.

32 Everyone simply went to work.

QUESTIONS FOR ANALYSIS AND DISCUSSION

1. At what point in your reading did you realize that this is a humorous piece? What, exactly, is Montville making fun of?
2. What are the chief characteristics of the parable format?
3. Why do parables often teach better than lectures?
4. What details in the story contribute to its humor?
5. Montville mentions the brand names of one kind of shirt, six kinds of jeans, and three kinds of shoes. How many of the other brands can you name from their logos or designs? What would the effect of the parable be if we were unfamiliar with these brands?
6. What seem to be the reasons why people get pleasure from wearing designer-labeled clothes? What needs do these clothes help satisfy?
7. Do you like to buy clothes with recognizable logos or brand names on them? Why or why not? Do you think people who buy designer-labeled clothes have been suckered by advertising? Influenced by peer groups? Moved by a desire for quality clothes?

How Not To Aid African Nomads

BLAINE HARDEN

Blaine Harden's current position as the Washington Post's *foreign correspondent stationed in Nairobi, Kenya, covering sub-Saharan Africa, has taken him a long way from home. Born in Washington State in 1952, he graduated from Gonzaga University in Spokane and then traveled east to obtain an M.A. in newspaper journalism from Syracuse University. After a year with the* Trenton *(New Jersey)* Times, *Harden started working for the* Washington Post *as a general assignment reporter, sometimes doing daily reporting, other times working on Sunday magazine features. A brief stint at the* Washingtonian *magazine led to a return to the* Post, *coverage of the Ethiopian famine in 1984, and a decision to become the* Post's *man in Kenya.*

Although "foreign correspondent" would be the appropriate label for Harden in his current position, he describes himself as a "feature writer." His bent toward feature writing is apparent in the following piece, printed in the Post *on April 5, 1986. Appearing in the world news section, "How Not to Aid African Nomads" is nonetheless a feature article, not the reporting of a single, specific event. After reading the article and thinking about the characteristics of a feature story, read Harden's reflections on the problems of audience and purpose he faced in writing the article.*

1 LAKE TURKANA, Kenya—In this jade-green sea in the moonlike desert of northwestern Kenya, the water boils with 12,000 crocodiles. Windstorms blast across the lake like artillery shells, swamping boats and drowning fishermen. Marauding tribesmen from the north routinely sweep down to steal cattle and burn villages. Near the lake's edge, where migratory Siberian shore birds diffidently tiptoe in the sand, skeletons of man's earliest ancestors have been unearthed. Every 30 years or so, parts of the lake disappear, desiccated in the equatorial sun.

2 It is here, in one of the more hallucinatory corners of the earth, that well-meaning, big-spending foreign donors have come to monumental grief trying to improve the lives of the Turkana people, a seminomadic tribe of cattle-, goat- and camel-herders chronically vulnerable to starvation.

3 The Turkana are a small tribe, numbering about 220,000 people. But their hard-scrabble existence and susceptibility to famine are typical

of the more than 20 million pastoral people spread across the semidesert heart of Africa south of the Sahara. When drought hits Africa, the pastoral people are usually the first to suffer and die.

4 As the continent recovers from its worst drought this century, padding margins of survival for pastoral people has become one of the overriding goals of foreign donors and African governments. In recent years, however, most "innovative" high-technology plans to help nomads have failed. Many have created more problems than they have solved—splitting up families, turning nomads into beggars, triggering environmental damage.

5 The Turkana district is the site of several spectacular, damaging failures. But after 20 years of learning by fouling up, it is also a center for a revised development approach that attempts to understand the limits of this dusty, unforgiving land and the traditions of people whose lives are centered around livestock.

6 The expensive lessons learned here have parallels across Africa, and those cumulative failures are forcing donors and African leaders to rethink the wisdom of imposing outside solutions on the problems of nomads.

7 "When it comes to pastoralists, where the sociocultural factors are so subtle and so alien to big-city people, in Washington, in Niamey [Niger], in Paris, then the odds are that the results of foreign development will not be good," said Robert J. Berg, an Africa specialist and senior fellow of Washington's private Overseas Development Council.

8 After participating last month in a closed-door conference in Nairobi attended by major international donors and senior ministers from nearly every drought-affected country in Africa, Berg said there has been a dramatic change in what these people see as the solution for drought in Africa. He said there is finally a consensus among policy makers that the survival of pastoral people must depend on the survival of their livestock, not on high-tech development projects.

9 Like Lake Turkana itself, which is a vast body of water encircled by denuded lava hills that look like shark fins, there is a nether-world quality to the many moldering monuments here to good intentions.

10 Consider the frozen fish plant. It was built to catapult the Turkana out of a centuries-old cycle of drought, destitution and famine and into a commercial venture that would rely on a renewable, environmentally neutral resource—fish.

11 A widespread fear among donor nations in the 1960s and 1970s

was that pastoral people and their herds were ruining their fragile lands by overgrazing. Fish, it was thought, would stop this scourge.

12 The government of Norway, where commercial fishing is a mainstay of the economy, spent $2 million on the "ice-making, freezing and cold-storage plant." It is a handsome, modernistic building with the understated, prosperous look of a suburban bank. Although surrounded by tin-roof shacks and desert, it would not look out of place on Wisconsin Avenue in Chevy Chase.[1]

13 The Norwegians, who divert about 1 percent of their gross national product to help the Third World, also built a road that connected the fish plant south to Kenya's road system and Nairobi. That cost $20 million.

14 The idea was for the Turkana Fishermen's Cooperative Society to sell lake fish—Nile perch and tilapia—in Kenya's cities. In the mid-1970s, when the frozen-fish scheme was hatched by visiting Norwegian consultants, local fishermen were netting record catches of these fish in a nearby cove of Lake Turkana known as Ferguson's Gulf.

15 By the time the plant was completed in 1980, however, it was clear that the fish plant was an ill-conceived idea.

16 For starters, to chill the fish from 100 degrees, the normal daytime temperature, to below freezing would have taken more electricity than was available in Turkana district.

17 "No one could have afforded to buy the fish that that plant would have produced," said Arne Dalfelt, senior program officer in Kenya for Norad, the Norwegian aid agency.

18 The frozen fish plant operated for a couple of days before the electricity was turned off, and it was converted into Africa's most handsome dried-fish warehouse.

19 Then, as it does every 30 years or so, part of Lake Turkana disappeared. The part that went away was Ferguson's Gulf, where 80 percent of the lake's fish were caught. The gulf disappeared because the Omo River, which flows out of southern Ethiopia into the north end of Lake Turkana and accounts for 90 percent of the lake's water supply, was running low due to severe drought.

20 According to a Norad report commissioned last year to figure what went wrong here, the Norwegian consultants who recommended building the frozen-fish plant were deceived by a "temporary boom" in the lake's fish catch.

[1]Chevy Chase is an affluent residential area of the District of Columbia. Wisconsin Avenue is a wide street through the area containing a mix of stores and low office buildings.—Ed.

21 "When we see a lake, we think in fairly static terms," said Dalfelt, trying to explain Norwegian thinking. "We see a lake, we assume it will be there for 100 million years."

22 The consultants need only have traveled about 35 miles to the town of Lodwar, where colonial district records show that Ferguson's Gulf also disappeared in 1954. Apparently, no one checked.

23 Many of the 20,000 Turkana whom the Norwegians had brought to the lake shore, given boats and nets and taught how to fish soon were stuck without a renewable, environmentally neutral resource. Destitute and without their livestock—which had died due to overcrowding and disease on the inhospitable banks of the lake—many Turkana turned to food aid.

24 Out in the middle of the gulf, which is now a big mudhole, lies the research vessel Iji, a Norwegian gift to the Kenyan Fisheries Department. The ship, according to the Norad report, "appears to be damaged beyond the possibility of repair."

25 Fishing, however, is only one line on the learning curve of pastoral development in Turkana District in the past 20 years. There also is irrigation.

26 Like fishing, irrigation was seen as a way of taking Turkana away from the hardships of pastoral life and offsetting the destructive effects of the desert's continuous encroachment.

27 The idea seized the U.N. Development Program and the Food and Agriculture Organization in the 1960s, when 30,000 Turkana were receiving famine assistance after one of the district's periodic droughts. Drought comes here one year in four.

28 The U.N. agencies built several irrigation developments near rivers in Turkana district. Into a largely roadless area that previously had supported wandering Turkana herds and a few guinea fowl, they brought water pumps, heavy farm machinery, generators, pesticides, fertilizers and irrigation specialists.

29 The problems began, as one might suspect in an arid region, with the rivers. The rivers are highly erratic. They shift course radically. They break their banks and, for about four months a year, they dry up. The equipment needed to build an irrigation system along such rivers is expensive, and it needs a lot of maintenance. For example, after the rivers flood, irrigation canals clog with sediment and have to be dug out by farmers. In drought years, when the rivers dry up, all crops die.

30 The Norwegians, who began funding the irrigation projects in 1980

when the U.N. programs ran out of money, recently estimated the cost of irrigation and its benefits to Turkana pastoral herders-turned-farmers. Their report, based on a project involving 10,000 people at a place called Katilu, found that $25,000 had been spent on each farmer so that he could earn, in a good year, about $100–about one-fourth of the average per capita income in Kenya.

31 "They make that much only if they are lucky," said Dalfelt. "If they are not lucky, then we have to go in and give them food aid."

32 Richard Hogg, a British social anthropologist who studies the pastoral tribes of northern Kenya, argues that the fish and irrigation fiascos were partly the result of donor and Kenyan government prejudice against the wandering ways of the Turkana.

33 "The donors thought it was their job to get as many people as possible out of the nomadic life," said Hogg, who works for the British relief agency Oxfam. "And, of course, it is attractive to African governments to settle these people into towns rather than have them wandering around across borders."

34 Even the Norwegians, who say they remain committed to being the major donor in Turkana District, are not prepared to spend much more money on fishing or irrigation. Dalfelt said Norad is searching for a way to pull out gracefully from both projects. As the money runs out and the schemes unravel, their effects on the Turkana people have become painfully clear.

35 "They are poverty traps that make it more difficult, rather than easier, for poor people to better themselves," said Hogg, whose conclusions are shared by many development officials.

36 One unintended effect of fishing and irrigation has been to render many Turkana unable to marry. Neither fishermen nor farmers have managed to make enough money in their new professions to buy the livestock traditionally given by a man to the bride's family. With no livestock for the "bride price" (normally about 60 goats), there could be no marriage.

37 In the fishing project, Norad found that only about 25 percent of the women got married. The rest had become "concubines" who had no legal or moral claim on the wealth of the men and whose children were not the responsibility of the father. When the fishing turned bad, some of the mothers turned to prostitution to survive.

38 After all this failure, the evolution of development thinking in Turkana can be summed up by Norwegian aid official Dalfelt in one sentence:

39 "If we could back them up with what is natural for them, it is far more efficient."

40 To that end, donors in the region have accepted, with some important reservations, the view that the best possible use of the region's scarce natural grasses and water can be made by limited numbers of roving herds.

41 One current development program, administered by Oxfam with food from the U.N. World Food Program, buys goats from herdsmen and gives them to destitute Turkana in relief camps. Some of the reborn herders are failed fishermen and farmers. Each family gets 70 goats, enough to begin a herd, along with food for a year and some pots, pans and clothes.

42 Norad has trimmed the irrigation projects, getting rid of tractors that could not be repaired and corrupt cooperative societies that drained away the farmers' limited profits. Now, Dalfelt said, "each man grows his own thing. Whatever he grows is his. They have all the responsibility and keep their own money."

43 Donors want to buttress what the Turkana know how to do with protection against what they cannot control—periodic drought. Hogg said the region needs effective early warning for drought and a way of marketing livestock so that prices do not collapse before each famine.

44 "You can increase the margins for survival, but you can't remake their lives," Hogg said.

45 But what is realistic to a relief and development agency like Oxfam still seems a bit too defeatist to donors like the Norwegians.

46 "There must be more to development than just sustaining life," said Dalfelt. "We are still experimenting in Turkana. We are looking into industrial production of 120,000 head of cattle. And there is still a lot of fish out there in the lake. Maybe we should think about fish cakes."

Comments on HOW NOT TO AID AFRICAN NOMADS

BLAINE HARDEN

For this piece on development foul-ups at Turkana, the idea was to find the most interesting way possible to pull readers through the problems the rich world has had in trying to help Africa's nomadic people. The frozen fish plant in the desert seemed a good way of galvanizing reader attention. Lake Turkana is one of the more unearthly places I have seen. I thought a strong sense of place at the beginning of the story would entice readers to hang on through a rather long newspaper feature.

The issues presented in this piece are among the most important in African development. Should rich nations continue to try to turn nomads into something that they are not, fishermen or farmers? Or should donors forsake "civilizing" these people, and use their money only to build safety nets that will keep nomads from starving in times of drought? While important, these issues can also be terrifically dull for American readers. I wanted this piece to be both important and readable.

QUESTIONS FOR ANALYSIS AND DISCUSSION

1. What is the effect of the article's opening two paragraphs? Why is the area described as "hallucinatory"?
2. What, specifically, is the problem being reported in this article?
3. What "solutions" have not worked? What solution are policy makers agreeing on now?
4. State the specific problems that doomed the fish factory on Lake Turkana. Why were the Norwegians unable to anticipate the lake's drying up? Why do we make these kinds of errors all too frequently?
5. Why did the irrigation solution fail?
6. What prejudice may have spurred the decision to try fishing and irrigation to help the Turkana? What attitude underlies the Norwegian desire to make the Turkana fishermen or farmers?
7. What attitude is held by those such as Oxfam who want to supply the herdsmen with goats?
8. Where do you stand on this issue? Why? Has reading this feature article helped to clarify your thinking?
9. Analyze Harden's organization. How does this article differ from news reporting?
10. Although Harden ends by representing the differing views of two donors and withholding his own, what do you think his attitude toward the problem is? How does Harden use organization, word choice, and humorous understatement to convey his attitude?
11. In his comments, Harden says he wanted his article to be both important and readable (Gans would say interesting). How successful has he been in achieving these dual goals of news stories?

Africa: Portrait of a Continent

DAVID LAMB

David Lamb (b. 1940), a Boston native with a degree in journalism from the University of Maine, went west in 1965 looking for a job. In Lamb's words: "My car broke down in Reno; I limped into Las Vegas on a bus, with $20 in my wallet, and hit paydirt: the city editor at the Las Vegas Review-Journal *gave me a reporting job for $90 a week. I've had fun at journalism every day since." In 1970 he joined the* Los Angeles Times, *and from 1976 to 1980 he was the paper's bureau chief in Nairobi. He returned to the United States to take a Nieman Fellowship at Harvard for a year; but by 1982 he was off again, this time to become the* Los Angeles Times's *bureau chief in Cairo. He left Cairo in 1985 and is now in Los Angeles on the paper's national staff. He has been nominated for a Pulitzer six times. Lamb's latest book,* The Arabs: Journeys Beyond the Mirage, *published in 1987, has received favorable reviews.*

During his four years in Nairobi, Lamb traveled through forty-eight African countries and kept numerous journals as background for The Africans, *published in 1983, from which the following excerpt is taken. Alan Cowell, in his* New York Times *review, said that the book was "essential reading for an understanding of modern-day Africa."*

Lamb represents a growing number of journalists, especially those who cover campaigns or become foreign correspondents, who turn their experiences into book-length studies. Although Lamb shows the influence of literary journalism in his use of personal experiences, his writing is more reserved than Joan Didion's, for example. The Africans *reflects the stance of a contemporary historian or sociologist rather than the intense personal reportage of the literary journalist. Lamb clearly feels that a concerned West's first step toward aiding Africa must be the eliminating of ignorance. His comments on writing, on Africa, and on the book's reception follow the excerpt.*

1 Carlos Miranda, former guerrilla fighter and one-time prisoner of war, sat with his friends in the barren little café, idling away the Saturday afternoon over a bottle of Portuguese wine and a few memories. There really wasn't much else to do, anyway. Cacheu, in Guinea-Bissau, is a small quiet town and the day was hot. So the men sat at their rickety wooden table, just talking quietly or doing nothing at all, expending

little energy except that needed to brush away the flies. The walls of the bar were bare save for a faded photograph of the president, Luis de Almeida Cabral,[1] and the stock of refreshments had dwindled to a dust-covered jug of rum, a case of Coca-Cola and an odd assortment of white wines, served lukewarm because the refrigerator, like the electricity in Caçheu, had long since broken down. The near-sighted bartender was propped like a broom against the refrigerator, squinting and sweating, and when a bottle slipped from his hands and shattered at his feet, he kicked the glass under the counter without a word and wiped his damp hands across his T-shirt. His family—a wife and seven young children—was sprawled out on the concrete floor nearby, fast asleep.

2 "Francisco broke another bottle," Miranda said. "No wonder there's nothing left to drink." Francisco had indeed been dropping too many precious bottles of Coke lately, and his carelessness had become a source of much annoyance.

3 Outside the bar, along the one sandy road that leads away, to Bissau, once the capital of Portuguese Guinea and since 1974 the capital of the independent West African state of Guinea-Bissau, the town was very still. Dogs lay panting in the shade of drooping palms; a solitary woman sat in the square with a dozen turnips spread out in the dirt before her. The ancient rusted cannon atop the fort at the edge of town pointed toward the Cacheu River estuary; downstream, a hundred yards from the fort, three abandoned patrol boats swayed to and fro in the lazy currents. Lingering there between the fort and the boats were three centuries of history, a history that spoke of the birth and death of the Portuguese empire in Africa and the dawn of Africa's own troubled independence.

4 The stone fort, built in 1647, had been the symbol of Portugal's might when its colonial rule stretched from Africa to South America to Asia. And the Soviet-made patrol boats, left to rot and sink in the muddy waters of the river, were the discarded tools of the longest and militarily most successful liberation war ever waged in black Africa against colonial authority.

5 Carlos Miranda had been a soldier, and later a prisoner of the Portuguese, in that war, which lasted from 1961 to 1974. His guerrilla movement, with significant help from the Soviet Union and Cuba, had fielded a 10,000-man army and eventually forced the 35,000

[1]Cabral was overthrown in November 1980 by his prime minister and accused, among other crimes, of murder and torture. He was later allowed to take up exile residence in Cape Verde.

Portuguese and African government troops to abandon the countryside and withdraw into fortified urban areas. Their victory directly influenced the coup d'état that brought down the Lisbon dictatorship on April 25, 1974.

6 "You ask what the difference between colonialism and independence means to me," the thirty-six-year-old Miranda said, filling my glass with wine. "Well, I will tell you. The difference is great. Now I go to bed at night and I sleep comfortably. I do not worry about the secret police. And I do not tip my hat to the *Tuga* [Portuguese].

7 "Now I speak to a white man without fear. Before, white and black did not talk. But now at this moment I have the pleasure of sitting with you, a white, and I speak to you like a man. That is all we fought for, the right to respect. We did not hate the Portuguese people, only the Portuguese government. Even if you were Portuguese, I would still be happy to sit with you, because now we are equals."

8 It was, I thought, an eloquent response. Miranda—a customs clerk with nine children and a salary of $50 a month—had not been a leader in the liberation war, only one of the foot soldiers. But it was for people like him that the war had been fought, and independence had given him a priceless reward: self-respect. For Guinea-Bissau as a whole, though, things had not gone particularly well since the first unfurling of the country's yellow and green flag with a black star on a red field. Only one person in twenty could read, life expectancy at birth was only thirty-five years, and 45 percent of the children died before the age of five. Shortages of everything from rice to soap were epidemic, and when a merchant in the capital put four hundred pairs of just imported shoes on display one day during my visit, such a mob showed up that the police had to be called to restore order. The country had a small peanut crop and some animal hides to export and bauxite reserves worth exploiting, but not much else to build an economic foundation on. In all of Guinea-Bissau (population 800,000) there were only 24,000 jobs, 82 percent of them in the public sector.

9 Unlike two other former Portuguese colonies, Mozambique and Angola, Guinea-Bissau had not been a white-settler colony. The Portuguese came only to administer and to save enough money to retire on back home. Within a few weeks of independence, all but 350 of the 2,500 Portuguese in Guinea-Bissau hurried home. Most departed with no sorrows. And what they left as a legacy of three hundred years of colonial rule was pitifully little: fourteen university graduates, an illiteracy rate of 97 percent and only 265 miles of paved roads in an area

twice the size of New Jersey. There was only one modern plant in Guinea-Bissau in 1974–it produced beer for the Portuguese troops–and as a final gesture before leaving, the Portuguese destroyed the national archives.

10 In many ways Guinea-Bissau is a microcosm of a continent where events have conspired against progress, where the future remains a hostage of the past, and the victims are the Carlos Mirandas of Africa. As setback followed setback and each modest step forward was no more effective than running in place, black Africa became uncertain of its own identity and purpose, divided by ideology and self-interests, perplexed by the demands of nationhood–and as dependent militarily and economically on foreign powers as it was during the colonial era. It moves through the 1980s as a continent in crisis, explosive and vulnerable, a continent where the romance of revolution cannot hide the frustration and despair that tears at the fiber of African society.

11 To many outsiders, Africa seems an intimidating and foreboding place. But remember, the changes that have swept Africa in less than a generation–forty-three new countries were born south of the Sahara between 1956 and 1980–have been as traumatic as those endured by any people anywhere in peacetime. Before we move on to examine these changes in detail, let's strip away a few mysteries and put the continent in a contemporary perspective.

12 Africa–its name may have come from the Latin word *aprica* ("sunny") or the Greek word *aphrike* ("without cold")–was once part of Gondwanaland, the hypothetical supercontinent that also included South America, Asia, India, Australia and Antarctica. Africa occupies 20 percent of the earth's land surface, or 11.7 million square miles. Only Asia is larger. Africa is 5,000 miles long, reaching from the God-forsaken deserts of the north to the lush wine country in the south, and 4,600 miles wide. Its coastline measures 18,950 miles–shorter than Europe's because of the absence of inlets and bays–and the equator cuts Africa just about in half. Africa's climate varies wildly, from temperate in the high plateaus, to tropical along the coastal plains to just plain intolerable in the sizzling deserts.

13 The coastal strip around Africa is narrow, and the interior plateaus are characterized by wide belts of tropical rain forest, wooded savannah and grassland plains. In the far north is the Sahara, the world's largest desert. It covers one quarter of the continent, an area as large as the United States mainland. In the far south is the Kalahari Desert, the world's seventh largest. The highest point in Africa is Mount Kilimanjaro

in Tanzania, 19,340 feet tall and snow-capped the year round, but with the exception of Antarctica, Africa is, in proportion to its size, the flattest continent in the world, something like the Great Plains of North America without corn, an endless champaign that flows from country to country, through the cities and back into the dusty look-alike villages, yielding just enough food to provide millions of subsistence farmers with the meagerest of existences.

14 Wandering through those empty spaces, you realize that ten thousand American farmers turned loose on African soil could transform the face—and the future—of the continent as surely as they did their own land. It seems so easy. Yet farming in black Africa is still a hoe-and-sickle enterprise, more primitive than any in the world. For example, there are but 7 tractors for every 25,000 farmed acres (compared to 45 in Asia, 57 in South America and 240 in the United States) and Africa uses only 4 pounds of fertilizer for every acre. (Asia and South America each use about ten times more; the United States, twenty times more.) Just as distressing, each year Africans are working less and less land as the desert advances like a plundering army, taking as its booty the lean hopes of helpless people and leaving in its wake barren wasteland.

15 The Sahara alone is growing at the rate of 250,000 acres a year, and in Northern Africa, once the grassy breadbasket of the Roman Empire, the process known as desertization is actually a visible phenomenon. Only a generation ago the capital of Mauritania (Nouakchott, meaning "the Place of the Winds") was many days' walk from the Sahara. Now it is *in* the Sahara. Vast, dead expanses of shifting, rolling sand dunes stretch as far as the eye can see and beyond. Blowing sand piles up against walls and fences like snowdrifts, and the city streets dead-end at the desert's doorstep a few hundred yards away. No longer able to support their livestock, thousands of Berbers have poured into Nouakchott, buying homes that they use for storage while living under tents in their backyards. A way of life—and the spirit of a people—has changed forever.

16 Scientists point out that desertization is not unique to Africa, for deserts are growing on all six inhabited continents. Some blame nature for climatic changes and drought. Others cite man's abuse of the environment, particularly overgrazing and the destruction of forests that hasten the erosion of topsoil. Still others believe the phenomenon is cyclic because ages-old deserts have always grown and shrunk and shifted at the mercy of nature's many forces. Whatever the reason, the ecological metamorphosis is a frightening one for Africa, where weather satellites have detected a constant cloud of fine, reddish particles blowing

toward India. The particles have been identified as topsoil, and it takes up to a thousand years to replace a layer of topsoil.

17 The irony of Africa's misfortunes is that this is the place where mankind originated—and this was a center of culture and sophistication long before the Europeans arrived. Fossils nearly 3 million years old found by the anthropologists Mary Leakey and her late husband, Louis, have shown that the evolution of man from his apelike ancestors probably took place in East Africa. And American and French scientists working in Ethiopia have discovered simple stone tools 2.5 million years old. The razor-sharp cutters and the fist-sized rock choppers, the oldest tools ever found, were used, they believe, to slice through animal skins and butcher carcasses.

18 As far back as 500 B.C., when the Nok culture flourished in Nigeria, furnaces were being used to smelt iron. The Nigerian state of Benin exchanged ambassadors with Portugal in 1486. At that time Timbuktu in Mali was a major trading center of international fame. The splendors of the Songhai Empire, which stretched from Mali to Kano, Nigeria, in the fifteenth and sixteenth centuries, were compared by early travelers with those of contemporary Europe. "As you enter it, the town appears very great," a Dutch visitor wrote about 1600 of Edo city in Benin. "You go into a great broad street, not paved, which seems to be seven or eight times broader than the Warmoes Street in Amsterdam . . . The houses in this town stand in good order, one close and even with the other, as the houses in Holland stand . . ." Now-priceless bronze busts were being cast in Nigeria's Ife state before Columbus set sail for America. Iron-age Africans started building stone structures in the area we call Zimbabwe as early as A.D. 1100, and sixteenth-century Portuguese maritime traders found that some West African textiles were superior to anything then being made in Europe.

19 Because the history of ancient Africa was passed from generation to generation by the spoken, not written, word, the origins, and sometimes the fate, of the old civilizations remain clouded in mystery. (One exception is Ethiopia, which did have a written language.) It was, though, intra-African warfare and not the arrival of the European that ensured the disintegration of Africa's early civilizations: the Ghana Empire was destroyed in the thirteenth century by Almoravid warriors from Senegal; the Mali Empire began to crumble in 1430 under pressure from the nomadic Tuaregs; the Songhai Empire was broken up in 1591 when its troops were defeated by an invading Moroccan army. With no written language, no way to store and exchange information,

Africa lacked the building blocks a civilization needs; it was defenseless against a new enemy from the north—the white man.

20 The Portuguese, in the fifteenth century, were the first Europeans to undertake systemic voyages of discovery southward along the African coast. Thus began six centuries of contact between African and European in which the African—until recently, when he learned how to turn the white man's feelings of guilt into a gold mine of international aid—always ended up second best. The Portuguese explorers opened the door for the slave traders, who in turn ushered in the missionaries, who were, in their own right, agents of colonialism. Each invader—slave, missionary, colonialist—sought to exploit and convert. Each came to serve himself or his God, not the African. With Europe looking for new markets and materials during the industrial revolution of the nineteenth century, the European powers scrambled for domination in Africa, Balkanizing the continent into colonies with artificial boundaries that ignored traditional ethnic groupings. By 1920 every square inch of Africa except Ethiopia, Liberia and the Union of South Africa was under European rule or protection or was claimed by a European country.

21 The manner in which colonial administrations governed virtually ensured the failure of Africa's transition into independence. Their practice of "divide and rule"—favoring some tribes to the exclusion of others—served to accentuate the ethnic divisiveness that had been pulling Africa in different directions for centuries. Before independence, the colonialist was the common enemy. When he left, the major tribal groups in each country had to confront one another for leadership roles, and on a continent where tribal loyalty usually surpasses any allegiance to the nation, the African's new antagonist became the African.

22 Tribalism is one of the most difficult African concepts to grasp, and one of the most essential in understanding Africa. Publicly, modern African politicians deplore it. Kenya's President Daniel arap Moi (*arap* means "the son of") calls it the "cancer that threatens to eat out the very fabric of our nation." Yet almost every African politician practices it—most African presidents are more tribal chief than national statesman—and it remains perhaps the most potent force in day-to-day African life. It is a factor in wars and power struggles. It often determines who gets jobs, who gets promoted, who gets accepted to a university, because by its very definition tribalism implies sharing among members of the extended family, making sure that your own are looked after first.

23 To give a job to a fellow tribesman is not nepotism, it is an obligation. For a politician or military leader to choose his closest advisers and

his bodyguards from the ranks of his own tribe is not patronage, it is good common sense. It ensures security, continuity, authority.

24 The family tree of William R. Tolbert, Jr., the assassinated Liberian president, provides an illuminating example of how African politicians take care of their own. Tolbert's brother Frank was president pro tempore of the senate; his brother Stephen was minister of finance; his sister Lucia was mayor of Bentol City; his son A.B. was an ambassador at large; his daughter Wilhelmina was the presidential physician; his daughter Christine was deputy minister of education; his niece Tula was the presidential dietician; his three nephews were assistant minister of presidential affairs, agricultural attaché to Rome and vice governor of the National Bank; his four sons-in-law held positions as minister of defense, deputy minister of public works, commissioner for immigration and board member of Air Liberia; one brother-in-law was ambassador to Guinea, another was in the Liberian senate, a third was mayor of Monrovia.

25 In its simplest form, one could compare tribalism to the situation in a city like Boston, where one finds a series of ethnic neighborhoods, with the blacks in Roxbury, the Italians in the North End, the Irish in South Boston, the Jews in the neighboring town of Brookline, the WASPs in the Wellesley suburbs. Each group is protective of its own turf, each shares a cultural affinity and each, in its own way, feels superior to the other. Africa has 2,000 such "neighborhoods," some of which cover thousands of square miles, and each of those tribes has its own language or dialect—usually unintelligible to another tribe that may be located just over the next hill—as well as its own culture, traditions and, in most cases, physical features that make one of its members immediately recognizable to an individual from another tribe.

26 In Lusaka, Zambia, a university student I knew applied for a job and was told to report to the personnel manager. My friend leaned over the receptionist's desk and asked, "What tribe is he?" Told that the manager was a Mashona, my friend, who belonged to another ethnic group, replied, "Then I'll never get the job." He didn't.

27 A live-in cook in Africa earns about $75 a month—a luxury most expatriates can easily afford—and shortly after arriving in Nairobi, I hired a cook from the Kikuyu tribe, a gardener and an *askari* (night watchman) from the Luo tribe. For the next three months our house was in turmoil as they fought and cussed and argued with one another for hours on end. We fired the watchman after he accused us of trying to poison him—he said we were prejudiced against the Luos—and we put

Dishun, the gardener, on indefinite sick leave when he accused the cook of bewitching him with evil spirits. We took Dishun to our British doctor, but the prescribed pills didn't help his stomach cramps. He returned to his village, where the witch doctor, using herbs and chants, quickly cured him. In the meantime we had hired a Kikuyu gardener and *askari*. They struck up an immediate friendship with the Kikuyu cook. Tranquillity returned to our home.

Comments on AFRICA: PORTRAIT OF A CONTINENT

DAVID S. LAMB

Writing a first book is a fearful experience—and a rewarding adventure to look back on. I still remember putting the first piece of paper into my typewriter when I started *The Africans* and wondering, Good Lord, what if I *can't* write a *book*? Slowly, though, the manuscript took form, a tone established itself, a theme developed. I even surprised myself in discovering a few original ideas and thoughts that lay dormant in my brain and needed only to be shaken loose to be transcribed to paper.

I particularly wanted to accomplish two things with *The Africans*. First, I wanted the book to be people-oriented rather than just a dry political and economic tome. Africa is a wonderfully vibrant and exciting place, and to capture the moods and the color of the continent, it was necessary to make the Africans themselves the centerpiece of the serious issues I was writing about. Second, I wanted to write about Africa as a single entity, a continent, not just a group of fifty-one disparate countries. So I looked for the common denominators that both united and separated the peoples of Africa. There were many, from the colonial heritage to the problem of today's failed economies.

My intent was to write a book that was both critical of and compassionate toward Africa. I didn't want to romanticize the continent, nor did I want readers to forget how new the African experience with independence is. After the book was published, I received many letters from Africans saying that I had focused on the continent's strengths and weaknesses in a healthy, constructive manner. But the reaction from African governments was quite different. Almost every one banned *The*

Africans, presumably on the premise that I was too critical and that some issues I raised—tribalism and inadequate leadership among them—were best left unstated.

QUESTIONS FOR ANALYSIS AND DISCUSSION

1. What is the effect of Lamb's beginning the chapter with his café conversation with Miranda?
2. List all the facts you learn about Guinea-Bissau in the next few paragraphs. Did you realize you were absorbing so many details?
3. From what paragraph do you learn that Lamb's subject is broader than Miranda or Guinea-Bissau? What is Lamb's subject? What is his thesis?
4. In paragraphs 12 and 13 Lamb provides many facts about Africa. Which facts did you find most surprising?
5. Explain the term *desertization.* What are the various reasons suggested for this process?
6. What irony does Lamb find in Africa's current unfortunate condition?
7. What major limitation in Africa's early civilization (except in Ethiopia) contributed to the continent's decline and its subjugation by Europeans? What characteristic of African society contributes to African problems today, slowing the process of nationalism?
8. What characteristics of this excerpt reveal Lamb's training as a reporter? What characteristics might mark him as a feature writer, a historian, or a social scientist?
9. In his comments, Lamb mentions that he wanted to accomplish two things in *The Africans.* In this excerpt, has he accomplished them?

Salvador

JOAN DIDION

For a biographical sketch of Didion, *see p. 32.* *Although introduced earlier as a writer of novels and short stories as well as essays, Didion is usually referred to as one of the new or literary journalists. The following excerpt from her short book* Salvador, *based on a two-week trip to El Salvador and published in*

1983, is a good example of both literary journalism and Didion's continual focus on the telling detail. Before reading Didion, you may want to review the characteristics of literary journalism presented in the introduction to this chapter.

1 The three-year-old El Salvador International Airport is glassy and white and splendidly isolated, conceived during the waning of the Molina "National Transformation" as convenient less to the capital (San Salvador is forty miles away, until recently a drive of several hours) than to a central hallucination of the Molina and Romero regimes, the projected beach resorts, the Hyatt, the Pacific Paradise, tennis, golf, waterskiing, condos, *Costa del Sol*; the visionary invention of a tourist industry in yet another republic where the leading natural cause of death is gastrointestinal infection. In the general absence of tourists these hotels have since been abandoned, ghost resorts on the empty Pacific beaches, and to land at this airport built to service them is to plunge directly into a state in which no ground is solid, no depth of field reliable, no perception so definite that it might not dissolve into its reverse.

2 The only logic is that of acquiescence. Immigration is negotiated in a thicket of automatic weapons, but by whose authority the weapons are brandished (Army or National Guard or National Police or Customs Police or Treasury Police or one of a continuing proliferation of other shadowy and overlapping forces) is a blurred point. Eye contact is avoided. Documents are scrutinized upside down. Once clear of the airport, on the new highway that slices through green hills rendered phosphorescent by the cloud cover of the tropical rainy season, one sees mainly underfed cattle and mongrel dogs and armored vehicles, vans and trucks and Cherokee Chiefs fitted with reinforced steel and bullet-proof Plexiglas an inch thick. Such vehicles are a fixed feature of local life, and are popularly associated with disappearance and death. There was the Cherokee Chief seen following the Dutch television crew killed in Chalatenango province in March of 1982. There was the red Toyota three-quarter-ton pickup sighted near the van driven by the four American Catholic workers on the night they were killed in 1980. There were, in the late spring and summer of 1982, the three Toyota panel trucks, one yellow, one blue, and one green, none bearing plates, reported present at each of the mass detentions (a "detention" is another fixed feature of local life, and often precedes a "disappearance") in the Amatepec district of San Salvador. These are the details—the models and colors of armored vehicles, the makes and calibers of weapons, the particular methods of dismemberment and decapitation

used in particular instances—on which the visitor to Salvador learns immediately to concentrate, to the exclusion of past or future concerns, as in a prolonged amnesiac fugue.

3 Terror is the given of the place. Black-and-white police cars cruise in pairs, each with the barrel of a rifle extruding from an open window. Roadblocks materialize at random, soldiers fanning out from trucks and taking positions, fingers always on triggers, safeties clicking on and off. Aim is taken as if to pass the time. Every morning *El Diario de Hoy* and *La Prensa Gráfica* carry cautionary stories. *"Una madre y sus dos hijos fueron asesinados con arma cortante (corvo) por ocho sujetos desconocidos el lunes en la noche"*: A mother and her two sons hacked to death in their beds by eight *desconocidos,* unknown men. The same morning's paper: the unidentified body of a young man, strangled, found on the shoulder of a road. Same morning, different story: the unidentified bodies of three young men, found on another road, their faces partially destroyed by bayonets, one face carved to represent a cross.

4 It is largely from these reports in the newspapers that the United States embassy compiles its body counts, which are transmitted to Washington in a weekly dispatch referred to by embassy people as "the grim-gram." These counts are presented in a kind of tortured code that fails to obscure what is taken for granted in El Salvador, that government forces do most of the killing. In a January 15 1982 memo to Washington, for example, the embassy issued a "guarded" breakdown on its count of 6,909 "reported" political murders between September 16 1980 and September 15 1981. Of these 6,909, according to the memo, 922 were "believed committed by security forces," 952 "believed committed by leftist terrorists," 136 "believed committed by rightist terrorists," and 4,889 "committed by unknown assailants," the famous *desconocidos* favored by those San Salvador newspapers still publishing. (The figures actually add up not to 6,909 but to 6,899, leaving ten in a kind of official limbo.) The memo continued:

> The uncertainty involved here can be seen in the fact that responsiblity cannot be fixed in the majority of cases. We note, however, that it is generally believed in El Salvador that a large number of the unexplained killings are carried out by the security forces, officially or unofficially. The Embassy is aware of dramatic claims that have been made by one interest group or another in which the security forces figure as the primary agents of murder here. El Salvador's tangled web of attack and vengeance, traditional criminal

> violence and political mayhem make this an impossible charge to sustain. In saying this, however, we make no attempt to lighten the responsibility for the deaths of many hundreds, and perhaps thousands, which can be attributed to the security forces. . . .

5 The body count kept by what is generally referred to in San Salvador as "the Human Rights Commission" is higher than the embassy's, and documented periodically by a photographer who goes out looking for bodies. These bodies he photographs are often broken into unnatural positions, and the faces to which the bodies are attached (when they are attached) are equally unnatural, sometimes unrecognizable as human faces, obliterated by acid or beaten to a mash of misplaced ears and teeth or slashed ear to ear and invaded by insects. *"Encontrado en Antiguo Cuscatlán el día 25 de Marzo 1982: camison de dormir celeste,"* the typed caption reads on one photograph: found in Antiguo Cuscatlán March 25 1982 wearing a sky-blue nightshirt. The captions are laconic. Found in Soyapango May 21 1982. Found in Mejicanos June 11 1982. Found at El Playón May 30 1982, white shirt, purple pants, black shoes.

6 The photograph accompanying that last caption shows a body with no eyes, because the vultures got to it before the photographer did. There is a special kind of practical information that the visitor to El Salvador acquires immediately, the way visitors to other places acquire information about the currency rates, the hours for the museums. In El Salvador one learns that vultures go first for the soft tissue, for the eyes, the exposed genitalia, the open mouth. One learns that an open mouth can be used to make a specific point, can be stuffed with something emblematic; stuffed, say, with a penis, or, if the point has to do with land title, stuffed with some of the dirt in question. One learns that hair deteriorates less rapidly than flesh, and that a skull surrounded by a perfect corona of hair is a not uncommon sight in the body dumps.

7 All forensic photographs induce in the viewer a certain protective numbness, but dissociation is more difficult here. In the first place these are not, technically, "forensic" photographs, since the evidence they document will never be presented in a court of law. In the second place the disfigurement is too routine. The locations are too near, the dates too recent. There is the presence of the relatives of the disappeared: the women who sit every day in this cramped office on the grounds of the archdiocese, waiting to look at the spiral-bound photo albums in which the photographs are kept. These albums have plastic covers bearing soft-focus color photographs of young Americans in

dating situations (strolling through autumn foliage on one album, recumbent in a field of daisies on another), and the women, looking for the bodies of their husbands and brothers and sisters and children, pass them from hand to hand without comment or expression.

> One of the more shadowy elements of the violent scene here [is] the death squad. Existence of these groups has long been disputed, but not by many Salvadorans. . . . Who constitutes the death squads is yet another difficult question. We do not believe that these squads exist as permanent formations but rather as ad hoc vigilante groups that coalesce according to perceived need. Membership is also uncertain, but in addition to civilians we believe that both on- and off-duty members of the security forces are participants. This was unofficially confirmed by right-wing spokesman Maj. Roberto D'Aubuisson who stated in an interview in early 1981 that security force members utilize the guise of the death squad when a potentially embarrassing or odious task needs to be performed.
>
> —*From the confidential but later declassified January 15, 1982 memo previously cited, drafted for the State Department by the political section at the embassy in San Salvador.*

8 The dead and pieces of the dead turn up in El Salvador everywhere, every day, as taken for granted as in a nightmare, or a horror movie. Vultures of course suggest the presence of a body. A knot of children on the street suggests the presence of a body. Bodies turn up in the brush of vacant lots, in the garbage thrown down ravines in the richest districts, in public rest rooms, in bus stations. Some are dropped in Lake Ilopango, a few miles east of the city, and wash up near the lakeside cottages and clubs frequented by what remains in San Salvador of the sporting bourgeoisie. Some still turn up at El Playón, the lunar lava field of rotting human flesh visible at one time or another on every television screen in America but characterized in June of 1982 in the *El Salvador News Gazette*, an English-language weekly edited by an American named Mario Rosenthal, as an "uncorroborated story . . . dredged up from the files of leftist propaganda." Others turn up at Puerta del Diablo, above Parque Balboa, a national *Turicentro* described as recently as the April–July 1982 issue of *Aboard TACA*, the magazine provided passengers on the national airline of El Salvador, as "offering excellent subjects for color photography."

9 I drove up to Puerta del Diablo one morning in June of 1982, past the Casa Presidencial and the camouflaged watch towers and heavy

concentrations of troops and arms south of town, on up a narrow road narrowed further by landslides and deep crevices in the roadbed, a drive so insistently premonitory that after a while I began to hope that I would pass Puerta del Diablo without knowing it, just miss it, write it off, turn around and go back. There was however no way of missing it. Puerta del Diablo is a "view site" in an older and distinctly literary tradition, nature as lesson, an immense cleft rock through which half of El Salvador seems framed, a site so romantic and "mystical," so theatrically sacrificial in aspect, that it might be a cosmic parody of nineteenth-century landscape painting. The place presents itself as pathetic fallacy: the sky "broods," the stones "weep," a constant seepage of water weighting the ferns and moss. The foliage is thick and slick with moisture. The only sound is a steady buzz, I believe of cicadas.

10 Body dumps are seen in El Salvador as a kind of visitors' must-do, difficult but worth the detour. "Of course you have seen El Playón," an aide to President Alvaro Magaña said to me one day, and proceeded to discuss the site geologically, as evidence of the country's geothermal resources. He made no mention of the bodies. I was unsure if he was sounding me out or simply found the geothermal aspect of overriding interest. One difference between El Playón and Puerta del Diablo is that most bodies at El Playón appear to have been killed somewhere else, and then dumped; at Puerta del Diablo the executions are believed to occur in place, at the top, and the bodies thrown over. Sometimes reporters will speak of wanting to spend the night at Puerta del Diablo, in order to document the actual execution, but at the time I was in Salvador no one had.

11 The aftermath, the daylight aspect, is well documented. "Nothing fresh today, I hear," an embassy officer said when I mentioned that I had visited Puerta del Diablo. "Were there any on top?" someone else asked. "There were supposed to have been three on top yesterday." The point about whether or not there had been any on top was that usually it was necessary to go down to see bodies. The way down is hard. Slabs of stone, slippery with moss, are set into the vertiginous cliff, and it is down this cliff that one begins the descent to the bodies, or what is left of the bodies, pecked and maggoty masses of flesh, bone, hair. On some days there have been helicopters circling, tracking those making the descent. Other days there have been militia at the top, in the clearing where the road seems to run out, but on the morning I was there the only people on top were a man and a woman and three small children, who played in the wet grass while the woman started and stopped a

Toyota pickup. She appeared to be learning how to drive. She drove forward and then back toward the edge, apparently following the man's signals, over and over again.

12 We did not speak, and it was only later, down the mountain and back in the land of the provisionally living, that it occurred to me that there was a definite question about why a man and a woman might choose a well-known body dump for a driving lesson. This was one of a number of occasions, during the two weeks my husband and I spent in El Salvador, on which I came to understand, in a way I had not understood before, the exact mechanism of terror. . . .

13 The place brings everything into question. One afternoon when I had run out of the Halazone tablets I dropped every night in a pitcher of tap water (a demented *gringa* gesture, I knew even then, in a country where everyone not born there was at least mildly ill, including the nurse at the American embassy), I walked across the street from the Camino Real to the Metrocenter, which is referred to locally as "Central America's Largest Shopping Mall." I found no Halazone at the Metrocenter but became absorbed in making notes about the mall itself, about the Muzak playing "I Left My Heart in San Francisco" and "American Pie" ("*. . . singing this will be the day that I die . . .*") although the record store featured a cassette called *Classics of Paraguay*, about the *pâté de foie gras* for sale in the supermarket, about the guard who did the weapons check on everyone who entered the supermarket, about the young matrons in tight Sergio Valente jeans, trailing maids and babies behind them and buying towels, big beach towels printed with maps of Manhattan that featured Bloomingdale's; about the number of things for sale that seemed to suggest a fashion for "smart drinking," to evoke modish cocktail hours. There were bottles of Stolichnaya vodka packaged with glasses and mixer, there were ice buckets, there were bar carts of every conceivable design, displayed with sample bottles.

14 This was a shopping center that embodied the future for which El Salvador was presumably being saved, and I wrote it down dutifully, this being the kind of "color" I knew how to interpret, the kind of inductive irony, the detail that was supposed to illuminate the story. As I wrote it down I realized that I was no longer much interested in this kind of irony, that this was a story that would not be illuminated by such details, that this was a story that would perhaps not be illuminated at all, that this was perhaps even less a "story" than a true *noche obscura*. As I waited to cross back over the Boulevard de los Heroes to the Camino Real I noticed soldiers herding a young civilian into a van, their guns at the

boy's back, and I walked straight ahead, not wanting to see anything at all. . . .

15 That the texture of life in such a situation is essentially untranslatable became clear to me only recently, when I tried to describe to a friend in Los Angeles an incident that occurred some days before I left El Salvador. I had gone with my husband and another American to the San Salvador morgue, which, unlike most morgues in the United States, is easily accessible, through an open door on the ground floor around the back of the court building. We had been too late that morning to see the day's bodies (there is not much emphasis on embalming in El Salvador, or for that matter on identification, and bodies are dispatched fast for disposal), but the man in charge had opened his log to show us the morning's entries, seven bodies, all male, none identified, none believed older than twenty-five. Six had been certified dead by *arma de fuego,* firearms, and the seventh, who had also been shot, of shock. The slab on which the bodies had been received had already been washed down, and water stood on the floor. There were many flies, and an electric fan.

16 The other American with whom my husband and I had gone to the morgue that morning was a newspaper reporter, and since only seven unidentified bodies bearing evidence of *arma de fuego* did not in San Salvador in the summer of 1982 constitute a newspaper story worth pursuing, we left. Outside in the parking lot there were a number of wrecked or impounded cars, many of them shot up, upholstery chewed by bullets, windshield shattered, thick pastes of congealed blood on pearlized hoods, but this was also unremarkable, and it was not until we walked back around the building to the reporter's rented car that each of us began to sense the potentially remarkable.

17 Surrounding the car were three men in uniform, two on the sidewalk and the third, who was very young, sitting on his motorcycle in such a way as to block our leaving. A second motorcycle had been pulled up directly behind the car, and the space in front was occupied. The three had been joking among themselves, but the laughter stopped as we got into the car. The reporter turned the ignition on, and waited. No one moved. The two men on the sidewalk did not meet our eyes. The boy on the motorcycle stared directly, and caressed the G-3 propped between his thighs. The reporter asked in Spanish if one of the motorcycles could be moved so that we could get out. The men on the sidewalk said nothing, but smiled enigmatically. The boy only continued staring, and began twirling the flash suppressor on the barrel of his G-3.

18 This was a kind of impasse. It seemed clear that if we tried to leave and scraped either motorcycle the situation would deteriorate. It also seemed clear that if we did not try to leave the situation would deteriorate. I studied my hands. The reporter gunned the motor, forced the car up onto the curb far enough to provide a minimum space in which to maneuver, and managed to back out clean. Nothing more happened, and what did happen had been a common enough kind of incident in El Salvador, a pointless confrontation with aimless authority, but I have heard of no *solución* that precisely addresses this local vocation for terror.

19 Any situation can turn to terror. The most ordinary errand can go bad. Among Americans in El Salvador there is an endemic apprehension of danger in the apparently benign. I recall being told by a network anchor man that one night in his hotel room (it was at the time of the election, and because the Camino Real was full he had been put up at the Sheraton) he took the mattress off the bed and shoved it against the window. He happened to have with him several bullet-proof vests that he had brought from New York for the camera crew, and before going to the Sheraton lobby he put one on. Managers of American companies in El Salvador (Texas Instruments is still there, and Cargill, and some others) are replaced every several months, and their presence is kept secret. Some companies bury their managers in a number-two or number-three post. American embassy officers are driven in armored and unmarked vans (no eagle, no seal, no CD plates) by Salvadoran drivers and Salvadoran guards, because, I was told, "if someone gets blown away, obviously the State Department would prefer it done by a local security man, then you don't get headlines saying 'American Shoots Salvadoran Citizen.' " These local security men carry automatic weapons on their laps.

20 In such a climate the fact of being in El Salvador comes to seem a sentence of indeterminate length, and the prospect of leaving doubtful. On the night before I was due to leave I did not sleep, lay awake and listened to the music drifting up from a party at the Camino Real pool, heard the band play "Malaguena" at three and at four and again at five A.M., when the party seemed to end and light broke and I could get up. I was picked up to go to the airport that morning by one of the embassy vans, and a few blocks from the hotel I was seized by the conviction that this was not the most direct way to the airport, that this was not an embassy guard sitting in front with the Remington on his lap; that this was someone else. That the van turned out in fact to be the embassy van, detouring into San Benito to pick up an AID official, failed

to relax me: once at the airport I sat without moving and averted my eyes from the soldiers patrolling the empty departure lounges.

21 When the nine A.M. TACA flight to Miami was announced I boarded without looking back, and sat rigid until the plane left the ground. I did not fasten my seat belt. I did not lean back. The plane stopped that morning at Belize, setting down on the runway lined with abandoned pillboxes and rusting camouflaged tanks to pick up what seemed to be every floater on two continents, wildcatters, collectors of information, the fantasts of the hemisphere. Even a team of student missionaries got on at Belize, sallow children from the piney woods of Georgia and Alabama who had been teaching the people of Belize, as the team member who settled down next to me explained, to know Jesus as their personal savior.

22 He was perhaps twenty, with three hundred years of American hill stock in his features, and as soon as the plane left Belize he began filling out a questionnaire on his experience there, laboriously printing out the phrases, *in obedience to God, opportunity to renew commitment, most rewarding part of my experience, most disheartening part.* Somewhere over the Keys I asked him what the most disheartening part of his experience had been. The most disheartening part of his experience, he said, had been seeing people leave the Crusade as empty as they came. The most rewarding part of his experience had been renewing his commitment to bring the Good News of Jesus as personal savior to all these different places. The different places to which he was committed to bring the Good News were New Zealand, Iceland, Finland, Colorado, and El Salvador. This was *la solución* not from Washington or Panama or Mexico but from Belize, and the piney woods of Georgia. This flight from San Salvador to Belize to Miami took place at the end of June 1982. In the week that I am completing this report, at the end of October 1982, the offices in the Hotel Camino Real in San Salvador of the Associated Press, United Press International, United Press International Television News, NBC News, CBS News, and ABC News were raided and searched by members of the El Salvador National Police carrying submachine guns; fifteen leaders of legally recognized political and labor groups opposing the government of El Salvador were disappeared in San Salvador; Deane Hinton said that he was "reasonably certain" that these disappearances had not been conducted under Salvadoran government orders; the Salvadoran Ministry of Defense announced that eight of the fifteen disappeared citizens were in fact in government custody; and the State Department announced that the Reagan administration believed

that it had "turned the corner" in its campaign for political stability in Central America.

QUESTIONS FOR ANALYSIS AND DISCUSSION

1. What general organization shapes the details in this piece? What element of literary journalism is introduced by this organization that is not characteristic of news reporting?
2. What details in the piece establish and remind us that this is nonfiction?
3. Which excursion reported by Didion did you find most moving, most gripping? Why?
4. What irony does Didion find in the Metrocenter supermarket? Why are these details not illuminating, not the *telling* details of her experience? Why does she include them anyway?
5. What irony can be found in the airport's location?
6. What dominant characteristic of life in El Salvador is established through Didion's comments (paragraph 1) about the airport? What is her primary sense of the place that she wants us to grasp?
7. Examine Didion's style: her word choice, sentence structure, sentence length. Consider, for instance, some of her paragraph openings:

   The only logic is that of acquiescence.
   Terror is the given of the place.
   The dead and pieces of the dead turn up in El Salvador everywhere.

   Find other similar sentences. How would you describe this writing? What tone is conveyed through her style?
8. Examine Didion's final paragraph as well. What tone is created? How is that tone achieved?
9. How do style and tone help convey Didion's vision of El Salvador and convey her attitude toward her subject?

STUDENT ESSAY

PHOTO CROPS—SHOWING SEXISM IN PHOTOGRAPHY

BRIAN R. KREUDEL

Suffrage was not granted to women in America until August 26, 1920. Since then, feminists have advanced their cause with considerable effort and have achieved much success, especially in the past decade. Sandra Day O'Connor was appointed to the Supreme Court in 1982. Geraldine Ferraro was a viable candidate for the vice-presidency in 1984. And Sally Ride became a national hero as the first woman on a space shuttle. Yet these gains seem to have had little influence on how we perceive women as individuals. Portrayal of women pictorially in the press remains stereotyped.

Sociologist Dane Archer (University of California at Santa Cruz) conducted a study from 1976 to 1977 on photographic bias of the sexes in magazines and newspapers. In an article in *Psychology Today* ("Face-ism," September 1978), he suggested that photographic stereotyping exists because we have different images of men and women. According to Archer, we "think of women in terms of their bodies and men in terms of their faces." Archer holds that this association is deep-seated in society and, "consciously or not," causes biased representation of women in photographs.

In light of the recent achievements of women, I decided it was pertinent to reevaluate photographic stereotyping. I evaluated recent photographs, using Archer's face-ism index. In each photograph studied, the subject's facial length was measured and the total body length (including the face) was measured. The index of facial representation was then calculated by dividing facial length by total body length. This yields a decimal equivalent of the percentage that the face represents the subject. Each photograph is given a "face" value, a potential measure of photographic bias.

For this reevaluation, I used the same three magazines, *Time, Newsweek,* and *Ms.*, that Archer had used in his study. But whereas Archer had used the *San Francisco Chronicle* and the *Santa Cruz Sentinel,* I used the *Washington Post,* the *Alexandria Journal,* and the *Arlington Journal,* the first representing a "major newspaper," the second and third "small-city papers."

My criteria for choosing samples varied slightly from the ones in Archer's study. Originally, photographs were limited to isolated subjects. I extended this to include samples in which a single subject was obviously the main focus of the photograph, with others in the background. Shadowy examples were excluded. Some photographs had an unmeasurable body length because dark clothing blended with the background. Because of the type of bias under consideration, samples of children were not used. As in Archer's study, photographs from advertisements and news stories were chosen, but shots that intentionally focused on a special part of the body were excluded. Thus the photograph for a coat advertisement would have a dictated "face" value, but the photograph for a shoe ad might not. These guidelines provided samples that would reflect a conscious or unconscious tendency to stereotype.

The results of the reevaluation were virtually identical to those of the original study. The average "face" value for men was nearly 20 percent higher than

Table 1. Face-ism Values by Source

Total Number of Samples: 131			
Female	53	Av. Female Value	.42
Male	78	Av. Male Value	.61
Time Samples: 36			
Female	10	Av. Female Value	.32
Male	26	Av. Male Value	.57
Ms. Samples: 15			
Female	11	Av. Female Value	.27
Male	4	Av. Male Value	.44
Newsweek Samples: 26			
Female	14	Av. Female Value	.48
Male	12	Av. Male Value	.62
Washington Post Samples: 31			
Female	9	Av. Female Value	.53
Male	22	Av. Male Value	.62
Journal Samples: 23			
Female	9	Av. Female Value	.50
Male	14	Av. Male Value	.71

that for women. Not only was my percentage difference the same as Archer's, but the mean values for men and women were only 4 and 3 percent lower than Archer's values, respectively. The results are summarized as a group and by publication in Table 1.

The values from the individual publications replicate findings from Archer's study. Newspapers tend to emphasize faces. They show higher values for both sexes relative to magazines. This discrepancy can be attributed to newspapers' devoting more space to print compared to magazines. Thus, photographs in newspapers are cropped more so than in magazines. The feminist *Ms.* magazine still shows stereotyping, even though it used the greatest number of female photos relative to the magazine's total photos. In my study, the actual percentage difference in "face" values between men and women is still the same as in Archer's study, about 20 percent; but the values from *Ms.* reflect a 10 percent decrease in values for both sexes. Perhaps magazines tailored to women are now showing more of both sexes' bodies.

The photographs fell into two distinct categories. Many showed extensive cropping. Other photographs presented an unposed view of the subject, or "action" shot. Often in such photos (designated "choice" samples) the subject is

Table 2. Face-ism Values in Uncropped Photos

Choice Samples: 51				
	Female	27	Av. Female Value	.32
	Male	24	Av. Male Value	.42

standing behind a desk or podium, yet a full representation of the subject is shown. Since these samples were not cropped, they were analyzed as a special category. The results are slightly different from the overall values, as illustrated in Table 2.

Cursory examination of these choice values shows little evidence of stereotyping. The women's average face value is only 10 percent lower than the men's. The proximity of values could be expected: these photos are uncropped. Most of these samples show men and women at full length. We might infer, then, that cropping is important in creating photographic bias. If this choice category represents a control category, then cropping creates the disparity of values that results in stereotyping. In cropping a photograph, someone, a photographer or an editor, makes that conscious or unconscious choice of stereotyping the sexes.

EXERCISES

I. Becoming Alert to Word Choice

A writer's choice of words is critical in the shaping of attitude. The best way to become aware of the effect of a writer's choice of words is to become alert to alternatives.

A. Levels of Diction

Label each of the following sentences as formal, technical, or informal and then rewrite each so that it illustrates a different level of diction than the one originally used.

1. Fourscore and seven years ago our fathers brought forth on this continent a new nation.
2. Today's athletes pit themselves against the odds and will do anything to win.
3. Investigators have looked for paw or limb preferences in animals as evidence of brain lateralization, and they have found that many species do show such preferences.
4. If you have kids, then you have all kinds of breakfast cereals in the house – and on the dining room chairs, too.
5. Farewell, my lovely, until we meet on the morrow.

B. Connotation

One of the best ways to be aware of the emotional impact of a writer's choice of connotative language is to consider what words could have been used instead.

1. For each of the following words or phrases, list at least two synonyms that have more negative connotations than the given word.
   a. child
   b. persistent
   c. willowy
   d. a large group
   e. tiff
   f. (politically) progressive
2. For each of the following words, list at least two synonyms that have more positive connotations than the given word.
   a. fat
   b. notorious
   c. drunk
   d. politician
   e. mediocre
   f. old (person)
3. Although many words have connotations to which we all respond automatically, some words affect us positively or negatively depending on the context in which they are used. First, for each of the following words, label its usual connotation as positive or negative. Then, for each word with a positive connotation, write a sentence in which the word would convey a more negative connotation. For each word with a negative connotation, write a sentence in which the word would convey a more positive connotation.
   a. natural
   b. old
   c. pig
   d. free
   e. chemical
   f. lazy

II. Controlling Attitude Through Details

Writing fables or parables to make a point about human character or morality can be fun. Try writing a fable or parable to make some point about advertising or what motivates humans to purchase particular products, or what motivates students to select particular colleges or careers. (You might think, for example, about the many different car models available and about the types—or stereotypes—of people drawn to each model. And surely the array of sports equipment, even running shoes alone, can spark some clever, fun-poking tales.)

Here are some guidelines to help you along:

1. Keep your story short, no more than two or three pages.
2. Make it a short story, not an essay, with characters and dialogue and a sequence of events.
3. Remember that "characters" do not have to be human.
4. Make it concrete, filled with specific details.
5. Avoid any direct statement of your story's point.

WRITING ASSIGNMENTS

1. To test Gans's analysis of news story structure, select from a daily newspaper one front-page article, one article from the life-style or society section, and one sports article, and analyze them. To what extent does each use a narrative structure containing conflict and resolution? Look at each article's organization or structuring of the event, presentation of participants, use of "color" to create interest. Write a comparative analysis; that is, analyze each of the articles but also examine their similarities and differences. (Instead of selecting three pieces from a newspaper, you may select three articles from a newsmagazine, one from the international or national news section, two from other sections.)
2. Much feature writing today is about people. Select a feature article about a person from *People* magazine, *Sports Illustrated,* or the *National Enquirer* and consider whether or not you think the article goes beyond the bounds of propriety and/or useful news reporting. How many facts are included? How much of the article is thoughtful analysis and opinion? How much is idle speculation or detail irrelevant to the person's public life? Support your judgment about the article with a detailed analysis.
3. Select three articles from newspapers and/or newsmagazines on a current political figure who is "handling" a current specific problem. Examine the articles to see if they focus primarily on the moral/political issues connected with the problem, or primarily on the politician's "handling" of the problem: his/her internal conflicts, conflicts with other politicians, and/or conflicts with the public. That is, are we encouraged to *learn* about the problem (as in Harden's article, p. 328), or are we encouraged to *watch* newsworthy people acting (or not acting)? Analyze the nature of the conflicts in the articles and evaluate each article's success in reporting on the issues.

4. Choose two newspaper or newsmagazine articles that differ in their discussion of the same event. Analyze differences in both content and presentation (connotative word choice, total context of the article, outright opinion, use of photographs or charts), and then consider why the two accounts differ. What differences in political bias might have led to the different handling of the event? (You might find it easiest to search for contrasting articles in sources known to have differing political biases. The *Nation* and *National Review* are examples.) Organize your contrast by points of difference, not by the two articles (to avoid summary only) and write for an audience not necessarily familiar with the articles.
5. Drawing from your study of this chapter, especially the introduction and the articles by Gans and Rosenblatt, write an essay on the topic that it is naive or foolish to seek the truth in journalism. Decide how you feel about this topic and make your position clear in your essay's thesis. You may draw on ideas and examples from your own reading of newspapers or newsmagazines, but make sure to acknowledge your sources by a clear attribution statement (e.g., "According to Herbert Gans in *Deciding What's News,* news stories are shaped into a conflict-resolution pattern similar to fiction"). Think of yourself as a journalism instructor preparing a lecture for a beginning course in journalism. Thus you will need to illustrate your views and keep tone reserved and analytic, not wildly attacking or defensive.
6. Travel writing that includes both details of prices and means of transportation as well as the writer's subjective responses to places and experiences can frequently be classified as literary journalism. If you have recently traveled and the experience left an impression on you, try your hand at a travel essay. Remember that details must be accurate (call the hotel for prices, check the map you used, etc.) but that you also want to re-create the atmosphere of the place and incorporate *telling* details of the trip. You will find examples of travel writing in magazines such as *Travel and Leisure* and *Gourmet,* and in the Sunday editions of most city newspapers.

Ben Shahn. Scott's Run, West Virginia. 1937. *Tempera on cardboard, 22¼" by 27⅞". Collection of the Whitney Museum of American Art, New York.*

CHAPTER 7

WRITINGS FROM THE SOCIAL SCIENCES AND ECONOMICS

Like historians and journalists, social scientists are interested in obtaining, organizing, and analyzing facts. If we think of historians as gathering and ordering evidence of past events and journalists as seeking and reporting the facts of current events, then we can usefully think of social scientists working in the "middle distance." For when social scientists study current behavior of people in groups, it is not with the same immediacy as the journalists. The journalist reports a single event or related cluster of events; the sociologist or economist seeks patterns or trends in the study of many facts, even if those facts are the demographics of this year's college applicants or last month's employment figures.

If in one sense social scientists fit between historians and journalists—in the kinds of facts they study—in another sense they fit between scholars in the humanities and those in the sciences. The psychologist, the sociologist, the anthropologist, the economist, when writing to other specialists in the field, will adhere to agreed-upon conventions for format, documentation, and style of writing. Social scientists seek the objectivity and logical rigor in their experiments or data collecting and analyzing that one finds in the sciences, and they convey that desire in their use of scientific writing: the voice of a disengaged, objective speaker, a review of previous research, detailed description of methodology, control for bias, careful and qualified conclusions. Thus one of the most damaging charges that can be made about a sociological study, for example, is the charge that there is a fundamental bias in the way data were collected or analyzed. In spite of their agreed-upon subject matter for study and a methodology for conducting research, the social scientists are not exactly like scientists because their subjects for study are elusive in their complexity and variety and because values and beliefs about what *should be* are forever bombarding the desired objectivity of the research scientist.

The elusiveness of scientific objectivity in these "middle distance" disciplines is both their frustration and their fascination. Many readers of social science research are annoyed by the dehumanizing jargon we associate with the worst writing in these fields. The jargon seems, unfortunately, to be produced by a desire for objectivity. But what readers need is confidence that the researcher has employed a rigorous objectivity and logic in his or her data collecting and analyzing. In their recognition of the deficiencies of previous studies and in their careful control for bias in their procedures for obtaining evidence, the authors of "Playing Dumb" demonstrate the values of a scientific approach to studying human behavior. Rubinstein's detailed review of research on the effects of television on children is fascinating if we want information, but frustrating if we want an answer to the problem. On the other hand, Neil Postman, writing to a general audience, offers the fascinating thesis that television has destroyed childhood, and in the process makes sociologists cringe at his lack of evidence to demonstrate that television is the single—or even the primary—cause of such dramatic social change. (Some sociologists might further disagree that childhood has in fact been lost—or that it has been significantly altered for a majority of children.)

Another "middle distance" characteristic of the social sciences lies in the variety of approaches within each discipline. In the sciences, a field emerges when the group working in one area of study achieves a paradigm, agreed-upon research methods and theories that will guide research in the area. The textbooks and lab exercises demonstrate the field's shared models for research, and students must learn them to be accepted into the field, whether it be botany or astrophysics. Much less agreement exists in the social sciences, however, as can be seen in texts and teaching methods. An introductory psychology text will present several distinct models for explaining and studying human behavior: probably the behavioral, the Freudian or psychoanalytic, and the Gestalt. Similarly, there are several incompatible and competing economic theories, as presented by Galbraith and illustrated in Murray's and Thurow's work excerpted in this chapter. Psychologists and economists do not have minor disputes over issues under investigation; they have major theoretical differences that affect the way they see and seek to solve problems.

Less fundamental, perhaps, but still important are the many research methods available to the social scientist. For to some extent, the way in which evidence is gathered and organized will affect the facts we obtain and our understanding of them. In the chapter's first selection, you will see that the sociologists used the questionnaire/interview process for obtaining data. Other possibilities include analyzing data gathered by government agencies, the Census Bureau or IRS, for example; setting up controlled experiments, such as observing the behavior of groups of children who have watched different types of television shows; and the field work or participant/observer method used by Herbert Gans in his study *Deciding What's News* (see Chapter 6). Which research techniques a student becomes skilled in will depend, to some degree, on the theoretical viewpoints of the professors he or she studies under.

Just as historians and scientists write both scholarly works and works addressed to nonspecialists, so do experts in the social sciences. In this chapter, as in others in the text, both scholarly and popular articles are presented. The differences in format and style to meet the needs and interests of differing audiences are nowhere better illustrated than in the two versions of "Playing Dumb" and in Michael Hughes's helpful analysis of those articles' differences. Differences of approach and purpose in addition to style can be seen in Rubinstein's and Postman's discussions of television viewing by children. Galbraith offers a brief but useful introduction to several key economic theories affecting social policy; Murray and Thurow continue the debate in their books and in Thurow's review of Murray's book.

Since economics and the social sciences are fragmented by opposing schools of thought, much student writing in introductory courses will call for summary, explication of competing theories, and application of various theories to specific problems. The book review, illustrated by Thurow and the student essay, is a popular assignment because it requires a blending of accurate reading and evaluation of both theory and evidence. Of course the reporting of results of your research will also be required. Chapter exercises, similar to those in Chapter 5, will acquaint you with reference works and procedures; assignments include the various writing tasks just discussed.

Playing Dumb: A Form of Impression Management with Undesirable Side Effects

WALTER R. GOVE, MICHAEL HUGHES, AND MICHAEL R. GEERKEN

Professor of sociology at Vanderbilt University, Walter R. Gove (b. 1938) is the senior member of the threesome who collaborated on "Playing Dumb." As director of graduate studies in Vanderbilt's Department of Sociology and Anthropology, he has directed a dozen Ph.D. dissertations, including those of Michael Hughes and Michael R. Geerken. Gove serves on the editorial board of several academic journals, including Social Science Research *and* Journal of Family Issues. *His list of published books, articles, and reviews, and of papers presented at conferences, runs to many pages. He edited* Labeling Deviant Behavior: Evaluating a Perspective *(2nd ed. 1980) and* Deviance and Mental Illness *(1982). With Michael Geerken, Gove wrote* At Home and at Work: The Family's Allocation of Labor *(1983). Gove and Michael Hughes have published* Household Crowding: Social and Structural Determinants of Its Effects *(1983) and have in progress* The Psychological and Behavioral Consequences of Living Alone.

Michael Hughes (b. 1944) completed his doctorate in sociology at Vanderbilt in 1979 and is associate professor of sociology at Virginia Polytechnic Institute and State University. Hughes has published articles in academic journals related to his field and concentrates his research efforts on the sociology of mental health.

Michael R. Geerken (b. 1949) was a research associate at Vanderbilt and an instructor at Tulane University before entering the criminal justice field in New Orleans. He is currently Orleans Parish criminal sheriff and continues as an adjunct lecturer at Tulane. In addition to the book coauthored with Gove, Geerken has published several professional articles on drug use, criminal deterrence, and crime rates.

The following article presents interesting data that challenge current assumptions about those who play dumb and the effects of doing so. The article, published in 1980 in Social Psychology Quarterly, *can in addition be examined as a typical academic paper in the social sciences. It is especially useful to compare it with the popular version published the following year in* Psychology Today.

INTRODUCTION

1 Approximately thirty years ago Komarovsky (1946) and Wallin (1950) published two studies showing that some female college students reported they had played dumb on dates. As Dean *et al.* (1975) have shown, these studies are widely cited as demonstrating a general tendency for women, in a variety of situations, to act less intelligent than they consider themselves to be, and that this is evidence of the pervasive and detrimental effect on women of their lower status in modern society. Given the fact that there are no comparative data for men and that the samples were small (the total combined n = 316), it is clear that the premise that cultural contradictions in sex-role expectations cause women to play dumb more frequently than men rests on a very tenuous empirical basis. The present paper will suggest that playing dumb is a form of impression management that in only very specific circumstances is linked to sex-role behavior. Furthermore, we will suggest that when persons feel strongly constrained to play dumb, such acts are related to alienation and poor mental health.

REVIEW AND IMPLICATIONS OF THE LITERATURE

Sex and Playing Dumb

2 Komarovsky (1946) studied 153 female students enrolled in sociology courses in 1942 and 1943 at an eastern college which provided a strong career orientation for its students. From autobiographical data provided by 73 of these students in family classes, and from interviews with 80 more in a social psychology class, she found that women experienced distress from the conflicting expectations produced by being simultaneously (1) a student preparing for a career and (2) a woman ostensibly looking forward to becoming married and establishing a family. This situation produced problems in two areas: with parents, and with potential or actual dating partners. Komarovsky reports that 26% of her subjects indicated some "grievance against their families for failure

to confront them with clear-cut and consistent goals" (i.e., parents expected them to work hard for a career, but not to become unfeminine and therefore unattractive to men, p. 185). In addition, 40% of the women in the study reported that they had occasionally played dumb on dates, that is, according to Komarovsky, that they hid their academic achievements, pretended ignorance, or allowed men to "win" in social situations involving intellectual or athletic competition. She also strongly implies, providing discursive excerpts from her data, that playing dumb was related to a significant amount of psychological strain and distress. Komarovsky's model appears to be that for women the requirements for academic and career achievement are in conflict with the attributes that make women attractive to men, and that this conflict causes women to behave in ways that are inconsistent with their self-images (i.e., to play dumb), and this in turn produces distress. This is an interesting idea; however, as Komarovsky has no control group, in even the weakest sense,[1] it is an idea that essentially rests on speculation.

3 Wallin (1950) is in basic agreement with Komarovsky, but suggests, on the basis of his somewhat more systematic questionnaire and interview data (163 female students selected randomly from a college population and all given *both* a questionnaire and an interview), that playing dumb due to cultural contradictions is less "momentous" than Komarovsky claims. He finds that women in college do report that their parents seem to promote inconsistent expectations ("be a career girl" and "don't be unfeminine"), and they do report in substantial numbers that they have played dumb on dates (41.3%). However, he indicates that in the interviews his subjects reported that they have few problems with the inconsistencies in the demands of their parents and little distress over playing dumb on dates. He suggests that they solve these contradictions easily, that playing dumb is likely a temporary phase in a dating relationship and accepted as part of conventionalized dating behavior which is dropped when the relationship becomes more serious. Furthermore, he suggests that if a particular woman would be upset by such pretenses she will avoid dating men for whom this is necessary. We confront the same basic problem with Wallin's analysis as with Komarovsky's; namely, he does not present any comparable data on men, nor does he look at those women who do not play dumb. His assertion that playing dumb

[1]There are women in her study who did not play dumb (60%) and there are women who reported no particular problems with inconsistent goals (74%), but she provided no analysis of these students' responses and no explanation of why most women confronted with cultural contradictions in sex roles have no problems with them at all.

does not seem to be problematic for those who do it is based on sketchy data which may be biased by the fact that the majority of the interviewers were college men whose gender may have affected the responses of the female subjects. He suggests that the women in his sample were probably less career-oriented than Komarovsky's subjects and therefore experienced fewer problems with playing dumb, a suggestion with which Komarovsky (1973) concurs.

4 Dean *et al.* (1975), using data collected from a sample of 287 female and 318 male students in introductory sociology classes in spring, 1972, show that playing dumb on dates is not characteristic of women only. Komarovsky, Wallin, and Dean *et al.*, each report percentages of women who *ever* played dumb on dates, and each finds that approximately half have done so. In addition, Wallin reports whether this had occurred very often, often, several times, or once or twice.[2] When persons who say that they have played dumb on dates only once or twice are classified with those who say they have never done so, Dean *et al.* find that the vast majority of women fall into this combined category, and that the rates are very similar across the different time periods. In short, evidence indicates that in both 1950 and 1970 college women rarely played dumb on dates. More important, Dean *et al.* also found that college males tend to play dumb and pretend inferiority in roughly the same proportions that college women do. Dean *et al.* concluded that playing dumb is not a common response to cultural contradictions in the sex roles occupied by college women in our society.

5 Komarovsky, Wallin, and Dean *et al.* all treat playing dumb as a form of impression management. Individuals presumably play dumb in

---

[2]Both Wallin (1950) and Dean *et al.* (1975) used the same set of survey questions with fixed alternatives to measure playing dumb, and Wallin (1950) supplemented this with interview data. The four questions they asked were: (1) When on dates, how often have you pretended to be inferior in artistic knowledge or taste (in music, art, literature, etc.)? (2) How often have you pretended to be intellectually inferior? (3) How often have you "played dumb" on dates because you thought the (man/woman) preferred you that way? (4) How often have you pretended to be athletically inferior when participating in some sport with a (man/woman)? Wallin's questions asked only about men, while Dean's were asked about both sexes. In contrast, Komarovsky (1946) read autobiographical accounts of her student's family histories and interviewed some others, presumably about their family and sex-role experiences. It is not completely clear in Komarovsky's case how it was determined whether persons played dumb or not. Furthermore, the 40% of women she reports as playing dumb include women who said that they had allowed men to win various games and athletic contests. While in this paper we do not discuss the results with all four questions in both Wallin's and Dean *et al.*'s articles, the findings are fairly consistent across all of the questions and, surprisingly, with Komarovsky; the differences are not substantively important with respect to the arguments we are making in this paper.

an effort to shape the image other persons have of them. Implicit in their analyses is the assumption that playing dumb will both give the other person a sense of superiority and put him or her at ease and that this will facilitate social interaction. Although none of these investigators has linked playing dumb to a theoretical perspective, the phenomenon clearly is rooted in symbolic interactionism. The process of playing dumb as a form of impression management is similar to the process described by Goffman (1959) regarding the presentation of self, and by Weinstein (1966) regarding alter casting. Where Komarovsky differs from Wallin and from Dean *et al.* is in the perception of the strength of the social constraints on the individual to play dumb. Komarovsky sees the constraints as strong; both Wallin and Dean *et al.* see the constraints as weak. Put in terms of exchange theory (Blau, 1964; Homans, 1961; Emerson, 1962), for Komarovsky the individual has few alternatives and the costs and benefits are substantial, whereas for Wallin, and for Dean *et al.*, the individual has clear alternatives and the costs and benefits are minimal.

Summary

6 From the literature reviewed it is clear that (1) there is no evidence that playing dumb on dates is a reaction to cultural contradictions in sex roles, (2) playing dumb on dates is probably not done with any greater frequency by college women than it is by college men, (3) playing dumb on dates is not done with particular frequency by either college men or college women, and (4) the evidence is unclear as to whether playing dumb is related to feelings of resentment, low self-esteem, and poor mental health, generally. It appears, therefore, that an adequate understanding of playing dumb must involve considering it as a general form of impression management that might occur in a variety of situations, and investigating its relationships with other variables using data from a representative sample of a normal adult population which includes systematic data on the mental health of persons who do and do not play dumb.

THE STUDY

7 For an analysis of playing dumb, we use data collected as part of a study on sex and marital roles and mental health drawn from a stratified probability sample of 2247 respondents aged 18 years and over who

were interviewed in the 48 contiguous states during the winter 1974–75. The interview schedule was developed by the lead author; the sampling, interviewing and coding were done by Leiberman, Inc. Besides the initial contact attempt there were two call-backs if no one was at home. The average interview lasted 80 minutes. Since the study was designed to investigate the relationship between sex roles, marital roles, and mental health, widowed and divorced persons (particularly men) were oversampled. We would note that the refusal rate was constant throughout the interview period and the marital status of the respondent had no bearing on their chances for being selected for the interview. An overall response rate of 65.6% was obtained. Potential respondents included in the nonresponse categories included households where no one was located after three consecutive attempts, persons who refused to respond to the screening interview, persons selected at the time of the screening interview who refused to be interviewed, as well as respondents who did not complete the interview. In our analysis we have corrected for the over-sampling of the widowed and divorced with a weighting procedure so that the data are representative of the nation as a whole. An analysis of the data without weighting produces a pattern identical to the one presented and yields identical conclusions.

8 The respondents were asked "Have you ever pretended to be less intelligent or knowledgeable than you really are?" If the respondent said "yes," we asked "How often have you pretended to be less intelligent or knowledgeable than you really are—very often, pretty often, not too often, or not at all often?" In addition, if the respondents reported they had ever played dumb, they were asked in what situations this had occurred. The categories were (1) with a date, (2) with your spouse, (3) with your boss, (4) with your co-workers, (5) with friends, (6) with strangers, and (7) with children.

9 The quality of our data is limited by the fact that the key independent variable is a single question for which individuals make somewhat different interpretations. In the analysis that follows, we assume that people who report playing dumb actually have played dumb both in the situations they report and with the frequency they indicate. We also assume that any errors are randomly distributed across categories of our independent variables and do not invalidate the patterns that we find. We would note that these are assumptions for which we have no proof and thus, as with most surveys, our results must be taken as suggestive and not definitive. We have analyzed the relationships between playing dumb and our independent variables controlling for social

desirability by using a version of the Crown-Marlow (1964) scale and for the respondents' tendency to yeasay or naysay. The same results are obtained as when the analysis is performed without controls. We would also note that the available evidence on response bias (e.g., see the reviews in Rorer, 1965; Sudman and Bradburn, 1974; Gove and Geerken, 1977) would suggest that it is unlikely that a systematic bias would be strong enough to have a substantive effect on our results and their interpretation.

RESULTS

Sex

10 The relationships between sex and playing dumb are presented in Table 1. Part A of the table contains the percentages of men and women who answered "yes" to the question, "Have you ever pretended to be less intelligent or knowledgeable than you really are?" As these data show, slightly over a quarter of the respondents report ever playing dumb, and men are much more likely to do so than women. Part A of the table also shows that among respondents who report playing dumb, there is a very slight tendency for women to report playing dumb more frequently than men, but the difference does not approach statistical significance. Turning to specific situations, we see that wives are more likely than husbands to report playing dumb with their spouses. The data suggest that males and females play dumb on dates at approximately the same rate. Consistent with the fact that the never-married and the divorced respondents are more likely than others to be dating, these respondents are the most likely to report playing dumb on dates. On the job, men are more likely than women to report playing dumb with their bosses and their co-workers. Men are also more likely to report playing dumb with friends and strangers. There is no difference between the sexes in the exent to which respondents report playing dumb with children.

11 Our data show that, contrary to the accepted view, men are more likely to report playing dumb than women. The ready acceptance of the view that women play dumb more than men and our finding that this is not the case has a parallel in the reaction to the early work of Horner (unpublished, 1970). Horner's work, which was also based on the assumption that women were expected to be submissive, argues that women are much more likely than men to fear success. This conclusion was rapidly incorporated into the sex-role literature. However, Horner's work suffered from serious methodological limitations, and subsequent

Table 1. Percent of Respondents Reporting "Playing Dumb" in Different Situations

PART A: IN ANY SITUATION

	EVER PLAY DUMB	SIG.	N	VERY OFTEN	PRETTY OFTEN	NOT TOO OFTEN	NOT AT ALL OFTEN	SIG.	N
All males	31.1	.001	1065	5.6	11.2	68.1	15.8	n.s.	330
All females	22.9		1182	4.6	14.8	69.8	10.8		260
Total	26.5		2247	5.1	12.7	68.8	13.4		590

PART B: WITH SPOUSE AND DATES

	WITH DATE	SIG.	WITH SPOUSE	SIG.	N
Male married	6.2	ns	7.2	.001	(783)
Female married	8.7		12.5		(795)
Male never-married	15.9	ns			(211)
Female never-married	14.7				(166)
Male widowed	1.3	ns	3.7	ns	(34)
Female widowed	3.8		7.4		(164)
Male divorced	12.8	ns	9.4	ns	(38)
Female divorced	12.4		13.3		(56)
All males	8.2	ns	6.0	.001	(1065)
All females	9.0		10.0		(1182)

PART C: ON THE JOB

	WITH ONE'S BOSS	SIG.	WITH ONE'S CO-WORKERS	SIG.	N
Males working	14.9	.001	17.0	.001	(786)
Females working	7.2		9.4		(406)
Males not working	8.3	.01	8.0	.05	(276)
Females not working	4.2		4.8		(775)
All males	13.1	.001	14.6	.001	(1065)
All females	5.2		6.3		(1182)

PART D: WITH FRIENDS, STRANGERS, CHILDREN

	WITH FRIENDS	SIG.	WITH STRANGERS	SIG.	WITH CHILDREN	SIG.	N
All males	12.6	.001	15.8	.001	8.7	ns	(1065)
All females	8.7		7.7		7.4		(1182)

NOTE: In all cases, significance levels were calculated with the F-test.

replications varying the situations and the method of coding "fear of success," give no clear indication that women fear success more than men (Levine and Crumrine, 1975).

Table 2. The Relationship between Demographic Variables and Playing Dumb in Various Situations; Zero-Order Correlation Coefficients and Standardized Regresson Coefficients

	IN ANY SITUATION		WITH DATE (NEVER-MARRIED ONLY)		WITH SPOUSE (MARRIED ONLY)		WITH BOSS (WORKING ONLY)	
	r	beta	r	beta	r	beta	r	beta
High Status Occupation	.117[c]	.070[b]	−.047	−.063	.010	.005	.108[c]	.111[b]
Sex	.093[c]	.076[c]	.021	.027	−.088[c]	−.075[b]	.126[c]	.117[c]
Never Married	.041[a]	−.046					.039	−.010
Widowed	−.087[c]	.003					−.061[a]	−.041
Divorced	.035[a]	.037					.007	.008
Age	−.177[c]	−.166[c]	−.136[b]	−.122[a]	−.124[c]	−.095[c]	−.063[a]	−.041
Ed'n.	.145[c]	.081[b]	.072	.088	.083[c]	.045	.035	.025
Income	.066[c]	−.027	−.011	−.051	.063[b]	.035	−.075[a]	−.124[b]
Black	−.000	.009	−.041	−.040	.017	.026	−.043	−.042
Oriental	.027	.018	−.019	−.027	−.018	−.022	−.023	−.014
Spanish	.017	.015	.055	.047	.026	.032	−.037	−.012
Jewish	.078[c]	.059[b]	.055	.051	−.019	−.023	.057[a]	.062
Foreign Born	−.021	−.005	−.015	−.000	−.009	−.002	.002	.021
Constant		.427		.143		.029		.346
R		.231[c]		.186[c]		.163[c]		.220[c]
N		2181		354		1552		835

NOTE: In all cases significance was calculated with the F-test. a< .05; b< .01; c< .001.

12 In terms of frequency of playing dumb, the data suggest—at least in a survey that does not sensitize the respondent to the issue of "playing dumb"—that most respondents do not report playing dumb. For those respondents who do report playing dumb, in most instances, it appears to be neither a very trivial aspect of their life (3.5% of the respondents report playing dumb "not at all often," n = 2247), nor does it appear to be a phenomenon that plays a dominant role in the life of many respondents (4.6% of the respondents report playing dumb "very" or "pretty" often, n = 2247). Thus our data suggest that playing dumb is a form of impression management that occurs among a quarter of the population and for those individuals it generally comprises a modest but clearly discernible aspect of their behavior.

Demographic Variables

13 A set of multiple regression analyses were run to look at the relationship between a particular independent variable and (a) ever playing

	WITH CO-WORKER (WORKING ONLY)		WITH FRIENDS		WITH STRANGERS		WITH CHILDREN	
	r	beta	r	beta	r	beta	r	beta
High Status Occupation	.071[b]	.036	.104[c]	.101[c]	.126[c]	.071[b]	.072[c]	.039
Sex	.108[c]	.111[c]	.061[b]	.043[b]	.129[c]	−.109[c]	.028	.021
Never Married	−.001	−.029	.023	−.034	.048[a]	−.002	−.008	−.052[a]
Widowed	−.047	−.022	−.048[a]	.003	−.074[c]	−.006	−.028	.013
Divorced	.026	.023	.029	.028	.012	.017	−.000	−.001
Age	−.041	−.032	−.116[c]	−.137[c]	−.103[c]	−.063[a]	−.071[c]	−.071[b]
Ed'n.	.098[c]	.089[b]	.051[b]	.001	.136[c]	.093[c]	.105[c]	.078[b]
Income	.003	−.066[a]	.004	−.055[a]	.065[c]	−.021	.052[b]	−.011
Black	−.025	.009	−.014	−.017	−.019	−.038	.008	.021
Oriental	−.029	−.029	.001	−.005	.044[a]	.036	−.016	−.021
Spanish	−.034	−.028	.013	.000	.018	.024	−.028	−.018
Jewish	.125[c]	.118[c]	.023	.013	.080[c]	.061[b]	.081[c]	.071[c]
Foreign Born	.034	.049	.003	.011	−.012	−.006	.016	.026
Constant		.233		.263		.172		.074
R		.211[c]		.171[c]		.220[c]		.153[c]
N		1164		2181		2181		2181

dumb and (b) playing dumb in specific situations, while controlling for the other independent variables. These data are presented in Table 2. For each situation reported in the table, the first column contains the zero-order correlation coefficient between each of the independent variables and playing dumb, while the second column contains the standardized regression coefficient for each of the independent variables controlling for all of the others. Occupational status is coded 1 = high status, 0 = low status or unemployed. Sex is coded 1 = male, 0 = female. Marital status is represented by dummy variables for never-married, widowed, and separated-divorced (married was left out). Ethnicity is represented by dummy variables for a number of ethnic groups (with those not Black, not Oriental, not Spanish-American, not Jewish, and not foreign-born left out). The dependent variable is coded 1 = reported playing dumb, 0 = did not report playing dumb.

14 Looking first at the zero-order relationships for "ever playing dumb" we find that the following are significantly related to playing dumb in descending order of magnitude (1) age (negatively), (2) education

(positively), (3) having high occupational status, (4) being male, (5) being widowed, (6) being Jewish, (7) family income (positively), (8) being never-married, and (9) being divorced. After controlling on the other demographic variables all the relationships with marital status become nonsignificant and the relationship with family income not only becomes nonsignificant but reverses sign. After controls the following variables remain significant, and again are presented in order of decreasing magnitude: (1) age (negatively), (2) education (positively), (3) being male, (4) having a high occupational status, and (5) being Jewish.

15 We now turn to playing dumb in specific situations, looking first at those relationships involving male/female interaction. The only demographic variable significantly related to dating and playing dumb is being young. Among the married, the only demographic variables that have significant relationships after controls are being young and being female. We would note that of the eight situations presented, only in the marital relationship are women rather than men more likely to play dumb.

16 Turning to relationships on the job, we look at the respondent's relationship to his or her (a) boss, and (b) co-workers. In analyzing the relationships with one's boss, we eliminated those relationships in which the respondent tended to be free from direct supervision, and thus eliminated most professionals, individuals who are self-employed, and other individuals who have a great deal of autonomy (e.g., cab drivers). After controls it is clear that having a high occupational status and being male are the two major variables positively related to playing dumb. Being Jewish is also related to playing dumb, although the relationship is not quite statistically significant ($p < .07$). It is worthy of note that after controls the strongest relationship in the analysis is with income, with low income associated with playing dumb. Turning to interaction with co-workers, we find after controls that being male, being highly educated, and being Jewish are related to playing dumb. Again, low income is also related to playing dumb. Turning to the remaining types of social interaction (with friends, strangers, children), after controls it is clear that age and education are again the variables most strongly related to playing dumb. Having high occupational status, being male, being Jewish, and having low income are also related to playing dumb.

17 Taken as a whole, the data presented in Table 2 suggest that playing dumb is associated with being young,[3] being highly educated, being

[3]One might feel that, unless playing dumb has increased drastically in our society in recent years, these data on age do not make sense. However, there is evidence that questions

male (except when dealing with one's spouse), having a high-status occupation, being Jewish, and having a relatively low income. Except for income, playing dumb tends to be associated with variables indicative of high prestige. Of particular note, given the sex-role literature on the behavior of women, is the fact that, overall, men tend to play dumb more than women. Perhaps equally noteworthy, given societal stereotypes of Blacks (and attempts to change them), is that in terms of playing dumb Blacks are virtually identical to Whites.

Frequency of Playing Dumb and Mental Health

18 In our analysis we look at the relationship between the frequency of playing dumb and the mental health of the respondent. We use two indices of positive mental health (a measure of self-esteem[4] and a measure of happiness[5]), and two measures of poor mental health (a measure of psychiatric symptoms,[6] and a measure of alienation[7]). The measure

---

asking whether a person has ever engaged in a particular behavior tend to be interpreted, either purposefully or because of faulty memory, as asking if it was done or if it occurred in the recent past. For example, if one decomposes the positive responses to the question, "Have you ever had a nervous breakdown?" into those who say they have had one in the last year and those who say they had one more than a year ago, the former category is much larger. The same thing happens when one asks about suicidal thoughts and suicidal attempts (data from present survey).

[4]This measure was composed of the following eight items selected from Rosenberg (1965): (1) I feel that I am a person of worth, at least equal to others; (2) At times I think I am no good at all; (3) I wish I could have more respect for myself; (4) I take a positive attitude toward myself; (5) I feel I do not have much to be proud of; (6) On the whole, I am satisfied with myself; (7) All in all, I feel I am a failure; (8) I feel worthless at times. In the interview the respondent was simply asked to indicate whether each item was true of himself or herself. The alpha coefficient was .62. Elsewhere it has been shown that this scale is not affected by response bias (Gove and Geerken, 1977).

[5]The respondent was asked: "Taking all things together, how happy are you these days—very happy, pretty happy, not too happy or not at all happy?"

[6]In the interview the respondent was asked if he or she had experienced the following symptoms often, sometimes, or never during the past few weeks: Feeling (1) anxious about someone or something; (2) that people were saying all kinds of things behind your back; (3) bothered by special fears; (4) so blue or depressed that it interfered with your daily activities; (5) that it was not safe to trust anybody; (6) bothered by nervousness, such as being irritable, fidgety or tense; (7) that you were in low spirits; (8) bothered by special thoughts; (9) so restless that you couldn't sit long in a chair; (10) as if nothing turned out the way you wanted it to; (11) somewhat apart or alone even among friends; (12) that personal worries were getting you down physically, that is, making you physically ill; (13) that nothing was worthwhile anymore. The alpha coefficient was .86. For a justification of this particular scale and a demonstration that it is not affected by response bias, see Gove and Geerken (1977).

[7]The items in the three alienation subscales are: *Powerlessness:* (1) the average citizen can have an influence on government decisions; (2) this world is run by a few persons in

of alienation is divided into three subscales dealing with powerlessness, normlessness, and belonginglessness.

19 The relationships between the frequency of playing dumb and the respondents' mental health are presented in Table 3. The data show that persons who play dumb "not at all often" tend to be in the best mental health, and those who never play dumb are in the next best mental health. The respondents who play dumb "not too often" are clearly in poorer mental health than those who never play dumb, but tend to be in slightly better mental health than those who play dumb "pretty often." Those who play dumb "very often" clearly have the poorest mental health. It is interesting that, of the alienation subscales, belonginglessness, which indicates that respondents perceive others as unfriendly and feel awkward and out of place, is the subscale most strongly related to playing dumb. Neither the pattern nor the strength of these relations are appreciably affected by controlling the standard demographic variables through the use of multiple classification analysis[8] (Andrews *et al.*, 1967).

20 These results are readily interpretable if we assume: (1) that respondents who play "not at all often" do so in casual interaction and are especially competent individuals, and that playing dumb in such situations will not have a negative effect on their mental health; and (2) respondents who play dumb more frequently are under strong social constraints to demean themselves, and playing dumb (or perhaps the situation that requires them to play dumb) has a negative effect on their mental health. The data on the respondents in fact tend to support these assumptions.

21 First, the data on the respondents' demographic characteristics suggests that the respondents who play dumb "not at all often" are less likely to be in situations that constrain them to play dumb, either because

---

power and there is not much the average person can do about it; (3) it doesn't matter how hard you try, what happens to you is just a matter of fate; (4) I seem to have very little control over what happens to me. *Normlessness:* (1) the trouble with the world today is that most people don't really believe in anything; (2) there are so many ideas of what is right and wrong these days it is hard to figure out how to live your life; (3) things are changing so fast these days we do not know what to expect from day to day. *Belonginglessness:* (1) most people really do care what happens to the next fellow; (2) most people are just naturally friendly and helpful; (3) I hardly ever feel awkward and out of place. In the interview the respondents were asked whether or not they agreed with each item. The alpha coefficient for the full scale was .53.

[8]The small changes that do occur after controlling for demographic variables generally have the effect of slightly increasing the extent to which persons who play dumb appear to be in poor mental health as compared to those who do not play dumb.

Table 3. Mental Health of Respondents and Frequency of Playing Dumb (Mean Scores)

	FREQUENCY OF PLAYING DUMB					
	Very often (n = 30)	Pretty often (n = 75)	Not too often (n = 406)	Not at all often (n = 78)	Never (n = 1637)	
Indices of Good Mental Health						
Self Esteem[a]	5.51	6.47	6.37	6.80	6.75	<.001
Happiness[a]	3.00	3.12	3.14	3.28	3.28	<.001
Indices of Poor Mental Health						
Psychiatric Symptoms[b]	8.79	7.51	7.18	5.49	5.99	<.001
Alienation[b]						
Powerlessness	1.42	1.28	1.19	1.03	1.23	ns
Normlessness	1.55	1.38	1.42	1.05	1.36	<.01
Belonginglessness	1.95	1.95	1.75	1.40	1.62	<.001
Full Scale	4.85	4.49	4.33	3.42	4.14	<.001

[a]The higher the score the better the respondent's mental health.
[b]The higher the score the worse the respondent's mental health.
NOTE: In all cases significance was calculated with the F-test.

they are more successful or because they are not in competitive situations. In particular, they have the highest education, income, and occupational status of any of the groups considered (i.e., the three other categories of persons who play dumb plus those who never play dumb). Furthermore, unlike the other respondents who play dumb, for those who do so "not at all often" having a low income is not related to playing dumb with one's boss or co-workers. The respondents who play dumb not at all often also tend to be older and, more important, the majority of them tend to be female.

22 Second, if we look at those situations where, as will be noted later, there are often clear social constraints to play dumb (i.e., with one's boss, co-workers, and spouse), and compare (1) those who play dumb not at all often with (2) all other respondents who play dumb, we find that the former do not tend to report playing dumb in any of these constraining situations, whereas the latter are very likely to report playing dumb in all three of these situations (the differences between these two types of respondents is statistically significant for each situation). In contrast, these two categories of respondents are both very likely to report playing dumb with friends, strangers, and children, and the small

Table 4. The Cluster of Personality Attributes that Respondents Indicate "Best" Describe Themselves

RESPONDENTS WHO PLAY DUMB "NOT AT ALL OFTEN"	RESPONDENTS WHO PLAY DUMB WITH SOME DEGREE OF FREQUENCY	RESPONDENTS WHO NEVER PLAY DUMB
logical	strong	sympathetic
helpful	self-confident	logical
intelligent	tough	flexible
considerate	persistent	considerate
sympathetic	ambitious	self-confident
hardworking	intelligent	intelligent
contented	competitive	competitive
self-confident	logical	helpful
well-organized	hardworking	persistent
		ambitious

differences between the two categories are not statistically significant for any of these three situations.[9]

23 Perhaps the best evidence to support these two assumptions comes from the personality attributes the respondents use to describe themselves. During the interview the respondents were given a list of 22 personality attributes and were asked to indicate which attributes described them. We analyzed the 22 personality attributes for respondents who played dumb (1) "not at all often," (2) "with a greater degree of frequency," and (3) "never," using the Quartermax factor analysis. The first factor explains the most variance in the respondents' personality attributes and the cluster of items that load strongly on this factor are the most highly intercorrelated items and may be taken as the cluster of personality attributes that best describes the key dimension common to the category of respondents under consideration.

24 These clusters of attributes are presented in Table 4; items are listed in the order of their importance. Among these three groups there are fairly distinct differences. Some of the attributes that stand out for the respondents who play dumb with some degree of frequency are "strong," "tough," "ambitious," and "competitive." One of the most striking things about this set of attributes is the total absence of items reflecting a concern with others. Persons who play dumb "not at all often," although clearly instrumentally oriented, appear to be very concerned with others

[9]We could not decide whether playing dumb on dates really fit in either a constrained or a nonconstrained situation. It is the case that respondents who play dumb not at all often are significantly less likely to do so than the other respondents who play dumb.

as well, as is indicated by the personality attributes of "helpful," "considerate," and "sympathetic." Their attributes also not only suggest a lack of concern with competitiveness but also a high degree of self-assurance, as indicated by the items "contented" and "self-confident." Respondents who never play dumb correspond most closely to those who play dumb not at all often, but appear to be more ambitious and competitive, consistent with the view that they would be unlikely to play dumb simply to put others at ease.

25 As the present study is cross-sectional, we cannot empirically establish the causal relationship between playing dumb and mental health. We feel in fact that the nature of the relationships is very complex and that the direction and strength of the relationship will vary greatly according to the unique characteristics of a particular situation. In most cases we feel that being in poor mental health will be associated with a sense of low self-confidence, a feeling of exclusion, and a desire to avoid interpersonal conflict, and that these variables will be causally linked to playing dumb. However, playing dumb is associated with a number of variables, in particular being male, being highly educated, and having high occupational status, and these variables in the present sample and in numerous other data sets are generally associated with good mental health. This leads us to suspect that among persons with these attributes, something about playing dumb and/or something about the constraints that cause them to play dumb affects their mental health. Schuessler *et al.* (1978:229) found that from a set of undesirable items included in their social desirability/undesirability scale, being socially constrained to "put on an act" was the *most* undesirable item—a finding that supports the supposition that having to play dumb under such constraints would have a negative effect on one's mental health. The cluster of self-described personality characteristics for respondents who play dumb with some frequency (Table 4) provides the strongest evidence that for these respondents, the causal relationship leads from playing dumb to poor mental health, rather than from poor mental health to playing dumb. As noted, these respondents are in poor mental health, yet their cluster of personal attributes suggest they have a strong instrumental orientation and there is nothing in these items to suggest that it is their emotional insecurity and lack of self-confidence that causes them to play dumb.

26 We view the relationship between playing dumb and mental health as complex, and believe that the parsimonious explanation of the positive association between (1) playing dumb "not at all often" and (2) being

in good mental health reflects a spurious relationship. It is our view that particularly competent individuals will (1) be inclined to play dumb in casual interactions to put the others at ease, and (2) be in particularly good mental health; and that the relationship between playing dumb and mental health is spurious, as both variables are determined by the competency of the individuals.

Sex, Playing Dumb, and Mental Health

27 Although the issue is never raised by Komarovsky (1946; 1973) it might be argued that while women and men are equally likely to play dumb, because playing dumb interacts with a woman's low status it would be more demeaning for women than for men, and thus women would be more affected by such behavior. To test this possibility we analyzed the relationship for men and women between playing dumb and the psychiatric symptom scale, using both overall measures of playing dumb and playing dumb in each of the specific situations. As before, these relationships are not affected by demographic controls. Both men and women who report ever playing dumb are in worse mental health than their counterparts who do not report this behavior. Of the seven specific situations, men who play dumb are significantly worse off in six of these (with dates, boss, co-workers, friends, strangers, and children) than those who do not. For women, only four comparisons are statistically significant (with dates, spouse, boss, and friends). Thus, overall, playing dumb is at least as strongly associated with poor mental health for men as it is for women. We would note, however, that the relationship between playing dumb with one's spouse and poor mental health is stronger for women than for men.

28 It is notable that in all situations, both for men and women, those who play dumb are worse off than those who do not. In fact, during the numerous analyses that were run, except for the category of respondents who played dumb "not at all often," we never were able to find a category of persons who were better off if they played dumb. It appears that the impression of Wallin (1950) and the tacit implication of Dean *et al.* (1975), that playing dumb is a psychologically insignificant phenomenon, is incorrect. The differences between their studies and our study are probably due partly to the fact that in our analysis we use a national probability sample while they used college students, and primarily to the fact that our question seems to pick up acts of playing dumb that are salient to the respondents whereas the other studies, by sensitizing their

respondents to the issue being studied, pick up acts that are much less salient to the respondents. This is suggested by the fact that in comparable categories of persons (age 18–25, never-married, student) we find many fewer persons playing dumb than do Wallin (1950) and Dean *et al.* (1975).

DISCUSSION

29 To most social scientists the results of our analysis will not be those anticipated. Drawing on the data presented, it is possible to develop a tentative *post factum* theoretical explanation of "playing dumb" that goes beyond what has previously been offered and which makes sense of the relationships we have found. Social interaction is largely based on the assumption that one is similar in capability to one's peers and/or superiors, and that one's superiors are more knowledgeable. If one in fact is clearly more knowledgeable and intelligent than one's peers and/or superiors, there will be considerable pressure to hide this fact, that is, to play dumb. If this is not hidden, a very basic expectation will be violated and the person will generally be negatively sanctioned and possibly excluded from the group.

30 As indicated, situations in which an individual plays dumb can be roughly divided into two types. In the first, the individual has a strong commitment to the relationship and is concerned with the other's evaluation of himself or herself, a type of situation that characteristically involves either primary interaction with significant others or interactions in which others have power over one. To be strongly committed to a situation and at the same time constrained to play dumb would be very frustrating and demeaning, and would likely have a negative effect on one's mental health.

31 The second type of situation in which a person may play dumb involves interaction in which the person is not concerned with the others' evaluation of him or her. This may occur in transitory interactions with strangers,[10] or with casual friends or acquaintances, in which the impression one makes is not important or in interactions

[10]Although it was not reported above, the few men (n = 34) and women (n = 18) who only report playing dumb with 'strangers', and in no other situations, are in identical mental health to the other respondents who report playing dumb with no one. Males who played dumb only with strangers had a mean ($\bar{X}$) psychiatric symptom score of 6.04; all other males had a $\bar{X}$ psychiatric symptom score of 5.95; p = .89. Females who played dumb only with strangers had a $\bar{X}$ psychiatric symptom score of 6.57; all other females had a $\bar{X}$ psychiatric symptom score of 6.57; p = 1.00.

between a superior and a subordinate in a social setting where the ranking is not relevant, and the superior wishes to put the subordinate at ease. We assume that in this second type of situation such acts are not frustrating and not demeaning the individual. In fact, since playing dumb in such situations is related to the ability to have control over social interactions, it might well be related to a sense of well-being. In this paper we are primarily concerned with playing dumb in the first situation, in which the relationship involves a strong commitment; we believe our measures are generally tapping such situations.[11]

32 In summary, we are trying to explain a behavior that occurs relatively infrequently, but in situations involving high commitment; and, that occurs with greater frequency among males, the young, those with a high level of education, those with a relatively low income, those with high-status occupations, and Jews. The following four factors are consistent with these findings and our assumptions:

1. The actor must be intelligent and knowledgeable or at least perceive this to be the case.
2. Knowledge and intelligence must be salient in the interaction.
3. The intelligence and knowledge of the actor must be taken seriously by others.
4. The gain from playing dumb must be greater than the cost incurred.

33 Unless the first two points apply in a situation, playing dumb is meaningless and would be nonexistent. Unless points three and four were true, it is difficult to imagine a motivation for playing dumb. According to societal stereotypes, both the first and second points (knowledge and saliency of knowledge) are attributes of the upper classes (particularly the educated), of males, and (among the ethnic groups) of Jews. Assuming that these widely held stereotypes tend to reflect real characteristics, albeit in somewhat distorted form, these attributes are thus more common in these groups, which explains why we find these categories of persons playing dumb.

[11] In the second situation we assume that many individuals are not particularly aware they are playing dumb as the behavior is infrequent, almost automatic, and has little significance to the individual. In short, in the second situation such acts are likely to be vastly underreported, especially in a general survey that does not probe such behavior. The few individuals who do report playing dumb in this second situation may be particularly skilled in and very sensitive to the subtle dynamics of social interaction.

34 Since in contemporary American society women are less likely than men to be channeled into situations in which all four criteria apply, it is not surprising that men have higher rates.[12] However, if a woman is interacting with males and is considered a serious competitor, there will probably be even more pressure for her to play dumb than there would be for a male in the same situation. Academic women are in such a situation, and this may be one reason some of them have so readily accepted Komarovsky's argument.

35 The one situation in which women are significantly more likely to play dumb, namely marriage, is also the only situation in which women clearly meet the four criteria we have suggested are necessary before a person is very likely to play dumb. Women's roles in marriage are subject to complex and often contradictory expectations and definitions, ranging from "superior status" (e.g., in issues related to homemaking and childrearing) through "equal status" (contemporary ideal, if not legal fact) to "subordinate status" (dependent; less worldly). That is, in a marriage situation a wife's opinion and knowledge are almost by definition salient, credible, and relevant, while at the same time she is expected to play a subordinate role. Thus in the marital relationship, women would frequently be constrained to play dumb. We would not, for example, expect a wife to play dumb on issues involving homemaking or childrearing, where she would be the assumed expert, but would expect a wife to play dumb on more general issues (e.g., "worldly affairs") where a display of superior knowledge would tend to undercut the husband's assumed superior status.

36 The strongest relationship found in our data was that younger persons are more likely to play dumb than older persons. This makes sense

---

[12]Given the present concern about equality between the sexes, a few words about the suggested explanation of the relationship with males is warranted. We are not implying that women are less intelligent than men. What we are implying is that because of the nature of socialization into sex roles in our society, males are channeled into situations that value knowledge and encourage competition, whereas females are not, and thus that males are both more aware of and more concerned about affairs outside the home. In contrast, because of socialization and because they are less likely to have careers outside the home, women tend to be less competitive and more concerned with the particularistic affairs and relationships whose nexus is the home. The attributes that make superior intelligence or knowledge in a woman seem unusual, therefore, are real societal characteristics which (a) tend to channel women away from intellectual competition, and (b) allow others to see her as having less general knowledge than men and to discount what she says. Thus, those attributes of the woman's role that others have perceived as making it necessary for women to play dumb are, we would argue, the very characteristics which keep women out of situations where they need to play dumb.

within our framework, since younger persons are somewhat more likely than are older persons (1) to be in situations where competition and ambition are important, (2) to be in lower-status positions in their occupations, and at the same time (3) to be more educated. Thus, as younger persons move into positions and situations where playing dumb may be beneficial, older persons are moving out of them and into situations where there are fewer persons to whom it is necessary to defer for any reason. The relationship between playing dumb and low income also fits into our framework, for it provides a motive to act in an ingratiating manner. This is especially true in the job setting, where the relationship is particularly strong, for ingratiating acts may lead to future occupational advancement.

REFERENCES

Andrews, F. M., J. N. Morgan, and J. A. Sonquist
1967 Multiple Classification Analysis. Ann Arbor: Institute for Social Research, University of Michigan.

Blau, Peter
1964 Exchange and Power in Social Life. New York: John Wiley.

Crowne, Douglas, and David Marlowe
1964 The Approval Motive. New York: John Wiley.

Dean, Dwight, Rita Braito, Edward Powers, and Bruce Brant
1975 "Cultural contradictions and sex roles revisited: A replication and reassessment." The Sociological Quarterly 16 (Spring):207–15.

Emerson, R.
1962 "Power-dependence relations." American Sociological Review 27: 31–41.

Goffman, Erving
1959 The Presentation of Self in Everyday Life. Garden City, N.Y.: Doubleday.

Gove, Walter R., and Michael Geerken
1977 "Response bias in surveys of mental health: An empirical investigation." American Journal of Sociology 82 (May):1289–1317.

Homans, George C.
1961 Social Behavior: Its Elementary Forms. New York: Harcourt, Brace and World, Inc.

Horner, Matina
Un-publ. "Sex differences in achievement motivation and performance in competitive and non-competitive situations." PhD dissertation, University of Michigan, 1968.
1970 "Femininity and successful achievement: A basic inconsistency." In J. Bardwick, E. M. Douvan, M. S. Horner and D. Butman (eds.), Feminine Personality and Conflict. Belmont, California: Brooks/Cole.

Komarovsky, Mirra

1946 "Cultural contradiction and sex roles." American Journal of Sociology 52 (November):184–89.

1973 "Cultural contradictions and sex roles: The masculine case." American Journal of Sociology 78 (January):873–91.

Levine, Adeline, and Janice Crumine

1975 "Women and the fear of success: A problem in replication." American Journal of Sociology 80 (January):964–974.

Rorer, Leonard

1965 "The great response bias myth." Psychological Bulletin 63 (March): 129–56.

Rosenberg, Morris

1965 Society and the Adolescent Self-Image. Princeton: Princeton University Press.

Schuessler, Karl, David Hittle, and John Cardascia

1978 "Measuring responding desirability with attitude–opinion items." Social Psychology 41:224–235.

Sudman, S., and N. Bradburn

1974 Response Bias in Surveys. Chicago: Aldine.

Wallin, Paul

1950 "Cultural contradictions and sex roles: A repeat study." American Sociological Review 15 (April):288–93.

Weinstein, Eugene

1966 "Toward a theory of interpersonal tactics." Pp. 394–95 in Carl W. Backman and Paul F. Secord (eds.), Problems in Social Psychology. New York: McGraw-Hill.

QUESTIONS FOR ANALYSIS AND DISCUSSION

1. What two points about playing dumb do the authors seek to demonstrate?
2. What four conclusions do the authors reach from a review of previous work on playing dumb?
3. Explain the concept "impression management."
4. In your own words, describe the study the authors conducted, including who was studied, what questions were asked, and what assumptions underlie the study.
5. What is the study's most significant result with regard to sex? What sex-role assumption does this result contradict?
6. The authors indicate in several places that the results of their study are not affected by "response bias." Looking at their discussion, determine what the term means and why it concerns social scientists.
7. What relationship did the authors find between playing dumb and mental health? What, if any, causal relationship seems to exist between playing dumb and mental health?

8. Why are men, the young, the highly educated, and lower-income people the most likely to play dumb?
9. Why are women more likely than men to play dumb with spouses?
10. Using this article as a model, describe the characteristics or conventions of academic writing in the social sciences. Consider details of format and organization as well as writing style.

Playing Dumb

MICHAEL HUGHES AND WALTER R. GOVE

Because of his significant role in the original study of playing dumb, Walter Gove appears as coauthor of the following article. Michael Hughes was, however, the principal writer of the article published in Psychology Today *in October 1981, as he makes clear in his short essay on preparing the popular version, an essay he wrote for* The Writer's Stance. *Read the* Psychology Today *article and analyze the differences between the academic and popular versions; then read Hughes's discussion and answer the remaining study questions.*

1 Several years ago, when we and our colleagues at Vanderbilt University put together a national survey of sex roles, marital roles, and mental health, we included a group of questions about playing dumb—that is, consciously deciding not to display one's knowledge or intelligence. The survey was designed to measure a number of factors that might make women more likely than men to develop mental problems. At least one previous study had suggested that having to feign inferiority in some social situations—particularly on dates—might be one of the major stresses on women. We wanted to find out if playing dumb could account for the differences researchers have found in the mental health of men and women.

2 The sample was sizable. The survey included 2,247 men and women, 18 years old and older, weighted to be representative of Americans living in the 48 contiguous states. We recently analyzed the data on playing dumb and found that they contradicted most common assumptions. On the basis of our sample, we conclude that, in fact,

more men than women play dumb in nearly every situation—with friends and strangers, with bosses and coworkers, with dates and children—and that such behavior is most common among people with more education and high-status jobs.

3 The widespread impression that women play dumb more often than men was created in part by two articles published by sociologists more than 30 years ago that have frequently been mentioned since in newspapers and popular magazines as well as in the psychological literature. In a 1946 piece in the *American Journal of Sociology,* Mirra Komarovsky reported that 40 percent of the female students she had interviewed at a prestigious eastern university admitted they had occasionally hidden their academic achievements from the men they dated, pretended ignorance, or allowed their dates to beat them in athletic or intellectual competition. Komarovsky concluded that for women in our society, the desire for academic and career achievement comes into conflict with the attributes that make women attractive to men; this conflict causes women to behave in ways that are inconsistent with their self-image, producing a significant amount of psychological distress.

4 After studying 163 female college students, Paul Wallin published an article in the *American Sociological Review* in 1950 that showed essentially the same thing—women occasionally play dumb on dates. Wallin suggested that the women did not think of playing dumb as particularly distressing but accepted it as part of conventionalized dating behavior, a ploy that they dropped when relationships became serious.

5 Those studies have been cited by behavioral scientists for more than 30 years to demonstrate that, because of their lower social status, women often act less intelligent than they are, not only on dates but in many other situations as well. Dwight Dean and his colleagues at Iowa State University reported in a 1975 article in *Sociological Quarterly* that a casual search of the sociological literature had turned up 20 uncritical citations of the two journal articles and none that questioned the validity of the studies, despite the fact that neither study considered cases of men who play dumb or women who don't.

6 Dean and his colleagues also told about a study of their own, in which about equal numbers of college men and women said they played dumb on dates. Indeed, the same researchers found that more than 90 percent of the students in their study—and in Wallin's—said either that they had never played dumb or that they had done so only a few times in their lives.

7 The Dean study had not been published when we designed and

conducted our original study at Vanderbilt University, although we did consider it in the analysis reported here. What we knew at the time was that some evidence showed that college women played dumb on dates and that Komarovsky claimed it produced psychological distress; that Wallin claimed that it did not, but that neither had any real indicators of the mental state that accompanied the behavior.

8 The question we decided to ask our respondents was: "Have you ever pretended to be less intelligent or knowledgeable than you really are?" Note that the wording of the question was such that people who answered yes were presumably not *feeling* dumb; that is, they were confident of their knowledge and intelligence and were only pretending to be ignorant in a given circumstance. If they answered yes, they were then asked how often they had pretended to be less intelligent or knowledgeable—very often, pretty often, not too often, or not at all often. We also asked them in what situations they had ever played dumb. The categories were: 1) with a date, 2) with your spouse, 3) with your boss, 4) with your coworkers, 5) with friends, 6) with strangers, 7) with children.

9 We were surprised by the answers, which showed that more men than women admitted to having played dumb—31 percent to 23 percent. Since the earlier research had led us to expect the opposite, we looked for an explanation. Perhaps more men play dumb at some time, but women do so more frequently. That idea proved false. Among those who had played dumb, only about 18 percent of both sexes said they had done so very often or fairly often.

10 Taking another tack, we wondered whether there were differences in *when* men and women played dumb. To find out, we analyzed the answers in each of the seven categories separately. For dates, we confirmed what Dean had found: no significant differences in the propensity of men and women to play dumb on dates. That is true of the never-married (16 percent of the men, 15 percent of the women); the divorced (13 percent, men; 12 percent, women); the widowed (1 percent, men; 4 percent, women); and the married—we presume their responses were completely retrospective (7 percent, men; 9 percent. women).

11 Men were roughly twice as likely to say that they have played dumb on the job as were women. That was true both with the boss (15 percent, men; 7 percent, women) and with their coworkers (17 percent, men; 9 percent, women).

12 The responses were similar with friends (13 percent, men; 9 percent, women); with strangers (16 percent, men; 8 percent, women); and

with children (9 percent, men; 7 percent, women). The only situation in which women were significantly more likely to report playing dumb was with their spouses. They were nearly twice as likely to say they play dumb with their husbands (13 percent) as men were to say they play dumb with their wives (7 percent).

13 We then decided to see what personal characteristics other than sex were involved. We looked at age, education, income, occupation, marital status, ethnicity, and mental health to see if any of those characteristics were related to the tendency to feign ignorance. We did two separate analyses: one to see how the characteristics related to ever having played dumb, and another to see how they related to playing dumb in each situation (with a date, with a friend, and so on).

14 We found that age was the strongest overall predictor, relating significantly to playing dumb with dates, spouses, friends, strangers, and children. Young people consistently play dumb more often than older people. People with more education are more likely to play dumb, particularly with coworkers, strangers, and children. In contrast, those with lower incomes play dumb more often, especially in dealing with bosses, friends, and coworkers. People in high-status occupations also play dumb more often, especially with the boss, with friends, and with strangers. Whether people are married or not doesn't seem to matter, but ethnicity does, in one case. Jews reported playing dumb more often than blacks, Hispanics, Orientals, and non-Jewish white Americans.

15 We were particularly interested in whether mental health and playing dumb were related, since Komarovsky, Wallin, and Dean had disagreed on the point. We looked at several indicators of mental health—self-esteem, happiness, psychiatric symptoms, and alienation—as shown by answers to questions in the survey. Without exception, we found that those who played dumb very often were worst off, while people who said they played dumb "not at all often" were in the best mental health. In between, going from poorer to better mental health, were those who said they feigned ignorance "pretty often," "not too often," or never. Apparently the willingness to seem dumb occasionally—to ingratiate yourself with others, perhaps, or to tease information out of them subtly—is consistent with good psychological adjustment.

16 Most of our findings contradicted our original suppositions. To account for both the findings and the contradictions, we must start with one of the basic tenets on which American society and democracy is based: that we are similar in intelligence to most of those around us. If you are—or feel you are—clearly more intelligent or knowledgeable

than those around you, you will feel considerable pressure to hide that fact. People play dumb when they have a strong commitment to a relationship with others and are concerned with how others will evaluate them. But they may also play dumb in another kind of situation, when they do not particularly care about the others involved. Then they may pretend to be dumb simply to promote smooth social interaction and to avoid situations embarrassing to themselves or others.

17 In our study, we were primarily concerned with playing dumb in relationships that involve a strong commitment—to dates, spouses, friends, bosses, and coworkers. That means we were trying to explain behavior that occurs relatively infrequently but is usually important when it does occur. As we've mentioned, we have found that it occurs most often among males, the young, and the highly educated; among Jews, people with relatively low income, and people in high-status occupations. There are four factors or conditions consistent with our findings that we feel provide a framework for understanding why and in what situations people play dumb:

1. They must be intelligent and knowledgeable, or at least believe they are.
2. Knowledge and intelligence must be valued by everyone involved.
3. Their intelligence and knowledge must be taken seriously by others involved in the situation.
4. What they gain from playing dumb must be greater than what it costs them.

18 Unless the first two points apply to a situation, playing dumb has no point. Unless the second two points apply, it is difficult to imagine any motivation for playing dumb. According to social stereotypes, distorted as they may be, the first and second points are attributes of those with a good education and high-status jobs, of males, and (among ethnic groups) of Jews—the same groups who, according to our study, play dumb the most.

19 Within our framework, it makes sense that young people play dumb more often than old people, since they are more likely to meet situations in which competition and ambition are important; to hold low-status positions at work, and, at the same time, to be more educated than their elders. As a result, they face more situations in which playing dumb may be useful, compared with older people, who generally meet few persons to whom they find it necessary to defer.

20 The relationship between playing dumb and low income is also consistent with our framework; it provides a motive for acting in an ingratiating manner. That is especially true where the relationship between low income and playing dumb was particularly strong—on the job.

21 Since in America today women are less likely than men to encounter situations in which all four criteria apply, it is not surprising that men play dumb more often. The situation is changing as more women reach responsible positions in the working world, but a higher percentage of men are still channeled into situations that value knowledge and competition.

22 Our interpretation is strengthened by what happens in marriage, the one situation in which women are more likely than men to play dumb. It is also the one situation in which women consistently meet our four criteria for playing dumb. In some areas of marriage, such as homemaking and childrearing, women are considered particularly intelligent and knowledgeable and are valued for their special ability (factors 1 through 3). In other areas—financial matters or world affairs, for example—women are frequently constrained to play dumb to avoid undercutting their husband's supposed special competence (factor 4).

23 We have provided some evidence that disputes the belief that women play dumb more than men because of social stereotypes and pressures. But what does that tell us? Given our analysis, the fact that fewer women pretend to do so simply means that women have less opportunity or reason to play dumb. Even among the majority of women who work, many are channeled into low-status, low-paying jobs. At home or at work, they are less likely than men to see themselves as intelligent, to meet others who value knowledge highly, or to be taken seriously by those in authority. Cold comfort for anyone who believes in sexual equality.

QUESTIONS FOR ANALYSIS AND DISCUSSION

1. How, exactly, does the popular version differ from the original academic study? Note specific differences in format, organization, and writing style.
2. What elements in the academic article have been totally eliminated? How does the academic article benefit from including these elements for its readers? Why do the authors assume that these elements can and should be eliminated from the popular version?

3. What observation has been added to the popular version? Why do you think it was added?
4. Comparing the two versions, what can you conclude about the demands for writing in popular magazines? What was the major change in the writer's stance required for a successful *Psychology Today* version?
5. Compare your analysis of differences with Michael Hughes's account of writing the popular piece. Did you overlook any differences he covers in his explanation?
6. Hughes asserts that the popular version is "a much better vehicle for communicating our major findings." In what way is it better? Why is it not better for the professional social psychologist and therefore not a substitute for the original "playdumb paper"?

Recasting a Piece of Sociological Research for a Popular Audience: The Case of "Playing Dumb . . ."*

MICHAEL HUGHES

When Walter Gove, Michael Geerken, and I wrote the paper that would ultimately be published in *Social Psychology Quarterly* as "Playing Dumb: A Form of Impression Management with Undesirable Consequences," we had a very narrow audience in mind: the editor and reviewers of *Social Psychology Quarterly.* Reviewers and editors of professional journals in sociology are concerned primarily with the substance of papers under review. That is, they are concerned with how the paper fits into or modifies existing theories and with the technical competence of the empirical research presented. Capturing and maintaining the interest of journal readers is clearly secondary: those who have a professional interest in the piece or must read it for its sociological importance will read it regardless of the style of writing.

A rarely stated but widely recognized principle of writing for scientific journals is that attention to stylistic considerations may be confined

*I would like to thank Carolyn J. Kroehler for comments on an earlier draft.

to avoiding only the worst: misspelled words, incorrect grammar, hackneyed phrases and metaphors, awkward constructions, and completely incomprehensible statements. Editors and reviewers have a negative reaction to lapses such as these, not so much for aesthetic reasons but because they may be signs of more serious problems, such as sloppy research practices and confused thinking. In writing what we came to call the "playdumb paper," we therefore paid more attention to the organization and presentation of the research and its importance than we did to entertaining the reader.

This avoidance of matters of style in writing for journals is further encouraged by (1) the fact that many social scientists use copy editors to correct major writing problems before sending papers for review, and virtually all are aware that copy editors at the better journals edit papers before publication; and (2) the assumption that, as a "gatekeeper," the journal's editor will also act as the reader's advocate and inform authors of what they should change stylistically.

When I wrote what we came to call the "*Psychology Today* paper," I was also writing for a very narrow audience. In this case, my audience was one editorial contact person who had invited me to write the paper and the editorial staff of *Psychology Today*. However, it was clear to me that because these editors wanted to maintain the interest of an audience of general readers, they would be very concerned about the writing style. Readers of *Psychology Today* simply would not bother with the article if it were boring or written in the sometimes awkward and/or convoluted style evident in many social science journals.

As a mass-market magazine, *Psychology Today* must convince advertisers that readers will be interested enough in what is published to read it and will ultimately be exposed to the magazine's advertisements. If articles are not interesting or are hard to wade through, pages will be skipped, along with the ads on them. Worst of all, readers having a bad experience with a magazine will simply ignore it in the future—subscriptions will not be renewed and future issues will gather dust on newsstands. My job on this version, therefore, was not so much to create an article that would make a big impact on social psychology through its significance and proficiency but to create an article that a general audience would read.

Psychology Today was concerned with the importance and competence of our research, to be sure, but they were apparently satisfied with our research before they asked us to write a version for them. After that point, their concern was to help me take a research article with some interesting findings and make it consumable.

And that is what they did. The editor I worked with did not tell me what to write and was true to his word in not changing anything I wrote without my permission. For my part, I resolved to be flexible and work to make the piece acceptable for publication in a mass-market magazine.

Here, specifically, is what I did.

First, I changed the whole tone of the piece by turning a research report into a kind of story. I scrapped the conventional organization for scientific articles and instead explained the process and experience of doing the research, saying, "We did this and we did that," "We wondered . . . ," "We were surprised . . . ," and so forth. The idea was to put the article into a more conversational, colloquial style and to get the reader to believe that something more was coming in the remainder of the article.

Second, I took care to eliminate sociological jargon and words that seem to creep into professional social science writing and almost nowhere else—terms like "actor," "sanction," "primary interaction," "salience," and others of their ilk.

Third, the lead was totally changed from one emphasizing the place of the research in the sociological literature to one that explained the original impetus for doing the study. The purpose of this was to give our study a context and provide a basis for the "story" to come—something that was unnecessary in, and even irrelevant to, the original playdumb paper. In the paragraph just following the lead, I summarized our anomalous findings, hoping to increase interest in what would follow.

Fourth, in the main body of the paper I decided to focus on the chief findings and interpretations that would be of most obvious reader interest and to eliminate everything that was not directly relevant to these. This resulted in major changes. The literature review in the playdumb paper was reduced from five long paragraphs and two footnotes to four short paragraphs. I took what was supposed to be a precise account of other studies and turned it into a general statement of what other studies had shown. I left out most of the hard data and specific questions from the other studies; I eliminated our qualifying phrases and parenthetical remarks; I eliminated the theoretical discussion; and I simplified the problem statement, making it more empirical and less theoretical.

By cutting out discussion of data limitations, response rates, and validity of measures, the data description was reduced to a presentation of the survey questions from which the data on playing dumb were obtained.

The analysis section, which in the playdumb paper consisted of seventeen paragraphs, seven footnotes, and four tables, became a mere seven paragraphs with no footnotes and no tables in the *Psychology Today* paper. I needed only the detail relevant to the major thrust of the new version, which had already been limited by earlier changes.

I did the least cutting in the discussion section, since much of that was necessary for explaining our major findings. However, I did rewrite it to conform to the style of the rest of the paper and cut three footnotes; and with direct help from *Psychology Today* editors, I added a snappy last sentence about sexual equality.

The article that appeared in *Psychology Today* is a much better vehicle for communicating our major findings than is that which appeared in *Social Psychology Quarterly.* In fact, I would hazard a guess that a higher proportion of readers of *Psychology Today* read the article than did readers of *Social Psychology.* However, to the professional social psychologist, the *Psychology Today* piece is only suggestive. There is a great deal of information in the original playdumb paper that is essential to an evaluation of the research and its contribution to the social psychological literature. Parts of the original paper, however, would easily put an only slightly drowsy "actor" to sleep. The two papers therefore are not substitutes for each other but serve different needs of different editors with an eye to serving different audiences.

Television and the Young Viewer

ELI A. RUBINSTEIN

Born in New York City in 1919, Eli A. Rubinstein graduated from City College of New York and then obtained a Ph.D. in psychology from Catholic University. From 1958 to 1971 he worked at the National Institutes of Mental Health in a variety of capacities, most recently as vice-chairman of the Surgeon General's Scientific Advisory Committee and coeditor of the research reports produced by the committee. From 1971 to 1978 Rubinstein was professor of psychiatry and psychology at the State University of New York at Stony Brook. In 1978 he became adjunct research professor of psychology at the University of North Carolina. A number of his published works on television are listed in the article's bibliography.

In his detailed review of research on the effects of television on the young viewer, published in the November/December 1978 issue of American Scientist, *Rubinstein establishes the issues of concern, examines the extent and nature of studies on those issues, provides an extensive bibliography for further reading, and concludes that no effective social policy has yet emerged.*

1 For *some* children, under *some* conditions, *some* television is harmful. For *other* children under the same conditions, or for the same children under *other* conditions, it may be beneficial. For *most* children, under *most* conditions, *most* television is probably neither particularly harmful nor particularly beneficial. [Schramm, Lyle, and Parker 1961, p. 1]

That assessment, made in 1961 by three leading Stanford researchers, was the general conclusion of one of the first major studies of television and children. Almost two decades and about two thousand studies later, their conclusion remains a reasonably accurate evaluation of the complex and differential impact of television on its millions of young viewers. The published research since 1961 has further confirmed the harmful effects to some children of some television under some conditions. At the same time, stronger evidence for the corollary has been found: for some children, under some conditions, some television is beneficial.

2 It is in the differentiation between *some* children and *most* children and in the distinction between *some* television and *most* television that the scientific findings are still not clear. As in so many other instances of exposure to persuasive messages, it is the cumulative impact over extended periods of time that should be the crucial test of consequences. It seems reasonable to assume that when millions of young viewers each spend on average about a thousand hours per year watching hundreds of television programs, such time spent must have some significant effect on their social development. It is equally reasonable to assume that if the effect is so tangible there should be little difficulty in identifying its characteristics or assessing its strength. Here, however, the evidence is less than definitive—thus the continued applicability of the Schramm, Lyle, and Parker generalization.

3 While the total impact of television on the young viewer is still unclear, the pursuit of evidence has attracted increasing interest on the part of social scientists. In the appendix to the 1961 report by Schramm et al., 52 earlier publications dealing with television and children are annotated, and they make up a fairly complete list of relevant prior research. By 1970 (Atkin, Murray, and Nayman 1971) that list of publications had grown to a total of almost 500 citations. By 1974 a total of

almost 2,400 publications were cited under the category of television and human behavior in a major review of the field by Comstock and Fisher (1975). Since 1974, research interest has continued unabated as new topics begin to be explored. The concern about televised violence has been augmented by a concern about sex on television, the persuasive power of television advertising on children, and, indeed, the effect of television on the entire socialization process of children.

4 Two events in the early 1970s provided the most compelling influence toward that growth of interest. One was the development of the program "Sesame Street," in which formative research was pursued in partnership with the production of the program itself. The other was the completion in 1972 of a major federally funded research program, now known as the Surgeon-General's program, to evaluate the relationship between TV violence and aggressive behavior in children. . . .

TELEVISED VIOLENCE

5 At about the same time that "Sesame Street" was being prepared for broadcast in 1969, a major federal research program was initiated to assess the effects of televised violence on children. The history of that research enterprise has been thoroughly described and evaluated from a variety of perspectives (Bogart 1972; Cater and Strickland 1975; Rubinstein 1975). The belief is fairly widespread that the body of research, published in five volumes of technical reports, provided a major new set of findings.

6 There is much less agreement about the report and conclusions of the advisory committee itself, because of the cautious language used. Even now, years after the report was published, the conclusions are debated. The debate was sparked initially because of a misleading headline in a front-page story in the *New York Times* ("TV Violence Held Unharmful to Youth") when the report was first released. A careful analysis of the subsequent press coverage revealed how influential that headline was in further confusing the interpretation of the findings (Tankard and Showalter 1977). The committee had unanimously agreed that there was some evidence of a causal relationship between televised violence and later aggressive behavior. However, the conclusion was so moderated by qualifiers that it was, and still is, criticized and misinterpreted by industry spokesmen as being too strong and by researchers as being too weak.

7 The effect of televised violence has been an issue of public concern

almost from the inception of television in the early 1950s. Periodically, over the past 25 years, a variety of congressional inquiries as well as commissioned reports have drawn attention to the problem of televised violence. In almost every instance concern was raised about harmful effects. In all these reports, however, relatively little new research on the problem was produced. Even the prestigious Eisenhower Commission, which was asked by President Johnson in 1968 to explore the question within its total inquiry into violence in America, devoted its attention primarily to a synthesis of existing knowledge rather than to collecting new scientific information. Its conclusions—that violence on television encourages real violence—were seen as less than persuasive and were largely ignored, especially since attention was then focused on the new Surgeon-General's Committee.

8 The Surgeon-General's program provided the first major infusion of new monies into research on television violence, which in turn has stimulated a "second harvest," as Schramm (1976) calls it, of new work on television and social behavior. The debate on the evidence from the five volumes of research reports produced in 1972 by the Surgeon-General's program is also still lively. The essence of the debate emerges from two contrasting approaches to assessing the evidence. The Surgeon-General's advisory committee, while acknowledging flaws in many of the individual studies, held that the *convergence* of evidence was sufficient to permit a qualified conclusion indicating a causal relationship between extensive viewing of violence and later aggressive behavior. This conclusion, without the qualifications, is endorsed by a number of highly respected researchers, some of whom participated in the Surgeon-General's program and some who were not directly involved.

9 A different and seemingly more rigorous approach to the evidence is adopted by some other experts in the field. This contrasting view is epitomized by Kaplan and Singer (1976), who conclude that the total evidence does no more than support the null hypothesis.

10 A brief explanation is appropriate here about the theoretical formulations most common in the research underlying the whole question of television and aggressive behavior. Quite simply, three possibilities exist—and all have their proponents. (1) Television has no significant relationship to aggressive behavior. (2) Television reduces aggressive behavior. (3) Television causes aggressive behavior; a variant on this possibility is that both television viewing and aggressive behavior are related not to each other but to a "third variable" which mediates between the first two variables.

11 The Kaplan and Singer position, to give one recent example, is that the research so far has demonstrated no relationship between televised violence and later aggressive behavior. They characterize this as the "conservative" assessment of the evidence and come to that conclusion by finding no study persuasive enough in its own right to bear the burden of significant correlation, let alone causal relationship. They are not the only ones to conclude "no-effect": Singer (1971) came to the same conclusion, as did Howitt and Cumberbatch (1975).

12 The second point of view has been espoused primarily by Feshbach (1961). The catharsis hypothesis holds that vicarious experience of aggressive behavior, as occurs in viewing TV violence, may actually serve as a release of aggressive tensions and thereby reduce direct expression of aggressive behavior. This view has not been supported by research evidence, although it emerges time and again as a "common-sense" assessment of the relationship between vicarious viewing of violence and later behavior. Indeed, the thesis itself goes back to Aristotle, who considered dramatic presentations a vehicle for discharge of feelings by the audience. The Surgeon-General's committee, in considering this thesis, made one of their few unequivocal assessments—that there was "no evidence that would support a catharsis interpretation."

13 The third general conclusion, and the one now prevailing, is that there is a positive relationship between TV violence and later aggressive behavior. This facilitation of later aggression, explained primarily by social learning theory, is endorsed by a number of investigators. The basic theoretical formulation is generally credited to Bandura (Bandura and Walters 1963), who began his social learning studies in the early 1960s, when he and his students clearly demonstrated that children will imitate aggressive acts they witness in film presentations. These were the so-called "bobo doll" studies, in which children watching a bobo doll being attacked, either by a live model or a cartoon character, were more likely to imitate such behavior. These early studies were criticized both because bobo dolls, made for rough and tumble play, tend to provoke aggressive hitting and because the hostile play was only against inanimate play objects. Later studies have demonstrated that such aggression will also take place against people (Hanratty et al. 1972).

14 Variations on the basic social learning theory are rather numerous. Kaplan and Singer make a useful schema by incorporating three related theoretical branches under the general label of "activation hypotheses." Bandura and his students are included in the category of social learning and imitation. A second branch is represented by Berkowitz and his

students, who follow a classical conditioning hypothesis, in which repeated viewing of aggressive behavior is presented to build up the probability of aggressive behavior as a conditioned response to the cues produced in the portrayal. A number of experiments by Berkowitz and his colleagues have shown that subjects viewing a violent film after being angered were more likely to show aggressive behavior than subjects, similarly angered beforehand, who saw nonaggressive films (Berkowitz 1965; Berkowitz and Geen 1966).

15 In still a third variation on the activation approach, Tannenbaum (1972) holds that a generalized emotional arousal is instigated by emotionally charged viewing material and that this level of arousal itself is the precursor of the subsequent behavior. Any exciting content, including erotic content, can induce this heightened arousal. The nature of response is then a function of the conditions that exist at the time the activation of behavior takes place. Thus, according to this theory, it is not so much the violent content per se that induces later aggressive behavior as it is the level of arousal evoked. Subsequent circumstances may channel the heightened arousal in the direction of aggressive behavior.

16 In an important examination of the utility of these various formulations, Watt and Krull (1977) reanalyzed data on 597 adolescents from three prior studies, involving both programming attributes (such as perceived violent content) and viewer attributes (such as viewing exposure and aggressive behavior) through a series of correlations. They contrasted three models, which they labeled catharsis model, arousal model, and facilitation model. The first two models are essentially as described above. The facilitation model is identified as a general social-learning model without regard to whether the process is primarily imitation, cueing, or legitimization of aggressive behavior. Thus, the Bandura and Berkowitz studies both fall into the facilitation model.

17 Through a series of partial correlations, Watt and Krull found (1) no support for the catharsis model; (2) support for a combination of the facilitation and arousal models; and (3) some differences due to age and/or sex, with the arousal model a somewhat better explanation for female adolescents, whereas the facilitation model better described the data for males. (Sex differences in results in many studies of television and behavior are quite common. One of the major studies in the field, by Lefkowitz et al., 1972, found significant correlations between TV violence and later aggressive behavior with boys but not with girls.)

18 What are the implications in this continuing controversy about the effects of television violence on aggressive behavior? As in so many other

social science issues it depends on what you are looking for. The dilemma is neatly characterized in a legal case in Florida in October 1977, in which the defense argued that an adolescent boy, who admittedly killed an elderly woman, was suffering from "involuntary subliminal television intoxication." (This term, which appears nowhere in the scientific literature, was introduced by the defense attorney.) In trying to show that the scientific evidence on television's effects on behavior was not directly pertinent to this murder trial, the prosecuting attorney asked an expert witness if any scientific studies indicated that a viewer had ever been induced to commit a serious crime following the viewing of TV violence. The (correct) answer to that question was "no." The judge thereby ruled that expert testimony on the effects of televised violence would be inadmissible and brought back the jury, which had been sequestered during the interrogation of the expert witness. On the basis of the evidence presented to it, the jury found the defendant guilty of murder and rejected the plea of temporary insanity by virtue of "involuntary subliminal television intoxication."

19 While there is indeed no *scientific* evidence that excessive viewing of televised violence can or does provoke violent crime in any one individual, it is clear that the bulk of the studies show that if large groups of children watch a great deal of televised violence they will be more prone to behave aggressively than similar groups of children who do not watch such TV violence. The argument simply follows from the basic premise that children learn from all aspects of their environment. To the extent that one or another environmental agent occupies a significant proportion of a child's daily activity, that agent becomes a component of influence on his or her behavior. In a recent comprehensive review of all the evidence on the effects of television on children, Comstock et al. (1978) conclude that television should be considered a major agent of socialization in the lives of children.

20 An important confirmation of the more general influence of television on the young viewer derives from research on the so-called "prosocial" effects of television. Stimulated by the findings of the Surgeon-General's program, a number of researchers began in 1972 to explore the corollary question: If TV violence can induce aggressive behavior, can TV prosocial programming stimulate positive behavior? By 1975, this question was of highest interest to active researchers in the field, according to a national survey (Comstock and Lindsey 1975).

21 A significant body of literature has now been generated to confirm these prosocial effects (Rubinstein et al. 1974; Stein and Friedrich 1975).

Research by network scientists (CBS Broadcast Group 1977) has confirmed that children learn from the prosocial messages included in programs designed to impart such messages. Because the effect of prosocial program content is so clearly similar in process to the effect of TV violence, confirmation of the former effect adds strength to the validity of the latter effect.

22 In all the intensive analysis of the effects of TV violence, perhaps the one scientific issue most strongly argued against by the network officials has been the definition and assessment of levels of violent content. The single continuing source of such definition and assessment has been the work of Gerbner and his associates (Gerbner 1972). Beginning in 1969 and continuing annually, Gerbner has been publishing a violence index which has charted the levels of violence among the three networks on prime time. The decline in violence over the entire decade had been negligible until the 1977–78 season (Gerbner et al. 1978), following an intensive public campaign against TV violence by both the American Medical Association and the Parent-Teacher Association.

23 Gerbner's definition of violence is specific and yet inclusive—"the overt expression of physical force against others or self, or compelling action against one's will on pain of being hurt or killed or actually hurting or killing." Despite criticism by the industry, the Gerbner index has been widely accepted by other researchers. An extensive effort by a Committee on Television and Social Behavior, organized by the Social Science Research Council to develop a more comprehensive violence index, ended up essentially endorsing Gerbner's approach (Social Science Research Council 1975).

24 Perhaps of more theoretical interest than his violence index is Gerbner's present thesis that television is a "cultural indicator." He argues that television content reinforces beliefs about various cultural themes—the social realities of life are modified in the mind of the viewer by the images portrayed on the television screen. To the extent that the television world differs from the real world, some portion of that difference influences the perception of the viewer about the world in which he or she lives. Thus, Gerbner has found that heavy viewers see the world in a much more sinister light than individuals who do not watch as much television. Gerbner argues that excessive portrayals of violence on television inculcate feelings of fear among heavy viewers, which may be as important an effect as the findings of increased aggressive behavior. Some confirmation of this feeling of fear was found in a national survey of children (Zill 1977): children who were heavy viewers were reported

significantly more likely to be more fearful in general than children who watched less television.

TV ADVERTISING

25 An area of research that has been increasing in importance since the work of the Surgeon-General's program has been concerned with the effects of advertising on children. One of the technical reports in the Surgeon-General's program described a series of studies on this topic by Ward (1972), which was among the first major published studies in which children's reactions to television advertising were examined in their relationship to cognitive development. That report provided preliminary findings on (1) how children's responses to television advertising become increasingly differentiated and complex with age; (2) the development of cynicism and suspicion about television messages by the fourth grade; (3) mothers' perceptions about how television influences their children; and (4) how television advertising influences consumer socialization among adolescents.

26 The entire field of research on effects of television advertising—at least academic published research—has only begun to develop in the 1970s. A major review of the published literature in the field was sponsored and published by the National Science Foundation in 1977 (Adler 1977). It is noteworthy that only 21 studies, all published between 1971 and 1976, were considered significant enough to be singled out for inclusion in the review's annotated appendix. The total body of evidence is still so small that no major theoretical formulations have yet emerged. Instead, the research follows the general social-learning model inherent in the earlier research on televised violence.

27 Despite the lack of extensive research findings on the effects of television advertising on children, formal concern about possible effects began to emerge in the early 1960s. Self-regulatory guidelines were adopted by the National Association of Broadcasters in 1961 to define acceptable toy advertising practices to children. Subsequently, published NAB guidelines were expanded to include all advertising directed primarily to children. An entire mechanism has been established within the industry, under the responsibility of the NAB Television Code Authority, through which guidelines on children's advertising—as well as other broadcast standards—are enforced. In addition, in 1974 the National Advertising Division of the Council of Better Business Bureaus established a Children's Advertising Review Unit to help in the self-regulation

of advertising directed to children aged eleven and under. That organization, with the assistance of a panel of social science advisors, developed and issued its own set of guidelines for children's advertising.

28 The role of research in helping to make those guidelines on children's advertising more meaningful is only now receiving some attention, thanks in part to the NSF review cited above. Two recent events have highlighted both the paucity and the relevance of research in this field. In 1975, the Attorney General of Massachusetts, in collaboration with Attorneys General of other states, petitioned the Federal Communications Commission to ban all drug advertising between 9 A.M. and 9 P.M., on the ground that such advertising was harmful to children. After a series of hearings in May 1976, at which researchers and scientists testified, the petition was denied for lack of scientific evidence to support the claim.

29 In 1978, the Federal Trade Commission formally considered petitions requesting "the promulgation of a trade rule regulating television advertising of candy and other sugared products to children." A comprehensive staff report on television advertising to children (Ratner et al. 1978) made recommendations to the FTC, citing much of the relevant scientific literature on advertising to children as evidence supporting the need for such a trade rule. At the time of this writing, the entire matter was still under active consideration.

30 What does the existing research in this area demonstrate? It is clear that children are exposed to a large number of television commercials. The statistics themselves are significant. Annually, on average, children between two and eleven years of age are now exposed to more than 20,000 television commercials. Children in this age group watch an average of about 25 hours of television per week all through the year. The most clichéd statistic quoted is that, by the time a child graduates from high school today, he or she will have spent more time in front of a television set (17,000 hours) than in a formal classroom (11,000 hours). Indeed, all the statistics on television viewing from earliest childhood through age eighteen show that no other daily activity, with the exception of sleeping, is so clearly dominant.

31 Just as was shown in the earlier research examining the effects of programming content, even the limited research now available on television commercials documents that children learn from watching these commercials. Whether it is the sheer recall of products and product attributes (Atkin 1975) or the singing of commercial jingles (Lyle and Hoffman 1972), the evidence is positive that children learn. More important, children and their parents are influenced by the intent of these

commercials. One study (Lyle and Hoffman 1972) showed that nine out of ten preschool children asked for food items and toys they saw advertised on television.

32 A number of studies have also revealed various unintended effects of television advertising. While a vast majority of the advertisements adhere to the guidelines that attempt to protect children against exploitative practices, a number of studies have shown that, over time, children begin to distrust the accuracy of the commercial message. By the sixth grade, children are generally cynical about the truthfulness of the ads. A recent educational film by Consumers Union, on some of the excessive claims in TV advertising, highlights the problem of disbelief (Consumers Union 1976). There have also been a number of surveys in which parents have indicated negative reactions to children's commercials. In one study (Ward, Wackman, and Wartella 1975) 75% of the parents had such negative reactions.

33 In the survey of the literature evaluated in the 1977 NSF review, the evidence is examined against some of the major policy concerns that have emerged in the development of appropriate guidelines on children's advertising. These concerns can be grouped into four categories: (1) modes of advertising; (2) content of advertising; (3) products advertised; and (4) general effects of advertising.

34 Studies of "modes of advertising" show, for example, that separation of program and commercial is not well understood by children under eight years of age. While these younger children receive and retain the commercial messages, they are less able to discriminate the persuasive intent of the commercial and are more likely to perceive the message as truthful and to want to buy the product (Robertson and Rossiter 1974).

35 The format and the use of various audio-visual techniques also influence the children's perceptions of the message. This influence is clearly acknowledged by the advertisers and the broadcasters, who have included explicit instructions in the guidelines, especially for toy products, to ensure that audio and video production techniques do not misrepresent the product. What little research there is on this entire aspect of format is still far from definitive. What is clear is that attention, especially among young children, is increased by active movement, animation, lively music, and visual changes. (All of this, and more, is well understood by the advertising agencies and those who develop the ads, and they keep such knowledge confidential, much as a trade secret.)

36 One other relatively clear finding on audio-visual technique relates to the understanding of "disclaimers" – special statements about the product that may not be clear from the commercial itself, such as "batteries

not included." A study of disclaimer wording and comprehension (Liebert et al. 1977) revealed that a standard disclaimer ("some assembly required") was less well understood by 6- and 8-year-olds than a modification ("You have to put it together"). The obvious conclusion—that wording should be appropriate to the child's ability to understand—is just one of the many ways in which this research can play a role in refining guidelines.

37 Studies on the content of advertising have shown that the appearance of a particular character with the product can modify the child's evaluation of the product, either positively or negatively, depending on the child's evaluation of the character. It is also clear that children are affected in a positive way by presenters of their own sex and race (Adler 1977). On a more general level, sexual stereotypes in advertising probably influence children in the same way they do in the program content.

38 Although there is relatively little significant research on the effects of classes of products, two such classes have been under intense public scrutiny in recent years: proprietary drug advertising and certain categories of food advertising. Governmental regulatory agencies are currently considering what kind of controls should be placed on such advertising to children.

39 Concerning the more general effects of advertising targeted to children, surveys suggest that parents have predominantly negative attitudes about such advertising because they believe it causes stress in the parent-child relationship. Studies on questions such as this, and on the larger issue of how such advertising leads to consumer socialization, are now being pursued. Ward and his associates (Ward, Wackman, and Wartella 1975) have been examining the entire question of how children learn to buy. The highly sophisticated techniques used by advertisers to give a 30-second or 60-second commercial strong impact on the child viewer make these commercials excellent study material for examining the entire process of consumer socialization. Much important research still remains to be done on this topic.

SEX ON TV

40 Of the many public concerns about television and its potentially harmful effects on children, the issue of sex on television is at present among the most visible and the least understood. If research on the effects of advertising is still in its early development, research on sex on television has hardly begun.

41 It has been found that children who watch large amounts of television (25 hours or more per week) are more likely to reveal stereotypic sex role attitudes than children who watch 10 hours or less per week (Frueh and McGhee 1975). Research has documented the stereotyping on television of women as passive and rule-abiding, while men are shown as aggressive, powerful, and smarter than women. Also, youth and attractiveness are stressed more for females than males. This evidence of stereotyping was included as one part of an argument by the U.S. Commission on Civil Rights that the Federal Communications Commission should conduct an inquiry into the portrayal of minorities and women in commercial and public television drama and should propose rules to correct the problem (U.S. Commission on Civil Rights 1977). Program content in 1977 and 1978 has given increased emphasis to so-called "sex on television," at the same time that violence on television is decreasing (Gerbner et al. 1978).

42 Despite all the public concern and attention, including cover stories in major newsweeklies, relatively little academic research has been done on sex on TV. Two studies reported in 1977 provided information on the level of physical intimacy portrayed on television (Franzblau et al. 1977 and Fernandez-Collado and Greenberg 1977). Franzblau, Sprafkin, and Rubinstein analyzed 61 prime-time programs shown on all three networks during a full week in early October 1975. Results showed that, while there was considerable casual intimacy such as kissing and embracing and much verbal innuendo on sexual activity, actual physical intimacy such as intercourse, rape, and homosexual behavior was absent in explicit form.

43 Fernandez-Collado and Greenberg examined 77 programs aired in prime time during the 1976–77 season and concluded that intimate sexual acts did occur on commercial television, with "the predominant act being sexual intercourse between heterosexuals unmarried to each other." An examination of the data, however, reveals that in this study, verbal statements—identified as verbal innuendo in the study by Franzblau et al.—served as the basis for the conclusion reached. In fact, explicit sexual acts such as identify an R- or an X-rated movie do not occur on prime-time network television.

44 Even though few published studies have so far examined the question of sex on television, at least two important issues have been highlighted by the two studies mentioned above. The most obvious point is the differences in interpretation of the data by the two reports—unfortunately not an uncommon occurrence in social science research. Labeling

and defining the phenomena under examination, let alone drawing conclusions from results, show variations from investigator to investigator. While this kind of difference is not unique to the social sciences, the more complex the data and the less standard the measurement—qualities often inherent in social science studies—the more likely these individual differences of interpretation.

45 The second point illustrated by these two studies of sex on TV is more intrinsic to the subject matter itself. The public concern about sex on TV suggests that the general reaction is much in keeping with the substitution of behavior for verbal statements, as is found in the study by Fernandez-Collado and Greenberg. And, in fact, there are no scientific data to indicate that verbal innuendo may not affect the young viewer as much—or as little—as explicitly revealed behavior. What is important here is that we do not know the effects of either the verbal description or the explicit depiction on the young viewer. Research findings of the Commission on Obscenity and Pornography in 1970 suggest that exposure to explicit sexuality seems harmless. Nevertheless, public sensitivities are clearly high; whether those sensitivities are justified by the facts still remains an open question. At the very least, studies should be undertaken to give some objective answers to these questions.

REFERENCES

McCombs, and D. Roberts. 1978. *Television and Human Behavior.* Columbia University Press.

Comstock, G., and M. Fisher. 1975. *Television and Human Behavior: A Guide to the Pertinent Scientific Literature.* Santa Monica, CA: Rand Corporation.

Comstock, G., and G. Lindsey. 1975. *Television and Human Behavior: The Research Horizon, Future and Present.* Santa Monica, CA: Rand Corporation.

Consumers Union. 1976. *The Six Billion Dollar Sell.* Mount Vernon, NY.

Cook, T. D., H. Appleton, R. F. Conner, A. Shaffer, G. Tomkin, and S. J. Weber. 1975. *Sesame Street Revisited.* New York: Russell Sage Foundation.

Dienstbier, R. A. 1977. Sex and violence: Can research have it both ways? *J. Communication* 27:176–88.

Fernandez-Collado, C., and B. S. Greenberg. 1977. *Substance Use and Sexual Intimacy on Commercial Television.* Report #5, Mich. State Univ.

Feshbach, S. 1961. The stimulating versus cathartic effects of a vicarious aggressive activity. *J. Abnormal and Soc. Psych.* 63:381–85.

Ford Foundation. 1976. *Television and Children: Priorities for Research.* New York.

Franzblau, S., J. N. Sprafkin, and E. A. Rubinstein. 1977. Sex on TV: A content analysis. *J. Communication* 27:164–70.

Frueh, T., and P. E. McGhee. 1975. Traditional sex-role development and amount of time spent watching television. *Devel. Psych.* 11:109.

Gerbner, G. 1972. Violence in television drama: Trends and symbolic functions.

In *Television and Social Behavior,* vol. 1. *Media Content and Control,* ed. G. A. Comstock and E. A. Rubinstein. U. S. Government Printing Office.

Gerbner, G., L. Gross, M. Jackson-Beeck, A. Jeffries-Fox, and N. Signorielli. 1978. *Violence Profile No. 9.* Univ. of Pennsylvania Press.

Hanratty, M. A., E. O'Neal, and J. L. Sulzer. 1972. Effect of frustration upon imitation of aggression. *J. Pers. and Soc. Psych.* 21:30–34.

Howitt, D., and G. Cumberbatch. 1975. *Mass Media Violence and Society.* Wiley.

Kaplan, R. M., and R. D. Singer. 1976. Television violence and viewer aggression: A reexamination of the evidence. *J. Soc. Issues* 32:35–70.

Katz, E. 1977. *Social Research on Broadcasting: Proposals for Further Development. A Report to the British Broadcasting Corporation.* British Broadcasting Corporation.

Kochnower, J. M., J. F. Fracchia, E. A. Rubinstein, and J. N. Sprafkin. 1978. *Television Viewing Behaviors of Emotionally Disturbed Children: An Interview Study.* New York: Brookdale International Institute.

Lefkowitz, M. M., L. D. Eron, L. O. Walder, and L. R. Huesmann. 1972. Television violence and child aggression: A follow-up study. In *Television and Social Behavior,* vol. 3. *Television and Adolescent Aggressiveness,* ed. G. A. Comstock and E. A. Rubinstein. U. S. Gov. Printing Office.

Lesser, G. S. 1974. *Children and Television: Lessons from "Sesame Street."* Random House.

Liebert, D. E., R. M. Liebert, J. N. Sprafkin, and E. A. Rubinstein. 1977. Effects of television commercial disclaimers on the product expectations of children. *J. Communication* 27:118–24.

Lyle, J., and H. Hoffman. 1972. Children's use of television and other media. In *Television and Social Behavior,* vol. 5. *Television in Day-to-Day Life: Patterns of Use,* ed. E. A. Rubinstein, G. A. Comstock, and J. P. Murray. U. S. Government Printing Office.

Ratner, E. M., et al. 1978. *FTC Staff Report on Television Advertising to Children.* Washington, DC: Federal Trade Commission.

Robertson, T. S., and J. R. Rossiter. 1974. Children and commercial persuasion: An attribution theory analysis. *J. Consumer Research* 1:13–20.

Rubinstein, E. A. 1975. Social science and media policy. *J. Communication* 25:194–200.

_____. 1976. Warning: The Surgeon General's research program may be dangerous to preconceived notions. *J. Soc. Issues* 32:18–34.

Rubinstein, E. A., J. F. Fracchia, J. M . Kochnower, and J. N. Sprafkin. 1977. *Television Viewing Behaviors of Mental Patients: A Survey of Psychiatric Centers in New York State.* New York: Brookdale International Institute.

Rubinstein, E. A., R. M. Liebert, J. M. Neale, and R. W. Poulos. 1974. *Assessing Television's Influence on Children's Prosocial Behavior.* New York: Brookdale International Institute.

Schaar, K. 1978. TV ad probe snags on Hill, researcher ire. *APA Monitor* vol. 9, no. 6, 1.

Schramm, W. 1976. The second harvest of two research-producing events: The Surgeon General's inquiry and "Sesame Street." *Proc. Nat. Acad. Educ.,* vol. 3.

Schramm, W., J. Lyle, and E. B. Parker. 1961. *Television in the Lives of our Children.* Stanford Univ. Press.

Silverman, L. T., J. N. Sprafkin, and E. A. Rubinstein. 1978. *Sex on Television: A Content Analysis of the 1977–78 Prime-Time Programs.* New York: Brookdale International Institute.

Singer, J. L., ed. 1971. *The Control of Aggression and Violence.* Academic Press.

Social Science Research Council. 1975. *A Profile of Televised Violence.* New York.

Stein, A. H., and L. K. Friedrich. 1975. *Impact of Television on Children and Youth.* Univ. of Chicago Press.

Surgeon-General's Scientific Advisory Committee on Television and Social Behavior. 1972. *Television and Growing Up: The Impact of Televised Violence.* U.S. Government Printing Office.

Tankard, J. W., and S. W. Showalter. 1977. Press coverage of the 1972 report on television and social behavior. *Journalism Quart.* 54:293–306.

Tannenbaum, P. H. 1972. Studies in film- and television-mediated arousal and aggression: A progress report. In *Television and Social Behavior,* vol. 5. *Television Effects: Further Explorations,* ed. G. A. Comstock, E. A. Rubinstein, and J. P. Murray. U. S. Government Printing Office.

U. S. Commission on Civil Rights. 1977. *Window Dressing on the Set: Women and Minorities in Television.* Washington, DC.

Ward, S. 1972. Effects of television advertising on children and adolescents. In *Television and Social Behavior,* vol. 5. *Television in Day-to-Day Life: Patterns of Use,* ed. E. A. Rubinstein, G. A. Comstock, and J. P. Murray. U. S. Government Printing Office.

Ward, S., D. B. Wackman, and E. Wartella. 1975. *Children Learning to Buy: The Development of Consumer Information Processing Skills.* Cambridge, MA: Marketing Science Institute.

Watt, J. H., and R. Krull. 1977. An examination of three models of television viewing and aggression. *Human Communications Research* 3:99–112.

Zill, N. 1977. *National Survey of Children: Preliminary Results.* New York: Foundation for Child Development.

QUESTIONS FOR ANALYSIS AND DISCUSSION

1. What assumption about the effects of television on children does it seem reasonable to make?
2. What other assumption seems reasonable but in fact has not been easily demonstrated? What view of the relationship between television and child viewers continues as a result?
3. What four topics regarding children and television currently interest researchers?
4. In 1969 a research project was initiated to examine television violence and aggression. What did the report conclude? Why has it irritated so many people?

5. What are the three possible relationships between televised violence and aggressive behavior? Which one is the prevailing view?
6. Explain the catharsis hypothesis. Is there any evidence for this hypothesis with regard to television viewing?
7. Explain the concepts of the arousal model and the facilitation model. What differences seem to exist between the responses of boy and girl viewers to TV violence?
8. After surveying the principal studies, what does Rubinstein conclude about the connection, if any, between TV violence and aggressive behavior? What seems to be the most important element in assessing the influence of television on children?
9. Besides perhaps increasing aggressive behavior, what other effect does TV violence have on youngsters who are frequent television viewers?
10. What, in summary, do the limited studies of television advertising reveal about its effect on children? Do young children seem to understand the intent of ads?
11. How much work had been done on television's influence on sex stereotyping when Rubinstein wrote? What has been learned about acquiring sex role stereotypes?
12. How much explicit sex appeared on television prior to 1978? What is one problem in determining how much appeared? Do you think, from your own viewing, that more recent studies would reveal an increase in explicit sex on television?
13. Which research results were you already familiar with? Do you find any of the new information surprising? Why or why not?
14. Who is Rubinstein's audience? What is his purpose in writing? Is it more useful to ask about his purpose than to ask about his thesis? Why?

Television and the Disappearance of Childhood

NEIL POSTMAN

Professor of media ecology at New York University, Neil Postman (b. 1931) is a well-known author of books and articles on teaching, language, and contemporary culture. He made his reputation initially with several books, coauthored with Charles Weingartner, calling for reforms in education, the most famous being Teaching as a Subversive Activity *(1969). Postman and Weingartner argued for change, initiated by students and teachers, from a stifling authoritarian environment of force-feeding facts to a process that would develop flexible, creative, innovative personalities. A decade later, in* Teaching as a Conserving Activity, *Postman reveals a conservative shift that he readily acknowledges. In this work he argues for schools that preserve and teach intellectual inquiry and the attributes of culture in a fragmented, media-oriented society.*

Two of his popular books on culture are Crazy Talk, Stupid Talk *(1976), in which Postman examines the ways we allow language to narrow our focus and limit our choices, and* The Disappearance of Childhood *(1982), from which the following selection is taken.*

Written in Postman's usual forceful, challenging style, The Disappearance of Childhood *seeks to demonstrate to a general readership one of the serious changes in contemporary culture, and to account for that change. Unhampered by the conventions of scholarship in the social sciences, Postman can write a lively popular work; but he frequently annoys scholars with his seeping, undocumented assertions. Annoying he may be, but boring he is not.*

1 The plain facts are that television operates virtually around the clock, that both its physical and symbolic form make it unnecessary—in fact, impossible—to segregate its audience, and that it requires a continuous supply of novel and interesting information to engage and hold that audience. Thus, television must make use of every existing taboo in the culture. Whether the taboo is revealed on a talk show, made into a theme for a soap opera or situation comedy, or exposed in a commercial is largely irrelevant. Television needs material. And it needs it in a way quite different from other media. Television is not only a pictorial medium, it is a present-centered and speed-of-light medium. The bias and therefore the business of television is to *move* information, not collect it. Television cannot dwell upon a subject or explore it deeply, an activity for which the static, lineal form of typography is well suited. There may, for example, be fifty books on the history of Argentina, five hundred on childhood, five thousand on the Civil War. If television has anything to do with these subjects, it will do it once, and then move on. . . .

2 Like alphabetic writing and the printed book, television opens secrets, makes public what has previously been private.[1] But unlike

[1]For an excellent treatment of how television makes available "back region" information, see Joshua Meyrowitz's *No Sense of Place: A Theory on the Impact of Electronic Media on Social Structure and Behavior*, unpublished doctoral dissertation, New York University, 1978.

writing and printing, television has no way to close things down. The great paradox of literacy was that as it made secrets accessible, it simultaneously created an obstacle to their availability. One must *qualify* for the deeper mysteries of the printed page by submitting oneself to the rigors of a scholastic education. One must progress slowly, sequentially, even painfully, as the capacity for self-restraint and conceptual thinking is both enriched and expanded. I vividly remember being told as a thirteen-year-old of the existence of a book, Henry Miller's *Tropic of Cancer,* that, I was assured, was required reading for all who wanted to know sexual secrets. But the problems that needed to be solved to have access to it were formidable. For one, it was hard to find. For another, it cost money. For still another, it had to be *read.* Much of it, therefore, was not understandable to me, and even the special passages to which my attention was drawn by a thoughtful previous reader who underlined them required acts of imagination that my experience could not always generate.

3 Television, by contrast, is an open-admission technology to which there are no physical, economic, cognitive, or imaginative restraints. The six-year-old and the sixty-year-old are equally qualified to experience what television has to offer. Television, in this sense, is the consummate egalitarian medium of communication, surpassing oral language itself. For in speaking, we may always whisper so that the children will not hear. Or we may use words they may not understand. But television cannot whisper, and its pictures are both concrete and self-explanatory. The children see everything it shows.

4 The most obvious and general effect of this situation is to eliminate the exclusivity of worldly knowledge and, therefore, to eliminate one of the principal differences between childhood and adulthood. This effect follows from a fundamental principle of social structure: A group is largely defined by the exclusivity of the information its members share. If everyone knew what lawyers know, there would be no lawyers. If students knew what their teachers know, there would be no need to differentiate between them. Indeed, if fifth graders knew what eighth graders know, there would be no point to having grades at all. G. B. Shaw once remarked that all professions are conspiracies against the laity. We might broaden this idea to say that any group is a "conspiracy" against those who are not in it by virtue of the fact that, for one reason or another, the "outs" do not have access to the information possessed by the "ins."

5 Of course, not every instance of role differentiation or group identity rests on access to information. Biology, for example, will determine

who will be a male and who a female. But in most instances social role is formed by the conditions of a particular information environment, and this is most certainly the case with the social category of childhood. Children are a group of people who do *not* know certain things that adults know. In the Middle Ages there were no children because there existed no means for adults to know exclusive information. In the Age of Gutenberg, such a means developed. In the Age of Television, it is dissolved.

6 This means more than that childhood "innocence" is lost, a phrase that tends to imply only a diminution of childhood's charm. With the electric media's rapid and egalitarian disclosure of the total content of the adult world, several profound consequences result. First, the idea of shame is diluted and demystified. So that the meaning I am giving to shame may be clearer, it is necessary to introduce a particularly relevant remark by G. K. Chesterton. "All healthy men," he observed, "ancient and modern, Eastern and Western, know that there is a certain fury in sex that we cannot afford to inflame and that a certain mystery and awe must ever surround it if we are to remain sane."

7 Although Chesterton is here talking about sexual impulses, his point has a wider meaning, and is, I think, a fair summary of Freud's and Elias's views on the civilizing process. Civilization cannot exist without the control of impulses, particularly the impulse toward aggression and immediate gratification. We are in constant danger of being possessed by barbarism, of being overrun by violence, promiscuity, instinct, egoism. Shame is the mechanism by which barbarism is held at bay, and much of its power comes, as Chesterton holds, from the mystery and awe that surround various acts. Included among these acts are thoughts and words, all of which are made mysterious and awesome by the fact that they are constantly hidden from public view. By hiding them, we make them mysterious; by making them mysterious, we regulate them. In some cases, adults may not even display their knowledge of such secrets to each other and must find relief in the psychiatrist's office or the Confessional Box. But in all cases it is necessary to control the extent to which children are aware of such matters. Certainly since the Middle Ages it has been commonly believed that the impulse toward violence, sexuality, and egoism is of particular danger to children, who, it is assumed, are not yet sufficiently governed by self-restraint. Therefore, the inculcation of feelings of shame has constituted a rich and delicate part of a child's formal and informal education. Children, in other words, are immersed in a world of secrets, surrounded by mystery and

awe; a world that will be made intelligible to them by adults who will teach them, in stages, how shame is transformed into a set of moral directives. From the child's point of view, shame gives power and authority to adulthood. For adults know, whereas children do not, what words are shameful to use, what subjects are shameful to discuss, what acts are deemed necessary to privatize.

8 I should like to be especially clear on this point. I do not argue that the content of shame is created by the information structure of society. The roots of shame lie elsewhere, go very deep into the history and fears of a people, and are far beyond the scope and point of this book. I am, however, claiming that shame cannot exert any influence as a means of social control or role differentiation in a society that cannot keep secrets. If one lived in a society in which the law required people to be nude on public beaches, the shame in revealing certain parts of the body would quickly disappear. For clothing is a means of keeping a secret, and if we are deprived of the means of keeping a secret, we are deprived of the secret. Similarly, the shamefulness in incest, in violence, in homosexuality, in mental illness, disappears when the means of concealing them disappears, when their details become the content of public discourse, available for examination by everyone in a public arena. What was once shameful may become a "social problem" or a "political issue" or a "psychological phenomenon," but in the process it must lose its dark and fugitive character, as well as some of its moral force. . . .

9 It is clear that if we turn over to children a vast store of powerful adult material, childhood cannot survive. By definition adulthood means mysteries solved and secrets uncovered. If from the start the children know the mysteries and the secrets, how shall we tell them apart from anyone else?

10 With the gradual decline of shame there is, of course, a corresponding diminution in the significance of manners. As shame is the psychological mechanism that overcomes impulse, manners are the exterior social expression of the same conquest. Everything from table manners to language manners to the manners of dress is intended to reveal the extent to which one has learned self-restraint; and it is at the same time a means of teaching self-restraint. As already noted, manners or civilité did not begin to emerge in elaborated forms among the mass of people until after the printing press, in large measure because literacy both demanded and promoted a high degree of self-control and delayed gratification. Manners, one might say, are a social analogue to literacy. Both require a submission of body to mind. Both require a fairly long

developmental learning process. Both require intensive adult teaching. As literacy creates a hierarchical intellectual order, manners create a hierarchical social order. Children must earn adulthood by becoming both literate and well-mannered. But in an information environment in which literacy loses force as a metaphor of the structure of human development, the importance of manners must decline. The new media make distinctions among age groups appear invidious, and thus are hostile to the idea of a hierarchical social order.

11 Consider, for example, the case of language manners. Within recent memory adults did not use certain words in the presence of children, who, in turn, were not expected to use them in the presence of adults. The question of whether or not children knew such words from other contexts was beside the point. Social propriety required that a public distinction be maintained between an adult's symbolic world and the child's. This custom, unknown in the Middle Ages, represented more than a pleasant social fiction. Linguistic restraint on the adult's part reflected a social idea, i.e., a disposition to protect children from the harsh, sordid, or cynical attitudes so often implicit in brutal or obscene language. On the children's part, restraint reflected an understanding of their place in the social hierarchy, and in particular, the understanding that they were not yet entitled to the public expression of such attitudes. But, of course, with the blurring of role distinctions such linguistic deference loses its point. Today, this custom has so rapidly eroded that those who practice it are considered "quaint." It would appear that we are moving back toward a fourteenth-century situation where no words were considered unfit for a youthful ear.

12 In the face of all this, both the authority of adulthood and the curiosity of childhood lose ground. For like shame and manners they are rooted in the idea of secrets. Children are curious because they do not yet know what they suspect there is to know; adults have authority in great measure because they are the principal source of knowledge. . . .

13 To a certain extent curiosity comes naturally to the young, but its development depends upon a growing awareness of the power of well-ordered questions to expose secrets. The world of the known and the not yet known is bridged by wonderment. But wonderment happens largely in a situation where the child's world is separate from the adult world, where children must seek entry, through their questions, into the adult world. As media merge the two worlds, as the tension created by secrets to be unraveled is diminished, the calculus of wonderment changes. Curiosity is replaced by cynicism or, even worse, arrogance.

We are left with children who rely not on authoritative adults but on news from nowhere. We are left with children who are given answers to questions they never asked. We are left, in short, without children.

14 We must keep in mind here that it is not television alone that contributes to the opening of adult secrets. As I have already noted, the process whereby information became uncontrollable—whereby the home and school lost their commanding place as regulators of child development—began with the telegraph and is not a new problem. Every medium of communication that plugs into a wall socket has contributed its share in freeing children from the limited range of childhood sensibility. The movies, for example, played a distinctive role in revealing to children the language and strategies of romance; those readers over the age of forty can testify to the fact that they learned the secrets of kissing from films. In today's world one can learn far more than that from a movie. But movies are not free, and it is still possible to bar children from those that display too much carnal knowledge or violence or adult madness. Except, of course, when they are shown on television. For with television there are no restrictions, economic or otherwise, and the occasional warning to parents that the "following program contains adult material . . . etc." only serves to ensure that more, not fewer, children will watch. What is it that they will see? What precisely are the secrets that will be revealed to them?

15 There are, as already mentioned, all of those matters that fall within the province of sexuality. Indeed, in revealing the secrets of sex, television has come close to eliminating the concept of sexual aberration altogether. For example, it is now common enough to see twelve- and thirteen-year-old girls displayed on television commercials as erotic objects. Some adults may have forgotten when such an act was regarded as psychopathic, and they will have to take my word for it that it was. This is not to say that adult males did not until recently covet pubescent girls. They did, but the point is that their desire was kept a carefully guarded secret, especially from the young themselves. Television not only exposes the secret but shows it to be an invidious inhibition and a matter of no special consequence. As in the Middle Ages, playing with the privy parts of children may once again become only a ribald amusement. Or, if that takes the matter too far, perhaps we may say that the explicit, albeit symbolic, *use* of children as material for the satisfaction of adult sexual fantasies has already become entirely acceptable. Indeed, conditioned by such use of children on television, the New York State of Appeals ruled in 1981 that no distinction may be made between

children and adults in addressing the question of a pornographic film. If a film is judged obscene, the court ruled, then a conviction can be sustained. But if it is not judged obscene, then any law that tries to distinguish between the status of children and adults is invidious.[2] One might say that such a ruling clears the way for continued exploitation of children. Or, from another point of view, that such a ruling merely reflects the realities of our new electric environment. . . .

16 I am well aware that the word *hypocrisy* is sometimes used to describe a situation where public knowledge and private knowledge are rigidly kept apart. But the better face of hypocrisy is, after all, a certain social idealism. In the case of childhood, for example, secrecy is practiced in order to maintain the conditions for healthy and ordered growth. Childhood, as we ideally think of it, cannot exist without a certain measure of hypocrisy. Let us take violence, for example. There can be no denying that human beings spend an inordinate amount of time and energy in maiming and killing each other. Along with symbol making and toolmaking, killing is among our most distinctive characteristics. I have estimated that in my lifetime approximately seventy-five million people have been killed by other people. And this does not include those killings that are done, as Russell Baker puts it, in the name of private enterprise, e.g., street killings, family killings, robbery killings, etc. Is it hypocrisy to keep this knowledge from children? Hypocrisy should be made of sterner stuff. We wish to keep this knowledge from children because for all of its reality, too much of it too soon is quite likely dangerous to the well-being of an unformed mind. Enlightened opinion on child development claims it is necessary for children to believe that adults have control over their impulses to violence and that they have a clear conception of right and wrong. Through these beliefs, as Bruno Bettelheim has said, children can develop the positive feelings about themselves that give them the strength to nurture their rationality, which, in turn, will sustain them in adversity.[3] C. H. Waddington has hypothesized that "one component of human evolution and the capacity for choice is the ability of the human child to accept on authority from elders the criteria for right and wrong."[4] Without such assurances children

---

[2]See "Sexual Portrayals Using Children Legal Unless Obscene, Court Rules," *The New York Times*, May 13, 1981, p. 1.

[3]Bruno Bettelheim, *The Uses of Enchantment: The Meaning and Importance of Fairy Tales* (New York: Knopf, 1976), p. 4.

[4]As quoted in Margaret Mead, *Culture and Commitment: A Study of the Generation Gap* (Garden City, N.Y.: Doubleday, 1970), p. 64.

find it difficult to be hopeful or courageous or disciplined. If it is hypocrisy to hide from children the "facts" of adult violence and moral ineptitude, it is nonetheless wise to do so. Surely, hypocrisy in the cause of strengthening child growth is no vice.

17 This is not to say that children must be protected from all knowledge of violence or moral degeneracy. As Bettelheim has demonstrated in *The Uses of Enchantment*, the importance of fairy tales lies in their capacity to reveal the existence of evil in a form that permits children to integrate it without trauma. This is possible not only because the content of fairy tales has grown organically over centuries and is under the control of adults (who may, for example, modify the violence or the ending to suit the needs of a particular child) but also because the psychological context in which the tales are told is usually reassuring and is, therefore, therapeutic. But the violence that is now revealed over television is not mediated by a mother's voice, is not much modified to suit the child, is not governed by any theory of child development. It is there because television requires material that comes in inexhaustible variety. It is also there because television directs everything to everyone at the same time, which is to say, television cannot keep secrets of any kind. This results in the impossibility of protecting children from the fullest and harshest disclosure of unrelenting violence.

18 And here we must keep in mind that the stylized murders, rapes, and plunderings that are depicted on weekly fictional programs are much less than half the problem. They are, after all, clearly marked as fiction or pseudo–fairy tales, and we may assume (although not safely) that some children do not take them to be representations of real adult life. Far more impressive are the daily examples of violence and moral degeneracy that are the staple of TV news shows. These are not mitigated by the presence of recognizable and attractive actors and actresses. They are put forward as the stuff of everyday life. These are real murders, real rapes, real plunderings. And the fact that they *are* the stuff of real life makes them all the more powerful.

19 Researchers have been trying for years to determine the effects on children of such knowledge, their principal question being, To what extent does violence, when depicted so vividly and on such a scale, induce violence in children? Although this question is not trivial, it diverts our attention from such important questions as, To what extent does the depiction of the world *as it is* undermine a child's belief in adult rationality, in the possibility of an ordered world, in a hopeful future? To what extent does it undermine the child's confidence in his or her future capacity to control the impulse to violence?

20 The secret of adult violence is, in fact, only part of a larger secret revealed by television. From the child's point of view, what is mostly shown on television is the plain fact that the adult world is filled with ineptitude, strife, and worry. Television, as Josh Meyrowitz has phrased it, opens to view the backstage of adult life. Researchers have paid very little attention to the implications of our revealing to children, in one televised form or another, the causes of marital conflict, the need for life insurance, the infinite possibilities of misunderstanding, the persistent incompetence of political leaders, the myriad afflictions of the human body. This list, which could be extended for a page, provides two items of particular interest as examples of how television is unsparing in revealing the secrets of adult life. The first, about which Meyrowitz has written with great insight, concerns the incompetence or at least vulnerability of political leaders. In its quest for material, especially of a "human interest" variety, television has found an almost inexhaustible supply in the private lives of politicians. Never before have so many people known so much about the wives, children, mistresses, drinking habits, sexual preferences, slips of the tongue, even inarticulateness of their national leaders. Those who did know at least some of this were kept informed by newspapers and magazines, which is to say that until television, the dark or private side of political life was mostly the business of adults. Children are not newspaper readers and never have been. But they are television viewers and therefore are continually exposed to accounts of the frailties of those who in a different age would have been perceived as without blemish. The result of this is that children develop what may be called adult attitudes—from cynicism to indifference—toward political leaders and toward the political process itself. . . .

21 I am sure I have given the impression to this point that all of the adult secrets made available to children through television concern that which is frightening, sordid, or confusing. But in fact television is not necessarily biased in this direction. If most of its disclosures are of that nature, it is because most of adult life is of that nature, filled with illness, violence, incompetence, and disorder. But not all of adult life. There is, for example, the existential pleasure of buying things. Television reveals to children at the earliest possible age the joys of consumerism, the satisfactions to be derived from buying almost anything—from floor wax to automobiles. Marshall McLuhan was once asked why the news on television is always bad news. He replied that it wasn't: the commercials are the good news. And indeed they are. It is a comfort to know that the drudgery of one's work can be relieved by a trip to Jamaica

or Hawaii, that one's status may be enhanced by buying a Cordoba, that one's competence may be established by using a certain detergent, that one's sex appeal may be enlivened by a mouthwash. These are the promises of American culture, and they give a certain coherence to adult motivations. By age three our children have been introduced to these motivations, for television invites everyone to share in them. I do not claim that these are mature motivations. . . . The point here is simply that the "good news" on television is *adult* good news, about which children are entirely knowledgeable by age seven.

22 Neither do I claim that children in an earlier period were entirely ignorant of the material of the adult world, only that not since the Middle Ages have children known so much about adult life as now. Not even the ten-year-old girls working in the mines in England in the eighteenth century were as knowing as our own children. The children of the industrial revolution knew very little beyond the horror of their own lives. Through the miracle of symbols and electricity our own children know everything anyone else knows—the good with the bad. Nothing is mysterious, nothing awesome, nothing is held back from public view. Indeed, it is a common enough observation, particularly favored by television executives when under attack, that whatever else may be said about television's impact on the young, today's children are better informed than any previous group of youngsters. The metaphor usually employed is that television is a window to the world. This observation is entirely correct, but why it should be taken as a sign of progress is a mystery. What does it mean that our children are better informed than ever before? That they know what the elders know? It means that they have become adults, or, at least, adult-like. It means—to use a metaphor of my own—that in having access to the previously hidden fruit of adult information, they are expelled from the garden of childhood.

QUESTIONS FOR ANALYSIS AND DISCUSSION

1. What do both books and television offer? How do they differ?
2. What is a significant difference between adults and children? How does television contribute to the altering of this difference?
3. Is Postman's point about groups (that "a group is largely defined by the exclusivity of the information its members share") a new idea for you? Does it seem to make sense? Should it be qualified in any way?
4. What brought childhood into existence?

5. Television dissolves childhood because it dilutes and demystifies what? Explain Postman's points about controlling impulses and teaching their control.
6. How are literacy and manners similar? How has television affected the learning and use of manners?
7. Do you perceive a decline in manners in our society? If so, is it a problem or an improvement—or irrelevant? Why?
8. Postman asserts that as the media eliminate secrets, and thus childhood, young people lose their curiosity, their desire to learn adult secrets. If Postman is right, might this be a cause for declining reading skills as children feel less pressure to become good readers?
9. What justification does Postman offer for hypocrisy, for keeping some realities from children? (If you do not know who Bettelheim is, find out and then explain his contribution to Postman's argument.)
10. In paragraph 19, Postman introduces the issue of the effect of TV violence on behavior that Rubinstein examines at length. How does Postman alter the principal question sociologists ask? Explain, in your own words, the differing issues raised by these questions. Do you agree that Postman is asking an equally important, if not more important, question?
11. In addition to showing violence, what else does television reveal about adult life? What are the dangers of showing adult ineptitude and immorality?
12. Explain Postman's concluding metaphor (end of paragraph 22).
13. One argument used to support informing children of adult weaknesses is that they then avoid foolish hero worship. Is this an adequate counter to Postman's analysis of television's damaging effects? Why or why not?
14. Both Postman and Rubinstein examine the effects of television on children, yet their articles are quite different. Analyze their differences in style and explain how those differences serve each writer's audience and purpose.

How to Get the Poor off Our Conscience

JOHN KENNETH GALBRAITH

One of the most influential of contemporary economists, John Kenneth Galbraith (b. 1908) was educated at the Universities of Toronto and California and was, for many years, the Paul M. Warburg Professor of Economics at Harvard. Galbraith has also served as ambassador to India (1961–1963), national chairman of Americans for Democratic Action, and presidential adviser to both Kennedy and Johnson. Galbraith has a long list of books and articles to his credit, but perhaps best known are The Affluent Society *(1959),* The New Industrial State *(1967), and* Economics and the Public Purpose *(1973).* The Affluent Society, *standard reading in college courses, has been translated into a dozen languages.*

Galbraith has been called the noneconomist's economist, probably because his most popular books are written to nonspecialists and because he is a broad-scope or philosophical economist. He raises moral issues and questions social priorities, asking how, for example, wealth should be divided. In the following article, adapted from several speeches and published in the November 1985 issue of Harper's, *he examines some contemporary philosophies for coping with society's poor and then offers his views.*

1 I would like to reflect on one of the oldest of human exercises, the process by which over the years, and indeed over the centuries, we have undertaken to get the poor off our conscience.

2 Rich and poor have lived together, always uncomfortably and sometimes perilously, since the beginning of time. Plutarch was led to say: "An imbalance between the rich and poor is the oldest and most fatal ailment of republics." And the problems that arise from the continuing coexistence of affluence and poverty—and particularly the process by which good fortune is justified in the presence of the ill fortune of others—have been an intellectual preoccupation for centuries. They continue to be so in our own time.

3 One begins with the solution proposed in the Bible: the poor suffer in this world but are wonderfully rewarded in the next. Their poverty is a temporary misfortune; if they are poor and also meek, they eventually will inherit the earth. This is, in some ways, an admirable solution. It allows the rich to enjoy their wealth while envying the poor their future fortune.

4 Much, much later, in the twenty or thirty years following the publication in 1776 of *The Wealth of Nations*—the late dawn of the Industrial Revolution in Britain—the problem and its solution began to take on their modern form. Jeremy Bentham, a near contemporary of Adam Smith,[1] came up with the formula that for perhaps fifty years was extraordinarily influential in British and, to some degree, American thought. This was utilitarianism. "By the principle of utility," Bentham said in

[1] Author of *The Wealth of Nations.*—Ed.

1789, "is meant the principle which approves or disapproves of every action whatsoever according to the tendency which it appears to have to augment or diminish the happiness of the party whose interest is in question." Virtue is, indeed must be, self-centered. While there were people with great good fortune and many more with great ill fortune, the social problem was solved as long as, again in Bentham's words, there was "the greatest good for the greatest number." Society did its best for the largest possible number of people; one accepted that the result might be sadly unpleasant for the many whose happiness was not served.

5 In the 1830s a new formula, influential in no slight degree to this day, became available for getting the poor off the public conscience. This is associated with the names of David Ricardo, a stockbroker, and Thomas Robert Malthus, a divine. The essentials are familiar: the poverty of the poor was the fault of the poor. And it was so because it was a product of their excessive fecundity: their grievously uncontrolled lust caused them to breed up to the full limits of the available subsistence.

6 This was Malthusianism. Poverty being caused in the bed meant that the rich were not responsible for either its creation or its amelioration. However, Malthus was himself not without a certain feeling of responsibility: he urged that the marriage ceremony contain a warning against undue and irresponsible sexual intercourse—a warning, it is fair to say, that has not been accepted as a fully effective method of birth control. In more recent times, Ronald Reagan has said that the best form of population control emerges from the market. (Couples in love should repair to R. H. Macy's, not their bedrooms.) Malthus, it must be said, was at least as relevant.

7 By the middle of the nineteenth century, a new form of denial achieved great influence, especially in the United States. The new doctrine, associated with the name of Herbert Spencer, was Social Darwinism. In economic life, as in biological development, the overriding rule was survival of the fittest. That phrase—"survival of the fittest"—came, in fact, not from Charles Darwin but from Spencer, and expressed his view of economic life. The elimination of the poor is nature's way of improving the race. The weak and unfortunate being extruded, the quality of the human family is thus strengthened.

8 One of the most notable American spokespersons of Social Darwinism was John D. Rockefeller—the first Rockefeller—who said in a famous speech: "The American Beauty rose can be produced in the splendor and fragrance which bring cheer to its beholder only by sacrificing the early buds which grow up around it. And so it is in economic life. It is merely the working out of a law of nature and a law of God."

9 In the course of the present century, however, Social Darwinism came to be considered a bit too cruel. It declined in popularity, and references to it acquired a condemnatory tone. We passed on to the more amorphous denial of poverty associated with Calvin Coolidge and Herbert Hoover. They held that public assistance to the poor interfered with the effective operation of the economic system—that such assistance was inconsistent with the economic design that had come to serve most people very well. The notion that there is something economically damaging about helping the poor remains with us to this day as one of the ways by which we get them off our conscience.

10 With the Roosevelt revolution (as previously with that of Lloyd George in Britain), a specific responsibility was assumed by the government for the least fortunate people in the republic. Roosevelt and the presidents who followed him accepted a substantial measure of responsibility for the old through Social Security, for the unemployed through unemployment insurance, for the unemployable and the handicapped through direct relief, and for the sick through Medicare and Medicaid. This was a truly great change, and for a time, the age-old tendency to avoid thinking about the poor gave way to the feeling that we didn't need to try—that we were, indeed, doing something about them.

11 In recent years, however, it has become clear that the search for a way of getting the poor off our conscience was not at an end; it was only suspended. And so we are now again engaged in this search in a highly energetic way. It has again become a major philosophical, literary, and rhetorical preoccupation, and an economically not unrewarding enterprise.

12 Of the four, maybe five, current designs we have to get the poor off our conscience, the first proceeds from the inescapable fact that most of the things that must be done on behalf of the poor must be done in one way or another by the government. It is then argued that the government is inherently incompetent, except as regards weapons design and procurement and the overall management of the Pentagon. Being incompetent and ineffective, it must not be asked to succor the poor; it will only louse things up or make things worse.

13 The allegation of government incompetence is associated in our time with the general condemnation of the bureaucrat—again excluding those concerned with national defense. The only form of discrimination that is still permissible—that is, still officially encouraged in the United States today—is discrimination against people who work for the federal government, especially on social welfare activities. We have great corporate bureaucracies replete with corporate bureaucrats, but they are

good; only public bureaucracy and government servants are bad. In fact, we have in the United States an extraordinarily good public service—one made up of talented and dedicated people who are overwhelmingly honest and only rarely given to overpaying for monkey wrenches, flashlights, coffee makers, and toilet seats. (When these aberrations have occurred, they have, oddly enough, all been in the Pentagon.) We have nearly abolished poverty among the old, greatly democratized health care, assured minorities of their civil rights, and vastly enhanced educational opportunity. All this would seem a considerable achievement for incompetent and otherwise ineffective people. We must recognize that the present condemnation of government and government administration is really part of the continuing design for avoiding responsibility for the poor.

14 The second design in this great centuries-old tradition is to argue that any form of public help to the poor only hurts the poor. It destroys morale. It seduces people away from gainful employment. It breaks up marriages, since women can seek welfare for themselves and their children once they are without their husbands.

15 There is no proof of this—none, certainly, that compares that damage with the damage that would be inflicted by the loss of public assistance. Still, the case is made—and believed—that there is something gravely damaging about aid to the unfortunate. This is perhaps our most highly influential piece of fiction.

16 The third, and closely related, design for relieving ourselves of responsibility for the poor is the argument that public-assistance measures have an adverse effect on incentive. They transfer income from the diligent to the idle and feckless, thus reducing the effort of the diligent and encouraging the idleness of the idle. The modern manifestation of this is supply-side economics. Supply-side economics holds that the rich in the United States have not been working because they have too little income. So, by taking money from the poor and giving it to the rich, we increase effort and stimulate the economy. Can we really believe that any considerable number of the poor prefer welfare to a good job? Or that business people—corporate executives, the key figures in our time—are idling away their hours because of the insufficiency of their pay? This is a scandalous charge against the American businessperson, notably a hard worker. Belief can be the servant of truth—but even more of convenience.

17 The fourth design for getting the poor off our conscience is to point to the presumed adverse effect on freedom of taking responsibility

for them. Freedom consists of the right to spend a maximum of one's money by one's own choice, and to see a minimum taken and spent by the government. (Again, expenditure on national defense is excepted.) In the enduring words of Professor Milton Friedman,[2] people must be "free to choose."

18 This is possibly the most transparent of all of the designs; no mention is ordinarily made of the relation of income to the freedom of the poor. (Professor Friedman is here an exception; through the negative income tax, he would assure everyone a basic income.) There is, we can surely agree, no form of oppression that is quite so great, no constriction on thought and effort quite so comprehensive, as that which comes from having no money at all. Though we hear much about the limitation on the freedom of the affluent when their income is reduced through taxes, we hear nothing of the extraordinary enhancement of the freedom of the poor from having some money of their own to spend. Yet the loss of freedom from taxation to the rich is a small thing as compared with the gain in freedom from providing some income to the impoverished. Freedom we rightly cherish. Cherishing it, we should not use it as a cover for denying freedom to those in need.

19 Finally, when all else fails, we resort to simple psychological denial. This is a psychic tendency that in various manifestations is common to us all. It causes us to avoid thinking about death. It causes a great many people to avoid thought of the arms race and the consequent rush toward a highly probable extinction. By the same process of psychological denial, we decline to think of the poor. Whether they be in Ethiopia, the South Bronx, or even in such an Elysium as Los Angeles, we resolve to keep them off our minds. Think, we are often advised, of something pleasant.

20 These are the modern designs by which we escape concern for the poor. All, save perhaps the last, are in great inventive descent from Bentham, Malthus, and Spencer. Ronald Reagan and his colleagues are clearly in a notable tradition—at the end of a long history of effort to escape responsibility for one's fellow beings. So are the philosophers now celebrated in Washington: George Gilder,[3] a greatly favored figure of the recent past, who tells to much applause that the poor must have the cruel spur of their own suffering to ensure effort; Charles Murray,[4]

---

[2] President Reagan's first chairman of the Council of Economic Advisers. —Ed.

[3] Author of *Wealth and Poverty* (1981), a book that has influenced the economic thinking of the Reagan administration. —Ed.

[4] A senior research fellow at the Manhattan Institute for Policy Research and author of *Losing Ground: American Social Policy, 1950–1980* (1984). —Ed.

who, to greater cheers, contemplates "scrapping the entire federal welfare and income-support structure for working and aged persons, including A.F.D.C., Medicaid, food stamps, unemployment insurance, Workers' Compensation, subsidized housing, disability insurance, and," he adds, "the rest. Cut the knot, for there is no way to untie it." By a triage, the worthy would be selected to survive; the loss of the rest is the penalty we should pay. Murray is the voice of Spencer in our time; he is enjoying, as indicated, unparalleled popularity in high Washington circles.

21 Compassion, along with the associated public effort, is the least comfortable, the least convenient, course of behavior and action in our time. But it remains the only one that is consistent with a totally civilized life. Also, it is, in the end, the most truly conservative course. There is no paradox here. Civil discontent and its consequences do not come from contented people—an obvious point. To the extent that we can make contentment as nearly universal as possible, we will preserve and enlarge the social and political tranquillity for which conservatives, above all, should yearn.

QUESTIONS FOR ANALYSIS AND DISCUSSION

1. Galbraith says that he wants to reflect on the ways we explain (and thus justify) the discrepancy between rich and poor. How do you know that his purpose is not only to analyze economic theories but to express an attitude about the appropriate way to respond to the poor? From the first two paragraphs, what clues do you get about his attitude?
2. State, in your own words, the specific explanations and justifications for poverty in Galbraith's historical review, beginning with the Bible.
3. What made the Roosevelt era's view of the poor different from previous periods?
4. State, in your own words, the five contemporary designs for getting the poor off our conscience.
5. How does Galbraith challenge each modern attitude?
6. Do you share the antibureaucratic attitude Galbraith refers to? Do you agree that the view is widespread? Does Galbraith offer good reasons for rejecting the attitude?
7. The novelist F. Scott Fitzgerald once said that the rich are different from the poor, to which Ernest Hemingway responded that yes, they have more money. What is the difference that Fitzgerald understood and that Galbraith also emphasizes?

8. What does Galbraith want us to feel and to do about the poor? What kind of argument does he offer in support of his views?
9. Galbraith's essay is neatly organized. Analyze his organization and prepare, from your analysis, a detailed outline.

Education: Incentives to Fail and Proposals for Change

CHARLES MURRAY

Born and raised in Newton, Iowa, Charles Murray obtained his undergraduate degree from Harvard and his Ph.D. in political science from MIT. Murray spent six years in Thailand, first with the Peace Corps and then as a researcher. He then spent seven years (1974–1981) at the American Institutes for Research, a nonprofit social science research organization. In his last two years at AIR, Murray was chief scientist, responsible for the research program. At AIR Murray conducted or supervised a number of experimental programs designed to aid inner-city youths. Currently a senior research fellow at the Manhattan Institute for Policy Research, Murray has published articles in the New York Times, Harper's, Atlantic, *and* The Public Interest; *contributed to James Q. Wilson's* Crime and Public Policy *(1983); and written two books,* Beyond Probation, *a study of juvenile corrections procedures, and* Losing Ground: American Social Policy, 1950–1980 *(1984), from which the following selection is taken.*

In his chapter on education in Losing Ground, *Murray argues that our schools are not doing the job they once were and that policies need changing to allow them once again to provide instruction in an orderly environment.*

1 The basic problem in education has not changed. Persuading youngsters to work hard against the promise of intangible and long-deferred rewards was as tough in 1960 as in 1970. The challenge of creating adequate incentives was no different. But . . . the disincentives for a certain type of student changed.

2 We are not considering children whose parents check their homework every night, or children who from earliest childhood expect to go to college, or children with high IQs and a creative flair. Rather, we are

considering children with average or below-average abilities, with parents who ignore their progress or lack of it, with parents who are themselves incompetent to help with homework. We are not considering the small-town school with a few students, but the large urban school. Such children and such schools existed in 1960 as in 1970. Yet among those who stayed in school, more students seemed to learn to read and write and calculate in 1960 than in 1970. How might we employ an incentives approach to account for this?

3 While learning is hard work, it should be exciting and fun as well. But most large urban schools, though they may try to achieve that ideal, have other concerns that must take priority. They must first of all maintain order in the classroom and secondly make students try to do the work even if they do not want to. With students who come from supportive home environments, these tasks are relatively easy for the school; a bad grade or a comment on a report card is likely to trigger the needed corrective action. But with students who have no backup at home, these tasks are always difficult. Sanctions are required. In 1960, such sanctions consisted of holding a student back, in-school disciplinary measures, suspension, and expulsion. By the 1970s, use of all these sanctions had been sharply circumscribed.

4 During the same period, the incidence of student disorders went from nowhere to a national problem. Robert Rubel, who has compiled the most extensive data on this topic, divides the history of school disorders into three periods. From 1950 to 1964, disorders were of such low levels of frequency and seriousness that they were hardly worth mentioning. From 1964 to about 1971, disorders exploded, especially those that Rubel calls "teacher-testing." After 1971, the disorders were less patterned, but they continued to exist at the high levels they had reached during the late 1960s.[1] Why should disorders have increased at that time? Rubel points to the generally chaotic nature of the times. Another answer is that we began to permit them.

5 In part, the intellectual climate altered behavior. Books such as *Death at an Early Age* led the way for educational reforms that deemphasized the traditional classroom norms in favor of a more open, less disciplined (or less repressive and ethnocentric, depending on one's

[1] Robert J. Rubel, *The Unruly School: Disorders, Disruptions, and Crimes* (Lexington, Mass.: Lexington Books, 1977), 60–66. His book includes a comprehensive bibliography. The federal government's data on the school crime problem is detailed in *Violent Schools – Safe Schools: The Safe School Study Report to the Congress*, Department of Health, Education and Welfare (Washington, D.C.: Government Printing Office, 1978).

ideology) treatment of the learning process.[2] The black pride movement added voices claiming that traditional education was one more example of white-middle-class values arbitrarily forced on blacks.[3] But there were more concrete reasons for students and teachers alike to change their behavior.

6 In part, the federal offices that dispensed government help had a hand. They could establish projects implementing preferred strategies, which in the 1960s invariably favored a less traditional, less white-middle-class attitude toward education. They could support efforts to limit the use of suspension and expulsion. They could make imaginative use of the provisions of Title VI of the 1964 Civil Rights Act (enabling them to withdraw federal funds if a school system was found to be discriminating on grounds of race) to bring reluctant school systems around to their point of view.

7 In part, the judiciary had a hand. The key event was the Supreme Court's *Gault* v. *Arizona* decision in 1967. The case involved a juvenile court, but the principle enunciated by the Court applied to the schools as well, as the American Civil Liberties Union was quick to point out to school systems nationwide.[4] Due process was required for suspension, and the circumstances under which students could be suspended or otherwise disciplined were restricted. Teachers and administrators became vulnerable to lawsuits or professional setbacks for using the discretion that had been taken for granted in 1960.[5] Urban schools gave up

---

[2]Jonathan Kozol, *Death at an Early Age* (Boston: Houghton Mifflin, 1967). For the best account of the ferment in ideology during the late 1960s, see Diane Ravitch, *The Troubled Crusade: American Education 1945–1980* (New York: Basic Books, 1983), chapter 7.

[3]For variations on the theme that black culture is unique and mostly superior to white middle-class culture, see Joyce A. Ladner, ed., *The Death of White Sociology* (New York: Random House, 1973). The theme, while less common in the 1980s, has not disappeared altogether. See H. Morgan, "How Schools Fail Black Children," *Social Policy* 10 (January 1980): 49–54, which applies an elaborate psychological rationale for arguing that schools should adjust their behavior to lower-class black norms of behavior, rather than the other way around.

[4]See, for example, the influential booklet *Academic Freedom in the Secondary Schools* (New York: American Civil Liberties Union, 1968). For a discussion of the role of the courts and children in general (with emphasis on education), see Edward A. Wynne, "What Are the Courts Doing to Our Children?" *The Public Interest* no. 64 (Summer 1981): 3–18; the reply to Wynne by Julius Menacker, "The Courts Are Not Killing Our Children," *The Public Interest* no. 67 (Spring 1982): 131–36; and Wynne's rejoinder in the same issue, pp. 136–39.

[5]The abolishment of penalties and neglect of scholastic achievement was most extreme in the early and mid-1970s. By 1980, the pendulum had started to swing back, and some large school systems were already reinstituting stricter codes. The description in the text

the practice of making a student repeat a grade. "Social promotions" were given regardless of academic progress.

8 For all these reasons and many more, a student who did not want to learn was much freer not to learn in 1970 than in 1960, and freer to disrupt the learning process for others. Facing no credible sanctions for not learning and possessing no tangible incentives to learn, large numbers of students did things they considered more fun and did not learn. What could have been more natural?

9 A concomitant to these changes in incentives was that teachers had new reasons *not* to demand high performance (or any performance at all). In the typical inner-city school, a demanding teaching style would be sure to displease some of the students—as indeed demanding teachers have done everywhere, from time immemorial. But now there was this difference: The rebellious students could make life considerably more miserable for the teacher than the teacher could for the students—through their disruptive behavior in class, through physical threats, or even through official channels, complaining to the administration that the teacher was unreasonable, harsh, or otherwise failing to observe their rights. In the 1960s and into the 1970s, teachers who demanded performance in an inner-city school were asking for trouble.

10 The dramatic problems of confrontation were combined with the less dramatic ones of absenteeism, tardiness, and failure to do homework. Jackson Toby describes the results:

> When only a handful of students attempt to complete homework, teachers stop assigning it; and of course, it is difficult to teach a lesson that depends on material taught yesterday or last week when only a few students can be counted on to be regularly in class. Eventually, in these circumstances, teachers stop putting forth the considerable effort required to educate.[6]

Toby traces the rest of the chain: Teachers take the maximum number of days off to which they are entitled. Substitute teachers are hard to recruit for the same reasons that the teachers are taking days off. The

---

was still accurate in 1980, however, if for no other reason than that court decisions following from *Gault* v. *Arizona* still sharply limited a local school district's discretion in many of the practices taken for granted in the 1950s. For a discussion of current practice, see Gerald Grant, "Children's Rights and Adult Confusions," *The Public Interest* no. 69 (Fall 1982): 83–99.

[6]Jackson Toby, "Crime in the Schools," in James Q. Wilson, ed., *Crime and Public Policy* (San Francisco: ICS Press, 1983), 73–74.

best students, both black and white, transfer to private or parochial schools, making it that much more difficult to control the remainder. Absent teachers and loss of control lead to more class-cutting. More class-cutting increases the noise in the halls. "In the classrooms, teachers struggle for the attention of the students. Students talk to one another; they engage in playful and not-so-playful fights; they leave repeatedly to visit the toilet or to get drinks of water."[7] Learning does not, cannot, occur.

11 School administrators in the last half of the 1960s had to finesse the problem of the gap between white and black achievement. Pushing hard for academic achievement in schools with a mix of blacks and whites led to embarrassment and protests when the white children always seemed to end up winning the academic awards and getting the best grades and scoring highest on the tests. Pushing hard for academic achievement in predominantly black urban schools led to intense resentment by the students and occasionally by parents and the community. It was not the students' fault they were ill-prepared—racism was to blame, the system was to blame—and solutions that depended on the students' working doubly hard to make up their deficits were accordingly inappropriate, tantamount to getting the students to cover for the system's mistakes.

12 As in the case of work effort, marital behavior, and crime, the empirical evidence is accumulating that the changes in incentives in the classroom are causally linked to the trends in educational outcomes.[8] . . . But perhaps the most persuasive evidence is one's own answer to the question, "What would *I* do given the same situation?" Given the changes in risks and rewards: If you were a student in the inner-city school of 1970, would you have behaved the same as you would have in 1960? If you were a teacher, would you have enforced the same standards? If you really loved teaching, would you have remained a teacher in the public schools?

---

[7]Ibid., 74.

[8]For the role of the learning environment—discipline, demands on the student, and so forth—in contrast to teaching technology and facilities as an explanation for educational outcomes, the material is just beginning to burgeon, as of 1983. The most ambitious data base was accumulated by James S. Coleman, of "Coleman Report" fame in the mid-1960s. This time, he and his colleagues surveyed 58,000 students in 893 public and 122 private high schools. They found that the typical private school, with larger classrooms, lower-paid teachers, and fewer resources, was producing substantially better academic achievement than its public counterpart. The reason was not much more complicated than the ones I included under the heading of incentives. The most thorough discussion of the findings, along with replies to the fierce criticism of their first publications on this topic, can be found in James S. Coleman, Thomas Hoffer, and Sally Kilgore, *High School Achievement: Public, Catholic, and Private Schools Compared* (New York: Basic Books, 1982).

A PROPOSAL FOR EDUCATION

13 There is no such thing as an undeserving five-year-old. Society, in the form of government intervention, is quite limited in what it can do to make up for many of the deficiencies of life that an unlucky five-year-old experiences; it can, however, provide a good education and thereby give the child a chance at a different future.

14 The objective is a system that provides more effective education of the poor and disadvantaged without running afoul of the three laws of social programs. The objective is also to construct what is, in my view, a just system—one that does not sacrifice one student's interests to another's, and one that removes barriers in the way of those who want most badly to succeed and are prepared to make the greatest effort to do so. So once again let us put ourselves in the position of bureaucrats of sweeping authority and large budgets. How shall we make things better?

15 We begin by installing a completely free educational system that goes from preschool to the loftiest graduate degrees, removing economic barriers entirely. Having done so, however, we find little change from the system that prevailed in 1980. Even then, kindergarten through high school were free to the student, and federal grants and loans worth $4.4 billion *plus* a very extensive system of private scholarships and loans were available for needy students who wanted to continue their education. By making the system entirely free, we are not making more education newly accessible to large numbers of people, nor have we done anything about the quality of education.

16 We then make a second and much more powerful change. For many years, the notion of a voucher system for education has enjoyed a periodic vogue. In its pure form, it would give each parent of a child of school age a voucher that the parent could use to pay for schooling at any institution to which the child could gain admittance. The school would redeem the voucher for cash from the government. The proposals for voucher systems have generally foundered on accusations that they are a tool for the middle class and would leave the disadvantaged in the lurch. My proposition is rather different: A voucher system is the single most powerful method available to us to improve the education of the poor and disadvantaged. Vouchers thus become the second component of our educational reforms.

17 For one large segment of the population of poor and disadvantaged, the results are immediate, unequivocal, and dramatic. I refer to children whose parents take an active role in overseeing and encouraging

their children's education. Such parents have been fighting one of the saddest of the battles of the poor—doing everything they can within the home environment, only to see their influence systematically undermined as soon as their children get out the door. When we give such parents vouchers, we find that they behave very much as their affluent counterparts behave when they are deciding upon a private school. They visit prospective schools, interview teachers, and place their children in schools that are demanding of the students and accountable to the parents for results. I suggest that when we give such parents vouchers, we will observe substantial convergence of black and white test scores in a single generation. All that such parents have ever needed is an educational system that operates on the same principles they do.

18 This is a sufficient improvement to justify the system, for we are in a no-lose situation with regard to the children whose parents do not play their part effectively. These children are sent to bad schools or no schools at all—just as they were in the past. How much worse can it be under the new system?

19 This defect in the voucher system leaves us, however, with a substantial number of students who are still getting no education through no fault of their own. Nor can we count on getting results if we round them up and dispatch them willy-nilly to the nearest accredited school. A school that can motivate and teach a child when there is backup from home cannot necessarily teach the children we are now discussing. Many of them are poor not only in money. Many have been developmentally impoverished as well, receiving very little of the early verbal and conceptual stimulation that happens as a matter of course when parents expect their children to be smart. Some arrive at the school door already believing themselves to be stupid, expecting to fail. We can be as angry as we wish at their parents, but we are still left with the job of devising a school that works for these children. What do we do—not in terms of a particular pedagogical program or curriculum, but in broad strokes?

20 First, whatever else, we decide to create a world that makes sense in the context of the society we want them to succeed in. The school is not an extension of the neighborhood. Within the confines of the school building and school day, we create a world that may seem as strange and irrelevant as Oz.

21 We do not do so with uniforms or elaborate rules or inspirational readings—the embellishments are left up to the school. Rather, we install one simple, inflexible procedure. Each course has an entrance test.

Tenth-grade geometry has an entrance test; so does first-grade reading. Entrance tests for simple courses are simple; entrance tests for hard courses are hard. Their purpose is not to identify the best students, but to make sure that any student who gets in can, with an honest effort, complete the course work.

22 Our system does not carry with it any special teaching technique. It does, however, give the teacher full discretion over enforcing an orderly working environment. The teacher's only obligation is to teach those who want to learn.

23 The system is also infinitely forgiving. A student who has just flunked algebra three times running can enroll in that or any other math class for which he can pass the entrance test. He can enroll even if he has just been kicked out of three other classes for misbehavior. The question is never "What have you been in the past?" but always "What are you being as of now?"

24 The evolving outcomes of the system are complex. Some students begin by picking the easiest, least taxing courses, and approach them with as little motivation as their counterparts under the current system. Perhaps among this set of students are some who cannot or will not complete even the simplest courses. They drop by the wayside, failures of the system.

25 Among those who do complete courses, *any* courses, five things happen, all of them positive. First, the system is so constructed that to get into a course is in itself a small success ("I passed!"). Second, the students go into the course with a legitimate reason for believing that they can do the work; they passed a valid test that says they can. Third, they experience—directly—a cause-effect relationship between their success in one course and their ability to get into the next course, no matter how small a step upward that next course may be. Fifth, all the while this is going on, they are likely to be observing other students *no different from them*—no richer, no smarter—who are moving upward faster than they are but using the same mechanism.

26 What of those who are disappointed, who try to get into a class and fail? Some will withdraw into themselves and be forever fearful of taking a chance on failure—as almost all do under the current system anyway. But there is a gradation to risk, and a peculiar sort of guarantee of success in our zero-transfer system. Whatever class a student finally takes, the student will have succeeded in gaining entrance to it. He will go into the classroom with official certification—based on reality—that

he will be able to learn the material if he gives it an honest effort. The success-failure, cause-effect features of the system are indispensable for teaching some critical lessons:

- Effort is often rewarded with success.
- Effort is not *always* rewarded with success.
- Failure in one instance does not mean inability to succeed in anything else.
- Failure in one try does not mean perpetual failure.
- The better the preparation, the more likely the success.

27 None of these lessons is taught as well or as directly under the system prevailing in our current education of the disadvantaged. The central failing of the educational system for the poor and disadvantaged, and most especially poor and disadvantaged blacks, is not that it fails to provide meaningful ways for a student to succeed, though that is part of it. The central failing is not that ersatz success—fake curricula, fake grades, fake diplomas—sets the students up for failure when they leave the school, though that too is part of it. The central failing is that the system does not teach disadvantaged students, who see permanent failure all around them, *how to fail.* For students who are growing up expecting (whatever their dreams may be) ultimately to be a failure, with failure writ large, the first essential contravening lesson is that failure can come in small, digestible packages. Failure can be dealt with. It can be absorbed, analyzed, and converted to an asset.

28 We are now discussing a population of students—the children of what has become known as "the underclass"—that comes to the classroom with an array of disadvantages beyond simple economic poverty. I am not suggesting that, under our hypothetical system, all children of the underclass will become motivated students forthwith. Rather, some will. Perhaps it will be a small proportion; perhaps a large one. Certainly the effect interacts with the inherent abilities of the children involved. But some effect will be observed. Some children who are at the very bottom of the pile in the disadvantages they bear will act on the change in the reality of their environment. It will be an improvement over the situation in the system we have replaced, in which virtually none of them gets an education in anything except the futility of hoping.

QUESTIONS FOR ANALYSIS AND DISCUSSION

1. What, according to Murray, are the major changes that took place in schools between 1960 and 1970? What, for Murray, are the causes for the decrease in learning by 1970?
2. Do you see the problems Murray describes continuing in schools today? Do you think there may be causes that Murray has not considered? If so, what are they?
3. Explain Murray's justification for a voucher system. Does his argument seem reasonable to you? Why or why not?
4. Explain the details of Murray's proposals for the remaining students—the disadvantaged urban poor who will presumably be the ones left in public schools. How will they get in and out of classes? What will the system teach them? Why will this be an improvement?
5. Does Murray seem to have a good grasp of the behavior and attitudes of weak students? Is he, from your experience, leaving out any types of students or types of student behavior?
6. Can you generalize regarding Murray's views about what motivates people, not just students? What seems to be his psychological model for motivation?

Of Grasshoppers and Ants (A Review of Charles Murray's Losing Ground)

LESTER C. THUROW

A Phi Beta Kappa graduate of Williams College and a Rhodes Scholar, Lester C. Thurow (b. 1938) earned his Ph.D. at Harvard. He then taught at Harvard and was a research associate at the Kennedy School of Government and a member of the Institute of Politics. Thurow is now Gordon Y. Billard Professor of Management and Economics at MIT and consultant to various government agencies and private companies. He is also a productive writer, having contributed to a long list of collections on economics and public policy, written more than sixty articles for both professional journals and popular magazines, and authored more than a half-dozen books, among them The

Political Economy of Income Redistribution Policies *(1977),* The Zero-Sum Society *(1980), and* Dangerous Currents *(1984). An excerpt from* Dangerous Currents *follows later in the chapter.*

In the following review of Charles Murray's Losing Ground, *Thurow challenges both Murray's statistics and the conclusions Murray draws from them. The review appeared in the July–August 1985 issue of the* Harvard Business Review.

1 The purpose of *Losing Ground* is to help President Reagan shoot a silver bullet into the heart of the monster called social welfare spending. In the author's view, social welfare programs are demonic, not because they are not effective but precisely because they are: they encourage the poor to quit working and to rely on government aid. As a result, those groups who are supposed to be helped by social welfare spending are actually hurt by it. Their income with transfer payments is less than it would be without such payments. To kill the beast that social welfare has become, Charles Murray proposes the elimination of all spending for such programs. With the monster dead, poverty would once again start declining in America.

2 When it comes to human nature, Murray, a political scientist, is a believer in Theory X. Everywhere he looks he sees lazy people who must be forced to work under threat of harsh penalties for failure and with the lure of large rewards for success. Any organized efforts to improve poor people's conditions or to reduce the disparity in rewards and punishments among individuals, no matter how well intentioned, become counterproductive, since the poor simply work less the more they are helped.

3 Murray believes in the Aesop's fable of the improvident grasshopper who fiddled rather than work in the summertime and as a consequence froze to death for lack of food and shelter in the winter. From his perspective, the grasshopper's death was necessary to keep the ants working in the summer. If the grasshopper had been fed in the winter with social welfare programs, the ants would have quit working in the summer and become grasshoppers.

4 According to *Losing Ground,* American ants are becoming American grasshoppers because of the social welfare programs of the late 1960s and 1970s. Therefore, no one should worry about hurting people when cutbacks are made in the social safety net. If cut off from public largesse, most grasshoppers will return to their antlike ways and those few who starve are necessary to set an example for the many who might be reluctant to return to antdom.

5 Murray seeks to demonstrate that the Theory Y view of human nature is utterly wrong—that human beings in no way resemble a colony of ants or beavers who work without the benefit of whips and large rewards because they just naturally like to work.

6 We can look at the evidence that Murray amasses in *Losing Ground* in two ways. A charitable interpretation is that he so firmly believes in Theory X that he cannot distinguish a grasshopper from an ant—that he just cannot see successful social welfare programs even when they exist all around him. A less charitable view is that he knows about the ants and the positive effects of social welfare programs but he chooses to ignore or distort them. Not knowing Murray personally, I cannot judge which hypothesis is correct, but I do know that *Losing Ground* presents a very selective collection of "evidence."

7 For example, the book contains only three words concerning the elderly: "I shall be discussing the working-age poor and discriminated against, not the elderly." Thus he does not tell us that poverty among the elderly has declined from 25.3% (twice the national average) in 1969 to 14.1% (less than the national average) in 1983. Nor does he tell us that although the elderly used to have median per capita incomes well below those of the nonelderly, their median per capita incomes are now equal to—and perhaps even slightly superior to—those of the nonelderly. In other words, the biggest social welfare success story isn't in the analysis.

8 At the same time, Murray fails to remind us that most (86% of federal income transfer payments in 1983) of the government's spending on social welfare has gone to programs to help the elderly. Nor does he tell us that he often includes spending on the elderly in his data on social welfare spending. If the elderly are to be left out of the analysis of benefits, they must also be left out of the analysis of costs. And if they are left out of the analysis of costs, the federal government ends up not having spent much money on social welfare programs, so no one should be surprised if the effects are small. Instead, readers of *Losing Ground* are left to believe that our government has spent massive amounts of money and that the only result is rising poverty.

9 At the same time, we are supposed to believe that the relatively small amounts spent on the nonelderly have corrupted Americans in every conceivable way. Thus Murray blames social welfare programs for high crime rates among black teenage males despite the fact that no social welfare programs give any money to that group. Apparently he believes that the attitudes that lead to social welfare programs also lead to high crime rates.

10 Page after page is devoted to illegitimate births, especially among blacks, but nowhere does he tell us that infant mortality rates have declined sharply, especially for poor black families, as a result of Medicaid and nutrition programs for pregnant mothers and children. Murray sees Medicaid as simply a failure without redeeming virtues, which should be abolished.

11 While the book purports to talk about human nature, it says nothing about the rest of the world. If social welfare systems lead to illegitimate births, Europe—which has much more generous social welfare systems than ours—should have very high rates of illegitimate births. In fact, European illegitimate birth rates are far below those of America. Presumably this means that something other than generous social welfare systems causes high illegitimacy rates. If not, one is forced to argue that there is something wrong with American genes or with the American environment, since Americans respond as grasshoppers to social welfare programs while Europeans respond as ants.

12 Murray talks as if only Americans have been experimenting with social welfare systems, although the United States in fact spends less on such programs than any other developed nation. As a result, Murray never has to ask himself two important questions: "If social welfare spending is so stupid, why do all those smart people in other countries do it?" and "If social welfare spending creates all these bad effects, such as high central city crime rates, why don't these other countries have all these bad side effects?"

STATISTICAL SWAMP

13 Misleading graphs abound. On page 57, a graph shows the pattern of cash public assistance and the number of people in poverty over time. It purports to demonstrate that poverty was falling faster before spending on social programs began than it was once they were fully under way.

14 Cash public assistance is, of course, only one of many social welfare programs. If the GI Bill is included as social welfare spending, the late 1940s and early 1950s are years of very high, not low, social welfare spending. The GI Bill was, of course, America's largest and most successful antipoverty, income-raising, social welfare program for the non-elderly. Veterans are in the working-age group—supposedly the age group Murray examines—but like success among the elderly, success among veterans is ignored.

15 The other part of the graph is also visually cooked. In measuring the rates of decline in poverty, the graph fails to take account of great

disparities in the population bases. If 1% of the population leaves poverty in 1949 when 46 million people are in poverty, that obviously leads to a much bigger decline in the number of people leaving poverty than if the same percentage leaves poverty in 1971 when 25 million people are poor. The incidence of poverty did quit falling after 1973, but the shift is not as dramatic as the curve indicates.

16 Murray also dismisses the rapid rate of decline in poverty from 1964 to 1968 as not germane because the poverty programs hadn't started spending much money back then. One could just as easily argue that it isn't money alone that makes antipoverty programs work but the attitudes behind them – prevalent from 1964 to 1968 – that a good society simply does not tolerate poverty. The rise in poverty after 1978 was caused by the fact that attitudes changed in the 1970s but the spending continued. Antipoverty spending does not work unless Americans are willing to change their institutional and sociological practices to accommodate new groups. In the 1960s they were willing to; in the 1970s they were not.

17 Murray does not mention that poverty did not start to rise until increases in real cash public assistance stopped and that the most rapid increases in poverty have occurred in the 1980s when cash public assistance was falling. Close inspection of the last six years of his graph shows that cutting public assistance leads to a rapid increase in poverty.

18 He does not state that transfer payments account for about half of all of the income going to the bottom 20% of the American population. If transfer payments were abolished, that segment of the population would have their incomes cut in half. In fact, most of the money spent got to the people who needed it, and without that money they would be much poorer than they are now.

19 Poor people could of course give up their current grasshopper ways and return to antdom, but what does being an ant mean for the 11.8 million poverty-stricken people who are under the age of 15 and the 3.7 million who are over 65? How are these Americans supposed to put bread on the table and work their way out of poverty?

20 In education, as in crime, Murray blames all declines in performance on social welfare spending. But no correlation exists between the location of declines and the target of the spending. From 1966 to 1981, average test scores on the Scholastic Aptitude Test given to college-bound high school seniors declined from 478 to 424 on the verbal and from 502 to 466 on the mathematical section of the test. But scores at the top of the distribution declined even more. While verbal scores were falling an average of 11% and math scores 7%, the number of students

scoring higher than 600 (out of a possible total of 800) declined 39% on the verbal exam and 19% on the math exam.

21 In fact, scores at the bottom of the distribution fell less steeply than scores at the top, which might indicate some measure of relative success —but not to Murray. From his point of view, educational spending on poor slum kids led to test score declines for rich suburban kids. On the face of it a preposterous argument, but one Murray implicitly makes.

22 Nowhere does Murray mention demography and the impact it has had on elementary and secondary education and will have on higher education. Think about the problem at the college level. Between 1984 and 1996, the population 18 to 22 years of age will fall 28%. This means that every college must become smaller or about one-quarter of all U.S. colleges must close their doors. Who manages decline well? Name a success story in a declining industry! The best people bail out. Good people won't enter the industry. There are no rewards.

23 Every year people are going to be laid off regardless of the quality of their performance. With schools closing, opportunities for promotion disappear. With plenty of warm bodies available, relative salaries fall. Morale and esprit de corps disappear. And in the wake of such events, the quality of the product not surprisingly falls.

24 How much of the decline in U.S. education should be traced to demography, how much to the loss of self-confidence suffered during the Vietnam War, and how much to television sets that are now on more than seven hours a day in the average home? These are all interesting and relevant questions that Murray has left unasked. For him, all the ills of American education can be traced to social welfare spending.

25 At times the book contradicts itself. On page 195, he tells us, "In the early years of the Reagan administration we witnessed exceedingly bitter disputes about the passage of what were, at bottom, reductions in the rate of increase in social spending and parings from a nearly unchanged array of social programs." The graph on page 57 shows that, after correction for inflation, cash public assistance had started to fall rapidly in the Carter administration and if updated would show continuing declines in the Reagan administration. Social welfare spending rises in the 1980s only if you include social security expenditures as social welfare spending, and Murray supposedly excludes the elderly from his analysis.

26 Concerning blacks, we learn that highly educated blacks and black women have been catching up with their white counterparts, but Murray dismisses this fact as if it somehow has nothing to do with antidiscrimination laws and social welfare spending. If such spending were turning

anyone into grasshoppers, it should be black women. It is they who are eligible for the programs, but it is also they who have reached parity with white women. Black males, who are ineligible for the social programs, are precisely the group who have difficulty in catching up. A moral might have been drawn from these data, but not the one Murray draws.

27 Many of those highly educated blacks would also not in fact have been educated were it not for social welfare scholarship funds, and they would have found no reason for education if affirmative action programs had not opened up opportunities previously closed. Murray points out that highly educated blacks for the first time made it into white collar jobs in the 1960s and 1970s and that more than half of these jobs were in government. A success story? Not in Murray's eyes. The fact that the jobs were government jobs means that "blacks have not been integrated into the woof and warp of the American economy to the degree that the trend lines may suggest."

28 Nor does it occur to Murray that private industry still might be discriminating against educated blacks and that new efforts are needed to open those doors. Government did its job and opened its management suites to blacks, but private industry did not. A reasonable inference, perhaps, but not one that Murray draws.

CONTRADICTORY ARGUMENTS

29 Finally, if you believe Murray's arguments in his first 194 pages, you must reject what he says in the last 46 pages on rethinking social policy. His proposal for public welfare consists of "scrapping the entire federal welfare and income support structure for working-age persons, including AFDC, Medicaid, food stamps, unemployment insurance, workers compensation, subsidized housing, disability insurance, and the rest. It would leave the working-age person with no recourse whatsoever except the job market, family members, friends, and public or private locally funded services" (page 228).

30 But if federally funded services lead to such bad results, why would anyone want to continue public or private locally funded services? He has not argued that federal government-funded services were poorly run. He has said that social services bring bad results regardless of how they are run. Local or federal, public or private, gifts lead to laziness.

31 Murray also doubles back and decides he does not really want to abolish unemployment insurance after all. But why this exception? His reason, "They need something to tide them over while finding a new

place in the economy" (page 230), does not make sense. Elsewhere, he argues that unemployment insurance leads people to seek unemployment longer than they otherwise would, and short periods of unemployment are a known possibility (much like the possibility of winter) that everyone should be prepared to meet out of personal resources.

32 Murray says that "hungry children should be fed; there is no argument about that" (page 233) but his arguments lead to the opposite conclusion. He says the federal government should not feed hungry children but his own reasoning also would compel those who believe his arguments to call for abolition of all private and public local charities for feeding hungry children. In fact, if one believes the Murray Theory X, the system needs a few hungry children to keep adults working. Every once in a while, a grasshopper must die to prove to the ants that they must remain ants. And if the dead grasshopper happens to be a child, so be it.

QUESTIONS FOR ANALYSIS AND DISCUSSION

1. Thurow begins his review with general remarks. What is the purpose of *Losing Ground*? What is Murray's view of social welfare programs? Of incentives for human effort?
2. Explain Theories X and Y. What are the two possible explanations for Murray's adherence to Theory X in spite of evidence to the contrary? Do these two possibilities seem the logical alternatives for this and similar situations?
3. When Thurow places quotation marks around the word *evidence* in paragraph 6, what is the effect?
4. How, according to Thurow, does Murray distort evidence with regard to the elderly? With regard to social welfare costs? Is Thurow's objection valid?
5. What facts and key questions does Murray avoid by not relating U.S. welfare programs to those in Europe?
6. In blaming social welfare spending (removing incentives) for declines in education, what does Murray overlook?
7. Thurow offers several possible causes for declines in U.S. education that Murray did not consider. What are they? Did you think of any of these when you read the selection on education from *Losing Ground*? Who in this chapter would agree that television viewing is a significant influence on students?
8. If social welfare spending eliminates incentive to work, how well should black women and black men be doing economically? How are they in fact doing? What would Thurow like readers to conclude from this?

9. What examples does Thurow offer of contradictions in Murray's book?
10. What seem to be the most damaging elements of Thurow's review, damaging even though you recognize that Thurow and Murray do not share social philosophies? Would Thurow's criticisms keep you from reading Murray's book? Why or why not?
11. Thurow is a respected economist, and his review has been printed in a respectable journal. What can you conclude, then, about characteristics of a good review?

Rebuilding the Foundations of Economics

LESTER C. THUROW

For a biographical sketch of Thurow, see pp. 440–441. The following excerpt is from Thurow's Dangerous Currents *(1984). In it Thurow explains Theory X and Theory Y, theories he refers to in his review of Murray's* Losing Ground. *The excerpt enlarges our understanding of that review, gives some context for evaluating student Gary Isom's review of* Dangerous Currents, *which follows, and provides some thought-provoking ideas in its own right.*

1 One of the peculiarities of economics is that it still rests on a behavioral assumption—rational utility maximization—that has long since been rejected by sociologists and psychologists who specialize in studying human behavior. Rational individual utility (income) maximization was the common assumption of all social science in the nineteenth century, but only economics continues to use it.

2 Contrary behavioral evidence has had little impact on economics because having a theory of how the world "ought" to act, economists can reject all manner of evidence showing that individuals are not rational utility maximizers. Actions that are not rational maximizations exist, but they are labeled "market imperfections" that "ought" to be eliminated. Individual economic actors "ought" to be rational utility maximizers and they can be taught to do what they "ought" to do. Prescription dominates description in economics, while the reverse is true in the other social sciences that study real human behavior.

3 Besides, the world is a complicated place, which means you can see

pretty much what you want to see. An industrial psychologist, Douglas McGregor, once constructed what he called theory X and theory Y.[1] A theory X person believes that people are rational utility maximizers motivated by a calculus of individual economic costs and benefits. As in the child's nursery tale, man is basically a grasshopper with a limited, short-time horizon who, liking leisure, must be forced to work and save enticed by rewards much greater than those he gets from leisure. Wherever a theory X person looks, according to McGregor, he sees people who confirm his prior belief that harsh economic whips and large economic carrots are required to keep individuals working and saving.

4 A theory Y person believes that man is basically a social, working, tool-using animal. It is possible to create disincentives big enough to stop him from working and saving, but relatively mild rewards and punishments will keep him at work in a world of social interaction. Man, for a theory Y person, is a beaver living in a colony with other beavers—a social animal motivated by many factors other than self-interested utility or income. Wherever a theory Y person looks, he sees social, industrious people having a variety of motives, who work without harsh whips and large carrots.

5 Proponents of both theory X and theory Y can easily observe real people who confirm their theories. There are lazy, self-interested individuals and also industrious social beings. The basic problem is one of proportion, and according to McGregor, top business managers (and economists?) are programmed to see mostly grasshoppers wherever they look, even if they happen to be looking at a colony of beavers.

6 Utility maximization in economics survives despite the lack of empirical support for it. Why? Because it has assumed a sophisticated form in which it has been emptied of empirical content. Every elementary economics textbook has several chapters on the theory of consumer choice. The utility maximizing consumer must insure that the marginal utility of the last dollar spent on each good and service is equal if individuals are to maximize their total utility, given some budget (income) constraint. Yet when it comes to empirical analysis of consumer choice, economists retreat to the doctrine of "revealed preferences" and do not attempt to specify the procedure by which marginal utility is determined or measured. Revealed preferences, however, is just a fancy way of saying that individuals do whatever individuals do, and whatever they do,

---

[1]Douglas Murry McGregor, *The Human Side of Management* (New York: McGraw-Hill, 1960).

economists will call it "utility maximization." Whether individuals buy good X or good Y they are still rational individual utility maximizers. By definition, there is no such thing as an individual who does not maximize his utility.[2] But if a theory can never be wrong, it has no content. It is merely a tautology.

7 The same problem exists on the earnings side of individual behavior. Income maximization is postulated, but then vanishes via a presumed nonobservable variable, psychic income. This notion tautologically makes everyone an income maximizer whatever his observed behavior. A person takes a job that pays less money than some other job, but economists still describe that person as a rational utility maximizer, since his total income (money plus psychic income) must be greater than jobs paying more money, or he wouldn't have taken the job. Again, by definition, no one can ever make a mistake and accept the wrong job.

8 Attempts have been made to rescue the postulates of consumption and income maximization with analogies based on natural selection—economic Darwinism. Firms and individuals who survive economically must be better maximizers than others, or they would not have survived. "Survival of the fittest" makes maximization a reasonable postulate.

9 But as recent work on the biology of natural selection shows, "survival of the fittest" is not synonymous with "individual maximization." Survival is instead a group process where random changes in the environment can turn survival into random good or bad luck. To prove that a species is optimal, you must be able to point to the specific characteristics that permit one to survive and another to become extinct. And this no one has been able to do. Whenever a given characteristic is asserted to be the reason for a species' becoming extinct, another species that survived can be found with that same characteristic. Survival, therefore, cannot be taken to mean maximization.

10 And even if survival approximated maximization, the theory of the second best has shown that simply being somewhere close to a maximizing path does not permit you to use deductive reasoning based on maximizing price-auction theory.[3] What would make for "market imperfections" on an optimal path may not be that on something less than optimal. In other words, the best actions in the world of the second best

---

[2]For an attempt to break out of this dilemma, see: Lester D. Taylor, "A Model of Consumption and Demand Based on Psychological Opponent Processes." Mimeo; and Tibor Scitovsky, *The Joyless Economy* (London: Oxford University Press, 1978).

[3]R. Lipsy and K. Lancaster, "The General Theory of the Second Best," *Review of Economic Studies,* Vol. 24 (1956–57), p. 12.

cannot be deduced from the theory of the first best, but need empirical justification.

11 Among economists, the failure or inability to move from rational optimization to a concept more refined and complicated reflects a number of realities within the profession. But probably none is more important than the fact that maximization can be mathematized while the alternatives—often labeled "satisficing"—cannot.[4] There is a seeming intellectual rigor to individual maximization, and a seeming "softness" to social satisficing. But the appearance of rigor is useless if economic actors don't maximize in the manner called for by the theory. Perhaps economic actors could be taught to be individual maximizers and forget social factors like relative income, but that is irrelevant unless the transformation actually takes place.

12 "Satisficing" may not be the right word, but each of us knows that we have made mistakes in our own decisions to spend money and often knowingly fail to be maximizers. Moreover, individual and group actions dictated by habit rather than optimization are pervasive. Many of our decisions are large irreversible decisions rather than the small reversible marginal decisions assumed by economic analysis. Ignorance is often greater than knowledge, and human preferences are not exogenous,[5] given unchanging reference points, but continually form and re-form as people engage themselves in economic activity. The basic problem of economics is to find a way to model this reality, even if the model cannot be neatly mathematized.

13 As things now stand, the price-auction model is silent about how preferences are formed. In theory they simply exist—fully developed and immutable. This of course in no way tells us anything about how the real world works. What we want and like constantly evolves as we experience life. We will often do something deliberately, take a music appreciation course, for example, to explore or even alter our preferences. So some real theory of preference formation has to lie at the heart of the rebuilding effort in economics. No one knows where a reformulation of the behavioral assumptions of economics would lead, but it is clear that the current assumptions neither conform with what we know about human behavior nor produce models with much predictive power.

---

[4]Herbert Simon, *Models of Man: Social and Rational: Mathematical Essays on Rational Human Behavior in a Social Setting* (New York: John Wiley, 1957).

[5]Obtained externally or formed by external elements.—Ed.

14 Consider a deliberate and pervasive effort to alter preferences: advertising. Not wanting to recognize what is happening, the economics profession has a very ambivalent attitude toward it. Advertising is divided into good advertising (informational) and bad advertising (persuasive), but most advertising is clearly designed to persuade, not to inform. Some economists see advertising as a pernicious attempt to distort perfectly good "home-grown" preferences, while others consider it a not very successful attempt to alter those same perfectly good "home-grown" preferences and therefore not anything worth worrying about. In either case, if true preferences are being "distorted," advertising is a market imperfection that must be eliminated.

15 Neither view of advertising confronts the real problem. Preferences are not being distorted by advertising, but are instead being formed endogenously in the market by a wide variety of *social* forces that include deliberate advertising. There is no such thing as "true" independent individual preferences. Human preferences are like an onion, because when the layers of social influence are peeled away, nothing is left. So the rock of stable preferences on which equilibrium price-auction markets are founded is in fact little more than quicksand.

16 If we concede that advertising is effective (and if it isn't, why does anyone bother with it?), the problem of preference formation becomes visible to anyone interested. If the demand for cigarettes is man-made, then human beings can unmake that preference, and rules that require health warnings on cigarettes become as legitimate as the advertising that created the initial demand. No one is distorting true preferences; it is just a matter of who has the *power* to create individual preferences. On the other hand, if preferences are fixed and fully formed, a clear argument exists for limiting any government intervention that tries to distort those fully formed preferences. But if we use social preferences to alter individual preferences, we immediately admit that the real world is much more complicated than the one traditionally studied by economists.

17 The desire for power, economic and otherwise, clearly motivates many people, but the desire for power is also left out of economic analysis because in the price-auction model there is no such thing as economic power. And a rational man cannot desire what cannot exist. Yet in the world most of us live in, we see many people working to get economic power, to get rich, and some are thought to have it, both by those who possess it and those who don't.

18 If you do not admit to economic power, problems are created for the conventional analysis of capital (wealth) accumulation. According to

the dictates of the price-auction model there is only one reason for accumulating wealth—future consumption. A person saves to consume in the future. So eventually everyone wakes up one morning and starts to "dis-save" because no one wants to die with a lot of unused consumption privileges.

19 If the rational individual knew when he was going to die, if he had, in the language of the economist, "perfect knowledge," he would die with zero assets. Lacking such knowledge, the rational individual buys annuities to yield the same result, which is to say, bringing lifetime consumption and production into equilibrium. But this model is at variance with the facts—many people die with a very substantial accumulation of wealth; at no age above sixty-five are Americans on average dis-saving (the average American saves until the day he dies), and the society at large is gradually accumulating a larger capital stock (something it would not do if everyone's lifetime consumption equaled his lifetime income). Why?

20 The standard way out of the problem expands consumption desires to take into account the bequest motive. But the desire to make consumption gifts to your children after you are dead constitutes an ad hoc addition to the theory that only seems sensible because we have heard it so often. It means you have to believe that a person gets more pleasure from providing for his children's consumption after he is dead than he would get from watching them consume while alive. Also ignored are American tax laws under which less tax is paid if income is given away before one dies rather than after one dies. So if a person has a strong desire to provide for his children, why doesn't he give his money away, in a way minimizing the tax bite? But those who choose low gift taxes over high inheritance taxes are few.

21 Moreover, children who know that they will receive bequests will usually accumulate less themselves. If all are arranging their lifetime consumption possibilities optimally, a bequest can neither change that pattern of consumption nor increase savings at any point in time. A bequest can only have an effect if it is unexpected and alters individual estimates of lifetime budget constraints. And even here the effect is only short-run. No increase in capital accumulation results over time. The bequest motive is also peculiar in a world without "power" motives because it effectively transfers income from the poor (this generation) to the rich (the next generation). Why should a rational individual utility maximizer want to shift money from someone presumably having a high marginal utility of income (the poor, himself) to those with a low marginal utility of income (the rich, his children)?

22 You can get a realistic model of capital accumulation more in line with what happens in the real world if you assume that human beings want to accumulate economic power. But as we've said, the standard economic model rules that out because there is no such thing as economic power in an equilibrium price-auction economy, within which no individual can affect market outcomes. No individual decisions to buy or sell can affect the market rate of return.

23 But even if market economic power does not exist, presumed wealth undeniably allows one to exercise power within the family and the society at large. Studies show that people don't take advantage of the gift tax because they feel that with fewer resources they will lose authority and respect within the family. Upon death you will give your money and assets to your children, but until that time you will keep them so that you can use them to wield family power. Economic clout also gives one access to the political and cultural affairs of a society that one would not otherwise have. At the extreme, economic power can be used to buy political power to change the rules of the economic game. In short, one can become a very important person with the judicious use of economic resources. Individuals want to become wealthy for many reasons other than considerations of future consumption.

QUESTIONS FOR ANALYSIS AND DISCUSSION

1. What is meant by "rational utility maximization"?
2. How, according to Thurow, does economics differ from the other social sciences? Why is this difference a problem for the study of economics?
3. Explain McGregor's Theory X and Theory Y. How do people reinforce their belief in one theory or the other? Which theory seems to be preferred by most economists? By Thurow?
4. How do economists maintain belief in utility maximization when empirical evidence is lacking? What is a "tautology"?
5. What is incorrect about the economic analogy to the biological "survival of the fittest"?
6. How does Thurow account for economists retaining maximization theory when it does not seem to account for economic behavior? Explain the term "satisficing."
7. What, for Thurow, is the basic problem for economics?
8. What is the central weakness of price-auction theory? What is it about human preferences that determine economic activity that the theory fails to consider?

9. How does the price-auction model account for the desire for economic power?
10. What is Thurow illustrating in his discussion of saving money, seeking wealth, and not giving money away before we die?
11. What is Thurow's purpose in this selection from *Dangerous Currents*? If you were to treat this excerpt as an essay, what would you say is Thurow's thesis? How does he develop and support his thesis?
12. Has Thurow convinced you of the many limitations in current economic thinking? Why or why not?

STUDENT ESSAY

SAILING AGAINST THE TIDE
(A Review of Lester C. Thurow's *Dangerous Currents*)
GARY ISOM

For Lester C. Thurow, an MIT professor of economics and syndicated columnist, the world economy is a ship sailing through oceans of uncertainty. In *Dangerous Currents,* Thurow finds the flaws in the prevailing economic theories that have allowed the world's economic ship to capsize in the past.

The two prevailing economic theories are the Keynesian theory and the price-auction theory, which noneconomists call the supply and demand theory. Economists have favored the price-auction theory since they began their science, but they embraced the Keynesian theory only when the price-auction theory failed to predict or alleviate the Great Depression. Economists used the Keynesian theory to analyze large-scale problems—inflation, unemployment, and low productivity. They called this new branch of study macroeconomics. The U.S. government based its policies on macroeconomic theory from the Depression era until the 1980s. Economists kept the price-auction theory to examine small-scale problems—the behavior of individual markets—and renamed this theory microeconomics.

Microeconomics disagrees with macroeconomics in its most basic assumption. Microeconomics assumes that real wages and prices—wages and prices minus the influence of inflation—can change instantly, without limit, whereas macroeconomics assumes that real wages and prices can never drop. Large-scale economic behavior is just the aggregate of all small-scale economic behavior. Microeconomics must jibe with macroeconomics for macroeconomics to provide a useful analysis of the U.S. economy.

This disagreement between the two prevailing economic theories has led, Thurow claims, to the failure of macroeconomic policies in the years since

World War II. The high inflation and high unemployment that have plagued the U.S. economy since World War II have inspired popular support for a return to government policies based on the price-auction theory. The Reagan administration has tried to put such policies into force.

Thurow, who sees nothing but trouble in the popular resurgence of the price-auction theory, seeks to defend Keynesian economics. In the first chapter, he points out the major flaw in the price-auction theory: in the real world, real wages and prices cannot change instantly, without limit. The price-auction theory always fails to predict real-world results.

Chapter 2 concerns the influence of political pressures on the U.S. government's economic plans. The expense of the unpopular war in Vietnam, for example, caused U.S. leaders to pursue poor economic policies. Thurow blames politicians, not Keynesian economic theory, for post–World War II economic failure. "Inflation," the title and subject of the third chapter, results when the government sacrifices long-term planning for short-term relief from political pressures. Thurow believes that the public worries too much about inflation: "a 12 percent rate of inflation and a 15 percent interest rate are equivalent to a zero inflation rate and a three percent interest rate."

In Chapter 4, "Econometrics," and Chapter 5, "Rational Expectations," Thurow examines two attempts to make the price-auction theory produce accurate, real-world predictions. Econometrics uses the power of the modern computer to shape economic equations around volumes of data. These equations should predict economic behavior in the real world, but as Thurow demonstrates, they don't.

Rational expectationists don't even try to predict real-world economic behavior. They believe that the economy will adjust to any economic prediction and cancel that prediction out. Rational expectationists also believe that the economy always works as efficiently as it can work. If high unemployment and high inflation occur, they occur because the economy can do no better. Thurow does not, of course, accept this view, since it verges on a complete denial of the worth of economics.

In Thurow's view, a new microeconomic theory, one without the price-auction theory's flaws, must support any renewal of Keynesian theory. The last two chapters, "The Labor Market" and "Rebuilding the Foundations of Economics," emphasize human behavior as the starting point of a new microeconomic theory. Rates of inflation and unemployment depend upon rates of productivity, which in turn depend upon the degree of worker cooperation and satisfaction.

Thurow demonstrates well the inadequacies of the price-auction theory. Other economists will not, unfortunately, show much interest in his emphasis on human behavior as the foundation for a new economic theory. The study of human behavior does not submit to much mathematical precision. Thurow himself admits that academic economists favor the price-auction theory because it works so well with calculus. Political difficulties will also hamper the acceptance of Thurow's ideas. Rugged individualism has become the favorite popular myth of the Reagan era. Politicians will find it difficult to sell their voters on an economic theory based on cooperation and mutual goodwill. The lack of an index (an absolute necessity for an economics text) will not help Thurow's case either.

What will help Thurow's case is the failure of economic policies based on the price-auction theory. One clear sign of this failure is the huge federal budget deficit. Voters will soon begin paying for this deficit, and these payments will no doubt squash the current surge of economic prosperity. With emptier pockets, and more open minds, voters might withdraw their support for price-auction economics and consider other views. With luck, they will remember *Dangerous Currents.*

EXERCISES

1. Rubinstein reviews the research on television and children to 1978. If you wanted to update this work, your task would be to prepare a complete bibliography and then start reading. Using both the *Reader's Guide to Periodical Literature* and the *Social Sciences and Humanities Index,* prepare a bibliography from 1979 to the present for one of the following subjects:
   a. Television advertising and children
   b. The effect of television violence on children
   c. Sex on television
2. Select ten articles from your extensive bibliography (or find ten since 1979 in the indexes listed above, if you did not do exercise 1), read them, and prepare an annotated bibliography of those ten articles. Make each annotation no more than two or three sentences, focusing on what the article contains, not on what it says—that is, on what a researcher would find useful in it.
3. In his article, Galbraith mentions five early economists whose theories continue to influence economic thought: Adam Smith, Jeremy Bentham, David Ricardo, Thomas Robert Malthus, and Herbert Spencer. Selecting one writer, prepare a bibliography that will include works by the writer, biographies and other books about the writer, articles about the writer, and published bibliographies, if any. Organize your items under these headings.
4. Select a field of the social sciences you are interested in—sociology, psychology, anthropology, economics—and examine the journals in that field

subscribed to by your library. Look at several issues of each journal, and then prepare a brief account of each journal in the form of an annotated bibliography. That is, list the journals alphabetically and, following each title, briefly describe the journal: Who publishes it? When is it published? What kinds of articles does it contain, and thus who is the intended audience? What other features (book reviews, etc.) are noteworthy?

WRITING ASSIGNMENTS

1. Select a recent article from one of your library's scholarly journals in the social sciences and prepare a detailed, accurate summary of 200 words. Simplify language when possible but do not eliminate necessary technical terms. Your goal is to demonstrate understanding. Then, using the "Playing Dumb" articles as your guide, prepare a popular version of the article for an appropriate magazine, as if you were the author of the original. Make your 500-700 word article lively and eliminate the research report format; but retain significant parts of the study and keep it accurate. Submit a copy of the original article, your summary, and your popular version.
2. Select one of the books listed below (or select another book in the social sciences approved by your instructor) and prepare a book review of 500 words to be published in an appropriate journal. Your review should contain an explanation of the type of book reviewed, a sampling of content, and a fair evaluation that will be helpful to possible readers.

   Bettelheim, *The Uses of Enchantment: The Meaning and Importance of Fairy Tales*

   Gilder, *Wealth and Poverty*

   Galbraith, *The Affluent Society*

   Postman, *The Disappearance of Childhood*

   Postman, *Crazy Talk, Stupid Talk*

   Schumacher, *Small Is Beautiful: Economics as if People Mattered*

   Etzioni, *Capital Corruption: A New Attack on American Democracy*

3. Conduct your own research on one of the topics listed below and report results in a scientific manner. Begin by stating your research question; explain methodology in detail (how many ads, from what sources, how analyzed, etc.); present evidence, analyzing and illustrating for your reader; state conclusions. Include, in your presentation of evidence, at least one chart or graph that visually presents some of your results. (Your model is the student essay in Chapter 6.)

a. Study print ads in magazines for one type of product (cars, cosmetics, cigarettes) and draw inferences about the dominant techniques used to sell that product. Study at least twenty-five ads, but when presenting evidence use several representative ads for detailed analysis; include all, however, when generalizing about techniques used.

b. Study print ads for one type of product as advertised in different types of magazines clearly directed to different audiences to see how (or if) selling techniques change with a change in audience. Again, study at least twenty-five ads. Remember that to conclude that no changes in technique occur can be just as interesting as finding changes.

c. Spend at least ten hours watching television shows directed specifically to children and study the advertising that occurs. Catalogue types of products advertised and/or techniques used to sell products to a child audience. A VCR might help so that you can see the ads several times, especially if you want to examine techniques. Another approach is to prepare in advance a list of possible techniques to aid in quick, simple classifications, e.g., testimonials, appeal to popularity. If you are interested in how frequently a type of product was advertised, be sure to count repeats of the same ad.

Vincent Van Gogh, Starry Night, 1889. *Approx.* 29″ × 36¼″. *Collection, the* Museum *of* Modern Art, *New York (bequest of* Lillie P. Bliss).

CHAPTER 8

WRITINGS FROM THE SCIENCES

When a scientist writes, that is, when a scientist writes as a professional for an audience of colleagues, the writer's personality is almost entirely submerged, content is dominant, and the audience, although theoretically without limit, is actually a small but captive one. Let's look at each one of these assertions. When nonscientists read scientific reports, they usually describe them as cold or impersonal. This does not mean, of course, that scientists are cold people or unfeeling about their work. Rather, they are adhering to the conventions of writing in the sciences, conventions that require use of a standard format for reporting the results of research, the use of precise, unemotional terms, and the avoidance of first person pronouns and other indicators of voice or personality. Ironically, the persona created by the scientist as writer is an impartial, objective "nonperson."

For scientists as writers and readers, content is what matters; not the shaping of content into a finely structured work but the actual data gathered and conclusions reached. To aid the reader's understanding of content, scientific articles, like those in the social sciences, adhere to an agreed-upon structure that is usually highlighted by subheadings to mark the standard parts of the report. Graphs, charts, diagrams, or other visuals are used not to enliven the presentation but rather to clarify content.

How does the scientist manage to find an audience for writing that is clear but impersonal, predictably structured, and often lacking grace or sparkle? The answer is the same as for social scientists. As Michael Hughes explains in Chapter 7, professionals are obliged to keep up in their fields, to read the articles relevant to their specializations if they want to participate in the ongoing work of the group. The botanist may not have as many readers as journalist Ellen Goodman, but the botanist does not have to create and hold an audience each time he or she writes for colleagues. If the content is worthwhile, the botanist will have readers, but not as many as might be interested, potentially, in the botanist's information. Why not? Consider the following sentence:

> Begoniacae, by their anthero-connectival fabric, indicate a close relationship with anonaceo-hydrocharideo-nymphaeoid forms, an affinity confirmed by the serpentarioid flexuosonodulous stem, the liriodendroid stipules, and cissoid and victorioid foliage of a certain Begonia, and if considered hypogynous, would, in their triquetrous capsule, alate seed, apetalism and tufed stamination, represent the floral fabric of Nepenthes, itself of aristolochioid affinity, while, by its pitchered leaves, directly belonging to Sarracenias and Dionaceas.

To a botanist, the content of that sentence is quite clear; to the average reader, it is hopelessly obscure.

In theory, the less personal, connotative, and allusive a piece of writing, the more easily it can be read by many people. Scientific writing, for example, can be readily translated into other languages, whereas much literature and nonfiction that is highly personal, metaphoric, or based on shared cultural knowledge cannot be translated, exactly, into other languages. But the fact is that science in the twentieth century has become so detailed and complex that an ever smaller portion of educated people can read scientific articles written for specialists. The sentence quoted above is perfectly clear only to those familiar with the language and ways of thinking of a botanist.

The way we teach the sciences today both reflects the amount and complexity of subject matter to be learned and accounts for—in the view of many—the rapid expansion of information and knowledge in these fields. In the arts, students learn primarily by practice and guidance in the presence of artists; texts are secondary, when used at all. In the humanities and social sciences, texts are more important, but they present competing, often incompatible, theories and ways of solving problems. Students are encouraged to analyze and evaluate differing approaches. In the sciences, however, students rely on textbooks until graduate school. (Students go to the lab to practice standard procedures and redo famous experiments, not to be creative.) The texts vary only slightly in the presentation of the information and theories currently accepted in a given field.

To join a group of specialists, students learn the vocabulary, methods of research, core information, and accepted theories of a field—whether geology, biochemistry, or astrophysics—what Thomas S. Kuhn calls "normal science." "Abnormal science," Kuhn argues in *The Structure of Scientific Revolutions,* is the work that leads to the rejecting of a once-accepted theory for a new one, frequently radically new. When the theory is radically new, the result is a revolution in the field of study and, often, in world view for nonspecialists as well. Examples of scientific revolutions include a shift from the earth-centered (and man-centered) universe of Ptolemy to the sun-centered solar system of Copernicus, or the shift from the orderly Newtonian universe of fixed laws to the relative universe of Einstein.

The teaching of science seems to encourage the progress of normal science, the adding of new information that fits within accepted theories; yet the emphasis on uniform training has not restricted the development of new theories and new fields of specialization. Howard Gruber addresses the fascinating issue of creativity, particularly in the sciences, in the chapter's opening selection. Studying Darwin's development of the theory of evolution, Gruber provides insight into the creative interaction of facts and ideas.

The realities of science training and specialized writing have led to an array of books and articles on science for nonspecialists. Although the most up-to-date information and most current debates will be found in the scholarly journals of the specialists, several journals—*Scientific American,* for example—offer articles from all fields written by specialists for a knowledgeable but nonspecialist audience. Dale Russell's review of the dinosaur-extinction issue for *Scientific American* readers represents this type of science article. Scientists and well-educated nonscientists with an interest in paleontology will form Russell's audience. However, if you flip through a current issue of *Scientific American,* or the British journal *Nature,* you may find many incomprehensible articles—for instance, those that require a knowledge of advanced calculus.

Once a specialist, a physicist for example, shifts from an audience of physicists to a nonspecialized audience, he or she faces—and must solve—the problems facing any writer: Who is my audience? What is my purpose in writing? How will the answers to these questions shape my presentation? John Gribben and Nancy Andreasen are both writing primarily to inform nonspecialists; they rely on patterns of organization and visuals they are accustomed to, but they provide background information and adjust vocabulary to accommodate their readers. Realizing, however, that in this instance they do not have a captive audience but must entice and hold readers, the best writers about science provide more than accurate and clear accounts. They seek to engage readers in the mystery or excitement of their subjects. Both Isaac Asimov and Stephen Jay Gould succeed in engaging their readers; that is why they are so well known among educated readers.

John Noble Wilford, writing for a general audience, the newspaper reader, reminds us that scientists do debate, that science is controversial. But then Wilford is a journalist, so you might expect him to focus on controversy, for that is what makes news (as you explored in Chapter 6). We learn, from his comments on writing *The Riddle of the Dinosaur,* that Wilford is a writer first, a student of science second. He gives good advice to the studentwriter, who also must juggle learning the subject matter and planning the paper.

We have examined both the training that students of science receive and the writing that scientists do for colleagues and nonspecialists. These concerns come together in the questions that follow each article and in the chapter's exercises and writing assignments. Reading some of the chapter's selections just once may not prepare you to answer all the questions that follow; you will have to study the selections to master the facts and understand the concepts. Similarly, you will need to work with reference materials to prepare exercises and writing assignments, for you cannot practice academic writing without appropriate content. But as you practice organizing, analyzing, and contrasting data and concepts, you will become a better studentwriter, and you will learn from your reading.

Scientific Creativity: A Study of Darwin

HOWARD E. GRUBER

A native of Pittsburgh, Howard Gruber (b. 1922) has a Ph.D. in experimental psychology from Cornell University and is a professor of psychology at Rutgers University and director of the university's Institute for Cognitive Studies. Gruber specializes in the study of the creative process in both scientific and artistic work. He is best known for Darwin on Man: A Psychological Study of Scientific Creativity *(1974), written with Paul H. Barrett, from which the following excerpt is taken.* Darwin on Man *contains not only Gruber's study but an edition of Darwin's early Notebooks. (Although Gruber and Barrett are technically coauthors, Gruber prepared the study and Barrett edited the Notebooks.) Gruber's other books include* Perception of Slanted Surfaces *(1956),* The Psychologist at Work: An Introduction to Scientific Psychology *(1972), and, as a coauthor,* The Essential Piaget *(1977).*

"Scientific Creativity" provides a brief but valuable look at Gruber's study of Darwin and the creative process—a process that, in Gruber's view, is a conscious, determined effort not limited to a few geniuses who have occasional flashes of insight. The integrity of creative individuals is maintained, Gruber argues, by their choosing their life's work, determining what they can do and what they want to do, and then devoting a sustained effort over time to those choices. In his study of Darwin's notebooks, letters, and published works, Gruber reveals this creative process at work.

1 In his life work Darwin carried forward two distinct but closely related aims: first, to propose a theory that would explain how evolution occurs; and second, to marshal the evidence that evolution had in fact occurred. The *Origin of Species* is organized in a way that reflects these twin themes. The first five chapters give the basic theory. The topics dealt with are variation under domestication and under nature, the struggle for existence, natural selection, and the laws of variation. The next four chapters deal with difficulties confronting the theory. One of these difficulties was the enormous strain placed on nineteenth-century thought by the proposal that mental functions had evolved in a thoroughly natural fashion; in the *Origin* Darwin treated only the subject of instinct, leaving the higher mental functions for his later works. The next four chapters marshal the evidence for the occurrence of evolution:

"the geological succession of organic beings, geographical distribution, mutual affinities of organic beings, morphology,[1] embryology,[2] rudimentary origins."[3]

2 Beyond a doubt, the *Origin* is a master work precisely because of Darwin's beautiful orchestration of these two themes. For those who were not entirely persuaded by Darwin's theory of natural selection, the fact that *any* reasonably plausible theory could be advanced gave weight to the evidence that evolution occurs. For those who saw gaps in the factual evidence, the theory explained just why such gaps must necessarily occur, so that they almost became evidence for the theory rather than reasons to doubt it.

3 The construction of the theory and the marshaling of the evidence entailed somewhat different activities on Darwin's part. Theory construction is a matter of rumination[4] and schematization;[5] it is primarily an internal effort, involving play with ideas—information and generalizations—already incorporated in existing schemes of thought; its end product is the alteration of those schemes.

4 The marshaling of evidence and the construction of general laws from particular facts is largely a matter of observation and data collection, the noting of similarities among events, and the drawing of general conclusions. But this marshaling of evidence is not simply "induction" if that term means a theoretically neutral activity or an activity preceding the construction of a theory. The whole point is that information can *only* be incorporated in existing schemes of thought. When we notice a similarity between events or processes that seem superficially different, we are being guided by a point of view that makes some characteristics important, certain comparisons possible and meaningful. This is what Hanson meant when he wrote, "Observation is a theory-laden undertaking."[6]

5 The two kinds of task, theoretical and evidential, entail different activities, and in the long run they may yield distinguishable products for our consideration. But *in vivo,*[7] in the life of the thinking person,

---

[1]The study of the form and structure of plants and animals.—Ed.

[2]The study of the formation, development, and structure of embryos.—Ed.

[3]These phrases are from the chapter headings of the *Origin.*

[4]Pondering.—Ed.

[5]Organizing into a plan or pattern.—Ed.

[6]N. R. Hanson, *Patterns of Discovery* (Cambridge University Press, 1958).

[7]Within a living organism.—Ed.

they are thoroughly intertwined. The most speculative "castle in the air" is triggered off by a simple observation or a friend's remark about his dog. Hard work amassing the facts on a special point is guided by a long theoretical argument with which it may have only a tenuous logical relationship: the theory does not absolutely depend on the facts, nor could the facts ever guarantee the theory. The relation of theory and evidence is not simply logical but psychological.

6 For example, Darwin's experimental work on the germination of seeds in sea water . . . clearly did *not* bear a relationship of necessity and sufficiency to any theory of evolution. He wanted to show that some facts of geographical distribution could be harmonized with the idea of evolution—i.e., a widespread species of plant might have had a single origin and then become diffused if its seeds could have been floated across the sea. This argument requires that certain seeds soaked in sea water must then germinate. But if the seeds do not germinate, Darwin can find other mechanisms of diffusion—indeed, there are many. If the seeds do germinate, it increases the plausibility of the notion of a single origin—but only to someone who is already prepared to reject the notion of creation. To another, an undoubting believer in God's power to create the same species in as many places as He wishes, the appearance of the same creature in widely separated loci[8] presents no special problem, and the germination of sea-soaked seeds is only an isolated curiosity.

7 The relation between theory and experiment would be somewhat different if the entire debate were public. After all, a theory is not simply an argument of one man with nature; it is an argument *among* men *about* nature—or, in Darwin's case, about the relation of God and nature. If Darwin had shown how the theory of evolution had led him to the experiment on sea-soaked seeds, his positive results might have changed the structure of the public debate. From the private 1837–39 notebooks we know how theory led to experiment. But in his published papers on this subject, begun in 1843 and printed in 1855 and 1857, Darwin restricted himself to the bare facts, biding his time until 1859 before revealing the full connection of these facts with his evolutionary theory.

8 He did, however, indicate that the facts bore on "a very interesting problem, . . . whether the same organic being has been created at one point or on several on the face of our globe." He ended the same article on the successful generation of seeds after floating across a salt-water

---

[8]Places.—Ed.

barrier: "But when the seed is sown in its new home then as I believe, comes the ordeal; will the old occupants in the great struggle for life allow the new and solitary immigrant room and sustenance?"[9]

9 The sense in which experiments form part of an argument among people is neatly conveyed in a letter Darwin wrote to his close friend, the botanist Joseph Hooker. Hooker was one of the very few who knew all along about Darwin's theories and the complex interrelationships among Darwin's many projects and varied levels of thought. In 1855 the two men had been corresponding about the seed-soaking experiments. In answer to a letter from Hooker, Darwin wrote, "You are a good man to confess that you expected the cress would be killed in a week, for this gives me a nice little triumph. The children at first were tremendously eager, and asked me often, 'whether I should beat Dr. Hooker!' The cress and lettuce have just vegetated well after twenty-one days' immersion." (*LL* 2, 155. Letter writen April 14, 1855)

10 Darwin was certainly thinking not only of seeds but of the unity of man, his single origin, and his subsequent dispersal through countless small migrations. In his account of the *Beagle* voyage he alluded to the similarity between seeds and canoes washed up on shores far from their origins. (*Voyage,* 1839, p. 542) Just a few pages before his first mention of the "curious experiment" of soaking seeds in sea water (*B* 125e), he wrote of human migrations, "In first settling a country, people very apt to be split up into many isolated races!" (*B* 119) He, of course, had first-hand knowledge of the sea-faring exploits of the creature he described as "the most dominant animal that has ever appeared on this earth"; in his survey of human inventions he wrote, "He has made rafts or canoes for fishing or crossing over to neighboring fertile islands." (*Descent,* 48) Even in the *Origin,* one chapter of his lengthy treatment of geographical distribution closes with an analogy between man and other sea-borne creatures carried from one habitat to another: "The various beings thus left stranded may be compared with savage races of man, driven up and surviving in the mountain-fastnesses of almost every land, which serve as a record, full of interest to us, of the former inhabitants of the surrounding lowlands." (*Origin,* 382)

11 I have concentrated almost entirely on Darwin's first strategic aim, theory construction. This leads to an oversimplification which may make

---

[9]Charles Darwin, "Does Sea-Water Kill Seeds?" *Gardeners' Chronicle and Agricultural Gazette,* 1855. Darwin's papers on the germination of sea-soaked seeds are reprinted in Barrett, *op cit.* The *Origin* has several pages summarizing these experiments.

it appear as though Darwin's thought was a purely endogenous[10] process. But during the summer of 1837 he was engaged in a great variety of activities related to the subject of the notebooks. Most of his time was probably spent in writing the *Journal of Researches* describing the voyage of the *Beagle.* This work required him to go over his notes and specimens in all fields of natural history. He also completed the practical arrangements for government support of the *Zoology of the Voyage of the Beagle,* which eventually ran to five volumes. The B notebook, for the period from July to September 1837, refers to at least seven conversations, twenty-one books and twenty scientific articles—all used in thinking through the problem Darwin had set himself.

12 From a methodological point of view, . . . facts are ambiguous unless linked by a plausible and coherent theory; a theory is weak and empty if it does not unite many important facts; and a new theory is pointless if it does not do its appointed job better than its predecessors.

13 From a psychological point of view, the individual's engagement in more than one enterprise permits him to continue productive work on one front when he is forced to a halt on another. When these enterprises are related, continued progess in one of them may eventually permit him to move forward in the others. Let us see how this feature of the total economy of thought worked out in Darwin's case.

14 When he began the transmutation notebooks, clearly he was aiming at a theory that would explain evolution. At the same time, he believed that evolution taken as a *premise* could explain many of the peculiarities of geographical distribution and taxonomic[11] relationships he had come to know so well.

15 After a few months of hard theoretical work, Darwin had given up the monad theory[12] and had come to doubt the effectiveness of the theory of perpetual becoming.[13] At about the same time, he began to see that if he could not advance on the theoretical front, it was still extremely useful to group facts together under general empirical laws which could best be accounted for by assuming that evolution had occurred. Darwin had actually begun to do this work much earlier, but

---

[10] Proceeding from within.—Ed.

[11] Organism classification.—Ed.

[12] Darwin's first theory of evolution: simple life forms (monads) appear from inanimate matter, evolve as a result of environmental influences, and then all species created from the monad die to make room for the progeny of new monads.—Ed.

[13] A revision of the monad theory: a species lives on only if it gives rise to new species—that is, if it changes. This thinking led to Darwin's search for the causes of change.—Ed.

his first explicit statement of this methodological goal is the remark: "Absolute knowledge that species die and others replace them. – Two hypotheses: fresh creations is mere assumption, it explains nothing further; points gained if any facts are connected." (*B* 104)

16 Accordingly, the notebooks devote much attention to the searching out of these empirical connections. But Darwin leaves no doubt that his ultimate goal is the construction of an explanatory theory, a theory having the same universality and deductive structure as Newtonian physics.

17 In a passage summarizing the progress he has made by January or February of 1838, the entire weight of emphasis is on the variety of facts that will be explained if one assumes the correctness of the concept of an irregularly branching tree of nature. But he concludes that all these studies of special groups of facts will "lead to laws of change, which would then be main object of study. . . ." (*B* 228)

18 As Darwin searched vainly for the causes of variation, he began to think that if he did not find them, his theory of evolution might not get much further than a clear organization of the many facts that the assumption of branching evolution could explain. If so, his theory would be only a small advance over previous efforts. Although he is aware of many differences between himself and Lamarck, now he likens himself to his precursor: "What the Frenchman did for *species* between England and France I will do with *forms*." (*C* 123)

19 A few months later, on September 7, 1838, just three weeks before his recognition of the evolutionary significance of natural selection, he wrote: "Seeing what Von Buch (Humboldt) G. St. Hilaire, & Lamarck have written I pretend to no originality of idea – (though I arrived at them quite independently & have used them since) the line of proof & reducing facts to law only merit if merit there be in following work." (*D* 69)

20 In his beautiful book *Productive Thinking*, Max Wertheimer, founder of Gestalt psychology, focused his attention on the kind of direct thinking that goes to the heart of the problem under attack. In Darwin's long and twisting path, however, there are several striking examples of important steps toward the theory of evolution through natural selection being taken as by-products of efforts that seemed to move in other directions. Let us review briefly some of these by-productive moves.

21 The theory of coral reefs was based on an extrapolation from what Darwin had learned about the formation of continental mountain chains; if mountains are up-raised, he reasoned, the adjacent sea bed must sink; from this slow subsidence of the sea bed, the coral-reef theory followed. That theory does not deal at all with organic evolution, but it

does provide a formal model quite analogous to Darwin's eventual theory. Darwin did not have a five-year *plan* to move through this important sequence of ideas. It evolved.

22 The monad theory, itself short-lived in Darwin's thought and not entirely original, led him to his branching model of evolution. This became a cornerstone of his thought. During the difficult months when he had dropped the monad theory without yet discovering the natural-selection theory, the branching model guided him in a searching critique of the Quinarian system of classification. The essence of this mystical approach to taxonomy was the notion that there are five major groups of animals, that each group has five subgroups, etc., and that at all levels of classification the groups are ordered in perfect circles of affinity—in other words, a closed arrangement in which each group could be placed between two neighboring groups most resembling it.

23 It was, of course, important for Darwin to reject the mystical insistence on fives. But more fundamental was his criticism of the closed, regular system of nature. Darwin's system was irregular, open-ended, uncertain in number. His critique of Quinarianism and his development of the branching model stimulated him to organize his ideas about taxonomic affinities, and to reinterpret much of the information then known.

24 The branching model contains within it the very same formal structure which is the kernel of the Malthusian[14] idea of explosive population growth. The branching diagram depicts an exponential growth function because it shows a series of successive branchings with an increasing number of possible branches as distance from the origin (measured in number of generations) increases. Darwin never explicitly used this way of showing exponential population growth; rather, he used the branching model to show that most of the species that were in some sense possible did not in fact exist—either they were extinct or they never had existed. Thus, although its substance was entirely different, the form of Darwin's early image of the irregularly branching tree of nature foreshadowed his use of the Malthusian principle over a year later.

25 Darwin's long wrestling match with hybridization did not lead him to a clear explanation of the causes of variation, as he hoped it would. But it did serve to acquaint him with the field of plant and animal breeding

[14]The theory of population growth argued by English economist Thomas Malthus, a contemporary of Darwin.—Ed.

and thus with artificial selection, which gave him the nearest thing he had to an experimental version of natural selection.[15]

26 Similarly, Darwin's abiding preoccupation with the influence of function on form was also part of his search for the causes of variation. It led him to the study of behavior and mind, and the marshaling of the material which gave him the confidence to write his chapter on "Instinct" in the *Origin,* and later the *Descent of Man* and the *Expression of Emotions.* In short, by-productive thinking led him in 1838 to begin the notebooks on man and mind.

27 I do not intend to suggest that the concept of "by-productive thinking" contradicts Wertheimer's major thesis, which is not so much that thinking is direct as that it is *organized.* . . . But something does emerge in this picture which Wertheimer neglected. Thinking about complex subjects is *organized over time,* over long periods of time; it is organized in major sub-groupings or enterprises; at any given moment, any one of these may wholly occupy the consciousness of the thinking person. Holding the entire complex together, disciplining oneself so that every by-productive moment does not threaten the integrity of the larger structure of enterprise—this struggle for coherence and identity does not come simply from direct perceptual contact with the materials of nature. On the contrary, those materials are so fascinating, and at each moment they lead to such engrossing thoughts and so many enchanting tangents, that we need to introduce another conception to explain how the individual maintains his sense of direction.

28 That other concept is the individual's sense of purpose: his ability to imagine himself outside the perspective of the moment, to see each sub-task in its place as part of the larger task he has set himself. This abstract purposefulness and perspective, this *standing outside,* is an activity undertaken in quite a different spirit from that in which the creative person immerses himself, loses himself in the material of nature. To accomplish his great synthesis Darwin had to be able to alternate between these two attitudes. To see more deeply into nature, he needed the perceptual, intuitive direct contact with the material. To understand what

[15]See Robert M. Young, "Darwin's Metaphor: Does Nature Select?" *The Monist,* Vol. 55, 1971, pp. 442–503. In Young's view Darwin began his studies of domestic breeding in order to demonstrate the tenuousness of the distinction between species and varieties. Young bases his account on Darwin's recollections as given in the *Origin.* The interpretation given above is based mainly on Darwin's early notebooks. While the two views differ, they are not mutually exclusive. In any case, Darwin's knowledge of artificial selection was a by-product of other theoretical interests.

he had seen, and to construct a theory that would do it new justice, he had to re-examine everything incessantly from the varied perspectives of his diverse enterprises.

QUESTIONS FOR ANALYSIS AND DISCUSSION

1. What were the two aims reflected in Darwin's life work? How did these two aims unite to make *Origin of Species* a masterwork?
2. What is the relationship between theory construction and evidence gathering? How does Gruber qualify the concept of induction as the scientific method?
3. How did Darwin's experiment with sea-soaked seeds connect to his theory of evolution? How does this connection illustrate Gruber's point about the interweaving of theory and data?
4. What theories did Darwin reject on his way to developing the theory of evolution? Explain each theory. (Use appropriate reference works as needed.)
5. What is important about Darwin's branching model? How did this metaphor help to state some of the components of evolutionary theory?
6. Explain the concept of by-productive thinking. How, according to Gruber, is our thinking organized?
7. How can by-productive thinking contribute to creative effort? For by-productive thinking to contribute, what must the creative person be able to do?
8. Does Gruber's emphasis on the interweaving of fact and theory to make both meaningful (see paragraph 12) make sense to you? Think about your study of the sciences. Hasn't it involved the learning of both facts and theories, data and principles for organizing them? Has your study of subjects in the humanities (history, literature, art) been different? If so, how?
9. Just as Gruber rejects the "genie-in-the-bottle" concept of creativity, he seems also to reject the idea of spontaneity, the "eureka" theory of discovery. What is appealing about the "genie" theory of creativity? The "eureka" theory? The "conscious, sustained effort over time" theory? What are the problems with or less appealing features of each theory?
10. Which view of the creative process did you hold before reading Gruber? Do you see creativity in scientific discoveries and in the arts as different processes? If so, why? Has Gruber altered your thinking about creativity? If so, how?

Were Dinosaurs Dumb?

STEPHEN JAY GOULD

Born in New York and educated at Antioch College and Columbia University, Stephen Jay Gould (b. 1941) has been a professor of geology at Harvard since 1973. Trained in the study of fossil records, Gould is also an expert on the history of science. He draws on his wide-ranging knowledge of science to write a monthly column for Natural History *magazine. Four collections of these columns have been published, including* The Panda's Thumb *(1980)—an American Book Award winner in 1981—from which the following essay is taken. Gould has also contributed over 100 articles to scholarly journals and is the author of* The Mismeasure of Man *(1981), a historical study of the generally foolish (or dangerous) attempts to measure human intelligence and rank people thereby.*

In all his writing, Gould seeks to debunk foolish or pernicious ideas presented in the name of science and to remind readers that scientific investigation always takes place in a cultural and political context. This means that the facts of science must necessarily be understood in the light of the ideas, values, and myths of a given time—and must be reevaluated in succeeding times.

1 When Muhammad Ali flunked his army intelligence test, he quipped (with a wit that belied his performance on the exam): "I only said I was the greatest; I never said I was the smartest." In our metaphors and fairy tales, size and power are almost always balanced by a want of intelligence. Cunning is the refuge of the little guy. Think of Br'er Rabbit and Br'er Bear; David smiting Goliath with a slingshot; Jack chopping down the beanstalk.[1] Slow wit is the tragic flaw of a giant.

2 The discovery of dinosaurs in the nineteenth century provided, or so it appeared, a quintessential case of the negative correlation of size and smarts. With their pea brains and giant bodies, dinosaurs became a symbol of lumbering stupidity. Their extinction seemed only to confirm their flawed design.

3 Dinosaurs were not even granted the usual solace of a giant—great physical prowess. God maintained a discreet silence about the brains of behemoth, but he certainly marveled at its strength: "Lo, now, his

[1]All are examples of "the little guy" triumphing over a much bigger enemy.—Ed.

strength is in his loins, and his force is in the navel of his belly. He moveth his tail like a cedar. . . . His bones are as strong pieces of brass; his bones are like bars of iron [Job 40:16–18]." Dinosaurs, on the other hand, have usually been reconstructed as slow and clumsy. In the standard illustration, *Brontosaurus*[2] wades in a murky pond because he cannot hold up his own weight on land.

4 Popularizations for grade school curricula provide a good illustration of prevailing orthodoxy. I still have my third grade copy (1948 edition) of Bertha Morris Parker's *Animals of Yesterday*, stolen, I am forced to suppose, from P.S. 26, Queens (sorry Mrs. McInerney). In it, boy (teleported back to the Jurassic[3]) meets brontosaur:

> It is huge, and you can tell from the size of its head that it must be stupid. . . . This giant animal moves about very slowly as it eats. No wonder it moves slowly! Its huge feet are very heavy, and its great tail is not easy to pull around. You are not surprised that the thunder lizard likes to stay in the water so that the water will help it hold up its huge body. . . . Giant dinosaurs were once the lords of the earth. Why did they disappear? You can probably guess part of the answer—their bodies were too large for their brains. If their bodies had been smaller, and their brains larger, they might have lived on.

5 Dinosaurs have been making a strong comeback of late, in this age of "I'm OK, you're OK." Most paleontologists are now willing to view them as energetic, active, and capable animals. The *Brontosaurus* that wallowed in its pond a generation ago is now running on land, while pairs of males have been seen twining their necks about each other in elaborate sexual combat for access to females (much like the neck wrestling of giraffes). Modern anatomical reconstructions indicate strength and agility, and many paleontologists now believe that dinosaurs were warmblooded.[4]

6 The idea of warmblooded dinosaurs has captured the public imagination and received a torrent of press coverage. Yet another vindication of dinosaurian capability has received very little attention, although I regard it as equally significant. I refer to the issue of stupidity and its correlation with size. The revisionist interpretation, which I support in this column, does not enshrine dinosaurs as paragons of intellect, but it

---

[2]One of the largest of the dinosaurs, measuring over sixty feet long.—Ed.

[3]A geologic period of the Mesozoic era, extending from 180 million to 135 million years ago.—Ed.

[4]See John Noble Wilford's "Hot Times over Warm Blood," pp. 481–494.—Ed.

Triceratops (Gregory S. Paul)

does maintain that they were not small brained after all. They had the "right-sized" brains for reptiles of their body size.

7 I don't wish to deny that the flattened, minuscule head of large-bodied *Stegosaurus* houses little brain from our subjective, top-heavy perspective, but I do wish to assert that we should not expect more of the beast. First of all, large animals have relatively smaller brains than related, small animals. The correlation of brain size with body size among kindred animals (all reptiles, all mammals, for example) is remarkably regular. As we move from small to large animals, from mice to elephants or small lizards to Komodo dragons,[5] brain size increases, but not so fast as body size. In other words, bodies grow faster than brains, and large animals have low ratios of brain weight to body weight. In fact, brains grow only about two-thirds as fast as bodies. Since we have no reason to believe that large animals are consistently stupider than their smaller relatives, we must conclude that large animals require relatively less brain to do as well as smaller animals. If we do not recognize this relationship, we are likely to underestimate the mental power of very large animals, dinosaurs in particular.

8 Second, the relationship between brain and body is not identical in all groups of vertebrates. All share the same rate of relative decrease in brain size, but small mammals have much larger brains than small reptiles of the same body weight. This discrepancy is maintained at all

[5] The largest lizard in the world, growing to ten feet long. —Ed.

Brachiosaurus (Gregory S. Paul)

larger body weights, since brain size increases at the same rate in both groups—two-thirds as fast as body size.

9 Put these two facts together, all large animals have relatively small brains, and reptiles have much smaller brains than mammals at any common body weight—and what should we expect from a normal, large reptile? The answer, of course, is a brain of very modest size. No living reptile even approaches a middle-sized dinosaur in bulk, so we have no modern standard to serve as a model for dinosaurs.

10 Fortunately, our imperfect fossil record has, for once, not severely disappointed us in providing data about fossil brains. Superbly preserved skulls have been found for many species of dinosaurs, and cranial capacities can be measured. (Since brains do not fill craniums in reptiles, some creative, although not unreasonable, manipulation must be applied to estimate brain size from the hole within a skull.) With these data, we have a clear test for the conventional hypothesis of dinosaurian stupidity. We should agree, at the outset, that a reptilian standard is the only proper one—it is surely irrelevant that dinosaurs had smaller brains than people or whales. We have abundant data on the relationship of brain and body size in modern reptiles. Since we know that brains increase two-thirds as fast as bodies as we move from small to large living species,

we can extrapolate[6] this rate to dinosaurian sizes and ask whether dinosaur brains match what we would expect of living reptiles if they grew so large.

11 Harry Jerison studied the brain sizes of ten dinosaurs and found that they fell right on the extrapolated reptilian curve. Dinosaurs did not have small brains; they maintained just the right-sized brains for reptiles of their dimensions. So much for Ms. Parker's explanation of their demise.

12 Jerison made no attempt to distinguish among various kinds of dinosaurs; ten species distributed over six major groups scarcely provide a proper basis for comparison. Recently, James A. Hopson of the University of Chicago gathered more data and made a remarkable and satisfying discovery.

13 Hopson needed a common scale for all dinosaurs. He therefore compared each dinosaur brain with the average reptilian brain we would expect at its body weight. If the dinosaur falls on the standard reptilian curve, its brain receives a value of 1.0 (called an encephalization quotient, or EQ—the ratio of actual brain to expected brain for a standard reptile of the same body weight). Dinosaurs lying above the curve (more brain than expected in a standard reptile of the same body weight) receive values in excess of 1.0, while those below the curve measure less than 1.0.

14 Hopson found that the major groups of dinosaurs can be ranked by increasing values of average EQ. This ranking corresponds perfectly with inferred speed, agility and behavioral complexity in feeding (or avoiding the prospect of becoming a meal). The giant sauropods, ***Brontosaurus*** and its allies, have the lowest EQ's—0.20 to 0.35. They must have moved fairly slowly and without great maneuverability. They probably escaped predation by virtue of their bulk alone, much as elephants do today. The armored ankylosaurs and stegosaurs come next with EQ's of 0.52 to 0.56. These animals, with their heavy armor, probably relied largely upon passive defense, but the clubbed tail of ankylosaurs and the spiked tail of stegosaurs imply some active fighting and increased behavioral complexity.

15 The ceratopsians rank next at about 0.7 to 0.9. Hopson remarks: "The larger ceratopsians, with their great horned heads, relied on active defensive strategies and presumably required somewhat greater agility than the tail-weaponed forms, both in fending off predators and in

[6]Infer what is not known from what is known.—Ed.

intraspecific combat bouts. The smaller ceratopsians, lacking true horns, would have relied on sensory acuity and speed to escape from predators." The ornithopods (duckbills and their allies) were the brainiest herbivores, with EQ's from 0.85 to 1.5. They relied upon "acute senses and relatively fast speeds" to elude carnivores. Flight seems to require more acuity and agility than standing defense. Among ceratopsians, small, hornless, and presumably fleeing *Protoceratops* had a higher EQ than great three-horned *Triceratops.*

16 Carnivores have higher EQ's than herbivores, as in modern vertebrates. Catching a rapidly moving or stoutly fighting prey demands a good deal more upstairs than plucking the right kind of plant. The giant theropods (*Tyrannosaurus* and its allies) vary from 1.0 to nearly 2.0. Atop the heap, quite appropriately at its small size, rests the little coelurosaur *Stenonychosaurus* with an EQ well above 5.0. Its actively moving quarry, small mammals and birds perhaps, probably posed a greater challenge in discovery and capture than *Triceratops* afforded *Tyrannosaurus.*

17 I do not wish to make a naive claim that brain size equals intelligence or, in this case, behavioral range and agility (I don't know what intelligence means in humans, much less in a group of extinct reptiles). Variation in brain size within a species has precious little to do with brain power (humans do equally well with 900 or 2,500 cubic centimeters of brain). But comparison across species, when the differences are large, seems reasonable. I do not regard it as irrelevant to our achievements that we so greatly exceed koala bears—much as I love them—in EQ. The sensible ordering among dinosaurs also indicates that even so coarse a measure as brain size counts for something.

18 If behavioral complexity is one consequence of mental power, then we might expect to uncover among dinosaurs some signs of social behavior that demand coordination, cohesiveness, and recognition. Indeed we do, and it cannot be accidental that these signs were overlooked when dinosaurs labored under the burden of a falsely imposed obtuseness. Multiple trackways have been uncovered, with evidence for more than twenty animals traveling together in parallel movement. Did some dinosaurs live in herds? At the Davenport Ranch sauropod trackway, small footprints lie in the center and larger ones at the periphery. Could it be that some dinosaurs traveled much as some advanced herbivorous mammals do today, with large adults at the borders sheltering juveniles in the center?[7]

---

[7]Elephants, for example.—Ed.

19 In addition, the very structures that seemed most bizarre and useless to older paleontologists—the elaborate crests of hadrosaurs, the frills and horns of ceratopsians, and the nine inches of solid bone above the brain of *Pachycephalosaurus*—now appear to gain a coordinated explanation as devices for sexual display and combat. Pachycephalosaurs may have engaged in head-butting contests much as mountain sheep do today. The crests of some hadrosaurs are well designed as resonating chambers; did they engage in bellowing matches? The ceratopsian horn and frill may have acted as sword and shield in the battle for mates. Since such behavior is not only intrinsically complex, but also implies an elaborate social system, we would scarcely expect to find it in a group of animals barely muddling through at a moronic level.

20 But the best illustration of dinosaurian capability may well be the fact most often cited against them—their demise. Extinction, for most people, carries many of the connotations attributed to sex not so long ago—a rather disreputable business, frequent in occurrence, but not to anyone's credit, and certainly not to be discussed in proper circles. But, like sex, extinction is an ineluctable part of life. It is the ultimate fate of all species, not the lot of unfortunate and ill-designed creatures. It is no sign of failure.

21 The remarkable thing about dinosaurs is not that they became extinct, but that they dominated the earth for so long. Dinosaurs held sway for 100 million years while mammals, all the while, lived as small animals in the interstices[8] of their world. After 70 million years on top, we mammals have an excellent track record and good prospects for the future, but we have yet to display the staying power of dinosaurs.

22 People, on this criterion, are scarcely worth mentioning—5 million years perhaps since *Australopithecus*, a mere 50,000 for our own species, *Homo sapiens.* Try the ultimate test within our system of values: Do you know anyone who would wager a substantial sum, even at favorable odds, on the proposition that *Homo sapiens* will last longer than *Brontosaurus*?

QUESTIONS FOR ANALYSIS AND DISCUSSION

1. Given that Gould's subject is dinosaurs, what is the purpose of his opening paragraph? What does his opening suggest to you about Gould's audience and purpose?

---

[8]Nooks and crannies. Early mammals were very small animals that probably escaped predation by hiding from the carnivorous dinosaurs.—Ed.

2. What used to be the view of the dinosaur's intelligence? How was its extinction used to support this view?
3. What new views of the dinosaur's physical, physiological, and intellectual characteristics are now being advanced by paleontologists? Which new view does Gould develop and support in his article?
4. Review Gould's argument. What is his first point in support of the dinosaur's intelligence? What is his second point? Given these two points, what kind of brain should we expect in a dinosaur?
5. Explain, in your own words, the method and results of Hopson's study of dinosaur brain size. (You might want to make a chart or graph to aid your understanding.)
6. Why does Gould think Hopson's study "counts for something"? With what qualification should we view Hopson's results?
7. How does the dinosaur's extinction actually help demonstrate its considerable abilities? What is important to remember about extinction?
8. Gould's revisionist view of the dinosaur's skills and social complexity is not based primarily on new discoveries. On what is it based? What blocks to new ideas can hinder scientists as well as the rest of us?
9. Analyze Gould's style. Consider vocabulary, sentence structure, the use of examples and modern expressions, the explanation of Hopson's study. Then describe Gould's audience. What degree of scientific knowledge does Gould assume? What level of general education? What degree of interest in scientific topics?

Hot Times over Warm Blood

JOHN NOBLE WILFORD

John Noble Wilford (b. 1933) was born in Kentucky and educated at the University of Tennessee and Syracuse University, with additional graduate study at Columbia. He began his career in journalism as a reporter for the Wall Street Journal, *moved to* Time *magazine, and then settled in at the* New York Times *as a science reporter. Since 1979 he has held the title "science correspondent" for the* Times.

Wilford's primary focus has been on space. He has covered the U.S. space program, and he wrote We Reach the Moon *in 1969, publishing it seventy-six hours after Apollo 11 landed on the moon. In 1979 he gathered his* New

York Times *articles on scientists into the book* Scientists at Work; *his history of cartography,* The Mapmakers, *appeared in 1981; and* The Riddle of the Dinosaur, *from which the following chapter is excerpted, was published in 1985. Wilford's awards for science writing include a Pulitzer Prize in 1984.*

Wilford's comments following the excerpt offer insights into the writing process, provide helpful hints for long projects, and further illustrate his skill in writing, whatever his subject. Consider, especially, why his opening sentences are so effective.

1 Late one afternoon in August 1964, John Ostrom and his assistant, Grant E. Meyer, walked a slope in south central Montana, near the town of Bridger. This was prairie, grasslands interrupted by eroded mounds and set among hills of pine and juniper. Ostrom and Meyer were winding up the third Yale University field expedition aimed at collecting fossil vertebrate remains from the early Cretaceous.[1] Ostrom called this a "twilight zone" of Mesozoic[2] life; because of the rarity of terrestrial deposits from that time, and thus a paucity of fossils to work with, paleontologists had long had trouble seeing patterns of evolutionary change that occurred in this 25-million-year interval. To rectify this, Ostrom had reconnoitered most of the early Cretaceous strata exposed along the flanks of mountain ranges in northern Wyoming and southern Montana. He and his teams of scientists and students had traversed and inspected some 1,500 kilometers of outcrops, digging here and there and finding the skeletons of several hitherto unknown species of animals, some of which were dinosaurs. Ostrom and Meyer had just examined one possible site for next year's excavations and were moving along the slope of an eroded mound to another site several hundred meters away when they came upon the claws reaching out.

2 "We both nearly rolled down the slope in our rush to the spot," Ostrom recalled. "In front of us, clearly recognizable, was a good portion of a large-clawed hand protruding from the surface. My crew had missed it. I saw their footprints just a few feet away."

3 The bones had lain there, unrecognized, for years and years. Ostrom could tell this by their weathered condition. He could also tell that the hand was something unusual. "I knew from the fragments there on the surface," he said, "that this was the most important thing we'd found so far."

---

[1]A period of the Mesozoic era, from 135 million to 70 million years ago, during which the dinosaurs became extinct. —Ed.

[2]A geologic era, from 220 million to 70 million years ago. —Ed.

4 Ostrom and Meyer fell to their hands and knees and brushed away the soil from around the fossils. Not expecting to do any digging that day, they had left their picks, chisels, and shovels back at the truck, but in their excitement, they dug the best they could with jackknives. They knew what it must feel like to discover a lost treasure. Within minutes they uncovered other parts of the hand. The several finger bones were somewhat larger than those of an adult human. The claws were large and sharp. Ostrom and Meyer had found a powerful, three-fingered grasping hand. They also came across some teeth, the sharp, serrated teeth of what had been a carnivore.

5 Returning the next day, equipped this time with tools more substantial than jackknives, the two paleontologists resumed digging and made an even more breathtaking discovery, the perfectly preserved bones of a foot. They looked at the foot in amazement. In all other carnivorous dinosaurs the foot is rather birdlike, with three main toes and one smaller toe at the inner side or at the back of the foot. The three principal toes are usually alike, with the middle toe the longest and the other two of equal length and diverging from the middle one. All in all, birdlike. But the foot of the creature they had found differed from this basic plan. The outside and middle toes were equal in length, and the innermost of the principal toes stuck out, Ostrom said, "like a sore thumb." And quite a "thumb" it was. This inner toe was longer than the others. Instead of having a short, pointed, triangular claw like the other toes, it bore a long, thin claw in the sharply curved shape of a sickle. Ostrom had never seen anything to compare with this terrible claw, but he could well imagine the uses to which it had been put and how this instrument surely marked the character and vitality of its owner. To this creature that had lived more than 125 million years ago Ostrom would give the name *Deinonychus,* meaning "terrible claw."

6 *Deinonychus* is one of the most remarkable dinosaurs ever discovered. Nearly everything about the animal, its arms and legs, its terrible claws and stiff tail, was soon to be introduced as Exhibit A in the case for the swift, agile, dynamic Bakkerian[3] dinosaurs. The evidence, as seen by many paleontologists, seemed compelling, but the ensuing debate polarized dinosaur paleontology. Were dinosaurs as a group warm-blooded the way birds and mammals are? Was their metabolism more like that of mammals than that of other reptiles, giving them the

[3]Robert Bakker, a student of Ostrom's, has argued strongly for active, warm-blooded dinosaurs. – Ed.

capacity to lead more active lives? Ostrom, in his initial examination of *Deinonychus,* began to suspect that this might be the case. But the very idea contradicted the traditional view of dinosaurs as sluggish creatures in the reptilian mode. Traditional scientists held that dinosaurs, which were classified as reptiles on the basis of their skeletal anatomy, must have been cold-blooded. Modern reptiles are cold-blooded, dinosaurs were reptiles, and, therefore, dinosaurs must have been cold-blooded. This logic had not been seriously disputed until the new generation of paleontologists began taking a new look at dinosaurs and, in particular, at *Deinonychus.* For too long too many paleontologists, it seemed, had been blind to the apparent nonreptilian attributes of dinosaurs. Just because a fossil animal is assigned to a particular class, it does not follow that it possesses all the characteristics of the modern members of that class.

7 John Ostrom, who was thirty-three years old at the time, made a brief announcement to newspapers in the fall of 1964, calling the fossils a "startling discovery" but refraining from further assessment. He had yet to name the animal or appraise its importance. Ostrom and his associates returned to the discovery site the next two summers. They dug deeper into the sides of the bald Montana hill, a sixty-meter-high mound resembling a scoop of ice cream melting a little at the base. Their intensive quarrying recovered more than a thousand bones representing at least three individual animals, each one a *Deinonychus.* There followed three more years of skeletal reconstruction and analysis back in Ostrom's laboratory at the Peabody Museum. . . .

8 Examining the skeletons, Ostrom concluded that *Deinonychus* was relatively small, as dinosaurs go, and lightly built. It stood approximately one and a half meters high and measured more than two and a half meters from the snout to the tip of its tail. Judging by the limb bones and vertebrae, the fully grown animal weighed no more than 80 kilograms, 175 pounds. Judging by the teeth, it was a carnivore and so classified with the saurischian[4] dinosaurs in the same suborder as the tyrannosaurs. The structure of the fore limbs and hands clearly showed that the animal was an obligatory biped; it could not have walked on all fours even if it wanted to. Like most reptiles, *Deinonychus* had a rather long tail that accounted for about half its length, but the tail had a feature unlike anything Ostrom had seen. The entire length of the tail was

[4]Any dinosaur of the order *Saurichia,* characterized by having a three-pronged pelvis like a crocodile.—Ed.

encased in thin, parallel bony rods—ossified tendons, like those Dollo[5] had noted in the Belgian iguanodonts. This mystified Ostrom at first, until he came to realize that a rigidized tail, presumably made possible by the bony rods, must have been important to *Deinonychus.* As Ostrom visualized it, the rigid tail could be moved up and down, sideway, and all-around-the-clock. The tail, he concluded, was used as a dynamic stabilizer, a counterbalance for an active, mobile bipedal animal. This and other skeletal evidence indicated to Ostrom that the posture of this biped was much like that of an ostrich, with the trunk held in a near-horizontal position, the neck curving upward, and the tail sticking straight out behind. "In my opinion," Ostrom wrote in 1969 in *Discovery,* "this is a much more natural-looking posture than the 'kangaroo' pose that is commonly illustrated for other carnivorous dinosaurs such as *Allosaurus* or *Tyrannosaurus.*" Indeed, he added, if the skeletons of these giants were as well preserved as those of *Deinonychus,* scientists would probably find that they, too, often held their tails out as rigid counterbalances rather than dragging them through the mud. Other paleontologists in interpreting other dinosaurs have now largely abandoned the tail-dragging image, which had never been good for the reputation of dinosaurs.

9 If *Deinonychus* walked and ran on its hind limbs, this made the terrible claw on each foot all the more remarkable. One might expect this type of claw on a grasping hand, Ostrom reasoned, but not on a toe that came in contact with the ground, where it could be easily broken or dulled, leaving the animal helpless. Each claw stuck out about ten or twelve centimeters, surely an effective weapon of defense and probably also for killing and dismembering prey. "Common sense tells us that a sharp, thin, recurved sickle-like blade is for cutting or slashing and not for digging, tree-climbing or providing traction on the ground," Ostrom observed. But how did the animal wield such a lethal weapon? How was it protected from damage while running? To the latter question the fossils provided an apparently straightforward answer. The two main joints of the inner toe, the one with the claw, were found to be unusual in that they permitted the claw to be lifted back and far off the ground. The joints in the other toes were nonretractile. Answering the other question—how the animal wielded its sharp claw—led Ostrom to some inferences that pointed up the importance of *Deinonychus* to revisionist paleontologists.

[5]Louis Dollo (1857–1931), a French paleontologist who studied the genus *Iguanodon* for most of his life.—Ed.

10 "It does not surprise us to see an eagle or hawk slash with its talons, or stand on one foot and lash out with the other," Ostrom wrote, explaining his reasoning and how it flew in the face of the usual views of dinosaurian behavior. "But to imagine a lizard or a crocodile—or any modern reptile—standing on its hind legs and attacking is ridiculous. Reptiles are just not capable of such intricate maneuvers, such delicate balance, poise and agility—such demanding (metabolically) activity. As we all know, reptiles are sluggish, sprawling animals that are boringly inactive most of the time."

11 Yet the bladelike claw required that *Deinonychus* do just that, attack with one or both feet. It had nothing whatsoever to do with standing or walking, but it could explain the utility of the tail as a counterbalance. It suggested an unreptilian bioenergetic system that could sustain such combat. Ostrom concluded: "The creature thus must have stood or leaped about on one foot or the other while it slashed with the opposite foot. Such extraordinary balance and agility is unknown in any living reptile."

12 Further examination of the creature's arms and long, grasping hands seemed to strengthen Ostrom's contention that *Deinonychus* was a clever and fierce predator. The wrist joints rotated to enable the hands to turn in toward each other. The animal could thus seize prey by both hands working together. Only humans and certain other mammals can do this. Only *Deinonychus* and one related species of all the dinosaurs are known to have had such wrist mobility.

13 Ostrom made known his description and interpretation of this unusual dinosaur in 1969. Bob Bakker, who had been with Ostrom as a

The agile *Deinonychus*, from a drawing by Bakker

student-member of the 1964 expedition, had anticipated and embellished many of Ostrom's arguments in his 1968 article on the "superiority" of dinosaurs. But he was the young Turk whose views could be dismissed by established paleontologists. Ostrom, however, could not be ignored. He was a member in good standing of the establishment, a professor at Yale and curator of vertebrate paleontology at the Peabody Museum. The reverberations from Ostrom's 1969 reports on *Deinonychus* and dinosaurian metabolism still echo through dinosaur studies.

14 In a report in the *Bulletin* of the Peabody Museum, Ostrom summarized the inferences he felt able to make from the skeletons he had discovered in Montana. He wrote: "The foot of *Deinonychus* is perhaps the most revealing bit of anatomical evidence pertaining to dinosaurian habits and must have been anything but 'reptilian' in its behavior, responses and way of life. It must have been a fleet-footed, highly predaceous, extremely agile and very active animal, sensitive to many stimuli and quick in its responses. These in turn indicate an unusual level of activity for a reptile and suggest an unusually high metabolic rate. The evidence for these lies chiefly, but not entirely, in the [foot]."

15 Ostrom raised the issue of dinosaurian metabolism even more explicitly and forcefully in a paper he delivered that year in Chicago at the first North American Paleontological Convention. He was nervous beforehand, knowing that what he had to say would be controversial, which it was. Everyone agreed that Ostrom was the meeting's most provocative speaker. The title of his paper, "Terrestrial Vertebrates as Indicators of Mesozoic Climates," gave no hint of its radical message.

16 It is well known, Ostrom noted, that modern fish, amphibians, and reptiles are so-called cold-blooded creatures. The term "cold-blooded," used by laymen more than scientists, has nothing to do with the temperature of the blood itself. Rather, it means that the animal's body temperature fluctuates with that of its surroundings. The cold-blooded animal lacks internal mechanisms to raise or lower body temperature much above or below environmental temperatures. Most reptiles are inactive in the cool of night and must bask in the sun to warm up for the day's hunt. Since their main source of heat is external, reptiles and other cold-blooded animals are, to be more scientific in the terminology, ectotherms. When ectotherms begin to get too hot, they must seek the shade; they are always having to do something about the weather. In contrast, warm-blooded animals, mammals and birds, have internal regulating mechanisms that maintain their body temperatures at approximately the same level, regardless of external conditions. They are known

as endotherms. Humans, unless sick, maintain a temperature of 37.1 degrees Celsius, or 98.4 degrees Fahrenheit. Most other mammals operate at comparable temperatures, while birds generally have higher temperatures, averaging about 40 degrees Celsius. Many endotherms perspire and pant to help keep cool or have layers of hair or feathers to cut heat loss. But the primary mechanism of endothermy is a high basal metabolism: all living cells generate small amounts of heat as a by-product of the chemical processes occurring within them, and in mammals and birds these processes, known as metabolism, are at least four times as active as in ectotherms of comparable body size and temperature. Accordingly, endotherms can spring into action under almost any climatic conditions, whereas ectotherms are more severely influenced and restricted by the environment. It is this "climate dependency" of ectotherms, Ostrom said, that makes them useful for paleoclimatic interpretations. This was the point he was building up to.

17 If dinosaurs were ectotherms, according to the prevailing assumptions, then the millions of years during which they lived must have been a time of generally mild climate worldwide. Only in an equable environment could these reptiles have prospered in such number and over a range that seemed to run to the higher latitudes approaching the polar regions. They presumably could not have survived extreme seasonal changes. However, although pollen and invertebrate fossils tend to support the idea of a mild Mesozoic climate, Ostrom argued that paleontologists could not look to the dinosaurs as corroborating evidence. Dinosaurs, he said, were useless as thermal indicators because there was reason to question the assumption of their low reptilian metabolisms, their ectothermy. Throwing down the gauntlet, Ostrom declared: "There is considerable evidence, which is impressive, if not compelling, that many different kinds of ancient reptiles were characterized by mammalian or avian[6] levels of metabolism."

18 Ostrom's analysis of *Deinonychus* had made him more conscious of the potential significance of dinosaurian posture. Dinosaurs were not sprawlers, as are the living reptiles—a distinction scientists had been aware of (but had made surprisingly little of) since the time of Huxley. *Deinonychus* and apparently most other dinosaurs, biped and quadruped alike, held themselves erect with their feet directly under their bodies. No living ectotherms have such postures. If they did, they would presumably

[6]Birdlike.—Ed.

be able to run faster and over greater distances than they do. At least some dinosaurs were apparently fleet of foot. The long limbs of *Deinonychus* and some other dinosaurs, as well as many fossil tracks, indicated that they could be swift runners. The evidence, Ostrom said, suggests that "erect posture and locomotion probably are not possible without high metabolism and high, uniform body temperature." He did not state flatly that dinosaurs were endotherms. They might have been homeothermic, which is to say that they maintained a constant body temperature by whatever means, internal or external. Whether homeothermic or possibly even endothermic, Ostrom affirmed, dinosaurs were extremely active and extraordinary animals whose bioenergetic mechanisms seemingly set them apart from the usual run of reptiles.

19 Many paleontologists found the idea of warm-blooded dinosaurs unthinkable. Others thought it liberating, offering as it did a model of dinosaurian physiology that could explain their long success and perhaps even their extinction. Debate among scientists raged for years over the question of whether dinosaurs may have been ectothermic, endothermic, something in between, or something entirely different.

20 Reconstructing the thermal physiology of extinct animals is no simple matter. Nothing about the fossils affords a direct measure of how the dinosaurs regulated their body temperatures. There can be no thought of some brave scientist putting a thermometer under the tongue or up the rectum of a dinosaur. All the evidence introduced to support or challenge the endothermic hypothesis was of necessity derived from the inferences scientists extracted from the dinosaur bones. The results were bewildering. Different interpretations of the same bones produced conflicting hypotheses and guesses. . . .

21 Ostrom continued to base his case on the fact that erect posture and gait occur only in endotherms, mammals and birds. But he acknowledged that his critics had a point when they argued that no cause-and-effect relationship between posture and physiology has ever been established. Still, he insisted, "the correlation between posture and endothermy or ectothermy is virtually absolute and surely is not merely coincidental." He also advanced another line of indirect evidence related to upright posture. Citing the research of Roger S. Seymour, a zoologist at the University of Adelaide in Australia, Ostrom noted that the greater the vertical distance between an animal's heart and brain, the greater the required blood pressure. A giraffe's blood pressure is double that of a human's. In the case of *Brachiosaurus,* to take an extreme dinosaurian

example, the heart-brain distance was approximately six meters. To pump blood such distances, or even lesser distances, in an animal with upright posture, Ostrom said, would require an advanced four-chambered heart that is a hallmark of endotherms. Owen, in 1841, had wondered if dinosaurs had not had four-chambered hearts, but he never pursued such thinking. Crocodiles have imperfect versions of a four-chambered heart, indicating that such a feature was not out of the question among archosaurs. The heart-brain distance does not prove that dinosaurs were endothermic, as Seymour observed, but it helped make the case that many of them had need of and, therefore, must have possessed a heart and circulatory system capable of maintaining an endothermic physiology.

22 In contrast to Ostrom's cautious inferences and concessions to his critics, his former student Robert Bakker asserted flatly that the case for dinosaur endothermy was conclusive. To the usual arguments for endothermy he added a new and ingenious one: the relative abundance of dinosaurian prey with respect to dinosaurian predators.

23 Warm-blooded animals pay a high price for the metabolism that keeps them in an almost constant state of readiness. They must eat more, and this means spending extra time grazing or hunting. A lion consumes its weight in food every seven to ten days, whereas the Komodo dragon, a carnivorous lizard, eats its weight in food only every sixty days. This means that a given quantity of meat will not supply nearly as many endothermic carnivores as it would ectothermic ones. Bakker, therefore, decided to tote up the relative sizes of populations of prey and predators as revealed in fossils from the late Cretaceous. Surveying several collections of fossils, separating the predators from the prey by their teeth and jaws and calculating probable body weights, Bakker sought to determine the percentage of predators in the whole fossil population. A small percentage of predators would mean that they must have had hearty, endothermic appetites; in some African habitats today, predators constitute only 1 to 6 percent of the total animal population. For the dinosaurs in his fossil samples, Bakker found, the predators represented 1 to 3 percent of the total. The predator-prey ratios of pre-Mesozoic reptiles, which were unquestionably ectothermic, ranged from 35 to 60 percent.

24 These data became the keystone in Bakker's increasingly aggressive campaign for dinosaurian endothermy. By 1975 he had left Yale and was working on his Ph.D. at Harvard. He took his case to the public in an article in *Scientific American* entitled "Dinosaur Renaissance," in which he asserted: "Predator-prey ratios are powerful tools for paleophysiology

because they are the direct result of predator metabolisms." In the same year, a Harvard colleague, Adrian J. Desmond, a historian of science, published *The Hot-Blooded Dinosaurs,* and to the dismay of the more conservative paleontologists, the general public joined the spirited debate and tended to side with Bakker's warm-blooded forces. People liked their dinosaurs lively, not languid. In drawings for Desmond's book and other publications, Bakker, who is a skilled artist as well as paleontological provocateur, portrayed dinosaurs that did not stand idly about, but were zippy, ferocious speedsters, chasing down little mammals for lunch or stalking one another and pouncing for the kill like lions. These were the "new and improved" dinosaurs. . . .

25 Telling shots were fired at Bakker's predator-prey argument. The opposition doubted the reliability of the fossil record he had used to calculate the ratios. How could Bakker or anyone know if the fossils gave an accurate indication of the proportion of predators among the living animals of the time? Because of the nature of their bones or the conditions of the habitat, some types of animals may have become fossilized more readily than others. The collectors may have had biases in the fossils they looked for and gathered up. Nor is there any way of knowing whether the herbivores in a given fossil community were all preyed upon by the carnivores there. Even if such interpretations of the fossil record were accepted as accurate reflections of predator-prey ratios, Pierre Beland and Dale Russell, both of the National Museum of Natural Sciences in Ottawa, questioned Bakker's calculations for the dinosaur community in Alberta. By their estimates, the ratio there was about four times greater than that calculated by Bakker, which, if true, weakened his argument that the predators must have been ravenous endotherms. Bakker insisted, however, that the corrected ratio still did not put the animals out of the endothermic range.

26 Another argument against Bakker revolved around the large size of most dinosaurs. Dinosaurs may have behaved like warm-blooded animals not because they were endotherms but because they were large. They may have owed their success to their sheer bulk.

27 If there is one thing beyond dispute about dinosaurs, it is their size. Hotton determined that 80 percent of living mammals are smaller than the smallest dinosaur, which weighed about ten kilograms, and that more than half of the dinosaurs weighed more than two tons, a size attained by only 2 percent of modern mammals. Large size, it would seem, was in some way critical to dinosaur survival and so the bigger individuals of a species would be more likely to reproduce, leading to

the evolution of species of even larger animals—at least up to some point of diminishing advantage.

28 Several scientists, including Hotton, Beland, and Russell,[7] presented data suggesting that ectotherms and endotherms become more similar with increasing size. Their metabolic requirements and hence predator-prey ratios may be very similar if both are large. Indeed, as Spotila[8] contended, a large body mass results in a fairly constant body temperature. The dinosaurs could have been inertial homeotherms, animals that can maintain a constant body temperature by any means, including those dependent on the environment. Colbert[9] and his colleagues, in their earlier experiments with Florida alligators, had shown that these animals, descendants of archosaurs, heat up more slowly when exposed to sunlight and cool off more slowly than do smaller animals. They thus can keep the temperature of their bodies fairly constant without endothermic mechanisms or any outside insulation like fur or feathers. The larger the alligator, Colbert found, the slower the rate of heat absorption and heat loss. In the warmer climate of the Mesozoic, moreover, the variations in the animal's body temperature would presumably be minimal. Dinosaurs, therefore, could have had most of the attributes of warm-bloodedness without endothermy.

29 Hotton summed up the implications of what he believed was the dinosaur's inertial homeothermy in this way: "Dinosaurs, like mammals, enlarged their capacity for continuous activity by reducing their dependence on the physical environment as a source of body heat. They did so, however, at low cost, by a system of heat conservation that shaped life-styles which were very different from those conditioned by the high-cost, heat-generating system of mammals. Locomotor mechanisms and size illustrate a fundamental difference: the activity of dinosaurs was more sedate than that of mammals. The basic strategy of dinosaurs in general was 'slow and steady,' and what it lacked in mammalian elan, it made up in economy."

30 One part of the strategy, Hotton further suggested, probably involved seasonal migrations over distances upward of 3,200 kilometers. In North America, dinosaur fossils have been found as far north as

---

[7]Participants in a symposium on dinosaurs at the 1978 meeting of the American Association for the Advancement of Science.—Ed.

[8]James Spotila of the State University of New York at Buffalo opposed the view of dinosaurs as endotherms.—Ed.

[9]Edwin Colbert of Columbia University, who viewed dinosaurian physiology as cold-blooded.—Ed.

Yukon Territory, seventy degrees north latitude; even in the mild Mesozoic, the arctic was probably not a fit place for a dinosaur in the winter because of the chill and the darkness that suspended the growth of vegetation. The migrations may have begun with random drift in the course of everyday foraging. Large dinosaurs, herbivores and predators alike, would have had to be wanderers in order to gather enough food to keep themselves going, even at modest rates of ectothermic metabolism. Hotton offered two other reasons. The activity of migration would have provided a reliable source of internal heat. Second, the travels would have kept them exposed to approximately the same temperatures year-round, which was a vital consideration if, as ectotherms, the dinosaurs' tolerance of thermal fluctuation was restricted by a relatively narrow margin of heat output from resting metabolism. The concept that some dinosaurs, like many living birds, migrated north and south, season by season, is appealing and not implausible, but it was only speculation and probably not provable with direct evidence in the rocks and fossils. . . .

31 Although the arguments favoring large size and inertial homeothermy as the controlling features of dinosaurian physiology seemed to satisfy many paleontologists, Bakker did not retreat. Such a thermoregulatory system, he pointed out, would not give rise to endothermic bone histology or the low predator-prey ratios or the success of many small dinosaur species with an adult weight of between five and fifty kilograms. The smaller dinosaurs were among the most agile and liveliest of the breed, more like endotherms. . . .

32 No clear winners emerged from the debate. The question of dinosaur warm-bloodedness remains unanswered, perhaps unanswerable. In their introduction to the published proceedings of the symposium,[10] the editors, Everett C. Olson and Roger D. K. Thomas, concluded: "No . . . resolution of the controversy over whether dinosaurs were scaled-up, cold-blooded reptiles or warm-blooded surrogate 'mammals' is reached here, although the weight of current opinion lies between the extremes."

33 The consensus seemed to be that there was no single thermoregulatory strategy for all dinosaurs. The largest dinosaurs, sauropods like the brontosaurs, were probably most nearly ectothermic. Their bones suggest that they were not swift or active, and it is difficult to imagine how sauropods could have found food to maintain a high metabolism.

[10]At the 1978 meeting of the American Association for the Advancement of Science. – Ed.

Most dinosaurs, because of their large size and the mild climate, probably maintained fairly constant body temperatures. They were inertial homeotherms. The smaller dinosaurs, with bones suggesting a capacity for speed and agility, may have been true endotherms. Indeed, the smallest ones, such as *Compsognathus,* which was a contemporary of *Archaeopteryx,* were probably too small to be inertial homeotherms.

34 John Ostrom now has doubts that all dinosaurs were endothermic. "If any of the dinosaurs were endotherms," he said, "the most probable candidates were the small carnivores." *Compsognathus,* for example, and *Deinonychus,* among others. He still feels, as he did in 1969, that *Deinonychus* must have led a vigorous warm-blooded kind of life as a fierce, swift, and agile predator. It was a most unreptilian dinosaur, and so perhaps were many others. Ostrom observed: "There is a lot of suspicion out there that some or most of these animals were physiologically very different from any living reptiles, perhaps more like mammals or birds. Unhappily, we'll never know."

35 The wonder of dinosaurs also is that they are an enigma seemingly beyond solution. Science has explained so much: the divisibility of atoms and the nature of subatomic particles; the decipherable code of heredity contained in DNA; the earth's restless crust; gravity, electromagnetism, and the age of the solar system. Science has identified hundreds of species of dinosaurs, assembling their bones and dating their time on earth, but so much about the lives of these strange and monstrous creatures defies explication. It is reassuringly human of scientists that, when it comes to dinosaurs, they can be just as stricken with puzzlement as the next person and find themselves with little more to work with than their imaginations. Yet they persist in their search for solutions to the riddle, knowing they will never fully succeed but believing they will learn something about the greater mysteries of life. This is the wonder of humans, their faith that there is much about dinosaurs worth knowing.

36 Scientists came away from the warm-blooded debates with, if nothing else, a new appreciation of the dinosaur enigma. Bakker, though he failed to prove that dinosaurs were endotherms, inspired a host of paleontologists to explore the ecology and community structure of these unusual reptiles and seek to understand their place in the evolution of life. Even Nicholas Hotton, Bakker's staunchest adversary in the debates, had to concede: "Alternative thermal strategies and life-styles available to dinosaurs may well have been as exotic as their body form, the like of which no man has ever seen."

Comments on THE RIDDLE OF THE DINOSAUR

JOHN NOBLE WILFORD

The sight of some dinosaur bones lying in a dry wash somewhere in southern Utah dispelled any doubts I had about the subject of my next book. I was spending a week in the field with Jim Jensen, an indefatigable dinosaur hunter. Then and there, in the summer of 1981, I decided to write a popular narrative of how dinosaurs were discovered in the first place and how they have been rediscovered in recent years and examined more thoroughly in light of new findings and a clash of theories.

You will note that I did not set out to write a book *about* dinosaurs, of which there were many already. Instead, I wanted to write a story of people. While children may find endless descriptions of dinosaurs to be fascinating, adults are probably more interested in the discoverers of dinosaurs and how their work is important to understanding the history of life on earth. At least this was my assumption, and I was writing a book for adults.

In library research and interviews with scientists, I sought always to identify the leading figures in each important discovery and learn something about their lives and their motivations for getting involved in dinosaurs. I organized the book roughly in chronological order, which seems most natural for the narrative form. Each chapter advances the story by describing new discoveries or the debates prompted by new discoveries and new hypotheses, and central to the story in each chapter is one paleontologist or other scientist.

After the first few months of general research necessary for determining the scope and outline of the book, my practice is to alternate research and writing. Spend a few weeks reading and interviewing for one or two related chapters and then write a draft. Do some more research, and then more writing. Finally, work through the manuscript from beginning to end, revising, polishing, and making sure the tone and style are consistent throughout and that it reads like the narrative intended. I'm not saying this is the best way; it's my way.

Well into the writing of a book, I have found, the material has a way of asserting itself, taking on a life of its own, and carrying the author beyond his original idea. This happened about halfway through my work on the dinosaur book. Out of the narrative emerged some themes I had not set out consciously to develop. How wondrous it is that humans can reach back so far into the past and in their minds resurrect these strange creatures. How science advances slowly through the give-and-take of those with conflicting views of what discoveries mean. It is better to let the themes emerge naturally than to impose them on the material.

When I am writing I have in mind an audience of one: myself. I write about science, but I am not a trained scientist. I write for a general, educated lay audience. And if I can shape the material so that I can understand it and find it interesting, I have succeeded to my satisfaction. When there are any doubts about how well I have described or interpreted something, I have a scientist read the section for scientific accuracy. I don't want to get it wrong, and I want to maintain the trust of scientists who may be the sources of stories for my next book.

QUESTIONS FOR ANALYSIS AND DISCUSSION

1. Wilford devotes five paragraphs to presenting the discovery of a new dinosaur. What dinosaur did Ostrom and Meyer uncover? What is the purpose of Wilford's rather long introduction?
2. What conclusions about general appearance and life style did Ostrom reach from studying the bones of *Deinonychus*?
3. These conclusions led Bakker to proclaim and Ostrom to consider what important revisionist view of dinosaurs?
4. Summarize the arguments for endothermy. Summarize the arguments for ectothermy. Explain the compromise position.
5. Having studied Wilford's history of the controversy, which position do you find most convincing? Why?
6. Gould examines a resistance to viewing dinosaurs as "appropriately smart." Wilford examines the controversy over endothermy. Does part of this controversy seem to result from the same resistance to change that Gould finds throughout the history of science? Why would paleontologists feel so strongly, one way or another, about dinosaur metabolism?
7. Notice that the "warm blood" controversy is also tied to dinosaur extinction. What seems to be, for both specialist and nonspecialist, the critical question about the dinosaurs?
8. Analyze Wilford's article as science reporting. What characteristics of content, organization, and style may be generated by his purpose and audience and by his training as a journalist? What differences do you note between Gould's article and Wilford's?

The Mass Extinctions of the Late Mesozoic

DALE A. RUSSELL

Dale A. Russell was born in San Francisco in 1937 and educated at the University of Oregon and the University of California at Berkeley before traveling east to acquire a Ph.D. in geology from Columbia University. After a postdoctoral fellowship at Yale, Russell in 1977 became Curator of Fossil Vertebrates at Canada's National Museum of Natural Sciences in Ottawa. Russell's obligation to the museum, he explains, "consists of carrying out original research on fossil reptiles of the Mesozoic age, of conducting field work in pursuit of original research and for the purpose of augmenting museum collections, and of serving the public by writing popular articles, assisting in the preparation of displays, and giving lectures." When asked how he ended up making his career choice, Russell explained: "Dinosaurs have a very broad appeal, and when I was very young they appealed to a sense of wonder and discovery in me as well." Russell adds further comments on his work in an interview following his article.

Russell's article, published in Scientific American *in January 1982, completes the chapter's survey of our continuing fascination with the world of dinosaurs. Because he is writing in an interdisciplinary journal for scientists (not exclusively geologists) and educated nonspecialists, Russell uses a style and writing conventions that differ from Gould's or Wilford's. His approach and style are different because his audience and purpose are different.*

1 One of the most striking events in the record of life on our planet is the simultaneous disappearance at the end of the Mesozoic era, some 63 million years ago, of many kinds of reptiles, certain kinds of marine invertebrates and certain kinds of primitive plants. For generations scholars have sought unsuccessfully to explain this event. New evidence, however, has now led to a novel hypothesis: The disappearances were the result of a catastrophic disruption of the biosphere by an extraterrestrial agency.

2 Catastrophism is not a new doctrine in efforts to account for episodes in the history of the earth, but it has not been a particularly popular one. Early in the 19th century, when geology was in its infancy, the French anatomist Georges Cuvier suggested that the past had been

marked by a series of environmental "revolutions," or catastrophes. In his view such disruptions would account for three animal disappearances: that of the mammoths at the end of the ice age, that of the many primitive mammals fossilized in rocks lying deeper than the ice-age gravels and that of the giant reptiles fossilized in chalk beds lying deeper still. In the decades that followed, however, the work of such pioneer geologists as Charles Lyell made it apparent that the processes of change in earth history were of far greater duration than Cuvier had believed. Catastrophism fell from favor, to be replaced by the doctrine of gradualism. For more than a century now paleontologists have generally agreed that whatever may have caused the disappearances at the end of the Mesozoic era, it could not have been a worldwide catastrophe.

3 The principal casualties among the reptiles were the dinosaurs. As an example, late in the Cretaceous period, the closing chapter of the Mesozoic, at least 15 separate families of dinosaurs, possibly representing between 50 and 70 distinct species, inhabited North America. In the rocks that were formed immediately after the Cretaceous not one dinosaur skeleton has been found. That is why the end of the Mesozoic is generally characterized as the time when the dinosaurs became extinct. The dinosaurs were not, however, the only organisms to disappear. Among the 33 other families of reptiles that inhabited North America late in the Cretaceous there were the following losses. All four of the families of marine turtles died out (although three of the four survived elsewhere). One of the three families of crocodilians, the Goniopholidae, also died out. So did two pterosaur (flying reptile) families, the Ornithocheiridae and a family still unnamed, two ichthyosaur (marine reptile) families, the Platypterygiidae and another family still unnamed, and all three of the plesiosaur (also marine reptile) families, the Elasmosauridae, the Polycotylidae and the Cimoliasauridae. And so did two of the eight families of lizards, the Polyglyphanodontidae (primitive skinklike land forms) and the Mosasauridae (large marine forms).

4 What happened? Was there a gradual or a catastrophic extinction? My own interest is primarily in the larger reptiles of the Mesozoic in North America, and so the examination of these questions I shall undertake here will focus mainly on the disappearance of those animals. Among the many hypotheses put forward to account for their disappearance are disruptions of the food chain, both at sea and on land, a general alteration of the environment as the sea level began to drop at the end of the Mesozoic, a sharp rise in temperature, a fall in temperature caused by volcanic dust in the atmosphere, and so on. None of these

phenomena, however, would seem by itself to be a convincing cause of the reptilian extinctions.

5 In 1979 paleontologists interested in the problem were presented with a new possibility. A group of workers at the University of California at Berkeley—the geologist Walter Alvarez, his father, the physicist Luis W. Alvarez, and two physical chemists, Frank Asaro and Helen V. Michel—announced the discovery of abnormally large traces of the heavy element iridium in a marine formation near Gubbio in the Apennine mountains of Italy. The iridium was concentrated in a layer of clay, one centimeter to two centimeters thick, that separates marine limestone of late Cretaceous age from an overlying marine limestone of early Paleocene age. The limestone below the clay contains fossil marine organisms typical of the latest part of the Cretaceous. No organisms are preserved in the clay. In the limestone above the clay the Cretaceous organisms are absent; they have been replaced by other organisms typical of the Paleocene.

6 Iridium is one of several elements geologists call siderophiles, "iron lovers." It is rarely present in the rocks of the earth's crust but is comparatively abundant in meteorites. The steady rain of micrometeorites on the surface of the earth (more than 70 percent of which fall into the oceans) results in modest concentrations of iridium and other siderophilic elements in the sediments that accumulate in the ocean basins.

7 In 1977 Walter Alvarez was working with an international group of scholars, including the paleontologist Isabella Premoli Silva of the University of Milan, who were examining the marine strata near Gubbio that include the layer of clay. Because the infall of micrometeoritic material is thought to be more or less constant, Luis Alvarez suggested that by measuring the amount of iridium in the clay it would be possible to calculate how much time had passed during the deposition of the layer. When Asaro and Michel did so, they discovered to their surprise that the iridium in the clay layer was 30 times more abundant than it was in clays from adjacent limestone strata.

8 If this excess of iridium had somehow been derived from terrestrial sources, the clay should have shown comparable enhancements in the other elements normally associated with the minerals that form clay. The Berkeley group's analysis disclosed a different pattern of enhancement, closer to that of the relative abundances of the elements found in meteorites. Could the surplus iridium have come from the oceanic reservoir of elements derived from micrometeorites, suddenly precipitated by

some chemical event? Evidently not; neither above nor below the clay stratum was there any evidence that the normal rate of siderophile accumulation had fallen off as it should have if a precipitation had occurred. In this connection Charles J. Orth of the Los Alamos Scientific Laboratory and his collaborators have found a similar surplus of iridium at the top of Cretaceous sedimentary strata that are continental in origin; precipitation from an oceanic reservoir cannot, of course, have caused this.

9 By the time its report was published in 1980 the Berkeley group could add to the Gubbio datum the discovery of strata containing surplus iridium in late Cretaceous marine rocks in Denmark, Spain and New Zealand. (They were later able to add to the list iridium anomalies in deep-sea cores from both the Atlantic and the Pacific.) The report concluded with the suggestion that at the time of the mass extinction of certain marine microorganisms (and by inference at the time many reptiles disappeared) some 500 billion tons of extraterrestrial material had been abruptly deposited on the surface of the earth.

10 Where might the material have come from? The question is pertinent to further elaboration of the Berkeley group's hypothesis. If, on the one hand, the influx came from within the solar system, the mechanism of its arrival on the earth can be sought in the large body of data on this region of space. If, on the other hand, it came from outside the solar system, where there are comparatively few data on the enormous range of environments, the search for a mechanism would call for much speculation.

11 Consider the possibility that the extraterrestrial material was produced outside the solar system by a gigantic stellar explosion: a supernova. In support of such a hypothesis Malvin A. Ruderman of Columbia University and James W. Truran, Jr., of the University of Illinois at Urbana-Champaign have proposed that a gigantic burst of gamma rays from such an explosion could have blown micrometeoritic material off the surface of the moon and the earth could have swept it up. They subsequently noted, however, that gamma-ray flashes from supernovas have yet to be observed and furthermore that the transfer of iridium to the earth by such a mechanism would probably fall short of the required amount.

12 Another potential source of support for the supernova hypothesis is a continuing study being done by Paolo Maffei of the Astrophysical Observatory at Catania in Italy. Maffei is evaluating astronomical evidence for a gigantic explosive event some 1,000 light-years distant from the solar system at the end of the Mesozoic. The hypothesis is considered

unlikely, however, by Wallace H. Tucker of the Center for Astrophysics of the Harvard College Observatory and the Smithsonian Astrophysical Observatory. In his opinion the interstellar material swept up by even a very large supernova would not accumulate in sufficiently dense concentrations to account for the amount of iridium in the zone of siderophile enhancement that caps late Mesozoic strata.

13 The sequence of events in a supernova explosion begins with an initial implosion. In the course of this collapse the nuclei of heavy elements at the core of the star rapidly capture neutrons. Among the new nuclear species formed is plutonium 244. The subsequent explosion distributes this radioactive isotope throughout an enormous volume of space. The chemists in the Berkeley group searched for Pu-244 in the iridium-rich clay, reasoning that if the iridium had been produced by a supernova, the plutonium should be present in detectable amounts. None was found.

14 They further reasoned that the two isotopes of iridium, Ir-191 and Ir-193, would be produced in different proportions by different supernova explosions because of variations in neutron fluxes and reaction times. When they analyzed the iridium-rich clay, they found that the two isotopes were present not in any exotic proportion but in the proportion that is typical of iridium in the solar system. The same is true of the proportion of the two isotopes of osmium, as has been discovered by workers in two separate laboratories: J. Hertogen of the University of Louvain in Belgium and Ramachandran Ganapathy of the J. T. Baker Chemical Company in Phillipsburg, N.J. Therefore it seems improbable that the extraterrestrial material present in the clay stratum was the product of a supernova explosion (other than the one that may have been responsible for the formation of the solar system).

15 If the material came from within the solar system, how did it reach the surface of the earth? Two possibilities immediately suggest themselves: an encounter with a meteorite of asteroid size or an encounter with a comet. Concerning the first possibility the Berkeley group has estimated that the amount of exotic material in the iridium-rich stratum worldwide could have been contained in an asteroid some 10 kilometers in diameter. One problem with the asteroid hypothesis is that material of terrestrial origin in the iridium-rich stratum is not present in the large amounts that should have been gouged out of the earth's crust by the impact of a body of that size. Richard A. F. Grieve of the Canadian Department of Energy, Mines and Resources has suggested a way around

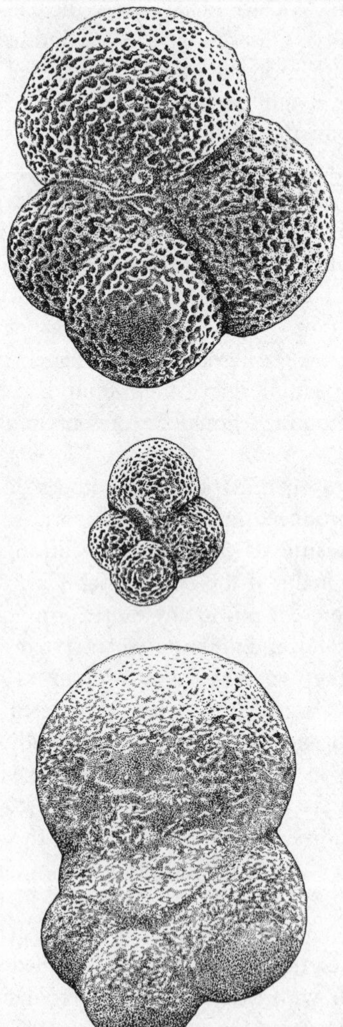

Foraminifera of the late Mesozoic and the very early Cenozoic are seen in these drawings based on scanning electron micrographs enlarged to the same scale (200 diameters). Members of the Globigerinacea, they are, from the top, *Eoglobigerina*, an early Paleocene specimen from Denmark, an *Eoglobigerina* specimen of earliest Paleocene age from a North Pacific deep-sea core and an eroded *Rugoglobigerina* of late Cretaceous age from an oil-well core in Libya. The abnormally small size of the second specimen is taken to reflect a stage of gradual recovery from the environmental stresses that caused most late Mesozoic foraminifera to die out.

this problem. The iridium could have been deposited after the impact in the form of a fallout of relatively pure meteoritic material reinjected into the stratosphere by the force of the collision. Both the Berkeley group and Jan Smit of the University of Amsterdam, a geologist who has studied late Mesozoic limestone strata in Spain, see still another way around the problem. If the asteroid fell into the sea, which is statistically likely, only a small amount of crustal material would have been excavated by the impact.

16 As for the possibility of an encounter with a comet, comets are low-density bodies composed largely of water ice. It is therefore estimated that a comet containing siderophiles in quantities large enough to account for the observed enrichment would have to be twice as massive as the hypothetical asteroid and therefore very much larger. This, of course, raises the excavation problem again. To counter it Frank Kyte of the University of California at Los Angeles and his colleagues Zhiming Zhou and John Watson have proposed that as the hypothetical comet approached the earth it was disrupted by gravitational forces. The earth would then have been showered with cometary debris that would not have excavated any major crater or craters.

17 Either of these hypothetical events might cause extreme short-term stresses within the biosphere. For example, S. V. M. Clube and William M. Napier of the Royal Observatory in Edinburgh estimate that the shock wave generated by the impact of such a big asteroid on land would not only destroy all the earth's forests but also kill all the larger land-dwelling animals. And if the impact were at sea, it would generate tidal waves eight kilometers high.

18 Extreme stresses such as these, in the opinion of Walter Alvarez and the other members of his group, might not have been enough to have caused the late Mesozoic extinctions. They suggest that the impact would also have injected an enormous quantity of dust-size particles into the stratosphere. These, the Alvarez hypothesis proposes, would render the atmosphere much less transparent and strike at the very foundations of the biosphere by diminishing photosynthesis.

19 What light does the fossil record throw on this new hypothesis? A considerable amount, but it must be remembered that the fossil record contains a limited quantity of information and is not easy to interpret. For example, although paleontologists have been collecting the remains of Mesozoic animals for more than a century, the total number of known fragments of dinosaur skeletons is only about 5,000. This is largely owing to simple economics: the high cost of collecting dinosaur bones.

As a comparison, much useful environmental information can be gleaned from the study of Mesozoic plant pollens. It costs about $500 (including a week's working time) to extract 20,000 pollen grains and mount them for microscopic examination. To collect and prepare the same number of dinosaur bones would cost about $400 million (including a million weeks' working time).

20 The point is relevant to an important factor in the study of biological extinctions: sample size. For example, one of the most recent Mesozoic dinosaur assemblages, the remains of animals that roamed the interior plains of the U.S. and Canada some 63 million years ago, is characterized by large horned herbivores, such as the genus *Triceratops*, and giant carnivores, such as the genus *Tyrannosaurus*. Strata that are 12 million years older, at Dinosaur Provincial Park in Alberta, have yielded a far greater variety of dinosaurs than the more recent rocks.

21 Does this mean, as some have suggested, that the dinosaurs were declining in variety as the end of the Mesozoic approached? Were they already heading for extinction millions of years before the hypothetical catastrophe? Not at all. The Alberta fossils show a greater variety because many specimens have been collected there: more than 300, compared with fewer than 75 and even as few as six or seven at the more recent locales.

22 The fact is that the diversity of dinosaurs in Europe as the end of the Mesozoic drew near remained about the same; in Mongolia the diversity actually increased. In other areas of the world the samples are too small to reveal trends. In summary, evidence of a long-term decline in the diversity of dinosaurs before the time of extinction is simply not available.

23 Nowhere else in the world has the fossil record of land organisms over the final 1.75 million years of the Cretaceous been as fully sampled as it has in the 100-meter-thick exposures of grayish brown sediments around the southern edge of the Fort Peck Reservoir in northeastern Montana. The lower, earlier half of the formation is dominated by river-deposited sands, the upper, later half by alluvial silts and clays. The change in depositional patterns presumably reflects environmental changes that would have caused a change in the distribution of the animals, dinosaurs included, that inhabited this former coastal plain. In the lower levels the large predatory genus *Tyrannosaurus* and the duck-billed herbivorous genus *Amatosaurus* predominate. In the upper levels the herbivorous genus *Triceratops* and small browsing dinosaurs of the genus

Thescelosaurus are more abundant. Similar changes in the plant community are documented by studies of fossil spores and pollen by Robert Tschudy of the U.S. Geological Survey.

24 An extraordinary pattern of change seems to occur at the top of the 100-meter formation. Here, along one horizon, the relative abundances lower in the sequence are reversed and the remains of large dinosaurs locally outnumber those of small ones. Large animals normally have lower birth and death rates than small animals. Hence an imbalance of this kind, with more large dinosaurs preserved as fossils than small ones, suggests some kind of mass death. (My interpretation is tentative, but further work at Fort Peck Reservoir will surely clarify the situation.)

25 Above this horizon near the top of the formation the sediments begin to take on a more laminated appearance. The only dinosaur bones are a few fragments that appear to have been eroded from older strata and deposited secondarily in stream beds. At first there is no comparable change in the plant community. Then, at a level about five meters above the horizon that holds the last unredeposited dinosaur skeletal material, the fossil pollen and spores become poorly preserved. David M. Jarzen of the National Museum of Natural Sciences in Ottawa has studied the plant evidence. He and I estimate that the five-meter interval represents a depositional period several tens of thousands of years long.

26 Above the level of poor plant preservation, beds of low-grade coal alternate with laminated siltstones. This separation of the highest occurrence of dinosaurs from the lowest occurrence of coal was first observed some years ago by William A. Clemens of the University of California at Berkeley. Tschudy, who has also studied the spores and pollen in the coal-bearing strata, reports that these evidences of plant life are only a third as abundant as they were in the dinosaur-bone strata below. The age of mammals had begun.

27 The limestones Smit and his colleagues have been studying in Spain record a remarkable series of events. They were deposited on the floor of an open tropical sea that intruded into southern Spain in late Mesozoic times. The formations are composed almost entirely of the calcium carbonate shells and platelets of tiny foraminifera: free-floating protozoan members of the sea's zooplankton. Here for more than 10 million years planktonic productivity remained high and there was no significant change in the character of the organic debris deposited on the sea floor.

28 Then within a layer of rock no more than five millimeters thick

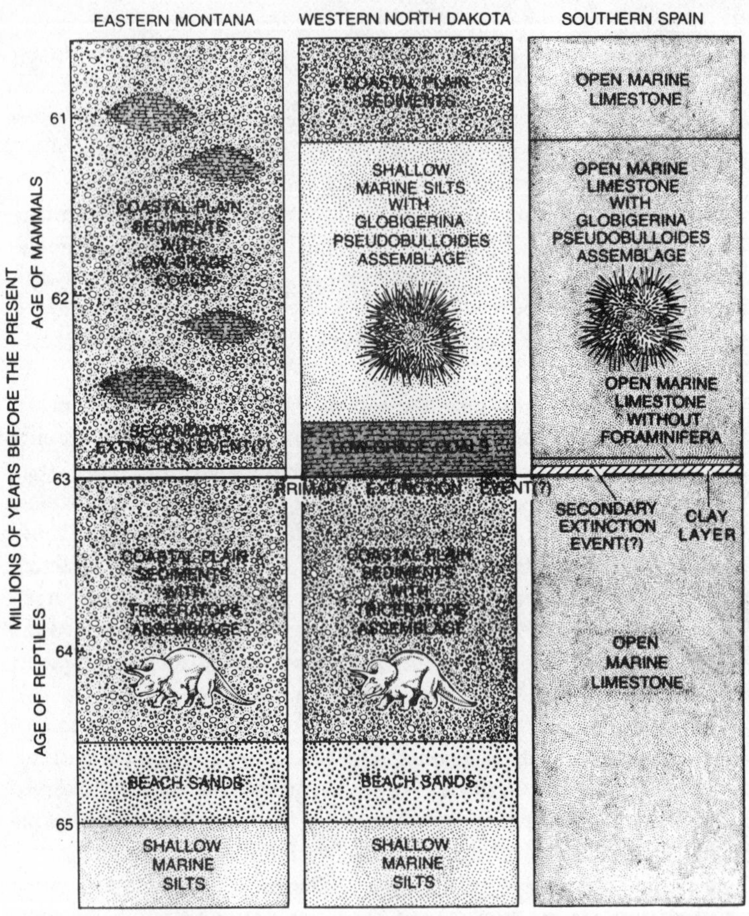

Sequence of events at two land sites in North America and a marine site in Spain at the close of the Mesozoic and the opening of the Cenozoic is presented in this table. The presence of the same replacement foraminiferan, *Globigerina pseudobulloides*, in North Dakota and Spain in the Cenozoic suggests a coincidence of marine and terrestrial extinctions.

(representing less than 200 years of deposition) nearly 90 percent of the foraminifera species found lower in the formation simply vanish. Those protozoans that survived attained only a tenth the size of their predecessors. As the rain of shells and platelets nearly ceased so did the burrowing activity of bottom-dwelling invertebrate animals. A blanket of laminated red and green clays accumulated on the sea floor, reaching a thickness of about 10 centimeters. Conditions apparently remained stable for perhaps 20,000 years; by then all but one species of the surviving foraminifera had dwindled to extinction.

29 Thereafter life began to proliferate once more. The deposition of sediments resumed, and the ocean floor was once again plowed by bottom-dwelling invertebrates. A new assemblage of foraminifera arose and was soon followed by another, characterized by the presence of, among others, the species *Globigerina pseudobulloides.* The resurgent protozoans inhabited the ancient Spanish sea for the next two million years.

30 Half a world away, in what is now North Dakota, a great interior sea spread westward at this same time, flooding a delta area where the remains of *Triceratops* had become fossilized and had been covered by coal-bearing strata. The marine siltstones that were laid down on top of the coal hold the shells of foraminifera species belonging to the same *G. pseudobulloides* assemblage that appeared in the Spanish sea after the great foraminiferan extinction. Given the uncertainties in estimating elapsed time from the thickness of sedimentary deposits, it seems possible that the story told by the sediments here, at Fort Peck Reservoir and in southern Spain is the same. If that is the case, the extinction of the dinosaurs on land and of the foraminifera at sea would have coincided.

31 The foraminifera were not the only marine organisms to die out at the end of the Mesozoic. As I have noted above, so did a number of marine reptiles. So did various mollusks: the coiled-shell cephalopods known as ammonites, the squidlike cephalopods known as belemnites and the peculiar coral-like bivalves known as rudists. Most of the major families of marine animals survived, but they lost many genera and species.

32 The fossil record at this crucial boundary is not as well understood with respect to larger marine animals as it is with respect to the microfauna such as the foraminifera. The reason is that the larger animals are numerous and diverse and the number of paleontologists is finite. As one example, even in such relatively well-studied formations as the chalks of Denmark the survival rate among such important animal groups as sponges, lampshells, marine snails and crustaceans remains uncalculated. As another example, the record of animal life in the tropical regions of the globe at this time is still poorly known. In view of the paucity of

Big-brained dinosaur of the late Cretaceous, *Stenonychosaurus inequalus*, measured some three meters from the tip of its snout to the tip of its tail. This drawing is based on a restoration at the National Museum of Natural Sciences in Ottawa. Its ratio of brain weight to body weight equaled that of early mammals. Had such predators lived on they might have halted the rise of the mammals.

data it is no wonder that the issue of gradualism v. catastrophism is so vigorously debated.

33 A crude tabulation is helpful in suggesting the magnitude of the extinctions. Compare the number of animal genera in the fossil record some 10 million years before the end of the Cretaceous with the number of genera in the record in a comparable period after the crisis. It is obvious how insecure these numerical values are. Nevertheless, the numbers appear to reflect a 50 percent decline in generic diversity worldwide. When one repeats this numbers game, counting the number of species recorded for certain plant and animal genera before and after the crisis, the result is similar. In a sample that includes mammals as representative land animals, chitinous marine algae as representative plants, and sand dollars, starfishes and oysters as representative marine animals,

the decline in species during the extinction interval is from about three species per genus to 1.5. Therefore it seems reasonable to estimate that the biological crisis associated with the extinction of the dinosaurs also caused 75 percent of the previously existing plant and animal species to disappear. Indeed, this estimate is probably somewhat conservative.

34 The record of extinctions shows certain anomalies. For example, no land animal weighing more than about 25 kilograms (55 pounds) survived, and many of those that disappeared were considerably smaller. Again, the terrestrial plants of the northern regions of the Temperate Zone suffered more losses than those farther south. Yet the plants and animals of freshwater communities were scarcely affected. Much the same was probably true of deep-water marine mollusks in the opinion of Arthur H. Clarke of Ecosearch, Inc., of Mattapoisett, Mass. Shallow-water marine life, however, particularly the fauna of tropical reefs, was much more profoundly altered.

35 Even animals that shared the same environment were not identically affected. As Eric Buffetaut of the University of Paris has pointed out, crocodiles that occupied shallow marine waters survived the extinctions but the mosasaurs that occupied the same habitat did not. Whatever the agents of biological stress were, disturbances in food chains included, the ability of the biosphere to resist them was evidently varied.

36 What is the significance of the apparently dual nature of animal and plant extinctions at the end of the Mesozoic? Were the extinctions truly separate events, with the land animals dying out first and then plants second? If they were, was the second extinction the result of stresses as severe as those that caused the first, or was it simply a quasi-successional phenomenon of biology? Whatever the answer to these questions is, mankind may have been the long-term beneficiary of the evident catastrophe. As the Mesozoic drew to a close certain small carnivorous dinosaurs had achieved the ratio of brain weight to body weight that is characteristic of early mammals. If these presumably more intelligent reptiles had survived, their descendants might conceivably have continued to suppress the rise of the mammals, thereby preempting our own position as the brainiest animals on the planet.

QUESTIONS FOR ANALYSIS AND DISCUSSION

1. Explain the difference between catastrophism and gradualism as scientific models. Which model has been the more popular among modern scientists?

2. What are some of the hypotheses offered to explain the animal extinctions at the end of the Mesozoic era?
3. Explain the significance of the discovery of iridium deposits at the end of the Cretaceous period.
4. By what reasoning does Russell reject a supernova as the cause of the iridium deposits?
5. By what reasoning could either an asteroid or a comet have caused mass extinctions? Does Russell argue specifically in favor of either cause?
6. If Russell doesn't know *exactly* what caused the extinctions, what *type* of cause is he convinced of? How does the fossil record support his view?
7. Are you convinced that a terrestrial catastrophe of some sort wiped out the dinosaurs? If not, why not?
8. Russell avoids one convention of scholarly writing—documentation of sources. How does he get around this convention and yet include the work of other scientists?
9. Analyze Russell's style. What is his stance—his relation to subject and audience? How do his style and stance differ from Gould's discussion of dinosaurs?

An Interview with DALE A. RUSSELL

What are your particular research interests?

In particular, I am interested in dinosaurian ecology, evolution, and systematics. In general, I am interested in the identification of large-scale evolutionary trends that may indicate large-scale trends in the evolution of multicellular organisms wherever they may occur in the cosmos.

What responses did you have to your article?

There was a very large number of reprint requests, many of them from physicians. I also received a few letters expressing a desire for more information or offering a different point of view. Perhaps the most significant effect of the article, as far as my own work was concerned, was to legitimize somewhat a rather unusual paleontological point of view.

Can you account for the response from physicians?

My guess is that physicians form a large portion of *Scientific American*'s readership. Physicians may also be drawn to paleontological topics as intellectually stimulating but free of the concerns they face in their daily practice.

If you were to revise your article, what if any changes would you make?

Recent studies have revealed at least two paleontological errors in the article. The late Cretaceous material thought to have been ichthyosaurian has since been determined by Donald Baird of Princeton University to be plesiosaurian, so that ichthyosaurs became extinct during middle Cretaceous time, and Michael Spoon and Greg Retallack of the University of Oregon have suggested that a change in soil acidity in early postextinction time induced a change in the fossil record in eastern Montana. Thus the putative two-phase extinction is more likely to have been the result of a secondary change in quality of bone preservation. Since the article was published, much interesting information has appeared that would have been mentioned if it had been available. However, the original manuscript benefited greatly from the counsel of colleagues working on the extinction problem, and it fairly accurately reflects the "state of the art" of the catastrophic school early in 1982.

Where do you think the gradualism/catastrophe conflict stands today?

The question has been rather accurately addressed in articles by Browne (*New York Times*, 29 October 1985: 21–22) and by Hoffman and Nitecki (*Geology* 13 [1985]: 844–887). Although a very good case in support of an asteroid impact at the end of Cretaceous time has been made on the basis of paleontological, physical, and chemical evidence, some paleontological data have been cited to suggest that such an impact had little biological effect. This has promoted a general interest in the asteroid impact hypothesis, but it has also discouraged its acceptance. Although the majority of paleontologists still hold to gradualistic hypotheses, the catastrophe hypothesis is gaining converts.

What is your position today?

My view continues to be that the paleobiological record strongly supports the hypothesis that the dinosaurs were eliminated in a general and extremely catastrophic extinction event, but that ordinary and well-understood sedimentary processes have blurred the record somewhat. I am aware of no evidence implying that the correct extinction mechanism has not yet been identified. Research is fascinating because nature continues to hold so many surprises for us. Thus, I wish to go on record that I am capable of changing my position in the face of new evidence, for example, on the "warm-bloodedness" of dinosaurs. Some dinosaurs almost certainly possessed a metabolism similar to that of mammals.

Do you have any advice for science students?

I think that in addition to the emphasis schools place on getting the facts right, we should also encourage students to speculate and to place their research in a larger philosophical framework. The study of our evolutionary history and contemplation of future prospects should be an exciting, joyous experience, as well as an experience in logic.

The Origin of Earth

JOHN GRIBBEN

Born 1946 in Maidstone, Kent, in England, John Gribben holds two degrees from Sussex University and a Ph.D. in astrophysics from Cambridge University. A respected scientist, Gribben has written several science fiction novels and numerous articles and books on topics that include meteorology, geology, and astronomy. Among his books are Our Changing Climate *(1975),* Our Changing Universe *(1976),* Timewarps *(1979),* Spacewarps *(1983), and* Genesis: The Origins of Man and the Universe *(1981), from which the following excerpt on our solar system is taken.*

Gribben has also been a staff writer for the English scientific journal Nature *and is currently physics consultant to the English journal* New Scientist. *Clearly his primary profession now is science writer, not scientist, and he has been quoted as asserting that his "ambition is to write more nonfiction books than Isaac Asimov." That's a tall order, but one that Gribben may be able to fill. His writing, like Asimov's, is clear and lively, though his books are sometimes aimed at a somewhat more knowledgeable audience than are Asimov's general guides and introductions. In the following pages, Gribben describes the earth's formation and characteristics.*

1 The origin of our Solar System is intimately connected with the nature of our Galaxy, just as the origin of our Galaxy resulted from the underlying structure of the whole Universe. At every step down the chain from Big Bang to man himself we will find this close relationship with what has gone before; and ultimately this tells us that the kind of creatures we are depends not just on the kind of planet we live on or the Sun that is in our sky, but on the detailed physical nature of the Big Bang—the origin of the Universe—itself. We are creatures of our Universe, and creatures like us could not have evolved without the Universe being what it is. . . .

2 The nature of the Solar System, as it condensed out of a collapsing cloud of gas, was determined by rotation. Just as a collapsing cloud of gas, on a much larger scale, was held up by its rotation into a disk which became the flattened Milky Way system in which we live, so the rotation of the presolar gas cloud held up some of the collapsing material into a disk. A great deal of material did indeed settle into a more or less

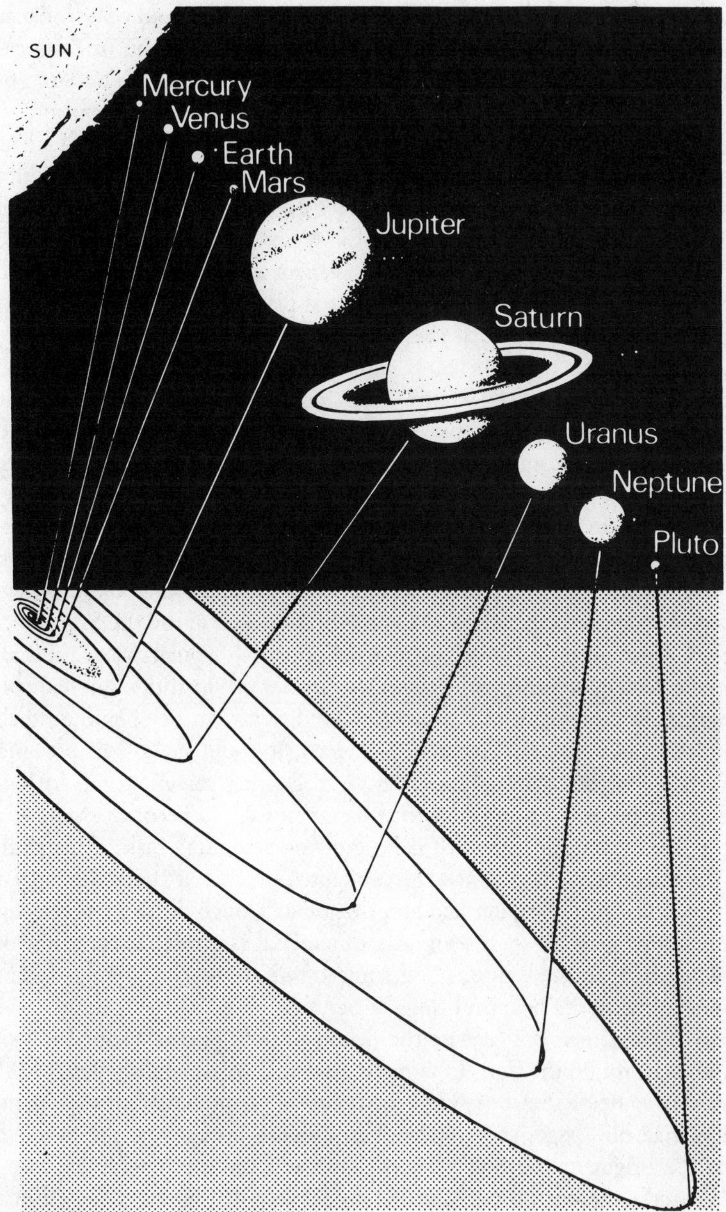

The planets of our Solar System, shown approximately to scale, and the positions of their orbits in the disk of material surrounding our Sun.

spherical ball at the center—the Sun itself—but this could only collapse to such an extent because the angular momentum of the original gas cloud was spread over the remaining material in the disk. The Sun got most of the mass, but the disk got most of the angular momentum.

3 It might seem an exaggeration to describe the Sun's family of planets as a disk, but in terms of the Solar System as a whole there is no doubt about the validity of the description. It's not as if we just had one small body orbiting around another, like the Moon around the Earth. In the Solar System, there are nine known planets, all of which move around the Sun in the same way; most of these planets have moons, and the overwhelming majority of these orbit their planets in the same sense that the planets orbit the Sun, while the planets themselves, with the exception of Venus and Uranus, turn on their axes in the same sense again. This dominant rotation sense of all the material in the disk is also the direction of rotation of the Sun itself, which turns on its axis once every 25.3 days. And, finally, all of this material rotating the same way about the Sun is indeed concentrated in a thin disk, the plane of the ecliptic. This evidence very clearly shows the intimate relationship between the Sun and planets, and leaves no room to doubt that they formed together. If the planets had somehow been picked up by the Sun on its travels around the Galaxy, they would not be so regularly arranged, all in the same plane and with essentially circular orbits; if the Sun had collapsed on its own from a great gas cloud, it would be spinning much more rapidly than we see today—indeed, it could never collapse into such a compact ball as it is today. A collapsing gas cloud has to lose angular momentum in order to collapse enough to become a star, and the best way to do the trick is by growing a rotating disk of material. The material in the disk can then collapse into planets, with the biggest planets (especially Jupiter and Saturn) going through the same process in miniature, growing their own disks of material as they contract, some of which have formed moons and some of which remain as rings today, most notably the beautiful rings of Saturn.

4 Astronomers still debate the details of how planets formed out of the disk around the Sun. In a major academic work published in 1978[1] twenty-eight of the most eminent theorists of modern times spent no less than 668 pages covering the best modern thought on the problem of the origin of the Solar System, and still came out with no single "answer"—there is no one detailed model accepted by everybody. But a

[1] S. F. Dermott, ed., *The Origin of the Solar System* (New York: Wiley, 1978).

great deal of the disagreement between the theories *is* over detail, and does not represent any fundamental dispute over the evidence that Sun and planets formed together, going through a Sun plus disk stage as the original gas cloud collapsed. So although the following simplification of the current thought on the problem cannot be presented as correct in every detail, it does give a broad outline of the ideas that are becoming increasingly accepted today, and within which the details, although still being debated, are likely to be filled in in the not too distant future.

5 From this point of view there is one basic feature of the Solar System—apart from its existence!—that is of crucial importance to human life and must be explained by any satisfactory theory. Why is the Solar System made up of two kinds of planets—small, rocky planets near the Sun (including the Earth) and large, gaseous planets further out?[2] This can certainly be explained satisfactorily in terms of the evolution of a disk of material around the Sun, heated by the young star at its heart. The heating is of key importance, driving material out and away from the nebula in which the Sun formed. In order to explain the slow spin of the Sun, most modern theories require not just the transfer of angular momentum to the disk, but a lot of material—as much as remains in the Sun itself—blown out of the system altogether by the fiery furnace at its heart. Long before this furnace switched on, however, the processes that led to the formation of the planets had already begun.

6 Tiny grains of dust which existed in the original gas cloud (nebula) would begin to stick together to form little fluffy "supergrains," perhaps a few millimeters across, as the nebula started to contract and the grains collided with one another more and more often in the increasingly dense cloud. Constantly bombarded by the atoms of gas in the collapsing cloud, these supergrains would be very susceptible to the processes which transfer angular momentum, and would settle rapidly into the disk as it began to grow around the bulging, flattened ball of the embryonic Sun. This concentrated the supergrains into a still smaller volume of space, giving them ample opportunity to come into contact with one another and to interact through gravity. The result was that they clumped

---

[2]Pluto, generally regarded as the farthest known planet, is an exception to this pattern, being both far out and small and rocky. But Pluto doesn't seem to be a "proper" planet at all, since it follows an elongated orbit which brings it closer to the Sun than Neptune for some of the time, including from January 1979 to March 1999. In all probability, Pluto is a moon that has escaped from one of the gas giants, so that the "real" planets divide rather neatly into two groups of four, separated by a belt of cosmic rubble between Mars and Jupiter, the asteroid belt.

together into bigger lumps, building up to pieces a kilometer or more across, rather like meteors or the rubble that remains in the asteroid belt today, and forming the first respectably sized solid objects in the Solar System. As this process of clumping together (accretion) continued, eventually planet-sized objects were built up—although the details of the accretion process and the reasons for the exact positions of the planets from the Sun are among the puzzles still being debated by the experts. . . .

7 The most important thing we know about the origin of the Earth is that our home planet formed at the same time as the Sun, with the rest of the Solar System, from a collapsing cloud of gas in interstellar space. . . . Our form of life needs a planet with a star like the Sun, which inevitably was the product of a galaxy which itself formed from fireball fluctuations in the expanding Universe. . . .

8 The cloud of dust and gas within the Solar System which collapsed to form Planet Earth was probably composed chiefly of silicon compounds, iron oxides, and magnesium oxides, with just a trace of all the other chemical elements we now find in our terrestrial environment. This debris itself represented just a tiny fraction of heavier material left behind in the inner Solar System, with lighter elements driven outward by the activity of the Sun as it formed. As the Earth formed, it warmed up through three processes. First, as particles collided with one another and stuck together, their energy of motion (kinetic energy) was converted into heat. This continued well after the planet had grown to a respectable size, with the "particles" doing the colliding then being large meteorites smashing into the surface of the planet—as still happens occasionally today. Then, as a planet proper began to grow by this accretion, the interior was pressed ever tighter by the increasing weight of material above. Just as a gas cloud or star warms up as it contracts, releasing gravitational potential energy as heat, so did the proto-Earth. Unlike a gas cloud or star, however, the heat from the interior could not escape easily into space, but was largely trapped by the solid barrier of the crust above, helping to keep the interior of the Earth hot to the present day. And, thirdly, some of the elements in the mixture of heavy materials that made up the core of the young planet were radioactive—the heavy products of the nearby supernova that triggered the birth of the Solar System—and have since been decaying, giving up energy of nuclear fission as a further contribution to the heat of the Earth's interior. The radioactive heat was produced in greater quantities when the Earth was young, since many, many atoms have now decayed and relatively few are left to contribute to the warmth of the Earth today. Almost certainly

this early radioactive heating was a major factor in melting the iron-rich Earth, perhaps a few hundred million years after a planet began to form from the cloud of material circling the proto-Sun. But because the melting temperature of a solid is increased if the solid is under pressure, melting did not begin at the center of the Earth, but between 400 and 800 km depth, where the combination of slightly lower pressure than in the middle but distinctly higher temperature than at the surface provided an appropriate balance.

9 Molten globules of iron, formed in this way, would then have sunk through the material around them toward the center of the Earth, giving up more gravitational energy as heat in the process, with almost the whole of the interior eventually melting. At this stage, heavier elements could settle freely into the deep interior, while lighter elements could float toward the surface. So the Earth began to approach its present structure, with a molten interior rich in iron and a surface layer of lighter material, dominated by silicon. Just as the composition of the whole Earth is not typical of the composition of the cloud from which the Solar System formed, so the material of the crust on which we live is not typical of the material which makes up the bulk of the Earth. But at every stage along the way that separation of elements from one another has occurred, it has followed straightforward physical laws. There is nothing peculiar about the separation of materials which led up to the environment present today at the surface of the Earth, and any planet forming in the same way would end up in a very similar state. Our terrestrial environment is very much a product of the Universe we live in, right back to the fireball of the Big Bang itself.

10 So today the crust of the Earth contains just 6 percent iron, whereas the planet as a whole contains 35 percent iron, while the crust is made up of 28 percent silicon, which only makes up 15 percent of the mass of the whole planet. Some heavy elements, such as uranium and thorium, never got a chance to settle deep into the Earth's interior, because they easily combine with light elements such as oxygen and silicon, making light compounds (oxides and silicates) which happily floated up into the surface layers. One result of this is that after the initial melting a great deal of the radioactive heat was produced in the surface layers, where it could easily be radiated away into space. Indeed, once the surface layers of light material had formed, and very little hot material from the interior was rising to the surface, cooling was able to produce the solid crust of the Earth that established more or less the kind of surface we know today, but without the atmosphere or oceans we now know, and certainly

without life. Instead, as the crust solidified, the Earth's surface was covered with hot rock and a wealth of active volcanoes, pouring out both molten rock (lava) and gases. These gases played a crucial part in the subsequent evolution of the surface of our planet. . . . But since it was at the stage of cooling and solidifying that the main feature of the crust, its division into continents and what were to become ocean basins, must have occurred, first let's take a look at how the structure of our planet, from crust to deep interior, stabilized.

11 The continents are made of light rock, chiefly granite, while the material of the crust beneath the oceans, chiefly basalt, is rather heavier, so that to the very end the lighter materials were rising higher than the denser materials, in line with the simple laws of physics. We can even put a date on when all this happened, since the oldest rocks known on Earth are 3,900 million years old, and the age of the Solar System is about 4,500 million years. So, in round terms, it took about 600 million years for the proto-Earth to develop a hot, molten interior, for "differentiation" of light and heavy material to take place, and for the crust to begin to solidify—just about 13 percent of the history of our planet to date.

12 What was produced after all that activity was a layered planet, with several shells wrapped around one another. And what we know about this layering today is a result of the study of earthquake waves, which pass right through the Earth and can be monitored by seismic detectors. Seismologists measure the time it takes the waves to pass through the Earth from a known earthquake to different points around the globe, and this tells them something about the nature of the material inside the Earth that the waves have passed through. In all honesty, unraveling a picture of the Earth's structure from this information is as much an art as a science, and one eminent geophysicist described it as like trying to analyze the structure of a piano by listening to the noise it made as it was pushed down a flight of stairs. It is therefore remarkable how much seismologists have determined about the structure of the Earth.

13 Starting from the surface, we have a rocky ball with an average radius of 6,371 km, slightly flattened at the poles. The outer shell or crust makes up only 0.6 percent of the volume of the planet, and its thickness varies from a fairly uniform 5 km below the oceans to 35 km under flat continental surfaces and as much as 80 km under great mountain ranges like the Himalayas. At least we know something about the crust from direct observation. It is made up mainly of silicon and aluminum, plus oxygen, combined in various compounds to make granite

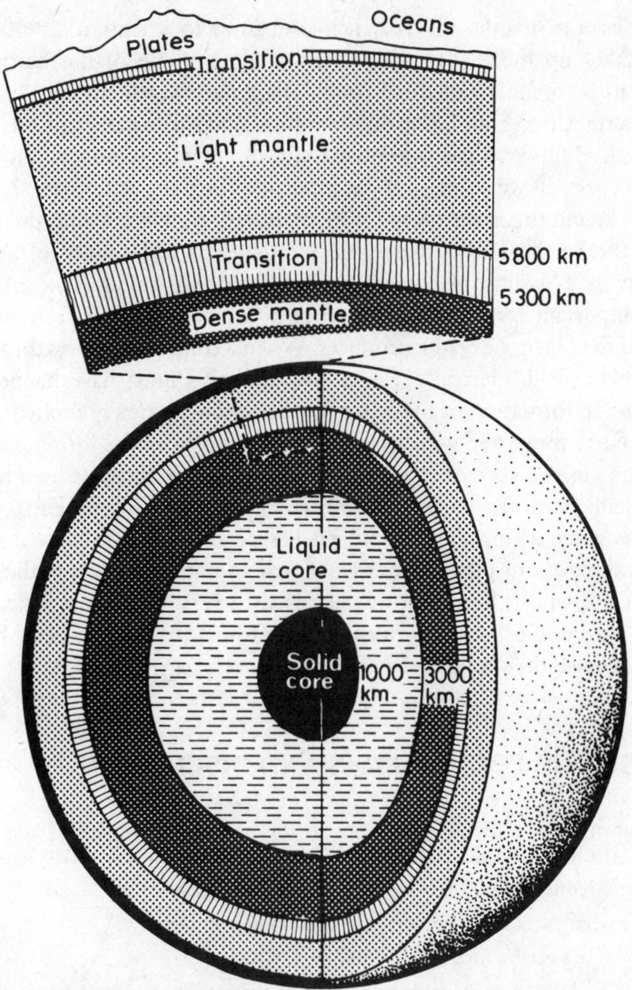

The layered structure of the Earth today.

rocks, solidified lava, and sedimentary deposits. Overall, the name given to the continental crust material is sial, from the first letters of silicon and aluminum; because oceanic crust also contains large amounts of magnesium, in various compounds, it is sometimes referred to as sima.

14 Below the crust there is a very pronounced change in structure, marked by a boundary called the Mohorovicic discontinuity (or simply Moho for short), after the Yugoslav seismologist who first identified it.

Below lies the mantle, a layer which goes down to a depth of 2,900 km and makes up more than 82 percent of the volume of the Earth. It seems to be made up of three zones, the upper mantle about 370 km thick, a transition zone some 600 km thick, and the lower mantle 1,900 km thick—but very little is known about its chemical composition.

15 Deeper still we come to the core, divided into the outer core, 2,100 km thick, and the inner core, 1,370 km in radius, which lies at the center of the Earth. This is the region which seems to be made of liquid iron, with a mixing of something else—probably sulfur. One of the most important results of the existence of a core of molten iron in the Earth is the magnetic field it produces. When a conductor moves through a magnetic field, electric currents flow, and this must have happened early in the formation of the Solar System when the newly molten core of the Earth interacted with stray magnetic fields from the forming Sun. Once an electric current is set up in this way, it produces its own magnetic fields, and, fed by the rotation energy of the spinning Earth, the result is a self-acting dynamo which has persisted to the present day. This feature of our planet may have played an important part in the history of life, and it has also provided us with very useful magnetic evidence, frozen into the rocks of the crust, of how the surface layers have changed since they solidified 3,900 million years ago.

QUESTIONS FOR ANALYSIS AND DISCUSSION

1. Gribben devotes several paragraphs to the process by which our sun and planets formed. State more briefly and in your own words the basic parts of the disk concept and the process of planet formation.
2. Over what parts of this process do astronomers disagree?
3. Why is the earth's interior still hot?
4. What enables scientists to describe with confidence the process of our earth's formation? How can they be so sure of a process that occurred so long ago?
5. Describe the earth's structure. Think about ways this description can be organized effectively. Which organization does Gribben use? If you choose a different organization, explain why.
6. What is important about the earth's core of molten iron? How has this characteristic helped determine the nature of our planet?
7. Analyze Gribben's style of writing. How technical is his word choice? What terms does he define and what background does he supply? What is Gribben's tone—his attitude toward his subject that he conveys to readers?

8. Why are Gribben's style and tone appropriate for a general audience but inappropriate for an audience of astronomers or geologists?
9. What specific details about the earth's formation and structure did you learn from Gribben? Which details do you find most fascinating? Why?

Black Holes

ISAAC ASIMOV

Born in Russia in 1920, Isaac Asimov came to the United States in 1923 and became a U.S. citizen in 1928. Asimov obtained three degrees from Columbia University while already at work on science fiction stories. His teaching career in biochemistry has been with the Boston University School of Medicine, where he became a full professor in 1979, after some stormy sessions over how he would spend his time when not teaching. He now makes his home in Manhattan – although one could say that he makes his home at his typewriter.

Some readers know Asimov primarily as a science fiction writer, others as a writer about science, but few have not bumped into at least one of his more than 200 books or too-many-to-count short stories and articles. Asimov has written fiction, literary criticism, humor, juvenile books, his autobiography, and explanations of scientific material from almost every science field. Indeed, Asimov may have written more books about more subjects than any other writer, and he has accomplished this feat doing all his own research, writing, typing, indexing, and proofreading.

Asimov's particular skill as a writer about science for nonspecialists lies in his ability to clarify complex principles and enliven dull details. He brings the same imaginative, witty, colorful style to his writings about science as we find in his science fiction works. His short explanation of black holes, originally published in the London Daily Telegraph *in 1979 also appears in* The Roving Mind *(1983), a collection of Asimov's essays about science.*

1 Of all the odd creatures in the astronomical zoo, the "black hole" is the oddest. To understand it, concentrate on gravity.

2 Every piece of matter produces a gravitational field. The larger the piece, the larger the field. What's more, the field grows more intense the closer you move to its center. If a large object is squeezed into a smaller

volume, its surface is nearer its center and the gravitational pull on that surface is stronger.

3 Anything on the surface of a large body is in the grip of its gravity, and in order to escape it must move rapidly. If it moves rapidly enough, then even though gravitational pull slows it down continually it can move sufficiently far away from the body so that the gravitational pull, weakened by distance, can never quite slow its motion to zero.

4 The minimum speed required for this is the "escape velocity." From the surface of the earth, the escape velocity is 7.0 miles per second. From Jupiter, which is larger, the escape velocity is 37.6 miles per second. From the sun, which is still larger, the escape velocity is 383.4 miles per second.

5 Imagine all the matter of the sun (which is a ball of hot gas 864,000 miles across) compressed tightly together. Imagine it compressed so tightly that its atoms smash and it becomes a ball of atomic nuclei and loose electrons, 30,000 miles across. The sun would then be a "white dwarf." Its surface would be nearer its center, the gravitational pull on that surface would be stronger, and escape velocity would now be 2,100 miles per second.

6 Compress the sun still more to the point where the electrons melt into the nuclei. There would then be nothing left but tiny neutrons, and they will move together till they touch. The sun would then be only 9 miles across, and it would be a "neutron star." Escape velocity would be 120,000 miles per second.

7 Few things material could get away from a neutron star, but light could, of course, since light moves at 186,282 miles per second.

8 Imagine the sun shrinking past the neutron-star stage, with the neutrons smashing and collapsing. By the time the sun is 3.6 miles across, escape velocity has passed the speed of light, and light can no longer escape. Since nothing can go faster than light, *nothing* can escape.

9 Into such a shrunken sun anything might fall, but nothing can come out. It would be like an endlessly deep hole in space. Since not even light can come out, it is utterly dark–it is a "black hole."

10 In 1939, J. Robert Oppenheimer first worked out the nature of black holes in the light of the laws of modern physics, and ever since astronomers have wondered if black holes exist in fact as well as in theory.

11 How would they form? Stars would collapse under their own enormous gravity were it not for the enormous heat they develop, which keeps them expanded. The heat is formed by the fusion of hydrogen nuclei, however, and when the hydrogen is used up the star collapses.

12 A star like our sun will eventually collapse fairly quietly to a white dwarf. A more massive star will explode before it collapses, losing some of its mass in the process. If the portion that survives the explosion and collapses is more than 1.4 times the mass of the sun, it will surely collapse into a neutron star. If it is more than 3.2 times the mass of the sun, it must collapse into a black hole.

13 Since there are indeed massive stars, some of them have collapsed by now and formed black holes. But how can we detect one? Black holes are only a few miles across after all, give off no radiation, and are trillions of miles away.

14 There's one way out. If matter falls into a black hole, it gives off X-rays in the process. If a black hole is collecting a great deal of matter, enough X-rays may be given off for us to detect them.

15 Suppose two massive stars are circling each other in close proximity. One explodes and collapses into a black hole. The two objects continue to circle each other, but as the second star approaches explosion it expands. As it expands, some of its matter spirals into the black hole, and there is an intense radiation of X-rays as a result.

16 In 1965, an X-ray source was discovered in the constellation Cygnus and was named "Cygnus X-1." Eventually, the source was pinpointed to the near neighborhood of a dim star, HD-226868, which is only dim because it is 10,000 light-years away. Actually, it is a huge star, 30 times the mass of our sun.

17 That star is one of a pair and the two are circling each other once every 5.6 days. The X-rays are coming from the other star, the companion of HD-226868. That companion is Cygnus X-1. From the motion of HD-226868, it is possible to calculate that Cygnus X-1 is 5 to 8 times the mass of our sun.

18 A star of that mass should be visible if it is an ordinary star, but no telescope can detect any star on the spot where X-rays are emerging. Cygnus X-1 must be a collapsed star that is too small to see. Since Cygnus X-1 is at least 5 times as massive as our sun, it is too massive to be a white dwarf; too massive, even, to be a neutron star.

19 It can be nothing other than a black hole; the first to be discovered.

QUESTIONS FOR ANALYSIS AND DISCUSSION

1. Examine Asimov's sentence structure, word choice, and use of definitions, and then describe his audience. How do you know that his article is not written for scientists?

2. Asimov provides a clear and precise definition of a black hole without relying on many complex scientific terms. How does he do it? List, as precisely as you can, his techniques. Consider how the explanation is organized, how numbers are presented, and again his sentences, word choice, and use of such terms as "escape velocity" and "neutron star."
3. Asimov's explanation of a black hole does depend on his reader having a knowledge of atomic structure. Explain, in three or four sentences, for a nonspecialist, the structure of the atom.
4. In the process of defining a black hole, Asimov also defines a "white dwarf" and a "neutron star." Can you now explain these "astronomical creatures" to a nonspecialist? Write a brief definition of each.

Competing Models of Mental Illness: Psychodynamic, Behavioral, and Biological

NANCY C. ANDREASEN

A native of Lincoln, Nebraska, Nancy C. Andreasen (b. 1938) has had two careers, first as a college English instructor, now as a professor of psychiatry. After obtaining degrees in English from Radcliffe College and the University of Nebraska, Andreasen taught English at the University of Iowa—until she decided to attend medical school after the birth of her first child, an experience that made her realize how little she knew and how few good books on medicine exist for the nonspecialist. She completed her M.D. at Iowa in 1970, did residency in psychiatry until 1973, and then became a professor of psychiatry at Iowa, where she works today.

Andreasen contributes articles to medical journals, is editor of "Book Forum," a regular feature in the American Journal of Psychiatry, *and has published* Understanding Mental Illness: A Layman's Guide *(1974) and* The Broken Brain: The Biological Revolution in Psychiatry *(1984), from which the following excerpt comes.*

In "Competing Models of Mental Illness," Andreasen provides, for nonspecialists, a clear analysis and contrast of the three dominant theories of human psychology. Her contrast also incorporates a historical perspective, demonstrating the current revolution in the treatment of mental illness. Most important for writing students, Andreasen provides a good example of organizing by points of difference and presenting a clear, accurate summary of complex theories.

1 Freud, Kraepelin, and Watson[1] represent three competing models of how mental illnesses are caused, how they should be defined and studied, and how they should be treated. These are the psychodynamic (or psychoanalytic) model, the biological (or medical) model, and the behavioral model. Each of these models has very different practical implications about how patients are understood and treated. The shift from a psychodynamic or behavioral to a biological model will lead to very major changes in the clinical care of mental illness in the 1980s and 1990s. What are the practical implications of these three competing models? How do they affect the way doctors perceive their patients—and the way patients perceive their doctors? The differences between these three models are summarized in table 1.

THE PSYCHODYNAMIC MODEL

2 The *psychodynamic model* derives from the writings of Freud. Since Freud's time, however, many other psychoanalytic writers have added to or modified Freud's original ideas. These include such figures as his daughter, Anna Freud; Ernst Kris; Melanie Klein; Heinz Hartmann; Carl Jung; Erich Fromm; and Heinz Kohut, to mention only a few. Any summary of the work of so diverse a group of thinkers is inevitably an oversimplification. Nevertheless, several generalizations about the nature of the psychoanalytic model are probably true.

3 As mentioned earlier, although Freud began his medical career by studying the structure and workings of the brain (a physical part of the body), most of his life was devoted to studying the nature and workings of the *mind.* While the brain is something that can be seen, felt, and studied under a microscope, the mind is an abstract concept that usually refers to the activities the brain generates. Although Freud originally hoped that he would be able to relate his theories concerning the mind to scientific knowledge about the brain, he gradually abandoned this idea as his study of the mind consumed more and more of his time and effort.

---

[1]Sigmund Freud (1856–1939), an Austrian neurologist; Emil Kraepelin (1856–1926), a German psychiatrist; and John B. Watson (1878–1958), an American psychologist.—Ed.

Table 1. Three Models of Mental Illness

	Psychodynamic	Behavioral	Biological
emphasis	Mind	Behavior	Brain
causes of illness	Disturbed dynamics Childhood experiences	Learned habits	Biological imbalances
methods of study	Introspection (free association, dream analysis)	Controlled experiments (use of conditioning, animal research)	Neurosciences (neurochemistry, behavioral genetics)
types of illness	Mild (neuroses, personality disorders)	Mild to severe (neuroses, personality disorders, addictions)	Moderate to severe (depression, mania, schizophrenia)
method of treatment	Psychotherapy	Behavior modification	Medication

4 Freud's early thinking was heavily influenced by the physics of his time, especially that of the Helmholtz School. He was imbued with this point of view during the five years he spent there as a medical student working with Ernst von Brücke, a Viennese neurophysiologist who founded a scientific movement known as the Helmholtz School of Medicine. One of the fundamental principles that influenced Freud's thinking was the notion of the conservation of energy promulgated by Mayer and Helmholtz. According to this theory, every isolated system has a constant amount of energy that can be discharged, and discharges in various parts of any system tend to remain in equilibrium or homeostasis. Freud applied these ideas to his thinking about the workings of the mind, which he wrote out in an essay during the 1890s, titled "Project for a Scientific Psychology," published only after his death. In Freud's thinking, the mind, like any other system, contained a certain amount of psychic energy. The human mind could be understood through examining the interplay of psychic forces striving to maintain an equilibrium. That is why Freudian psychology is called "psychodynamic."

5 From this physiological framework, Freud gradually developed a variety of theories that formed the foundation of classical psychoanalysis. While his contemporary neurologists, neuroanatomists, and psychiatrists were describing the structure of the brain, Freud described the structure of the psyche or mind. He divided psychic functions into three regions: the unconscious, the preconscious, and the conscious. The

unconscious is characterized by primitive forms of thinking that Freud called "primary process thinking." This thinking is not directly available to consciousness and is expressed indirectly only through dreams or when censorship is relaxed during the process of free association. The unconscious is the repository of repressed ideas and unfulfilled wishes. According to Freud's thinking, much of the mental illness that he observed was due to an imbalance in the psychic equilibrium. Patients were using excessive amounts of psychic energy to keep primitive ideas under control, to ignore unfulfilled wishes that were unacceptable to their consciousness, and to repress unpleasant memories. When these unconscious drives were released and made conscious, a cure often occurred.

6 The unconscious could be made conscious in several different ways. Early in his career, Freud explored the use of hypnosis. Later, he discovered that when the patient relaxed on a couch and described without censorship any thoughts that came into his mind (the process of "free association"), this also led to the recovery of unconscious material. Using this approach and this foundation, Freud went on to evolve the psychoanalytic theories so familiar to many of us today, such as the Oedipus complex, the theory of infantile sexuality, and the division of the mind into id, ego, and superego.

7 The concern of this chapter is not to review the content of psychoanalytic theory, which is available from many different sources, but to examine its implications as a model for understanding mental illness and to compare it with two other major competing models, the behavioral model and the biological (or medical) model.

8 The psychodynamic model implies a certain set of assumptions about how mental illness should be approached, evaluated, and treated.

9 *The subject matter explored by the psychodynamic model is the human mind (or psyche).* The mind is an abstract or theoretical concept. Presumably, it ultimately represents the workings of the brain; but after Freud, psychodynamic thinkers made no effort to relate psychic function to brain function—they devoted their energies to defining a set of ideas that describe psychic functions. Their work has given us a group of terms and concepts that are widely used in both psychoanalysis and ordinary language: id, ego, superego; unconscious, preconscious, and conscious; primary and secondary process; libido, complex, drive, and dynamic conflict. These are terms and concepts that are useful descriptively and theoretically, but they have no known roots in physical reality.

10 *As a scientific endeavor, its techniques involve the careful study of individual cases or a small series of similar cases in order to understand the mental mechanisms that lead to malfunction.* Psychoanalytic research tends to be an intuitive and creative process. Following Freud's example, the psychoanalytic researcher is a careful observer who tries to understand what lies beneath the surface. He does not take things at face value and is in fact inclined to think that what seems most obvious is least likely to be true.

11 *Its tools involve the use of introspection and the reporting of subjective experiences.* In a clinical setting, the patient may free-associate, think aloud, or answer questions. Psychological tests of the type called "projective," such as the Rorschach (or "inkblot") test, may also be used as a vehicle to explore unconscious material, but the subject matter that is studied is always the verbal productions (or, in the case of children, play activity) of a human being.

12 *The psychodynamic model tends to emphasize the study of milder mental illnesses and the enhancement of adaptive functioning in individuals who are essentially healthy.* Sometimes these are referred to as "neuroses," "personality disorders," and "problems in daily living." When the model is applied narrowly, the ideal patient is an individual who is young, intelligent, and able to function reasonably well in everyday life, but who has a narrowly defined yet persistent psychological problem, such as difficulty in dealing with authority figures. More broadly defined, the psychodynamic model is used to treat patients with a wide variety of neuroses, such as difficulties with anxiety or mild depression, and more ingrained personality problems, such as difficulty in maintaining long-term relationships. The psychodynamic model has been applied to more-serious mental disorders, such as schizophrenia, but the results have not usually been very successful.

13 *As a treatment technique, the psychodynamic model emphasizes the use of psychotherapy.* When the model is applied narrowly, treatment sessions must occur several times a week. When it is applied more broadly, sessions can be less frequent, perhaps weekly or even every other week. Some psychodynamically oriented therapists see medication as inappropriate, since it may interfere with psychological treatment. Other psychodynamically oriented therapists are willing to prescribe medications occasionally.

14 Psychodynamic theories are not provable or testable to the same extent that other scientific theories may be. In their present form, they tend to be more philosophical than quantitative. Nevertheless, in developing

psychoanalytic theory, Freud and his successors founded one major branch of the modern sciences of psychology and psychiatry. Psychodynamic theories have been used effectively to understand the workings of the human mind and to treat a variety of disorders, such as obsessions, compulsions, or anxiety. They continue to provide useful explanations of the origins of some neuroses, and insights concerning methods of treating them. During coming years, as more emphasis is placed on the medical orientation in psychiatry, psychoanalysts will probably begin to apply scientific methods and experimental designs to the study of psychodynamic principles. This approach will further strengthen the psychodynamic perspective.

THE BEHAVIORAL MODEL

15 Behaviorism was launched by John B. Watson shortly after the introduction of Freud's ideas to this country. Followers of Watson presented their theories and research in reaction to the Freudian psychodynamic approach. Behaviorists such as Skinner, Wolpe, and Eysenck argue that the model used by Freud and his followers to understand the human mind is "unscientific"; only that which can be objectively observed and measured is allowed as evidence in understanding or treating mental illness. In contrast to the psychodynamic model, the tenets of the behavioral model are as follows:

16 *The proper study of mankind is human behavior rather than the mind.* Unlike psychodynamic theorists, behaviorists assume that the only things that are real (or at least worth studying) are the things we can see and observe. We cannot see the mind, the id, or the unconscious, but we can see how people act, react, and behave. From behavior we may be able to make inferences about the mind or brain, but they are not the primary focus of investigation. What people *do,* not what they *think* or *feel,* is the object of study. Likewise, the behaviorist does not look to the mind or brain to understand the causes of abnormal behavior. He assumes that such behavior represents learned habits, and he attempts to determine how they were learned.

17 *As a scientific technique, the behavioral model emphasizes the use of carefully controlled experiments on animals and human beings.* Experiments are defined in advance in order to explore a narrowly defined problem. For example, an investigator may choose to explore how frequently positive reinforcement must be given in order to maintain a behavior; thus, his experiment might compare rats pressing bars in Skinner boxes in order

to obtain food pellets when the pellet is given each time the rat presses the bar *versus* every fifth time *versus* random reward as determined by the use of a random number table. In such an experiment, numerical data are generated that can be compared statistically. Little can be learned from the study of single cases. In order to permit measurement and quantification, reasonably large samples must be investigated.

18 *The material that is studied is always behavior.* Because behaviorists are not interested in the mind, or its more rarefied equivalents such as psyche or soul, inferences about the conditions that maintain and reinforce human behavior can be made from the study of animal behavior. While psychodynamic theories have occasionally attempted to use animal models, this approach has not been very fruitful. On the other hand, animal research has provided a very important foundation for the behavioral approach. Human behavior is, of course, another very important subject of study for the behaviorists. Like the psychodynamic investigator, the behaviorist is interested in understanding the mechanisms underlying the behavior of both normal individuals and those with problems that might be referred to as "mental illness."

19 *When the behavioral model is applied to mental illness, it tends to be used for a wide variety of patients.* It is perhaps most effective in treating behavioral disorders and disorders of impulse control, such as excessive drinking, obesity, or sexual problems. Behavioral approaches may also be quite useful in the treatment of anxiety and have occasionally been helpful in the management of more severe mental disorders such as schizophrenia. From the point of view of a behaviorist, the schizophrenic tends to withdraw and to hallucinate because he has learned that by behaving in this way he will either gain positive effects or avoid negative ones. Treatment consists simply of teaching this patient new behavior. Behavior therapists feel they can teach a schizophrenic patient to function more effectively in society by reinforcing normal behavior, such as participation in social activities, through giving rewards like access to cigarettes or good desserts, and by extinguishing abnormal behavior, such as social withdrawal, through giving the patient less appetizing meals or depriving him of cigarettes.

20 *The primary methods of treatment involve teaching a patient new ways to modify his behavior.* These are sometimes called "conditioning." One approach may involve negative conditioning, the techniques of which involve putting the patient in a situation that he wishes to learn to dislike and then training him to dislike it. For example, the alcoholic might be given liquor to drink and then be given an unpleasant stimulus, such

as a drug that will make him vomit. After a series of such treatments, the patient no longer finds alcohol appealing. Unfortunately, the effects of negative conditioning tend to wear off rather quickly, and so this type of treatment is not used very often.

21 Positive reinforcement tends to be more effective. One common type, known as "reciprocal inhibition," is often used for phobias or anxiety. The patient is taught relaxation therapy—how to systematically and consistently relax various muscle groups in his body until he feels a pleasant state of total relaxation. After he has learned the techniques for relaxation, he is placed near the situation or stimulus that evokes his fear or anxiety and he is asked to assume the relaxed state of mind and body that he has learned to produce himself. Gradually he learns to gain control of the fear or anxiety through consciously relaxing himself in its presence. Behavior therapists, like the psychodynamically oriented therapists, tend to avoid the use of medication whenever possible, since they are concerned that it might interfere with the patient's ability to learn new behavioral controls.

22 Like psychodynamic theory, behaviorism has enriched our understanding of why people do the things they do and even how they think and feel. Narrowly applied, behaviorism can be arid and mechanistic. Like all potentially good things, it can be perverted to serve bad ends or used mindlessly and unimaginatively. Nevertheless, it provides a wholesome corrective to the sometimes ethereal theorizing of psychoanalysis. Its methods of treatment are helpful for some types of mental illnesses, such as alcoholism and other addictions.

THE BIOLOGICAL MODEL

23 The biological model, sometimes referred to as the "medical model," derives from Kraepelin and other psychiatrists and neurologists of the late nineteenth and early twentieth centuries. In fact, however, its roots go back much farther. It represents the mainstream of medical traditions for understanding mental illness. From the time of the classical Greeks, mental illnesses have been assumed to be due to some type of aberration in body function. In classical times, when the theory of the four humors prevailed, mental illness was thought to be due to an imbalance in the body fluids. Depression (or melancholia), for example, was thought to be due to an excess of black bile.

24 In more recent times the biological model has been shaped by the

growth of the discipline "neuroscience" or the neurosciences. Neuroscience is a combination of a set of related disciplines that share the common goal of understanding the relationship between brain structure and function, and human thoughts, feelings, and behavior. These disciplines include neuroanatomy (the study of brain structure), neuropathology (the study of disease processes caused by disorders of brain structure), neuropharmacology (the study of the effects of drugs on the brain), neurochemistry (the study of the chemical processes that control function), neuropsychology (the study of the relationship between various psychological or mental functions and brain structure), and neuroendocrinology (the study of the relationship between glandular function and brain function). Neurology and psychiatry are the two medical specialties that draw from and contribute to the neurosciences.

25 The boundaries between neurology and psychiatry are sometimes blurred. When these two specialties evolved in the nineteenth century, doctors tended to move freely between them, as Freud for example did. With increasing specialization, however, neurologists have tended to assume responsibility for diseases caused by precisely defined brain abnormalities, such as Parkinson's disease, or obvious large areas of injury, such as those caused by stroke or brain tumor. Usually these diseases are clinically manifested by such obvious signs as paralysis, shaking, or weakness. Psychiatry, on the other hand, has assumed responsibility for diseases that manifest themselves primarily by abnormalities in behavior, emotions, and thinking. Much of the time these abnormalities cannot be traced to a distinct area of damage in the brain, although the biological model assumes that as our knowledge progresses, some type of malfunction in the brain will be found. The current biological revolution in psychiatry places great emphasis on the search for the physical causes of mental illness.

26 The evolution of our understanding concerning a common neurological disorder, Parkinson's disease, helps us to understand both the problems and the purposes of the biologically oriented psychiatrist. Parkinson's disease was described by James Parkinson in 1817. It was called the "shaking palsy" because its victims suffered from a tendency to shake, especially noticeable in their hands, as well as a tendency to become stiff and rigid, sometimes so severe that they were nearly paralyzed. As techniques to study brain structure were developed, it was noted that victims of this disease had a loss of nerve cells in one particular quite small part of their brains. This area—called the "substantia nigra" because it is the only part of the brain that contains a dark pigment

(*nigra* = black)—is located deep inside the brain and is considered a part of the group of brain structures governing body movement, the "motor system."

27 Neurochemistry then added another perspective. The neuroanatomist's discovery of atrophy in the substantia nigra suggested to the neurochemists that they should look in this area for possible neurochemical abnormalities. When they did, they noted that patients suffering from Parkinson's disease had a deficiency of a particular substance usually found in the substantia nigra, a chemical known as dopamine. Neuropharmacologists then suggested that a form of dopamine known as L-dopa could be given to people with Parkinson's disease to correct their chemical deficiency. The material was made available to neurologists, who began prescribing it for their patients approximately fifteen years ago. The availability of L-dopa has revolutionized the treatment of Parkinson's disease. Patients who receive L-dopa have a marked decrease in their troublesome symptoms, particularly rigidity. Many patients who were nearly incapacitated are now able to live nearly normal lives.

28 The case of Parkinson's disease illustrates that the neurosciences are indeed a group of related disciplines: They truly serve and interact with one another, and discoveries in one branch are often used by researchers or clinicians in another branch. Further, while a neuroscientist may work within a particular discipline, such as neurology or neurochemistry, he must be aware of developments in all the other neurosciences because their interactions are so close. Modern psychiatry is progressing rapidly toward discovering the anatomic and biochemical abnormalities that underlie mental illnesses and toward developing pharmacological methods for treating them. Although none of the mental illnesses is as yet as fully understood as Parkinson's disease, biologically oriented psychiatrists hope that during the next ten to twenty years a similar logical progression from understanding structure to understanding cause to developing treatment will unfold for major mental illnesses such as depression or schizophrenia. The modern biologically oriented psychiatrist is truly the descendant of Emil Kraepelin, whose Department of Psychiatry in Munich was composed of clinicians, neuroanatomists, and neuropathologists. What are the tenets of the biological model, and how will it affect the treatment of mental illness during the 1980s?

29 *The major psychiatric illnesses are diseases.* They should be considered medical illnesses just as diabetes, heart disease, and cancer are. The emphasis in this model is on carefully diagnosing each specific illness from which the patient suffers, just as an internist or neurologist would.

When an internist listens to a patient complain of shortness of breath, he immediately begins to think of a "differential diagnosis," enumerating in his mind the various diseases that might cause the patient's complaint. The psychiatrist who follows the biological model works in the same way. When a patient complains of such symptoms as low energy, insomnia, or hearing voices, the psychiatrist assumes that the patient has a specific illness and proceeds through a detailed history and physical examination in order to determine what type of illness the patient has.

30 *These diseases are caused principally by biological factors, and most of these factors reside in the brain.* The brain is the organ of the body that serves to monitor and control the rest of the bodily functions, as well as providing the source and storehouse of all psychological functions, such as thoughts, memories, feelings, interests, and personality.

31 *As a scientific discipline, psychiatry seeks to identify the biological factors that cause mental illness.* This search involves all aspects of the neurosciences. A large amount of evidence has been amassed suggesting that mental illness is caused by biochemical abnormalities, neuroendocrine abnormalities, structural brain abnormalities, and genetic abnormalities.

32 *Clinical evaluation of patients involves careful history-taking, observing the course of symptoms over time, physical examination, and sometimes laboratory tests.* This model assumes that each different type of illness has a different specific cause. Therefore, making the correct diagnosis is very important. The understanding of each specific disease, the search for its cause, and the decision about appropriate treatment is aided by carefully observing the symptoms of the illness, its course over time, and the extent to which other members of the patient's family have had similar problems.

33 *The biological model tends to emphasize the study and management of more serious or severe mental illnesses.* These include depression, inappropriate elevations of mood (or mania), schizophrenia, severe anxiety disorders, and illnesses leading to senility (or the dementias). These diseases are emphasized because they are the ones thought most likely to have biological causes.

34 *The treatment of these diseases emphasizes the use of "somatic therapies."* The term *somatic therapies* refers to a diverse group of treatments whose common feature is that they are all physical in nature. The somatic therapies used most frequently are medications and electroconvulsive therapy (ECT). Because these diseases are considered to be biological in origin, the therapy is seen as correcting an underlying biological imbalance. Nevertheless, like any good physician, a biologically oriented

psychiatrist also recognizes that mental illness may affect social and economic functioning and addresses his attention to these problems as well. For example, a patient who is depressed and has no sex drive may develop marital problems. Ideally, the biologically oriented psychiatrist will recognize that he is treating the whole patient and that his emphasis should include helping the patient with all aspects of his or her life.

35 The return of many psychiatrists to the biological model is likely to dramatically change the nature of health care in the 1980s. Patients who go to a psychiatrist expecting to talk with him for a "fifty-minute hour" at each visit will be surprised to discover that visits are sometimes much shorter. Rather than free-associating, the patient will be asked a series of detailed questions about his symptoms, his family history of illness, and his general medical history. The psychiatrist may not even ask what the patient thinks about his mother or about traumatic early life experiences. Instead, after spending an hour or two taking a careful history of the patient's symptoms, the doctor may pull out a prescription pad, briefly explain his diagnosis and the reason for the prescription, outline the side effects and dose regimen of the drug, and ask the patient to come back in one or two weeks. When the patient returns, the doctor may spend only fifteen to thirty minutes determining whether or not the patient is getting better and how his symptoms have been affecting his work and his family and social life.

36 Patients who expect a psychiatrist to spend considerable amounts of time listening or talking often feel hurt or neglected when they see a biologically oriented psychiatrist, at least until they realize that the biological approach is quite different from the psychodynamic one that they are accustomed to equating with psychiatry. On the other hand, once they become accustomed to it, many patients feel quite comfortable with the biological model. It also carries implications about the nature of mental illness that may be very beneficial.

37 *Mental illnesses are not due to "bad habits" or weakness of will.* Because they are illnesses, they cannot be cured by acts of will. Many patients suffering from illnesses such as severe depression or mania feel guilty about their symptoms and responsible for experiencing them. Their guilt only makes them feel worse. When patients realize that their illnesses are probably caused by chemical or other types of physical abnormalities, they are relieved of feeling guilty. They no longer see themselves as inherently bad or worthless because they have a mental illness.

38 *Mental illnesses are not caused by bad parenting or bad "spousing."* Just as the patient is relieved from guilt about his symptoms, so are his friends

and relatives. The parent of a child with depression or schizophrenia no longer needs to agonize over what he or she did wrong. The husband or wife of a patient suffering from depression no longer needs to feel that he or she brought on the illness by being too demanding, or not demanding enough.

39 *The somatic therapies are very effective methods for treating many mental illnesses.* As biological psychiatry has progressed during the past twenty years, various specific kinds of medication have been developed to treat the different specific illnesses that have been recognized. Many of these medications are almost miraculously effective. The patient complaining of insomnia, low mood, and loss of appetite (usually feeling miserable and hopeless and convinced that his symptoms can never be cured) is frequently astonished to find that antidepressant medication relieves the symptoms almost completely within several weeks.

40 Not all biological treatments are miraculous cures, of course, and it is important that neither doctor nor patient has excessively high expectations. Most medical illnesses can be ameliorated by medication, but very few are eradicated by medication. Penicillin is truly a "miracle drug" that destroys the bacteria causing pneumonia, but except for infectious diseases and a few diseases that are treated surgically, most of the illnesses that afflict human beings are improved by doctors but not cured by them. Aspirin relieves the pain of arthritis, and nitroglycerine relieves the pain of angina. Antidepressant medications are somewhat closer to providing a "cure" for depression than either aspirin for arthritis or nitroglycerine for angina, but it is important not to expect too much. Psychiatry in the past has tended to oversell what it is able to do for people. Biological psychiatry promises some help, and often a great deal of help, but it does not guarantee a miraculous cure for every patient.

QUESTIONS FOR ANALYSIS AND DISCUSSION

1. Comment on Andreasen's opening paragraph. What does it accomplish? What does it reveal about her identified audience and her purpose in writing?
2. What did Freud's work concentrate on? How did he think the human mind could best be understood?
3. Since the mind is an abstraction, Freud's explanation of psychic forces striving for equilibrium must be understood as what kind of statement?
4. What are the methods and tools of psychoanalytic research? What kinds of

illnesses does the psychoanalytic model encourage concentration on? What assumptions of the model and the methodology might account for this?

5. What treatment do psychoanalysts use? With what kinds of illnesses are they generally most successful?
6. Watson and his followers leveled what charge against Freudian psychology? What do behaviorists think one should study to understand human psychology?
7. Why is it important to know what each group's emphasis is or assumptions are?
8. What are the behaviorist's methods of treatment? With what kinds of illness do they have the most success? How can this approach be misused?
9. What are the origins of the biological model? What disciplines shape the biological model today?
10. For the biological model, where will the causes of mental illness be found? What research concerns and research methods does this model encourage?
11. How will mental illness be treated primarily, according to the biological model? What else will a biologically oriented psychiatrist address?
12. According to Andreasen, how will the biological model affect the treatment of mental illness in the future? How will it affect attitudes toward mental illness?
13. Andreasen repeats the same steps in her analysis of each model. Which model does she embrace? How do you know?
14. Does the fact that she has a bias mean that her analysis is flawed? How many writers in this text write without any bias or attitude toward their subject? From your "statistics," what conclusions can you draw about writers—and writing?

STUDENT ESSAY

CAN YOU FEEL THE EARTH MOVE?

KRISTINA B. MURMANN

Did you know that just as snakes and people are constantly renewing their skins, so does the earth? Like so many changes in nature, this molting of the earth's crust is so gradual that we never notice it. That doesn't mean that there aren't constant and obvious signs of it happening all around us. The Great Rift Valley, the splitting of a tectonic plate, is evidence that can be seen on any map of Africa.

But what is the Rift Valley? What are tectonic plates? And why do they move? We tend to think of the earth as a big ball of solid mass, but it isn't. Only a crust or shell surrounding the earth is hard rock. Inside, there lies nothing solid, only molten rock and gases. Even the crust has its weak spots. There are cracks and holes all over the shell. Just like slabs of ice floating on the arctic waters, the cracks connect to become plates that can float individually on the liquid of rock and gases below. The Rift Valley is one of these giant cracks, plowing through Eastern Africa, trying to join a comrade to form a separate plate.

Though called the Great Rift Valley, it really isn't a valley like the ones we associate with mountains. The banks of the Rift rise slightly, but the surrounding country is flat. When the plates separated, the ground collapsed as if someone had pulled a plug, causing a strip of land to be slowly swallowed down the drain. The ravine left behind filled with water, forming some of the deepest lakes in the world and the Red Sea.

One day, give or take a million years, Mozambique, Tanzania, Uganda, Kenya, Somalia, and part of Ethiopia will be an island just like Madagascar. The gap will happen so gradually it will be as if it had always been there. If people still exist on the earth, they may find the gap as hard to believe as we do that once there was only one land mass that split into the seven continents.

Even since before the time when we could draw a map of the whole world, scientists set out to prove that once the earth had only one continent. Like pieces of a puzzle, it seemed obvious that South America and Africa fit together, Denmark fits up under Norway and Sweden, and Saudi Arabia matches perfectly with northeastern Africa. The Atlantic Ridge, almost the same as the Great Rift Valley, shows the possible result of the Valley. The Ridge, however, differs from the Valley in that it spurts out molten rock or magma to form more of the earth's crust, thus pushing the plates and the continents further apart. On the other side of the world, while more crust bubbles out along the Atlantic Ridge, the western part of the Pacific plate dives under its neighbor to return once again to molten rock. These are only a few examples of tectonic movement that resemble that of the Rift Valley.

With the Great Rift Valley being so large—about 5,000 km long and between 25 and 80 km wide—you would think its movement would be apparent; but if we can't feel the earth rotate at just over 1,600 km per hour, why should we feel it split apart at a rate of a few meters per century?

EXERCISES

1. Of all the ways scientists classify and categorize data, one of the most important in the biological sciences is the ordering of life forms. Complete the chart begun below by filling in the names (taxons) of the various categories for *Homo sapiens* and by listing the chief characteristics for each taxon.

You might begin by seeing how many you know and then use a biology text or reference work such as *Asimov's Guide to Science* to complete the table.

CATEGORY	TAXON	CHARACTERISTICS
Kingdom		
Phylum		
Subphylum		
Superclass		
Class		
Order		
Family		
Genus	*Homo*	
Species	*Homo sapiens*	

2. Frequently we can best understand the basis for a category or grouping by studying the group's characteristics in contrast to other relevant groups, as Andreasen does when she contrasts three models of mental illness. Select one category from the chart in question 1 – other than Superclass – and contrast the human taxon with two others of that same category level. For example, the subphylum to which we belong is subdivided into two superclasses, ours and the superclass Pisces. What are the contrasting characteristics of the two superclasses? To make contrasting traits clear, we need to present those traits in an organized way. Prepare a chart to show differences by organizing *points* of difference, as Andreasen does on p. 526 or as the model below illustrates.

CHARACTERISTICS	PISCES	TETRAPODA
Limbs	None	Four (at birth or by adulthood)
Type of heart	Two-chambered	Three- or four-chambered
Method of breathing	Gills	Lungs (at birth or by adulthood)
Environment	Water	Land (at birth or by adulthood)

3. Listed below are the mammals of East Africa of greatest interest to visitors on safari. If you were to prepare a book about these animals, how would you organize them into chapters and within each chapter? You might begin by trying several groupings, but then decide on and be prepared to justify a specific outline by chapter. (Note: Check on the family of animals that you think are related.)

African elephant	black rhinoceros
wildebeest or gnu	zebra
African buffalo	Masai giraffe

eland
dik-dik
topi
Grant's gazelle
jackal
vervet monkey
cheetah
Thomson's gazelle
baboon
impala
wart hog
leopard
hartebeest
lion
Rothschild's giraffe
spotted hyena
waterbuck
reticulated giraffe

WRITING ASSIGNMENTS

1. Define or explain one of the following terms or concepts for an entry in a reference work for nonscientists. Read several sources, take notes, and then write your own entry. List, after your entry, the works you studied. Your entry should be about one page—longer than a dictionary entry, shorter than an essay. Your purpose is to inform nonspecialists; your goals are accuracy and clarity.

   reptiles
   marsupials
   dinosaurs
   white dwarfs
   Freudian division of the mind into id, ego, superego
   quasars
   DNA
   the solar system
   natural selection

2. Select one of the terms or concepts from the assignment above and write a two- or three-page definition or explanation that will be part of a book that seeks to engage nonspecialists in the fun/mystery/excitement of your study. You still want to inform—to be accurate and clear—but you want to inform with sparkle and enthusiasm. Asimov's "Black Holes" is your model. Again, list as bibliography the sources you studied.
3. Describing a process is similar to defining a term, except that organization is determined by the steps in the process. Select one of the following and write a textbook entry for a high school text. Diagrams, charts, etc. may accompany your text as appropriate. List as bibliography the sources studied.

   The process of continent formation
   The formation of our sun
   Photosynthesis
   The extinction of the dinosaur (Remember that if scientists do not agree, a textbook must present the several most widely held views.)

4. Select one of the pairs below and prepare an article that contrasts the two items so that essential differences are clear. Give thought to organization and to the use of charts, tables, etc. as appropriate. Your audience will be readers of a science magazine for nonspecialists such as *Natural History.*

   Two members of the ape family: the gorilla and the chimpanzee
   Freudian and Jungian psychoanalytic theories
   Lamarckian and Darwinian theories of evolution

5. Using the articles in this chapter and other works in your library for information, take a stand on the "warm-bloodedness of dinosaurs" issue and argue for your position. You are a paleontologist writing in *Scientific American* or presenting a paper at an interdisciplinary meeting. Thus you want to present evidence and reason from it in a clear and orderly manner.

INDEX

"Africa: Portrait of a Continent," 335–344
"Alcohol Awareness," 116–117
analysis, 9–10, 128–129
Andreasen, Nancy C., 464, 524–537
Asimov, Isaac, 6, 464, 521–524
"Autobiographical Notes," 44–49

Baldwin, James, 44–49
Barthelme, Donald, 186–190
"Beauty: When the Other Dancer Is the Self," 91–97
"Black Holes," 521–523
"Bobcats," 104–108
Brooks, Gwendolyn, 192–201
Browning, Robert, 191, 195–197
Buckley, William F., 56–61, 64
"Business of Writing, The," 61–63

Camus, Albert, 157–169, 213–214, 280–284
"Can You Feel the Earth Move?" 537–538
"Cavalry Crossing a Ford," 209
character
  analysis of, 124–125
  conflicts, 124–125
Chopin, Kate, 148–151
"Competing Models of Mental Illness," 524–536
"Content to Be in My Place," 102–103
Cooper, Jeffrey, 68, 104–109
"Cyclical Time: Reinventing the Wheel," 109–114

"Desert Places," 198
Didion, Joan, 32–38, 65, 118, 303, 344–354
Dillard, Annie, 73–81, 129–135
Donne, John, 191, 194–195
dramatic monologue, 191
"Dream Deferred," 200
"Dulce et Decorum Est," 199
Dunbar, Paul Lawrence, 207
"Duty: The Forgotten Virtue," 275–279

"Education," 98–100
"Education: Incentives to Fail and Proposals for Change," 431–439
epistemology, 214
ethics, 214
Etzioni, Amitai, 213–214, 275–280
explication, 128

"Fiction Writer's Materials, The," 129–134
"Flea, The," 194–195
"Foreign Policy and the American Character," 243–259
"Foreword" to *The Essays of E. B. White*, 71–72
"Free Man's Worship, A," 284–292
free verse, 191

from *The Womanhood*–"the children of the poor #2," 201
Frost, Robert, 192, 198

Galbraith, John Kenneth, 424–431
Gans, Herbert J., 301–302, 304–316, 359–360, 365
Geerken, Michael, 366–388
Gould, Stephen Jay, 464, 474–481, 496, 510
Gribben, John, 464, 512–521
Gruber, Howard E., 463, 465–473
Godwin, Gail, 38–41, 64
Goodman, Ellen, 22–23, 42–44, 68, 101–104
Gove, Walter R., 366–394
Goya, Francisco, 203–205
"Guest, The," 157–169

Harden, Blaine, 300, 328–334
Herrick, Robert, 208
Hite, Kevin, 293–295
"How Not to Aid African Nomads," 328–333
"How to Get the Poor Off Our Conscience," 424–430
"Hot Times Over Warm Blood," 481–496
Hughes, Langston, 192, 200
Hughes, Michael, 365–397
hyperbole, 126

"I Think (and Write in a Journal), Therefore I Am," 29–31
"I Wandered Lonely as a Cloud," 207–208
"In Search of History," 215–227
"Indispensable Opposition, The," 260–267
"Inquiry into the Persistence of Unwisdom in Government, An," 228–241
"Interview with Dale A. Russell," 510–511
irony, 126
"Is Phoenix Jackson's Grandson Really Dead?" 144–147
Isom, Gary, 455–457

Jones, J. Penn, 61–63
journal, 27
"Journalism and the Larger Truth," 316–319

Kraft, Joseph, 13–14, 320–323
Krauthammer, Charles, 213–214, 268–275
Kreudel, Brian, 354–357

Lamb, David, 335–344
Lessing, Doris, 7, 8, 68, 81–90, 211
"Life in a Bundle of Letters," 42–44
Lippman, Walter, 213, 260–268
literary journalism, 303

"Made in Heaven," 324–327
"The Magic Barrel," 170–185
Malamud, Bernard, 170–185
Martin, Clark, 203–205
"Mass Extinctions of the Late Mesozoic," 497–509
Merwin, W. S., 193, 201–202
Metaphysics, 213–214
Metaphor, 69–70, 127–128, 205–208
"Mirror," 202–203
Montville, Leigh, 6–7, 18, 324–327

Murmann, Kristina B., 537–538
Murray, Charles, 431–448
"My Father," 82–89
"My Last Duchess," 195–197
"Myth of Sisyphus, The," 280–283

"Of Grasshoppers and Ants," 440–447
Oliphant, Pat, 323–324
"On Moral Equivalence," 268–273
"On the Exact Location of the Soul," 50–55
"Origin of the Earth, The," 512–520
Owen, Wilfred, 192, 199–200

personal essay, 26–27, 67–70, 122
"Photo Crops: Showing Sexism in Photography," 354–357
Plath, Sylvia, 193, 202–203
"Playing Dumb," 388–393
"Playing Dumb: A Form of Impression Management with Undesirable Side Effects," 366–387
plot structure, 122–124, 301–302
poetry, 121–122
point of view, 122
Postman, Neil, 364, 413–424
Potter, Penny M., 116–117
"Prayer in School" (cartoon), 324
"Promise," 207

reading skills, 10–21
"Rebuilding the Foundations of Economics," 448–454
"Recasting a Piece of Sociological Research for a Popular Audience: The Case of Playing Dumb," 394–397
"Report," 186–190
Reynolds, Joseph, 29–31, 63
Rosenblatt, Roger, 316–320, 360
Rubinstein, Eli A., 397–413
Russell, Bertrand, 214, 284–293
Russell, Dale A., 463, 497–511

"Sailing Against the Tide," 455–457
"Salvador," 344–354
Schlesinger, Arthur Jr., 243–260
"Scientific Creativity: A Study of Darwin," 465–473
"Secret Life of Walter Mitty, The," 151–156
"Seeing," 74–80
"Selecting the News: Story Suitability," 304–315
Selzer, Richard, 50–56, 64–65
Shakespeare, William, 191, 193–194, 206
sonnet, 190–191
"Sonnet 18," 206
"Sonnet 73," 193
"Sports Craze, The," 320–322
"Story of an Hour, The," 148–150
Stuart, Floyd C., 68, 109–116
student writer, 3, 7–8, 464
style in writing, 27–29, 69, 118–119
symbol, 127

"Television and the Disappearance of Childhood," 413–423
"Television and the Young Viewer," 397–412
thesis, 14–18
"The Third of May, 1808," 204
Thurber, James, 151–156
Thurow, Lester C., 440–457
"To Daffodils," 208
"Tool," 201–202
Tuchman, Barbara W., 213, 215–242, 295–296

understatement, 126

"View of War's Horrors, A," 203–205

Walker, Alice, 68, 90–98
"The Watcher at the Gates," 39–41
Welty, Eudora, 135–147
"Were Dinosaurs Dumb?" 474–480
"When I Heard the Learn'd Astronomer," 197
White, E. B., 67, 70–73, 98–101
Whitman, Walt, 191–192, 197–198, 209
"Why I Write," 32–38
Wilford, John Noble, 464, 481–496
"Wisdom," 293–295
"With All Deliberate Speed: What's So Bad About Writing Fast?" 56–61
Wordsworth, William, 207–208
"A Worn Path," 135–143
writer's stance, 18–20, 67–69, 121–122, 299, 363–365, 461–462
writing anxiety, 3–6, 28

ABOUT THE AUTHOR

Dorothy U. Seyler is Professor of English at Northern Virginia Community College at Annandale. With degrees from the College of William and Mary, Columbia University, and the State University of New York at Albany, she taught at Ohio State University, the University of Kentucky, and Nassau Community College before moving on to Northern Virginia. She has coauthored *Introduction to Literature* and *Language Power,* now in its second edition, and is the author of *Read, Reason, Write,* also in its second edition. In addition, Professor Seyler has published articles in professional journals and popular magazines. She enjoys tennis and traveling, and writing about both.